ANNUAL REVIEW OF

INFORMATION SCIENCE AND TECHNOLOGY

VOLUME **26** 1991

ISBN: 0-938734-55-5
ISSN: 0066-4200
CODEN: ARISBC
LC No. 66-25096

ANNUAL REVIEW OF

INFORMATION SCIENCE AND TECHNOLOGY

Volume 26, 1991

Edited by

Martha E. Williams
University of Illinois
Urbana, Illinois, USA

asis

Published on behalf of the
American Society for Information Science
by Learned Information, Inc.

1991

Learned Information, Inc.
Medford, New Jersey

ISBN: 0-938734-55-5
ISSN: 0066-4200
CODEN: ARISBC
LC No. 66-25096

Published and distributed by:
Learned Information, Inc.,
143 Old Marlton Pike
Medford, NJ 08055-8750
for the
American Society for Information Science
8720 Georgia Avenue, Suite 501
Silver Spring, MD 20910-3602, U.S. A.

Distributed outside North America by:
Learned Information Ltd.
Woodside, Hinksey Hill
Oxford OX1 5AU
England

ARIST Production staff, for ASIS:
Charles & Linda Holder, Graphic Compositors
Cover design by Sandy Skalkowski
Printed in the U.S.A.

Contents

I
Planning Information Systems and Services   1

1   **Cognitive Research in Information Science: Implications for Design**
Bryce L. Allen   3

2   **Information Pricing**
Fran Spigai   39

II
Basic Techniques and Technologies   75

3   **Information Technology Standards**
Michael B. Spring   79

4   **Expert Systems as Information Intermediaries**
Hilary Drenth, Anne Morris, and Gwyneth Tseng   113

5   **The Human–Computer Interface for Information Retrieval**
Debora Shaw   155

Preface

PUBLISHING HISTORY

This is the 26th volume of the *Annual Review of Information Science and Technology (ARIST)*. It was produced for the American Society for Information Science (ASIS) and published by Learned Information, Inc. ASIS initiated the series in 1966 with the publication of Volume 1 under the editorship of Carlos A. Cuadra, who continued as Editor through Volume 10. Martha E. Williams has served as Editor starting with Volume 11. ASIS is the owner of *ARIST*, maintains the editorial control, and has the sole rights to the series.

Through the years several organizations have been responsible for publishing and marketing *ARIST*. Volumes 1 and 2 were published by Interscience Publishers, a division of John Wiley & Sons. Volumes 3 through 6 were published by Encyclopaedia Britannica, Inc. Volumes 7 through 11 were published by ASIS itself. Volumes 12 through 21 were published by Knowledge Industry Publications, Inc. Volumes 22 through 25 were published by Elsevier Science Publishers B.V., Amsterdam, The Netherlands. With Volume 26 Learned Information, Inc., assumed the role of publisher of *ARIST* for ASIS.

POLICY

ARIST is an annual publication that reviews numerous topics within the broad field of information science and technology. No single topic is treated on an annual basis; it is the publication of the book that occurs annually. Inasmuch as the field is dynamic, the contents (chapters) of the various *ARIST* volumes must change to reflect this dynamism. *ARIST* chapters are scholarly reviews of specific topics as substantiated by the published literature. Some material may be included, even though not backed up by literature, if it is needed to provide a balanced and complete picture of the state of the art for the subject of the chapter. The time period covered varies from chapter to chapter, depending on whether the topic has been treated previously by *ARIST* and, if so, on the length of the interval from the last treatment to the current one. Thus, reviews may cover a one-year or a multiyear period. The reviews aim to be critical in that they provide the author's expert opinion regarding developments and activities within the chapter's subject area. The review guides the reader to or from specific publications. Chapters aim to be scholarly, thorough within the scope defined by the chapter author, up to date, well written, and readable by an audience that goes beyond the author's immediate peer group to researchers and practitioners in information science and technology, in general, and ASIS members, in particular.

PURPOSE

The purpose of *ARIST* is to describe and to appraise activities and trends in the field of information science and technology. Material presented should be substantiated by references to the literature. *ARIST* provides an annual review of topics in the field. One volume is produced each year. A master plan for the series encompasses the entire field in all its aspects, and topics for each volume are selected from the plan on the basis of timeliness and an assessment of reader interest.

REFERENCES CITED IN TEXT AND BIBLIOGRAPHY

The format for referring to bibliographic citations within the text involves use of the cited author's name instead of reference numbers. The cited author's surname is printed in upper case letters. The reader, wishing to find the bibliographic references, can readily locate the appropriate reference in the bibliography (alphabetically arranged by first author's last name). A single author appears as SMITH; coauthors as SMITH & JONES; and multiple authors as SMITH ET AL. If multiple papers by the same author are cited, the distinction is made by indicating the year of publication after the last name (e.g., SMITH, 1986), and if a further distinction is required for multiple papers within the same year, a lower case alpha character follows the year (e.g., SMITH, 1986a). Except for the fact that all authors in multi-authored papers are included in bibliographic references, the same basic conventions are used in the chapter bibliographies. Thus, the reader can easily locate in the bibliography any references discussed in the text.

Because of the emphasis placed on the requirement for chapter authors to discuss the key papers and significant developments reported in the literature, and because *ARIST* readers have expressed their liking for comprehensive bibliographies associated with the chapters, more references may be listed in the bibliographies than are discussed and/or cited in the text.

The format used for references in the bibliographies is based on the *American National Standard for Bibliographic References*, ANS Z39.29. We have followed the ANSI guidelines with respect to the sequence of bibliographic data elements and the punctuation used to separate the elements. Adoption of this convention should facilitate conversion of the references to machine-readable form as need arises. Journal article references follow the ANSI guide as closely as possible. Conference papers and microform publications follow an *ARIST* adaptation of the format.

STRUCTURE OF THE VOLUME

In accordance with the *ARIST* master plan, this volume's nine chapters fit within a basic framework: I. Planning Information Systems and Services; II. Basic Techniques and Technologies; III. Applications; and IV. The Profession. Chapter titles are provided in the Table of Contents, and an Introduction to each section highlights the events, trends, and evaluations given by the chapter authors. An Index to the entire volume is provided to help the user locate material relevant to the subject content, authors, and organizations cited in the book. An explanation of the guidelines employed in the Index is provided in the Introduction to the Index. A Keyword and Author Index to this and all prior volumes follows the Index.

DATABASES AND ABSTRACTING AND INDEXING SERVICES COVERING *ARIST*

ARIST as a whole and/or individual chapters are included in a number of abstracting and indexing (A&I) journals both within the United States and internationally. Databases that both cover *ARIST* and are available through major online services in the United States are:

> INSPEC (Computer and Control Abstracts)
> Social SciSearch (Social Sciences Citation Index)
> LISA (Library and Information Science Abstracts)
> Information Science Abstracts
> BIOSIS (Biological Abstracts)
> Library Literature
> Current Contents
> CompuMath Citation Index

Publishers of other A&I journals and databases who would like to include *ARIST* in their coverage are encouraged to contact the publisher for a review copy and notify the editor who will add the database name(s) to this list when appropriate.

Acknowledgments

Appreciation should be expressed to many individuals and organizations for their roles in creating this volume. First and foremost are the authors of the individual chapters who have generously contributed their time and efforts in searching, reviewing, and evaluating the large body of literature on which their chapters are based. The *ARIST* Advisory Committee Members and *ARIST* Reviewers provided valuable feedback and constructive criticism of the content. DIALOG Information Services generously provided the authors with online access to databases. Appreciation is expressed to all of the members of the editorial staff and *ARIST* technical support staff who are listed on the Acknowledgments page.

Martha E. Williams

Acknowledgments

The American Society for Information Science and the Editor wish to acknowledge the contributions of the three principals on the editorial staff and the technical support staff.

Mary W. Rakow, Copy Editor

Debora Shaw, Index Editor

Linda C. Smith, Bibliographic Editor

Technical Support Staff

El-Siddig At-Taras, Technical Advisor

Laurence Lannom, Technical Advisor

Scott E. Preece, Technical Advisor

Linda C. Smith, Technical Advisor

Sheila Carnder, Word Processing

Joy Ligon, Word Processing

Linda Holder, Compositor

Advisory Committee for *ARIST*

Nicholas J. Belkin

Martin Dillon

Raya Fidel

Jeffrey Katzer

Donald H. Kraft

Donald A.B. Lindberg

W. David Penniman

John Regazzi

Linda C. Smith

Contributors

Bryce L. Allen
University of Illinois
Graduate School of Library and
    Information Science
1407 W. Gregory Drive
Urbana, IL 61801

Eugenia K. Brumm
University of Texas
Graduate School of Library and
    Information Science
Education Bldg., Room 564
Austin, TX 78712-1276

Hilary Drenth
Loughborough University of
    Technology
Dept. of Library and Information
    Studies
Leicestershire Loughborough
LE11 3TU
England

Michael B. Eisenberg
Syracuse University
School of Information Studies
4-216 Center for Science and
    Technology
Syracuse, NY 13244-4100

Kerry Grosser
Royal Melbourne Institute of
    Technology
Victoria University of Technology
Department of Information Services
GPO Box 2476V
Melbourne, Victoria 3001
Australia

Anne Morris
Loughborough University of
    Technology
Dept. of Library and
    Information Studies
Leicestershire Loughborough
LE11 3TU
England

Debora Shaw
Indiana University
School of Library and
    Information Science
Bloomington, IN 47405

Fran Spigai
Database Services International
P.O. Box 366
The Marketplace at Salishan
Gleneden Beach, OR 97388

Kathleen L. Spitzer
Library and Information
    Consultant
8072 Ginger Road
Liverpool, NY 13090

Michael B. Spring
University of Pittsburgh
Department of Informaiton
    Science
727 LIS Building
Pittsburgh, PA 15260

Helen R. Tibbo
University of North Carolina
School of Information and
    Library Science
100 Manning Hall, CB #3360
Chapel Hill, NC 27599-3360

Gwyneth Tseng
Loughborough University of
    Technology
Dept. of Library and
    Information Studies
Leicestershire Loughborough
LE11 3TU
England

Chapter Reviewers

Marcia Bates	Jeffrey Katzer
David Becker	Donald H. Kraft
Nicholas J. Belkin	Donald A.B. Lindberg
Christine Borgman	Lois F. Lunin
Wesley T. Brandhorst	W. David Penniman
Bonnie Carroll	John Regazzi
Martin Dillon	Peter Schipma
Martha Evens	Elliot Siegel
Raya Fidel	Linda C. Smith
Glynn Harmon	Amy Warner
Mary Ellen Jacob	Herbert S. White

I

Planning Information Systems and Services

Section I includes two chapters, a chapter on "Cognitive Research in Information Science: Implications for Design" by Bryce L. Allen of the University of Illinois, and a chapter on "Information Pricing" by Fran Spigai of Database Services International.

Allen traces the history and development of the cognitive perspective in information science and surveys current research that relies on this perspective. Information systems that make use of the insights of cognitive research are examined, including experimental and proposed systems. Examples include systems that are designed to make appropriate demands on user cognitive processing.

In his chapter Bryce Allen points out that cognitive research in information science has focused primarily on users of information systems and to a lesser extent on information intermediaries. The object of these investigations has been to understand the knowledge that is employed during information retrieval and the cognitive processes that can have an impact on the success of information retrieval. Design initiatives deriving from this research have been directed toward developing information technology that can adapt to the knowledge, abilities, and styles of individual users and that make efficient use of the knowledge base and cognitive processes of groups of users.

Fran Spigai's chapter on "Information Pricing" is the first chapter devoted to this topic in the history of *ARIST*. Fran covers the subject of information pricing of scholarly, research, and professional publications from the viewpoint of the library market. With few exceptions, the literature covered is from the last five years (1986-1990). The chapter traces pricing events of the past decade for serials, monographs, online databases, and CD-ROM databases and shows how similar library responses are to apparently high prices or large price increases for each price format. Unfortunately, it appears price is merely one reflection of the perhaps outdated system of scholarly and research communication, of competing publishing formats using old and new technologies, of monopolist practices by publishers, of new electronic formats (with many new value-added features) using old price models, and of libraries limited by collection-building requirements. During the present transition from print to electronic publishing as the dominant medium for current information, it appears that all the forces mentioned above have joined to render the research library, as we know it, less effective at information acquisition and local information access than in the past. The conclusion is that a new paradigm is needed for research publishing, one that fosters creative pricing that will permit transfer of knowledge using the library as the main exchange agent.

1 Cognitive Research in Information Science: Implications for Design

BRYCE L. ALLEN
University of Illinois, Urbana-Champaign

INTRODUCTION

The development of cognitive research in information science can be traced to the International Workshop on the Cognitive Viewpoint held in Ghent in 1977 (BELKIN, 1990). At that workshop, the conceptual systems of information users were identified as the focus for research in this area (DE MEY). Since 1977 a number of researchers in information science have adopted this focus in their studies. As a result of the increasing number of research projects that identify themselves as sharing the cognitive perspective, the term "cognitive" has been applied to so many different kinds of research that its precise meaning has been lost. This chapter reviews cognitive research in information science and provides an outline that may clarify the relationships among the different types of investigations that have been called "cognitive."

Cognitive research in information science derives from methodologies and explanatory frameworks developed in cognitive science. Readers who would like a general introduction to these methodologies and frameworks can consult general textbooks on cognitive science. For example, a good survey of the processes studied by cognitive science, including learning, remembering, understanding, problem solving and decision making, can be found in the text of BOURNE ET AL. The raw materials of cognitive processes are mental "objects" such as concepts, ideas, and knowledge.

Annual Review of Information Science and Technology (ARIST), Volume 26, 1991
Martha E. Williams, Editor
Published for the American Society for Information Science (ASIS)
By Learned Information, Inc., Medford, N.J.

MCCLELLAND & RUMELHART's Parallel Distributed Processing model is based on a great deal of research on mental representations and cognitive structures and underlies much current research in cognitive science and artificial intelligence (AI). This model was analyzed from an information science perspective by MONSELL. As with any process, it is possible to have a high (or low) level of skill or ability in performing that process. The nature of these cognitive skills is the topic of the text edited by ANDERSON. Cognitive styles (stable preferences in the ways people think, learn, and solve problems) are sometimes seen as constructs of cognitive skills, but in other research they appear to be closely related to personality traits or to measures of general ability such as intelligence. GOLDSTEIN & BLACKMAN provide a good overview of research on cognitive styles.

Excellent discussions of the applications of cognitive research in design can be found in the *Handbook of Human–Computer Interaction*, edited by HELANDER. Particularly recommended are the chapters on cognitive systems engineering (by WOODS & ROTH), mental models (by CARROLL & OLSON), and individual differences (by EGAN).

Since 1977 when cognitive research in information science began, there has been a design agenda explicitly associated with such research. In his paper at the Ghent workshop, BELKIN (1977) identified this agenda: to improve information transfer, specifically by producing models of users' knowledge (or "conceptual systems" in De Mey's terminology) that are compatible with the conceptual frameworks used in information systems. INGWERSEN saw two independent strands of research and development coming together to create a cognitive focus in the design of information systems. The first strand is the traditional development of information systems—i.e., the work that has given information practitioners a wide range of useful products. In most of these systems, the user must adapt to the system in order to use it successfully. The second strand is what is generally known as "user studies"—i.e., investigations into information needs and problems, information-seeking behavior, and the interactions between users and intermediaries. The synthesis of system development with user studies, labeled the "cognitive paradigm" by Ingwersen, is the topic of this chapter. In this paradigm, information system design focuses on knowledge-based, interactive information systems that take into account the functions of information systems as well as the functions of those who are using the systems.

This agenda has been expressed in different ways. For example, GREGORY introduced the idea of a "normalized" user interface, in which there is no cognitive dissonance between users' experience times refer to the knowledge that users have about information systems and sometimes to the knowledge that information systems have about users. WHITEFIELD, in his survey of mental models, presents a classification in which users may have models of systems and programs, systems may have models of users, and researchers and designers may have models of users, systems, and programs. In the following discussion, the knowledge that users have about information systems is called "knowledge," and systems that attempt to encode some of the users' knowledge or some knowledge about the users are said to be implementing "cognitive models."

There are a number of different typologies of user knowledge in the literature. For example, SUTCLIFFE & OLD distinguished between the users' conceptual knowledge, task knowledge, and their visual or verbal image of the system they are using. Modifying this typology slightly to make it more applicable to information science, it seems that users of information systems are knowledgeable (in varying degrees) about their world, the topic they are searching, the task they are trying to complete via the search, and the information retrieval system they are using. These categories may not exhaust the range of user knowledge that is applied to information retrieval, and they are not always mutually exclusive. Nevertheless, they do provide a convenient framework for discussing research into user knowledge and the design implications of that research.

The main impact of research on user knowledge for the design of information technology occurs when representations of this knowledge are incorporated into the system. DANIELS surveyed the state of user modeling in information retrieval, and this chapter updates her survey.

One way to implement user models in information systems is to incorporate stereotypes of users into the system; users can then select a stereotype that seems to match their own level of knowledge. Alternatively, analysis of user input can lead to an algorithmic selection of a stereotype. PEJTERSEN described a search system for retrieving citations to fictional literature in which analysis of users' search behavior served this function. GILBERT identified a number of problems with models built on stereotypes and suggested that a more appropriate strategy is to allow the system to tell the user about itself and allow the user to adapt to it.

Other experimental information systems include user modeling. The CODER system (Composite Document Expert/Extended/Effective Retrieval) described by FOX, the MONSTRAT project detailed by BELKIN ET AL. (1984), and the I³R system of CROFT ET AL. all model some of the types of knowledge considered below.

World Knowledge

The most general kind of knowledge that can influence information retrieval is the knowledge that individuals have about the world. This world knowledge can affect how people choose to search for information. For example, BARNETT & SIEGEL showed that potential users of information technology understand the world differently from those who are not likely to use the technology. Using a semantic differential questionnaire (a questionnaire that asks people to identify the similarity or difference between pairs of words or terms), they found that potential users associated the "self" with information technology more than those who were not potential users.

The world knowledge of users may be determined partly by demographic factors such as ethnicity and gender. ALLWOOD & WANG, for example, demonstrated that ethnic background can influence people's attitudes about computers. For example, Swedish scholars tended to place a higher value on computers (as compared to humans) than their Chinese counterparts. KRENDL ET AL., PARASURAMAN & IGBARIA, and TEMPLE & LIPS documented the effect of gender on attitudes toward computers. These researchers showed that males tend to be more comfortable and confident, and females more anxious, in dealing with computers. Therefore, how individuals view their world, determined at least in part by ethnicity and gender, can influence the way they use information technology. In his comments on the practical applications of cognitive models of users, R. B. ALLEN suggested that such models should include general predictors of information behavior such as ethnicity and gender. If this idea were implemented in information technology, it could result in information systems that responded differently to people who, for reasons of background or demographics, view the world differently. Although ZWEIZIG & DERVIN concluded that demographic characteristics are not strong predictors of information-seeking behavior, it seems reasonable to model all types of knowledge, including world knowledge, in designing flexible information systems.

At this point, research into how a user's world knowledge can influence information retrieval is incomplete, and there are few clear indications as to how world knowledge can be effectively modeled in an information system. One main design suggestion that emerges from the literature is to incorporate demographic factors into stereotype-based cognitive models so that different interfaces and/or search functions can be presented to users who are likely to be more or less favorably disposed toward information technology.

System Knowledge

Users of information systems also know something about these systems. This knowledge is frequently crucial to the success of the information retrieval. KATZEFF (1990) used think-aloud protocols to determine the knowledge that users of a full-text database had about the information system.

Another way to investigate the effects of users' system knowledge is to assess the effects of knowledge possessed by expert users of information technology. In the early 1980s, WANGER ET AL., FENICHEL, and HOWARD showed that experience and training can affect the quality of searching, while more recently, FIDEL and HEWETT & SCOTT have provided evidence of how different searching styles can be discerned in experienced searchers.

CHEN & DHAR (1990) took a different approach to system knowledge by examining the misconceptions that permeate users' knowledge of information systems, in this case a library online public access catalog (OPAC). Similarly, JORRAMS-SMITH analyzed the errors made by users of UNIX and modeled these errors in an error-detection system that offered the users advice when an error was detected.

Another aspect of system knowledge is shown in the expectations the user has about search success. MACGREGOR ET AL. and FISCHHOFF & MACGREGOR found that users tend to overrate their probability of finding what they want from an information system, and these authors suggested that information technology be designed to give users a realistic expectation of their probability of success.

System knowledge is sometimes structured metaphorically—i.e., different users may think of the same system in different ways. BORGMAN (1986b) showed that different ways of structuring users' knowledge of systems can affect the quality of information retrieval, and she emphasized the importance of designing a system so that users can develop a consistent metaphor to express their knowledge of it. The role of these metaphors or analogies in the cognitive process of learning an information system is discussed below in the section on learning as a cognitive process.

On the other hand, LIEBSCHER & MARCHIONINI reported that different types of system knowledge used by students searching a full-text CD-ROM encyclopedia had no effect on search outcomes. Students trained with a simple browse strategy did as well as students trained with a more sophisticated analytical strategy. This suggests that some current information technology may be relatively insensitive to differences in how system knowledge is organized. Despite the inconsistency of these findings, MCDONALD & SCHANEVELDT argued convincingly a guiding principle for interface design—viz., interfaces should reflect the system knowledge of users and the ways that users have organized that knowledge. For this design principle to be achieved, more research into the system knowledge of users is essential.

Perhaps the most fruitful research into system knowledge is the analysis of command sequences employed by users. As mentioned above, these sequences can be used to detect errors and thus to offer advice that is tailored to users' situations. CANTER ET AL. derived a number of simple searching styles by analyzing command sequences and suggested that these styles could be reflected in different interfaces. User knowledge of commands can also be used to organize these commands in menus, as DUMAIS & LANDAUER and SNYDER ET AL. have shown.

Various investigative techniques have provided insights into what users know and how they organize that knowledge. Design initiatives based on that understanding include the modeling of system knowledge in "typical" search styles, identifying errors and misconceptions and providing immediate remedial action (including instruction), and fostering productive metaphors to organize users' system knowledge through online instruction and interface design.

Task Knowledge

In addition to their general knowledge about the world and practical knowledge about the functioning of information systems, users have specific goals for their information-seeking behavior. This task knowledge can have important effects on search performance. Accordingly, some cognitive research in information science has been directed toward identifying and systematizing user goals and plans. For example, BELKIN ET AL. (1990) described the methodology they used to study the tasks and goals of users of OPACs. DESMARAIS ET AL. and DESMARAIS & PAVEL have worked on recognizing the plans of users in text editors and in the UNIX operating system (based on a knowledge network of system commands), and they suggested that advice could be offered by the system based on the plans so identified.

WILSON investigated the information tasks performed by professionals in a variety of settings. Research of this sort provides background on the information-seeking behaviors of users. This knowledge is necessary for any design effort.

Perhaps the greatest amount of research on task knowledge has been on analyzing users' problem descriptions. Clearly problem descriptions, which are statements of information need, are essential inputs from users into the information retrieval process. Of the research into users' knowledge of problems or needs, probably the best known is the ASK (Anomalous State of Knowledge) research. These studies have been widely reported and surveyed, and BELKIN (1987) has given an overview of the research. The original ASK research now forms a part of a much more ambitious integrated view of information technology. As described by BELKIN & KWASNIK, the ASK (or problem description) is seen as being constructed through an interactive dialog between the user and the computer. This problem description module is part of a distributed expert information retrieval system, which includes components to identify problem modes and problem states as well as problem descriptions and which incorporates user models similar to those discussed above. This modular approach to information system design was described in some detail by BROOKS ET AL. and by BELKIN ET AL. (1983). BROOKS provided a detailed overview of the theory and practice of identifying problem descriptions.

A different approach to modeling users' problems is represented by the THOMAS system (ODDY; OFORI-DWUMFUO), in which a searcher's intent is modeled by a pruned and weighted segment of a world model that includes associations among documents, authors, and terms.

KUHLTHAU (1988a) and KUHLTHAU ET AL. provided a different emphasis on task knowledge. In their research, they emphasized not only the knowledge of the task demonstrated by users of information systems but also the feelings of the users as they moved from one part of the search to another. Although no specific design implications were drawn from this research, Kuhlthau suggested that designers can use an understanding of the feelings of users to create appropriate system interventions at each stage of the search.

In summary, some aspects of task knowledge, particularly problem statements, have been investigated by cognitive research in information science. A number of experimental information retrieval systems have been developed that work in part by building models of that task knowledge and using these models either to retrieve materials directly or to assist the user in working with the systems.

Domain Knowledge

Knowledge that users have of the topic being searched, or of the general subject area from which that topic is drawn, can also affect information retrieval. This knowledge is called domain knowledge, and there are two ways of looking at it. The first is to focus on the level of user domain knowledge; the second is to consider the different ways that domain knowledge can be organized. B. L. ALLEN (1991) demonstrated that the amount of knowledge users have about a topic affects the way they create search expressions with an online catalog. Similarly, SHUTE examined the effects of domain knowledge on search tactics in online bibliographic systems. Although the generalizability of his research was limited by the fact that he studied only two searchers, his dissertation is of considerable interest because of the knowledge-based topic-refinement mechanisms he designed and tested. One mechanism was based on a semantic network of terms relating to pollution that suggested alternative vocabulary to refine search expression. For example, the term "nitrite" was suggested as an alternative term for a search on the effects of nitrates. LINDE & WAERN showed how the domain knowledge of users can affect information retrieval by demonstrating that prior knowledge about a topic is used to infer answers to questions from records seen in a database search.

One way to model domain knowledge is through semantic association networks. In this technique, expert knowledge of a domain is represented by the vocabulary of that domain, arranged according to the semantic distance between words. This network can be activated to identify vocabulary that is close to the search terms entered by searchers. SMITH ET AL. described a system that used such semantic modeling of user knowledge to suggest search areas and keywords. CROFT described how users' domain knowledge can be encoded in a thesaurus (another version of a semantic association network) as part of the I^3R system.

The research of KOUBEK & SALVENDY added a qualification to the idea that information systems can model the domain knowledge of users. They found that domain knowledge varies according to the expertise of the user. Experts appear to have a relatively narrow, task-specific knowledge of a domain, while superexperts have an abstract, generalized knowledge. These differences mean that superexperts may require a much broader network of semantic associations. Since broader semantic networks are more difficult to build and to use than narrow networks, implementing models of superexpert knowledge is likely to be more difficult than working with models of expert knowledge.

The amount of domain knowledge users possess differs from one person to another. The ways that this knowledge is organized may also differ in ways that can affect information retrieval. PIEKARA &

STRUBE pointed out that users' organization of knowledge may be different from that adopted by information retrieval systems. In particular, a system may organize its thesaurus or semantic network quite differently from the ways the users have organized their knowledge of the topic or of the field. One possible design implication is to enable individualized descriptor structures to be used in retrieval, along the lines suggested by PEJTERSEN ET AL. In such a system, descriptors suggested by users and relationships between descriptors revealed by investigating the semantic associations of users would replace the standard thesaurus. In theory, it would be possible for a database to be indexed by a large number of alternative thesauri suggested by different user groups.

In related research, CHIGNELL suggested that a conceptual model of the domain, derived from users' organization of their knowledge of that domain, can serve as the basis for a query-by-example interface. The organization of domain knowledge revealed by a concept sorting task was subsequently applied by TESHIBA & CHIGNELL to designing a HyperCard browsing mechanism and by BORGMAN ET AL. to designing a prototype interface for a children's information retrieval system.

Domain knowledge is obviously important for information retrieval. The design focus has been on modeling domain knowledge in a way that will help users find the information they need. A simple thesaurus can serve as a crude model of domain knowledge, while more sophisticated semantic networks using (for example) spreading-activation techniques have the potential to guide users to precise topic areas, to suggest additional topics of interest, and to place individual search topics within larger subject domains.

COGNITIVE PROCESSES

Cognitive processes are mental activities such as thinking, imagining, remembering, and problem solving. It seems self-evident that the activities associated with seeking information and finding it through an information system use these processes. Information science research into cognitive processes has investigated how these processes figure in information-related behavior and how the ways these processes occur can affect the results of a search. The design goal that emerges is to create systems that are compatible with efficient cognitive processing—in effect, systems that are easier to use.

Research into cognitive processes is complementary to research into knowledge. Knowledge is both the raw material and the end result of cognitive processing. A focus on knowledge tends to be primarily static, while research on the process emphasizes the dynamic nature of human thinking. Thus, the design implications of investigations into cognitive processes parallel those of knowledge modeling. Some aspects of research on cognitive processes are grouped together under the term "psychometrics." RORVIG surveyed in considerable detail the research on one particular cognitive process, magnitude estimation. The following discussion is more general in focus, surveying a broader range of phenomena in less detail.

General Cognitive Processes

Cognitive load.   At the most general level, research into cognitive processes indicates that mental activity is hard work. DAS ET AL. identified a limit on the number of cognitive processes that can occur simultaneously. Building on this research, VIGIL suggested a means of using Boolean negation (*NOT*) to reduce the cognitive load in conventional online searching. The idea was that searchers could use this means of combining sets to reduce the number of "active" sets and thus reduce the number of simultaneous cognitive processes. A more detailed consideration of the implications of cognitive load for information system design was presented by GARG-JANARDAN & SALVENDY (1986). They suggested such mechanisms as saving the context of the search (thus enabling the user to view the steps that led to a particular outcome) and giving reminders about alternative strategies or commands.

Cognitive behaviors.   Researchers who examine the cognitive behaviors that occur during a search also provide insights into cognitive processes. For example, HALPERN & NILAN identified a sequence of behavior that occurs, beginning with defining the information need, then defining the help that is expected from the information system. After connecting with sources of information, the result is evaluated, and the information source may be changed. Different cognitive processes are involved, so different assistance is required at various stages of this process. Accordingly, a single approach to providing assistance to users is inadequate.

Other researchers have analyzed the sequence of events in information seeking by recording the interaction between users and intermediaries. SARACEVIC ET AL. (1990) identified a sequence of interactions, with a variety of options at each stage. Each stage involves a different relationship between user and intermediary, although the overall goal of the process is to reduce the variety and range of possible solutions to the information need. WETTLER & GLÖCKNER-RIST analyzed recorded interviews between intermediaries and users and identified a similar sequence of events. According to their analysis, this clear thematic structure in the events of the search reflects an underlying consistent problem-solving activity.

Using observation, interviewing, and think-aloud protocol analysis, HANCOCK-BEAULIEU (1987; 1990) found evidence that searching is an adaptive process that proceeds through a number of stages. These results led her to suggest that information systems should provide more opportunities for interaction between systems and users, including search-formulation aids and contextual aids. In-depth interviews also led ELLIS to the conclusion that different approaches to information retrieval were appropriate to different stages in the information seeking patterns of social scientists. BATES (1989) based some suggestions for information system design on the idea that searches evolve over time. These involve multiple access points and devices for scanning and browsing through an area. Information system design, to take account of the different stages of searching, will clearly require a substantial increase in complexity, particularly in the user interface.

It is also important to identify how users move from one stage in the information retrieval process to another if appropriate assistance is to be offered by the system. HORNE found that people ask different numbers of questions and different types of questions at various stages of a search. By monitoring query behavior, we may provide a way to track the progress of users.

The implications for design of these investigations of cognitive behaviors in information retrieval are clear. If there is a standard sequence of behaviors, then systems can be designed to track the transition from one type of behavior to another and to provide appropriate help at each stage. If, as one suspects, the standard sequences of behaviors are too stereotyped to be realistic, the challenge for design is greater. To be able to determine from input provided by users the kind of information-related behavior being performed by the user requires a high degree of sophistication in user modeling. This seems a realistic long-range design goal but somewhat unattainable in the near term.

Specific Cognitive Processes

It is also possible to analyze specific cognitive processes to determine their effects on information seeking behavior. Clearly people learn when they use information systems, they comprehend some or all of the information presented, they interpret what they learn in the context of existing knowledge in memory, and they engage in problem solving and decision making. Once an understanding of the role of these functions in information retrieval is achieved, a design imperative will become clear. It may be possible to supplant specific cognitive processes by delegating those processes to the information system. For example, some aspects of the decision-making process that determines the relevance of citations retrieved in a bibliographic retrieval system might be taken over by the information system. If this is not a realistic alternative, it may still be possible to design systems in such a way that human cognitive processes are facilitated by the system.

Learning. One of the most important tasks is learning how to use information technology. CARROLL & ROSSON emphasized the importance of designing computer-based systems for ease of learning. Learning is one of the more heavily researched cognitive processes, particularly in educational psychology, and different effects have been investigated in information science research. For example, DAVIS & SHAW showed that highlighting key terms in instructions can reduce errors in performance, and LEUTNER & SCHUMACHER found that placing a limit on response time in interactive instruction increased learning. In both of these studies, relatively minor changes in the way instruction was presented had a significant effect on the results.

POLSON suggested another relatively simple change that could lead to significant improvements in learning. Consistent user interfaces, in which the interfaces of similar systems used similar menu or command structures, led to large positive transfer effects when users were learning a new system. As Polson pointed out, consistency in interfaces is currently the exception rather than the rule, although standardizing command and query languages may be a step in effecting consistency. However, GRUDIN pointed out that an emphasis on consistency for ease of learning can conflict with an emphasis on ease of use. Standardization must not become an excuse for ignoring user-centered task analysis and design.

CARROLL & THOMAS suggested that mental models constructed by the learner of a system can act as metaphors that substantially affect the learning process. These metaphors, in which users represent their knowledge of the information system in a structured manner, are discussed above in the section on system knowledge. Information systems can be designed to increase the ease of learning by use of appropriate metaphors: images of the system that are congruent with the way the system works yet conducive to appropriate emotional attitudes and learning strategies of the user. Similarly, different models or metaphors can be used at different stages of learning to facilitate user understanding of the system.

A general model of cognitive processes in computer-based instruction was given by HANNAFIN & RIEBER, who argued for learner-mediated instruction. In other words, flexibility should be built into each stage of instructional systems so that the users can select instructional mechanisms appropriate for learning preferences. Investigations of learning styles, discussed below, provide additional impetus toward this type of flexibility in the design of instructional modules.

Explanation can also have a learning function. HOLLNAGEL suggested that information systems should contain models of their own functioning and assist user learning by explaining or describing what is going on in the information system. Similarly, BELKIN (1988) speculated that explanation by intelligent information retrieval systems could be modeled on the kinds of explanation provided by human intermediaries.

Memory. An understanding of how learning works has obvious application to information technology. It may be less clear how an understanding of human memory processes can influence the design of information technology. In fact, research into the role of memory in information retrieval is in its early stages, and there are only a few indications of how it could be applied in design.

PRASSE ET AL. began from the well-known limitation of short-term or working memory, and reasoned that this limitation would make it difficult for users to read and understand textual data spread across several screens. They devised a system of presenting text to make optimal use of limited short-term memory. Single cognitive units (in this case, single paragraphs) were displayed, and tables of contents and index entries were used as navigational aids for the reader.

DALRYMPLE started from memory research that showed that detailed knowledge is sometimes recalled by a strategy called "reformulation"—i.e., reorganizing encoded memories in such a way as to derive from them the detailed knowledge that is needed. She investigated whether this kind of reformulation could be useful as a mechanism for searching library catalogs. Although she was unable to reach a conclusive answer, her research is typical of attempts to apply research to cognitive processes in an information retrieval context.

B. L. ALLEN (1990) showed that the organizational structure used to encode information about a topic could influence the expression of information needs on that topic. Specifically, people who used a particular organizational device produced a more complete description of the topic when they were presented with questions that used an organizational structure different from their personal one.

The research of Dalrymple and Allen suggests that how people remember information may influence how they seek additional information. How this influence functions is unclear in detail. Therefore, current memory research cannot serve as a reliable basis for the design of information systems. Perhaps research into knowledge structures (as detailed above) may be more fruitful than research into memory processes for the design of information technology.

Problem solving. Problem solving is a complex cognitive process, and much of the psychological research in this area has been restricted to relatively narrow contexts such as solving games, puzzles, or mathematical problems. However, some research shows how problem solving works in the information retrieval setting. For example, KATZEFF (1986) found that users who were faced with a query that was more complex than those for which they had been trained sought various kinds of information to formulate a database query. In other words, users applied various strategies to solve this problem. Thus, online help should be made available in a flexible manner; the same details may not be equally helpful to all individuals facing the same problem. It is also possible that sophisticated models of domain knowledge, such as those described above, can meet the problem-solving challenge raised by WORMELL: to help users to ask better-defined questions and to stimulate knowledge states to shift from one form of problem representation to another. In other words, knowledge about the domain as well as about the information system may be very useful in helping users in problem solving associated with information retrieval.

Search tactics can be seen as problem-solving techniques. BATES (1987) discussed a variety of tactics for use in searching online bibliographic databases. CHEN & DHAR (1991) took a similar approach to problem solving during searching. By examining the search logs and think-aloud protocols associated with searches of an online library catalog, they identified five specific strategies used during these searches: (1) known-item instantiation, (2) search-option heuristics, (3) thesaurus browsing, (4) screen browsing, and (5) trial and error. They were then able to incorporate features that supported some of these strategies into a redesigned system that produced better search results. However, the strategies observed for one online catalog may not be appropriate for other information systems. This is a general problem in cognitive research in information science: research that focuses on existing systems may lack generalizability, but research into more general cognitive processes may lack applicability. A combination of these types of research is necessary to overcome the weaknesses of each: general cognitive research tested and applied in working systems, and system-based research informed by cognitive theory.

Users of information systems also face the problem of evaluating a list of citations. O'SHAUGHNESSY ET AL. found that the amount of information used to identify those citations that are relevant or useful is limited. Users can read through a list of citations presented by a bibliographic retrieval system and make instantaneous decisions based on very limited information. If this problem-solving process could be adequately modeled, perhaps it could be done by the information system rather than the user. Contributions to modeling this process may be found in the research into task and domain knowledge discussed above.

As with investigations of memory processes, our understanding of problem solving in information retrieval is limited. Additional research is needed to reveal how people solve problems during information seeking, retrieval, and use. The implications for design of such research may be considerable. Strategies and heuristics for problem solving may well form the basis for expert systems in information retrieval, as GARG-JANARDAN & SALVENDY (1988) suggested in their interesting article.

Comprehension. Another complex cognitive process is the understanding of textual materials. People can read lengthy documents and extract the gist with little apparent effort. As HUTCHINS suggested, if this human process were thoroughly understood, perhaps it could be modeled by a computer to generate summaries or other text surrogates—in other words, a relatively intelligent form of automatic indexing or abstracting. Hutchins outlined the research in this area and progress in applying the research to the generation of document surrogates. BEGHTOL surveyed much of the same research, primarily in the area of text linguistics, and suggested an interpretation of the cognitive processes involved in indexing and classification. Again, research is incomplete in this area, and much basic understanding must be achieved before successful applications of the research in information technology design can be achieved.

COGNITIVE ABILITIES

Cognitive processes, like other human activities, are performed differently by individuals who have different levels of ability. Accordingly, some cognitive research in information science has focused on how individual differences in cognitive abilities can affect information retrieval. The design considerations that emerge from this research relate to helping different users with different abilities make optimal use of information technology. In general, this goal requires systems with a variety of interfaces, help, or instructional modules and search mechanisms so that users can select that version of the information system that matches their particular ability.

TEITELBAUM-KRONISH, in an interesting dissertation, found that there is a significant relationship between cognitive ability and online searching success. People who reason logically—i.e., can reason from premise to conclusion or can evaluate the correctness of a conclusion—did better in online searches than did those with poor logical skills. Similarly, people who did better in integrative processes—i.e., can keep in mind simultaneously or combine several conditions, premises, or rules in order to produce a correct response—were more successful than those who could not do this. GREENE ET AL. found that in addition to the logical reasoning and integrative processes, visual memory (the ability to remember the configuration, location, and orientation of images) and induction (the ability to form and test hypotheses that will fit a set of data) affected a user's ability to use logical operators such as *AND, OR,* and *NOT*. Taking this research one step further, they tested a system that did not require users to use logical operators and found improved performance. They recommended that this interface without Boolean operators be used, particularly for complex queries.

Other investigations using different types of information technology have added to the body of findings that indicate the importance of cognitive abilities in information work. In examining a user's ability to learn to use a text editor, EGAN & GOMEZ found differences related to visual memory (thus confirming the findings of Greene et al.) and to associational fluency (the ability to produce words that share a given area of meaning or some other common semantic property). VICENTE ET AL. showed that vocabulary skills and visualization abilities account for 45% of the variation in the time that users take to find items when searching a hierarchical filing system. ULICH surveyed a number of experiments that demonstrated individual differences in human-computer interaction and showed the need for flexibility in system design. More specifically, WILLIGES suggested that visual augmentation be built into an interface to help users who are not adept at spatial visualization.

There are, however, concerns about this body of research that may lead to reservations about its design implications. The first concern is methodological. All of the studies cited relied on tests included in the Kit of Factor-Referenced Cognitive Tests (EKSTROM ET AL.). This kit contains 72 tests to assess 23 cognitive factors. Only a few of these factors have been tested in an information retrieval context. Also, some of the research cited above ignored the explicit recommendation of the publishers (Educational Testing Service) to use at least two tests to assess each cognitive ability.

The second reservation was expressed by HOCKEY, who maintained that these tests fail to distinguish between abilities and styles. The truth of this criticism can be found in the fact that some researchers have used the cognitive factor called "flexibility of closure" as the equivalent of the cognitive style called "field independence." Another criticism by Hockey is even more important. Hockey notes that these tests were developed primarily in the educational domain and may have only limited application to an area like information retrieval. He recommends that a series of tests of cognitive abilities that specifically relate to the human–computer interaction domain be developed. This suggestion has much merit, but it would require a substantial investment of research time and effort.

There appears to be sufficient replication of findings from a number of studies to confirm that cognitive abilities can affect information retrieval performance. Taking account of these individual differences in information system design necessitates alternative interfaces and search mechanisms and providing augmentation devices for individuals with weak abilities in logical reasoning, visual memory, or vocabulary skills. These alternative interfaces and system devices will make systems more complex. The design challenge is to implement devices that meet the needs of individual users without making systems so complex that no one can use them.

COGNITIVE STYLES

As Hockey indicated, the distinction between cognitive abilities and cognitive styles is frequently fuzzy. VAN DER VEER provided a useful criterion for distinguishing among different kinds of individual differences—viz., the dimension of changeability. Personality traits are relatively unchanging, as are cognitive styles. Cognitive abilities differ from cognitive styles in that they can be learned and so are relatively changeable. Most changeable are knowledge structures because learning continually affects them. According to this definition, cognitive styles are relatively stable preferences in the ways people think, learn, and solve problems.

Research has shown that people who have different cognitive styles perform differently in information-related tasks. One commonly tested cognitive style is field dependence. People who are field dependent tend to respond uncritically to environmental cues, while those who are field independent will tend to orient themselves correctly in spite of environmental cues. Field dependence is associated with passivity, field independence with an active coping style. Some research shows that computer proficiency is predicted by this cognitive style. For example, CAVIANI found that field-independent students did better in diagnosing logical errors in a programming task than field-dependent students. COUNTRY found that field-independent students were more likely to use a trial-and-error approach to learn a computer system, and field-dependent students were more likely to use help facilities.

In research more applicable to information technology design, AMBARDAR tested field-independent and field-dependent subjects on three different information retrieval interfaces and discovered that field-dependent subjects preferred a highly structured approach that featured sequential browsing, while field-independent subjects preferred a more flexible approach using keyword searching. Interestingly, this research also suggested that field-independent subjects were unable to adapt to the structured approach: their preference was so fixed that it constituted a disability. YOO tested library school students and found that field-independent searchers had a higher success rate than field-dependent searchers. Other aspects of information behavior also seem to be determined partly by differences of cognitive style. COOPER & RIBBLE found that differences in cognitive complexity (as measured by the Paragraph Completion Test) were associated with differences in individuals' perceptions of documents, although DAVIDSON found that tests for cognitive style were not associated with differences in relevance judgments.

A number of studies involving information professionals confirm that cognitive styles can influence performance. For example, BELLARDO found that personal characteristics measured by the Khatena-Torrance Creative Perception Inventory had some effect on the recall achieved by online searchers. Recall achieved on their searches was affected by whether intermediaries were "artistic scholars" or "analytical individualists." LOGAN, SARACEVIC & KANTOR, and WOELFL all found differences in online searching performance associated with different learning styles as revealed by the Learning Styles Inventory. In particular, it appears that the learning style called "Concrete Experience" is associated with lower precision and recall.

This research demonstrated that cognitive styles affect information retrieval performance. As BORGMAN (1989) suggested, all users of information retrieval systems are not created equal. Several implications from this research for information technology design were suggested in the literature. FOWLER & MURRAY suggested that some users of information systems prefer system-guided dialogs, while others prefer to have a more active role in using the system. In terms of gender differences among users, they suggested that women are more likely to prefer the system-guided approach and men to prefer the more active approach. Similarly, RIDING ET AL. pointed out the importance of matching computer-based training with the learning styles of users.

It is also possible to include cognitive styles in models of the user in addition to representations of users' knowledge. NEAL described a user model for a text editor that includes learning strategies and risk aversion of users along with representations of their level of knowledge of computer programming. BRAJNIK ET AL. suggested that, in addition to the knowledge of the user (as indicated by education, professional background, information retrieval background, and experience), personal traits, such as communication preferences and attitudes should be included in user models for intelligent information retrieval. The design imperative is to create systems that are flexible enough in their search capabilities, indexing, and interfaces to ensure that users with different cognitive styles use them effectively.

CONCLUSIONS

This chapter has demonstrated that the process of merging system development with user studies is beginning to produce results, but substantial research gaps remain. Researchers have only begun to understand how some cognitive processes contribute to information-related behavior. The ways that memory, problem solving, and comprehension function in information retrieval need much more detailed study before such knowledge can be used in designing information systems. In other areas, however, research has produced a modest base of understanding, and experimental systems designed on that understanding are being built. This is most noticeable in the area of knowledge-based information retrieval. In interface design, knowledge about the domain and about the system can be used to guide search formulation and to tutor users. There is also an impact on the design of storage and retrieval mechanisms. Models of domain knowledge and task knowledge (particularly problem descriptions) of users are being used in experimental systems to increase the quality of information retrieval.

Many of the gaps in cognitive research have been identified, and ongoing research to fill those gaps is an important element of the research agenda in information science. Equally important is the application of cognitive research in system design. The ideal that is driving the design efforts outlined in this chapter seems unimpeachable: to improve the usability and effectiveness of information retrieval systems. This ideal can be achieved by enhancing existing design initiatives and extending the results from laboratory systems to mass market applications.

BIBLIOGRAPHY

ALLEN, BRYCE L. 1990. Knowledge Organization in an Information Retrieval Task. Information Processing & Management. 1990; 26(4): 535-542. ISSN: 0306-4573.

ALLEN, BRYCE L. 1991. Topic Knowledge and Online Catalog Search Formulation. Library Quarterly. 1991 April; 61(2): 188-213. ISSN: 0024-2519.

ALLEN, ROBERT B. 1990. User Models: Theory, Method and Practice. International Journal of Man-Machine Studies. 1990 May; 32(5): 511-543. ISSN: 0020-7373.

ALLWOOD, CARL MARTIN; WANG, ZHONG-MING. 1990. Conceptions of Computers among Students in China and Sweden. Computers in Human Behavior. 1990; 6(2): 185-199. ISSN: 0747-5632.

AMBARDAR, A. KAK. 1988. User-Computer Interaction: Analysis of Individual Differences and Information Retrieval. In: Proceedings of the 1988 IEEE International Conference on Systems, Man, and Cybernetics: Volume 2; 1988 August 8-12; Beijing/Shenyang, China. New York, NY: IEEE; 1988. 1246-1249. ISBN: 7-80003-039-3.

ANDERSON, JOHN R., ed. 1981. Cognitive Skills and Their Acquisition. Hillsdale, NJ: Lawrence Erlbaum Associates; 1981. 386p. ISBN: 0-98959-093-0.

BARNETT, GEORGE A.; SIEGEL, GARY. 1988. The Diffusion of Computer-Assisted Legal Research Systems. Journal of the American Society for Information Science. 1988 July; 39(4): 224-234. ISSN: 0002-8231.

BATES, MARCIA J. 1987. How to Use Information Search Tactics Online. Online. 1987 May; 11(3): 47-54. ISSN: 0146-5422.

BATES, MARCIA J. 1989. The Design of Browsing and Berrypicking Techniques for the Online Search Interface. Online Review. 1989 October; 13(5): 407-424. ISSN: 0309-314X.

BEGHTOL, CLARE. 1986. Bibliographic Classification Theory and Text Linguistics: Aboutness Analysis, Intertextuality and the Cognitive Act of Classifying Documents. Journal of Documentation. 1986 June; 42(2): 84-113. ISSN: 0022-0418.

BELKIN, NICHOLAS J. 1977. Internal Knowledge and External Information. In: CC77. International Workshop on the Cognitive Viewpoint; 1977 March 24-26; Ghent, Belgium, University of Ghent. Ghent, Belgium: University of Ghent; 1977. 187-194.

BELKIN, NICHOLAS J. 1987. Discourse Analysis of Human Information Interaction for Specification of Human-Computer Information Interaction. Canadian Journal of Information Science. 1987; 12(3-4): 31-42. ISSN: 0380-9218.

BELKIN, NICHOLAS J. 1988. On the Nature and Function of Explanation in Intelligent Information Retrieval. In: Chiaramella, Yves, ed. Proceedings of the 11th International Conference on Research and Development in Information Retrieval; 1988 June 13-15; Grenoble, France. Grenoble, France: Presses Universitaires de Grenoble; 1988. 135-195. ISBN: 2-7061-0309-4.

BELKIN, NICHOLAS J. 1990. The Cognitive Viewpoint in Information Science. Journal of Information Science: Principles and Practice. 1990; 16(1): 11-16. ISSN: 0165-5515.

BELKIN, NICHOLAS J.; CHANG, SHEN-JU; DOWNS, TRUDY. 1990. Taking Account of User Tasks, Goals and Behavior for the Design of Online Public Access Catalogs. In: Henderson, Diane, ed. ASIS '90: Information in the Year 2000: From Research to Applications: Proceedings of the American Society for Information Science (ASIS) 53rd Annual Meeting: Volume 27; 1990 November 4-8; Toronto, Canada. Medford, NJ: Learned Information, Inc. for ASIS; 1990. 69-73. ISSN: 0044-7870; ISBN: 0-938734-48-2.

BELKIN, NICHOLAS J.; HENNINGS, RALF-DIRK; SEEGER, THOMAS. 1984. Simulation of a Distributed Expert-Based Information Provision Mechanism. Information Technology: Research Development Applications. 1984; 3(3): 122-141. ISSN: 0144-817X.

BELKIN, NICHOLAS J.; KWASNIK, BARBARA H. 1986. Using Structural Representations of Anomalous States of Knowledge for Choosing Document Retrieval Strategies. In: Rabitti, Fausto, ed. Association for Computing Machinery (ACM) Conference on Research and Development in Information Retrieval; 1986 September 8-10; Pisa, Italy. Baltimore, MD: ACM; 1986. 11-22. ISBN: 0-89791-187-3.

BELKIN, NICHOLAS J.; SEEGER, THOMAS; WERSIG, GERNOT. 1983. Distributed Expert Problem Treatment as a Model for Information System Analysis and Design. Journal of Information Science: Principles and Practice. 1983; 5: 153-167. ISSN: 0165-5515.

BELLARDO, TRUDI. 1985. An Investigation of Online Searcher Traits and Their Relationship to Search Outcome. Journal of the American Society for Information Science. 1985 July; 36(4): 241-250. ISSN: 0002-8231.

BLAIR, DAVID C. 1990. Language and Representation in Information Retrieval. Amsterdam, The Netherlands: Elsevier; 1990. 335p. ISBN: 0-444-88437-8.

BORGMAN, CHRISTINE L. 1984. Psychological Research in Human-Computer Interaction. In: Williams, Martha E., ed. Annual Review of Information Science and Technology: Volume 19. White Plains, NY: Knowledge Industry Publications, Inc. for the American Society for Information Science; 1984. 33-64. ISSN: 0066-4200; ISBN: 0-86729-093-5.

BORGMAN, CHRISTINE L. 1986a. Human-Computer Interaction with Information Retrieval Systems: Understanding Complex Communication Behavior. In: Dervin, Brenda; Voigt, Melvin J., eds. Progress in Communication Sciences: Volume 7. New York, NY: Ablex; 1986. 91-122. ISSN: 0173-5689; ISBN: 0-89391-325-1.

BORGMAN, CHRISTINE L. 1986b. The User's Mental Model of an Information Retrieval System: An Experiment on a Prototype Online Catalog. International Journal of Man-Machine Studies. 1986; 24(1): 47-64. ISSN: 0020-7373.

BORGMAN, CHRISTINE L. 1989. All Users of Information Retrieval Systems Are Not Created Equal: An Exploration into Individual Differences. Information Processing & Management. 1989; 25(3): 237-251. ISSN: 0306-4573.

BORGMAN, CHRISTINE L.; CHIGNELL, MARK H.; VALDEZ, FELIX. 1989. Designing an Information Retrieval Interface Based on Children's Categorization of Knowledge: A Pilot Study. In: Katzer, Jeffrey; Newby, Gregory B., eds. ASIS '89: Proceedings of the American Society for Information Science (ASIS) 52nd Annual Meeting: Volume 26; 1989 October 30-November 2; Washington, DC. Medford, NJ: Learned Information, Inc. for ASIS; 1989. 81-95. ISSN: 0044-7870; ISBN: 0-938734-40-7.

BOURNE, LYLE E.; DOMINOWSKI, ROGER L.; LOFTUS, ELIZABETH F. 1979. Cognitive Processes. Englewood Cliffs, NJ: Prentice-Hall; 1979. 408p. ISBN: 0-13-139634-X.

BRAJNIK, GIORGIO; GUIDA, GIOVANNI; TASSO, CARLO. 1987. User Modeling in Intelligent Information Retrieval. Information Processing & Management. 1987; 23(4): 305-320. ISSN: 0306-4573.

BROOKS, HELEN M. 1986. Developing and Representing Problem Descriptions. In: Brookes, Bertram C., ed. Intelligent Information Systems for the Information Society: Proceedings of the 6th International Research Forum in Information Science (IRFIS 6); 1985 September 16-18; Frascati, Italy. Amsterdam, The Netherlands: North-Holland; 1986. 141-161. ISBN: 0-444-70070-1; LC:86-13585.

BROOKS, HELEN M.; DANIELS, PENNY J.; BELKIN, NICHOLAS J. 1986. Research on Information Interaction and Intelligent Information Provision Mechanisms. Journal of Information Science: Principles and Practice. 1986; 12(1-2): 37-44. ISSN: 0165-5515.

BURT, PATRICIA V.; KINNUCAN, MARK T. 1990. Information Models and Modeling Techniques for Information Systems. In: Williams, Martha E., ed. Annual Review of Information Science and Technology: Volume 25. Amsterdam, The Netherlands: Elsevier Science Publishers for the American Society for Information Science; 1990. 175-208. ISSN: 0066-4200; ISBN: 0-444-88531-5.

CANTER, DAVID; RIVERS, ROD; STORRS, GRAHAM. 1985. Characterizing User Navigation through Complex Data Structures. Behaviour & Information Technology. 1985 April-June; 4(2): 93-102. ISSN: 0144-929X.

CARROLL, JOHN M.; OLSON, JUDITH REITMAN. 1988. Mental Models in Human-Computer Interaction. In: Helander, Martin, ed. Handbook of Human-Computer Interaction. Amsterdam, The Netherlands: North-Holland; 1988. 45-65. ISBN: 0-444-70536-8.

CARROLL, JOHN M.; ROSSON, MARY BETH. 1987. Paradox of the Active User. In: Carroll, John M., ed. Interfacing Thought: Cognitive Aspects of Human-Computer Interaction. Cambridge, MA: MIT Press; 1987. 80-111. ISBN: 0-262-03125-6; LC: 86-20974.

CARROLL, JOHN M.; THOMAS, JOHN C. 1982. Metaphor and the Cognitive Representation of Computing Systems. IEEE Transactions on Systems, Man and Cybernetics. 1982 March-April; 12(2): 107-116. ISSN: 0018-9472.

CAVIANI, THOMAS P. 1989. Cognitive Style and Diagnostic Skills of Student Programmers. Journal of Research on Computing in Education. 1989 Summer; 21(4): 411-420. ISSN: 0888-6504.

CHEN, HSINCHUN; DHAR, VASANT. 1990. User Misconceptions of Information Retrieval Systems. International Journal of Man-Machine Studies. 1990 June; 32(6): 673-692. ISSN: 0020-7373.

CHEN, HSINCHUN; DHAR, VASANT. 1991. Cognitive Process as a Basis for Intelligent Retrieval Systems Design. Information Processing & Management. 1991. ISSN: 0306-4573. (In press).

CHIGNELL, MARK H. 1987. Computer Interfaces for the Humanities. In: Salvendy, Gavriel, ed. Cognitive Engineering in the Design of Human-Computer Interaction and Expert Systems: Proceedings of the 2nd International Conference on Human-Computer Interaction: Volume 2; 1987 August 10-14; Honolulu, HI. Amsterdam, The Netherlands: Elsevier; 1987. 273-280. ISBN: 0-444-42848-8.

COOPER, HARRIS; RIBBLE, RONALD. 1985. Influences on the Outcome of Literature Searches for Integrative Research Reviews. Columbia, MO: University of Missouri, Center for Research in Social Behavior; 1985. 36p. Available from: ERIC Document Reproduction Service. ERIC: ED-266 802.

COUNTRY, JENNIFER. 1989. Some Effects of Cognitive Style on Learning UNIX. International Journal of Man-Machine Studies. 1989 September; 31(3): 349-365. ISSN: 0020-7373.

CROFT, W. BRUCE. 1986. User-Specified Domain Knowledge for Document Retrieval. In: Rabitti, Fausto, ed. Association for Computing Machinery (ACM) Conference on Research and Development in Information Retrieval; 1986 September 8-10; Pisa, Italy. Baltimore, MD: ACM; 1986. 201-206. ISBN: 0-89791-187-3.

CROFT, W. BRUCE; LUCIA, T. J.; CRIGEAN, JANEY K.; WILLETT, P. 1989. Retrieving Documents by Plausible Inference: An Experimental Study. Information Processing & Management. 1989; 25(6): 599-614. ISSN: 0306-4573.

DALRYMPLE, PRUDENCE W. 1990. Retrieval by Reformulation in Two Library Catalogs: Toward a Cognitive Model of Searching Behavior. Journal of the American Society for Information Science. 1990 June; 41(4): 272-281. ISSN: 0002-8231.

DANIELS, PENNY J. 1986. Cognitive Models in Information Retrieval: An
    Evaluative Review. Journal of Documentation. 1986 December; 42(4):
    272-304. ISSN: 0022-0418.
DAS, J. P.; KIRBY, JOHN R.; JARMAN, RONALD F. 1979. Simultaneous
    and Successive Cognitive Processes. New York, NY: Academic Press;
    1979. 247p. ISBN: 0-12-203150-4; LC: 78-20039.
DAVIDSON, DAVID. 1977. The Effect of Individual Differences of Cogni-
    tive Style on Judgments of Document Relevance. Journal of the
    American Society for Information Science. 1977 September; 28(5): 273-
    284. ISSN: 0002-8231.
DAVIS, CHARLES H.; SHAW, DEBORA. 1989. Comparison of Retrieval
    System Interfaces Using an Objective Measure of Screen Design Effec-
    tiveness. Library and Information Science Research. 1989 October-
    December; 11(4): 325-334. ISSN: 0740-8188.
DE MEY, MARC. 1977. The Cognitive Viewpoint: Its Development and Its
    Scope. In: CC77. International Workshop on the Cognitive Viewpoint;
    1977 March 24-26; Ghent, Belgium, University of Ghent. Ghent, Bel-
    gium: University of Ghent; 1977. xvi-xxxii.
DERVIN, BRENDA; NILAN, MICHAEL. 1986. Information Needs and
    Uses. In: Williams, Martha E., ed. Annual Review of Information
    Science and Technology: Volume 21. White Plains, NY: Knowledge
    Industry Publications, Inc. for the American Society for Information
    Science; 1986. 3-33. ISSN: 0066-4200; ISBN: 0-86729-209-1.
DESMARAIS, MICHEL C.; LAROCHELE, SERGE; GIROUX, LUC. 1987.
    The Diagnosis of User Strategies. In: Bullinger, Hans-Jorg; Shackel,
    Brian; Kornwachs, Klaus, eds. Human-Computer Interaction: INTER-
    ACT '87: Proceedings of the 2nd IFIP Conference; 1987 September 1-4;
    Stuttgart, West Germany. Amsterdam, The Netherlands: North-Hol-
    land; 1987. 185-189. ISBN: 0-444-70304-7.
DESMARAIS, MICHEL C.; PAVEL, MICHAEL. 1987. User Knowledge
    Evaluation: An Experiment with UNIX. In: Bullinger, Hans-Jorg;
    Shackel, Brian; Kornwachs, Klaus, eds. Human-Computer Interac-
    tion: INTERACT '87: Proceedings of the 2nd IFIP Conference; 1987
    September 1-4; Stuttgart, West Germany. Amsterdam, The Netherlands:
    North-Holland; 1987. 151-156. ISBN: 0-444-70304-7.
DUMAIS, SUSAN T.; LANDAUER, THOMAS K. 1984. Describing Catego-
    ries of Objects for Menu Retrieval Systems. Behavior Research Meth-
    ods, Instruments, and Computers. 1984 April; 16(2): 242-248. ISSN:
    0743-3808.
EASON, K.D.; OLPHERT, C.W.; NOVARA, F.; BERTAGGIA, N.;
    ALLAMANO, N. 1987. The Design of Usable IT Products: The
    ESPRIT/HUFIT Approach. In: Salvendy, Gavriel, ed. Cognitive Engi-
    neering in the Design of Human-Computer Interaction and Expert
    Systems: Proceedings of the 2nd International Conference on Human-
    Computer Interaction: Volume 2; 1987 August 10-14; Honolulu, HI.
    Amsterdam, The Netherlands: Elsevier; 1987. 147-154. ISBN: 0-444-
    42848-8.

EGAN, DENNIS E. 1988. Individual Differences in Human-Computer Interaction. In: Helander, Martin, ed. Handbook of Human-Computer Interaction. Amsterdam, The Netherlands: North-Holland; 1988. 543-568. ISBN: 0-444-70536-8.

EGAN, DENNIS E.; GOMEZ, LOUIS M. 1985. Assaying, Isolating and Accommodating Individual Differences in Learning a Complex Skill. In: Dillon, Ronna F., ed. Individual Differences in Cognition. Orlando, FL: Academic Press; 1985. Volume 2: 174-217. ISBN: 0-12-216402-4; LC: 82-22738.

EKSTROM, RUTH B.; FRENCH, JOHN W.; HARMAN, HARRY H. 1976. Manual for Kit of Factor-Referenced Cognitive Tests. Princeton, NJ: Educational Testing Service; 1976. 224p. LC: 77-156260.

ELLIS, DAVID. 1989. A Behavioural Approach to Information Retrieval System Design. Journal of Documentation. 1989 September; 45(3): 171-212. ISSN: 0022-0418.

FENICHEL, CAROL HANSEN. 1981. Online Searching: Measures That Discriminate among Users with Different Types of Experiences. Journal of the American Society for Information Science. 1981; 32(1): 24-32. ISSN: 0002-8231.

FIDEL, RAYA. 1990. Online Searching Styles. In: Henderson, Diane, ed. ASIS '90: Information in the Year 2000: From Research to Applications: Proceedings of the American Society for Information Science (ASIS) 53rd Annual Meeting: Volume 27; 1990 November 4-8; Toronto, Canada. Medford, NJ: Learned Information, Inc. for ASIS; 1990. 98-103. ISSN: 0044-7870; ISBN: 0-938734-48-2.

FISCHER, GERHARD C.; LEMKE, ANDREAS C. 1988. Constrained Design Processes: Steps towards Convivial Computing. In: Guindon, Raymonde, ed. Cognitive Science and Its Applications for Human-Computer Interaction. Hillsdale, NJ: Lawrence Erlbaum Associates; 1988. 1-58. ISBN: 0-89859-884-2; LC: 87-36523.

FISCHHOFF, BARUCH; MACGREGOR, DONALD. 1986. Calibrating Databases. Journal of the American Society for Information Science. 1986 July; 37(4): 222-233. ISSN: 0002-8231.

FOWLER, C. J. H.; MURRAY, D. 1987. Gender and Cognitive Style Differences at the Human-Computer Interface. In: Bullinger, Hans-Jorg; Shackel, Brian; Kornwachs, Klaus, eds. Human-Computer Interaction: INTERACT '87: Proceedings of the 2nd IFIP Conference; 1987 September 1-4; Stuttgart, West Germany. Amsterdam, The Netherlands: North-Holland; 1987. 709-714. ISBN: 0-444-70304-7.

FOX, EDWARD A. 1987. Development of the CODER System: A Testbed for Artificial Intelligence Methods in Information Retrieval. Information Processing & Management. 1987; 23(4): 341-366. ISSN: 0306-4573.

FROHMANN, BERND. 1990. Rules of Indexing: A Critique of Mentalism in Information Retrieval Theory. Journal of Documentation. 1990 June; 46(2): 81-101. ISSN: 0022-0418.

GARG-JANARDAN, CHAYA; SALVENDY, GAVRIEL. 1986. Contribution
    of Cognitive Engineering to the Effective Design and Use of Informa-
    tion Systems. Information Services and Use. 1986; 6(5-6): 235-252.
    ISSN: 0167-5265.
GARG-JANARDAN, CHAYA; SALVENDY, GAVRIEL. 1988. The Contri-
    butions of Cognitive Engineering to the Design and Use of Expert
    Systems. Behaviour & Information Technology. 1988 July-September;
    7(3): 323-342. ISSN: 0144-929X.
GILBERT, G. NIGEL. 1987. Cognitive and Social Models of the User. In:
    Bullinger, Hans-Jorg; Shackel, Brian; Kornwachs, Klaus, eds. Human-
    Computer Interaction: INTERACT '87: Proceedings of the 2nd IFIP
    Conference; 1987 September 1-4; Stuttgart, West Germany. Amsterdam,
    The Netherlands: North-Holland; 1987. 165-169. ISBN: 0-444-70304-7.
GOLDSTEIN, KENNETH M.; BLACKMAN, SHELDON. 1978. Cognitive
    Style: Five Approaches and Relevant Research. New York, NY: Wiley;
    1978. 279p. ISBN: 0-471-31275-4.
GREENE, SHARON L.; DEVLIN, SUSAN J.; CANNATA, PHILIP E.;
    GOMEZ, LOUIS M. 1990. No IFs, ANDs or ORs: A Study of Database
    Querying. International Journal of Man-Machine Studies. 1990 March;
    32(3): 303-326. ISSN: 0020-7373.
GREGORY, KEITH. 1987. Methodology for Designing a Normalized User
    Interface. In: Salvendy, Gavriel, ed. Cognitive Engineering in the
    Design of Human-Computer Interaction and Expert Systems: Pro-
    ceedings of the 2nd International Conference on Human-Computer
    Interaction: Volume 2; 1987 August 10-14; Honolulu, HI. Amsterdam,
    The Netherlands: Elsevier; 1987. 139-146. ISBN: 0-444-42848-8.
GRUDIN, JONATHAN. 1989. The Case Against User Interface Consis-
    tency. Communications of the ACM. 1989 October; 32(10): 1164-1173.
    ISSN: 0001-0782.
HALPERN, DAVID; NILAN, MICHAEL. 1988. A Step toward Shifting the
    Research Emphasis in Information Science from the System to the
    User: An Empirical Investigation. In: Borgman, Christine L.; Pai,
    Edward Y. H. eds. ASIS '88: Information & Technology: Planning for
    the Second 50 Years: Proceedings of the American Society for Informa-
    tion Science (ASIS) 51st Annual Meeting: Volume 25; 1988 October 23-
    27; Atlanta, GA. Medford, NJ: Learned Information, Inc. for ASIS;
    1988. 169-176. ISSN: 0044-7870; ISBN: 0-938734-29-6.
HANCOCK-BEAULIEU, MICHELINE. 1987. Subject Searching Behaviour
    at the Library Catalogue and the Shelves: Implications for Online
    Interactive Catalogues. Journal of Documentation. 1987 December;
    43(4): 303-321. ISSN: 0022-0418.
HANCOCK-BEAULIEU, MICHELINE. 1990. Evaluating the Impact of an
    Online Library Catalogue on Subject Searching Behaviour at the Cata-
    logue and at the Shelves. Journal of Documentation. 1990 December;
    46(4): 318-338. ISSN: 0022-0418.
HANNAFIN, MICHAEL J.; RIEBER, LLOYD R. 1989. Psychological
    Foundations of Instructional Design for Emerging Computer-Based

Instructional Technologies. Educational Technology Research and Development. 1989; 37(2): Part 1: 91-101, Part 2: 102-114. ISSN: 1042-1629.

HELANDER, MARTIN, ed. 1988. Handbook of Human-Computer Interaction. Amsterdam, The Netherlands: North-Holland; 1988. 1167p. ISBN: 0-444-70536-8.

HEWETT, THOMAS T.; SCOTT, SARI. 1987. The Use of Thinking-Out-Loud and Protocol Analysis in Development of a Process Model of Interactive Database Searching. In: Bullinger, Hans-Jorg; Shackel, Brian; Kornwachs, Klaus, eds. Human-Computer Interaction: INTERACT '87: Proceedings of the 2nd IFIP Conference; 1987 September 1-4; Stuttgart, West Germany. Amsterdam, The Netherlands: North-Holland; 1987. 51-56. ISBN: 0-444-70304-7.

HEWINS, ELIZABETH T. 1990. Information Needs and Use Studies. In: Williams, Martha E., ed. Annual Review of Information Science and Technology: Volume 25. Amsterdam, The Netherlands: Elsevier Science Publishers for the American Society for Information Science; 1990. 145-172. ISSN: 0066-4200; ISBN: 0-444-88531-5.

HOCKEY, G. ROBERT J. 1990. Styles, Skills and Strategies: Cognitive Variability and Its Implications for the Role of Mental Models in HCI. In: Ackermann, D.; Tauber, M. J., eds. Mental Models and Human-Computer Interaction 1. Amsterdam, The Netherlands: North-Holland; 1990. 113-129. ISBN: 0-444-88453-X; LC: 89-70977.

HOLLNAGEL, ERIK. 1987. Cognitive Models, Cognitive Tasks, and Information Retrieval. In: Wormell, Irene, ed. Knowledge Engineering: Expert Systems and Information Retrieval. London, England: Taylor Graham; 1987. 34-52. ISBN: 0-947568-30-1.

HOLLNAGEL, ERIK; WEIR, G. 1989. Principles for Dialogue Design in Man-Machine Systems. In: Ranta, J., ed. Analysis, Design and Evaluation of Man-Machine Systems 1988. Selected Papers from the 3rd IFAC/IFIP/IEA/IFORS Conference; 1988 June 14-16; Oulu, Finland. Oxford, England: Pergamon; 1989. 145-149. ISBN: 0-08-036226-5.

HORNE, ESTHER E. 1990. An Investigation into Self-Questioning Behavior during Problem-Solving. In: Henderson, Diane, ed. ASIS '90: Information in the Year 2000: From Research to Applications: Proceedings of the American Society for Information Science (ASIS) 53rd Annual Meeting: Volume 27; 1990 November 4-8; Toronto, Canada. Medford, NJ: Learned Information, Inc. for ASIS; 1990. 86-90. ISSN: 0044-7870; ISBN: 0-938734-48-2.

HOWARD, HELEN. 1982. Measures That Discriminate among Online Searchers with Different Training and Experience. Online Review. 1982 August; 6(4): 315-327. ISSN: 0309-314X.

HUTCHINS, JOHN. 1987. Summarization: Some Problems and Methods. In: Jones, Kevin P., ed. Informatics 9: Meaning: The Frontier of Informatics: Proceedings; 1987 March 26-27; Cambridge, England. London, England: Aslib; 1987. 151-173. ISBN: 0-85142-223-3.

INGWERSEN, PETER. 1987. Towards a New Research Paradigm in Information Retrieval. In: Wormell, Irene, ed. Knowledge Engineering: Expert Systems and Information Retrieval. London, England: Taylor Graham; 1987. 150-189. ISBN: 0-947568-30-1.

JORRAMS-SMITH, JENNIFER. 1989. An Attempt to Incorporate Expertise about Users into an Intelligent Interface for UNIX. International Journal of Man-Machine Studies. 1989 September; 31(3): 269-292. ISSN: 0020-7373.

KATZEFF, CECILIA. 1986. Dealing with a Database Query Language in a New Situation. International Journal of Man-Machine Studies. 1986 July; 25(1): 1-17. ISSN: 0020-7373.

KATZEFF, CECILIA. 1990. System Demands on Mental Models for a Fulltext Database. International Journal of Man-Machine Studies. 1990 May; 32(5): 483-509. ISSN: 0020-7373.

KOUBEK, RICHARD J.; SALVENDY, GAVRIEL. 1989. The Implementation and Evaluation of a Theory for High Level Cognitive Skill Acquisition through Expert Systems Modeling Techniques. Ergonomics. 1989 November; 32(11): 1419-1430. ISSN: 0014-0139.

KRENDL, KATHY A.; BROIHIER, MARY C.; FLEETWOOD, CYNTHIA. 1989. Children and Computers: Do Sex-Related Differences Persist? Journal of Communication. 1989 Summer; 39(3): 85-93. ISSN: 0021-9916.

KUHLTHAU, CAROL COLLIER. 1988a. Developing a Model of the Library Search Process: Cognitive and Affective Aspects. RQ. 1988 Winter; 28: 232-242. ISSN: 0033-7072.

KUHLTHAU, CAROL COLLIER. 1988b. Longitudinal Case Studies of the Information Search Process of Users in Libraries. Library and Information Science Research. 1988 July; 10: 257-304. ISSN: 0740-8188.

KUHLTHAU, CAROL COLLIER; TUROCK, BETTY J.; BELVIN, ROBERT J. 1988. Facilitating Information Seeking through Cognitive Models of the Search Process. In: Borgman, Christine L.; Pai, Edward Y. H., eds. ASIS '88: Information and Technology: Planning for the Second 50 Years: Proceedings of the American Society for Information Science (ASIS) 51st Annual Meeting: Volume 25; 1988 October 23-27; Atlanta, GA. Medford, NJ: Learned Information, Inc. for ASIS; 1988. 70-75. ISSN: 0044-7870; ISBN: 0-938734-29-6.

LEUTNER, DETLEV; SCHUMACHER, GERD. 1990. The Effects of Different Online Adaptive Response Time Limits on Speed and Amount of Learning in Computer Assisted Instruction and Intelligent Tutoring. Computers in Human Behavior. 1990; 6(1): 17-29. ISSN: 0747-5632.

LIEBSCHER, PETER; MARCHIONINI, GARY. 1988. Browse and Analytical Search Strategies in a Full-Text CD-ROM Encyclopedia. School Library Media Quarterly. 1988 Summer; 16(4): 223-233. ISSN: 0278-4823.

LINDE, LENA; WAERN, YVONNE. 1985. On Search in an Incomplete Database. International Journal of Man-Machine Studies. 1985 May; 22(5): 563-579. ISSN: 0020-7373.

LOGAN, ELISABETH. 1990. Cognitive Styles and Online Behavior of Novice Searchers. Information Processing & Management. 1990; 26(4): 503-510. ISSN: 0306-4573.

LONG, JOHN. 1989. Cognitive Ergonomics and Human-Computer Interaction. In: Long, John; Whitefield, Andy, eds. Cognitive Ergonomics and Human-Computer Interaction. Cambridge, England: Cambridge University Press; 1989. 4-34. ISBN: 0-521-37179-1.

MACGREGOR, DONALD; FISCHHOFF, BARUCH; BLACKSHAW, LYN. 1987. Search Success and Expectations with a Computer Interface. Information Processing & Management. 1987; 23(5): 419-432. ISSN: 0306-4573.

MCCLELLAND, JAMES L.; RUMELHART, DAVID E. 1986. Parallel Distributed Processing: Explorations in the Microstructure of Cognition. Cambridge, MA: The MIT Press; 1986. 2 volumes. ISBN: 0-262-18123-1; LC: 85-24073.

MCDONALD, JAMES E.; SCHANEVELDT, ROGER W. 1988. The Application of User Knowledge to Interface Design. In: Guindon, Raymonde, ed. Cognitive Science and Its Applications for Human-Computer Interaction. Hillsdale, NJ: Lawrence Erlbaum Associates; 1988. 289-338. ISBN: 0-89859-884-2; LC: 87-36523.

MONSELL, STEPHEN. 1981. Representations, Processes, Memory Mechanisms: The Basic Components of Cognition. Journal of the American Society for Information Science. 1981 September; 32(5): 378-390. ISSN: 0002-8231.

NEAL, LISA RUBIN. 1987. User Modeling for Syntax-Directed Editors. In: Bullinger, Hans-Jorg; Shackel, Brian; Kornwachs, Klaus, eds. Human-Computer Interaction: INTERACT '87: Proceedings of the 2nd IFIP Conference; 1987 September 1-4; Stuttgart, West Germany. Amsterdam, The Netherlands: North-Holland; 1987. 131-133. ISBN: 0-444-70304-7.

NORMAN, DONALD A. 1987. Cognitive Engineering, Cognitive Science. In: Carroll, John M., ed. Interfacing Thought: Cognitive Aspects of Human-Computer Interaction. Cambridge, MA: MIT Press; 1987. 325-336. ISBN: 0-262-03125-6; LC: 86-20974.

ODDY, ROBERT N. 1977. Information Retrieval through Man-Machine Dialogue. Journal of Documentation. 1977; 33(1): 1-14. ISSN: 0022-0418.

OFORI-DWUMFUO, G. O. 1984. Using a Cognitive Model of Dialogue for Reference Retrieval. Journal of Information Science: Principles and Practice. 1984 August; 9(1): 19-28. ISSN: 0165-5515.

O'SHAUGHNESSY, MARK P.; COSKUNTUNA, SEMRA; KANTRO, ELLEN. 1987. Multiple Attribute Decision Making and On-Line Information Systems. In: Salvendy, Gavriel, ed. Cognitive Engineering in the Design of Human-Computer Interaction and Expert Systems: Proceedings of the 2nd International Conference on Human-Computer Interaction: Volume 2; 1987 August 10-14; Honolulu, HI. Amsterdam, The Netherlands: Elsevier; 1987. 61-66. ISBN: 0-444-42848-8.

PARASURAMAN, S.; IGBARIA, M. 1990. An Examination of Gender Differences in the Determinants of Computer Anxiety and Attitudes toward Microcomputers among Managers. International Journal of Man-Machine Studies. 1990 March; 32(3): 327-340. ISSN: 0020-7373.

PEJTERSEN, ANNELISE MARK. 1984. Design of a Computer-Aided User-System Dialogue Based on an Analysis of Users' Search Behavior. Social Science Information Studies. 1984 April/July; 4(2/3): 167-183. ISSN: 0143-6236.

PEJTERSEN, ANNELISE MARK; OLSEN, SVEND ERIK; ZUNDE, PRANAS. 1987. Development of a Term Association Interface for Browsing Bibliographic Data Bases Based on End Users' Word Associations. In: Wormell, Irene, ed. Knowledge Engineering: Expert Systems and Information Retrieval. London, England: Taylor Graham; 1987. 92-112. ISBN: 0-947568-30-1.

PIEKARA, FRANK HENRY; STRUBE, GERHARD. 1987. Data-Base Organization and Cognitive Structure: Using Information Systems Organized by Oneself and by Others. In: Bullinger, Hans-Jorg; Shackel, Brian; Kornwachs, Klaus, eds. Human-Computer Interaction: INTERACT '87: Proceedings of the 2nd IFIP Conference; 1987 September 1-4; Stuttgart, West Germany. Amsterdam, The Netherlands: North-Holland; 1987. 93-98. ISBN: 0-444-70304-7.

POLSON, PETER G. 1988. Consequences of Consistent and Inconsistent User Interfaces. In: Guindon, Raymonde, ed. Cognitive Science and Its Applications for Human-Computer Interaction. Hillsdale, NJ: Lawrence Erlbaum Associates; 1988. 59-108. ISBN: 0-89859-884-2; LC: 87-36523.

PRASSE, MICHAEL J.; DILLON, MARTIN; GORDON, MARTHA J.; MORTLAND, BRUCE; REPKA, ANTHONY. 1988. F-TAS: A Full-Text Access System. In: Williams, Martha E.; Hogan, Thomas H., comps. Proceedings of the 9th National Online Meeting; 1988 May 10-12; New York, NY. Medford, NJ: Learned Information; 1988. 327-332. ISBN: 0-938734-26-1.

RAMSEY, H. RUDY; GRIMES, JACK D. 1983. Human Factors in Interactive Computer Dialog. In: Williams, Martha E., ed. Annual Review of Information Science and Technology: Volume 18. New York, NY: Knowledge Industry Publications, Inc. for the American Society for Information Science; 1983. 29-59. ISSN: 0066-4200; ISBN: 0-86729-050-1.

RICH, ELAINE. 1983. Users Are Individuals: Individualizing User Models. International Journal of Man-Machine Studies. 1983 March; 18(3): 199-214. ISSN: 0020-7373.

RIDING, RICHARD J.; BUCKLE, CHRISTOPHER F.; THOMPSON, STEWART; HAGGER, EDWARD. 1989. The Computer Determination of Learning Styles as an Aid to Individualized Computer-Based Training. Educational and Training Technology International. 1989 October; 26(4): 393-398. ISSN: 0954-7304.

RORVIG, MARK E. 1988. Psychometric Measurement and Information Retrieval. In: Williams, Martha E., ed. Annual Review of Information Science and Technology: Volume 23. Amsterdam, The Netherlands: Elsevier Science Publishers for the American Society for Information Science; 1988. 157-189. ISSN: 0066-4200; ISBN: 0-444-70543-0.

SARACEVIC, TEFKO; KANTOR, PAUL. 1988. A Study of Information Seeking and Retrieving. Part II: Users, Questions, and Effectiveness. Journal of the American Society for Information Science. 1988 May; 39(3): 177-196. Part III: Searchers, Searches and Overlap. Journal of the American Society for Information Science. 1988 May; 39(3): 197-216. ISSN: 0002-8231.

SARACEVIC, TEFKO; KANTOR, PAUL; CHAMIS, ALICE Y.; TRIVISON, DONNA. 1988. A Study of Information Seeking and Retrieving. Part I: Background and Methodology. Journal of the American Society for Information Science. 1988 May; 39(3): 161-176. ISSN: 0002-8231.

SARACEVIC, TEFKO; MOKROS, HARTMUT; SU, LOUISE. 1990. Nature of Interaction between Users and Intermediaries in Online Searching: A Qualitative Analysis. In: Henderson, Diane, ed. ASIS '90: Information in the Year 2000: From Research to Applications: Proceedings of the American Society for Information Science (ASIS) 53rd Annual Meeting: Volume 27; 1990 November 4-8; Toronto, Canada. Medford, NJ: Learned Information, Inc. for ASIS; 1990. 47-54. ISSN: 0044-7870; ISBN: 0-938734-48-2.

SHAW, DEBORA. 1991. The Human-Computer Interface for Information Retrieval. In: Williams, Martha E., ed. Annual Review of Information Science and Technology: Volume 26. Medford, NJ: Learned Information, Inc. for the American Society for Information Science; 1991. 155-195. ISSN: 0066-4200; ISBN: 0-938734-55-5.

SHUTE, STEVEN JOSEPH. 1990. An Empirical Investigation of Knowledge-Based Search Tactics in the Topic Refinement Behavior of Online Bibliographic Searchers. Columbus, OH: Ohio State University; 1990; c1989. 375p. (Ph.D. dissertation). Available from: University Microfilms International, Ann Arbor, MI. (UM order no. 90-11264).

SMITH, LINDA C. 1987. Artificial Intelligence and Information Retrieval. In: Williams, Martha E., ed. Annual Review of Information Science and Technology: Volume 22. Amsterdam, The Netherlands: Elsevier Science Publishers for the American Society for Information Science; 1987. 41-77. ISSN: 0066-4200; ISBN: 0-444-70302-0.

SMITH, PHILIP J.; SHUTE, STEVEN J.; CHIGNELL, MARK H.; KRAWCZAK, DEBORAH A. 1989. Bibliographic Information Retrieval: Developing Semantically-Based Search Systems. In: Rouse, William B., ed. Advances in Man-Machine Systems Research: Volume 5. Greenwich, CT: JAI Press, Inc.; 1989. 93-152. ISBN: 1-55938-011-X.

SNYDER, KATHLEEN M.; HAPP, ALAN J.; MALCUS, LAWRENCE; RAAP, KENNETH R.; LEWIS, JAMES R. 1985. Using Cognitive Models to Create Menus. In: Swezey, Robert W., ed. Proceedings of the Human Factors Society 29th Annual Meeting; 1985 September 29-October 3;

Baltimore, MD. Santa Monica, CA: Human Factors Society; 1985. 655-658. ISSN: 0163-5182.

SUTCLIFFE, A. G.; OLD, A.C. 1987. Do Users Know They Have User Models? Some Experiences in the Practice of User Modeling. In: Bullinger, Hans-Jorg; Shackel, Brian; Kornwachs, Klaus, eds. Human-Computer Interaction: INTERACT '87: Proceedings of the 2nd IFIP Conference; 1987 September 1-4; Stuttgart, West Germany. Amsterdam, The Netherlands: North-Holland; 1987. 35-41. ISBN: 0-444-70304-7.

TEITELBAUM-KRONISH, PRISCILLA. 1985. Relationship of Selected Cognitive Aptitudes and Personality Characteristics of the Online Searcher to the Quality of Performance in Online Bibliographic Retrieval. New York, NY: New York University; 1985; c1984. 171p. (Ph.D. dissertation). Available from: University Microfilms International, Ann Arbor, MI. (UM order no. 85-10778).

TEMPLE, LINDA; LIPS, HILARY M. 1989. Gender Differences and Similarities in Attitudes toward Computers. Computers in Human Behavior. 1989; 5(4): 215-226. ISSN: 0747-5632.

TESHIBA, KENNETH; CHIGNELL, MARK. 1988. Development of a User Model Evaluation Technique for Hypermedia Based Interfaces. In: Riding the Wave of Innovation: Proceedings of the Human Factors Society 32nd Annual Meeting; 1988 October 24-28; Anaheim, CA. Santa Monica, CA: Human Factors Society; 1988. 323-327. ISSN: 0163-5182.

ULICH, EBERHARD. 1987. Individual Differences in Human-Computer Interaction: Concepts and Research Findings. In: Salvendy, Gavriel, ed. Cognitive Engineering in the Design of Human-Computer Interaction and Expert Systems: Proceedings of the 2nd International Conference on Human-Computer Interaction: Volume 2; 1987 August 10-14; Honolulu, HI. Amsterdam, The Netherlands: Elsevier; 1987. 29-36. ISBN: 0-444-42848-8.

VAN DER VEER, GERRITT C. 1989. Individual Differences and the User Interface. Ergonomics. 1989 November; 32(11): 1431-1449. ISSN: 0014-0139.

VICENTE, KIM J.; HAYES, BRIAN C.; WILLIGES, ROBERT C. 1987. Assaying and Isolating Individual Differences in Searching a Hierarchical File System. Human Factors. 1987 June; 29(3): 349-359. ISSN: 0018-7208.

VIGIL, PETER J. 1983. The Psychology of Online Searching. Journal of the American Society for Information Science. 1983 July; 34(4): 281-287. ISSN: 0002-8231.

WANGER, JUDITH; MCDONALD, DENNIS; BERGER, MARY C. 1980. Evaluation of the On-Line Search Process: A Final Report. Santa Monica, CA: Rockville, MD: Cuadra Associates; King Research Associates; 1980. 266p. NTIS: PB 81 132565.

WETTLER, MANFRED; GLÖCKNER-RIST, ANGELIKA. 1990. Empirical Study of the Reference Interview in Bibliographic Online Retrieval. In: Ackermann, D.; Tauber, M. J., eds. Mental Models and Human-Computer Interaction 1. Amsterdam, The Netherlands: North-Holland; 1990. 177-192. ISBN: 0-444-88453-X; LC: 89-70977.

WHITEFIELD, ANDY. 1987. Models in Human Computer Interaction: A Classification with Special Reference to Their Uses in Design. In: Bullinger, Hans-Jorg; Shackel, Brian; Kornwachs, Klaus, eds. Human-Computer Interaction: INTERACT '87: Proceedings of the 2nd IFIP Conference; 1987 September 1-4; Stuttgart, West Germany. Amsterdam, The Netherlands: North-Holland; 1987. 57-63. ISBN: 0-444-70304-7.

WILLIGES, ROBERT C. 1987. Adapting Human-Computer Interfaces for Inexperienced Users. In: Salvendy, Gavriel, ed. Cognitive Engineering in the Design of Human-Computer Interaction and Expert Systems: Proceedings of the 2nd International Conference on Human-Computer Interaction: Volume 2; 1987 August 10-14; Honolulu, HI. Amsterdam, The Netherlands: Elsevier; 1987. 21-28. ISBN: 0-444-42848-8.

WILSON, THOMAS D. 1984. Cognitive Approach to Information-Seeking Behaviour and Information Use. Social Science Information Studies. 1984 April/June; 4(2/3): 197-204. ISSN: 0143-6236.

WOELFL, NANCY N. 1984. Individual Differences in Online Search Behavior: The Effect of Learning Styles and Cognitive Abilities on Process and Outcome. Cleveland, OH: Case Western Reserve University; 1984. 180p. (Ph.D. dissertation). Available from: University Microfilms, Ann Arbor, MI. (UM order no. 85-03614).

WOODS, D. D.; ROTH, E. M. 1988. Cognitive Systems Engineering. In: Helander, Martin, ed. Handbook of Human-Computer Interaction. Amsterdam, The Netherlands: North-Holland; 1988. 3-43. ISBN: 0-444-70536-8.

WORMELL, IRENE. 1984. Cognitive Aspects in Natural Language and Free-Text Searching. Social Science Information Studies. 1984 April/July; 4(2/3): 131-141. ISSN: 0143-6236.

YOO, JAE-OK. 1990. Field Dependence/Independence and the Performance of the Online Searcher. Bloomington, IN: Indiana University; 1990. 225p. (Ph.D. dissertation). Available from: University Microfilms, Ann Arbor, MI. (UM order no. 90-30439).

ZWEIZIG, DOUGLAS; DERVIN, BRENDA. 1977. Public Library Use, Users, Uses: Advances in Knowledge of the Characteristics and Needs of the Adult Clientele of American Public Libraries. In: Voigt, Melvin J.; Harris, Michael L., eds. Advances in Librarianship: Volume 7. New York, NY: Academic Press; 1977. 231-255. ISBN: 0-12-785007-4.

2 Information Pricing

FRAN SPIGAI
Database Services International

INTRODUCTION

This is the first time that information pricing has been the subject of an *ARIST* chapters, although pricing has been discussed in *ARIST* before, most recently by REPO. Whereas Repo covered 20 years of research and development, this chapter's scope is narrower in some respects and broader in others. The focus here is on the events and the literature surrounding the pricing of research and professional materials for libraries. The intent is to capture the historical transitions between outright sale and licensing of information and between the older philosophy of the need for collection building and the emerging library philosophy of access to information (the "virtual" collection). The literature shows a future in which electronic publications are becoming equal partners with print and in which librarians will be asked to manage a growing complex of published knowledge with tight budgets. Although many of these transitions and trends have been evolving for two decades, their effects have only recently come to a head.

Thus, this chapter concentrates on the literature of 1986–1990. The focus is on the library as information agent because it is charged with obtaining information, regardless of format, publisher, location, and, often, price. Thus, it is the first to encounter the full range of single-copy acquisition problems for both print and electronic formats.

Annual Review of Information Science and Technology (ARIST), Volume 26, 1991
Martha E. Williams, Editor
Published for the American Society for Information Science (ASIS)
By Learned Information, Inc., Medford, N.J.

Certain topics that have a major impact on library pricing policies for patrons are not included—e.g., the whole area of library charges for (usually online) information and the philosophies surrounding fees for access to information. Rather, this chapter treats the "list" prices paid by libraries to publishers or their distributors, gateways, vendors, or agents.

"Follow the money" is a common phrase in business. It means that if one looks at the source of major funds in any enterprise, he will find the answers to the mysteries of underlying incentives and relationships between buyers and sellers. This chapter intends to unravel many of the mysteries surrounding pricing.

THE SERIALS CRISIS IN PRINT

Background

The years 1986 and 1987 saw serials price increases that finally exceeded the serials budgets of the North American academic libraries. Price studies and price indexes for those years tell the story. For instance, a study using the Faxon Co.'s title, subscription rate, and client source databases showed that in 42 of 59 subject categories, serial prices increased by 10% or more in average price (YOUNG)— a rate far above inflation. After a decade of rising serials prices, following other decades of rising prices (BAUMOL & MARCUS; DEGENNARO; SIMORA; SOMERS), librarians finally took action.

The Gathering Storm

In 1988 and 1989 a series of studies and analyses emerged from within the library community; they were accompanied by some counterclaims by publishers (CLACK, 1989b; COX) and even a lawsuit by Gordon and Breach against an author of a pricing study (TURNER). A new column called "Serials Prices" in *Serials Review* (IVINS, n.d.) became the center for reporting research and news on the serials pricing crisis as did the electronic publication, *NEWS-LETTER ON SERIALS PRICING ISSUES*. The linchpin for academic library proactivity was probably the ARL report on serials prices (ASSOCIATION OF RESEARCH LIBRARIES), which consists of two meaty, fact-filled, commissioned reports, an ARL overview, and ARL member resolutions and recommendations for further action. The first report (ECONOMIC CONSULTING SERVICES, IN-CORPORATED) targeted four large publishers having demonstrable dominance in ARL serials budgets—Elsevier, Pergamon, Plenum (Consultants Bureau), and Springer-Verlag—for a review of price data vs. estimated publisher costs (1973–1987) and resultant profits. Selected statistics cited by the study show that publishers' profits (as estimated) rose from 40% to 137% from 1973–1987. During that same period, average funding support to ARL libraries rose 234% (vs. a 182% rise in the U.S. Consumer Price Index (CPI)), average percent of expenditures for materials rose from 29% in 1973 to 33% in 1987, percent spent for serials (of total budget) rose from 40% to 52%, and average serials holdings of the estimated universe of serials dropped from 32% to 26%. In the second report, OKERSON provides a historical and current overview of the serials pricing issue and recommends various actions to ARL.

Questions addressed by these various studies and articles fall into two categories: (1) What are the causes for these extraordinary price increases? and (2) What can be done to stem these prices in order to ensure the survival of the research library? Some possible causes are exchange rates, rising costs of doing business (especially due to journal page growth), inflation, and rampant profiteering; all were hotly debated in the literature (OKERSON). So too were suggested solutions—viz., boycott certain publishers, cancel subscriptions, negotiate with publishers, educate faculty (authors and readers), justify larger budgets, stimulate competition and alternative technologies, and share resources (DOUGHERTY & BARR; OKERSON).

Pricing Studies and Price Indexes

Journal/serial pricing has been addressed statistically and from an economic perspective by a number of studies over the past five years. The majority of these studies function as price indexes or price tracers for serials over a period of time, often comparing price increases to consumer price indexes (CPI) or currency exchange rates.

Economics of pricing   BEBENSEE ET AL. showed that the average price of a one-year journal subscription increased 190% in the period 1978–1987, causing the journal segment of academic library budgets to rise from 28% to 45% over this same decade. How can publishers continue to increase prices and expect librarians to continue to subscribe? Bebensee et al. posit that publishers understand well that libraries simply must subscribe in order to provide current/ essential information to faculty and to maintain collection continuity. This demand inelasticity is common when products have few substitutes; buyers believe that the product is needed regardless of cost. Even if there are a few cancellations resulting from an increase in price, publisher costs decrease, profits increase, and total revenues often increase as well. The authors conclude that econometric studies are needed to estimate demand curves and elasticities for various scholarly and professional journals. They contend that publishers could use such information to maximize profits, and librarians could forecast the leveling-off prices of particular journals. Perhaps in anticipation of this latest serials pricing crisis, the National Science Foundation (NSF) commissioned a rigorous report from BAUMOL ET AL. in which the authors "describe some principles of pricing [for publishers of sci/tech journals] which are designed to increase publication revenues while not disregarding either ability to pay or the desirability of stimulating the circulation of the journals" (p. 1).

Exchange rate effects.   A spate of papers address the impact of exchange rates on serials pricing (HEPFER; MADDOX; SOMERS; STRAUCH & STRAUCH). Hepfer reports a presentation by John Tagler of Elsevier Science Publishers, who reviewed factors influencing journal pricing, and concluded that "there is simply more information available than librarians can afford to buy" (HEPFER, p. 143).

Maddox points out that despite price increases over the decade, librarians have questioned pricing policies only in the past two to three years and that the price data gathered have been used to justify budgets rather than confront publishers. She suggests that a routine cost evaluation, which involves faculty, be done to help drive prices down. However, there is a problem in evaluating prices of foreign publications and monitoring the effects of exchange rates on prices. Publishers have responded to the U.S. market, where library budgets are heavily weighted toward buying U.S. publications or toward the convenience of purchasing foreign publications from U.S. distributors in U.S. dollars. Thus, it is difficult if not impossible to identify many truly "foreign" publishers.

Somers states that "the library budget is held hostage by our science collection" (p. 178). She highlights 1987 as a year when the *rate* of price increases was much higher than in previous years. She suggests that libraries first study the pricing patterns of the few large publishers with offices in both Europe and the United States as a way to control future price changes (since the dollar has been devalued). First, results should be disseminated widely in order to influence those publishers; smaller publishing houses will then fall in line. Second, libraries must cancel titles.

Strauch and Strauch appear to expose the practice of differential pricing, which is sometimes claimed to be solely a byproduct of exchange rates by foreign publishers. These authors suggest the use of what they call "exposure management" to manage the foreign exchange risks experienced by publishers and distributors. Four basic strategies are recommended for publishers: (1) invoice publications in native currency, (2) use "lead and lag strategy", (3) borrow in the currency of the buyer, and (4) buy foreign exchange options.

Differential pricing. GRINELL documents the differential pricing practices of Springer-Verlag (New York) in 1988–1989 by which non-U.S. librarians were charged higher prices than U.S. librarians. TUTTLE discusses the practice of British publishers' selling scholarly journals to North American libraries at a rate higher than that charged to British libraries. The practice of pricing in U.S. dollars to the U.S. market appears to contribute to this discrimination.

Other causes of serials price increases.   H. C. PETERSEN studied a random sample of 439 journals to determine those attributes that contribute to variations in journal prices. Significant regression results on noncost factors showed that prices are highest for journals: (1) in the physical sciences, (2) published by for-profit, governmental, or nonprofit institutions (vs. society journals), and (3) published outside the United States and Canada. Petersen concludes that shipping may account for a small amount of the difference, "but the rest reflects exchange rates and, perhaps, price discrimination by foreign journal publishers" (p. 8). SALT published two lists of top 20 journal titles rated by cost-per-page for the 20 most inflationary and the 20 least inflationary from a total sample of 95 journals in the geosciences. He could find no overall patterns to explain the price increases.

Price indexes.   YOUNG updates price analyses from the Faxon Co. databases for 1987–1989 for more than 200,000 unique serialized titles. Eight multipart tables include: (1) percent of total subscriptions and expenditures within 16 price ranges for public and academic libraries; (2) average price and annual percent change by seven types of libraries; (3) title rate and data; and (4) price comparisons by 36 abstracting and indexing (A&I) services, country of publication, and selected Library of Congress (LC) class.

The "bible" for price indexes for library materials is the *Library and Book Trade Almanac* (formerly the *Bowker Annual*). The most recent edition (SIMORA) contains: (1) price indexes for school and academic library acquisitions (p. 406-410); (2) average prices for hardcover books above and below $81; (3) prices for mass market paperbacks and trade paperbacks; and (4) average and median prices for novels, biographies, and history books (p. 479-489). More detailed breakouts by 32 broad subject categories are available for eight media and formats, including periodicals and U.S. serial services. Most of these indexes appear in earlier years of the *Library and Book Trade Almanac* as well.

Faxon Co.'s periodical and serials database (as of January 31, 1990), which contains more than 200,000 titles from U.S. and foreign publishers, is the source of subscription prices for 3,942 selected print periodicals in the 1990 price index study sponsored by a division of the American Library Association (ALA) (YOUNG & CARPENTER). Of 25 subject categories, average subscription prices ranged from $17.51 (children's periodicals) to $678.09 (Soviet translations). The average price of a journal (excluding Soviet translations) was $93.45, and the average annual price increase has been 9.2% over the past seven years. The 1986–1989 U.S. periodicals price indexes increased at substantially higher rates than the CPI (using 1977 as the base year). Young and Carpenter conclude that rising subscription prices continue to be a significant trend, although the average annual price increase dipped slightly from 10% early in the 13-year period (1977–1990) to the 9.2% mentioned above.

KRONENFELD & GABLE examine price increases for 188 journals in the *Brandon/Hill Selected List of Books and Journals for the Small Medical Library*. They show that the buying power of the 1987 dollar (vs. the 1975 dollar) spent on Brandon/Hill journals is 59% of a dollar spent in the general economy; in 1983 it was 64%. Further evidence shows that while inflation slowed, the buying power of libraries dwindled.

ANDERSON presents a similar picture for veterinary serials for 1977–1989. Inflation rates for titles on her list (comprised of core, adjunct core, and A&I reference categories) are: 25.08% for adjunct core (80% of which are from commercial publishers) and 16.75% for core (approximately 25% of which are commercial publishers).

GREENE reviewed representative library collections from a junior college, a Fortune 500 company, a mid-sized state university, and a mid-sized private university. Each case was detailed for 1981–1985 for total dollar expenditures, total dollar increases, total percentage increases, average line-item price, with dollar increase, and percent increase (broken out for U.S. titles, non-U.S. titles, and all titles). The actual average cost of foreign titles ($142.05) was nearly 40% higher than that of American titles ($96.54). Greene forecasts that if the 8.4% inflation rate of 1981–1985 is maintained, serials titles in 1994 will be double the price of those in 1986.

Consensus from the Library Community

Following the ARL report mentioned earlier, a consensus of opinion appeared to form in the library community regarding causes of and solutions to the increase in serials prices: (1) the major price increases appear to be emanating from a few large, commercial, mostly European, STM (scientific, technical, medical) publishers; (2) price increases from these publishers are much higher than from other publishers, and much of the increase seems directed to maximizing profits rather than being attributable to exchange rates or rising costs; (3) the scholarly community should be informed about the pricing dilemma and be encouraged to form a lasting partnership with librarians to help manage the problem; and (4) competition and publishing alternatives should be encouraged.

The Publishers Speak

An additional component of rising prices seems to be based on the following scenario. Publishers, particularly STM publishers, have been increasing coverage to correspond to the accelerating increase in the growth of knowledge (or at least growth of authors' output). This, of course, increases total publication size and increases costs of production and distribution. Sometimes this activity is done in the name of responding to the marketplace's request (by authors, scholars, and librarians) for comprehensive coverage and/or sometimes to meet the competition (BYRD; MERRIMAN). Increased prices cause cancellations, which diminish total revenues for a title, and cause prices to spiral. Another activity, "twigging," the proliferation of journals in narrower and narrower subject areas, exacerbates the situation; competition erodes the subscription base of existing titles.

Bob Miranda of Pergamon (CLACK, 1989b, p. 4) contends that "only the essence of the scientific discipline is ultimately published" by commercial publishers and that STM journals reject 50%–75% of submissions after first review (more after second and third reviews); society journals, however, accept most of their members' papers. Rowe, of Faxon Co. (CLACK, 1989b, p. 6,7,10), asserted that it is the library's responsibility as consumer to delineate the publisher/library relationship. WHITE (p. 63) suggests that librarians tell publishers what they plan to spend "as our own decision and not as part of a begging posture with our administration on the publishers' behalf." Rowe (CLACK, 1989b) believes that libraries are shifting from a collection orientation to an access orientation (not necessarily in conflict with the oft-stated need for a "collection of record"). In his concluding comments on differential pricing, Rowe explains that price differences are instituted to compensate for the multiple-user copy for the institution vs. the single-user copy for the individual.

In an earlier paper, BAUMOL ET AL. show a positive effect of "discriminatory" pricing: potentially lower prices for all subscribers.

Further, an issue of *Serials Review* explores the role of the serials agent and agency discounts in serials pricing (BARKER; IVINS, 1990). COX (p. 137) contends that Pergamon sets different prices in different parts of the world (formerly they sold at one worldwide price) in order to avoid large price increases in any one area of the world. John Tagler (CLACK, 1989b, p. 7–9) called attention to the recent dropoff in the launch of new journal titles at Elsevier—48 in 1979, 26 in 1983, and only 10 in 1988. In addition, fewer new journals survive, and the probable number of subscribers for a new journal is much smaller than the number for those that were started 20 years ago. Finally, journals such as those in clinical medicine would cost seven to eight times their present price if advertising were not included, Tagler added. (The startling phenomenon of a decrease in the rate of new serial titles appears to have begun in 1987 and the growth of the mean number of current serial titles in ARL libraries was stagnant in the mid-80s (HUNTER; OKERSON, p. 10, 12).

Some Final Words from the Library Community

DOUGHERTY & JOHNSON take a hard line and state that libraries simply don't have sufficient budgets to buy new journals while contending with rising prices. The alternative is to look at other options, including working with scholars and bibliographic utilities to "become more directly involved in the communication, publication and distribution of scholarly information" (p. 29). HOUBECK (p. 117) believes that journal publishers are still responding to article producers, and as controllers of the precious resource of outlets for manuscripts are commanding high prices. He suggests that libraries: (1) set aside serials funds to spend on new journals from smaller publishers in order to encourage competition; (2) inform the faculty about serials price increases; (3) create price-evaluation and -review tools and disseminate the findings widely and rapidly; and (4) confront publishers about exchange rates. In an analogy between rising prices at the gas pump and rising prices at the serials pump the author remembers that lowered gas prices came about when people changed their behavior and used alternatives.

The Need for a New Paradigm of Scholarly Publishing

BYRD (1990), in an excellent and compelling essay, is also concerned about changes in behavior within the scholarly publishing community. He concludes that cooperative, not competitive, strategies are keys to a new information order. To make his point, he relates a well-known economic fable (The Tragedy of the Commons) in which each herdsman in a community that shares a grazing commons decides to add more cattle for personal profit, thereby contributing to overgrazing and the subsequent demise (the "tragedy") of the commons. Michael PORTER might say that publishers are unwittingly milking the cash cow of a declining business—print. However, they are also contributing to the demise of the library commons, abetted by librarians who have been savaging collections in social sciences and humanities as a consequence of concentrating book and serial acquisitions in the scientific disciplines. It should be clear that the oft-touted electronic networks cannot be part of a solution to this "commons" problem without concomitant changes in the behavior of all the players in the scholarly communication system. A paradigm shift with new roles for librarians, scholars, and publishers may be the only way to save the library commons.

HUNTER of Elsevier fingers changes in electronic information retrieval and document delivery (aids to resource sharing) as the first two parts of a three-part strategy to solve the problem of high serials prices. The third part is to devise and implement a new economic model for journal publishing to help shed the remnants of print-only, collection limitations and to be receptive to the characteristics of a library based on access to information (wherever it might be housed). Prices will probably continue to rise under the present system, Hunter concludes. In fact, Faxon projects that serials prices will inflate by 20% in 1991. Elsevier's increases for 1991, when converted to U.S. dollars, may be as high as 35%, much of which is said to be due to a decline of the dollar relative to the Dutch guilder (*NFAIS NEWSLETTER*). Licensing agreements may play a large part in the future, addressing some of the pricing problems influenced by copyright (HOGEWEG-DE HAART) as might a pay-as-you-go policy of charging for information. Most significantly, Hunter believes that the very structure of the professional journal will have to change if pricing issues are to be addressed appropriately by the publishers. She also thinks it will be necessary to "attract advertising to subsidize reader access" (p. 125).

THE BOOK CRISIS

Introduction

Much early evidence suggests that the serials crisis has contributed substantially to a similar crisis for the publishing, purchasing, and pricing of monographs.

Background

DUCHIN, who is affiliated with Blackwell N.A. science publishers, presents a set of 1987, 1988, and 1989 statistics for scholarly publications. The average prices of titles imported into the United States and sold through U.S. sources increased during those years at twice the rate of domestic titles—i.e., from $53.68 to $62.44 (16.6%) for the former and from $48.53 to $52.52 (8.2%) for the latter. Blackwell, a major book jobber, observed 14% increases in scholarly publishing list prices. Highest average prices were in science: $66.00 (prices for chemistry and microbiology subsets were $88 and $91, respectively). Only law and sci-tech titles averaged more than $50 in the scholarly set.

One hundred booksellers, librarians, and publishers convened in London in April 1989 to discuss rising book prices and their effects on British library buying practices. *THE BOOKSELLER* gives a pithy, well-documented commentary (including 11 tables and graphs illustrating average book prices, prices of STM (scientific, technical, and medical) books adjusted for inflation, price breakouts for selected STM publisher titles, and library expenditures). The article concludes that more titles, especially English-language titles, are being produced and distributed in a depressed library market (33,000 in 1972, double that in 1986) in order to keep up with the accelerated growth of knowledge and to capture the growing English-reading markets. Monograph prices are increasing faster than inflation to cover smaller unit sales; this phenomenon seems particularly pronounced for STM titles from the United States. Academic libraries are spending a larger percentage of their budgets on journals, and public libraries are spending more on paperbacks and "cheaper books" to sustain title growth—but not necessarily for good quality collection development.

The Somerset Studies

Case study. In a renowned case, STOAKLEY traced the activities of the Library Committee of the Somerset County Council (U.K.) in its attempts to determine why prices for books were increasing at rates so much above inflation for books purchased by public libraries in its territory. First, the council required reports on the efficiency of library suppliers (vs. local booksellers) and on the Net Book Agreement relative to library price discounts and publisher subsidies. Frustrated by the lack of an answer, since it appeared that neither the Net Book Agreement nor library purchasing practices was the apparent culprit, the council had its external auditors make a comprehensive study of the council's book-purchasing practices and book suppliers. The study "confirmed that given the current national book trading arrangements, the County Council was indeed acquiring its public library books in the most expeditious and economic way" (STOAKLEY, p. 11). Finally, an additional report on the publishing industry was commissioned, and it concluded: "On the basis of this analysis, the major influences forcing up prices of books are the changes in the number of titles produced, with the consequent effects on the average print runs and industry's cost structure, as well as the large investments made in promoting books" (p. 11). The report also cast a shadow over the Net Book Agreement for preventing competition which might counter rising prices. In the face of eroding support for the Net Book Agreement, Stoakley concludes that we are witnessing "the ravages of commercialism, in an industry with its roots in philanthropy" (p. 12). He implores members of the book trade to share the "responsibility to society, of ensuring the widest possible access to ideas, knowledge, information and enlightenment, through the printed medium" (p. 13).

Price Discrimination

MONTAG identifies two kinds of price discrimination practiced against libraries: (1) institutional vs. individual subscription pricing (e.g., Pergamon Press's 1988 "surcharges" ranged from 1,474% to 1,590%) and (2) pricing based on the geographic location of the library or the library's supplier relative to the country of publication (e.g., many U.S. publishers require substantial surcharges (an average of 47% in 1987 in the U.K.) for books ordered by a foreign bookseller directly from them). The latter problem is compounded since some catalogs from multinational publishers don't indicate the country in which books were published; thus, a wrong choice can cost up to 70% more. Self-education of librarians with respect to pricing and international and/or national negotiations with publishers by librarians or library associations may be the solutions to these discriminatory practices.

Some titles appear in both American and "foreign" editions, each with its own price. DUCHIN suggests that publishers may be "pricing by targeted market." A survey of 200 titles revealed that: "(1) only about half the titles are even close to being published simultaneously, and (2) the pricing of the U.S. edition was totally inconsistent from publisher to publisher and even within the same publisher" (DUCHIN, p. 117).

Price Structures

ABEL suggests that service be the primary criterion for choosing a book vendor but notes that cost-plus pricing (delivered cost from the publisher plus a percentage of that cost) offers a simple formula for comparing prices among vendors. MARSH & LOCKMAN present examples of how one identifies the "net" price of a book (cost plus an additional dollar amount) and determines the accuracy of the costs.

Impacts and Potential Solutions

WELSCH "examines the assumptions behind the use of book price increases in budget calculations and suggests a new measure of collection development needs that factors the change in percent of coverage and in size of the literature into funding cost" (p. 159). For example, there were 619 volumes of business books in 1975 and 1,048 in 1985, and the average price for a business book increased from $16.54 to $28.89 during that same period (p. 161). The total cost increase (to the library attempting to maintain *comprehensive* coverage) is thus about 193% over 1975, not just the 74% price increase (WELSCH, p. 161, table). LYNDEN (1990) reviews the monograph and serials price crisis and possible actions to solve the pricing problem. He focuses on providing better data for selection and cancellation decisions, and he concentrates on the data-gathering process. Lynden provides an excellent summary of where to find domestic and foreign price indexes as the basis for budget presentations. He concludes that "any solution requires more substantial data on the costs of library materials" (p. 37).

An earlier paper by LYNDEN (1988b) seeks standard and reliable sources of data on the costs of foreign library materials and provides a dozen conclusions. Foremost among these is that book "vendors are the best source of information on foreign price trends for 'academic' titles" (p. 225).

HAMAKER & GRINELL attempt to answer the question: What are the implications of major increases in library materials expenditures with declines in volumes added during the same period "for the concept of a collection of record created by our nation's libraries?" The trend is toward a decreasing percentage of coverage, which may be irreversible. LYNDEN (1990) thus concludes that a "serious consequence of the decline in book purchasing has been the effect on the social sciences and humanities" (p. 38). Once again, data by Hamaker and Grinell point to the fact that it is only a few publishers that seriously affect all Association of College and Research Libraries (ACRL) and Association of Research Libraries (ARL) library collections. While the book "crisis" is several years behind the serials crisis and is taking a back seat in terms of library action, its impact on collection development may be even more serious.

THE ONLINE REVOLUTION IN ELECTRONIC PUBLISHING

Introduction

By the early 1980s online searching had become recognized as a respectable function and powerful research tool in most libraries of size and budget in the developed countries. Unfortunately, the pricing is complex (though usually manageable) within any one service; across services, it is downright perplexing. Although the value of online searching is usually recognized, the cost of one search is now in the tens and sometimes hundreds of dollars and is often difficult to estimate in advance. Further, since searches are not easily defined information units, there is no standard unit cost for a search, even the same search; thus, pricing for online searching is open ended. Finally, when the intermediary (usually library staff) has finished doing an online search for a patron, what does the library have to show for the effort? The collection has not been enhanced; no tangible assets remain with the library. Each "purchased" search is a customized information package probably unlike any other and probably with little value to others. These properties and pricing characteristics set online databases apart from print counterparts and allow them to compete so well (yet so little) with print. Online vendors have struggled for two decades to reach a pricing structure that is appealing, simple, and technologically current. The literature reflects this condition but offers few solutions.

Fortunately, an omnibus review article on online information pricing was done by HAWKINS. He reviews the history and shortcomings of connect-time pricing for online information services and reviews other pricing structures that were tried over time: (1) computer resource units (by Mead Data Central and Chemical Abstracts Service (CAS)), (2) flat-rate pricing (Telebase Systems' EasyNet), (3) Unlimited Access (BRS/After Dark) (4) time (of day) differential (Dow-Jones and NewsNet), (5) baud rate differential (Dow-Jones and others), and (6) hit charges (CAB Abstracts). Output formats with no hit charges, downloading, telecommunications fees, up-front fees, minimums, discounts, credit card billing, two-tier pricing, and database leasing are also addressed. Sidebars cover: (1) likely pricing for gateway services from Regional Bell Operating Companies (use-sensitive pricing) and (2) aspects of the "fee vs. free" debate. Hawkins concludes that major changes in online pricing schemes are due and that the search for ideal pricing can be successful only with cooperation among users, database producers, and online vendors.

Trends

Pricing models and trends for a variety of information products are presented in the *Information Industry Factbook* (FLEMING ET AL.). For example, the 1990/91 edition discusses prices and the price model for online consumer services such as Delphi, Genie, and Prodigy, comparing their pricing to pricing by novel publishers selling "many copies at a relatively low price" (p. 289). Included in the five basic pricing techniques popular in 1989/90 (and different from online reference services) are two new options.

First is the option of unlimited use for a flat monthly fee; this is available from the fastest-growing of the general-interest services—viz., Prodigy. However, a sudden increase in their fees (from $9.95 to $12.95 per month) and the addition of message fees for major E-mail and bulletin board users (imposed to offset expenses incurred by frequent users) created a revolt by price-sensitive heavy users (SCHNEIDAWIND). Some of Prodigy's cost-based problems with pricing may be modified if advertising dollars become its major source of revenue.

The second option is tiered pricing (similar to cable TV pricing)—i.e., basic services for a flat fee, and additional charges for "premium" services. Genie's STAR Service boasts a low (after hours) minimum, with unlimited access to 100 services at $4.95/month. Standard Genie rates are $6/hour (evening) and $18/hour (daytime). Delphi's similar pricing is $6/hour (evening) and $15/hour (daytime), but for heavy users the 20/20 Advantage Plan offers 20 hours of use for $20/month. CompuServe has just instituted a $1.50/month minimum (FLEMING ET AL., p. 288-294).

On a different note, a new service from Dow-Jones, DowVision, does not permit users to interact with the "online" host computer but does allow interaction with the information distributed to the user's organization's computer(s). DowVision is intended for professional users of news and financial information and may be a major force in future corporate information distribution. DowVision is also "a package of real-time news feeds priced at a flat rate for distribution over internal corporate networks" (FLEMING ET AL., p. 309). It costs $1,000 for the first ten users each month, with additional charges for each additional user, or \$3,000 for the first 100 users a month, with additional charges for additional users.

Old Services, New Prices

BRS.   A decade after being established, BRS, which was noted for starting with subscription-based pricing for online services, moved into a new price structure and level in January 1987. In six tables, WILLIAMS compares the new volume discount scheme with the old one (both are based on connect time). He concludes "that BRS has simply raised their prices overall" and "simplified their offline price structure by incorporating the old per page charge into the new citation charge" (WILLIAMS, p. 68).

Chemical Abstracts Service.   CAS recently set forth its novel plan to move away from connect-hour pricing for its online databases and toward "search term" pricing—i.e., the more complex the query is, the more the search costs (*CAS REPORT*). For example, CAS will now charge 10 cents for each text search term and \$20 for each structure or substructure in a search statement. Record-extraction fees for data elements (such as Registry Numbers), used as the basis for occurrence analysis, will now be charged for as will partial records that can be linked to answer sets (vs. partial records indicating relevance). "Query import" fees were also being considered for search statements formulated online but outside of CAS databases. CAS believes that this pricing formula will "relate the return to the database producer more closely to the value delivered to the customer and open up the possibility of mixing databases of various database producers, with each producer receiving fair payment for the use of [its] data" (p. 4).

O'LEARY sees the new CAS license and pricing as a first step toward a new definition of the value of online information. In interviews with online industry leaders, publishers agree that online revenues are not growing fast enough, baud-rate price differentials should be considered and online prices do not reflect the producers' contributions and database value, and the intent of the CAS move may remedy some of these problems. Online vendors believe that the new CAS charges will result in online price increases. O'Leary concludes that the CAS pricing changes will bring higher and more complex prices.

PEMBERTON (1988a; 1988b) conducted a lengthy interview with Harry Boyle, Project Manager, Online Services, Chemical Abstracts Service, about CAS's pricing policy; the article was preceded by an editorial recognizing "winds of change" in online pricing structure (PEMBERTON, 1988b). An editorial in *MONITOR* stirred the pot of speculation by suggesting that CAS would be delighted if all six vendors that distribute its databases refused to sign the new CAS licensing agreement. Earlier speculation from another European publication said: "Chemical Abstracts very clearly has it in mind to become their own host" (*INFOTECTURE*), p. 9). Suits and countersuits filed in 1990 and 1991 between DIALOG Information Services and the American Chemical Society have muddied the water over pricing structures, although the accounting procedures used by DIALOG to compute royalties are central to CAS's position.

The reaction of a user of CAS Online to the new CAS pricing structure is voiced by WITIAK. While she expects business as usual (no confusing price schemes for the user; no price decreases), she recognizes that "the mechanism for change is being set into place" (p. 95). Despite earlier attempts by CAB (Commonwealth Agricultural Bureaux) Abstracts to structure its prices according to content vs. process and NLM's (National Library of Medicine) intent to "equalize system cost of our users," Witiak recounts that in 1977 the average search cost $20; by 1987 it cost $130 (a 550% increase that makes the serials crisis look good). Subsidized, subscription-based and value-based models of pricing for online databases are described briefly.

ESA-IRS. Just as Chemical Abstracts Service surprised the online world with its 1987 announcement of a new price structure, the Italian host ESA-IRS (European Space Agency-Information Retrieval Service) effected a unique pricing policy in January 1989—viz., connect-hour charges are virtually eliminated; charges are concentrated in information extracted or viewed (offline or online record charges). There is also a session charge applied to each database according to its royalty level. Marino Saksida, director of ESA-IRS, related in a lengthy interview (GARMAN, 1990b) that this new pricing structure is intended to open up and enlarge the end-user market. Preliminary reports (*INFOR-MATION WORLD REVIEW*, 1989b) quoted Saksida as saying that "use and revenue are now higher than they were twelve months ago" (p. 16). However, it was also reported that Saksida planned to raise prices in January or April of 1990, "but only by a little." The German host DIMDI (Deutsches Institut für Medizinische Dokumentation und Information) established a similar pricing scheme in October 1989 in partial response to changes in user behavior: "More and more people have started to access at 9600 bps, thereby acquiring much more information in a given time. This trend will continue," stated Hans-Eberhard Kurzwelly of DIMDI (*INFORMATION WORLD REVIEW*, 1989a, p. 16).

End-user KITLEY is critical of the CAS price structure change and the subsequent complementary change by ESA-IRS. He believes that the future will be filled with noncomparable pricing across hosts. Kitley characterizes the ESA move as a "revenue-boosting exercise" (p. 290). The move away from connect-time charges is expedient as other appealing pricing schemes (e.g., flat rate for X searches, or unlimited searches for a flat rate) compete. The ever-increasing baud rate is another major factor as telecommunications architectures, such as the proposed National Research and Education Network (NREN), aim to reach a 3 gigabit/second capacity by 1996 (PARKHURST, p. 3). It is unlikely that the move away from connect-time pricing is temporary. TENOPIR summarizes the challenges to connect-time pricing (e.g., baud rates, downloading to PCs, front-end software) and includes anecdotal evidence for NLM, Mead Data Central (who moved first to use-based, then to per-search-based prices), CAS, and EasyNet (with fixed-price, unlimited access pricing) to illustrate some of the moves away from a connect-time basis for online charging.

Comparative Studies

Two studies compare ESA-IRS and DIALOG pricing following the ESA price change (JACK; SORMUNEN). The tables in the article by JACK list ESA session rates ranging from $2.37 to $11.94 (although a statement reveals that the theoretical maximum is supposed to be $5.92). The online hourly rate (the housekeeping charge) is a flat $11.84, and full-record charges range from 37 cents to $1.44. JACK (from the United States) intentionally ignores telecommunications costs in the comparisons. He concludes that (without factoring in a session charge), in general, ESA is less expensive at 1,200 baud, and DIALOG is less expensive at 2,400 baud.

SORMUNEN (from Finland) includes both telecommunications costs and session charges and concludes that, in general, ESA-IRS is cheaper because telecommunications costs from Helsinki favor ESA. When telecommunications costs are ignored, "DIALOG is more economic in cases where the search is brief but with a lot of output. . .or in cases where it is necessary to carry out small separate searches in several databases, such as the bibliographic checking of documents" (SORMUNEN, p. 33).

A more ambitious study by ESKOLA & SORMUNEN (from Finland) compares prices of six databases (BIOSIS, Chemical Abstracts, COMPENDEX, FSTA, INSPEC, and NTIS) across four hosts (DataStar, DIALOG, ESA-IRS, and STN). The authors chart the average online and display charges under various conditions (e.g., 1,200 and 2,400 baud rates) and give high marks to ESA-IRS, which frees end users from time restrictions and makes it easier for them to estimate the total cost of a search before searching. With telecommunications costs included, at 2,400 baud, DIALOG has the lowest cost in three of six sample database searches, ESA the lowest cost in the other three; STN has the highest prices in four of the six, and DIALOG and ESA have the highest in the other two. At 1,200 baud ESA is the most economical in all six cases.

HOLMES conducted an experiment in 1979 to investigate a change in the price structure for the British Library's system, BLAISE (British Library Automated Information Service). The intent was to encourage charging for time and output rather than just connect-time. The results were inconclusive but indicated that users didn't understand how this change would benefit them.

ROBINSON identifies six types of business databases on DIALOG (abstracts, indexes, full text, index/abstract linked to full text, directories, and numeric) and gives the prices of these files within each category. He then speculates about the reasons for discrepancies in price within categories.

Although there were no true price indexes for online services, the "International Comparative Price Guide to Databases Online" (*ONLINE REVIEW*) used to supply discount schedules for nine U.S. and European hosts and a list of minimum and maximum online prices and offline and online record charges converted to U.S. dollars for 103 databases available from more than one of the nine vendors serving the library market. Exchange rates were said to favor the European hosts for the list compiled in mid-1986. A wide variety of prices existed for most databases. For example, COMPENDEX minimums ranged from $71/ hour (BRS) to $93/hour (DIALOG and SDC) over six hosts, no two having the same per-hour maximum. Likewise, for CA Search on seven hosts, minimums ranged from $66 (ESA-IRS) to $94 (the high on CAS Online (precursor of CA on STN) and for nonsubscribers to the print). Scanning the list, the price spread for databases on different hosts seems to be about 20%. Of course, no attempt is made to factor in the differences among the vendors for their individual treatment of value added to that database. One may have three years available for searching; another, eight years. One may have all years in one file, another may have the years split into two files.

Pricing Structures, Pricing Strategies

ELIAS & UNRUH provide some useful definitions for terms of sale for publications and a case study of pricing strategy for a database product line comprised of five components: print, online,

CD-ROM, microform and floppy disk (p. 81-93). The case study follows each delivery format (i.e., print) to illustrate how the price is determined once a base cost and profit are established. The strategy for pricing among different media is worth reading even though the costing portion of the example is missing a paragraph, which may cause some confusion. Remarks and examples are written (appropriately) within the context of a typical NFAIS (National Federation of Abstracting and Information Services) publisher: large, established, not-for-profit, database publisher to the library market.

FISCHER offers ten rules for successful pricing strategies for electronic information. She includes such useful advice as: "Price as a line of goods, not as a basic database with spin-off products based on incremental revenue" (Rule 1) (p. 74). "The price will change once a price has been established and used in the marketplace" (Rule 10) (p. 78).

ARNOLD (1989b) points out the complexity of online pricing strategies by online vendors to the consumer and the harsh techniques vendors use to control database producers and pricing. In a more polished piece, ARNOLD (1989c) discusses the United States as an overdeveloped country—viz., one in which the economy shifts from a manufacturing base to a base that depends on electronic information products (EIP); he also covers EIP life cycles and EIP pricing. This humorous but thoughtful essay includes a useful pricing exercise that illustrates unwanted migration from print to CD-ROM.

GARMAN (1988) provides additional fuel for arguments that online pricing is too complex, too confusing, and too volatile. Two main problems are identified: (1) as searchers learn of techniques and technologies to save money, vendors and producers "move to protect their income" (p. 7), and (2) it is difficult to estimate online search costs in advance and just as difficult to determine the final billable cost after the search is completed but before billing.

KOSTENBAUDER (of the IBM Technical Information Center) asks why information should cost him more simply because he gets greater value from it. Fixed fees are preferable to current pricing structures, but "fixed prices quoted are often too high" (p. 87). He goes on to say that "organizations indicate that a reasonable base license fee with a sliding scale of rates as the volume increases is usually easier to sell to upper management" (p. 87). He contends that all prices become negotiable if there is no acceptable price structure. Bulk (volume) pricing will be necessary to open up the end-user market.

TRUDELL presents DIALOG's pricing strategy for long-term growth: "maintaining current pricing levels on [the] expectation of faster development of volume potential" (p. 80). She discusses the effects of new technology from the viewpoint of user satisfaction, search efficiency, and increased use and revenues. Examples of four values added to DIALOG's service over a two-year period are described. Trudell's pricing philosophies are: increase value and apply simple, predictable pricing.

Roger K. Summit, president of DIALOG, considers databases as the raw materials that DIALOG then finishes (GARMAN, 1990a). It is DIALOG's value added for two functions within the online database industry—access to information and delivery of information—that determines its value in the pricing formula. Summit's perspective is that DIALOG licenses copyright from the database supplier after negotiating forms and amounts of royalty with them. Pricing to the customer is based on perceived value to the customer; the price must be sufficient to recover DIALOG's costs, pay royalties, and return profit. Summit suggests that user institutions can negotiate with DIALOG for basically unlimited use (with flat fee, site licenses) of individual databases. DIALOG delivery of unlimited use could take the place of dealing directly with only the database supplier and setting up an expensive retrieval service on site. In fact, Summit expects more flat-fee pricing in the future and believes that "the extent to which database suppliers will accommodate to the notion of a flat fee may determine if we can really move online searching to the masses" (GARMAN, 1990a, p. 43). BIOSIS has written its latest site license agreement to reflect delivery by tape from BIOSIS or delivery through a host; the pricing structure is not flat fee, however (ELIAS, 1990b).

Discounts and Resellers

Little is written about those who resell information or about the effect of discounts on pricing policies. A news article detailing CAS use (*INFORMATION WORLD REVIEW*, 1990) reveals: "more and more clients attract academic discount; nowadays virtually a third of all use of the CA file on STN" (p. 4). Library networks (such as AMIGOS, CLASS, and INCOLSA) resell both online and CD-ROM services and provide some customer support for members as well. MORRIS describes surcharges, dues, and markups to OCLC prices by 16 networks during 1985–1986. Some pricing variations are said to depend on location, level of state support, or affiliation. The author cannot uncover significant reasons for the many differences in price for the same OCLC services.

Marketing material from OCLC ONLINE COMPUTER LIBRARY CENTER describes FirstSearch (previously named MAX), a service to be available late in 1991. FirstSearch is said to be designed for library patrons and is priced in blocks of "searches" (any search statement after which one presses "ENTER"). The price per "search" ranges from 45 cents if a library pays for 80,000 at one time (160 blocks) to 90 cents for the purchase of just one block of 500 searches. The service is to be available to a limited group of OCLC participating libraries, and it is to be offered via OCLC dedicated-line terminals and Internet. If these prices hold, academic reselling of online searches may become as common as key cards for copying.

THE CD-ROM REVOLUTION IN ELECTRONIC PUBLISHING

Introduction

CD-ROM products are just over five years old, but they have already made an impression on the library market. Their fixed price and unlimited access—similar to single copies of books and journals—make budgeting simple. They also offer a real price advantage over online "equivalents" when use is high. The value added of CD-ROM over print is recognized as high, but the dependence on PCs as readers (as with online) adds a cost that has been transferred neatly to the consumer. Too, some libraries treat CD-ROM subscriptions as complementary to the print collection, while others consider them as substitutes and cancel equivalent or comparable print subscriptions; all of this affects pricing and packaging. In addition, one can purchase very different products bearing the same title. Update frequency options, coverage (usually by date), and searching capabilities are some of the major choices that will affect price. Unless advertising becomes an integral part of electronic publication (as it is with print), the pricing problem will become even more severe than it is now. With all this, the library views CD-ROM prices as beyond reach except on a limited basis. Finally, once again, the bibliographic unit (a paper, an abstract, an issue, a paragraph) must be established for intellectual property rights issues and for purposes of identification and pricing formulas.

Agents and Price Indexes

Online databases have only one true retailer that buys in bulk at discount and resells by the search: EasyNet, which routinely offers online access to information from more than 800 databases.

The fledgling CD-ROM industry already has several agents for CD-ROM purchasing and support (e.g., CD-ROM Inc., Bureau of Electronic

Publishing, UPDATA, Inc.). Some serials jobbers, such as EBSCO, also advertise that they are agents for CD-ROM publications. However, directories such as Meckler's *CD-ROMs in Print* (DESMARAIS) and the Cuadra/Elsevier *Directory of Portable Databases* (BARG) are among the few places you can locate extensive price lists. Apparently the first rigorous attempt at a price index for CD-ROM titles was accomplished by MASON. Her index surveys 100 titles, listing them in the most general LC classifications also used for price indexes for U.S. periodicals. Data are for 1988 and 1989 and show virtually no change in price for the two years (-0.1%). Mason identifies some fundamental issues to be addressed before a formal, more comprehensive index is developed: (1) Should data include prices for the full set or only for the current subscription? (2) How should scope changes (usually increasing content for a title available from more than one publisher) be handled? (3) What about multiple price options for the same title (e.g., network vs. single subscription, quarterly vs. annual versions)? (4) What is the unit of measurement to be (cost per disc, cost per megabyte, dollar total)? Mason concludes: "Perhaps the price index's greatest usefulness might be in the area of prices based on subject classification, for example, knowing the average cost of a CD-ROM title in medicine" (p. 182).

Trends and Pricing Strategies

The price of CD-ROM readers has dropped, but CD-ROM prices are rising slowly for established titles yet have come down in some markets—i.e., the average price of CD-ROM titles in the reference market has dropped almost 25% since 1987, 65% in industry-specific markets, and 17% overall. The average price of a CD-ROM title (across all markets) was $2,067 in 1987; by 1990 it had declined to $1,708. Of 232 CD-ROM titles, 153 did not change price from 1989 to 1990; 35 increased in price, and 42 lowered in price (FLEMING ET AL.). Based on fall 1988 prices for nearly 200 products (28% cost less than $500, 26% cost more than $2,500, and 46% were between $500–$2,500), ARNOLD (1989a) speculates that publishers have adopted one of three CD-ROM pricing strategies: (1) "Charge a low price and try to move units" (market share); (2) "Charge as much as possible" (market skimming); or (3) "Sit on the fence and offer prices that are neither too high nor too low." He believes that: "For the foreseeable future, prices will be downward bound" (p. 6) because design and production costs have dropped significantly, CD-ROM drive prices are dropping (a price of $500 is seen as appealing for the market to grow), and competition will force lower prices, at least in the library market.

RIETDYK (of Silver Platter) struggles with the problems of striking a balance between compensation and fair pricing. Aside from pricing level, he highlights the predictable, fixed, budgetable cost of CD-ROM publications as a major advantage. Networked CDs, however, are not analogous to single copies of print publications (which permit multiple but rarely simultaneous access). New pricing schemes will be necessary for networked CD products; perhaps "value pricing" via site licenses will permit a customized price for the library that wants to serve many users yet preserve predictable, fixed, and budgetable characteristics.

GIBBINS discusses pricing of the software component of CD-ROM publications and the dilemma software publishers face in pricing equitably for high-value products for mass volume and for low-volume, mid-value products. His conclusions focus on the life cycle of the CD-ROM product: "Each new product. . .has to test the price sensitivity of its market" (p. 180). He criticizes the price wars of the public domain databases (e.g., ERIC, MEDLINE) and their less-than $1,000 CD-ROM prices—one can purchase a CD-ROM and use it for an unlimited number of searches for a price that is "equivalent to the [total] revenue that would be earned from 25 hours of online searching" (p. 180). Finally he states: "Until the CD-ROM business. . .[sees] products selling in thousands rather than hundreds, both software suppliers and publishers will continue to struggle with the problem of how to price their products" (p. 180). Four years later, we are approaching these sales milestones.

Library Responses

The Canadian Library Association CD-ROM Special Interest Group surveyed libraries about prices of CD-ROMs, and the unanimous response was that they are too high (NEAME). Libraries were critical of: (1) the price of full cumulations for each update, (2) the annual repurchase of expensive databases, and (3) one user—one workstation limitations. The cost of upkeep for machines and paper is a side problem: "At the University of Calgary, a debit card system has been installed on public machines in order to defray the costs of maintenance and supplies" (p. 96).

DONEL presents criteria for libraries to use in selecting and cancelling compact disc databases: (1) the price should be competitive with comparable products, (2) preference will be given to products with no additional cost for networking versions, (3) preference will be given to products if the discs can be kept (owning vs. leasing), and (4) cancellation will be considered if there is a significant increase in the price of a product or if a competing product has higher value (e.g., lower price, superior quality of information). Prices for CD-ROMs and their print equivalents which were purchased by the Oregon State University Libraries are compared for 23 databases, eight of which are being networked.

Licensing, Leasing, and Buying

Just as online pricing permits the local acquisition of very small segments or of any portion of a publication—usually via a user contract agreement—CD-ROM "sales" can permit the local acquisition of very large publications via a licensing agreement. Unlike their printed counterparts, some electronic versions are not owned by the organizations that acquire them; they are leased, usually for one-year periods. Since libraries are often judged by the size and quality of their holdings, the concept of and rewards for leasing information are often new and foreign. Leased information, the use of which is further controlled by the terms of the licensing agreement, is the mode most online services have used with both suppliers and customers since the late 1960s. Now with the advent of optical publishing, the leasing and licensing of information is growing as publishers attempt to limit their risks by offering their publications in new formats such as CD-ROM.

Of the recent publications dealing with information licensing, one of the best is *CD-ROM Licensing and Copyright Issues for Libraries.* (NISSLEY & NELSON). Ten sample licensing agreements are appended. In the opening chapter, NISSLEY contends that the cost of current CD-ROM products sets up barriers to information access and that there are shortages of value-added CD-ROM products. She notes that until recently few products for libraries have had restrictive licensing or use agreements, and she attributes this new requirement to publishers' desires "to prevent use of the information for purposes other than its original format" (p. 6). Specifically, licensing is meant to prevent republishing and resale "without compensation to the copyright holder" (p. 6), and the publisher is the one to benefit from such agreements. Some publishers, however, (WLN (Western Library Network) and H.W. Wilson, for example) have distributed discs without restrictions except there can be no resale involved. Network versions of CD-ROM publications (when available) are often priced for 50% more than a single-user subscription price. Cost of replacing lost discs can range from no charge to as much as $200. Nissley concludes that the use of licensing agreements for distributing information via new technologies will continue to rise.

In the same volume DOBB points out that "the law of copyright in relation to electronic media is still very much in flux" (p. 28) and that as copyright law fails electronic publishers, they will use "locally tailored contracts" and will lobby to plug loopholes that permit copyright "infringement" by state entities such as universities and state agencies.

POOLEY sketches the evolution of licensing for CD-ROM products and posits that often the terms of the license are the basis for CD-ROM selection and acquisition. Pooley discusses database ownership and suggests that users must be educated to the reasons for licensing CD-ROM serials (i.e., giving away a large amount of a database to any subscriber in CD-ROM format might threaten revenues from existing formats such as print or online). Competition among publishers that offer public domain databases such as ERIC and MEDLINE lowered the prices for many early CD-ROM products. These lower prices helped to stimulate the library market for CD-ROM purchases.

GOLDSTEIN focuses on the problems and opportunities of selling CD-ROMs for use in networks. He draws the differences in values and vulnerability between CD-ROM and software in order to indicate what might be feasible to include in a "site license" (a license permitting many users to share one copy or reproduce it). For CD-ROM, copying of the entire database is not a current problem, and updating and timeliness provide much of the value (and therefore, the protection) for serials databases on this medium. Goldstein states that because his company (IAC) is both a producer and a distributor of its own information and because its market (mostly libraries) has great integrity with respect to protecting intellectual property against copyright infringement, IAC has not found a license agreement necessary. However, because a new IAC product, the Reference Center, offers network access to information from other publishers as well, IAC created its own license agreements. Pricing for this product consists of a subscription for access via four workstations, with discounts for additional stations. Goldstein suggests that producers/distributors and librarians need to work toward "licenses that will enable users the greatest freedom of access in a network yet will adequately compensate the database developers" (p. 54).

BOWERS asserts that legal issues have a predominant role in pricing CD-ROM products today. Publisher concerns about protection of information and continuing revenue streams have led to the licensing of information rather than its sale. Further, lawyers and publishers tend to be cautious in most product situations and react conservatively in uncertain situations; this attitude may result in very high license fees. Bowers points out that because CD-ROM information must be copied to be used, just as online information must, fair use may have to be redefined for electronic information (fair use concerns the amount of a publication that may be copied freely without infringing copyright laws). Bowers contends that because there is no formula established for pricing CD-ROM (in contrast to printed publications), publishers must focus on "the 'value' of information, in convenient form, to the consumer" (p. 62). Current CD-ROM prices are said to include what amounts to an insurance policy for potential risks to publisher investment. This "risk insurance" should decrease with time. (Perhaps we are already seeing this decrease together with competitive pressures and a better understanding of product value since average CD-ROM prices decreased from $2,067 per title in 1987 to $1,708 per title in 1989 (FLEMING ET AL.)). Bowers suggests that the music industry's method of recovering revenue for ad hoc professional use (via American Society of Composers, Authors and Publishers) might be a model worth examining for CD-ROM.

Advertising

In 1989 advertising made up 61% of the information industry's revenue but less than 1% of the revenue for electronic services (FLEMING ET AL.). The examples below illustrate the small trickle of services that offer publications subsidized by suppliers.

The Satellite Energy Service (Senergy), offered by Bonneville Market Information, plans to distribute (by satellite to very small earth stations) daily wholesale and pump prices for petroleum from suppliers to 12,000 wholesalers. Suppliers would finance the network, and the service would be offered free to wholesalers that use at least four suppliers (*DATA BROADCASTING REPORT*). McGraw-Hill's *Sweet's Catalog File* has long been a printed bible of specifications and illustrations for building material products, paid for mostly by supplier ads and used by architectural and engineering firms. Electronic Sweet's on CD-ROM is now to be distributed free to some of its 33,000 subscribers (FLEMING ET AL.). The consumer online information service called Prodigy, a joint venture of IBM and Sears, plans for ad revenues from its shopping and other services to be the backbone of its pricing strategy. Audiotex services (voice information delivered by phone) expect ad-supported revenue to grow to $150 million in 1990 (FLEMING ET AL.). In 1989 these revenues accounted for $125 million of an estimated $623 million in revenue for dial-it services.

CONCLUSION

One has only to read a few of the references cited in the Bibliography (e.g., ARNOLD (1989c), BYRD, KOSTENBAUDER, NEAME, and STOAKLEY) to understand that pricing is a passionate subject. Inflation has toppled governments; why shouldn't information inflation topple the publishing system that appeared to spawn it? However, the issue should not be whether publishing profits are too large, or whether information products have enough value added; the issue is that price is a major component in today's information product and that these products are no longer being designed for the library budget. The current marketplace is breaking down. Is this bad? Of course, those who cannot provide expected services or those who may lose business might say yes. But there is much more going on than "greedy publishers" or librarians out for the blood of commercial publishers. The story of the effect of the competitive forces of electronic publications on print publishers is yet to be told as is the story of life cycles of information technologies as a force on information pricing.

This is a time to build a new structure with electronic information access to a variety of formats and media as the core. It is a time for librarians to rethink and translate their service goals into the contexts of new technologies, new economics, and new customer requirements. It is a time for publishers to cooperate with libraries on library budget limits and to find creative ways to work with libraries as the main agents of information access. Finally, it is a time to look at the whole system of research authoring, publishing, and information requirements and weigh rewards and costs against contributions.

Libraries have survived internal automation which has reduced operating costs and added value to library services. Now it's time to turn serious attention to electronic publications, which are responsible for increasingly large portions of library budgets and services. New infrastructures must be built for electronic publications so that they can be brought into and through libraries for conventional processing and access (e.g., catalog records, price indexes, bibliographic control listings). Information units have to be redefined for pricing, licensing, and identification. Will libraries be paying for subscriptions to journals, for full-text articles as needed, and/or for sections of articles? How will output be labeled for its source identification and marked for use restrictions? These are questions from a new paradigm of research publishing, and solutions will require a new toll of library capital investment in human and machine resources. Librarians will be in a strong position in the research publishing scheme (and thus will be able to exert some control on prices) only if they are active in seeking solutions early; however, library capital expenditures for these activities have only begun to be allocated.

BIBLIOGRAPHY

ABEL, RICHARD. 1988. Cost-Plus Pricing: An Old Nag with a Second Wind? Library Acquisitions: Practice & Theory. 1988; 12(2): 201-202. ISSN: 0364-6408.

ANDERSON, DAVID C. 1989. Journals for Academic Veterinary Medical Libraries: Price Increases, 1977, 1988 and 1989. The Serials Librarian. 1989; 16(3/4): 81-91. ISSN: 0361-526X.

ARNOLD, STEPHEN E. 1989a. CD-ROM Pricing: Bound Down. Laserdisk Professional. 1989 March; 2(2): 6-10. ISSN: 0896-4149.

ARNOLD, STEPHEN E. 1989b. Online Pricing: Where It's At Today and Where It's Going Tomorrow. Online. 1989 March; 13(2): 6-8. ISSN: 0146-5422.

ARNOLD, STEPHEN E. 1989c. Stormy Weather in the Datasphere: The Problems of Pricing and Marketing Electronic Information. The Electronic Library. 1989 October; 7(5): 309-314. ISSN: 0264-0473.

ASSOCIATION OF RESEARCH LIBRARIES. 1989. Report of the ARL Serials Prices Project. Washington, DC: Association of Research Libraries; 1989. 114p. Available from: ERIC Document Reproduction Service. ERIC: ED-311922.

BARG, JEFFREY, ed. 1990. Directory of Portable Databases: Volume 2. New York: Cuadra/Elsevier; 1990 December. 642p. ISBN: 0-444-01596-5.

BARKER, JOSEPH W. 1990. Unbundling Serials Vendors' Service Charges: Are We Ready? Serials Review. 1990 Summer; 16(2): 33-43. ISSN: 0098-7913.

BASCH, N. BERNARD (BUZZY). 1988. Pricing. Library Acquisitions: Practice & Theory. 1988; 12(2): 203-205. ISSN: 0364-6408.

BAUMOL, WILLIAM J.; BRAUNSTEIN, YALE M.; FISHER, DIETRICH M.; ORDOVER, JANUSZ A. 1980. Manual of Pricing and Cost Determination for Organizations Engaged in Dissemination of Knowledge. New York, NY: New York University; 1980. 112p. Available from: U.S. National Technical Information Service, Springfield, VA. PB: 81-131856.

BAUMOL, WILLIAM J.; MARCUS, MATITYAHU. 1973. Economics of Academic Libraries. Washington, DC: American Council on Education; 1973. 98p. ISBN: 0-8268-1257-0; LC: 73-10244.

BEBENSEE, MARK; STRAUCH, BRUCE; STRAUCH, KATINA. 1989. Elasticity and Journal Pricing. The Acquisitions Librarian. 1989; 2(2): 219-227. ISSN: 0896-3576.

THE BOOKSELLER. 1989. Markets and Prices; Part One of a Report of a Seminar on Publishers' Prices. The Bookseller. 1989 May 12; (4351): 1620-1626. ISSN: 0006-7539.

BOWERS, RICHARD A. 1990. The Impact of Legal Issues on the Acceptance of CD-ROM in the Marketplace. In: Nissley, Meta; Nelson, Nancy Melin, eds. CD-ROM Licensing and Copyright Issues for Libraries. Westport, CT: Meckler Corp.; 1990. 57-64. ISBN: 0-88763-701-1; LC: 90-35109.

BULLARD, SCOTT R. 1989. Collection Development in the Electronic Age: Selected Papers and Complementary Reports. Library Acquisitions: Practice & Theory. 1989; 13(3): 209-212. ISSN: 0364-6408.

BYRD, GARY D. 1990. An Economic "Commons" Tragedy for Research Libraries: Scholarly Journal Publishing and Pricing Trends. College & Research Libraries. 1990 May; 51(3): 184-195. ISSN: 0010-0870.

CAS REPORT. 1987. Moving Away from Connect Hours: CAS Announces New Approach to Pricing Electronic Services. CAS Report. 1987 Special Issue; (23): 1-4. ISSN: 0162-7112.

CLACK, MARY ELIZABETH. 1989a. Price Index for 1989: U.S. Serial Services. Library Journal. 1989 April 15; 114(7): 50. ISSN: 0363-0277.

CLACK, MARY ELIZABETH. 1989b. Serials Pricing: A Dialogue between Librarians and Publishers. Library Acquisitions: Practice & Theory. 1989; 13(1): 3-10. ISSN: 0364-6408.

CLINE, GLORIA S. 1987. The High Price of Interlibrary Loan Service. RQ. 1987 Fall; 27(1): 80-86. ISSN: 0033-7072.

COX, BRIAN. 1987. Scholarly Journal Prices. The Serials Librarian. 1987 October/November; 13(2/3): 135-138. ISSN: 0361-526X.

DATA BROADCASTING REPORT. 1990. Bonneville Unveils Senergy VSAT Network for Sending Data to Petroleum Wholesalers. Data Broadcasting Report. 1990 September; 6(4): 1-2. ISSN: 0882-5726.

DAVIES, ROY. 1987. Non-Price Competition and the Structure of the Online Information Industry: Q-Analysis of Medical Databases and Hosts. Journal of Documentation. 1987 September; 43(3): 236-260. ISSN: 0022-0418.

DEGENNARO, RICHARD. 1977. Escalating Journal Prices: Time to Fight Back. American Libraries. 1977 February; 8(2): 70. ISSN: 0002-9769.

DESMARAIS, NORMAN, comp. 1991. CD-ROMs in Print 1991: An International Guide. Westport, CT: Meckler Corp.; 1991. 450p. ISSN: 0891-8198; ISBN: 0-88736-587-6.

DOBB, LINDA. 1990. Recent Developments in Copyright Law for New Information Technologies. In: Nissley, Meta; Nelson, Nancy Melin, eds. CD-ROM Licensing and Copyright Issues for Libraries. Westport, CT: Meckler Corp.; 1990. 19-30. ISBN: 0-88763-701-1; LC: 90-35109.

DONEL, JOHN. 1991. Evaluating CDs. Handout distributed at Online Northwest 91; 1991 January 25; Corvallis, OR. 12p. Available from: Author, Oregon State University, Kerr Library, Corvallis, OR 97330.

DOUGHERTY, RICHARD M.; BARR, NANCY E. 1988. Paying the Piper: ARL Libraries Respond to Skyrocketing Journal Subscription Prices.

Journal of Academic Librarianship. 1988 March; 14(1): 4-9. ISSN: 0099-1333.

DOUGHERTY, RICHARD M.; JOHNSON, BRENDA L. 1988. Periodical Price Escalation. Library Journal. 1988 May 15; 113(9): 27-29. ISSN: 0363-0277.

DOWNES, ROBIN N. 1990. Electronic Technology and Access to Information. Journal of Library Administration. 1990; 12(3): 51-61. ISSN: 0193-0826.

DUCHIN, DOUGLAS. 1989. The Apparently Automatic Self-Inflating Price of Books. Library Acquisitions: Practice & Theory. 1989; 13(2): 115-118. ISSN: 0364-6408.

ECONOMIC CONSULTING SERVICES, INCORPORATED. 1989. A Study of Trends in Average Prices and Costs of Certain Serials Over Time. In: Association of Research Libraries. Report of the ARL Serials Prices Project. Washington, DC: Association of Research Libraries; 1989. 1-43. Available from: ERIC Document Reproduction Service. ERIC: ED-311922.

ELIAS, ARTHUR W. 1990a. Copyright, Licensing Agreements and Gateways. Online Review. 1990 August; 14(4): 225-237. ISSN: 0309-314X.

ELIAS, ARTHUR. 1990b. Site Licensing Visited—Real or Imagined Fears. NFAIS Newsletter. 1990 December; 32(12): 1,3. ISSN: 0090-0893.

ELIAS, ART; UNRUH, BETTY. 1990. Economies of Database Production. Philadelphia, PA: The National Federation of Abstracting and Information Services; 1990. 116p. ISBN: 0-942308-29-8.

ESKOLA, PIRKKO; SORMUNEN, EERO. 1990. Cost Comparison of Online Searching in Four Hosts: Data-Star, Dialog, ESA-IRS and STN. Online Review. 1990 October; 14(5): 303-316. ISSN: 0309-314X.

FISCHER, MARGARET T. 1988. Overview of Pricing Strategies in the Electronic Information Industry. Information Services & Use. 1988; 8(2/3/4): 73-78. ISSN: 0167-5265.

FLEMING, MAUREEN; SILVERSTEIN, JEFF; ELWELL, CHRIS; KELLY, ROBERT D.; SIMPSON, BARBARA J.; FLEMING, LEE, eds. 1991. Information Industry Factbook. 1990/91 edition. Stamford, CT: Digital Information Group; 1991. 670p. ISBN: 0-927252-04-X.

GARMAN, NANCY. 1988. Online Pricing: A Complex Maze Not for Timid Mice. Database. 1988 April; 11(2): 6-7. ISSN: 0162-4105.

GARMAN, NANCY. 1990a. DIALOG Discusses Pricing: An Interview with DIALOG's President Roger K. Summit. Online. 1990 January; 14(1): 40-43. ISSN: 0146-5422.

GARMAN, NANCY. 1990b. Online Pricing: An Interview with Marino F. Saksida of ESA-IRS. Online. 1990 January; 14(1): 30-34. ISSN: 0146-5422.

GIBBINS, PATRICK. 1987. Pricing Software and Information on CD-ROM. Electronic and Optical Publishing Review. 1987 December; 7(4): 176-180. ISSN: 0951-7154.

GOLDSTEIN, MORRIS. 1990. Site Licensing Policies and CD-ROM Networks in Libraries. In: Nissley, Meta; Nelson, Nancy Melin, eds. CD-

ROM Licensing and Copyright Issues for Libraries. Westport, CT: Meckler Corp.; 1990. 45-55. ISBN: 0-88763-701-1; LC: 90-35109.

GRANNIS, CHANDLER B. 1989. Titles and Prices, 1988; Final Figures. Publishers Weekly. 1989 September 29; 236(13): 24-27. ISSN: 0000-0019.

GREENE, PHILIP E. N. 1987. Serials Prices: An Historical Perspective. The Serials Librarian. 1986 December/1987 January; 11(3/4): 19-29. ISSN: 0361-526X.

GRINELL, STUART F. 1989. Pricing by Geography: Springer-Verlag New York Journal Pricing, 1988 and 1989. Serials Review. 1989 Summer; 15(2): 11, 13, 33. ISSN: 0098-7913.

HAMAKER, CHARLES A.; GRINELL, STUART. 1990. Cost Analysis of Monographs and Serials. Journal of Library Administration. 1990; 12(3): 41-49. ISSN: 0193-0826.

HAWKINS, DONALD T. 1989. In Search of Ideal Pricing. Online. 1989 March; 13(2): 15-30. ISSN: 0146-5422.

HEPFER, CINDY. 1988. Serials Pricing: The Impact of Exchange Rates and Currency Trends. The Serials Librarian. 1988; 15(3/4): 141-143. ISSN: 0361-526X.

HOGEWEG-DE HAART, H. P. 1986. The Impact of Copyright on the Price and Availability of Scientific Information: A Review of Some Recent Literature. International Forum on Information and Documentation. 1986 January; 11(1): 10-14. ISSN: 0304-9701.

HOLMES, P. L. 1985. An Experiment in Pricing Mechanisms for Online Retrieval. Information Services & Use. 1985 October; 5(5): 269-275. ISSN: 0167-5265.

HOUBECK, ROBERT L. 1987. If Present Trends Continue: Forecasting and Responding to Journal Price Increases. The Serials Librarian. 1987 October-November; 13(2/3): 113-127. ISSN: 0361-526X.

HUDSON, ROSEMARY. 1988. What Price Interloans? New Zealand Libraries. 1988 June; 45(10): 221-222. ISSN: 0028-8381.

HUNTER, KAREN. 1990. Economic and Technological Trends in Journal Publishing. Library Acquisitions: Practice & Theory. 1990; 14(1): 121-126. ISSN: 0364-6408.

INFORMATION WORLD REVIEW. 1989a. Positive Responses. Information World Review. 1989 December; (43): 16. ISSN: 0950-9879.

INFORMATION WORLD REVIEW. 1989b. Usage Up Since Tariff Changes. Information World Review. 1989 December; (43): 16. ISSN: 0950-9879.

INFORMATION WORLD REVIEW. 1990. CAS Usage Detailed. Information World Review. 1990 June; (49): 4. ISSN: 0950-9879.

INFOTECTURE. 1982. Infotecture (European edition). 1982 May 19; (11): 9. ISSN: 0241-2640.

IVINS, OCTOBER, ed. Serials Prices. Serials Review. (Column). ISSN: 0098-7913.

IVINS, OCTOBER. 1988. Serials Prices. Serials Review. 1988; 14(3): 61-66. ISSN: 0098-7913.

IVINS, OCTOBER. 1989a. Serials Prices: ARL Series Pricing Study Completed. Serials Review. 1989 Summer; 15(2): 53-54. ISSN: 0098-7913.

IVINS, OCTOBER. 1989b. Serials Prices: Column 6. Serials Review. 1989 Winter; 15(4): 65-71. ISSN: 0098-7913.

IVINS, OCTOBER. 1990. Do Serials Vendor Policies Affect Serials Pricing? Serials Review. 1990 Summer; 16(2): 7-27, 80. ISSN: 0098-7913.

IVINS, OCTOBER; GRINELL, STUART. 1988. Serials Prices. Serials Review. 1988 Winter; 14(4): 55-59. ISSN: 0098-7913.

JACK, ROBERT F. 1990. The New ESA-IRS Pricing Scheme: A Comparison with DIALOG. Online. 1990 January; 14(1): 35-39. ISSN: 0146-5422.

KABACK, STUART. 1989. Free Formats Are Valuable, But Should Remain Free. Online. 1989 July; 13(4): 5. (Letter to the Editor). ISSN: 0146-5422.

KITLEY, ROY. 1988. 1P on the Price of a Loaf: A Look at Online Charging Development. Aslib Information. 1988 November/December; 16(11-12): 288-290. ISSN: 0305-0033.

KOSTENBAUDER, SCOTT. 1988. Pricing Issues: User Perspectives of Database Pricing, Deep Pockets and Empty Wallets. Information Services & Use. 1988; 8(2/3/4): 85-90. ISSN: 0167-5265.

KRONENFELD, MICHAEL R.; GABLE, SARAH H. 1989. Update on Inflation of Journal Prices: Medical Journals, U.S. Journals, and Brandon/Hill List Journals. Bulletin of the Medical Library Association. 1989 January; 77(1): 61-64. ISSN: 0025-7338.

LYNDEN, FREDERICK C. 1988a. Prices and Discounts. Library Acquisitions: Practice & Theory. 1988; 12(2): 255-258. ISSN: 0364-6408.

LYNDEN, FREDERICK C. 1988b. Prices of Foreign Library Materials: A Report. College & Research Libraries. 1988 May; 49(3): 217-231. ISSN: 0010-0870.

LYNDEN, FREDERICK C. 1990. Cost Analysis of Monographs and Serials. Journal of Library Administration. 1990; 12(3): 19-39. ISSN: 0193-0826.

MADDOX, JANE. 1988. Exchange Rate and Inflation. Library Acquisitions: Practice & Theory. 1988; 12(2): 181-185. ISSN: 0364-6408.

MARSH, CORRIE V.; LOCKMAN, EDWARD. 1988. Net Book Pricing. Library Acquisitions: Practice & Theory. 1988; 12(2): 169-176. ISSN: 0364-6408.

MASON, PAMELA R. 1990. CD-ROM Price Index: An Update. Library Acquisitions: Practice & Theory. 1990; 14(2): 179-182. ISSN: 0364-6408.

MERRIMAN, JOHN B. 1989. Publishing and Perishing. Nature. 1989 September 28; 341(6240): 349-350. ISSN: 0028-0836.

MILLER, EDWARD P.; O'NEILL, ANN L. 1990. Journal Deselection and Costing. Library Acquisitions: Practice & Theory. 1990; 14(2): 173-178. ISSN: 0364-6408.

MOLHOLT, PAT; HOHENBERG, PAUL M. 1987. What Price the Information Age: A Model for Fair Payment for the Use of Information. In:

Zunde, Pranas; Agrawal, Jagdish C., eds. Empirical Foundations of Information and Software Science IV: Proceedings of the 4th Symposium on Empirical Foundations of Information and Software Science; 1986 October 22-24; Atlanta, GA. New York, NY: Plenum Press; 1987. 479-486. ISBN: 0-306-42817-2.

MONITOR. 1987. Users, Vendors and Producers: First Reactions to the New Chemical Abstracts Licence. Monitor. 1987 August; (78): 1,5. ISSN: 0260-6666.

MONTAG, ULRICH. 1989. Differential Pricing in the International Book Market. IFLA Journal. 1989; 15(1): 37-43. ISSN: 0340-0352.

MORRIS, LESLIE R. 1987. Network Prices: Let the Buyer Beware. Technical Services Quarterly. 1987 Summer; 4(4): 57-66. ISSN: 0731-7131.

NEAME, LAURA. 1989. View from Canada: CD-ROM Pricing Issues. Laserdisk Professional. 1989 May; 2(3): 94-96. ISSN: 0896-4149.

NEWSLETTER ON SERIALS PRICING ISSUES. Tuttle, Marcia, ed. Chapel Hill, NC: University of North Carolina. ISSN: 0098-7913. (Electronic newsletter available on BITNET, ALANET, EBSCONET, DATALINX).

NFAIS NEWSLETTER. 1990. Serials Prices to Peak in 1991. NFAIS Newsletter. 1990 December; 32(12): 150. ISSN: 0090-0893.

NISSLEY, META. 1990. CD-ROMs, Licenses and Librarians. In: Nissley, Meta; Nelson, Nancy Melin, eds. CD-ROM Licensing and Copyright Issues for Libraries. Westport, CT: Meckler Corp.; 1990. 1-17. ISBN: 0-88763-701-1; LC: 90-35109.

NISSLEY, META; NELSON, NANCY MELIN, eds. 1990. CD-ROM Licensing and Copyright Issues for Libraries. Westport, CT: Meckler Corp.; 1990. 95p. ISBN: 0-88763-701-1; LC: 90-35109.

OCLC ONLINE COMPUTER LIBRARY CENTER, INC. 1991. Get Ready to Go. . .When We're Ready to Go. Dublin, OH: OCLC; 1991. 4p. (Marketing brochure). Available from: OCLC, 6565 Frantz Rd., Dublin, OH 43017.

OKERSON, ANN. 1989. Of Making Many Books There Is No End. Report on Serials Prices. In: Association of Research Libraries. Report of the ARL Serials Prices Project. Washington, DC: Association of Research Libraries; 1989. 1-55. Available from: ERIC Document Reproduction Service. ERIC: ED-311922.

OLAISEN, JOHAN L. 1989. Pricing Strategies for Library and Information Services. Libri. 1989 December; 39(4): 253-274. ISSN: 0024-2667.

O'LEARY, MICK. 1988. Price Versus Value for Online Data. Online. 1988 March; 12(2): 26-30. ISSN: 0146-5422.

ONLINE LIBRARIES AND MICROCOMPUTERS. 1988. H.W. Wilson Announces Licensing Agreement and Pricing for Leasing Its Databases on Magnetic Tape. Online Libraries and Microcomputers. 1988 May; 6(5): 4-7. ISSN: 0737-7770.

ONLINE REVIEW. 1986. International Comparative Price Guide to Databases Online. Online Review. 1986 April; 10(4): 249-260. ISSN: 0309-314X.

PARKHURST, CAROL A. 1990. Library Perspectives on NREN: The National Research and Education Network. Chicago, IL: Library and Information Technology Association; 1990. 75p. ISBN: 0-8389-7477-5.

PASCARELLI, ANNE M. 1990. Coping Strategies for Libraries Facing the Serials Pricing Crisis. Serials Review. 1990 Spring; 16(1): 75-80. ISSN: 0098-7913.

PEMBERTON, JEFFERY K. 1988a. ONLINE Interviews Harry Boyle on CA's New License Policy ... Effects on Searching/Prices. Online. 1988 March; 12(2): 19-25. ISSN: 0146-5422.

PEMBERTON, JEFFERY K. 1988b. Winds of Change in the Online World. (Editorial). Online. 1988 March; 12(2): 7-9. ISSN: 0146-5422.

PETERSEN, CLARENCE. 1975. The Bantam Story; Thirty Years of Paperback Publishing. 2nd edition, revised and updated. New York, NY: Bantam Books; 1975. 167p.

PETERSEN, H. CRAIG. 1989. Variations in Journal Prices: A Statistical Analysis. The Serials Librarian. 1989; 17(1/2): 1-9. ISSN: 0361-526X.

POOLEY, CHRISTOPHER G. 1990. CD-ROM Licensing Issues. In: Nissley, Meta; Nelson, Nancy Melin, eds. CD-ROM Licensing and Copyright Issues for Libraries. Westport, CT: Meckler Corp.; 1990. 31-43. ISBN: 0-88763-701-1; LC: 90-35109.

PORTER, MICHAEL E. 1980. Competitive Strategy: Techniques for Analyzing Industries and Competitors. New York, NY: The Free Press, A Division of Macmillan Publishing Co.; 1980. 396p. ISBN: 0-02-925360-8; LC: 80-652.

REPO, AATTO J. 1987. Economics of Information. In: Williams, Martha E., ed. Annual Review of Information Science and Technology (ARIST): Volume 22. Amsterdam, The Netherlands: Elsevier Science Publishers for the American Society for Information Science; 1987. 1-35. ISSN: 0066-4200; ISBN: 0-444-70302-0.

RIETDYK, RON. 1990. When Is the Price Right? CD-ROM Enters New Territory. NFAIS Newsletter. 1990 November; 32(11): 1,3,4. ISSN: 0090-0893.

ROBINSON, MARK L. 1990. Dialog Business Databases: An Informal Survey of Prices. Online Review. 1990 October; 14(5): 318-326. ISSN: 0309-314X.

SALT, DAVID P. 1989. Serials Price Increases: A Canadian Perspective. Canadian Library Journal. 1989 December; 46(6): 391-394. ISSN: 0008-4352.

SCHNEIDAWIND, JOHN. 1990. Prodigy Fees Ignite Customers' Revolt. USA Today, Final Edition. 1990 November 2; 2B.

SHUSTER, HELEN M. 1989. Fiscal Control of Serials Using dBASE III+. Serials Review. 1989 Spring; 15(1): 7-20. ISSN: 0098-7913.

SIMORA, FILOMENA, ed. 1990. Library and Book Trade Almanac. 35th edition. New York, NY: R.R. Bowker; 1990. 795p. ISSN: 0068-0540; ISBN: 0-8352-2943-2.

SOMERS, SALLY W. 1988. The Exchange Rate and Inflation: A Study of Sacred Cows, Lemmings, and Other Assorted Things. Library Acquisitions: Practice & Theory. 1988; 12(2): 177-180. ISSN: 0364-6408.

SORMUNEN, EERO. 1990. Price Comparison ESA-Dialog. Online Review. 1990 January; 14(1): 33-34. ISSN: 0309-314X.

STOAKLEY, ROGER. 1990. The Price of Books. Public Library Journal. 1990 January/February; 5(1): 9-13. ISSN: 0268-893X.

STRAUCH, BRUCE; STRAUCH, KATINA. 1989. Foreign Exchange Rates and Journal Pricing. Library Acquisitions: Practice & Theory. 1989; 13(4): 417-422. ISSN: 0364-6408.

TAYLOR, ROBERT S. 1986. Value-Added Processes in Information Systems. Norwood, NJ: Ablex Publishing Corp.; 1986. 257p. ISBN: 0-89391-273-5; LC: 85-18677.

TENOPIR, CAROL. 1988. Is Connect-Time Pricing Obsolete? Library Journal. 1988 March 1; 113(4): 48-49. ISSN: 0363-0277.

TREADWELL, JANE. 1989. Determining a Fair Price for Lost Books: A Case Study. Library and Archival Security. 1989; 9(1): 19-26. ISSN: 0196-0075.

TRUDELL, LIBBY. 1988. Pricing Online Information in the 90's: An Online Service Viewpoint. Information Services & Use. 1988; 8(2/3/4): 79-83. ISSN: 0167-5265.

TURNER, JUDITH AXLER. 1989. Critics Say Publisher's Suit Inhibits Inquiries into Rising Journal Costs. Chronicle of Higher Education. 1989 October 25; 36(8): A6. ISSN: 0009-5982.

TUTTLE, MARCIA. 1987. Discriminatory Pricing of British Scholarly Journals for the North American Market: An Overview. The Serials Librarian. 1987 January/1986 December; 11(3-4): 157-161. ISSN: 0361-526X.

WELSCH, ERWIN K. 1988. Price versus Coverage: Calculating the Impact on Collection Development. Library Resources & Technical Services. 1988 April; 32(2): 159-163. ISSN: 0024-2527.

WHITE, HERBERT S. 1988. The Journal That Ate the Library. Library Journal. 1988 May 15; 113(9): 62-63. ISSN: 0363-0277.

WILLIAMS, BRIAN. 1987. A Comparison of the New and the Old BRS Prices. Online. 1987 July; 11(4): 65-68. ISSN: 0146-5422.

WITIAK, JOANNE. 1988. It's All a Question of Price: An Expert Searcher Looks at the New CAS Pricing Scheme. Database. 1988 April; 12(2): 95-96. ISSN: 0162-4105.

YOUNG, PETER R. 1989. Periodical Prices 1987-1989 Update. The Serials Librarian. 1989; 17(1/2): 11-37. ISSN: 0361-526X.

YOUNG, PETER; CARPENTER, KATHRYN HAMMELL. 1990. Price Index for 1990: U.S. Periodicals. Library Journal. 1990 April 15; 115(7): 50-56. ISSN: 0363-0277.

II

Basic Techniques and Technologies

Section II includes four chapters, a chapter on "Information Technology Standards" by Michael B. Spring of the University of Pittsburgh, one on "Expert Systems as Information Intermediaries" by Hilary Drenth, Anne Morris, and Gwyneth Tseng all of Loughborough University in England, a chapter on "The Human-Computer Interface for Information Retrieval" by Debora Shaw of Indiana University, and a chapter entitled "Optical Disc Technology for Information Management" by Eugenia K. Brumm of the University of Texas at Austin.

In his chapter on "Information Technology Standards" Michael B. Spring addresses the problem of research on standards and standardization rather than looking at specific standards per se.

Spring defines standards and specifications and explains the immense scope of standardization. He broadly classifies their scope as: organizational, industry-wide, national, multinational, and international. He discusses the organizations that develop standards in the access of information processing, telecommunications, and information management and homes in on the U.S. national bodies central to many of the international standards. The Accredited Standards Committees (ASCs) X3 for information processing, T1 for telecommunications, and X12 for information management, together with the National Information Standards Organization (NISO) and the Institute of Electrical and Electronics Engineers (IEEE) are studied closely.

Spring looks at important standards and areas of standardization, which in his view are: open systems interconnection (OSI), human-computer interaction, application portability, data format and interchange, and what are called standards "profiles." His discussion of research on standards and standardization covers research methods, research on the emergence of standards, research on technology choice in standardization, research on the consensus standardization process, and the future of standards research. He concludes by pointing out that the time needed to develop stable standards is being eclipsed by the rate of technological development. He notes that more abstract standards permit technological evolution but lack specificity that could provide for interoperability with other products that also conform to the same "abstract" standard. Standards permitting products and processes to work together are essential. Research is needed to determine what standards should be developed and how to develop them efficiently and economically.

Hilary Drenth, Anne Morris, and Gwyneth Tseng, in their chapter on expert systems as information intermediaries, point out that expert systems have great potential to enhance access to information retrieval systems as they use expertise to carry out tasks such as diagnosis and planning and make expertise available to nonexperts. Potential end users of online information retrieval systems are frequently deterred by the complexity of these systems. Expert systems can mediate between the searcher and the information retrieval system and might be the key both to increasing end user searching and to improving the quality of searches overall.

This review describes expert intermediary systems which have been developed over the past decade, concentrating on recent work. It begins with a brief overview of expert system design and then considers the types of expertise used by intermediaries in retrieving information from online services. A major part of the review describes prototype expert intermediary systems developed in a research environment: search advisors, intelligent front ends, systems that adopt intelligent approaches to the entire retrieval process, and systems which handle specific intermediary roles or tasks, such as query formulation, database selection, searching in specific subject domains, and user modeling. Knowledge acquisition and evaluation of these systems are also considered. The review then examines, from an expert systems perspective, some online search aids currently in use. These include front ends, gateways, and user-friendly interfaces developed to assist searching of commercial online services. The review concludes with an assessment of the future of expert intermediary systems.

In a related chapter Debora Shaw discusses the human–computer interface for information retrieval. Shaw notes that research on human-computer interface design has generated many widely-accepted principles of interface design which should be of interest and value to designers of information retrieval systems. Work on display features such as highlighting, color, icons, and windows has received considerable attention. Research has also focused on how the user interacts with the system, whether by commands, menus, or direct manipulation. Help and related system messages can also affect user performance. Studies of interfaces for information retrieval systems reveal that online searching has emphasized development of front ends, with some novel uses of graphics. CD-ROM and optical media are characterized by interface diversity, again with some inclusion of graphic interfaces. Online catalogs and full-text databases have provided interesting comparisons of mode of interaction. Shaw also discusses standards and guidelines for information system interfaces. Shaw concludes by itemizing a set of resources for keeping up in the field and making a plea for the multidisciplinary work required to develop smarter interfaces.

In her chapter on "Optical Disc Technology for Information Management" Eugenia K. Brumm argues in favor of optical disc (OD) technology for the management of information because the paperless office has not been achieved—over 21 trillion documents are on file in the United States and companies continue to create about a million documents per minute per business day. She points out that we are plagued with a plethora of paper-based systems and the cost of managing them is huge though undocumented. The time, cost, and investment required for paper-based solutions are the driving force behind many organizations' consideration of OD as an alternative to paper for the management of their information.

Brumm directs the reader to important literature sources for those who wish to follow the literature of OD. In discussing vendors and products she segments them by size and price and by levels of integration where integration refers to the bringing together of text, data, voice, and images in a system that also permits access to word processing, E-mail, database applications, and spreadsheets. Advantages of OD include: (1) high-density storage, (2) ease of access, (3) speed of access and delivery, (4) document integrity and security, (5) the fact that images can be replicated electronically, transferred to users at different sites, and viewed simultaneously, and (6) data-document integration and cooperative processing.

In discussing standards Brumm bemoans the fact that little standardization of OD equipment and media exists despite the fact that the need and importance of standards are widely acknowledged. No standard exists for measuring the longevity of optical discs, and this is important because it affects the legal consideration of the acceptability of the medium as it relates to the legally mandated retention periods for certain documents. Data standardization is more difficult because it involves comprehensive software standards, but the most important issue in the long run, and the most difficult one, is application software standards, which include standardized formats for document images, document processing activities, database structures, document indexes, and user interfaces.

Brumm discusses software (operating systems, driver software, database software, and utility software), legal issues, the justification of OD systems, the records management aspects of OD (retention, security and vital records, and indexing), networks (for routing, annotating, and transmitting images for use in data and word processing), conversion products, user evaluation, and applications (government, aerospace/aviation, archives, insurance services, and pharmaceuticals). She concludes the chapter by pointing out that the area is ripe for research and she looks forward to a profound change: the ability of organizations to fully integrate the management of their information because documents will scanned, digitized, read onto optical discs and accessed together with pertinent electronic data and information from other sources in the system "...no longer will it be necessary to piece together paper documents. . .retrieved from physical storage, with electronic data that are logically unconnected to the documents."

3 Information Technology Standards

MICHAEL B. SPRING
University of Pittsburgh

INTRODUCTION

Over the years, many *ARIST* chapters have referred to information technology standards, but this is the first entire chapter dedicated to the topic of standards. It does not address the standards themselves as much as the research on standards and standardization, with particular attention to information technology standardization. For purposes of this chapter, information technology standards are the basic technology standards for computation, telecommunications, and information management. The chapter provides background on the field, an overview of important standards, and a review of the current state of research.

Information technology standards are an area of growing interest to academic researchers. This interest is the result of several developments. First, the number of information technology standards being developed has increased dramatically in recent years. Second, the number and kinds of organizations that are developing standards or playing a role in standards specification has increased. In fact, there is significant discussion about whether the increase in standards and standards-developing organizations is healthy for the information technology industries. Third, standards today have a greater impact on people, organizations, and nations than ever before. From the standards set by the Occupational Safety and Health Administration (OSHA) to the Federal Information Processing Standards (FIPS) to the American

Annual Review of Information Science and Technology (ARIST), Volume 26, 1991
Martha E. Williams, Editor
Published for the American Society for Information Science (ASIS)
By Learned Information, Inc., Medford, N.J.

National Standards Institute (ANSI) standards to the International Organization for Standardization (ISO) standards, what we buy and how we work is to an increasing extent determined by standards. Fourth, standards are becoming ever more costly to develop and maintain. It has been estimated that more than $4 billion has been spent developing the ISO suite of standards known popularly as OSI or Open Systems Interconnection and that $250 million more are being spent every year (ROBINSON, 1989). Fifth, there is a growing concern that standards are currently and will increasingly be used in the international marketplace as a mechanism to control or restrict free trade.

This review is divided into four parts. First, definitions of and the framework for the development of voluntary consensus standards are set out. Next, major standards and areas of standardization are described. Then, the research on standards and standardization is reviewed. Finally, some important research questions are outlined.

BACKGROUND

On the surface, standards would appear to be a rather simple matter. When a certain product or practice has achieved stability or market dominance, it is codified and then, by policy or by practice, widely used by some group. In practice, standards emerge from many different sources and by many different mechanisms. Various definitions of standards are contrasted below, and the more important developers of information technology standards are set out.

Definitions

Generally a standard is "the deliberate acceptance by a group of people having common interests or background of a quantifiable metric that influences their behavior and activities by permitting a common interchange" (CARGILL, 1989, p. 13). A standard may be developed to ensure some public good—e.g., working conditions. Standards that are promulgated by a legislative body are considered de jure standards. The definition of a standard put forward by the National Standards Policy Advisory Committee in 1979 has this flavor:

> A standard is a prescribed set of rules, conditions, or requirements concerning definition of terms; classification of components; specification of materials, performance, or operations; delineation of procedures; or measurement of quantity and quality in describing materials, products, systems, services, or practices. (CERNI, 1984, p. 9-10)

This definition does not explicitly specify the force-of-law condition that normally accompanies de jure standards. At the national level, many federal regulations constitute de jure standards. At the international level, many of the standards arising from the International Telecommunications Union (ITU), in particular the Consultative Committee on International Telephony and Telegraphy (CCITT), constitute de jure standards pertaining to the assignment of frequencies for international radio, tariffs for telegraphy and telephony, and standards for interconnection of national systems.

Standards can also emerge when products, services, or practices achieve market dominance. These are called de facto standards:

> Standards generally describe, define, or document an already existing reality (or problem solution) so that others can easily reproduce this reality (or solve a similar problem), thereby avoiding a duplication of effort. (CERNI, 1984, p. 9)

Information technology standards in this category would include the Postscript Page Description Language, which is used by many different laser printers and laser typesetters, and the IBM PC and many of its components, such as the Industry Standard Architecture (ISA) bus. (A bus is the electronic pathway between the various components of a computer across which address, control information, and data are transferred.)

Finally, many standards in the United States emerge out of discussion and compromise in one of the organizations accredited by ANSI. More than 250 bodies are either Accredited Standards Committees (ASCs) or Accredited Organizations (AOs) that develop standards under ANSI guidelines. The standards that emerge from these bodies are generally referred to as voluntary consensus standards. Such a standard may be characterized as:

> a technical specification or other document, available to the public, drawn up with the cooperation and consensus or general approval of all the interests affected by it, based on the consolidated results of science, technology, and experience, aimed at the promotion of optimum community benefits, and approved by a body recognized in the national, regional, or international level. (KEMMLER)

Recent work by CARGILL (1989) and BONINO & SPRING suggests that modern information technology standards may be more proactive than traditional information technology standards. Traditionally, standards such as the FORTRAN language standard are developed from experience with a number of different existing versions. More recent standards, such as the Fiber Distributed Data Interface, were developed before the particular products to which they apply. They have the impact of defining or changing the market and the products that will develop in the future. In this way the standards anticipate the market. According to CARGILL (1989, p. 41-42):

> A standard, of any form or type, represents a statement by its authors, who believe that their work will be understood, accepted, and implemented by the market. This belief is tempered by the understanding that the market will act in its own best interests, even if these do not coincide with the standard. A standard is also one of the agents used by the standardization process to bring about market change.

Although this analysis categorizes standards according to their origin or function, the reality is not quite so simple. Voluntary consensus standards may have their origin in de facto standards, and they may in time be used as the basis for de jure standards. For example, Ethernet technology had achieved market dominance before it was approved as an IEEE standard (INSTITUTE OF ELECTRICAL AND ELECTRONICS ENGINEERS, 1988). Similarly, the adoption of voluntary consensus standards by governmental organizations gives them selected characteristics of de jure standards. This has become an increasingly common practice in the European Community. Federal Information Processing Standards such as FIPS 146 (NATIONAL INSTITUTE OF STANDARDS AND TECHNOLOGY, 1988a) specify that all federal agency purchases of computer equipment will comply with the Government Open Systems Interconnection Profile (GOSIP), which is based on the ISO Open Systems Interconnection—Basic Reference Model (INTERNATIONAL ORGANIZATION FOR STANDARDIZATION, 1984). While a FIPS standard is not the same as an OSHA or FCC regulation, which establishes a de jure standard for all concerned parties in the public and private sector, it is a significant factor in that it affects all relevant federal purchases. It is worth noting that GOSIP does not affect all computer purchases, only those for which interconnection is a concern. Further, it is a phased implementation with greater levels of specification being provided at each phase.

The Scope of Standardization

The scope of standardization is immense. Almost every organization produces some standards that govern internal operations. Many groups of organizations produce standards that make it easier for them to work together. Virtually every nation produces standards, as do regional groups of countries and international organizations. Thus, as CRAWFORD points out, standards can be classified by their scope—organizational, industry-wide, national, multinational (or regional), and international. It should be noted that multinational efforts, as the term is used here, are a recent phenomenon. The efforts of the European Community (discussed later) are a commonly used example of a multinational or regional effort that includes less than the full international community.

CARGILL (1989) proposes a model of the standards environment that indicates that standards are actually developed at five levels: (1) reference models, (2) industry standards, (3) functional profiles, (4) system profiles, and (5) application implementations. He notes that the types of standards differ significantly in such aspects as level of abstraction, time required for development, and lead time required. Elaboration of the five-stage model provides a complex picture of the standards environment. For providers of information technology, a single reference standard yields multiple industry standards, each of which supports multiple profiles, and so forth. For users of information technology, the perspective is reversed. A particular process or product is based on multiple application standards, each of which is based on multiple system profiles, each of which in turn is based on multiple industry standards, and so on.

The research reported below is concerned primarily with information technology standards developed by voluntary consensus at the national level in the United States. Generally, this means the standards developed under the auspices of ANSI through Accredited Standards Committees such as X3, T1, and X12 and Accredited Organizations such as the Institute of Electrical and Electronics Engineers (IEEE), the National Information Standards Organization (NISO), and the Association for Information and Image Management (AIIM). This leaves out a significant number of standards and standards developing organizations (SDOs). It excludes de facto and industry standards that develop outside the voluntary consensus process; further it excludes the standards developed by other U.S. national standards bodies that do not directly concern information or information technology. Thus, it ignores the work of more than 200 ANSI accredited SDOs that work on standards in areas other than information technology. It also excludes most of the standards developed by other national standards bodies such as the Canadian Standards Association (CSA), the Deutsches Institut für Normung E.V. (DIN), the Association Française de Normalisation (AFNOR), and the Japanese Industrial Standards Committee (JISC).

While some consideration is given below to international standardization, the research largely ignores the interrelationship of voluntary consensus standards development in the United States and the work of the major international and regional standards bodies, such as ISO, the International Electrotechnical Commission (IEC), ITU, the European Computer Manufacturers Association (ECMA), Comitè Europèen de Normalisation (CEN), and Comitè Europèen de Normalisation Electrotechnique (CENELEC). (The discussion does address the work of these organizations to the extent that they represent a forum in which much of the work begun in X3, T1, X12, NISO, and IEEE is carried forward to the international arena.)

Standards-Developing Organizations

In the information technology industry, there are three focal areas of standards development: information processing, telecommunications, and information management. Standards in these areas are being developed at three levels—national, regional, and international. As indicated above, each country has its own national standards body, but the historical preeminence of the United States has made the efforts of the U.S. national bodies central to many of the international standards. Thus, Accredited Standards Committees (ASCs) X3 (for information processing), T1 (for telecommunications), and X12 (for information management) along with the work of NISO and IEEE deserve close scrutiny.

At the regional level, the most extensive standards efforts are those related to the emergence of the European Commission. FRENKEL (1990a) points out that these efforts began almost 30 years ago with the establishment of the European Common Market and have received tremendous impetus from the creation of the European Commission and the 1987 passage of the Single Europe Act, which promises the removal of barriers to trade in Europe by December 31, 1992. At this regional level, CENELEC develops standards for both information processing and information management. The European Telecommunications Standards Institute (ETSI) provides for telecommunications standards.

At the international level, information processing concerns have been handled historically by ISO Technical Committee 97 and IEC

Technical Committees 47B and 83. Information management as it pertains to information and documentation (parallel to NISO) is handled by ISO TC 46. Information management as it pertains to electronic data interchange (parallel to ANSI ASC X12) is the concern of ISO TC 154, which has developed the standard for Electronic Data Interchange for Administration, Commerce, and Transport (EDIFACT).

The efforts of ISO and IEC technical committees involved in information processing standards were coordinated in 1987 by formation of Joint Technical Committee 1 (JTC 1). The international efforts in the area of telecommunications that parallel the efforts of ANSI T1 and ETSI are carried out by CCITT under the auspices of the International Telecommunications Union (ITU). Unlike the other organizations discussed, ITU is not a voluntary standards group but a formal treaty organization under United Nations auspices. FRENKEL (1990b) analyzes the relationships among the various European regional bodies and their equivalent organizations at the international and U.S. national level.

HILL offers one of the earliest overviews of the information technology SDOs and their work. CERNI (1984) also provides an overview of the various organizations and processes with an eye to assessing the development of two significant standards efforts, Integrated Services Digital Network (ISDN) and Open Systems Interconnection (OSI). More recent treatments of this environment are provided by CARGILL (1989) and CRAWFORD. Cargill's book also introduces the concept of anticipatory standards—i.e., standards developed prior to product development. Crawford's treatment emphasizes library and publishing standards. Most recently, MACPHERSON reviews those organizations involved internationally in the development of telecommunications standards.

SAVA surveys the operation of ANSI. The oldest of ANSI's information technology SDOs is Z39, now NISO. WOOD reviews the history of Z39, beginning with its founding as an American Standards Association Committee in 1939. ROBINSON(1986) provides a brief review of X3. BUCKLEY provides an overview of the IEEE standards development process. LIFCHUS reviews the origin and outlines the scope and goals of the newest ANSI committee, ASC T1, which was created in large part as a forum for consensus telecommunications standards development after the divestiture of AT&T. Of increasing importance in the United States is the development of more than 150 standards for information processing in the federal government. J.L. BERG reviews the efforts of the National Computer Systems Laboratory (NCSL) at the National Institute of

Standards and Technology (NIST) (formerly the National Bureau of Standards) that is responsible for these standards.

SOCHATS outlines the scope of CCITT efforts, the structure of the organization, and its relationship to various other SDOs. FITZGERALD provides an exceptionally clear and concise analysis of the two European regional standards organizations concerned with information technology standards—CENELEC and ETSI.

IMPORTANT STANDARDS AND AREAS OF STANDARDIZATION

To understand the importance of research on information technology standards, the scope of the efforts currently under way needs to be reviewed. Although it is not comprehensive, the review below provides a sample of those efforts and an indication of the scope. We begin with the rather well-developed efforts to develop standards for the interconnection of equipment that makes multivendor systems possible. Next comes a brief discussion of recent efforts to specify a reference model for human–computer interaction standards. Major standards for data exchange are also discussed. The section concludes with a discussion of recent efforts to "standardize standards" through "functional standards" or "profiles."

Open Systems Interconnection (OSI)

For many, the Open Systems Interconnection (OSI) standards have taken on a somewhat mystical stature. They hold out the promise of vast networks of machines capable of interconnection and interoperation. Implementation of OSI is dependent on more than 70 interrelated standards that are related conceptually via the Basic Reference Model of OSI (INTERNATIONAL ORGANIZATION FOR STANDARDIZATION, 1984). CERNI (1984) provides one of the earliest overviews of OSI, which is particularly significant in its comparison of OSI with the emerging Integrated Services Digital Network (ISDN) standard. OSI standards have been the subject of a number of recent books. HENSHALL & SHAW provide one of the earliest treatments of the upper-layer standards of OSI—i.e., the application, presentation, session, and transport layers—giving an extended introduction to the then evolving standards for File Transfer, Access and Management (INTERNATIONAL ORGANIZATION FOR STANDARDIZATION, 1988a), Directory Services (INTERNA-TIONAL ORGANIZATION FOR STANDARDIZATION, 1988b), and

Message Oriented Text Interchange Service (INTERNATIONAL ORGANIZATION FOR STANDARDIZATION, 1988c).

ROSE has been intimately involved in the development and testing of applications for OSI based on the use of the Internet Transmission Control Protocols/Internet Protocols, widely used in the United States and commonly known as TCP/IP. Rose's work on the ISO Development Environment (ISODE) makes significant contributions to the development of OSI applications in a TCP/IP environment. Rose also provides one of the clearest explanations, short of reading the standards themselves, of the Abstract Syntax Notation One (ASN.1) (INTERNATIONAL ORGANIZATION FOR STANDARDIZATION, 1987c), the Basic Encoding Rules for ASN.1 (INTERNATIONAL ORGANIZATION FOR STANDARDIZATION, 1987d), and the extensions and addenda to the standards (INTERNATIONAL ORGANIZATION FOR STANDARDIZATION, 1987a, 1987b). The impact of these rules on compliance with the upper-layer intents of the OSI model is significant, making Rose's contribution in this area very important.

MACKINNON ET AL. also focus on the upper-layer standards but treat two emerging areas of concern with the use of OSI—namely, the development of International Standardized Profiles (ISPs) in accord with the efforts of Joint Technical Committee 1's Special Group on Functional Standards. They also review progress on the development of a Basic Reference Model for Open Distributed Processing (ODP) currently being developed by a Working Group within SC 21 of Joint Technical Committee 1.

Human–Computer Interaction

Over the past few years display technology has made it possible to move from text-only displays to bit-mapped or graphic displays. As a result, there has been an increase in the number of Graphical User Interfaces (GUIs) with Xerox's Viewpoint, Macintosh, Microsoft's Windows, NeXT, X Window System, and SunView being only a few. These multiple approaches have raised concerns about the ability to move people and software easily among various environments. (While many now view the X Window System as a de facto standard for windowing, windowing is simply a subset of the concerns in human–computer interaction. Various aspects of human–computer interaction have been the subject of standardization efforts for a number of years.) ABERNETHY traces the origins of a number of the important standards for human–computer interfaces and the organizations involved in their development. As of January 1991, at least nine committees were actively engaged in work on standards for human–computer interaction (BILLINGSLEY). Among the most comprehensive efforts are the following:

- ISO TC159/SC4/WG5 is developing a 19-part standard detailing the Ergonomic Requirements for Office Work with Visual Display Terminals (INTERNATIONAL ORGANIZATION FOR STANDARDIZATION, 1990);
- IEEE P1201 is working on a standard for application and user portability that would provide a standard application programmer interface as well as a set of recommendations defining optimal design for interface components (INSTITUTE OF ELECTRICAL AND ELECTRONICS ENGINEERS, 1990); and
- ISO/IEC JTC1 SC18 WG9 is working on a series of standards that will address keyboard layouts, dialog interaction, and symbols.

In 1990, SPRING ET AL. proposed a reference model for human–computer interaction that seeks to place the various ongoing efforts in a context that would minimize duplication of effort.

Application Portability

Application portability standards are concerned with the development of a standard execution platform viewed from the perspective of application software. Currently, software written for the PC has to be rewritten to be run on a UNIX workstation. The same holds true for software run on minicomputers and mainframes. If software producers could write only one version of an application that would run on multiple machines, development costs would be greatly reduced. The most significant standard for application portability is the IEEE POSIX Standard, a multipart standard currently under development that provides a Portable Operating System Interface for Computer Environments. An early published version of the standard has been widely circulated (INSTITUTE OF ELECTRICAL AND ELECTRONICS ENGINEERS, 1988). The work of IEEE on P1201 mentioned above also contributes to application portability by providing a standard approach to interface aspects of application programs.

Data Format and Interchange

While standards for system interconnection, human–computer interaction, and application portability are essential to achieving the goal of interoperability, little real progress can be made without the ability to freely create, manipulate, disseminate, store, and access data across the various systems. At the level of defined data types, such as "printable strings" or "integers," these concerns are addressed by the presentation level of the Open Systems Interconnection model. With the extensions provided to the Abstract Syntax Notation (INTERNATIONAL ORGANIZATION FOR STANDARDIZATION, 1987a), it becomes possible to describe objects of arbitrarily complex construction. However, in order to make meaningful use of the data at an information level, standards for data interchange are needed. Although multiple standards already exist for data interchange, there is still much discussion and evolution in this area as standards of increasingly limited scope are developed to meet specialized needs. There are literally hundreds of standards for data representation and interchange. A few of the more important ones are discussed in the overview below. These include standards for bibliographic data interchange, graphics, databases, records, and documents.

Among the earliest data interchange standards were those in the library field. Interest in the exchange of machine-readable records containing bibliographic information goes back to the 1950s. Indeed, while the American National Standard Format for Bibliographic Information Interchange on Magnetic Tape was not established until 1971, work on the MARC (Machine-Readable Cataloging) format goes back to the late 1950s, early 1960s (AVRAM, 1975; 1988). Work on extensions to the MARC format continues to be developed (WEBER, 1990).

Another area in which data representation and data interchange standards emerged early is the area of computer graphics. The Graphic Kernel System (GKS) allows for device independence by defining a standard data representation to be used in the interface between application programs and graphical devices (AMERICAN NATIONAL STANDARDS INSTITUTE, 1985). The Computer Graphics Metafile (CGM) defines a standard for the exchange of graphical information between systems (AMERICAN NATIONAL STANDARDS INSTITUTE, 1986a). While these standards are widely implemented, technological developments in displays and in the complexity and the nature of the graphical information being exchanged has resulted in several new standards, including the Initial Graphics Exchange Specification (IGES) and the Programmer's Hierarchical Interactive Graphics System (PHIGS) (AMERICAN NATIONAL STANDARDS INSTITUTE, 1990a). Beyond these specific graphics standards, the matter has been further confused by the use of the Postscript Page Description Language and the X Window System to specify graphics in selected situations.

Database standards have begun to solidify around a structured query language—SQL (AMERICAN NATIONAL STANDARDS INSTITUTE, 1986c) and the Network Data Language standard (AMERICAN NATIONAL STANDARDS INSTITUTE, 1986b). EVEREST ET AL. provide a detailed comparison and analysis of the strengths and weaknesses of the two languages. With a new standard called SQL2, or Extended SQL, currently being prepared, there is a growing consensus that some form of SQL will serve as the base standard. Perhaps more importantly, extensive work is nearing completion in the United States on a set of standards for an Information Resource Dictionary System (IRDS) (AMERICAN NATIONAL STANDARDS INSTITUTE, 1988b). This standard is designed to support the management of the information efforts of an enterprise (an enterprise is defined as the collective efforts of multiple organizations engaged in some activity—e.g., the automotive industry). WINKLER reviews the relationship between the U.S. national and international efforts toward IRDS. ALTOMARE ET AL. provide a more detailed description of prototype IRDSs implemented to provide a comparison of U.S. and international efforts directed at a standard for IRDS.

Efforts to define standards for Electronic Data Interchange (EDI) have intensified in the last few years. U.S. efforts in this area are the responsibility of Accredited Standards Committee X12, which has released more than 40 standards to define the process. The X12 Design Rules and Guidelines provide an overview of the process, which details the electronic formats of typical business transactions, such as a request for quotation, purchase order, shipping notice/manifest, and invoice (AMERICAN NATIONAL STANDARDS INSTITUTE, 1988a). U.S. efforts are closely coordinated with the international efforts of the United Nation's Electronic Data Interchange for Administration, Commerce and Transport (EDIFACT) (INTERNATIONAL ORGANIZATION FOR STANDARDIZATION, 1988c).

Another set of data interchange standards of interest are those for document interchange. There are two basic types of document interchange standards—revisable and final form. The revisable form standards for exchange of documents are the best known. The Standard Generalized Markup Language (SGML) became an International Standard in 1986 (INTERNATIONAL ORGANIZATION FOR STANDARDIZATION, 1986) and is supported by several related standards, one of the most interesting of which is the Standard for Electronic Manuscript Preparation and Markup prepared by

NISO (AMERICAN NATIONAL STANDARDS INSTITUTE, 1989). While SGML has been the first document interchange standard to be widely accepted, there is also significant support for the Office Document Architecture (ODA) approach (INTERNATIONAL ORGANIZATION FOR STANDARDIZATION, 1989). More recently, there has been an effort to standardize the format for final form document interchange. Several de facto standards have emerged in this area, including Adobe's Postscript and Hewlett Packard's HPGL for low-end laser printers and Xerox's Interpress for high-speed laser printers. ROBINSON & STRASEN describe the current efforts to specify a Standard Page Description Language (SPDL), which looks as if it will integrate the best features of Postscript and Interpress.

As the various standards for data interchange grow to maturity, users of information technology standards have had to find appropriate combinations of the base standards to meet their needs. WALCH describes the role of standards in the archival management of electronic records and discusses how many of the data interchange standards described above play a role in the archiving of electronic records. The Department of Defense has specified a subset of these standards under the Computer-Aided Acquisition and Logistical Support (CALS) initiative (U.S. DEPARTMENT OF DEFENSE).

Standards Profiles

As information technology standards have proliferated and become more complex, it has become more difficult to ascertain whether a functional system that conforms to one subset of standards will interoperate with another functional system that conforms to a different subset or even to the same subset with different options implemented. To address this problem, several user organizations have formed consortia to specify the specific standards and the options within those standards that would constitute a viable system. These specifications are commonly called "profiles." Among the earliest profiles is the Manufacturing Automation Protocol specified by General Motors Corp. and other manufacturing organizations. Concerns about the proliferation of these profiles led to the formation of a Special Group on Functional Standards as a part of ISO/IEC JTC 1. CERNI (1989) describes the background of the effort and the formation of the Special Group on Functional Standards responsible for what are now called International Standardized Profiles (ISP). The work of these various consortia and committees to develop profiles led to a need for organizations that could develop tests that would ensure that a vendor could indeed meet the specifications set out. MACPHERSON provides a comprehensive review of the various consortia currently engaged through "Feeder's Forums" in the specification of ISPs as well as the corresponding groups engaged in the development of conformance test suites. LEDRICK & SPRING review the ISP process and discuss potential sources of incompatibility in ISPs as well as offer suggestions for ensuring interoperability.

RESEARCH ON STANDARDS AND STANDARDIZATION

The literature on information technology standards can be divided into three groups. First, the standards themselves represent a significant corpus and, to some extent, represent an historical record of the development of information technology. Second, there is significant commentary in the popular and professional literature on various standards. This literature may be subdivided further into commentaries on standards and explanations of standards. Third, there is a growing number of studies of standards and the standardization process. Much of this literature involves case studies and focuses on the process of standardization or the nature of the standards rather than the content of a particular standard. This third body of literature is the main focus of this review.

As indicated, standards are agreements or conventions about the substance or form of some product or service. From this perspective, standards may be viewed as simple instruments for cooperation that are forged as needed. So why bother to study standards? The basis of most answers is financial—i.e., in many ways, standards have a significant financial impact on the information technology industry. Standards grow out of the efforts of individuals, often many individuals over many years, and their development may cost millions of dollars. Further, despite the high cost, not all standards are correct. Finally, standards are sometimes developed before they are needed and sometimes well after they they are needed. Therefore researchers have begun in the past decade to explore the nature of standards and the process by which they are developed.

Researchers have set out to answer three basic questions. First, how do we know when a standard needs to be developed? For example, in the area of public safety, how many accidents must occur before a standard is promulgated? In the case of compatibility standards, when do the costs of incompatibility become so great that products or services converge on a standard? What causes a group to decide to come to consensus on the need for a standard? Second, what factors affect the choice of a given process or product as a standard? If these were known, it might be possible to ensure that the best product or service be adopted as the standard. At the very least, it might be possible to ensure that what becomes the standard is what the group truly intends, even if it is less than optimal by some other measure. Third, what is the best way to develop a standard—e.g., how can it be done in less time or with more involvement or with less contention? When standards cost millions of dollars, improvements in the development process become important. Below is a presentation of what has been discovered about standards and the process of developing standards.

Standards Research Methodologies

Most of the research studies on standards have been economic studies of technology adoption by end users. The work, as pointed out by WEISS, may be classified as:

- Microeconomic and game theory research, which includes the work of ARTHUR, S.V. BERG (1987; 1988; 1989), BRAUNSTEIN & WHITE, DAVID (1985; 1987), FARRELL & SALONER (1985; 1986; 1987), and KATZ & SHAPIRO (1985; 1986a; 1986b). Berg, Braunstein, and White, and David have illustrated their hypotheses with prior cases in standardization;
- Case study research, which includes the work of BESEN & JOHNSON, CRANE, SIRBU & HUGHES, SIRBU & STEWART, and SIRBU & ZWIMPFER. Sirbu and Stewart have validated prior hypotheses by examining particular cases; and
- Macroeconomic research using highly aggregated statistics, such as the work of GRANT, LECRAW, LINK, and LINK & TASSEY.

Research on the Emergence of Standards

LINK and LECRAW have conducted research on the relationship between markets and standards. Link found that the more concentrated a market is, the more likely it is to have standards. Link's probit model examines whether the standards development process will be initiated for a particular market, given various market concentrations, levels of technological complexity, and percentage of unionization. Lecraw uses a discriminant analysis to predict whether a market will have a standard or not according to the independent variables of buyer concentration, seller concentration, proportion of government sales, product safety role, elasticity of demand, advertising intensity, R&D intensity, product complexity, and producer good/consumer good. These studies do not indicate, even at a macroeconomic level, how many standards are enough in a market given various conditions but only whether standards will exist.

An alternative analytical approach has been taken in several papers by Sirbu. SIRBU & STEWART examined market structures that promote the emergence of standards. They developed a model that is useful in determining the market conditions under which a standard is likely to emerge. In their taxonomy, the degree of centralization of purchase and manufacture was a critical factor. Thus, it was shown that standards are likely to exist when unrelated purchasers specified similar products that had to work together. This was also the case when diverse manufacturers produced products that had to interconnect. In contrast, products that are purchased by a single entity are not as likely to be standardized. These authors examined the data modem market to obtain evidence for their taxonomy. Sirbu and Stewart do not discuss the mechanism by which standards emerge—i.e., they do not differentiate between de facto and voluntary consensus standards.

SIRBU & HUGHES examine the standards setting process for local area networks and conclude that standards participation involves more than just an exercise in economic interests; it involves education as well. Some participants in a standards committee are there to learn about the technologies, whereas others are there to promote their technology. These authors believe that "the motivation to support standards can be understood through an examination of the problems of contingency contracting with and without a standard." In general, they indicate that a firm will support a standard when it will enhance profits. Basically, support for a standard reduces the investment and risk that would be faced without a standard. Sirbu and Hughes support this argument by using lessons from the local area network standardization process. This research supplies additional support for the hypotheses of Sirbu and Stewart.

Research on Technology Choice in Standardization

ARTHUR studied technology choice under increasing returns, modeling the initial choice of technologies by consumers as a random process. One technology emerges as a market leader as a result of the preferences or arbitrary choice of the initial consumers. Once established as a market leader, the technology will attract subsequent consumers who do not have strong preferences regarding the alternative technology. Later, even consumers with strong preferences regarding the alternative will feel compelled to adopt the dominant technology. The early technology, therefore, becomes the de facto standard. Thus, the ultimate technology chosen as the standard by consumers is the result of "small events" occurring in the early stages of technology deployment.

DAVID (1985) successfully explained the case of the development of the typewriter keyboard from this point of view. He further abstracted from this case three characteristics of technical "lock-in" based on this case: (1) technical interrelatedness, (2) economies of scale, and (3) quasi-irreversibility of investment. Lock-in for David is equivalent to the emergence of a de facto standard. Subsequent work by DAVID (1987) supports Arthur's analysis, showing increased lock-in under increasing returns. In the absence of some mechanism, which David calls a gateway, it becomes difficult for new technologies to emerge and displace the embedded technology even if there are benefits to switching and minimal costs. This observation led David to suggest that the policy objective of a public agency is to prevent premature standardization. This requires nonmarket support of the technologies that appear to be disadvantaged until a socially optimal choice can be made.

KATZ & SHAPIRO (1985; 1986a) formalize the notions developed by Arthur and by David into a theoretical model that describes consumer choice and producer behavior with regard to standards when "network externalities" exist and firms behave strategically. Network externalities describe the benefits a consumer receives when other consumers purchase products that are compatible. For example, a consumer who purchases a VHS video recorder benefits from others who purchase compatible recorders. The benefit is in the form of a greater diversity of add-on products and services at lower costs that results from increased competition to serve a larger market. Network externality is therefore a function of the installed base of the product or technology.

Katz and Shapiro use traditional economic constructs, such as rational consumer behavior and profit-maximizing firms, and assume a market-mediated (i.e., de facto) standards development process. They model consumer choice between competing standards-based products, such as personal computers and video cassette recorders. A static economic model (KATZ & SHAPIRO, 1985) shows that the social incentive to achieve full compatibility in a market is greater than the industry incentive. That is, left to producers alone, fewer standards would emerge in such a static market than is socially desirable in the welfare economic context. KATZ & SHAPIRO

(1986b) consider a dynamic market in which technical progress is occurring and reach several conclusions:

- The technology that is currently superior will likely dominate the market unless an inferior technology is actively promoted;
- If only one of two rival technologies is sponsored, the sponsored technology is likely to be adopted, even if it is technically inferior to the unsponsored one; and
- All else being equal, the technology that will be superior in the future has a strategic advantage over the technology that is currently superior.

KATZ & SHAPIRO (1986a) extend this model to study the private and social incentives to achieve compatibility through standardized interfaces. Here they find that firms often have socially excessive collective compatibility incentives. This is particularly true in the case of new markets. In a new market, firms may elect to standardize in order to reduce the competition required to establish an installed base, and, hence, a significant network externality. By standardizing early, firms can collectively build an installed base of compatible products. These incentives may be socially excessive because consumers may not have the opportunity to select the optimal technology, as they would in a purely competitive case. These authors show that this excess incentive diminishes later in the dynamic model because later consumers derive more benefit (surplus) from compatibility, so the private compatibility incentives may be too low.

FARRELL & SALONER (1985; 1986) also examine issues related to de facto standardization but are more concerned with industry effects, such as innovation, inertia, and predation. They identify various situations that can result from de facto standardization. For example, "stranding" occurs when there is bias against a new and perhaps superior technology because users of the old technology are tied to the installed base. Another type of situation, which they call the "penguin effect," occurs when no user wants to be the first to change to a new technology but all users quickly adopt the new technology once any one user changes. Just as penguins are reluctant to be the first in the water for fear of predators, users are reluctant to be the first to adopt a new technology for fear of being stranded with a new technology that no one else adopts. These fears can be used to anticompetitive ends. For example, an announcement of a forthcoming product may prevent consumers from adopting an available technology as they wait for the announced product to become available. Similarly, predatory pricing can be used to commit consumers to one technology, creating an aversion to being stranded with a competing technology.

FARRELL & SALONER (1987) are the first researchers to study voluntary consensus standards explicitly. In this analytical study using game theory, they compare market-mediated standardization processes and committee-mediated processes. They conclude that the committee-mediated processes provide superior payoffs to the participants than do market-mediated processes. Intuitively, the cost of failure to prevail in the marketplace is greater than the cost of participation in the standards process. The payoff for prevailing in the marketplace with a de facto standard is greater than the payoff from the voluntary consensus standard, but this difference in payoff is smaller than the difference in costs. These results explain why standards committees are normally the method of choice to develop standards.

BESEN & JOHNSON further validate the basic conclusions of Arthur, David, Katz and Shapiro, and Farrell and Saloner by developing several cases of standardization in the broadcast industry. Their research focuses on the market adoption of standards, whether they are mediated by the free market, the government, or a standards committee. Standards in the broadcast industry almost always involve an interplay among these three sources. The authors found that the following factors are important in the successful adoption of a technology: (1) sponsorship, (2) the behavior of firms with large market shares, (3) promotional pricing, and (4) cost.

BRAUNSTEIN & WHITE provide an analytical framework for the setting of compatibility standards. They separate consumers into "specialized" and "portfolio" consumers. Specialized consumers are loyal to a particular brand or implementation of a product and therefore consider interproduct compatibility irrelevant. Portfolio consumers are interested in consuming a type of product and do not favor a particular brand or implementation; these consumers are very interested in standards. Braunstein and White show that the dominant firm is most likely to dictate the outcome of the compatibility standard in both cases, although the time it takes to standardize the product might vary considerably. This segmentation of consumers is consistent with the work of SIRBU & STEWART and provides analytical support for their work. Since the dominant firm is likely to dictate the outcome of a compatibility standard in a de facto standards process, it is possible to conclude that the dominant firm would also more strongly influence the outcome of a voluntary consensus standardization process.

S.V. BERG (1987; 1988; 1989) has conducted research into standards from the point of view of the producer's choice of technology. In contrast to other researchers, he considers the choice of technologies as a continuum. He analyzes the producer's decision-making process under a variety of alternative models of consumer demand. He postulates that the advantages and disadvantages of various institutional processes are functions of cost, demand, and strategic factors. BERG (1987) draws on the case of AM stereo standardization to illustrate his points. Several interesting concepts and conclusions emerge from this work:

- The technical externality should be based on choices made by producers rather than those made by consumers; this is in contrast to the network externality of KATZ & SHAPIRO (1985);
- Voluntary cooperation in standardization does not necessarily yield socially optimal outcomes; and
- Incentives to cooperate are greatest when the combined market under compatibility is greater than the sum of the individual markets under incompatibility.

Thus, while FARRELL & SALONER (1987) conclude that firms are better off in attempting to develop voluntary consensus standards, S.V. BERG (1987) shows that these standards are not necessarily socially optimal. KATZ & SHAPIRO (1985) show that the firms that develop these standards may have socially excessive incentives to do so, particularly when they come early in a product's life cycle.

ECONOMIDES studied the incentives for compatibility in the absence of network externalities. He considers the situation in which compatible subsystems (or components) can be used to construct a system. He finds that the equilibrium prices and the equilibrium profits under compatibility are higher than they would be under incompatibility, even in the absence of network externalities. This is very strong evidence of the trend toward compatibility that can be observed in the marketplace.

Taken collectively, the work of the researchers discussed above predicts that markets not dominated by single firms will produce excessive standards early in a product life cycle and that these standards are not necessarily socially optimal. Anecdotal evidence reported by STRAUSS generally supports this result. While the researchers do not as a rule explicitly discuss the emergence mechanisms for standards (i.e., the de facto and voluntary consensus processes), their work is at a sufficiently general level that this difference is not important.

Research on the Consensus Standardization Process

Little empirical research exists on the standardization process itself. WEISS & SIRBU conducted an empirical analysis of technological rivalry in voluntary standards committees. They found that committee outcome (i.e., the technological choice process in a committee) is influenced positively by: (1) the market power of the sponsors, (2) the net assets of the sponsoring coalition, and (3) the degree to which the sponsors support their technology.

SPRING & WEISS have proposed a framework for research on the standardization process. They suggest that such research requires cross comparison of the processes used by various information technology standards development organizations. They also suggest studies of the process across industries and across standard types— i.e., base standards, reference standards, and implementation standards. The standardization process has been the subject of intense study by the Strategic Planning Committee of X3 (AMERICAN NATIONAL STANDARDS INSTITUTE, 1991b). The model proposes a five-stage life cycle: (1) initial requirements, (2) base standards development, (3) profiles/product development, (4) testing, and (5) user implementation and feedback.

Several authors have offered guidelines for the development of standards in the context of organizations. ELLISON & SIMSON suggest procedures for developing internal company standards. CARGILL (1990) discusses the management structure required for effective participation in standards. MCNAMARA discusses participation in standardization activities from the perspective of the participating company. These authors bring a wealth of practical experience to the process, but their recommendations are based primarily on experience.

THE FUTURE OF STANDARDS RESEARCH

A number of unanswered questions about standards and standardization will be addressed by researchers in the coming years. Fundamental questions about methodology still need to be considered. Some have suggested that although an economic paradigm provides a useful framework for the analysis of de facto standards, a political science, sociological, or anthropological framework may be more appropriate for studying the voluntary consensus standards development process. Whatever paradigm is used, better baseline data about standards and standardization efforts are needed. TOTH profiles standards activities in companies and across industries. His research provides one of the most comprehensive data-gathering efforts to date, and it can serve as the basis for further study. Before one can begin to compare the processes by which standards are developed, one must have some way of normalizing the efforts.

DAVID (1987) presents a taxonomy that classifies standards as behavioral or technical and, within those categories, as reference or definitional standards, minimum attribute standards, or interface/compatibility standards. SPRING & BEARMAN suggest that information technology standards, which fall almost exclusively in the technical interface/compatibility category, may be further classified according to the information process they support.

At a pragmatic level, organizations that support standards development and those that are developing the standards (SDOs) are concerned with several questions:

- How can the cost of developing standards be reduced?
- How can the cost of implementing standards be minimized?
- How can the time required to develop a standard be reduced?
- How can standards development best support conformance testing and certification?

It is expected that the standardization process can be streamlined without corrupting the due process requirements of the voluntary consensus standards development. Generally speaking, this can be accomplished by analysis of critical paths and unnecessary delays in the process. The problem to date with such studies, beyond the problem of normalizing the results (mentioned above), is that these data must be collected over a long period of time and at great expense before even tentative recommendations can be made.

It is also expected that the application of technology can aid the standards development process. Several SDOs have established plans to make better use of information technology to speed the standards development process. Notable are the efforts set out for ISO/IEC JTC 1 in the directives for their work as reported by MACPHERSON.

The development of appropriate reference models can help in the development of standards by identifying the need for standards further in advance, by avoiding duplicate efforts, and by better ensuring compatibility. SPRING & BEARMAN suggest models that are information oriented rather than technology oriented to help in this process. In addition to better models of standards to support a coherent set of reference models, better models of the standardization process are needed. In part this will be an outgrowth of the application of new research paradigms.

We need a better understanding of if and how standards can be used as a mechanism by which nations can restrict free trade. FRENKEL (1990b) and FITZGERALD address this concern with respect to the development of standards for the European Community. These concerns arise from the fact that CENELEC is not open to U.S. participation during the standards development process. This provides an edge to European corporations that participate in the CENELEC committees and thus have advance notice of the standards specifications that can be used by them to prepare products. There are also concerns about testing and certification. For example, if product testing must take place in Europe, U.S. manufacturers would be at a disadvantage.

CONCLUSIONS

Many users of information technology believe that standards will vastly expand the value of the systems at our disposal by allowing them to connect to and communicate with other systems. Standards developers and researchers are increasingly aware that true interoperability will not be achieved easily. The time required to develop stable standards is being eclipsed by the rate of technological development. More abstract standards allowing for technological evolution lack specificity and result in products that technically conform to the standards but nevertheless fail to interoperate with other products that also conform. Perhaps the most discouraging observation is that standardized profiles, which are essentially standards of standards, may not provide enough specificity to allow for true interoperability.

Academic researchers have begun to tackle some of the issues. Despite efforts to conduct controlled studies of standards or the standards development process, many studies find too many uncontrolled variables to be able to state generalizable conclusions. There is a paucity of baseline data for use in studies. For example, it has been theorized that traditional standards are developed by a process different from what CARGILL (1989) has called anticipatory stand ards. To determine whether the processes are indeed different, researchers must first develop criteria with which to identify anticipatory and traditional standards.

Over the next decade there will be significant changes in information technology. Over that same period, standards will be needed that permit producers of that technology to provide products and processes that can work together. To some significant extent, success in that venture will depend on research that will help us decide what standards need to be developed and research that helps us find the most economical and efficient way to develop them.

BIBLIOGRAPHY

ABERNETHY, CHARLES N. 1988. Human-Computer Interface Standards: Origins, Organizations and Comment. International Review of Ergonomics. 1988; 2: 31-54. ISSN: 0269-5839.

ALTOMARE, DANTE; CARULLI, MICHELE; CASANOVA, PIETRO; LIMONGELLI, DANIELE; TANGORRA, FILIPPO. 1989. A Prototype for the Integration of Information Resource Dictionary System and PCTE. Computer Standards & Interfaces. 1989; 9(1): 31-47. ISSN: 0920-5489.

AMERICAN NATIONAL STANDARDS INSTITUTE. 1985. Computer Graphics—Graphic Kernel System (GKS). New York, NY: American National Standards Institute; 1986. 129p. (X3.124-1985). Available from: ANSI, 1430 Broadway, New York, NY 10018.

AMERICAN NATIONAL STANDARDS INSTITUTE. 1986a. Computer Graphics Metafile (CGM). New York, NY: American National Standards Institute; 1986. 293p. (X3.122-1986). Available from: ANSI, 1430 Broadway, New York, NY 10018.

AMERICAN NATIONAL STANDARDS INSTITUTE. 1986b. Database Language NDL. New York, NY: American National Standards Institute; 1986. 136p. (X3.133-1986). Available from: ANSI, 1430 Broadway, New York, NY 10018.

AMERICAN NATIONAL STANDARDS INSTITUTE. 1986c. Database Language SQL. New York, NY: American National Standards Institute; 1986. 120p. (X3.135-1986). Available from: ANSI, 1430 Broadway, New York, NY 10018.

AMERICAN NATIONAL STANDARDS INSTITUTE. 1988a. ASCX12 Design Rules and Guidelines. New York, NY: American National Standards Institute; 1988. (ASCX12B/88-040). Available from: ANSI, 1430 Broadway, New York, NY 10018.

AMERICAN NATIONAL STANDARDS INSTITUTE. 1988b. Information Resource Dictionary System (IRDS). New York, NY: American National Standards Institute; 1988. 725p. (X3.138-1988). Available from: ANSI, 1430 Broadway, New York, NY 10018.

AMERICAN NATIONAL STANDARDS INSTITUTE. 1989. Electronic Manuscript Preparation and Markup. New York, NY: American National Standards Institute; 1989 September. 150p. (ANSI Z39.59). Available from: Transaction Publishers, New Brunswick, NJ 08903.

AMERICAN NATIONAL STANDARDS INSTITUTE. 1990a. Programmer's Hierarchical Interactive Graphics System (PHIGS). New York, NY: American National Standards Institute; 1990. 418p. (ISO 9592-199X; ISO 9592 Parts 1-3). Available from: ANSI, 1430 Broadway, New York, NY 10018.

AMERICAN NATIONAL STANDARDS INSTITUTE. 1990b. Programmer's Hierarchical Interactive Graphics System PLUS (PHIGS PLUS). New York, NY: American National Standards Institute; 1990. 171p. (ISO 9592-199X; ISO 9592 Part 4 (Amendments to 1-3)). Available from: ANSI, 1430 Broadway, New York, NY 10018.

AMERICAN NATIONAL STANDARDS INSTITUTE. 1991a. Strategic Planning Committee; Master Plan (Strategic). Washington, DC: American National Standards Institute; 1991 March. 32p. (X3/91-0635X). Available from: CBEMA, 311 First St. NW, Suite 500, Washington, DC 20001-2178.

AMERICAN NATIONAL STANDARDS INSTITUTE. 1991b. Strategic Planning Committee; Standards Life Cycle. Washington, DC: American National Standards Institute; 1991 April. 28p. (X3/91-0550). Available from: CBEMA, 311 First St. NW, Suite 500, Washington, DC 20001-2178.

ARTHUR, W. BRIAN. 1985. Competing Technologies and Lock-In by Historical Small Events: The Dynamics of Allocation Under Increasing Returns. Palo Alto, CA: Center for Economic Policy Research, Stanford University; 1985 January. (Technical Report 43). Available from: Center for Economic Policy Research, Stanford University, Palo Alto, CA.

AVRAM, HENRIETTE D. 1975. Machine-Readable Cataloging (MARC) Program. In: Kent, Allen, ed. Encyclopedia of Library and Information Science: Volume 16. New York, NY: Marcel Dekker; 1975. 380-413. ISBN: 0-8247-2016-4.

AVRAM, HENRIETTE D. 1988. Machine-Readable Cataloging (MARC): 1986. In: Kent, Allen, ed. Encyclopedia of Library and Information Science: Volume 43. New York, NY: Marcel Dekker; 1988. 136-160. ISBN: 0-8247-2043-1.

BATTEN, DAVID F. 1983. Spatial Analysis of Interacting Economies: The Role of Entropy and Information Theory in Spatial Input/Output Modeling. Boston, MA: Kluwer-Nijhoff Publishers; 1983. 306p. ISBN: 0-89838-109-6; LC: 82-15363.

BERG, JOHN L. 1990. Information about NCSL and Its Publications. Computer Standards & Interfaces. 1990; 10(3): 231-240. ISSN: 0920-5489.

BERG, SANFORD V. 1987. Public Policy and Corporate Strategies in the AM Stereo Market. In: Gabel, H. Landis, ed. Product Standardization and Competitive Strategy. New York, NY: North Holland; 1987. ISBN: 0-444-70232-6.

BERG, SANFORD V. 1988. Duopoly Compatibility Standards with Partial Cooperation and Standards Leadership. Information Economics and Policy. 1988; 3: 35-53. ISSN: 0167-6245.

BERG, SANFORD V. 1989. Technical Standards as Public Goods: Demand Incentives for Cooperative Behavior. Public Finance Quarterly. 1989 January; 17(1): 29-54. ISSN: 0048-5853.

BERG, SANFORD V. 1990. Technical Standards and Technological Change in the Telecommunications Industry. In: Link, A.L.; Smith, V.K., eds.; Advances in Applied Microeconomics: Volume 5. Greenwich, CT: JAI Press; 1990. ISSN: 0278-0984.

BESEN, STANLEY; JOHNSON, LELAND. 1986. Compatibility Standards, Competition, and Innovation in the Broadcasting Industry. 1986. 139p. Available from: Rand Corporation, Santa Monica, CA.

BILLINGSLEY, PAT. 1991. The Standards Factor: Catching up with Communities. SIGCHI Bulletin. 1991 January; 23(1): 6-10. ISSN: 0736-6906.

BONINO, MICHAL; SPRING, MICHAEL B. 1991. Standards as Change Agents in the Information Technology Market. Computer Standards & Interfaces. 1991; 11: (in press). ISSN: 0920-5489.

BRAUNSTEIN, YALE; WHITE, LAWRENCE J. 1985. Setting Technical Compatibility Standards: An Economic Analysis. The Antitrust Bulletin. 1985 Summer; 30(2): 337-355. ISSN: 0003-603X.

BUCKLEY, F.J. 1986. An Overview of the IEEE Computer Society Standards Process. In: Proceedings of the Computer Standards Conference: Striking a Balance between Technology, Economics, Politics, and Reality—For Substance, Not Form; 1986 May 13-15; San Francisco, CA. Washington, DC: IEEE Computer Society; 1986. 2-8. ISBN: 0-8186-0698-3.

CAMPBELL, JEREMY. 1982. Grammatical Man. New York, NY: Simon and Schuster; 1982. 319p. ISBN: 0-671-44062-4; LC: 82-3272.

CARGILL, CARL F. 1989. Information Technology Standardization: Theory, Process, and Organizations. Rockport, MA: Digital Press; 1989. 252p. ISBN: 1-5555-8022-X.

CARGILL, CARL F. 1990. Justifying the Need for a Standards Program. In: Toth, Robert B., ed. Standards Management: A Handbook for Profits. New York, NY: American National Standards Institute; 1990. 1-18. Available from: ANSI, 1430 Broadway, New York, NY 10018.

CERNI, DOROTHY M. 1984. Standards in Process: Foundations and Profiles of ISDN and OSI Studies. Boulder, CO: National Telecommunications and Information Administration, Institute for Telecommunications Sciences; 1984 December. 259p. (NTIA Report 84-170). NTIS: PB85-165041.

CERNI, DOROTHY M. 1989. Beyond OSI Standards: OSI Profiles. Communications Standards Management. 1989. 20p. Available from: Warren, Gorham & Lamont, Inc., 1 Penn Plaza, New York, NY 10119.

CRANE, RHONDA J. 1979. The Politics of International Standards: France and the Color TV War. Norwood, NJ: Ablex; 1979. 123p. ISBN: 0-89391-019-8; LC: 79-4231.

CRAWFORD, WALT. 1986. Technical Standards: An Introduction for Librarians. White Plains, NY: Knowledge Industry Publications; 1986. 299p. ISBN: 0-86729-192-3.

DAVID, PAUL A. 1985. Clio and the Economics of QWERTY. American Economic Review. 1985 May; 75(2): 332-337. ISSN: 0002-8282.

DAVID, PAUL A. 1987. Some New Standards for the Economics of Standardization in the Information Age. In: Dasgupta, Partha; Stoneman, Paul, eds. Economic Policy and Technological Performance. Cambridge, England: Cambridge University Press; 1987. 206-234. ISBN: 0-521-34555-3; LC: 87-9387.

DAVID, PAUL A.; BUNN, J.A. 1988. The Economics of Gateway Technologies and Network Evolution: Lessons from the Electricity Supply History. Information Economics and Policy. 1988; 3(2): 165-202. ISSN: 0167-6245.

DENENBERG, RAY. 1990. Data Communications and OSI. Library Hi Tech. 1990; 8(4): 15-32. ISSN: 0737-8831.

ECONOMIDES, NICHOLAS. 1989. Desirability of Compatibility in the Absence of Network Externalities. American Economic Review. 1989; 79(5): 1165-1181. ISSN: 0002-8282.

ELLISON, WILLIAM; SIMSON, VERNE H. 1990. Developing Internal Standards. In: Toth, Robert B., ed. Standards Management: A Handbook for Profits. New York, NY: American National Standards Institute; 1990. 163-190. Available from: ANSI, 1430 Broadway, New York, NY 10018.

EVEREST, GORDEN C.; MARCH, SALVATORE T.; HANNA, MAGDY S.; SASTRY, MARK N. 1990. An Analysis of the Data Representation Constructs of the ANSI NDL and SQL Standards. Computer Standards & Interfaces. 1990; 10(1): 3-27. ISSN: 0920-5489.

FARRELL, JOSEPH. 1989. The Economics of Standardization: A Guide for Non-Economists. In: Berg, J.L., ed. How Standards Succeed: Proceedings of the International Symposium on Information Technology Standardization. New York, NY: North-Holland; 1989. 189-198.

FARRELL, JOSEPH; SALONER, GARTH. 1985. Standardization, Compatibility, and Innovation. RAND Journal of Economics. 1985 Spring; 16(1): 70-83. ISSN: 0741-6261.

FARRELL, JOSEPH; SALONER, GARTH. 1986. Installed Base and Compatibility: Innovation, Product Preannouncements, and Predation. American Economic Review. 1986 December; 76(5): 940-955. ISSN: 0002-8282.

FARRELL, JOSEPH; SALONER, GARTH. 1987. Competition, Compatibility, and Standards: The Economics of Horses, Penguins, and Lemmings. In: Gabel, H. Landis, ed. Product Standardization and Competitive Strategy. New York, NY: North Holland; 1987. 1-21. ISBN: 0-444-70232-6.

FARRELL, JOSEPH; SALONER, GARTH. 1988. Coordination through Committees and Markets. RAND Journal of Economics. 1988; 19(2): 235-252. ISSN: 0741-6261.

FITZGERALD, KAREN. 1990. Global Standards: Facilitators or Barriers? IEEE Spectrum. 1990 June; 27(6): 44-46. ISSN: 0018-9235.

FRENKEL, KAREN. 1990a. The European Community and Information Technology. Communications of the ACM. 1990 April; 33(4): 404-411. ISSN: 0001-0782.

FRENKEL, KAREN. 1990b. The Politics of Standards and the EC. Communications of the ACM. 1990 July; 33(7): 40-51. ISSN: 0001-0782.

GRANT, ROBERT M. 1987. The Effects of Product Standardization on Competition: Octane Grading of Petrol in the UK. In: Gabel, H. Landis, ed. Product Standardization and Competitive Strategy. New York, NY: North Holland; 1987. 283-301. ISBN: 0-444-70232-6.

HENSHALL, JOHN; SHAW, SANDY. 1988. OSI Explained: End-to-End Computer Communication Standards. Chichester, England: Ellis Horwood Limited; 1988. 217p. ISBN: 0-470-21100-8.

HILL, MARJORIE F. 1972. The World of EDP Standards. Minneapolis, MN: Control Data Corporation; 1972. 156p. (Tech Memo TM 4). OCLC: 12858712.

INSTITUTE OF ELECTRICAL AND ELECTRONICS ENGINEERS. 1988. Carrier Multiplier Access with Collision Detection (CSMA/CD) Access Method and Physical Layer Specifications. New York, NY: Institute of Electrical and Electronics Engineers; 1988 June 9. (Std 802.3). Available from: IEEE, 345 East 47th Street, New York, NY 10017.

INSTITUTE OF ELECTRICAL AND ELECTRONICS ENGINEERS. 1990. Window Interface for User and Application Portability. New York, NY: Institute of Electrical and Electronics Engineers; 1990. (Project 1201; Draft Proposal 1990). Available from: IEEE, 345 East 47th Street, New York, NY 10017.

INTERNATIONAL ORGANIZATION FOR STANDARDIZATION. 1984. Information Processing Systems—Open Systems Interconnection: Basic Reference Model. Geneva, Switzerland: International Organization for Standardization; 1984. (International Standard 7498-1). Available from: OMNICOM, Inc., 115 Park Street S.E., Vienna, VA 22180.

INTERNATIONAL ORGANIZATION FOR STANDARDIZATION. 1986. Information Processing Systems—Text and Office Systems—Standard Generalized Markup Language (SGML). Geneva, Switzerland: International Organization for Standardization; 1986 October. (International Standard 8879). Available from: OMNICOM, Inc., 115 Park Street S.E., Vienna, VA 22180.

INTERNATIONAL ORGANIZATION FOR STANDARDIZATION. 1987a. Information Processing—Open Systems Interconnection—Abstract Syntax Notation One (ASN.1)—Draft Addendum 1: Extensions to ASN.1. Geneva, Switzerland: International Organization for Standardization and International Electrotechnical Committee; 1987. (Draft Addendum 8824/DAD 1). Available from: OMNICOM, Inc., 115 Park Street S.E., Vienna, VA 22180.

INTERNATIONAL ORGANIZATON FOR STANDARDIZATION. 1987b. Information Processing—Open Systems Interconnection—Abstract Syntax Notation One (ASN.1)—Draft Addendum 1: Extensions to ASN.1 Basic Encoding Rules. Geneva, Switzerland: International Or-

ganization for Standardization and International Electrotechnical
Committee; 1987. (Draft Addendum 8825/DAD 1). Available from:
OMNICOM, Inc., 115 Park Street S.E., Vienna, VA 22180.

INTERNATIONAL ORGANIZATION FOR STANDARDIZATION. 1987c.
Information Processing—Open Systems Interconnection—Specification
of Abstract Syntax Notation One (ASN.1). Geneva, Switzerland: In-
ternational Organization for Standardization; 1987. (International
Standard 8824). Available from: OMNICOM, Inc., 115 Park Street
S.E., Vienna, VA 22180.

INTERNATIONAL ORGANIZATION FOR STANDARDIZATION. 1987d.
Information Processing—Open Systems Interconnection—Specification
of Basic Encoding Rules for Abstract Syntax Notation One (ASN.1).
Geneva, Switzerland: International Organization for Standardization
and International Electrotechnical Committee; 1987. (International
Standard 8825). Available from: OMNICOM, Inc., 115 Park Street
S.E., Vienna, VA 22180.

INTERNATIONAL ORGANIZATION FOR STANDARDIZATION. 1988a.
Information Processing Systems—File Transfer, Access, and Management. Geneva, Switzerland: International Organization for Standardization; 1988 April. (Final Text of Draft International Standard 8571).
Available from: OMNICOM, Inc., 115 Park Street S.E., Vienna, VA
22180.

INTERNATIONAL ORGANIZATION FOR STANDARDIZATION. 1988b.
Information Processing Systems—Open Systems Interconnection—The
Directory—Overview of Concepts, Models, and Service. Geneva, Swit-
zerland: International Organization for Standardization; 1988 De-
cember. (International Standard 9594-1). Available from: OMNICOM,
Inc., 115 Park Street S.E., Vienna, VA 22180.

INTERNATIONAL ORGANIZATION FOR STANDARDIZATION. 1988c.
Information Processing Systems—Text and Office Systems—Electronic
Data Interchange for Administration, Commerce and Transport
(EDIFACT)—Syntax Rules. Geneva, Switzerland: International Orga-
nization for Standardization; 1988 July. (International Standard
9735). Available from: OMNICOM, Inc., 115 Park Street S.E., Vienna,
VA 22180.

INTERNATIONAL ORGANIZATION FOR STANDARDIZATION. 1988d.
Information Processing Systems—Text and Office Systems—SGML
Support Facilities—SGML Document Interchange Format (SDIF).
Geneva, Switzerland: International Organization for Standardization;
1988 September. (International Standard 9069). Available from:
OMNICOM, Inc., 115 Park Street S.E., Vienna, VA 22180.

INTERNATIONAL ORGANIZATION FOR STANDARDIZATION. 1988e.
Information Processing Systems—Text Communication—MOTIS—
Message Handling: System and Service Overview. Geneva, Switzer-
land: International Organization for Standardization; 1988 December.
(International Standard 10021-1). 1988 December. Available from:
OMNICOM, Inc., 115 Park Street S.E., Vienna, VA 22180.

INTERNATIONAL ORGANIZATION FOR STANDARDIZATION. 1989. Information Processing Systems—Text and Office Systems—Office Document Architecture (ODA) and Interchange Format—Part 1 to 8. Geneva, Switzerland: International Organization for Standardization; 1989 September. (International Standard 8613). Available from: OMNICOM, Inc., 115 Park Street S.E., Vienna, VA 22180.

INTERNATIONAL ORGANIZATION FOR STANDARDIZATION. 1990. Ergonomic Requirements for Office Work with Visual Display Terminals (VDTs). Geneva, Switzerland: International Organization for Standardization; 1990. (International Standard 9241). Available from: OMNICOM, Inc., 115 Park Street S.E., Vienna, VA 22180.

INTERNATIONAL ORGANIZATION FOR STANDARDIZATION. Information Processing Systems—Text and Office Systems—Documentation—Interlibrary Loan Protocol Definition. Geneva, Switzerland: International Organization for Standardization. (International Standard 10161). Available from: OMNICOM, Inc., 115 Park Street S.E., Vienna, VA 22180.

INTERNATIONAL ORGANIZATION FOR STANDARDIZATION. Information Processing Systems—Text and Office Systems—Documentation—Interlibrary Loan Service Definition. Geneva, Switzerland: International Organization for Standardization. (International Standard 10160). Available from: OMNICOM, Inc., 115 Park Street S.E., Vienna, VA 22180.

INTERNATIONAL ORGANIZATION FOR STANDARDIZATION. Information Processing Systems—Text and Office Systems—Documentation—Application Service for Information Systems—Search, Retrieve, and Update Service Definition. Geneva, Switzerland: International Organization for Standardization. (International Standard 10162). Available from: OMNICOM, Inc., 115 Park Street S.E., Vienna, VA 22180.

INTERNATIONAL ORGANIZATION FOR STANDARDIZATION. Information Processing Systems—Text and Office Systems—Documentation—Application Service for Information Systems—Search, Retrieve, and Update Protocol Specification. Geneva, Switzerland: International Organization for Standardization. (International Standard 10162). Available from: OMNICOM, Inc., 115 Park Street S.E., Vienna, VA 22180.

KATZ, MICHAEL L.; SHAPIRO, CARL. 1985. Network Externalities, Competition, and Compatibility. American Economic Review. 1985 June; 75(3): 424-440. ISSN: 0002-8282.

KATZ, MICHAEL L.; SHAPIRO, CARL. 1986a. Product Compatibility Choice in a Market with Technological Progress. Oxford Economic Papers. 1986 November; 38(Supplement): 146-165. ISBN: 0-19-828562-0.

KATZ, MICHAEL L.; SHAPIRO, CARL. 1986b. Technology Adoption in the Presence of Network Externalities. Journal of Political Economy. 1986 August; 94(4): 822-841. ISSN: 0022-3808.

KEMMLER, E.L. 1983. Codes, Standards, Accreditation, and Certification. ASTM Standardization News. 1983; 11(6): 28-31. ISSN: 0090-1210.

LECRAW, DONALD J. 1984. Some Effects of Standards. Applied Economics. 1984; 16: 507-522. ISSN: 0003-6846.

LEDRICK, DIANE P.; SPRING, MICHAEL B. 1991. International Standardized Profiles. Computer Standards & Interfaces. 1991; 11(2): 95-119. ISSN: 0920-5489.

LIFCHUS, I.M. 1985. Standards Committee T1—Telecommunications. IEEE Communications. 1985 January; 23(1): 34-37. ISSN: 0163-6804.

LINK, ALBERT. 1983. Market Structure and Voluntary Product Standards. Applied Economics. 1983; 15: 393-401. ISSN: 0003-6846.

LINK, ALBERT N.; TASSEY, GREGORY. 1987. The Impact of Standards on Technology-Based Industries: The Case of Numerically Controlled Machine Tools in Automated Batch Manufacture. In: Gabel, H. Landis, ed. Product Standardization and Competitive Strategy. New York, NY: North Holland; 1987. ISBN: 0-444-70232-6.

LYNCH, CLIFFORD A. 1990. Information Retrieval as a Network Application. Library Hi Tech. 1990; 8(4): 57-72. ISSN: 0737-8831.

MACKINNON, D.; MCCRUM, W.; SHEPPARD, D. 1990. Introduction to OSI Open Systems Interconnection. New York, NY: Computer Science Press; 1990. 254p. ISBN: 0-7167-8180-8.

MACPHERSON, A. 1990. International Telecommunication Standards Organizations. Norwood, MA: Artech House; 1990. 317p. ISBN: 0-89006-365-6; LC: 90-41620.

MCNAMARA, T.J. 1990. Company Participation in External Standards Activities. In: Toth, Robert B., ed. Standards Management: A Handbook for Profits. New York, NY: American National Standards Institute; 1990. 249-263. Available from: American National Standards Institute, 1420 Broadway, New York, NY 10018.

MILLS, KEVIN L. 1990. Government Open Systems Interconnection: Profile in Progress. Library Hi Tech. 1990; 8(4): 111-118. ISSN: 0737-8831.

NATIONAL INSTITUTE OF STANDARDS AND TECHNOLOGY. 1988a. Federal Information Processing Standard 146: Government Open Systems Interconnection Profile (GOSIP). Gaithersburg, MD: U.S. Department of Commerce, National Institute of Standards and Technology; 24 August 1988. 68p. Available from: National Technical Information Service, 5285 Port Royal Rd., Springfield, VA 22161.

NATIONAL INSTITUTE OF STANDARDS AND TECHNOLOGY. 1988b. POSIX: Portable Operating System Interface for Computer Environments. Gaithersburg, MD: U.S. Department of Commerce, National Institute of Standards and Technology; 1988 September 12. 324p. (IEEE 1003.1/Draft 12). Available from: National Technical Information Service, 5285 Port Royal Rd., Springfield, VA 22161.

NATIONAL INSTITUTE OF STANDARDS AND TECHNOLOGY. 1988c. Standard Generalized Markup Language (SGML). Gaithersburg, MD: U.S. Department of Commerce, National Institute of Standards and

Technology; 1988 September 26. 230p. Available from: National Technical Information Service, 5285 Port Royal Rd., Springfield, VA 22161.

NATIONAL INSTITUTE OF STANDARDS AND TECHNOLOGY. 1989. Information Resources Dictionary System. Gaithersburg, MD: U.S. Department of Commerce, National Institute of Standards and Technology; 1988 April 5. 801p. Available from: National Technical Information Service, 5285 Port Royal Rd., Springfield, VA 22161.

ROBINSON, GARY. 1986. Accredited Standards Committee for Information Processing Systems, X3. Computer Standards & Interfaces. 1986; 5(3): 189-193. ISSN: 0920-5489.

ROBINSON, GARY. 1989. The Application of Standards: Some Observations from a Practitioner. Pittsburgh, PA: University of Pittsburgh; 1989 June 26. 58p. (SLIS Colloquium Series). Available from: Department of Information Science, University of Pittsburgh, Pittsburgh, PA 15260.

ROBINSON, PETER J.; STRASEN, STEPHEN M. 1989. Standard Page Description Language. Computer Communications. 1989 April; 12(2): 85-92. ISSN: 0140-3664.

ROSE, MARSHALL T. 1990. The Open Book: A Practical Perspective on OSI. Englewood Cliffs, NJ: Prentice-Hall; 1990. 651p. ISBN: 0-13-643016-3.

SAVA, S.I. 1986. ANSI and Information Systems. In: Proceedings of the Computer Standards Conference: Striking a Balance between Technology, Economics, Politics, and Reality—For Substance, Not Form; 1986 May 13-15; San Francisco, CA. Washington, DC: IEEE Computer Society; 1986. 12-13. ISBN: 0-8186-0698-3.

SIRBU, MARVIN; HUGHES, KENT. 1986. Standardization of Local Area Networks. In: 14th Annual Telecommunications Policy Research Conference; Airlie, VA. 1986.

SIRBU, MARVIN; STEWART, STEVEN. 1986. Market Structures and the Emergence of Standards: A Test in the Modem Market WP-8. Cambridge, MA: MIT Research Program on Communications Policy; 1986 June.

SIRBU, MARVIN; ZWIMPFER, LAWRENCE. 1985. Standards Setting for Computer Communication: The Case of X.25. IEEE Communications Magazine. 1985 March; 23(3): 35-45. ISSN: 0163-6804.

SOCHATS, KENNETH. 1988. CCITT. In: Kent, Allen; Williams, James, eds. Encyclopedia of Microcomputers: Volume 2. New York, NY: Marcel Dekker; 1988. 226-230. ISBN: 0-8247-2701-0.

SPRING, MICHAEL B.; BEARMAN, TONI CARBO. 1988. Information Standards: Models for Future Development. Book Research Quarterly. 1988 Fall; 4(3): 38-47. ISSN: 0741-6148.

SPRING, MICHAEL B.; JAMISON, WESLEY; FITHEN, KATHERINE T.; THOMAS, PATRICIA M. 1990. Preliminary Notes: Human-Computer Interaction Reference Model (HIRM). Pittsburgh, PA: University of Pittsburgh; 1990 December. 41p. (SLIS Research Reports: LIS032/

IS90010). Available from: Department of Information Science, University of Pittsburgh, Pittsburgh, PA 15260.

SPRING, MICHAEL B.; WEISS, MARTIN B. 1989. Prospectus: Center for the Study of Information Technology Standardization. Pittsburgh, PA: Department of Information Science, University of Pittsburgh; 1989 July. 20p. (Working paper). Available from: Department of Information Science, University of Pittsburgh, Pittsburgh, PA 15260.

STRAUSS, P.R. 1988. The Standards Deluge: A Sound Foundation or a Tower of Babel? Data Communications. 1988 September; 17(10): 150-164. ISSN: 0363-6399.

TOTH, ROBERT B. 1990. Profiles of Company and National Standardization Activities. In: Toth, Robert B., ed. Standards Management: A Handbook for Profits. New York, NY: American National Standards Institute; 1990. 429-451. Available from: ANSI, 1430 Broadway, New York, NY 10018.

U.S. DEPARTMENT OF DEFENSE. 1987. Automated Interchange of Technical Information. 1987 December 22. (MIL-STD-1840A). Available from: Naval Publications and Forms Center (NPFC), 5801 Tabor Avenue, Philadelphia, PA 19120.

WALCH, VICTORIA I. 1990. The Role of Standards in the Archival Management of Electronic Records. The American Archivist. 1990 Winter; 53: 30-43. ISSN: 0360-9081.

WEBER, LISA B. 1990. The "Other" USMARC Formats: Authorities and Holdings. Do We Care to Be Partners in This Dance, Too? The American Archivist. 1990 Winter; 53: 44-51. ISSN: 0360-9081.

WEISS, MARTIN B.H. 1989. Compatibility Standards and Product Development Strategies: A Review of Data Modem Developments. Pittsburgh, PA: University of Pittsburgh, Department of Information Science; 1989 July. 23p. (Working paper LIS018/DIS89002). Available from: Department of Information Science, University of Pittsburgh, Pittsburgh, PA 15260.

WEISS, MARTIN B.H.; LEWIS, C. MICHAEL. 1990. Consumer Expectations and Telecommunications: The Case of the Operator Services Industry. Pittsburgh, PA: University of Pittsburgh, Department of Information Science; 1990 January. 18p. (Draft working paper). Available from: Department of Information Science, University of Pittsburgh, Pittsburgh, PA 15260.

WEISS, MARTIN B.H; SIRBU, MARVIN. 1990. Technological Choice in Voluntary Standards Committees: An Empirical Analysis. Economics of Innovation and New Technology. 1990; 1: 111-133. ISSN: 1043-8599.

WINKLER, JERRY. 1990. ISO IRDS Is an Oxymoron. Computer Standards & Interfaces. 1990; 9(1): 249-250. ISSN: 0920-5489.

WOOD, JAMES L. 1985. The National Information Standards Organization (Z39). In: Kent, Allen, ed. Encyclopedia of Library and Information Science: Volume 39. New York, NY: Marcel Dekker; 1985. 291-332. ISBN: 0-8247-2039-3.

4   Expert Systems as Information Intermediaries

HILARY DRENTH, ANNE MORRIS, and GWYNETH TSENG
Loughborough University of Technology

INTRODUCTION

Expert systems, sometimes called "knowledge-based systems," "knowledge systems," or even "intelligent systems," are a type of computer program that uses the knowledge-based techniques of artificial intelligence (AI). There have been many attempts to define the characteristics that distinguish expert systems from conventional computer programs, based on their performance, associated development techniques, and internal structure. For this review expert systems are computer programs that represent knowledge and apply expertise to manipulate that knowledge and to achieve (optimal) solutions (HAYWARD). They have been used to carry out tasks that trained, experienced humans might do, such as fault diagnosis, planning, and monitoring. Thus, scarce expertise can be stored and made available to other experts in the field and to nonexperts, which is not only cost effective but can improve performance.

Expert systems could be useful as online searching tools. Although long heralded as a wave about to break, mass end-user searching of online information services has yet to happen. Potential do-it-yourself searchers may be deterred by the complexity of online searching and the cost penalty of mistakes. Instead, most online searches are done by human intermediaries, creating both an information bottleneck and the possibility of misinterpretation of the

Annual Review of Information Science and Technology (ARIST), Volume 26, 1991
Martha E. Williams, Editor
Published for the American Society for Information Science (ASIS)
By Learned Information, Inc., Medford, N.J.

information need. The inaccessibility of online information retrieval systems to end users of information and dissatisfaction with their overall performance has been the mainspring of extensive research into intelligent information retrieval. This review does not, however, deal with the full gamut of knowledge-based techniques applied to this problem but looks at how one approach—the expert systems approach—has been used to explore and model the knowledge underlying the performance of the online search intermediary.

Expert intermediary systems were last described in *ARIST* by SMITH as part of her 1987 review of AI techniques in information retrieval. The current review describes these systems more fully, focusing on the application of intermediary expertise and tracing the development of "intelligent" commercial search aids. To provide a full picture of the development of expert intermediary systems, the review covers the relevant literature published over the past decade, concentrating on recent work where possible.

It begins with a brief overview of the components and types of knowledge representation used in expert systems. Work exploring the role of the intermediary in information retrieval and the knowledge that the intermediary brings to online retrieval is described next. This is followed by an examination of prototype expert systems developed to handle various intermediary roles and tasks. Finally, the review looks at operational intermediary systems from an expert systems perspective, covering front ends, gateways, and user-friendly interfaces for commercial online services. Where these systems are known to be currently available, this is indicated.

Earlier related work discussed the issues and problems in developing expert systems for intelligent information retrieval (BROOKS) and outlined the main research areas in intelligent information retrieval (CROFT); HAWKINS discussed the applications of AI and expert systems for information retrieval, especially online searching. VICKERY & BROOKS and ANDERSON considered the roles for expert systems in libraries and information services. Recent surveys relating to operational intermediary systems include the wide-ranging review of online search aids by EFTHIMIADIS and the discussion of intelligent gateway systems by HAWKINS ET AL.

EXPERT SYSTEMS—COMPONENTS AND KNOWLEDGE REPRESENTATION

Expert systems can stand alone or be embedded in another type of system such as a database management system (DBMS). Generally they are comprised of a knowledge base, an inference engine, a user interface, and some form of explanatory capability to show the reasoning behind their conclusions. The key components are the knowledge base and the inference engine. The knowledge base incorporates all the knowledge needed for problem solving, both problem-solving strategies, and the facts and entities relating to the problem. The inference engine applies the knowledge held in the knowledge base. While independent of the knowledge base, the form and operation of the inference engine depend on the size and structure of the knowledge base and the type of knowledge representation used (BROOKS).

Production rules in the form IF <antecedents> THEN <consequents> are the most common type of knowledge representation. Their operation is usually controlled by forward, data-driven chaining or backward, goal-driven chaining. Many types of knowledge are not amenable to rule-based representation, and increasing numbers of expert systems use a combination of knowledge representations. Well-classified domains, such as medicine, are particularly suited to representation by semantic networks. In semantic networks, objects, concepts, and descriptions are represented as nodes, while relationships among these entities are represented as arcs connecting the nodes. Nodes at lower levels of the network automatically inherit characteristics of "parent" nodes at higher levels, making the representation efficient and providing for default reasoning.

Frames can be viewed as complex semantic networks (RICH). They were developed to model the way in which humans analyze new situations by evoking stereotypical knowledge and modifying it as appropriate. Typically frames describe a class of objects, acts, or events and consist of slots describing various aspects of the frame. Scripts have a similar structure to frames but are used to describe a stereotyped sequence of events in a particular context, such as going to the bank or the library. Other types of knowledge representation include predicate logic, which permits a more precise expression of fact than the propositional logic embodied in production rules, nonmonotonic logic, probabilistic reasoning, and fuzzy logic for handling problems posed by uncertain and fuzzy knowledge.

Distributed expert systems architectures are being increasingly used for complex problem solving. In such architectures, a number of expert systems cooperate to solve problems and share their results. Communication among the systems is handled in one of three ways: (1) via an agenda (a list of tasks to be carried out), (2) with a blackboard (a list of hypotheses and/or current tasks), or (3) using the Δ-min search procedure to rank the hypotheses (RICH). Distributed expert systems allow the most appropriate knowledge representations to be used for the different components of a problem.

EXPERTISE AND THE INTERMEDIARY

Online searching involves various tasks, which can be summarized as:

- Identifying the information needed and the concepts associated with it;
- Identifying likely sources of information;
- Formulating a search strategy;
- Connecting to the appropriate online service(s) and database(s);
- Entering the query as a Boolean search statement;
- Reviewing the results;
- Reformulating the query as necessary; and
- Obtaining a hard copy of the results as necessary.

As HAWKINS pointed out, some of these tasks (fourth, fifth, and last above) are "mechanical"—i.e., do not require any complex knowledge or cognitive skills—and have therefore been successfully automated in commercial online search aids. Although descriptions and models of the online search process abound (BROOKS ET AL.; HAWKINS; INGWERSEN; MARCUS, 1983; PAICE; SARACEVIC ET AL.; VICKERY & VICKERY), relatively few of these go beyond defining the tasks involved. To build an expert intermediary system, however, a detailed understanding of the skills and knowledge underlying the "intellectual" components of the search process is essential.

In their groundbreaking work on the cognitive models that the human intermediary builds to support the development and selection of appropriate search strategies, BROOKS ET AL. identified some ten functions that an intelligent interface for document retrieval would need to perform. These include a user model builder, an input analyst, a retrieval strategist, and a function for building a description of the search problem. Further, the development of such an interface required detailed descriptions of intermediary knowledge and functions, the interaction among functions and of the intermediary–client dialog. Through discourse analysis of presearch interviews, Brooks and co-workers investigated user modeling and problem description. Problem description involved external knowledge resources (e.g., verbal information from the client and thesauri) and internal resources, including a knowledge of a particular subject domain and knowledge of users. Knowledge resources to support user modeling included some qualitative assessment of the user's state of knowledge and knowledge of likely user goals.

The conceptual knowledge identified by Brooks et al. constitutes for INGWERSEN just one aspect of intermediary knowledge. So-called IR knowledge—i.e., knowledge of retrieval systems, how to use them, and procedures and tactics for searching them—constitutes another. It is this type of intermediary knowledge, particularly that concerned with search formulation and execution, that has been the subject of most study to date. HARTER & PETERS identified six types of heuristics for search formulation, derived mostly from existing literature. These heuristics related to: (1) the intermediary's overall attitude and approach to searching, (2) description of the search problem, (3) the structure of the files and records being searched, (4) formulation and reformulation of search concepts, (5) increasing or decreasing recall and precision, and (6) achieving cost-effective searches. While the search formulation process comprises a number of separate tasks, as Harter and Peters noted, they did not suggest at what points in the process these heuristics come into play.

One of the sources drawn on by Harter and Peters was the influential paper by BATES, in which she distinguished search strategies (i.e., those ideas concerned with the overall plan of a search) from search tactics (i.e., those moves made to advance a strategy). In his review of search strategies, SORMUNEN (1989a, p.42) concluded that the knowledge required for selecting appropriate search strategies covers: (1) knowledge of various types of search problems, (2) knowledge of the search topic and databases, and (3) knowledge of "general searching principles"—presumably some of the heuristics identified by Harter and Peters and knowledge of various search strategies.

With regard to the knowledge used during a search, Bates identified 29 search tactics. These are related to monitoring the progress of a search, locating appropriate online sources, reformulating searches, and revising specific terms in a search statement. Fidel also identified heuristics for choosing search terms and descriptors (FIDEL, 1986; 1987), while other researchers have identified tactics for searching in specific subject domains (MORRIS ET AL., 1989; SMITH ET AL.). Although heuristics and tactics for online searching can be identified and incorporated into expert intermediary systems, more research at the level and of the type specified by Brooks et al. is clearly needed to build a coherent picture of the knowledge underlying them. For example, what cognitive processes and knowledge underlie the "spontaneous" generation of search tactics reported by Smith et al.?

In addition to the knowledge and skills acquired through training and on-the-job experience, intermediaries bring their own innate cognitive skills to online searching (SARACEVIC ET AL.;

SARACEVIC & KANTOR, 1988a, 1988b). Saracevic and co-workers looked at the effect of a range of variables on search outcomes, including the cognitive characteristics of intermediaries. They found that those intermediaries with strong language ability (measured by word association) were more likely to achieve high levels of relevance than intermediaries with a weak ability. Reasoning ability had no impact on search results, but the learning style of intermediaries was influential; a style that favored abstract over concrete thinking increased relevance and recall. FIDEL (1984; 1985) found that the tactics used by intermediaries depended on their searching styles. "Operational" searchers used system features to generate a set that matched the original query as closely as possible; "conceptual" searchers identified the main concept of a query and then created subsets representing its different aspects.

Plainly levels of expertise among intermediaries vary; INGWERSEN proposed four types of online searcher, ranging from elite to layman, with intermediaries being of two types, an elite with information retrieval knowledge and highly specialized conceptual knowledge, and an intermediary caste that conducts most searches but has less specialized conceptual knowledge. Whatever access to knowledge an intermediary has, that knowledge may not necessarily be used. OLDROYD & CITROEN found that once intermediaries have chosen a search strategy, they tend to continue using it even though they might search several databases with different properties. Intermediaries also tend to use a few favorite online sources, even though many are available (DRENTH ET AL.; TENOPIR). In fact, the range of sources available and their increasing numbers militate against the development of expertise in database selection by the intermediary, so that expertise in selection is limited to a few data-bases (BARKER). Given the understandable limits on the knowledge and skills of the typical intermediary, it is not unreasonable to suggest that future expert intermediary systems will outperform them. To achieve this, however, much more work in identifying and describing intermediary knowledge remains to be done. The next section looks at how intermediary knowledge has been harnessed so far in prototype expert intermediary systems.

PROTOTYPE INTERMEDIARIES

Since the late 1970s researchers have designed and developed prototype expert intermediaries that perform a variety of tasks. This section considers these systems in the context of both their role in relation to end users—that of search advisor, intelligent front end, or intelligent intermediary—and their role in the search process (as experts in search formulation, for example). Since some of the systems described, such as IIDA and CONIT, have been widely reported, the emphasis is on those systems that are less well known or that are recent.

Search Advisors

Search advisors are expert intermediary systems that aim not only to assist or advise end users but also to train them in online searching. Despite the clear potential for expert training aids in library schools and research centers, surprisingly few systems of this type have been developed and none is available commercially. The search advisors developed to date focus on search tactics, particularly on monitoring the progress of a search and on selecting or revising search terms.

The first of these systems was Individualized Instruction for Data Access System (IIDA) (MEADOW, 1979; MEADOW ET AL., 1982a, 1982b). It was designed to help scientists and technicians learn online bibliographic searching of DIALOG in order to obtain a few good references rather than attempting complex searches. IIDA was reactive, providing assistance only when the user made a mistake or when aid was specifically requested. In addition to dealing with syntactic errors, IIDA detected and offered advice on null sets retrieved, repetitive use of commands, unused sets, rapid shifts in search objectives, and the overuse of a single approach to a search. Feedback on the relevance of references was used to suggest new approaches to a search or, indeed, to finish the search.

Meadow continued his work on expert advisory systems for online bibliographic searching with the Online Access to Knowledge (OAK) project (MEADOW ET AL., 1989). OAK was developed for the U.S. Department of Energy DOE/RECON and BASIS online services. Again the approach was to allow the user primacy in formulating searches and evaluating results. OAK had two components, an assistant, OAKASSIST, and a tutor, OAKTUTOR. The tutor was intended to familiarize the user with the principles of searching before going online. OAKASSIST gave assistance during a search. To formulate a query with OAKASSIST, the user completed a form by entering search facets (e.g., the subject and author) and associated subject terms. Some facets (e.g., author) had associated scripts, used to elicit the correct details from the user. The completed query was translated into the appropriate command language and sent to the host. During browsing of the records retrieved by a search,

OAKASSIST requested an evaluation of usefulness and from this determined what actions to advise next. To provide a higher level of analysis of search results and more specific recommendations on how to proceed than OAKASSIST, Meadow developed OAKDEC, available as a menu option in OAK (MEADOW, 1988). OAKDEC was rule based and used factors such as the set size, the number of records reviewed by the user, and the user's evaluation of records to arrive at a recommendation.

Another recent search advisor was the Intelligent Database Enquiry Assistant (IDEA) developed by HOUGHTON ET AL. It was comprised of a Tutor, an Advisor, and a User Question Handler. The Tutor presented text describing the system and an interactive lesson. The Advisor offered advice on the choice of database and keywords, giving general advice such as "try more general terms," and suggesting alternative terms. The User Question Handler dealt with questions of why, what, and how, such as "How do I narrow a search?". The three components drew on knowledge of the task and the user. The task knowledge consisted of general search strategy principles and a knowledge of subject relationships held in a thesaurus. The records of knowledge of the user consisted of a log of the user's search strategies and progress in tutorials.

Of the systems described here, IDEA perhaps comes closest to an intelligent tutor. It not only incorporated instructional strategies and emphasized conceptual understanding, it also had some provision for student modeling. The operation of both IIDA and OAK tended toward "issue-based" tutoring, whereby the systems' recommendations are attached to specific issues observable in the student's behavior. This is an appropriate and powerful methodology, but it does not provide for the detailed levels of explanation that some student users might need. For this, a cognitive model of the search process is required, and although this has yet to be fully realized, there would seem to be scope for further development of expert systems as tutors in online searching.

Intelligent Front Ends

Expert intermediaries that act as intelligent front ends to online services are closely related to the advisory systems described above. Unlike reactive advisory systems, these front ends intervene in the search process to a greater or lesser extent, their primary aim being to provide trouble-free access to online services. In terms of the intermediary knowledge represented, early intelligent front ends focused on search tactics, especially those concerned with search formulation and the selection of terms. Lately, this approach has broadened to support a fuller intermediary role, incorporating knowledge relating to the selection of databases and search strategies.

Viewing the complexity and diversity of online search systems as deterrents to end-user searching, MARCUS & REINTJES developed the Connector for Networked Information Transfer (CONIT). This intermediary system gave user-friendly access to several hosts by means of a simple common-command language. In early versions of the system, CONIT suggested keyword/stem searching, but this function was subsequently automated. CONIT included some limited facilities for reformulating searches, such as automatically rerunning a search with exact terms only when too many references were retrieved. CONIT's rules were fired according to the point reached in a search and the current message (from the user or the host).

EXPERT, another system developed by Marcus, took a more active role in the search process than CONIT, suggesting suitable databases and prompting the user for terms and synonyms before translating them into Boolean search statements (MARCUS, 1981). Williams's OASIS also followed this "worksheet" approach to online searching, one of its major objectives being to reduce the amount of time spent online (WILLIAMS, 1984, 1985; WILLIAMS & GOLDSMITH). Both EXPERT and OASIS could suggest tactics for broadening or narrowing a search according to the number of postings found.

The evolution of expert systems as intelligent front ends was furthered by the use of natural-language user interfaces. With their Information Retrieval Natural Language Interface (IR-NLI), GUIDA & TASSO aimed to provide an intermediary system that could both comprehend a user's search request and identify the underlying information need. The first version was designed to operate offline, dealing with queries on one database in a single subject area. IR-NLI used a distributed expert systems architecture. One expert conducted the system-user dialog, semantically analyzed the user's request, created an internal representation of the request, and determined an appropriate search strategy; another expert applied domain-specific thesaural knowledge to fill out the request; a user modeler fine-tuned the dialog and the request. The overall operation of a search was controlled by a Strategy Generator, which activated the various experts as needed. Once a request was filled out sufficiently to allow generation of a search strategy, a Formalizer module translated the internal representation into the host command language, which was then presented to the user.

Natural-language processing was also used in the EURISKO prototype, reported by BARTHES ET AL., which searched scientific databases on the Questel and Cedocar online services. To search with EURISKO, the user selected the broad subject area from a menu, then typed the query in French, adding terms in English if required. EURISKO extracted the semantic components (e.g., subject, author, type of document required) and inserted proximity operators, asking the user about any prepositions or conjunctions that were not understood. The resulting interpretation of the query was displayed for the user to alter as necessary. Unlike IR-NLI, EURISKO could not suggest suitable search terms but otherwise came closer to fulfilling an intermediary role. It used knowledge derived from human intermediaries to suggest suitable databases according to the query subject and the types of document required and to generate a search strategy based on the position and operation of each term in the query. The developers of EURISKO are now working on the IMIS intelligent gateway (see Multi-User Gateways below).

Intelligent Intermediaries

This section covers systems developed to investigate intelligent approaches to the information retrieval process rather than to interface to existing online services. As such, they have integrated document collections and do not use the exact-match retrieval techniques found in conventional retrieval systems. Some of these systems, which are discussed first, draw on knowledge of users and search tactics to interpret and elaborate search requests. Other systems go beyond this in that they do not use knowledge to replicate expert behavior even though they are knowledge based. Instead, they use knowledge of the concepts represented in a document base to effect retrieval and thus sidestep many of the problem-solving tasks associated with human information intermediaries. Although they do not incorporate intermediary knowledge, these systems suggest new approaches to the intermediary function that might be integrated into expert intermediary systems.

The intelligent information retrieval systems that incorporate intermediary expertise have a distributed expert systems architecture. The system developed by CROFT & THOMPSON, the Intelligent Interface for Information Retrieval (I^3R), had experts for user modeling and modeling the search request, a domain knowledge expert that could infer related search concepts, a search controller that selected one of two available retrieval techniques, a browsing expert, and an explainer. The intention, however, was not to "do an accurate simulation of human intermediaries" but rather to use experts to structure and manage the search process (CROFT & THOMPSON, p. 390). A major criterion in the design of I³R was that it be flexible in response to user needs just as a human intermediary is flexible in handling search requests. In addition to supporting simple searches expressed as a Boolean combination of index terms or based on a known document, I³R could handle less well-defined searches, expressed in natural language, which the user could develop by evaluating retrieved documents and browsing documents. Retrieval was effected using a conventional probabilistic model; if this failed to retrieve any relevant documents or if the user model indicated that high-recall results were required, then cluster-based searching was used.

The Composite Document Expert/Extended/Effective Retrieval (CODER) of FOX, another distributed expert system, was developed as a testbed for analyzing, filing, and retrieving documents with widely differing contents and structures, such as those generated within electronic mailing systems. Query formulation in CODER was supported by browsing a lexicon of subject terms or documents, and retrieval was effected through a p-norm (extended Boolean) search, although a number of retrieval techniques, including cluster-based searching, were planned. CODER was unique in that it could be distributed over several machines and in that it included a temporal reasoning expert to identify, parse, and represent query expressions relating to time spans or dates.

Much of the recent R&D effort in intelligent information retrieval has concentrated on knowledge-intensive retrieval techniques. These are techniques that BELKIN & CROFT (p. 119) describe as typically relying on "a much richer representation of the knowledge in the subject domain covered by the documents and queries." In the IOTA information retrieval system developed by CHIARAMELLA & DEFUDE every component of a document—title and fragments of text—was indexed by noun phrases organized into a hierarchical tree representing the document content. As well as providing better semantic representation of documents, this structure allowed IOTA to be used for applications ranging from bibliographic retrieval to retrieval of sections from large complex documents. A query was entered into a subset of the natural language (French) to reduce ambiguity, parsed by pattern matching against Boolean expressions, and then displayed for confirmation. Additionally, the user could browse a thesaurus to indicate related terms. Once parsed, the query was mapped to the weighted indexing terms used in the document base. Retrieved references were evaluated, and if judged inappropriate, IOTA set a goal, such as "reduce the number of references," and reformulated the query.

Browsing is another knowledge-intensive retrieval technique in which the relationships among documents, terms, and other bibliographic information are represented as a network, which the searcher can examine and use to identify the documents required, as in the THOMAS system (ODDY). The CoalSORT prototype reported by MONARCH & CARBONELL used a frame-based semantic network of concepts in the subject domain of catalyst applications in coal liquefaction. This network was derived by consulting experts in catalysts and coal and was used to catalog some of the documents in the Pittsburgh Energy Center bibliographic database. Users constructed search statements by browsing terms in the network; each term had an associated frame that held details such as the term's meaning, its generic name, examples of its use, and whether it was used to index documents. This structure took the guesswork out of choosing relevant search terms since the user could display associated information as he browsed terms. It was also possible to browse terms within retrieved documents and use them to refine the search. A browsing interface is also planned for the KIWI system (KIWIS TEAM).

The graphical thesaurus-based information retrieval system described by MCMATH ET AL. also involved browsing, but documents were encoded as sets of thesaurus terms. To retrieve documents, the user selected a thesaurus, which was then loaded along with an associated document file. The document file held records of relevant document authors, titles, and keywords. The thesaurus was represented graphically, with a parent node shown surrounded by its children; when a node was selected, it was redisplayed as a parent surrounded by its own children. As the user moved down the hierarchy, a reduced picture of the parent node's position in the network was shown on the left of the screen so that the user could see up to four levels of the thesaurus at a glance. The rationale for this graphical user interface was that such displays augment short-term memory and therefore help users to present complex queries more effectively. Queries were formulated by selecting one or more nodes representing search terms. The conceptual distance between the terms selected and document keywords was then calculated, and those documents that most closely matched the query were retrieved. In a trial of the system using Medical Subject Headings (MeSH), all the users agreed that the graphical interface aided understanding of the thesaurus structure. While some subjects preferred more sophisticated query-construction facilities, many said they would sacrifice these for graphical representations of queries and documents.

Rule-Based Retrieval of Information by Computer (RUBRIC) was another knowledge-intensive information retrieval system (TONG ET AL., 1985; 1987); a commercial version of it is now available as Topic (CISLER). Topic's name derives from the way in which queries are formulated—i.e., as weighted, hierarchical topic outlines. The outline is used to infer the relevance of documents, which are then presented to the user in order of their likely relevance. Users can share topic outlines and use them as building blocks to create new queries. Topic also provides for Boolean searching and for browsing by hypertextual links. The Empty Software for Common Knowledge Transfer (ESOCKS), an expert system shell for document retrieval developed by Hitachi (YASUNOBU ET AL.), uses a technique similar to that of Topic. Knowledge describing the content of documents and associations among keywords is entered by the user, with assistance from ESOCKS, via worksheets. These worksheets are then processed into the rules and frames comprising the knowledge base. To retrieve documents, the user enters keywords that are automatically augmented with other suitable weighted keywords. On finding documents, ESOCKS assigns each one a relevance value so the user can decide which documents to display.

The systems described here represent a cross section of the many knowledge-intensive information retrieval systems that have been developed. By their nature, knowledge-intensive retrieval techniques are time-consuming to implement and therefore unsuitable for the large collections of documents that already exist. While they indicate approaches to the design of future information retrieval systems, they do not address the immediate problem of facilitating searches of online retrieval systems. For this, expert systems that can handle current intermediary search tasks, such as query formulation, are needed.

Experts in Query Formulation

Most prototype expert intermediary systems described in the literature offer some assistance in formulating queries because this task is viewed by some as the most expert one in online searching (HAWKINS), and in exact-match retrieval systems, it undoubtedly has considerable impact on search results. Query formulation comprises a number of subtasks (HARTER):

- Identify the major concepts of a query and the relationships among them;
- Select a search strategy;
- Identify suitable search terms;
- Enter the search in the appropriate command language; and
- Evaluate results and reformulate the search statement as necessary.

This section describes systems with special expertise inperforming some of these subtasks, beginning with elaboration of the search request.

The Comprehensive Information Retrieval Computer Environment (CIRCE) was one of the first systems to address the problem of elaborating the search topic prior to formal specification of the search (ARAGON-RAMIREZ & PAICE). It comprised a topic handler to construct a model of the user's request, a permissive search processor that identified appropriate terms, a dialog generator, and a topic picture to hold the terms that CIRCE found. The knowledge base comprised a thesaurus, dialog templates, and rules for term selection. The user entered a set of terms describing a query, and these were matched against thesaurus terms. Where some degree of match was found, terms were displayed for evaluation of their relevance. The dialog templates allowed CIRCE to ask questions to clarify, modify, and augment the set of terms comprising the final "topic picture." Aragon-Ramirez and Paice do not suggest how the concepts and terms comprising the search topic would be mapped to search statements.

SMITH ET AL. contend that using partial-match techniques to identify potentially relevant search concepts, as in CIRCE, does not support the interpretation of user queries and topic refinement sufficiently. In frame-based systems, such as their environmental pollution expert (EP-X), CoalSORT (MONARCH & CARBONELL), and the PLEXUS referral system (VICKERY ET AL.; VICKERY & BROOKS), topics and associated concepts and terms are represented explicitly, reflecting, in effect, the subject-based knowledge that a human intermediary brings to the interpretation of search topics. In PLEXUS, for example, entering a query activated a set of frames describing the search topic; these were used to identify any ambiguities and elicit the information needed to complete the problem description.

Once the search request is understood, an intermediary must decide on a suitable search strategy. Although studies show that intermediaries use a repertoire of search strategies (HARTER; HAWKINS & WAGERS), few expert intermediary systems incorporate expertise in their selection. Generally, a building-block strategy is assumed, with a consequent emphasis on identifying related concepts, terms, and synonyms and on "brute force" searching. Various approaches to the search process are provided by I^3R with its high-precision cluster-based retrieval and searches based on known items (CROFT & THOMPSON), and in IR-NLI, which can select strategies based on its knowledge of the search problem and the level of recall or precision required (GUIDA & TASSO). The impact of such factors as time and cost is seldom accounted for even though these have an obvious influence on an intermediary's search strategies (FENICHEL; HARTER; MORRIS ET AL., 1989).

The choice of suitable search terms in many systems amounts to term augmentation through the use of thesaural knowledge. The expert term selector of SHOVAL dealt specifically with this task although it did not use intermediary knowledge. Rather it used spreading activation in a network of terms, meanings, and associations to identify potentially relevant terms. These were evaluated according to the number of user-supplied terms involved in their selection and the extent of clustering with other terms. Suitable terms were then presented to the user.

To measure the success of a search and decide whether to reformulate the search statement, intermediaries frequently look at the number of references retrieved, the "correct" number being determined by user requirements or the cost of displaying and/or printing references (MORRIS ET AL., 1989). The reformulation of search strategies according to the number of references retrieved has been addressed by a number of systems, including those developed by MARCUS (1981), WILLIAMS (1984; 1985), BARTHES ET AL., GAUCH & SMITH, and SORMUNEN (1989b). Reformulation can be automatic (based on a target set size) or initiated by the user. The tactics used in all these systems were independent of the subject domain and focused on broadening or narrowing the search strategy.

The relevance of retrieved documents is another measure of search success and has been used in IIDA, OAKASSIST, I³R, and IOTA (CHIARAMELLA & DEFUDE; CROFT & THOMPSON; MEADOW, 1979; MEADOW ET AL., 1982a, 1982b, 1989). The Dow Jones News/ Retrieval commercial DowQuest service also uses relevance feedback techniques (WEYER).

Search tactics relating to specific subject domains, derived from observations of intermediaries at work, have been incorporated into an expert system for modifying online search strategies (MOSS) when searching business databases (MORRIS ET AL., 1989); they have also been used by EP-X, an intermediary system for searching environmental pollution literature (SMITH ET AL.). The MOSS system offered general advice when too many or too few references were retrieved. Once an initial set was retrieved, the domain knowledge-based tactics implemented in EP-X allowed the system to inform the user of the possibilities for refining a search or for increasing its thoroughness. PLEXUS used classic, domain-independent tactics for refining searches, such as using broader or narrower terms and excluding concepts from the search statement. Domain knowledge was used, however, where reformulation involved the dropping or adding of terms; PLEXUS determined the order for doing this, using its knowledge of subject indexing and of the importance of a term or concept to the overall meaning of a search.

EP-X and PLEXUS indicate the strength of the frame-based paradigm for representing the knowledge needed to support topic description and query formulation, although such an approach is not yet feasible in intermediary systems for searching large, heterogeneous document collections.

Experts for Database Selection

Apart from the database selector developed by WILLIAMS & PREECE, Marcus's work with automatic database selection in CONIT (MARCUS, 1981), and systems such as EURISKO that rank databases on the basis of subject coverage (BARTHES ET AL.), the problem of choosing suitable sources of online information has only recently received much attention. This is no doubt due in part to the burgeoning of online sources.

Expert systems for database selection are still at an early stage. The prototypes developed to date treat database selection apart from query formulation, and much of the research has been directed toward identifying the characteristics used by intermediaries to distinguish among databases. The expert selectors designed by THORNBURG, MORRIS ET AL. (1988), and DRENTH ET AL. drew on the expertise of human intermediaries in selecting databases for specific topic areas (the life science literature, company information, and marketing information, respectively). WANG has developed a database selector for business queries. TRAUTMAN and VON FLITTNER used printed guides to online sources for their expert system's knowledge, the intention being to develop a stand-alone aid to databases rather than to investigate the database-selection problem.

The operation of all the expert selectors mentioned above is data driven, with selection criteria elicited directly from the user for matching against database characteristics. For example, the selector developed by Trautman and Von Flittner requested information about the time period, language, geographical coverage, type and depth of coverage required, followed by the search subject. Using this information, the selector recommended databases that met the user's requirements as well as three other, successively broader sets. A human intermediary could infer much of this information from the search request and/or user model or use knowledge of databases to verify user requirements. The language required, for example, might be significant only when there were few native-language sources available for a particular subject.

Nonetheless, some useful selection criteria have been identified. Thornburg's LOOK used weighted variables, such as type of search, exhaustivity of search, type of material required, search fields, time span, geographical focus, and cost, in selecting databases for the life sciences. The currency, type, and quality of material needed and the search fields available were important criteria for choosing online sources of company information (MORRIS ET AL., 1988). More research to examine the relationships among the search request, search strategy development, and database characteristics is needed to build on these initial findings.

Acquisition of knowledge about how intermediaries select online databases is frustrated by the shifting nature of subject areas. TRAUTMAN & VON FLITTNER viewed their schema for the subject classification of databases, which used generic subject terms assigned by directory sources as facilitating the updating of their selector's knowledge base, and envisaged the distribution of updates via floppy disk or downloading, as in the IANI system (BERG HANSEN & ROTTBØLL ANDERSEN). The induction of rules for database selection from sample searches has not yet been investigated as a knowledge-acquisition technique for this domain and might indicate approaches to machine learning in future expert database selectors, as Thornburg suggested. The technique has been successfully used for knowledge acquisition in the closely related domain of reference inquiry work to develop AquaRef, which handles reference queries about aquaculture (HANFMAN). Several expert referral systems have been developed for library use, and the REFSIM system demonstrates how the criteria needed to select sources can be elicited as part of the reference interview (PARROTT, 1986, 1989; SARANGAPANI; WATERS).

Experts for Retrieval in Subject Domains

A number of expert systems for assisting searches in specific subject domains have been developed. These include NP-X (natural products chemistry), EP-X (environmental pollution), CANSEARCH (cancer therapy), and GENSEARCH (biomedical genetics) (POLLITT, 1987, 1988; SMITH ET AL.; SMITH & CHIGNELL). The strength of this approach, as Pollitt stated, is that domain-specific knowledge can be applied to improve the system's overall performance (as described for EP-X in the section, Experts in Query Formulation, above). The domain-specific knowledge incorporated in Pollitt's

CANSEARCH covered general knowledge of clinical cancer therapy, knowledge of the controlled vocabulary of terms used for indexing cancer therapy literature, and knowledge of the MeSH used to index the documents in the MEDLINE database, which CANSEARCH was designed to search. The hierarchical organization of MeSH was echoed in CANSEARCH's menus, from which the user built up search statements by choosing concepts that described the search topic. Touch screens were used to prevent the entry of ambiguous or incomplete phrases and to save time and avoid spelling mistakes. Once search concepts were chosen, CANSEARCH translated them into the appropriate query language and displayed the postings for each concept and combination of concepts. The user could then view document titles and revise the concepts as necessary. The CANSEARCH design was later applied to GENSEARCH for online searching of biochemical genetics literature on MEDLINE. As with CANSEARCH, the user indicated the subject of a query by choosing from menus, though GENSEARCH incorporated many more terms. Menus were improved by incorporating information on the number of references associated with each term.

User Modeling

Although not apparent to the casual observer, user modeling is an important intermediary task that has been incorporated in many of the intelligent information retrieval systems that use a distributed expert systems architecture—viz., I^{3}R, IR-NLI, IOTA, and CODER (CHIARAMELLA & DEFUDE; CROFT & THOMPSON; FOX; GUIDA & TASSO). By building a model of the user, an expert system can tailor its performance to a range of users. As PAICE noted, user interaction has a more central role in online IR than in typical expert systems applications, so establishing some picture of the user's background and information needs is particularly important if expert intermediary systems are to perform well. In their work on user modeling by human intermediaries, BROOKS ET AL. identified five user-modeling functions needed in an intelligent IR interface; these were determining the user's: (1) search goals, (2) status, (3) background, (4) familiarity with IR systems, and (5) state of knowledge about the search problem. This information about the user was important for structuring the user–system dialog, defining the search problem, and determining appropriate retrieval strategies. FOX describes a plan to base CODER's handling of user interaction on Brooks et al.'s findings, but in the initial implementation, information was gathered directly from the user rather than inferred from the user's responses to the system.

In designing the user modeling expert in IOTA, CHIARAMELLA & DEFUDE wanted to find out what was possible on the basis of inference alone. Consequently, their user modeler used indications of the level of the user's expertise in the query statement to infer whether the user was a "beginner," "average expert," or "expert." This somewhat coarse model was then used to evaluate search results before reformulating a search. Stereotypes have also been used by expert intermediaries to infer information about users. The user model builder in I³R collected information about the user (such as an interest in high recall) and then invoked the appropriate stereotype (CROFT & THOMPSON). This was not implemented as a frame but rather as a set of global parameters that determined the style of the system's interaction with the user and the goals of the retrieval session.

The user modeling done by IR-NLI was more complex, with an entire subsystem devoted to this task (GUIDA & TASSO). A user model was represented as a frame holding the user's profile details and details of the user's knowledge. Profile details covered the user's educational, professional, and information retrieval background, personal traits (e.g., communication style), and usual search requirements. The user's knowledge covered subject knowledge and knowledge of databases, online hosts, and retrieval strategies. The information for building and updating a user model was obtained from interviews with the user, from stereotypes, and from search histories for each user. The model was then used to refine the user–system dialog, interpret the user's responses, and complete the internal representation of the user's query. BRAJNIK ET AL. (1987; 1990) hoped to refine IR-NLI's model builder so that it could dynamically change the user model during a search just as a human intermediary might.

Knowledge Acquisition

Knowledge acquisition—i.e., the process of obtaining and organizing expert knowledge—is widely recognized as a bottleneck in the development of all expert systems. Once knowledge is acquired and incorporated into an expert system, there still remains the problem of keeping that knowledge current. Human experts can build on their expertise and restructure the way that they use it in the light of new experience; few expert systems are capable of this. The ability to acquire knowledge from new experiences is vitally important for expert intermediary systems since they not only interact with human users but also with rapidly changing retrieval systems and online sources.

A simple form of ongoing knowledge acquisition, or machine learning, involving the technique of learning by being told, has been used in IOTA, I³R, and PLEXUS (CHIARAMELLA & DEFUDE; CROFT & THOMPSON; VICKERY ET AL.; VICKERY & BROOKS). These systems acquire subject domain knowledge by asking the user for information about unrecognized terms and then incorporating this information into the thesaurus. The TEGEN research team has gone further, using a variant of learning by observation (GÜNTZER ET AL.). The TEGEN thesaurus-generating system observes searches by users and identifies possible thesaurus entries by analyzing the semantic relationships among search concepts. It then verifies the validity of these entries through implicit or explicit confirmation with subsequent users. The developers of IOTA have outlined the design of an expert task that would acquire subject domain knowledge through indexing documents (BRAUNDET). This would involve identifying significant terms, classifying the relationships among them, and finally incorporating this new indexing knowledge into the knowledge base.

There is clearly much scope for machine learning in expert intermediary systems. For example, search histories might be used to identify improvements to search strategies. Another application of machine learning might be inferring the possible uses of a new database from its structure and content. Another might be to use search histories to improve user modeling. However, several issues must be addressed with regard to machine learning in intelligent retrieval systems: identifying appropriate machine learning strategies, establishing a method of evaluating these strategies, and identifying the information that learning experts would use (GOKER).

Evaluation

Evaluation of expert systems is crucial for improving system design and performance, but it is "arguably the least well-developed area of expert systems research" (FORD). Aspects of expert system performance requiring evaluation include: (1) the quality of advice and decisions, (2) the correctness of reasoning techniques, (3) the quality of human–computer interaction, (4) system efficiency, and (5) cost effectiveness (GASCHNIG ET AL.). BERRY & HART point out that many evaluations have focused on the quality of system advice and on the reasoning techniques used rather than on aspects of system usability. Certainly this has been the trend in the few formal evaluations of expert intermediary systems that have been reported, in which expert system performance has been measured against that of human intermediaries. This was done by MEADOW ET AL. (1982b) for IIDA, by MARCUS (1983) for CONIT, and by POLLITT (1986b) for CANSEARCH.

The evaluation of IIDA found that users learned online search techniques just as well as they did through conventional training and were just as satisfied with the results obtained using IIDA as with those from professional intermediaries. In a similar experiment with CONIT, users achieved higher levels of recall than those assisted by professional intermediaries, but took 20% more time online. Although these evaluations indicate the overall worth of these expert systems, other factors, such as the relative subject domain knowledge of end users and intermediaries and differences in the user interfaces of the systems used in the evaluations, make it difficult to draw definite conclusions other than that the intermediary system's performance is good/acceptable/promising.

Pollitt examined CANSEARCH's performance in formulating queries (POLLITT, 1986b). Test queries were done by doctors using CANSEARCH, by intermediaries using all available resources to aid search formulation, and by intermediaries restricted to the same thesaurus resources as CANSEARCH. Although doctors occasionally produced better quality search formulations and better retrieval results than intermediaries, overall the two intermediary groups performed better (POLLITT, 1986a). More evaluations that consider a specific aspect of expert system performance are needed to pinpoint areas for improvement and to establish performance benchmarks.

WADE ET AL. ostensibly compared the performance of knowledge-based and statistical retrieval. PLEXUS, a referral expert that offers knowledge-based assistance in formulating conventional Boolean queries, and INSTRUCT, a statistically based reference retrieval system, were used to retrieve references about gardening queries. The results of PLEXUS, when compared with those of noninteractive best-match searching with INSTRUCT, were consistently better in terms of recall and precision. The use of INSTRUCT's query expansion, relevance feedback, and browsing options greatly improved its performance. The best results, however, were obtained by using the terms suggested by PLEXUS as the basis for an INSTRUCT search. This study indicates the value of knowledge-based query formulation and points toward the use of mixed retrieval techniques; however, like those done by MEADOW ET AL. (1982b) and MARCUS (1983), it does not go beyond demonstrating the value of an expert systems approach to IR. As intermediary expertise becomes better understood and as expert intermediary systems are used more widely, evaluations of these systems should take in a range of criteria, examine specific aspects of system performance, and produce findings on which to improve both system performance and utility.

OPERATIONAL INTERMEDIARY SYSTEMS

The prototype expert intermediary systems described above aim to represent and apply various aspects of intermediary knowledge to optimize online searches. In more recent prototypes this application of intelligence has been extended by exploring alternative retrieval techniques and user interfaces. In contrast, many intermediary systems available commercially are specifically intended to promote and facilitate the use of existing online services. Consequently, their emphasis is not on replicating an expert search but on producing acceptable search results. Intelligence is often claimed for commercial intermediary systems, but in most instances this reflects the degree to which searching has been automated, resulting in a simplification of the search process rather than in its elaboration through the use of knowledge-based techniques.

Two main types of intermediary systems are currently in operation: front ends and gateways. Front ends provide user-friendly access to specific information services. Generally they automate some intermediary tasks (e.g., connecting to a service and downloading results) and provide a simplified user interface. Some front ends incorporate functions for analyzing the information retrieved. Gateways provide access to a range of online and in-house information services. They may also act as front ends by providing a common user interface to the services accessed and an integrated environment for processing information. This section discusses some of the better-known front ends and gateways that offer high levels of functionality for information retrieval, sometimes described as "intelligent." It also considers some of the "friendly" online services that are targeted directly to the-end user sector and thus offer simple user interfaces.

Front Ends and Single-User Gateways

Although "front end" is commonly used to describe any product or service that offers an alternative user-friendly interface to online retrieval services, there are relatively few true front ends that offer simplified searching of a specific online service. Generally, front ends can be viewed as extended communications packages, with searches prepared offline and then uploaded as soon as the connection to the appropriate service and database is made. Search results are automatically downloaded, and some front ends offer facilities for formatting them, as in MicroDISCLOSURE and Current Contents Connection (EAGER; *LIBRARY MICROMATION NEWS*); others provide online accounting functions, as in Search Helper, Searchware and Duns Market Searcher (ENSOR & CURTIS; HUSHON; OJALA, 1989a; QUEENS BOROUGH CENTRAL LIBRARY STAFF; RENEAU). Functions for saving search strategies may also be provided. Extensive tutorial-style help and commentary are often available—e.g., in choosing databases in Search Helper and Duns Market Searcher (ENSOR & CURTIS; OJALA, 1989a; QUEENS BOROUGH CENTRAL LIBRARY STAFF) and in modifying a search in GRATEFUL MED (SNOW ET AL.); however, the overall approach is that of the cost-cutting "brief search," which, while enabling simple end-user searching, would seem to encourage a limited view and use of online search services.

Treatment of query formulation by front ends is varied and may use menus, forms, prompts, scripts or, as in WILSEARCH, may assume knowledge of Boolean logic and give assistance with tidying up a search statement—e.g., truncating terms and removing stop words (O'LEARY, 1986b). Menu-based searching on specific fields has been used by front ends that access non-full-text databases, as in Duns Market Searcher, whereas Dun and Bradstreet's business databases can be searched with a range of criteria (company location, type of business, and financial characteristics). Front ends for searching full-text databases are less opaque, and most guide the user through query formulation by prompts or form-filling.

Another class of online search aids often referred to as front ends are in fact microcomputer-based single-user gateways for searching multiple online services but not simultaneously. Well-known single-user gateways include Pro-Search for searching databases on DIALOG and BRS, SearchWorks for DIALOG, BRS, ORBIT, and NLM, and Sci-Mate Searcher for menu-driven and native-language searching of ISI, DIALOG, ORBIT, BRS, NLM, and Questel (COONS, 1986a, 1986b; HUSHON; QUINT; STOUT & MARCINKO; TESKEY ET AL.). These systems are more sophisticated than the front ends described above, providing for the preparation of searches offline and for interactive online searching. Both Pro-Search and Sci-Mate Searcher have menu-based directories of database descriptions to assist the user in choosing suitable online sources and offer help in choosing search terms. In Pro-Search, queries are prepared offline using worksheets; the user can display a list of available field qualifiers and select items for inclusion. Menu-driven online searching with Sci-Mate Searcher has options to browse index terms and search on named fields. All three gateways have functions for formatting search results and online accounting.

Pro-Search also provides cross emulation to allow searching of BRS with DIALOG commands and vice versa, and this common-language approach has been used recently in the IANI gateway. The Intelligent Access to Nordic Information (IANI) system provides user-friendly, common-language access to three Scandinavian hosts and native-language access to DIALOG, BRS, and ESA-IRS (BERG HANSEN & ROTTBØLL ANDERSEN; *INFORMATION WORLD REVIEW*). Descriptions of Scandinavian hosts are downloaded when they are first accessed and subsequently used by IANI to assist in selecting appropriate databases and search terms. They are also used to translate queries from IANI's common-command language. A session with IANI begins with the user choosing the database(s) required. IANI then logs on to the appropriate hosts, ready for the user to enter a query, which is then translated and transmitted to the host. Search results from different hosts can be sorted and edited, as with the SearchWorks gateway.

Other recent single-user gateways have been developed to assist searches in specific subject areas. ChemTalk Plus is for chemical information systems, with special emphasis on searching CAS Online (WARR & WILKINS). It does not provide any domain-specific knowledge but has facilities for drawing and modifying chemical structures offline, for importing drawings, and for drawing structures online. STN Express, for the scientific and technical databases on STN and Questel, has some "canned" domain knowledge—i.e., it provides several predefined search strategies for general subjects such as toxicology (WARR & WILKINS). The first true subject-domain expert to be made commercially available, however, was Tome Searcher, which evolved from PLEXUS (see above). It was used with ESA-IRS, STN, ORBIT, and DIALOG to answer queries on electrical engineering, computing, and information technology (GROSS; TOME; VICKERY). Like PLEXUS, Tome Searcher could handle natural-language queries and help in their formulation. At the beginning of a session, Tome Searcher asked questions to determine the user's experience (affecting the level of explanation offered), the type of search required (subject or author), any limitations on the search (e.g., language), the precision required, the number of items required, the format and form required for results, and the database to be searched. On entry of a query, Tome Searcher discarded any words not essential to the query and asked the user to clarify unrecognized words. Tome Searcher's dictionary included the number of postings; this was used to construct an appropriate search strategy based on the number of items and precision required. In constructing a strategy, Tome Searcher used a thesaurus to suggest terms for broadening or narrowing a query. No provision was made for any interaction online; once a suitable strategy had been built, Tome Searcher performed the search and downloaded or printed results as required.

Multi-User Gateways

Multi-user gateways are based on a central server to which users connect via modems to access a range of remote online services. While most gateways offer little functionality beyond this, some aim to provide an integrated environment for accessing and handling information and are the forebears of the "knowledge gateways" envisaged by HAWKINS ET AL.

Perhaps the best-known gateway for IR is EasyNet, which offers access to over 900 databases on 13 hosts, and has over 400,000 users (FOSTER & FOSTER). Business queries account for a half of its total use (DYCKMAN & O'CONNOR). EasyNet is mainly menu based and has three levels: (1) EasyNet I, for novice users, which gives access to the principal databases in any subject area (O'LEARY, 1985); (2) EasyNet II, which accesses the full range of databases; and (3) EasyNet III, which provides a common-command language for searching 12 host systems (EFTHIMIADIS; O'LEARY, 1988). EasyNet can select suitable databases for the user according to the topic and the type of material required. In her evaluation of database selection by the InfoMaster version of EasyNet, HU (p. 110) concluded that the selection of databases from a given category was random since several different databases were chosen for the same query. Overall, however, Hu found that "INFOMASTER could select databases as well as human intermediaries when the gateway user properly selected the subject area for a particular query." As an alternative to automatic database selection, users can use the Scan multifile search facility that shows the number of postings in databases for a given subject area (MEYER & RUIZ, 1990a; 1990b). EasyNet uses a simplified query language and offers menu-based searching of over 300 databases. Online help is available for formulating queries, or users can speak to trained intermediaries via EasyNet's 24-hour SOS facility. Once a query is entered, EasyNet translates it into the appropriate command language and modifies it to improve results (altering the adjacency of terms, for example). EasyNet also offers TrendTrac, which monitors media coverage of trends, and an Electronic Clipping Service for SDI (selective dissemination of information). The service is marketed under several names in the United States: EasyNet, InfoMaster, IQuest, EasySearch, ALANET Plus, and Einstein.

Other gateway systems address specific user audiences. The DoD Gateway Information System (DGIS) was developed to serve the DoD community (Department of Defense), the Livermore Intelligent gateway (TIS) for U.S. government users or contractors, the OCLC gateway for OCLC users (BURTON; HUSHON; KUHN; ZINN ET AL.). A common aim for these systems is the ability to customize the user's working environment; in DGIS the dialog with the user will be tailored, and TIS already provides for the integration of word processing, spreadsheet, and database software into the gateway so that users can create personalized information systems; users of the OCLC gateway will be able to customize menus for accessing services. Both DGIS and TIS provide tools for analyzing, formatting, and disseminating downloaded information. Work on intelligent functionality for DGIS is under way; intelligence in TIS seems to lie in its ability to select the optimum route to an information resource and its provision of a common-command language for searching multiple hosts simultaneously. Simultaneous access to multiple hosts is also planned for DGIS. A common-command language system (CCLS) will assist users in searching by using knowledge of users and databases. A user knowledge base will hold information relevant to a particular user or group of users, while the database knowledge base will contain the information needed to translate CCLS commands into native command languages and interpret hosts' responses. These knowledge bases are being developed by domain experts so that expert use of search commands is reflected in the CCLS behavior. Eventually the system will have a natural-language interface. The developers of DGIS were also considering implementing the CCLS as part of a windowed, desktop-style environment with a hypermedia link to databases on CD-ROM.

Two new gateways, the Intelligent Information Gateway and IMIS (under development), mark the introduction of highly featured, customized commercial gateways. The Intelligent Information Gateway offers access to databases loaded on 14 online services (INFOTAP). Tailored menu-based searching is available, with options for choosing databases and search terms and running searches automatically. For those who wish to choose a database themselves, a multilingual database directory, with examples of searching, is available online (*INFORMATION WORLD REVIEW*). Intelligent Information also allows more experienced searchers to search online services directly. IMIS, being developed by the creators of PLEXUS and Tome Searcher, and EURISKO (see above) will provide users with intelligent assistance in accessing four European online services and their own in-house databases (*INFORMATION WORLD REVIEW*). The system will have a natural-language, multilingual user interface based on the Tome Searcher software and incorporate a menu-based database selection aid to guide users to suitable online and internal sources of information.

Friendly Services

Online service providers have increasingly recognized the need to promote end-user searching by making their services easier to use. Some services, such as Financial Times (FT) Profile, provide simplified searching to cater to end users. Other services, notably DIALOG, with established user bases of professional searchers, have devised alternative user interfaces tailored to the needs of inexperienced searchers.

Most "friendly" services are menu-based; well-known examples include Dow Jones News/Retrieval's //TEXTM service for searching full-text news databases and DIALOG's Business, Medical and Corporate Connection services for searching specific types of databases on DIALOG (KWAN & DEENEY; OJALA, 1989b; O'LEARY, 1986a). DIALOG Corporate Connection (DCC) is the menu-based version of DIALOG's first friendly service, Knowledge Index. It offers simplified access to 30 databases and, unlike Knowledge Index, assumes no knowledge of online searching. Its screen design and extensive help are oriented to teaching search techniques. Databases are chosen by menu selection, and once a database is chosen, the user is presented with options for searching on fields specific to that database and prompted to enter appropriate search terms. After items have been retrieved, options for modifying a search include narrowing subject terms, widening them, replacing them, or selecting limits.

Two other menu-based search services are PaperChase (STIGLEMAN) and the bilingual interface developed by HALPERN & SARGEANT, which offers simplified searching of MEDLINE. Like the CANSEARCH expert intermediary, they exploit the MeSH used in indexing MEDLINE. PaperChase was designed for users with no knowledge of search commands or MeSH headings and guides the user through menus and prompts. Several features assist in the formulation of a query, such as automatically substituting MeSH entry points for the correct heading and permuting multiword headings. If PaperChase does not recognize a term, it retrieves references in which the term occurs and displays the most common MeSH headings associated with those references; the user can then choose appropriate headings. If many references are retrieved, the user is advised to narrow the search by using subheadings. The bilingual interface for searching MEDLINE is similar to PaperChase in that it offers searching by various criteria, such as time period, keywords, or a particular journal. It differs from PaperChase, however, in allowing the user to browse the MeSH thesaurus to select terms. It does not assist in formulating queries but does explode the thesaurus so that terms at lower levels are automatically included in a query. In addition to limiting the number of references retrieved by using MEDLINE subject headings, users are also encouraged to limit searches by specifying items in French only or clinical items only or by weighting some search terms.

Another approach to user-friendly service offers a simplified command language. This was done for DIALOG's Knowledge Index off-peak service that searches popular DIALOG databases (TESKEY ET AL.) and for the full FT Profile online full-text search service (NICHOLAS & ERBACH).

Other major online services are finally making their offerings more accessible to both end users and professional intermediaries. Maxwell Online is planning a new interface for its ORBIT and BRS services, which would support native-language searches, prompted searching, and a graphical environment (BASCH, 1990b). It is also investigating expert systems and knowledge-based search protocols. New interfaces are being developed by Data-Star, one of which will be menu driven. Such developments are an improvement, but online service providers still have some way to go before they meet the requirements of users, such as a natural-language interface and the ability to obtain information without having to search individual databases (BASCH, 1990a).

CONCLUSION

Current practice counsels expert system development only in narrow, well-defined, homogeneous domains; none of these attributes applies to online searching. The prototype expert intermediary systems have had little impact on commercial online offerings but have done much to define the knowledge used in online searching and to demonstrate the soundness of a distributed expert approach to solving complex problems. For the moment, however, the watchwords for expert intermediary systems are "more research."

Highly automated services such as EasyNet and IANI have been important in promoting the need for and benefits of "intelligent" information retrieval. As online services, products, and delivery media continue to proliferate, user friendliness will be vital in attracting and keeping end users. Techniques other than menus and simplified commands are needed, however, to circumvent the problem of friendly interfaces that lack search power. Expert systems are one such technique. IMIS will be one of the first commercial products to incorporate genuinely expert systems techniques to assist users, and it will be interesting to see how much systems like this influence the development of long-established online services.

Because retrieval performance is constrained as much by the type of information retrieval system as by the searcher's ability, future online systems will undoubtedly combine the best of human–computer interface design, expert systems, and mixed retrieval techniques. Although they have developed beyond infancy, it seems that information retrieval systems will not reach adulthood before the next century. There is much to be done with regard to standardizing platforms and formats, in developing and integrating information retrieval and AI techniques, and in introducing new technology, such as voice recognition, before consulting an information retrieval system is no more daunting and at least as rewarding as asking one's personal researcher for "Details about. . ."

BIBLIOGRAPHY

ANDERSON, P. F. 1988. Expert Systems, Expertise, and the Library and Information Profession. Library and Information Science Research. 1988 October-December; 10(4): 367-388. ISSN: 0740-8188.

ARAGON-RAMIREZ, V.; PAICE, CHRIS. 1985. Design of a System for the Online Elucidation of Natural Language Search Statements. In: Informatics 8: Advances in Intelligent Retrieval: Proceedings of a Conference Jointly Sponsored by Aslib, the Aslib Informatics Group, and the Information Retrieval Specialist Group of the British Computer Society; 1985 April 16-17; Wadham College, Oxford, England. London, England: Aslib, The Association for Information Management, Information House; 1985. 163-190. ISBN: 0-85142-195-4.

ARDIS, SUSAN B. 1990. Online Patent Searching: Guided by an Expert System. Online. 1990 March; 14(2): 56-62. ISSN: 0146-5422.

BARKER, FRANCES H. 1989. Which Database? Choosing an Organisational Cluster. In: Online Information 1989: Proceedings of the 13th International Online Information Meeting; 1989 December 12-14; London, England. Oxford, England: Learned Information Ltd.; 1989. 403-414. ISBN: 0-904933-72-5.

BARTHES, CHRISTINE; FRONTIN, J.; GLIZE, PIERRE. 1987. EURISKO: An Artificial Intelligence Tool for Automatic Online Information Retrieval. In: Online Information 1987: Proceedings of the 11th International Online Information Meeting; 1987 December 8-10; London, England. Oxford, England: Learned Information Ltd.; 1987. 431-442. ISBN: 0-904933-62-8.

BASCH, REVA. 1990a. Databank Software for the 1990s and Beyond. Part 1: The Users' Wish List. Online. 1990 March; 14(2): 15-21. ISSN: 0146-5422.

BASCH, REVA. 1990b. Databank Software for the 1990s and Beyond. Part 2: The Online Services Respond. Online. 1990 May; 14(3): 15-21. ISSN: 0146-5422.

BATES, MARCIA J. 1979. Information Search Tactics. Journal of the American Society for Information Science. 1979 July; 30(4): 205-214. ISSN: 0002-8231.

BELKIN, NICHOLAS J.; CROFT, W. BRUCE. 1987. Retrieval Techniques. In: Williams, Martha E., ed. Annual Review of Information Science and Technology: Volume 22. Amsterdam, The Netherlands: Elsevier Science Publishers for the American Society for Information Science; 1987. 109-145. ISSN: 0066-4200; ISBN: 0-444-70302-0.

BERG HANSEN, I.; ROTTBØLL ANDERSEN, T. R. 1988. IANI—Intelligent Access to Nordic Information. In: Online Information 1988: Proceedings of the 12th International Online Information Meeting; 1988 December 6-8; London, England. Oxford, England: Learned Information Ltd.; 1988. 705-713. ISBN: 0-904933-68-7.

BERRY, DIANNE C.; HART, ANNA D. 1990. Evaluating Expert Systems. Expert Systems. 1990 November; 7(4): 199-207. ISSN: 0266-4720.

BISWAS, GAUTAM; BEZDEK, JAMES C.; MARQUES, MARISOL; SUBRAMANIAN, VISWANATH. 1987a. Knowledge-Assisted Document Retrieval: I. The Natural Language Interface. Journal of the American Society for Information Science. 1987 March; 38(2): 83-96. ISSN: 0002-8231.

BISWAS, GAUTAM; BEZDEK, JAMES C.; MARQUES, MARISOL; SUBRAMANIAN, VISWANATH. 1987b. Knowledge-Assisted Document Retrieval: II. The Retrieval Process. Journal of the American Society for Information Science. 1987 March; 38(2): 97-110. ISSN: 0002-8231.

BRAJNIK, GIORGIO; GUIDA, GIOVANNI; TASSO, CARLO. 1987. User Modeling in Intelligent Information Retrieval. Information Processing & Management. 1987; 23(4): 305-320. ISSN: 0306-4573.

BRAJNIK, GIORGIO; GUIDA, GIOVANNI; TASSO, CARLO. 1990. User Modeling in Expert Man-Machine Interfaces: A Case Study in Intelligent Information Retrieval. IEEE Transactions on Systems, Man, and Cybernetics. 1990 January/February; 20(1): 166-185. ISSN: 0018-9472.

BRAUNDET, MARIE-FRANCE. 1987. Outline of a Knowledge Base Model for an Intelligent Information Retrieval System. In: Proceedings of the Association for Computing Machinery Special Interest Group on Information Retrieval (ACM-SIGIR) 10th Annual International

Conference on Research and Development in Information Retrieval; 1987 June 3-5; New Orleans, LA. New York, NY: ACM, Inc.; 1987. 33-43. ISBN: 0-89791-232-2.

BROOKS, HELEN M. 1987. Expert Systems and Intelligent Information Retrieval. Information Processing & Management. 1987; 23(4): 367-382. ISSN: 0306-4573.

BROOKS, HELEN M.; DANIELS, P. J.; BELKIN, NICHOLAS J. 1985. Problem Descriptions and User Models: Developing an Intelligent Interface for Document Retrieval Systems. In: Informatics 8: Advances in Intelligent Retrieval: Proceedings of a Conference Jointly Sponsored by Aslib, the Aslib Informatics Group, and the Information Retrieval Specialist Group of the British Computer Society; 1985 April 16-17; Wadham College, Oxford, England. London, England: Aslib, The Association for Information Management, Information House; 1985. 191-214. ISBN: 0-85142-195-4.

BURTON, HILARY D. 1989. The Livermore Intelligent Gateway: An Integrated Information Processing Environment. Information Processing & Management. 1989; 25(5): 509-514. ISSN: 0306-4573.

CHIARAMELLA, Y.; DEFUDE, B. 1987. A Prototype of an Intelligent System for Information Retrieval: IOTA. Information Processing & Management. 1987; 23(4): 285-303. ISSN: 0306-4573.

CISLER, STEVE. 1988. Searching for a Better Way: Verity Inc.'s TOPIC Software. Online. 1988 November; 12(6): 99-102. ISSN: 0146-5422.

CLANCY, STEPHEN. 1985. BRS/Saunders Colleague: An Information Service for Medical Professionals. Database. 1985 June; 8(2): 108-121. ISSN: 0162-4105.

COONS, BILL. 1986a. Frontiers in Front Ends and Gateways. In: Online '86 Conference Proceedings; 1986 November 4-6; Chicago, IL. Weston, CT: Online Inc.; 1986. 30-35. Available from: Online Inc., 11 Tannery Lane, Weston, CT 06883.

COONS, BILL. 1986b. SearchWorks: Does It Really Work? Database. 1986 December; 9(6): 62-68. ISSN: 0162-4105.

CROFT, W. BRUCE. 1987. Approaches to Intelligent Information Retrieval. Information Processing & Management. 1987; 23(4): 249-254. ISSN: 0306-4573.

CROFT, W. BRUCE; LEWIS, DAVID D. 1987. An Approach to Natural Language Processing for Document Retrieval. In: Proceedings of the Association for Computing Machinery Special Interest Group on Information Retrieval (ACM-SIGIR) 10th Annual International Conference on Research and Development in Information Retrieval; 1987 June 3-5; New Orleans, LA. New York, NY: ACM, Inc.; 1987. 26-32. ISBN: 0-89791-232-2.

CROFT, W. BRUCE; THOMPSON, ROGER H. 1987. I³R: A New Approach to the Design of Document Retrieval Systems. Journal of the American Society for Information Science. 1987 November; 36(6): 389-404. ISSN: 0002-8231.

DIBENIGNO, KATHRYN M.; CROSS, GEORGE R.; DEBESSONET, CARY G. 1986. COREL—A Conceptual Retrieval System. In: Proceedings of the Association for Computing Machinery Special Interest Group on Information Retrieval (ACM-SIGIR) 9th Annual International Conference on Research and Development in Information Retrieval; 1986 September 8-10; Pisa, Italy. New York, NY: ACM, Inc.; 1986. 144-148. ISBN: 0-89791-187-3.

DRENTH, HILARY J.; TSENG, GWYNETH; MORRIS, ANNE. 1991. Expert Selection of Marketing Databases. Business Information Review. 1991 April; 7(4): 24-32. ISSN: 0266-3821.

DYCKMAN, LISE M.; O'CONNOR, BRIAN T. 1989. Profiling the End-User: A Study of the Reference Needs of End-Users on Telebase System, Inc.'s EasyNet. In: Nixon, Carol; Padgett, Lauree, comps. Proceedings of the 10th National Online Meeting; 1989 May 9-11; New York, NY. Medford, NJ: Learned Information, Inc.; 1989. 143-152. ISBN: 0-938734-34-2.

EAGER, VIRGINIA W. 1984. MicroDISCLOSURE—Software for the IBM PC/XT Enduser. Database. 1984 June; 7(2): 79-84. ISSN: 0162-4105.

EFTHIMIADIS, EFTHIMIS N. 1990. Online Searching Aids: A Review of Front Ends, Gateways and Other Interfaces. Journal of Documentation. 1990 September; 46(3): 218-262. ISSN: 0022-0418.

ENSOR, PAT; CURTIS, RICHARD A. 1984. Search Helper: Low-Cost Online Searching in an Academic Library. RQ. 1984 Spring; 23(3): 327-331. ISSN: 0033-7072.

FENICHEL, CAROL H. 1980. An Examination of the Relationship between Searcher Behavior and Searcher Background. Online Review. 1980 August; 4(4): 341-347. ISSN: 0309-314X.

FIDEL, RAYA. 1984. Online Searching Styles: A Case-Study-based Model of Searching Behavior. Journal of the American Society for Information Science. 1984 July; 35(4): 211-221. ISSN: 0002-8231.

FIDEL, RAYA. 1985. Moves in Online Searching. Online Review. 1985 February; 9(1): 61-74. ISSN: 0309-314X.

FIDEL, RAYA. 1986. Towards Expert Systems for the Selection of Search Keys. Journal of the American Society for Information Science. 1986 January; 37(1): 37-44. ISSN: 0002-8231.

FIDEL, RAYA. 1987. Controlled Vocabulary and Free-text Searching: Searchers' Selection of Search Keys. In: Chen, Ching-Chih, ed. Information: The Transformation of Society: Proceedings of the American Society for Information Science (ASIS) 50th Annual Meeting: Volume 24; 1987 October 4-8; Boston, MA. Medford, NJ: Learned Information, Inc. for ASIS; 1987. 71-73. ISBN: 0-938734-19-9.

FLORIAN, D. 1987. SAFIR (Smart Assistant for Information Retrieval)—An Artificial Intelligence Impact on Information Retrieval. In: Online Information 1987: Proceedings of the 11th International Online Information Meeting; 1987 December 8-10; London, England. Oxford, England: Learned Information Ltd.; 1987. 423-429. ISBN: 0-904933-62-8.

FORD, NIGEL. 1991. European Research Letter: Knowledge-Based Information Retrieval. Journal of the American Society for Information Science. 1991 January; 42(1): 72-74. ISSN: 0002-8231.

FOSTER, PAMELA; FOSTER, ALAN, eds.   1990.   Online Business Sourcebook—Autumn 1990.   Cleveland, England: Headland Press Ltd.; 1990. 303p. ISSN: 0953-5055.

FOX, EDWARD A.   1987.   Development of the CODER System.   Information Processing & Management.   1987; 23(4): 341-366.   ISSN: 0306-4573.

FOX, M. S.; PALAY, A. J.   1979.   The BROWSE System: An Introduction. In: Tally, Roy D.; Deultgen, Ronald R., eds.   Information Choices and Policies: Proceedings of the American Society for Information Science (ASIS) 42nd Annual Meeting: Volume 16; 1979 October 14-18; Minneapolis, MN.   White Plains, NY: Knowledge Industry Publications, Inc. for ASIS; 1979.   183-193.   ISBN: 0-914236-47-4.

FREI, H. P.; JAUSLIN, J. F.   1983.   Graphical Representation of Information and Services: A User-Oriented Interface.   Information Technology: Research and Development.   1983 January; 2(1): 23-42.   ISSN: 0144-817X.

GASCHNIG, J.; KLAHR, P.; POPLE, E.; SHORTLIFFE, E.; TERRY, A. 1983.   Evaluation of Expert Systems: Issues and Case Studies.   In: Hayes-Roth, F.; Waterman, D.A.; Lenat, D.B., eds.   Building Expert Systems.   Reading, MA: Addison-Wesley; 1983.   241-282..   ISBN: 0-201-10686-8.

GAUCH, SUSAN; SMITH, JOHN B.   1988.   An Expert System for Searching in Full Text. Information Processing & Management. 1988; 25(3): 253-263.   ISSN: 0306-4573.

GOKER, AYSE.   1989.   Machine Learning for "Intelligent" Information Retrieval.   In: Pollitt, A. Steven, ed.   Proceedings of the British Computer Society Information Retrieval Specialist Group (IRSG) 11th Research Colloquium on Information Retrieval; 1989 July 5-6; Huddersfield, England.   Huddersfield, England: Huddersfield Polytechnic; 1989.   211-227.   Available from: Tony McCannery, Dept. of Computing, Lancaster University, LA1 4YR, UK.

GROSS, DANIEL.   1988.   Applications of AI Technology to Online Database Services.   Online Review.   1988 October; 12(5): 283-289.   ISSN: 0309-314X.

GUIDA, GIOVANNI; TASSO, CARLO.   1983.   An Expert Intermediary System for Interactive Document Retrieval. Automatica.   1983 November; 19(6): 759-766.   ISSN: 0005-1098.

GÜNTZER, U.; JÜTTNER, G.; SEEGMÜLLER, G.; SARRE, F.   1989. Automatic Thesaurus Construction by Machine Learning from Retrieval Sessions.   Information Processing & Management.   1989; 25(3): 265-276.   ISSN: 0306-4573.

HALPERN, J.; SARGEANT, H. A.   1988.   A New End-User Interface for Bilingual Searching of MEDLINE.   In: Online Information 1988: Proceedings of the 12th International Online Information Meeting; 1988 December 6-8; London, England.   Oxford, England: Learned Information Ltd.; 1988.   427-443.   ISBN: 0-904933-68-7.

HANFMAN, DEBORAH. 1989. AquaRef: An Expert Advisory System for Reference Support. Reference Librarian. 1989; 23: 113-133. (Special issue, Expert Systems in Reference Services). ISSN: 0276-3877.

HARTER, STEPHEN P. 1986. Online Information Retrieval: Concepts, Principles, and Techniques. Orlando, FL: Academic Press Inc.; 1986. 259p. ISBN: 0-12-328455-4.

HARTER, STEPHEN P.; PETERS, ANNE R. 1985. Heuristics for Online Information Retrieval: A Typology and Preliminary Listing. Online Review. 1985 October; 9(5): 407-424. ISSN: 0309-314X.

HAWKINS, DONALD T. 1988. Applications of Artificial Intelligence (AI) and Expert Systems for Online Searching. Online. 1988 January; 12(1): 31-43. ISSN: 0146-5422.

HAWKINS, DONALD T.; LEVY, LOUISE R.; MONTGOMERY, K. LEON. 1988. Knowledge Gateways: The Building Blocks. Information Processing & Management. 1988; 24(4): 459-468. ISSN: 0306-4573.

HAWKINS, DONALD T.; WAGERS, R. 1982. Online Bibliographic Search Strategy Development. Online. 1982 May; 6(3): 12-19. ISSN: 0146-5422.

HAYWARD, SIMON A. 1985. Is a Decision Tree an Expert System? In: Bramer, M. A., ed. Proceedings of the British Computer Society Specialist Group on Expert Systems 4th Conference; 1984 December 18-20; University of Warwick, England. Cambridge, England: Cambridge University Press; 1985. 185-192. ISBN: 0-521-30652-3.

HOOK, SARA ANNE. 1986. BRS/BRKTHRU: A Happy Medium. Online. 1986 January; 10(1): 97-101. ISSN: 0146-5422.

HOUGHTON, TONY; RICH, CLIVE; BASS, ANDREW. 1987. Front End Software to Online Database Searching: IDEA (Intelligent Database Enquiry Assistant). Given at a Conference on Knowledge Based Systems; 1987. Available from: the authors, BT Development and Procurement, BT Laboratories, Martlesham Heath, Ipswich, Suffolk, IPS 7RE, UK.

HU, CHENGREN. 1988. An Evaluation of a Gateway System for Automated Online Database Selection. In: Williams, Martha E.; Hogan, Thomas H., comps. Proceedings of the 9th National Online Meeting; 1988 May 10-12; New York, NY. Medford, NJ: Learned Information, Inc.; 1988. 107-114. ISBN: 0-938734-26-1.

HUSHON, JUDITH M. 1986. How Micro-CSIN, a New Gateway to Online Systems, Stacks Up. In: Williams, Martha, E.; Hogan, Thomas H., comps. Proceedings of the 7th National Online Meeting; 1986 May 6-8; New York, NY. Medford, NJ: Learned Information, Inc.; 1986. 203-210. ISBN: 0-938734-12-1.

INFORMATION WORLD REVIEW. 1989. Intelligent Front Ends. Information World Review. 1989 December; 43: 12-14. ISSN: 0950-9879.

INFOTAP. 1990. Intelligent Information. Luxembourg: Infotap; 1990. 2p. (Brochure). Available from: INFOTAP (Information Technology Applications), 2 rue A. Borschette, Boîte Postale 262, L-2012 Luxembourg.

INGWERSEN, PETER. 1986. Cognitive Analysis and the Role of the Intermediary in Information Retrieval. In: Davies, R., ed. Intelligent

Information Systems: Progress and Prospects.   Chichester, England: Ellis Horwood, Ltd.; 1986. 203-237. ISBN: 0-85312-896-0.

KIM, YOUNG WHAN; KIM, JIN H. 1990. A Model of Knowledge-Based Information Retrieval with Hierarchical Concept Graph. Journal of Documentation. 1990 June; 46(2): 113-136. ISSN: 0022-0418.

KIWIS TEAM. 1989. The KIWI(S) Projects: Past and Future. In: Commission of the European Communities, Directorate General Telecommunications, Information Industries and Innovation, ed. ESPRIT '89: Proceedings of the 6th Annual ESPRIT Conference; 1989 November 27-December 1; Brussels, Belgium. Dordrecht, The Netherlands: Kluwer Academic Publications; 1989. 594-603. ISBN: 0-7923-0592-2.

KRAWCZAK, DEBORAH A.; SMITH, PHILIP J.; SHUTE, STEVEN J.; CHIGNELL, MARK H. 1985. EP-X: A Knowledge-Based System to Aid in Searches of the Environmental Pollution Literature. In: The Engineering of Knowledge-Based Systems: [Proceedings of the] 2nd Conference on Artificial Intelligence Applications; 1985 December 11-13; Miami Beach, FL. Washington, DC: Institute of Electrical and Electronics Engineers (IEEE) Computer Society Press; 1985. 552-557. ISBN: 0-8186-0688-6.

KUHN, ALLAN D. 1988. DoD Gateway Information System (DGIS): The Development toward Artificial Intelligence and Hypermedia in Common Command Language. In: Online Information 1988: Proceedings of the 12th International Online Information Meeting; 1988 December 6-8; London, England. Oxford, England: Learned Information Ltd.; 1988. 691-704. ISBN: 0-904933-68-7.

KWAN, JULIE; DEENEY, KAY. 1987. DIALOG Medical Connection: An Evaluation. Online. 1987 November; 11(6): 32-38. ISSN: 0146-5422.

LARSEN, GITTE. 1986. Intelligent Gateways: An Evaluation of EasyNet— An End User Test. In: Online Information 1986: Proceedings of the 10th International Online Information Meeting; 1986 December 2-4; London, England. Oxford, England: Learned Information Ltd.; 1986. 131-135. ISBN: 0-904933-57-1.

LIBRARY MICROMATION NEWS. 1989. User-friendly Front End Software for Online Searchers. Library Micromation News. 1989 March; 23: 12-14. ISSN: 0262-7841.

MARCUS, RICHARD S. 1981. An Automated Expert System for Information Retrieval. In: Lunin, Lois F.; Henderson, Madeline; Wooster, Harold, eds. The Information Community: An Alliance for Progress: Proceedings of the American Society for Information Science (ASIS) 44th Annual Meeting: Volume 18; 1981 October 25-30; Washington, DC. White Plains, NY: Knowledge Industry Publications, Inc.; 1981. 270-273. ISBN: 0-914236-85-7.

MARCUS, RICHARD S. 1983. An Experimental Comparison of the Effectiveness of Computers and Humans as Search Intermediaries. Journal of the American Society for Information Science. 1983 November; 34(6): 381-404. ISSN: 0002-8231.

MARCUS, RICHARD S.; REINTJES, J. FRANCIS. 1981. A Translating Computer Interface for End-User Operation of Heterogeneous Retrieval Systems. I. Design. Journal of the American Society for Information Science. 1981 July; 32(4): 287-317. ISSN: 0002-8231.

MCMATH, CHARLES F.; TAMARU, ROBERT S.; RADA, ROY. 1989. A Graphical Thesaurus-Based Information Retrieval System. International Journal of Man-Machine Studies. 1989 August; 31(2): 121-147. ISSN: 0020-7373.

MEADOW, CHARLES T. 1979. The Computer as a Search Intermediary. Online. 1979 July; 3(4): 54-59. ISSN: 0146-5422.

MEADOW, CHARLES T. 1988. OAKDEC, a Program for Studying the Effects on Users of a Procedural Expert System for Database Searching. Information Processing & Management. 1988; 24(4): 449-457. ISSN: 0306-4573.

MEADOW, CHARLES T.; CERNY, BARBARA A.; BORGMAN, CHRISTINE L.; CASE, DONALD O. 1989. Online Access to Knowledge: System Design. Journal of the American Society for Information Science. 1989 March; 40(2): 86-98. ISSN: 0002-8231.

MEADOW, CHARLES T.; HEWETT, THOMAS T.; AVERSA, ELIZABETH S. 1982a. A Computer Intermediary for Interactive Database Searching. I. Design. Journal of the American Society for Information Science. 1982 September; 33(5): 325-332. ISSN: 0002-8231.

MEADOW, CHARLES T.; HEWETT, THOMAS T.; AVERSA, ELIZABETH S. 1982b. A Computer Intermediary for Interactive Database Searching. II. Evaluation. Journal of the American Society for Information Science. 1982 November; 33(6): 357-364. ISSN: 0002-8231.

MEYER, DANIEL E.; RUIZ, DEN. 1990a. End-User Selection of Databases—Part I: Science/Technology/Medicine. Database. 1990 June; 13(3): 21-29. ISSN: 0162-4105.

MEYER, DANIEL E.; RUIZ, DEN. 1990b. End-User Selection of Databases—Part II: Business/Law. Database. 1990 August; 13(4): 35-42. ISSN: 0162-4105.

MICCO, H. MARY; SMITH, IRMA. 1986. Designing an Expert System for the Reference Function Subject Access to Information. In: Hurd, Julie M., ed. ASIS '86: Proceedings of the American Society for Information Science (ASIS) 49th Annual Meeting: Volume 23; 1986 September 28-October 2; Chicago, IL. Medford, NJ: Learned Information, Inc. for ASIS; 1986. 204-210. ISBN: 0-938734-14-8.

MICCO, H. MARY; SMITH, IRMA. 1989. Designing a Workstation for Information Seekers. Reference Librarian. 1989; 23: 135-152. (Special issue, Expert Systems in Reference Services). ISSN: 0276-3877.

MONARCH, IRA; CARBONELL, JAIME. 1987. CoalSORT: A Knowledge-Based Interface. IEEE Expert. 1987 Spring; 2(1): 39-53. ISSN: 0885-9000.

MORRIS, ANNE; TSENG, GWYNETH; NEWHAM, GODFREY. 1988. The Selection of Online Databases and Hosts—An Expert System Approach. In: Online Information 1988: Proceedings of the 12th International Online Information Meeting; 1988 December 6-8; London, England. Oxford, England: Learned Information Ltd.; 1988. 139-148. ISBN: 0-904933-68-7.

MORRIS, ANNE; TSENG, GWYNETH; WALTON, KATHRYN P. 1989. Moss: A Prototype for Modifying Online Search Strategies. In: Online Information 1989: Proceedings of the 13th International Online Information Meeting; 1989 December 12-14; London, England. Oxford, England: Learned Information Ltd.; 1989. 691-704. ISBN: 0-904933-72-5.

NEALE, I. M.; MORRIS, ANNE. 1988. Knowledge Acquisition for Expert Systems: A Brief Review. Knowledge Acquisition. 1988; 1(3): 178-192. ISSN: 1042-8143.

NEWHAM, GODFREY; TSENG, GWYNETH; MORRIS, ANNE. 1988. Choosing a Business Database: The Expert Approach. Business Information Review. 1988 July; 5(1): 27-41. ISSN: 0266-3821.

NICHOLAS, DAVID; ERBACH, GERTRUD. 1989. Online Information Sources for Business and Current Affairs. London, England: Mansell Publishing Ltd.; 1989. 288p. ISBN: 0-7201-1878-6.

OBERMEIER, KLAUS K.; COOPER, LINDA E. 1984. Information Network Facility Organizing System (INFOS)—An Expert System for Information Retrieval. In: Flood, Barbara; Witiak, Joanne; Hogan, Thomas H., comps. Challenges to an Information Society: Proceedings of the American Society for Information Science (ASIS) 47th Annual Meeting: Volume 21; 1984 October 21-25; Philadelphia, PA. White Plains, NY: Knowledge Industry Publications, Inc.; 1984. 95-98. ISBN: 0-86729-115-X.

ODDY, R. N. 1977. Information Retrieval through Man-Machine Dialogue. Journal of Documentation. 1977; 33(1): 1-14. ISSN: 0022-0418.

OJALA, MARYDEE. 1989a. Searching Duns' Market Searcher. Database. 1989 April; 12(2): 90-94. ISSN: 0162-4105.

OJALA, MARYDEE. 1989b. What's on the Menu for Business Searchers? Database. 1989 February; 12(1): 66-76. ISSN: 0162-4105.

OLDROYD, BETTY K.; CITROEN, CHARLES L. 1977. Study of Strategies Used in On-line Searching. Online Review. 1977 December; 1(4): 295-310. ISSN: 0309-314X.

O'LEARY, MICK. 1985. EasyNet: Doing It All for the End-User. Online. 1985 July; 9(4): 106-113. ISSN: 0146-5422.

O'LEARY, MICK. 1986a. DIALOG Business Connection: DIALOG for the End User. Online. 1986 September; 10(5): 15-24. ISSN: 0146-5422.

O'LEARY, MICK. 1986b. WILSEARCH: A New Departure for an Old Institution. Online. 1986 March; 10(2): 102-107. ISSN: 0146-5422.

O'LEARY, MICK. 1988. EasyNet Revisited: Pushing the Online Frontier. Online. 1988 September; 12(5): 22-30. ISSN: 0146-5422.

PAICE, CHRIS. 1986. Expert Systems for Information Retrieval? Aslib Proceedings. 1986 October; 38(1): 343-353. ISSN: 0001-253X.

PARROTT, JAMES R. 1986. Expert Systems for Reference Work. Microcomputers for Information Management. 1986 September; 3(3): 155-171. ISSN: 0742-2342.

PARROTT, JAMES R. 1989. Simulation of the Reference Process, Part II: REFSIM, an Implementation with Expert System and ICAI Modes. Reference Librarian. 1989; 23: 153-176. (Special issue, Expert Systems in Reference Services). ISSN: 0276-3877.

PATEL-SCHNEIDER, PETER F.; BRACHMAN, RONALD J.; LEVESQUE, HECTOR J. 1984. ARGON: Knowledge Representation Meets Information Retrieval. In: Proceedings of the 1st Conference on AI Applications; 1984 December 5-7; Denver, CO. Washington, DC: Institute of Electrical and Electronics Engineers (IEEE) Computer Society Press; 1984. 280-286. ISBN: 0-8186-0624-X.

POLLITT, A. STEVEN. 1986a. An Expert Systems Approach to Document Retrieval. Huddersfield, England: Department of Computer Studies and Mathematics, Huddersfield Polytechnic; 1986. 349p. (Ph.D. dissertation). Available from: Huddersfield Polytechnic Library, Queensgate, Huddersfield HD1 3DH, UK.

POLLITT, A. STEVEN. 1986b. A Rule-Based System as an Intermediary for Searching Cancer Therapy Literature on MEDLINE. In: Davies, R., ed. Intelligent Information Systems: Progress and Prospects. Chichester, England: Ellis Horwood, Ltd.; 1986. 82-126. ISBN: 0-85312-896-0.

POLLITT, A. STEVEN. 1987. CANSEARCH: An Expert Systems Approach to Document Retrieval. Information Processing & Management. 1987; 23(2): 119-138. ISSN: 0306-4573.

POLLITT, A. STEVEN. 1988. A Common Query Interface Using MenUSE— A Menu-Based User Search Engine. In: Online Information 1988: Proceedings of the 12th International Online Information Meeting; 1988 December 6-8; London, England. Oxford, England: Learned Information Ltd.; 1988. 445-457. ISBN: 0-904933-68-7.

PREECE, SCOTT E. 1980. An Online Associative Query Modification Methodology. Online Review. 1980 August; 4(4): 375-382. ISSN: 0309-314X.

QUEENS BOROUGH CENTRAL LIBRARY STAFF. 1985. Search Helper: The Queens Borough Experience. Online. 1985 November; 9(6): 53-56. ISSN: 0146-5422.

QUINT, BARBARA. 1986. Menlo Corporation's Pro-Search: Review of a Software Search Aid. Online. 1986 January; 10(1): 17-25. ISSN: 0146-5422.

RENEAU, FRED W. 1986. Searchware for Online Access by Novice Users. Online Review. 1986 February; 10(1): 35-36. ISSN: 0309-314X.

RICH, ELAINE. 1983. Artificial Intelligence. New York, NY: McGraw-Hill, Inc.; 1983. 436p. ISBN: 0-07-052261-8.

ROBERTSON, D.; MUETZELFELDT, R.; PLUMER, D.; USCHOLD, M.; BUNDY, A. 1985. The ECO Browser. In: Merry, M., ed. Expert Systems '85: Proceedings of the British Computer Society Specialist

Group on Expert Systems 5th Technical Conference; 1985 December 17-19; University of Warwick, UK. Cambridge, England: Cambridge University Press; 1985. 143-156. ISBN: 0-521-32596-X.

SARACEVIC, TEFKO; KANTOR, PAUL. 1988a. A Study of Information Seeking and Retrieving. II. Users, Questions, and Effectiveness. Journal of the American Society for Information Science. 1988 May; 39(3): 177-196. ISSN: 0002-8231.

SARACEVIC, TEFKO; KANTOR, PAUL. 1988b. A Study of Information Seeking and Retrieving. III. Searchers, Searches, and Overlap. Journal of the American Society for Information Science. 1988 May; 39(3): 197-216. ISSN: 0002-8231.

SARACEVIC, TEFKO; KANTOR, PAUL; CHAMIS, ALICE Y.; TRIVISON, DONNA. 1988. A Study of Information Seeking and Retrieving. I. Background and Methodology. Journal of the American Society for Information Science. 1988 May; 39(3): 161-176. ISSN: 0002-8231.

SARANGAPANI, CHET. 1990. Development and Evaluation of a Reference Expert System in Chemistry. In: Williams, Martha E., ed. Proceedings of the 11th National Online Meeting; 1990 May 1-3; New York, NY. Medford, NJ: Learned Information, Inc.; 1990. 355-362. ISBN: 0-938734-44-X.

SHOVAL, PERETZ. 1985. Principles, Procedures and Rules in an Expert System for Information Retrieval. Information Processing & Management. 1985; 21(6): 475-487. ISSN: 0306-4573.

SMITH, LINDA C. 1987. Artificial Intelligence and Information Retrieval. In: Williams, Martha E., ed. Annual Review of Information Science and Technology: Volume 22. Amsterdam, The Netherlands: Elsevier Science Publishers for the American Society for Information Science (ASIS); 1987. 41-77. ISSN: 0066-4200; ISBN: 0-444-70302-0.

SMITH, PHILIP J.; CHIGNELL, MARK H. 1984. Development of an Expert System to Aid in Searches of the Chemical Abstracts. In: Flood, Barbara; Witiak, Joanne; Hogan, Thomas H., comps. Challenges to an Information Society: Proceedings of the American Society for Information Science (ASIS) 47th Annual Meeting: Volume 21; 1984 October 21-25; Philadelphia, PA. White Plains, NY: Knowledge Industry Publications, Inc. for ASIS; 1984. 99-102. ISBN: 0-86729-115-X.

SMITH, PHILIP J.; SHUTE, STEVEN J.; GALDES, DEB; CHIGNELL, MARK H. 1989. Knowledge-Based Search Tactics for an Intelligent Intermediary System. ACM Transactions on Information Systems. 1989 July; 7(3): 246-270. ISSN: 1046-8188.

SNOW, BONNIE; CORBETT, ANN L.; BRAHMI, FRANCES A. 1986. GRATEFUL MED: NLM's Front End Software. Database. 1986 December; 9(6): 94-99. ISSN: 0162-4105.

SORMUNEN, EERO. 1989a. An Analysis of Online Searching Knowledge for Intermediary Systems. Espoo, Finland: Technical Research Center of Finland; 1989. 81p. (Technical Research Center of Finland, Research Reports 630). ISBN: 951-38-3502-2.

SORMUNEN, EERO. 1989b. A Knowledge Base for the Search Profile Analysis and User Guidance. In: Online Information 1989: Proceedings of the 13th International Online Information Meeting; 1989 December 12-14; London, England. Oxford, England: Learned Information Ltd.; 1989. 435-446. ISBN: 0-904933-72-5.

SPARCK JONES, KAREN. 1988. Intelligent Interfaces for Information Retrieval Systems: Architecture Problems in the Construction of Expert Systems for Document Retrieval. In: Yeates-Mercer, P.A., ed. Future Trends in Information Science and Technology: Proceedings of the Silver Jubilee Conference of the City University's Department of Information Science; 1987 January 16; The City University, London. London, England: Taylor Graham; 1988. 47-73. ISBN: 0-947568-20-4.

STIGLEMAN, SUE. 1988. PaperChase: For MEDLINE Searching. Online Review. 1988 February; 12(1): 67-76. ISSN: 0309-314X.

STOUT, CATHERYNE; MARCINKO, THOMAS. 1983. Sci-Mate: A Menu-Driven Universal Online Searcher and Personal Data Manager. Online. 1983 September; 7(5): 112-116. ISSN: 0146-5422.

TENOPIR, CAROL. 1988. Database Selection Tools. Library Journal. 1988 November; 113(8): 52-53. ISSN: 0363-0277.

TESKEY, NIALL; HENRY, MALCOLM; CHRISTOPHER, SUE. 1987. A User Interface for Multiple Retrieval Systems. Online Review. 1987 October; 11(5): 283-296. ISSN: 0309-314X.

THORNBURG, GAIL E. 1987. LOOK: Implementation of an Expert System in Information Retrieval for Database Selection. Urbana, IL: University of Illinois at Urbana-Champaign; 1987. 103p. (Ph.D. dissertation). Available from: University Microfilms International, Ann Arbor, MI. (UMI order no.: 8803222).

TOME. 1988. Software Revolutionises Access to Databases. London, England: Tome; 1988. 2p. (Brochure). Available from: Tome Associates, IMO House, 222 Northfield Avenue, London W3 9SJ, UK.

TONG, RICHARD M.; APPELBAUM, LEE A.; ASKMAN, VICTOR N.; CUNNINGHAM, JAMES F. 1987. Conceptual Information Retrieval Using RUBRIC. In: Proceedings of the Association for Computing Machinery Special Interest Group on Information Retrieval (ACM-SIGIR) 10th Annual International Conference on Research and Development in Information Retrieval; 1987 June 3-5; New Orleans, LA. New York, NY: ACM, Inc.; 1987. 247-253. ISBN: 0-89791-232-2.

TONG, RICHARD M.; ASKMAN, VICTOR N.; CUNNINGHAM, JAMES F.; TOLLANDER, CARL J. 1985. RUBRIC: An Environment for Full Text Information Retrieval. In: Proceedings of the Association for Computing Machinery Special Interest Group on Information Retrieval (ACM-SIGIR) 8th Annual International Conference on Research and Development in Information Retrieval; 1985 June 5-7; Montreal, Canada. New York, NY: ACM, Inc.; 1985. 243-251. ISBN: 0-89791-159-8.

TRAUTMAN, RODES; VON FLITTNER, SARA. 1989. An Expert System for Microcomputers to Aid Selection of Online Databases. Reference Librarian. 1989; 23: 207-238. (Special issue, Expert Systems in Reference Services). ISSN: 0276-3877.

VICKERY, ALINA. 1988. The Experience of Building Expert Search Systems. In: Online Information 1988: Proceedings of the 12th International Online Information Meeting; 1988 December 6-8; London, England. Oxford, England: Learned Information Ltd.; 1988. 301-314. ISBN: 0-904933-68-7.

VICKERY, ALINA; BROOKS, HELEN M. 1987. Expert Systems and Their Applications in LIS. Online Review. 1987 June; 11(3): 149-165. ISSN: 0309-314X.

VICKERY, ALINA; BROOKS, HELEN M.; VICKERY, BRIAN C. 1986. An Expert System for Referral: The PLEXUS Project. In: Davies, R., ed. Intelligent Information Systems: Progress and Prospects. Chichester, England: Ellis Horwood, Ltd.; 1986. 154-183. ISBN: 0-85312-896-0.

VICKERY, BRIAN; VICKERY, ALINA. 1990. Intelligence and Information Systems. Journal of Information Science. 1990; 16(1): 65-70. ISSN: 0165-5515.

WADE, STEPHEN; WILLETT, PETER; ROBINSON, BRUCE; VICKERY, BRIAN C.; VICKERY, ALINA. 1988. A Comparison of Knowledge-Based and Statistically-Based Techniques for Reference Retrieval. Online Review. 1988 April; 12(2): 91-108. ISSN: 0309-314X.

WALTON, KENNETH R. 1986. SearchMaster—Programmed for the End-User. Online. 1986 September; 10(5): 70-79. ISSN: 0146-5422.

WANG, X. 1990. Knowledge-Based Selection of Databases: An Algorithm and Its Evaluation. College Park, MD: College of Library and Information Services, University of Maryland; 1990. 400p. (Ph.D. dissertation). Available from: the author, Library and Learning Resources, University of Wisconsin at Whitewater, Whitewater, WI 53190.

WARR, WENDY A.; WILKINS, MARTYN P. 1990. Graphics Front Ends for Chemical Searching and a Look at ChemTalk Plus. Online. 1990 May; 14(3): 50-54. ISSN: 0146-5422.

WATERS, SAMUEL T. 1986. Answerman, the Expert Information Specialist: An Expert System for Retrieval of Information from Library Reference Books. Information Technology & Libraries. 1986 September; 5(3): 204-212. ISSN: 0730-9295.

WATTERS, C. R.; SHEPHERD, M. A. 1987. A Logic Basis for Information Retrieval. Information Processing & Management. 1987; 23(5): 433-445. ISSN: 0306-4573.

WEYER, STEPHEN A. 1989. Questing for the "Dao": DowQuest and Intelligent Retrieval. Online. 1989 September; 13(5): 39-48. ISSN: 0146-5422.

WILLIAMS, MARTHA E.; PREECE, SCOTT E. 1977. Data Base Selector for Network Use: A Feasibility Study. In: Fry, Bernard M.; Shepherd, Clayton A., comps. Information Management in the 1980s: Proceedings of the American Society for Information Science (ASIS) 40th Annual Meeting: Volume 14; 1977 September 26-October 1; Chicago, IL. White Plains, NY: Knowledge Industry Publications, Inc.; 1977. 34. ISBN: 0-914236-12-1.

WILLIAMS, PHILIP W.   1984.   A Model for an Expert System for Automated Information Retrieval.   In: Online Information 1984: Proceedings of the 8th International Online Information Meeting; 1984 December 4-6; London, England.   Oxford, England: Learned Information Ltd.; 1984.   139-149.   ISBN: 0-904933-47-4.

WILLIAMS, PHILIP W.   1985.   Intelligent Access to Remote Computer Systems.   Library and Information Research News.   1985; 8(29): 5-10.   ISSN: 0141-6561.

WILLIAMS, PHILIP W.; GOLDSMITH, G.   1982.   A Completely Automatic Information Retrieval System for the Unskilled User.   In: Online Information 1982: Proceedings of the 6th International Online Information Meeting; 1982 December 7-9; London, England. Oxford, England: Learned Information Ltd.; 1982.   263-272.   ISBN: 0-904933-39-3.

YASUNOBU, CHIZUKO; ITSUKI, REI; TSUJI, HIROSHI; MORI, FUMIHIKO.   1989.   Document Retrieval Expert System Shell with Worksheet-based Knowledge Acquisition Facility.   In: Computer Software and Applications Conference: Proceedings of the 13th Annual International Conference; 1989 September 20-22; Orlando, FL.   Washington, DC: Institute of Electrical and Electronics Engineers (IEEE) Computer Society Press; 1989.   278-285.   ISBN: 0-8186-1964-3.

ZINN, S.; SELLARS, M.; BOHLI, D.   1986.   OCLC's Intelligent Gateway Service: Online Information Access for Libraries.   Library Hi Tech. 1986 Fall; 4(3): 25-29.   ISSN: 0737-8831.

5   The Human–Computer Interface for Information Retrieval

DEBORA SHAW
Indiana University, Bloomington

INTRODUCTION

The human–computer interface "is often the single most important factor in determining the success or failure of a system. It is also often one of the most expensive" (BAECKER & BUXTON, p. 1). Definitions of the human–computer interface begin with the "typical" conception noted by HANCOCK & CHIGNELL: "a physical structure composed mainly of screen and keyboard" (p. v). Many writers expand this definition to include additional input and output devices, the computer programs for interacting with the user, the system's modeling of the user, and the user's cognitive models of the system. For this review the human–computer interface is defined as what the user sees, hears, and touches in interacting with a computer system—i.e., primarily the VDT (video display terminal) screen and various input devices. CHIGNELL recently proposed a taxonomy of user interface terminology that divides this emerging interdisciplinary field into four broad categories: (1) the basic interface models, (2) cognitive engineering, (3) user interface engineering, and (4) applications. This chapter focuses on the basic interface models, topics related to user navigation, interaction styles, and screen design. Topics on user interface engineering, such as general guidelines, help facilities, and interface evaluation, are also covered. Under "applications," the emphasis here is on information technology and retrieval.

Annual Review of Information Science and Technology (ARIST), Volume 26, 1991
Martha E. Williams, Editor
Published for the American Society for Information Science (ASIS)
By Learned Information, Inc., Medford, N.J.

In this *ARIST* volume DRENTH ET AL. discuss expert systems as intermediaries, and B. ALLEN addresses cognitive aspects of information, including user models developed for interface systems. The reader is referred to these chapters for discussion of the topics mentioned. Other areas of information science relate to interface design, and they have also been covered in recent *ARIST* volumes. Reviews by L.C. SMITH on artificial intelligence (AI) and by WARNER on natural-language processing are germane.

The importance of the interface in information retrieval systems underlies the tool called The User Friendly Index proposed by MATTHEWS & WILLIAMS. The index is a somewhat tongue-in-cheek list, with descriptions for friendliness ranging from "user intimate" to "user vicious." This chapter examines the human–computer interface for information retrieval, a topic addressed most recently in *ARIST* by VIGIL (1986). Other *ARIST* chapters have discussed interfaces to information retrieval systems in the context of specific subjects or applications (e.g., FOX; LANCASTER ET AL.; LIPSCOMB ET AL.; MARTIN, 1988; MISCHO & LEE). This review emphasizes work from 1986 to 1990, with forays into earlier studies as needed to summarize developments.

The chapter begins with a review of advances in general interface design. Guidelines and fruitful areas of research are discussed, with emphasis on recent years during which considerable attention has been devoted to menu-based systems and direct manipulation interfaces. Information retrieval applications are examined in the second part of the chapter. Major application areas include online catalogs, online searching, and CD-ROM products. Here the emphasis is on working systems rather than prototypes and on comparisons and evaluations rather than descriptive reports of individual systems.

GENERAL PRINCIPLES OF INTERFACE DESIGN

Recent interest in human–computer interaction has spawned the publication of several textbooks and edited compilations of papers on interface design. BAECKER & BUXTON have compiled an intriguing collection of key papers on human–computer interaction, ranging from theoretical observations to specific applications. BØDKER takes a more theoretical view, emphasizing contributions from anthropology, psychology, cognitive science, software engineering, and computer science to interface design. Several texts emphasize psychological aspects of the human–computer interface (CARD ET AL.; GUINDON; HANCOCK & CHIGNELL; NORMAN & DRAPER; VAN DER VEER & MULDER; WAERN). Other authors place more emphasis on the practical aspects of interface design (BOOTH; BROWN; GALITZ; LAUREL; SHNEIDERMAN, 1987). HELANDER presents a comprehensive summary of research on topics grouped under seven headings: (1) models and theories of human–computer interaction, (2) user interface design, (3) individual differences and training, (4) applications of computer technology, (5) tools for design and evaluation, (6) artificial intelligence, and (7) psychological and organizational issues.

A decade ago the human–computer interface may well have been an afterthought in any computer-based system. The arrival of workstations and the proliferation of personal computers permitted and even encouraged the development of interfaces for specific applications packages such as word processing and spreadsheets. By the early 1980s designers recognized the need to devote more attention to the interface, but we do not yet have a consensus on how to evaluate the results. Guidelines and informed opinion from experienced designers are available, but several writers suggest that more general and widely applicable understanding is needed. SHNEIDERMAN (1987) holds that "the battle will not be won by angry argumentation over the 'user friendliness' of competing systems or biased claims that 'my design is more natural than your design'" (p. vi). He suggests five measurable criteria for evaluating a user interface: (1) time needed to learn it, (2) speed of performance, (3) rate of errors by users, (4) subjective satisfaction, and (5) retention over time.

BAECKER & BUXTON also stress the need for empirical evaluation of user interfaces. Citing RAY & RAVIZZA, they note that potential research methods vary along four major dimensions: (1) naturalistic observation vs. true (controlled) experiments, (2) field research vs. laboratory research, (3) scientist as participant vs. scientist as observer, and (4) few or many subjects. They conclude by noting that, as with all research, empirical studies of interfaces should lead to the development of predictive models and theories to explain the results of specific observations. The Questionnaire for User Interaction Satisfaction (QUIS), developed at the University of Maryland Human–Computer Interaction Laboratory, has been used in several system evaluations and has shown good reliability (CHIN ET AL.). QUIS can be administered in either electronic or paper form, and it provides an overall subjective assessment of the system while helping to identify its specific strengths and weaknesses.

Current interest in rapid prototyping encourages iterative design, with ongoing evaluation of the system and interface. HARTSON & HIX discuss this approach and describe computer systems for managing interface development and maintenance. A major part of rapid prototyping is user feedback. GOMOLL describes ten steps used at Apple Computer for observing users' interactions with computers and concludes with "use the results."

It is generally accepted that a good interface is internally consistent and that consistency among interfaces provides for greater transfer of skills to new applications. POLSON cites the Apple Macintosh as an example of a consistent interface for various applications. He uses psychological theories—GOMS rules (Goals, Operators, Methods, and Selection) (developed by CARD ET AL.) and CCT (Cognitive Complexity Theory)—to understand the retention of user skills from one interface to another. Systems that use consistent interfaces had significant reductions in training time.

Most work to date has featured descriptions of specific interfaces, often with relatively few users in each study; in only a few areas have attempts been made to synthesize and generalize findings. Research efforts are discussed below under the following headings: Display Features, Mode of Interaction (Command, Menu, Direct Manipulation), and Help/System Messages.

Display Features

Edward TUFTE (1983; 1989; 1990) provides lucid and challenging evaluations and critiques of the visual display of information, ranging from maps to statistical graphics to music animation. VAN NES stresses the need for visual clarity and legibility in screen displays. NOORDMAN holds that even when one reads from a VDT display, reading speed and quality of understanding are determined by higher-order information processing skills. Studies that report slower reading times for computer-displayed text vs. text printed in a book (e.g., 30% slower) attribute the slower speed to the fewer characters per line and lower resolution in computer displays than in print on paper. Specific display techniques that have received attention from system designers include highlighting, color, icons, and windows.

Highlighting. The use of highlighting in computer displays continues to be refined. FISHER & TAN report that the effectiveness of highlighting in reducing search time depends on the type of highlighting (blocked, random, or none), the reliability of highlighting (whether nontarget items are also highlighted), and the probability that the user will pay attention to highlighting. FISHER ET AL. present a model for determining which options to highlight for a given display in order to reduce users' search times. DAVIS & SHAW experiment with reverse video display to highlight key words and phrases in a weighted-term retrieval system and find that users of this system make significantly fewer keyboarding errors than users of the same interface without highlighting.

Color. Advances in display technology allow use of color without sacrificing resolution. However, DE WEERT cautions that technology alone does not ensure successful use of color. He discusses the differences in reactions to changes in color and luminance, noting that detailed information is better processed in terms of luminance than color. WRIGHT & LICKORISH examine color cues that aim to help readers remember and retrieve specific parts of a lengthy text. They find that for text presented on paper, color cues (colored paper for different topics) help users relocate the information requested. However, when the same text is presented on a CRT (cathode ray tube) display, color cues (different color displays for each topic) do not help in relocating information. They warn that caution should be used when transferring design principles across media.

SHNEIDERMAN (1987) describes several successful uses of color in computer displays for video games, power plant control, and realistic images of people, scenery, and three-dimensional objects. He notes that there is controversy about the use of color for alphanumeric displays and suggests guidelines, starting with the advice to use color conservatively. TUFTE (1990) laments the overuse of color to change "what should be a straight-forward tool into. . .a grim parody of a video game" (p. 88). VAN NES states that no more than three or, at most, four colors should be used on one screen of text. RICE provides "rules of thumb" for color in VDT displays, including:

- Establish and maintain adequate hue difference when color coding information;
- Use colors that are associated with the status or significance of the displayed information (e.g., red, green, and yellow for dangerous, safe, and cautionary situations, respectively);
- Use muted or neutral colors for the background to minimize interference with subject matter;
- Avoid overlapping or adjacent regions of highly saturated, highly bright red and blue;
- Consider color-monitor performance and ambient lighting;
- Limit the number of colors to prevent cluttering and confusion;
- Do not rely on color coding for small objects;
- Consider brightness coding to categorize or highlight information; and
- Adjust saturation to achieve desired effect and promote viewing comfort.

THORELL & SMITH provide a thorough discussion of underlying technical issues and also provide guidelines for color use.

Icons.   Icons are "images representing system commands, objects, states or results" (BAECKER & BUXTON, p. 302). Some writers have used the playful and slightly pejorative term WIMP to refer to interfaces that use windows, icons, menus/mice, and pointers/pull-down menus. A less partisan term is "graphic user interfaces" (GUIs). Graphic interfaces that incorporate icons are standard for many microcomputer applications, allowing the user to select a picture of the desired action rather than having to remember specific commands.

Baecker and Buxton discuss the difficulty of designing effective icons, noting the need for semantic, syntactic, and pragmatic effectiveness. They summarize the arguments for iconic interfaces: images are "natural" and more easily learned than commands; icons are more universal than a specific language, thus offering added benefits to systems for international use; the common properties of several objects can be differentiated by use of style and color; and icons reduce learning time and user errors. The arguments against iconic interfaces are also presented: they can be confusing and waste space; it is difficult to discriminate among many similar commands or concepts; many aspects of computer systems do not have obvious "pictographic equivalents"; and icons may not be as natural and direct as is sometimes claimed—i.e., their comprehension requires considerable perceptual learning, abstraction, and intelligence.

LANSDALE examines the use of icons as additions to documents to enhance subjects' recall of documents they had seen. Although the early work found that icons did not improve this sort of recall, a subsequent effort (LANSDALE ET AL.) finds that recall improves when subjects assign their own "enriching attributes" (icons or words) to documents. AREND ET AL. compare abstract and representational icons with word choices in a menu selection system. Abstract icons (e.g., a dashed square representing the current screen with a solid square pointed on one side to indicate scrolling) are searched and selected more quickly than either word commands or representational icons (e.g., a rectangle with lines symbolizing text, a small rectangular overlay and adjacent arrow to represent scrolling). It appears that the visually distinctive abstract icons are searched in parallel, reducing effects of menu size, while representational icons and words are so specific that each needs to be examined individually.

Windows.   Windows are used on-screen to display more than one application, file, or interaction. They are used extensively in the desktop metaphor, which sees the computer screen as a workspace on which the user arranges materials to correspond to complex task priorities. Among their advantages, windows allow users to transfer spatial management skills from desktop to computer, to change focus from one task to another easily, to resume an interrupted task with little effort to "reestablish context," to integrate information from various files, to monitor a secondary process, and to transfer information from one file to another (BILLINGSLEY). Research suggests that windowing systems may lose some of these advantages when users spend more time in display management (moving and resizing windows), and Billingsley suggests several aspects of window design that merit further study; among these are: window visibility, number of windows displayed, visual complexity, user vs. system control, interaction styles, and operations on windows (opening, closing, moving, resizing, scrolling, and designating active window).

Mode of Interaction

SHNEIDERMAN (1987) identifies and categorizes three major types of human–computer interaction: (1) command mode, (2) menu selection (including form fill-in), and (3) direct manipulation. Command mode has been the traditional form of interaction and is generally preferred by experienced users doing frequently performed tasks. However, user preference may not always indicate the "best" mode of interaction for a system. T.W. SMITH reports that a menu interface improves performance by both novice and experienced users even though experienced users are not more satisfied with it than with other interfaces.

Commands vs. menus. Several studies present conflicting findings about the effectiveness of various modes of interaction. SPAVOLD worked with children aged 9 to 11 to compile and search databases from the 1880 census. She reports that students rapidly understand menu choices and feel secure in navigating "their" databases. When the students switch to command mode, they have major problems with syntax and terminology; they are frustrated in attempting to translate a colloquial query into the command language. CANTER ET AL. report that a menu-based interface is more effective than command-mode or natural-language front ends for novice users navigating a full text database. On the other hand, M.E. WILLIAMS ET AL. compare three interfaces to a MEDLINE minidatabase. Novice users find the associative (natural-language) interface easiest to learn and remember, while the menu-driven interface is most helpful when the user is uncertain what to do next. PAAP & ROSKE-HOFSTRAND (1988) summarize several empirical comparisons of menu-based vs. command interfaces. These studies support the idea that novice users seem to find commands more natural than menu selection. Although menus require less learning than the other modes and provide context-appropriate prompts, they may present conceptual difficulties that interfere with ease of use. When TAYLOR offers users a choice between menu or command-mode searching, 60% choose the menu mode regardless of previous experience. In addition, being able to choose the mode of interaction results in more user satisfaction and better performance than if no choice is provided. The optimum interface, then, may not be strictly command mode or menu based but a combination of interaction modes with some user control of the choice.

Menus. SHNEIDERMAN (1986) offers a practical discussion of semantics and menu organization as well as screen design, response time, and selection mechanisms. The way in which the user approaches the menu should be considered in screen design. MACGREGOR & LEE (1987a) question whether menu options are read in order or at random and suggest that users appear to read sequentially. R.B. ALLEN reports that the vertical position of the target (top or bottom of the screen) affects response time, while left or right positioning affects error rates.

Early evaluations of menu-based systems note the tradeoff between depth and breadth in menu organization. LEE & MACGREGOR report a study of videotex users that finds that the optimum number of alternatives per page is four to eight. PAAP & ROSKE-HOFSTRAND (1986) suggest that users can handle more choices (16 to 78 per page) when random menu presentations are replaced by organized ones. They note that it is generally sufficient to develop categories that are "natural" to the user, even if the categories are unequal in size. HOLLANDS & MERIKLE find that menus that present options by category rather than by alphabetical or random organization improve the user's performance. They also report that subject experts' performance varies directly with performance in the categorized menu but not in the alphabetical or random presentations. PAAP & ROSKE-HOFSTRAND (1988) suggest frequency of use as one way to organize menus, and they cite ZIPF in observing that a certain few options are likely to be selected most often.

FISCHHOFF ET AL. examine various ways to organize the information in the *Statistical Abstract of the United States.* After looking for supercategories for the book's 33 chapters they find that the traditional chapter listing is consistently superior as an entry-level menu. They also report that performance is good when the additional menu categories and labels are chosen by individuals similar to the eventual users. PIEKARA ET AL. investigate users' understandings of menu terms on the German videotex system Btx and find that 25% of the keywords offered by system designers are considered "not informative" by users. MCDONALD & SCHVANEVELDT discuss various methods for developing groupings of options for menu-based systems.

The method of identifying and indicating a menu selection has also been studied. RAFAELI & ENGEL compare cursor movement with keying a number for both broad and narrow menus. They find that the fastest and most accurate responses occur with the broad menu, cursor-based interface. SHINAR & STERN report that selection by a meaningful letter (e.g., the first letter of the option) produces faster and more accurate responses than either a key-controlled cursor to highlight the desired item or keying a number to indicate the option choice.

FIELD & APPERLEY study selective retreat (back up to any previously selected screen) and restricted retreat (back to main menu only). When subjects are interrupted in their searches, those with restricted retreat are more likely to start over than to continue at the point of interruption. These authors report that videotex users benefit from an enhanced menu system that incorporates both selective retreat and additional contextual information. ENGEL ET AL. also provide videotex users with contextual information by creating a history facility showing the retrieval structure and the user's sequence of choices. An alternative approach is taken by KREIGH ET AL. They offer a "look ahead" feature, which presents upcoming alternatives for current options. The approach does not improve performance, although the authors suggest that this may be due to the rather simple selection tasks being performed.

In contrast to the novice's need to retrace steps through several menus, experienced users may be annoyed by the repetition of menus, which slows their progress with a system. MACGREGOR & LEE (1987b) say that menu systems are unsuitable for experienced users. They suggest menu keywords and even user-defined keywords as means of improving experienced users' performance and acceptance of the system. LAVERSON ET AL. compare two types of jump-ahead capabilities. They find the type-ahead option less successful than the direct access approach. With type-ahead, the user anticipates upcoming menus and selects the choices in advance. Users have lower error rates and faster learning times with the direct-access approach, in which each menu frame is assigned a unique name and can be reached directly (as with MacGregor and Lee's keyword approach).

VAN HOE ET AL. report several factors that influence user performance, including menu structure, depth, and the presence of escape (back-up) facilities. They also examine the personality characteristics of users and find differences between introverts and extroverts in their initial interactions with the system. These authors suggest that introverts will need more human and social support in times of trouble than extroverts, but because the differences appear to be short lived, the interface need not be adapted to the user's personality. In studying individual differences VICENTE ET AL. note that vocabulary and spatial visualization are the best predictors of performance, and experience alone is not a reliable predictor. Subjects with low spatial ability get lost in the menu structure and on the average take twice as long as other subjects to complete their tasks.

Direct manipulation. SHNEIDERMAN (1983) coined the term "direct manipulation interface." Direct manipulation emphasizes:

- Continuous representation of the object(s) of interest;
- Physical actions (e.g., movement and selection by mouse, joystick, touch screen) or labeled function keys;
- Rapid, incremental, reversible operations whose impact on the object of interest is immediately visible; and
- Layered or spiral approach to learning that permits usage with minimal knowledge.

In *Designing the User Interface* SHNEIDERMAN (1987) provides several examples of systems that use direct manipulation and discusses the advantages of such interfaces for reducing the operator's problem-solving load. JACOB notes that direct manipulation is especially effective for systems dealing with static, concrete objects, such as engineering drawings or typed reports. Here a WYSIWYG ("what you see is what you get") editor is easily understood. However, when the system operates on abstract objects, such as time sequence data, conditional statements, or data in a database, there is no direct graphic image and the utility of direct manipulation interfaces is less obvious.

In reviewing empirical investigations of direct manipulation interfaces, ZIEGLER & FÄHNRICH note consistent problems for novice users, especially with mouse manipulation. Various methods of instruction are being investigated to overcome what is apparently a steep initial learning curve. Subsequent learning may in fact be facilitated by the consistency of the interface. Experienced users generally complete tasks more quickly and report greater satisfaction with direct manipulation than with other types of interfaces.

Help/System Messages

SELLEN & NICOL ask why users avoid using help, and they suggest five reasons: (1) difficulty in finding information, (2) failure to obtain relevant information, (3) difficulty of switching between the help and the working context, (4) complexity of the help interface, and (5) the quality and layout of help information. They recommend different help interfaces for different kinds of help, from the basic "what can I do with this program?" to procedural and navigational questions. Instead of context, PAZ ET AL. emphasize the structure of the help tutorial in presenting help as a "graphic study tree."

SHNEIDERMAN (1987) recommends that error messages have a positive tone and address the problem in the user's terms. TRENNER proposes guidelines specifically for online help facilities, such as: use of language that is polite, constructive, and impersonal, and accommodation of both novice and experienced users.

The GOMS model (Goals, Operators, Methods, and Selection rules developed by CARD ET AL.) serves as the theoretical basis for design principles regarding online advice proposed by ELKERTON. Goal-level advice should describe what can be done with the system using task-oriented language. Operator-level advice is similar to most existing help systems, describing commands or providing tutorials. Method-level advice can provide procedures for solving specific problems. Selection rules can be presented, for example, to help the user decide when to use scrolling or a string search to locate a needed file. ELKERTON & PALMITER describe the use of the GOMS model for help with HyperCard authoring tasks. Users of the GOMS-based help module are significantly faster than users of the original help system designed by Apple Computer, especially in early uses. Over time, users of the original help system improve as they learn where help information is located.

T.W. SMITH compares online with written documentation for help messages. He finds that online help degrades performance since users require more time and make more references to the help documentation when it is available online. However, users are generally more satisfied with online than with written help.

INTERFACES FOR INFORMATION RETRIEVAL

Information retrieval systems provide special difficulties for users who are trying to discover something they do not know while interacting with what may be an unfamiliar computer system. LINDE & WAERN note major differences among individuals searching an incomplete database, one that requires users to make inferences from information retrieved in order to answer questions. The less efficient searchers are more likely to become confused by the different possibilities, forget information retrieved, and repeat searches. LIBERATORE ET AL. find that display features interact with task-related factors to affect interpretation accuracy. Work is still needed to provide a better understanding of how interface design can decrease stress or provide support.

Some information retrieval systems have been developed for what were at the time considered very different applications—e.g., library catalogs and abstracting/indexing service databases. Economic and technological constraints as well as custom have limited the interface options for some systems. In other cases, marketing demands or a sense of the technology "bandwagon" seem to have spurred diversity and competition in interface design, even yielding designs that contradict research and guidelines. The recent developments and findings of the studies described below are grouped by application: online searching, CD-ROM/optical media, online catalogs, and full-text databases.

Online Searching

Front ends.   The major online search services have traditionally been available through command-mode interfaces. Attempts to provide somewhat simplified "end user" interfaces such as BRS/After Dark, BRS Colleague, and DIALOG's Knowledge Index emerged in the 1980s. At the same time front-end software for microcomputers was developed to make online searching more accessible to the user, whether novice or expert, or a frequent or infrequent searcher. P. WILLIAMS discusses work on front-end systems in Britain, stressing the value of leading novices through the search process and of providing intelligent support for strategy revision by experienced searchers. M.E. WILLIAMS (1986) describes the advantages of and design requirements for these "transparent information systems" to provide unified multiple system access, automatic database selection and location, search facilitation, output reformatting, removal of duplicates from search output, automatic dial-up and logon, and protocol conversion. MISCHO & LEE document developments in front ends and related applications.

MEADOW ET AL. and BORGMAN ET AL. (1989a) describe the Online Access to Knowledge (OAK) system, a microcomputer-based front end for the U.S. Department of Energy's DOE/RECON database. CRAWFORD & EDWARDS describe a front-end package that emphasizes the Macintosh interface and use of a mouse to retrieve drug-related information from DIALOG files. CRAWFORD & BECKER report on the FIRSTUSER interface (Friendly Information Retrieval System User's interface), which is based on menus and the filling of forms and which can be used by novices without external documentation or training. The development of the Sci-Mate Searcher is recounted by TOLIVER, who notes the "online Babel" of the various modems, networks, and host system passwords as well as retrieval system language problems. The Common Command Language (CCL) is an attempt to standardize retrieval system languages. KLEMPERER gives a succinct and accessible summary of CCL.

Brown University's Institute for Research in Information and Scholarship (IRIS) has developed Intermedia, a multi-user hypermedia system (YANKELOVICH ET AL.). One part of Intermedia is InterBrowse, a uniform front end for online searching that reduces the complexities of different retrieval languages, controlled vocabularies, and bibliographic record formats. KAHN (1987; 1988a) describes the components of the system, and K.E. SMITH (1988a; 1988b) provides examples.

Menus.   While some front ends and gateways supply menus for initial topic selection, few systems can condense the entire subject content of a database to a menu structure. However, the Medical Subject Headings (MeSH) structure has served as a basis for some menu-based interfaces to medical literature. POLLITT describes a menu interface for CANSEARCH, an expert system to search cancer therapy literature from MEDLINE. While human intermediaries generally provide better searches, physicians using CANSEARCH are often able to search effectively and sometimes outperform trained intermediaries. The PDQ Cancer Information System of the National Library of Medicine (NLM) provides a menu-based subject searching capability. SHAW & CZAJA compare the NLM version with the same database accessible through the command-mode BRS Colleague interface. They find that physician searchers are more efficient with the menu-based system while intermediaries use fewer steps per question with the command-mode interface. The menu-based system encourages more complete retrieval from what is essentially a full-text database, with both the menu-structured search and predefined print formats assisting the searchers.

Graphics.   Graphic techniques are being adapted for online searching.   LIPSCOMB ET AL. describe such applications to the searching of chemical structures and substructures, which has received considerable attention and commercial development. PERCIVAL recounts the growth of graphic user interfaces and assesses possibilities for a HyperCard interface to commercial search services. MCMATH ET AL. develop graphic representations of MeSH for selection of search terms. They find that the interface adds to users' understanding of the MeSH thesaurus and eliminates incorrect entry of terms; however, users are unhappy with the lack of a "neighbor" facility (presentation of terms that are alphabetically close to a given term) to see related terms and are sometimes frustrated by their inability to locate a known MeSH term in the tree structure. ANICK ET AL. describe "visual Boolean semantics," which incorporates graphic display of search strategy with AI techniques of analysis. YERMISH provides an early approach to graphic representation of citation relations for information retrieval.

CD-ROM/Optical Media

Distributed databases on CD-ROM have been with us only since the mid-1980s. The diversity of applications and enhanced sound and graphics capabilities have led to considerable experimentation with interfaces; for example, NICHOLLS identifies 195 different retrieval software packages used with CD-ROM products. SCHWARTZ reviews trends in CD-ROM interfaces, emphasizing their use by untrained searchers. NICHOLLS ET AL. describe criteria for evaluating CD-ROM retrieval software, including the user interface. ROWLEY compares an online command-mode interface with menu-based access to the same database on CD-ROM. She finds that searchers are equally effective in both systems but that searches on CD-ROM are faster and that 12 of the 16 subjects rate the menu-based version easier to use. PUTTAPITHAKPORN observes students using ERIC on SilverPlatter and describes several syntactic and semantic errors and many "inefficiencies" that hinder productivity.

Interface diversity. NELSON & NICHOLLS identify 73 search software packages available in 200 products listed in Bowker's *Optical Publishing Directory 1988*. They compare the five most frequently used packages in terms of simplicity, consistency, speed, error rate, level of help available, and documentation. LI studies the search capabilities and ease of use of 20 CD-ROM systems. Systems vary greatly in ease of use, with the DIALOG products rated highest. There are major differences in use of Boolean operators, in truncation symbols, in limiting searches to a specific field, and in the use of function keys.

KAHN (1988b) studies six CD-ROM interfaces in terms of browsing, using menus, refining a search, accessing online versions of the databases, and printing and saving results. He concludes that CD-

ROM interfaces should make greater use of current interface design techniques, including graphical displays, windows, and pointing devices. PETERS also suggests that graphics will increase user acceptance of CD-ROM systems. These assertions are surprising given the general lack of understanding of how these techniques affect user performance, especially information retrieval.

BONHAM & NELSON compare four MEDLINE CD-ROM products and find that regardless of interface, users need to learn basic retrieval techniques and MeSH (Medical Subject Headings) vocabulary. WOODSMALL ET AL. provide a review of the evaluation of seven versions of MEDLINE on CD-ROM.

Standard interfaces from different CD-ROM producers seem to be an idea whose time has not yet come, and changes in technology coupled with attempts to achieve market advantage may outpace attempts at standardization. ROSEN suggests ways to ease the task of adjusting to various interfaces, including ready access to keyboard templates, "quick access" help cards, selection of systems with similar interfaces, and encouraging database producers to put their products on the interfaces that are most intuitive. The Library and Information Technology Association of the American Library Association has established a CD-ROM Consistent Interface Committee (CD-CINC), which identifies, names, and provides conceptual definitions for 13 basic functions in user interaction with CD-ROM systems (LIBRARY AND INFORMATION TECHNOLOGY ASSOCIATION (LITA). CD-ROM CONSISTENT INTERFACE COMMITTEE (CD-CINC)):

Top level functions
    Help (show explanatory information)
    Browse index (show terms in indexes)
    Search (look for information that satisfies a search statement)
    Display (show information on screen)
    Print (direct output to hardcopy device)
    Download (direct output to electronic media)
    Restart (go to beginning of application)
    Change (change discs or databases)
    Quit (end the application)
Operational functions
    Execute (alert application to begin processing)
    Break (interrupt an activity in program)
    Escape (back up one step at a time)
Navigational functions
    Navigation (movement within a database or search set)

Graphics. There have been some efforts to take advantage of CD-ROM's ability to store more than textual information. The BiblioFile Intelligent Catalog interface was an early attempt, with a subject search function that presented a spinning globe and allowed the user to zoom in to the "atomic" level or zoom out into the "universe" (HARRISON & MURPHY). The recent introduction of Compton's Multimedia Encyclopedia on CD-ROM makes major advances on this approach. The encyclopedia offers eight "entry paths" and includes 15,000 illustrations, 45 animated sequences, and 60 minutes of sound. For example, one can look up birds and see a full-color picture of a robin while listening to bird sounds (FRANKLIN).

Online Catalogs

MITEV looks at online public access catalogs (OPACs) as information retrieval mechanisms for the casual user. She summarizes research on human–computer interaction that can be used in the design and study of online catalogs. In their chapter on "User-System Interaction," ALURI ET AL. provide a useful review of how "friendliness" might be assessed in online catalogs. The article by TAGUE, "Negotiation at the OPAC Interface," is another recent review that emphasizes online catalogs and their human–computer interfaces. FOKKER also stresses a user orientation in online catalog design.

Historically, the Online Catalog Public Access Project, funded by the Council on Library Resources (CLR) in the early 1980s, provided an excellent overview of the status of online catalogs at that time (MATTHEWS ET AL.). While the project researchers lamented the problems associated with studying systems that are under constant modification, their reports laid the ground work for studying online catalogs.

In *Online Public Access Catalogs: The User Interface,* HILDRETH (1982) reviews and compares ten online catalog systems. He is optimistic that the then-current diversity of online catalog systems will encourage comparison and research that will yield empirical data and eventually optimal user interfaces. For this comparison he adapts the draft ANSI standard for information retrieval command languages to permit general comparison of the systems in terms of operational control, search formulation control, access points, output control, and user assistance, information, and instruction. Later HILDRETH (1985) reviews and summarizes the development of online catalogs for *ARIST.* His chapter closes with a list of research and design challenges, notably the need for more natural, helpful, and adaptive user-system interfaces.

BILLS & HELGERSON provide a thorough comparison of user interfaces for six online catalog products on CD-ROM; comparisons are made on the basis of basic screen design, user commands, and online user aids.

Mode of interaction.   In comparing the interfaces for seven academic institutions, one public library district, and two bibliographic utilities, HILDRETH (1982) finds that the menu/command distinction does not suffice to characterize the interfaces; he proposes a new classification for human–computer dialog: the computer-initiated/guided mode, which uses "directive prompts" and is generally characterized by simple instruction, menu selection, question/answer, and form filling. The user-initiated/guided mode employs, for example, simple queries, formatted queries, and ordinary-language queries. Of the ten systems reviewed, nine use user-initiated interaction as the primary interface; only three offer menu selection as supplementary modes, an approach seen as particularly helpful, as noted above.

EDMONDS ET AL. observe elementary school students using a CLSI (CL Systems, Inc.) touch-screen catalog. The interface requires selection of the term alphabetically preceding the term sought, meaning that the students have to perform "mental reverse alphabetization." While the students understand the concepts underlying such access and can generally find items in the card catalog, the younger ones in particular have limited success with the online catalog.

The development of the Okapi online catalog at the Polytechnic of Central London is summarized by WALKER. Okapi's evolution includes comparative evaluations using observed searches and interviews. Among the findings: users prefer an initial menu with several search mode options (e.g., searching by author, title, subject) rather than the "specific books/books about something" dichotomy, and they prefer full record displays but also want "everything on one screen" (bibliographic and location information). When GELLER & LESK compare users of an online catalog with users of a newswire service, they find that the relatively constant structure of the online catalog menu access is unnecessarily time consuming; however, in the rapidly changing current-events system, the menu provides valuable context to give the user an idea of the topics available.

Research questions. MATTHEWS & LAWRENCE report that the online catalog interfaces are generally well received by users in 13 libraries where surveys were conducted. User attitudes are grouped into seven categories, and each factor is tested for its correlation with user success. The only factor that correlates with user success across the different online catalogs is the "searching by subject."

Systems that automatically display subject headings before showing specific records are more effective than those that do not; user impatience is also reduced with these systems.

FAYEN notes that interface complexity increases both with the number of programs or modules in the interface and with the number of potential users anticipated for it. She suggests several research topics on screen design in general and for online catalogs in particular (p. 58):

- When specifying a menu choice, should the action precede or follow the explanation in the display? E.g.,

  "Type A"   "To search for an author"
  or
  "To search for an author Type A"

- What is the best place on the screen to use for error messages (if any)?
- Highlighting seems to be effective if not overused. How is it best employed?
- What about color displays? Is color just a frill? Does it have any value besides novelty?
- What indicators on the screen (e.g., leader dots, dashes, arrows, blank space) work best to connect menu choices with the appropriate actions?
- How is white space best used?
- What is the best way to handle a menu or screen display that is too big to fit on one screen?

Among the specific questions for online catalogs (p. 58-59):

- In what order should bibliographic records appear? Should it be the same for staff and for public users?
- What fields or data should appear for each bibliographic record? Should there be a default which users may change?
- What techniques work best to help users whose search strategy nets too few results or too many?
- How can one determine if a search that results in no hits represents a failure of the system or a failure of the database? [It should also be noted that a search with no hits may not be a failure at all.]

- What is the best way to explain the basic idea of retrieval sets to library users?

MATTHEWS suggests guidelines for screen layouts and design of
online catalogs according to current understanding of how online
catalogs are used. He sees a need for uniformity in labels, general text,
instructional text, and screen layouts. A standard nomenclature is
required to promote the use of names for bibliographic information in
ways that are most familiar to library patrons. He also encourages
research into which bibliographic elements users need and in what
sequence.

Special features, LYNCH (1987) discusses the potential addition of
algorithms to refine a search that yields thousands of hits or one with
zero results. He notes the importance of keeping the additional features
compatible with the existing interface and of telling the user what is
being done to "interpret" the query. As heuristics become more capable,
Lynch fears that users may rely on automated retrieval rather than
conduct informed searches.

The prospect of a direct manipulation interface for the library
catalog is intriguing. CHIANG compares this approach with menu-
selection and command-mode interfaces. She notes that direct manipulation techniques can overcome conceptual problems such as
database scope and access points, as well as mechanical problems
such as typographical errors, misspellings, and syntax difficulties.
LARSON discusses the value of rapid prototyping of direct manipulation front ends for online catalogs. The Book House database for
fiction uses icons to represent user category (child or adult), search
strategy (analytical search, search by analogy, or browsing), and
book subject (PEJTERSEN & GOODSTEIN).

Several libraries have created HyperCard library orientation tours,
and a few hypertext interfaces to online catalogs have been developed.
CHIANG & ENG report on a HyperCard front end for NOTIS
(Northwestern Online Total Integrated System) at Cornell University;
CASE & BORGMAN describe a similar approach to "hiding" the
native Orion catalog interface at UCLA. BORGMAN ET AL. (1989b)
describe the development of an interface using categories created by
children to develop menu structures. They find that if the children
can understand the words, they are generally able to categorize
them in a hierarchy. Subsequently BORGMAN ET AL. (1990) describe
use of the Dewey Decimal classification as the basis for a catalog
browsing structure implemented in HyperCard. Several projects
supported under the Apple Library of Tomorrow equipment grant
program include HyperCard or Macintosh front ends for library

catalogs (AMERICAN LIBRARIES). LIBLAB's HYPERCATalog brings the traditional library catalog into the age of hypertext and hyperdocuments. HJERPPE discusses the evolution of technology, documents, and access mechanisms that led to the HYPERCATalog, which is envisioned as connecting hyperdocuments and hypermedia.

SHAW & CULKIN describe extensions of the online catalog beyond traditional monographic and bibliographic data. DEBUSE and KOENIG suggest the inclusion of user-supplied data that evaluates items in the library's databases, what Koenig calls "online marginalia," as an aid to assessing the authoritativeness or relevance of library holdings. ACHLEITNER & WYATT explore potential implications of the emerging paradigms of information.

Full-Text Databases

DETEMPLE discusses potential developments in full-text databases, including host-based menu front ends, gateways and mailbox services, and microcomputer-based front-end software with expert systems for online retrieval and post-processing of downloaded search results.

Mode of interaction. KOVED & SHNEIDERMAN compare embedded vs. explicit menus for the TIES (The Interactive Encyclopedia System) online encyclopedia. With embedded menus, the selection and information display are integrated, users are able to answer more questions correctly, and fewer screens are consulted for each question; in addition, the subjects prefer embedded menus. As part of their evaluation of selection devices for an electronic encyclopedia, OSTROFF & SHNEIDERMAN review research on selection devices, noting that the touch screen has been found to be fastest in all trials in which it is included. Their study also finds the touch screen to be faster than arrow-jump keys, a jump-mouse, or number keys. The touch screen is also the least accurate selection device but still the favorite among study participants.

A specifically hypertext approach is taken with the Dynamic Medical Handbook Project (FRISSE). Limitations of the interface for the prototype lead to the observation that people interact with books in many ways beyond straight reading. To accommodate these uses, medical hypermedia should support easy-to-use mechanisms for highlighting and annotation, page flipping, query tracing and trail marking for future reference, a "smart bookmark" to reorient the reader and help cope with frequent interruptions that characterize medical life, a clipboard to serve as the electronic equivalent of the photocopy machine, and an "agenda keeper" to note future reading plans.

Comparison with hard copy. JOSEPH ET AL. compare print and online versions of an army manual. They find that new users rely on the table of contents and index, but after some experience most users prefer the keyword search mechanism. A tree-structured menu based on the manual's table of contents is effective only if the user is familiar with the print version. KOVED & SHNEIDERMAN analyze searches of an online maintenance manual using embedded menus. With this database it is necessary to add a "pruner" to trim irrelevant text. With this addition the embedded-menu approach allows searchers to find answers in less than half the time required by the traditional interface.

MARCHIONINI (1989a; 1989b) observes high school students using a printed encyclopedia and its equivalent full-text database. The students' ability to transfer from the printed to the online format is generally satisfactory; only a few develop distinct mental models of the electronic encyclopedia and use its special features. Problems with display methods are noted—for example, only a limited amount of text can be displayed on-screen, and the display starts in the first paragraph that contains search terms rather than at the beginning of the article; this feature causes many readers to skip the beginning paragraphs of an article. Searches in the electronic encyclopedia take twice as long as those in the print equivalent. MARCHIONINI & TEAGUE observe gifted and talented elementary school students using an online encyclopedia. The students make few typing errors but experience some "menu floundering"—i.e., trouble moving efficiently between menu options. The authors suggest that efficient menu traversal may require spatial visualization skills that some students have not yet developed.

EDYBURN studies how students with and without learning handicaps use a print encyclopedia, an electronic encyclopedia with a menu-based interface, and an electronic encyclopedia with a command-mode interface. He finds comparable rates of success with the print and menu-based encyclopedias, while the command-mode system significantly impairs retrieval. Reference skills and keyboarding ability are positively correlated with retrieval success, while there is no correlation between IQ or spelling ability and successful searches. Students with learning handicaps are significantly more positive about all three forms of encyclopedia than are the nonhandicapped students.

Standards, Guidelines, and Evaluation

Increasing use of electronic sources of information generates more contact with system interfaces. The diversity of user experience, user expectations, and overall "look and feel" of a system have led more than one writer to refer to the situation as a Tower of Babel.

SHNEIDERMAN (1990) emphasizes the importance of copyright or similar protection for the intellectual effort invested in interface design. He also suggests that excellent interfaces be recognized with an equivalent of the Emmy award or Pulitzer prize.

LINDEMAN (1989a) notes that standards and guidelines can reduce diversity and promote application of research results and insight from the experiences of others. On the other hand, diversity implies competition and hence the opportunity for the "best" interface(s) to emerge. HILDRETH (1982) hoped that the competition among online catalog interfaces would encourage comparison and research leading to the development of optimal interfaces. Almost a decade later variety abounds in OPAC interfaces, and users are likely to encounter more of these differences as computer networking extends access well beyond the local community.

LYNCH (1989) discusses some limitations of the ANSI Z39.50 Information Retrieval Protocol Standard, specifically noting that interfaces that are outside the protocol as well as those that are more sophisticated are not supported by the standard. S.L. SMITH (1986) holds that while standards may be appropriate for hardware design, interface software development will be more effectively assisted by flexible design guidelines.

BROWN provides interface design guidelines for display formats, wording, color, graphics, dialog, data entry, control and display devices, error messages, and online assistance. Guidelines can be used to raise the consciousness of system designers, but eventually an interface is a compromise, and many choices depend on the context in which the interface will be used (S.L. SMITH, 1988). DESOUZA ET AL. note that guidelines are a traditional way to transfer knowledge about human factors to designers, many of whom are not trained in this area. In an intriguing study they conduct a human factors analysis of human factors guidelines and identify various parts of the guidelines for interface design that are not interpreted correctly.

Calling for more research should be considered more than a handy way to conclude an article in this field. The textbooks and many journal articles include extensive literature reviews and attempts to synthesize previous research; SHNEIDERMAN (1987) concludes each chapter of his book with a "practitioner's summary" and a "researcher's agenda." NIELSEN & MOLICH assess the practicality of "heuristic evaluation" of user interfaces, finding that when an individual evaluator is asked to comment on an interface, from 20% to 51% of usability problems previously identified by experts are discovered (e.g., inconsistent use of the "#" key or overwriting search key entered by user). However, when the evaluators' examinations are aggregated, from 71% to 97% of the problems are identified. Nielsen and Molich note that heuristic evaluation is advantageous because it is cheap, intuitive, motivates participants, does not require advance planning, and can be used early in the development process.

For more formal evaluations, TAGUE & SCHULTZ (1988) cite work by G.C. Stevens in their proposed criteria for evaluating user interfaces for information retrieval:

- Length of training time to reach a specified level of competence;
- Number of errors competent users make per unit time of operation;
- Number of exasperation responses;
- Proportion of potential users who can learn in a specified time;
- Number of people who want to use the system;
- Habit-formation rate;
- Proportion of user vocabulary and syntax the system can recognize;
- Proportion of system vocabulary and syntax the user utilizes; and
- Number of system commands issued per unit time.

Several writers in the *Bulletin of the American Society for Information Science* suggest specific topics for research on human–computer interaction. PENNIMAN emphasizes the need for empirical studies and interim guidelines. In the same issue of the *Bulletin* SHNEIDERMAN (1982) calls for controlled, psychologically oriented experiments with evaluation during system development and actual use. Noting the prevalence of case studies in assessing human-computer interaction, MARTIN (1989) proposes that all accounts of such studies report the goals for the system, the characteristics of the user population, and the nature of tasks the system will be used to accomplish. LINDEMAN (1989b) stresses the need to examine the user, the task, the computer system itself, and changes in human-computer interaction as learning occurs.

While there have been empirical studies and development of guidelines since 1982, most work on interfaces for information retrieval has focused on case studies or comparisons of features without controlled observations. General research on interface design has highlighted the importance of testing systems with their intended users. Interfaces proliferate, but the competition has not yet weeded out the unfit. System designers should be encouraged to apply good interface design guidelines. Better guidelines can emerge only as careful research is done and reported and as findings coalesce into useful theories of human–computer interaction.

KEEPING UP WITH THE FIELD

Human–computer interaction is receiving considerable attention in computer science and psychology circles. The Association for Computing Machinery's (ACM) Special Interest Group on Computer and Human Interaction (SIGCHI) *Bulletin* and its annual Conference on Human Factors in Computing Systems are useful sources for reports of current research. *Resources in Human-Computer Interaction* (ACM PRESS) is a useful collection of reviews published since 1982 and bibliographic citations since 1986; indexes provide access by author, keyword subject, and proper noun. Subject areas covered are: user interface design, software development process, user interface design tools, analysis methods, empirical user studies, domain-specific designs, and group work. The proposed Computer Human Factors Information Service, with its interface designed "according to human factors principles" may be a useful source as well (PHILLIPS).

User interface issues related to information retrieval are also often covered by the library and information science abstracting and indexing services, especially *Library Literature* and *Library and Information Science Abstracts*. The Educational Resources Information Center (ERIC) provides access to fugitive materials, often with quite informative abstracts. The American Society for Information Science (ASIS) Special Interest Group on Human-Computer Interaction (SIG/HCI) and the Human/Machine Interfaces and Online Catalogs Interest Group of the American Library Association's Library and Information Technology Association have also presented programs in this area. As the importance of interface design becomes increasingly apparent, we should expect even more attention to the dissemination of this information.

The proliferation of terminology will no doubt continue. There seems to be an almost "mix and match" approach to naming this emerging field and its cross- and subdisciplines. Terms encountered in preparing this review include: cognitive engineering, cognitive ergonomics, computer–human interaction/interface (CHI), convivial computing, cooperative interface, human–computer interaction/interface (HCI), person–machine interface, software ergonomics, usability engineering, user friendly/cordial/oriented/centered, and user interface. While annoying, this proliferation attests to the vitality of the field.

At the 1990 CHI conference, significantly titled "Empowering People," DERTOUZOS urged that interfaces be "smarter so that they can anticipate even small portions of our intent, instead of brutally forcing us through a litany of repetitive and dumb rituals" (p. 1). While some promising first steps toward smarter interfaces have emerged, we find major gaps and inconsistencies in our understanding of how and why human–computer interfaces work. The sometimes heated disagreements about the benefits of graphic user interfaces and command–mode interaction may reflect basic differences in cognitive style as well as differences in hand–eye coordination and previous experience. More and careful studies are needed to clarify the interactions among users, tasks, and systems. The research reviewed here offers intriguing and at times contradictory findings. Insights and techniques from a variety of disciplines can help explore these opportunities to develop better, smarter interfaces. Surely by the time human–computer interfaces for information retrieval are next reviewed in *ARIST* there will be major progress to report.

BIBLIOGRAPHY

ACHLEITNER, HERBERT K.; WYATT, ROGER B.   1989.   The Post-Hegelian Dialectic: New Paradigm Applications and Transmedia Technology.   Paper presented at: American Society for Information Science 18th Mid-Year Meeting; 1989 May 21-24; San Diego, CA. 15p.   Available from: Herbert K. Achleitner, School of Library and Information Management, 1200 Commercial, Emporia State University, Emporia KS 66801-5087.

ACM PRESS. 1991.   Resources in Human-Computer Interaction.   New York, NY: ACM Press; 1991.   1197p.   ISBN: 0-89791-373-6; LC: 90-1108.

ALLEN, BRYCE. 1991.   Cognitive Research in Information Science: Implications for Design.   In: Williams, Martha E., ed.   Annual Review of Information Science and Technology: Volume 26. Medford, NJ: Learned Information, Inc. for the American Society for Information Science; 1991. 3-37.   ISSN: 0066-4200;   ISBN: 0-938734-55-5;   LC: 66-25096; CODEN: ARISBC.

ALLEN, ROBERT B.   1983.   Cognitive Factors in the Use of Menus and Trees: An Experiment.   IEEE Journal on Selected Areas in Communications. 1983 February; 1(2): 333-336.   ISSN: 0733-8716.

ALURI, RAO; KEMP, D. ALASDAIR; BOLL, JOHN J.   1991.   Subject Analysis in Online Catalogs.   Englewood, CO: Libraries Unlimited; 1991.   303p.   ISBN: 0-87287-670-5; LC: 90-49786..

AMERICAN LIBRARIES. 1990. Other Apple Library of Tomorrow 1989 Contest Winners. American Libraries. 1990 November; 21(10): 1000. ISSN: 0002-9769.

ANICK, PETER G.; BRENNAN, JEFFREY D.; FLYNN, REX A.; HANSSEN, DAVID R.; ALVEY, BRYAN; ROBBINS, JEFFREY M. 1990. A Direct Manipulation Interface for Boolean Information Retrieval via Natural Language Query. In: Vidick, Jean-Luc, ed. Proceedings of the 13th International Conference on Research and Development in Information Retrieval; 1990 September 5-7; Brussels, Belgium. New York, NY: Association for Computing Machinery; 1990. 135-150. ISBN: 0-89791-408-2.

AREND, UDO; MUTHIG, KLAUS-PETER; WANDMACHER, JENS. 1987. Evidence for Global Feature Superiority in Menu Selection by Icons. Behaviour & Information Technology (England). 1987 October-December; 6(4): 411-426. ISSN: 0144-929X.

BAECKER, RONALD M.; BUXTON, WILLIAM A.S., eds. 1987. Readings in Human-Computer Interaction: A Multidisciplinary Approach. Los Altos, CA: Morgan Kaufmann Publishers, Inc.; 1987. 738p. ISBN: 0-934613-24-9; LC: 87-12512.

BATES, MARCIA J. 1986. Subject Access in Online Catalogs: A Design Model. Journal of the American Society for Information Science. 1986 November; 37(6): 357-376. ISSN: 0002-8231; CODEN: AISJB6.

BILLINGSLEY, PATRICIA A. 1988. Taking Panes: Issues in the Design of Windowing Systems. See reference: HELANDER, MARTIN, ed. 413-436.

BILLS, LINDA G.; HELGERSON, LINDA W. 1988. User Interfaces for CD-ROM PACs. Library Hi Tech. 1988; 6(2): 73-113. ISSN: 0737-8831.

BØDKER, SUSANNE. 1991. Through the Interface: A Human Activity Approach to User Interface Design. Hillsdale, NJ: Lawrence Erlbaum Associates, Inc.; 1991. 186p. ISBN: 0-8058-0570-2; LC: 90-36038.

BOLC, LEONARD; JARKE, MATTHIAS, eds. 1986. Cooperative Interfaces to Information Systems. New York, NY: Springer-Verlag; 1986. 328p. ISBN: 0-387-16599-1.

BONHAM, MIRIAM D.; NELSON, LAURIE L. 1988. An Evaluation of Four End-User Systems for Searching MEDLINE. Bulletin of the Medical Library Association. 1988 April; 76(2): 171-180. ISSN: 0025-7338.

BOOTH, PAUL A. 1989. An Introduction to Human-Computer Interaction. Hillsdale, NJ: Lawrence Erlbaum Associates, Inc.; c1989. 268p. ISBN: 0-86377-122-X.

BORGMAN, CHRISTINE L.; CASE, DONALD O.; MEADOW, CHARLES T. 1989a. The Design and Evaluation of a Front-End Interface for Energy Researchers. Journal of the American Society for Information Science. 1989 March; 40(2): 99-109. ISSN: 0002-8231; CODEN: AISJB6.

BORGMAN, CHRISTINE L.; CHIGNELL, MARK H.; VALDEZ, FELIX. 1989b. Designing an Information Retrieval Interface Based on Children's

Categorization of Knowledge: A Pilot Study. In: Katzer, Jeffrey; Newby, Gregory B., eds. ASIS '89: Managing Information and Technology: Proceedings of the American Society for Information Science (ASIS) 52nd Annual Meeting: Volume 26; 1989 October 30-November 2; Washington, DC. Medford, NJ: Learned Information, Inc. for ASIS; 1989. 81-95. ISSN: 0044-7870; ISBN: 0-938734-40-7; CODEN: PAISDQ; LC: 64-8303.

BORGMAN, CHRISTINE L.; GALLAGHER, ANDREA L.; KRIEGER, DAVID; BOWER, JAMES. 1990. Children's Use of an Interactive Catalog of Science Materials. In: Henderson, Diane, ed. ASIS '90: Information in the Year 2000: From Research to Applications: Proceedings of the American Society for Information Science (ASIS) 53rd Annual Meeting: Volume 27; 1990 November 4-8; Toronto, Canada. Medford, NJ: Learned Information, Inc. for ASIS; 1990. 55-68. ISSN: 0044-7870; ISBN: 0-938734-48-2; CODEN: PAISDQ; LC: 64-8303.

BROWN, C. MARLIN "LIN." 1988. Human-Computer Interaction Design Guidelines. Norwood, NJ: Ablex Publishing Co.; 1988. 236p. ISBN: 0-89391-332-4; LC: 87-14473.

BURGESS, CLIFFORD; SWIGGER, KATHLEEN. 1986. A Graphical Database Interface for Casual, Naive Users. Information Processing & Management. 1986; 22(6): 511-521. ISSN: 0306-4573; CODEN: IPMADK.

CANTER, D.; POWELL, J.; WISHART, J.; RODERICK, C. 1986. User Navigation in Complex Database Systems. Behaviour & Information Technology (England). 1986 July-September; 5(3): 249-257. ISSN: 0144-929X.

CARD, STUART K.; MORAN, THOMAS P.; NEWELL, ALLEN. 1983. The Psychology of Human-Computer Interaction. Hillsdale, NJ: Lawrence Erlbaum Associates; 1983. ISBN: 0-89859-243-7; LC: 82-21045.

CASE, DONALD; BORGMAN, CHRISTINE L. 1989. Orion Online Catalog Interface. See reference: DILLON, MARTIN, ed. 32.

CHIANG, DUDEE. 1989. Comparison of Direct Manipulation, Menu Selection, and Command Language as Interaction Styles for Online Public Access Catalogs. See reference: DILLON, MARTIN, ed. 1.

CHIANG, KATHERINE; ENG, WING. 1989. Library Interfaces: NOTIS and Beyond. See reference: DILLON, MARTIN, ed. 5.

CHIGNELL, MARK H. 1990. Taxonomy of User Interface Terminology. SIGCHI Bulletin. 1990 April; 21(4): 27-34. ISSN: 0736-6906; CODEN: SGBUD4; OCLC: 8814572.

CHIN, JOHN P.; DIEHL, VIRGINIA A.; NORMAN, KENT L. 1988. Development of an Instrument Measuring User Satisfaction of the Human-Computer Interface. In: Soloway, Elliot; Frye, Douglas; Sheppard, Sylvia B., eds. Human Factors in Computing Systems CHI '88: Proceedings of the Association for Computing Machinery's Special Interest Group on Computer and Human Interaction (ACM/SIGCHI); 1988 May 15-19; Washington, DC. New York, NY: ACM Press; 1988. 213-218. ISBN: 0-89791-265-9; LC: 90-205485; ACM order no. 608880; OCLC: 18386652.

CHRISTIE, BRUCE. 1982. Psychology at the User-System Interface. In: Proceedings of the 6th International Online Information Meeting; 1982 December 7-9; London, England. Oxford, England: Learned Information; 1982. 39-47. ISBN: 0-90493-3339-3; LC: 84-114023; OCLC: 9589853.

CRAWFORD, R.G.; BECKER, H.S. 1986. A Novice User's Interface to Information Retrieval Systems. Information Processing & Management. 1986; 22(4): 287-298. ISSN: 0306-4573; CODEN: IPMADK.

CRAWFORD, R.G.; EDWARDS, MARY ELLEN. 1985. A Prototype Mouse-Based Interface to Drug-Related Information. Online Review. 1985 December; 9(6): 471-487. ISSN: 0309-314X.

DAVIS, CHARLES H.; SHAW, DEBORA. 1989. Comparison of Retrieval System Interfaces Using an Objective Measure of Screen Design Effectiveness. Library and Information Science Research. 1989 October-December; 11(4): 325-334. ISSN: 0740-8188.

DE WEERT, CHARLES M.M. 1988. The Use of Color in Visual Displays. See reference: VAN DER VEER, GERRITT C.; MULDER, GIJSBERTUS, eds. 26-40.

DEBUSE, RAYMOND. 1988. So That's a Book... Advancing Technology and the Library. Information Technology and Libraries. 1988 March; 7(1): 7-18. ISSN: 0730-9295.

DERTOUZOS, MICHAEL L. 1990. Redefining Tomorrow's User Interface. In: Chew, Jane Carrasco; Whiteside, John, eds. Empowering People: CHI '90 Conference Proceedings of the Association for Computing Machinery's Special Interest Group on Computer and Human Interaction (ACM/SIGCHI); 1990 April 1-5; Seattle, WA. New York, NY: ACM; 1990. 1. ISBN: 0-89791-345-0; ACM order no.: 608900.

DESOUZA, F.L.; LONG, J.B.; BEVAN, N. 1990. Types of Error and Difficulty in Using the Human-Factors Guidelines: The Case of Interface Menu Design. In: Lovesey, E.J., ed. Contemporary Ergonomics 1990: Proceedings of the Ergonomics Society's 1990 Annual Conference; 1990 April 3-6; Leeds, England. London, England: Taylor & Francis; 1990. 340-346. ISSN: 0267-4718; ISBN: 0-85066-851-4.

DETEMPLE, WENDELIN. 1989. Future Enhancements for Full Text Databases. Online Review. 1989 April; 13(2): 155-160. ISSN: 0309-314X.

DILLON, MARTIN, ed. 1989. The User Interface: Abstracts of Papers: American Society for Information Science (ASIS) 18th Mid-Year Meeting; 1989 May 21-24; San Diego, CA. Washington, DC: ASIS; 1989. 48p.

DRENTH, HILARY; MORRIS, ANNE; TSENG, GWYNETH. 1991. Expert Systems as Information Intermediaries. In: Williams, Martha E., ed. Annual Review of Information Science and Technology: Volume 26. Medford, NJ: Learned Information, Inc. for the American Society for Information Science; 1991. 113-154. ISSN: 0066-4200; ISBN: 0-938734-55-5; LC: 66-25096; CODEN: ARISBC.

ECHEVERRÍA, LUZ E.; PINO, JOSÉ A. 1989. An Intuitive Approach for the Expression of Boolean Queries. In: IEEE Workshop on Visual

Languages; 1989 October 4-6; Rome, Italy. Washington, DC: IEEE
Computer Society Press; 1989. 118-123. ISBN: 0-8186-2002-1; LC: 89-
46047.

EDMONDS, LESLIE; MOORE, PAULA; BALCOLM, KATHLEEN
MEHAFFEY. 1989. An Investigation of the Effectiveness of an Online
Catalog in Providing Bibliographic Access to Children in a Public
Library Setting. Research Report, 1986 Carroll Preston Baber Award.
Urbana, IL: University of Illinois; 1989. 2 microfiche; 98p.; 24X reduc-
tion. Available from: ERIC Document Reproduction Service. ERIC: ED-
311921.

EDYBURN, DAVE LEE. 1987. An Evaluation of the Information Retrieval
Skills of Students with and without Learning Handicaps Using Printed
and Electronic Encyclopedias. Urbana, IL: University of Illinois; 1987.
259p. (Ph.D. dissertation). Available from: University Microfilms
International (UM order no. 88-03029).

ELKERTON, JAY. 1988. Online Aiding for Human-Computer Interfaces.
See reference: HELANDER, MARTIN, ed. 345-364.

ELKERTON, JAY; PALMITER, SUSAN. 1989. Designing Help Systems
Using a GOMS Model: Part 1: An Information Retrieval Evaluation.
Ann Arbor, MI: Center for Ergonomics, College of Engineering, University of Michigan; 1989. 62p. (Technical Report C4E-ONR-3). Available
from: College of Engineering, University of Michigan, Ann Arbor, MI.

ELKERTON, JAY; WILLIGES, ROBERT C. 1984. Information Retrieval
Strategies in a File-Search Environment. Human Factors. 1984 April;
26(2): 171-184. ISSN: 0018-7208; CODEN: HUFAA6.

ENGEL, F.L.; ANDRIESSEN, J.J.; SCHMITZ, H.J. 1983. What, Where
and Whence: Means for Improving Electronic Data Access. International Journal of Man-Machine Studies. 1983 February; 18(2): 145-
159. ISSN: 0020-7373; CODEN: IJMMBC.

FAYEN, EMILY GALLUP. 1987. User Interfaces for Online Catalogs. In:
Lancaster, F. Wilfrid, ed. What Is User Friendly?: Papers Presented at
the 23rd Clinic on Library Applications of Data Processing; 1986 April
20-22; Urbana, IL. Urbana, IL: Graduate School of Library and Information Science, University of Illinois at Urbana-Champaign; 1987. 52-
60. ISSN: 0069-4789; ISBN: 0-87845-072-6.

FIELD, G.E.; APPERLEY, M.D. 1990. Context and Selective Retreat in
Hierarchical Menu Structures. Behaviour & Information Technology
(England). 1990 March-April; 9(2): 133-146. ISSN: 0144-929X.

FISCHHOFF, BARUCH; MACGREGOR, DONALD; BLACKSHAW, LYN.
1987. Creating Categories for Databases. International Journal of
Man-Machine Studies. 1987 July; 27(1): 33-63. ISSN: 0020-7373;
CODEN: IJMMBC.

FISHER, DONALD L.; COURY, BRUCE G.; TENGS, TAMMY O.; DUFFY,
SUSAN A. 1989. Minimizing the Time to Search Visual Displays: The
Role of Highlighting. Human Factors. 1989 April; 31(2): 167-182.
ISSN: 0018-7208; CODEN: HUFAA6.

FISHER, DONALD L.; TAN, KAY C. 1989. Visual Displays: The Highlight-
    ing Paradox. Human Factors. 1989 February; 31(1): 17-30. ISSN:
    00187208; CODEN: HUFAA6.
FOKKER, DIRK W. 1989. Requirements for a User-Friendly OPAC.
    Electronic Library. 1989 February; 7(1): 4-10. ISSN: 0264-0473.
FOX, EDWARD A. 1988. Optical Disks and CD-ROM: Publishing and
    Access. In: Williams, Martha E., ed. Annual Review of Information
    Science and Technology: Volume 23. Amsterdam, The Netherlands:
    Elsevier Science Publishers for the American Society for Information
    Science; 1988. 85-124. ISSN: 0066-4200; ISBN: 0-444-70543-0; LC: 66-
    25096; CODEN: ARISBC.
FRANKLIN, CARL. 1989. Hypertext Gets Practical. In: Online '89:
    Proceedings of the Online Inc. Conference; 1989 November 7-9; Chi-
    cago, IL. Weston, CT: Online, Inc.; 1989. 70-73. ISSN: 1051-9890;
    OCLC: 20720710.
FRISSE, MARK E. 1988. Searching for Information in a Hypertext Medical
    Handbook. Communications of the ACM. 1988 July; 31(7): 880-886.
    ISSN: 0001-0782.
GALITZ, WILBERT O. 1989. Handbook of Screen Format Design. 3rd
    edition. Wellesley, MA: QED Information Sciences, Inc.; 1989. 307p.
    ISBN: 0-89435-258-X; LC: 88-15849.
GARG-JANARDAN, CHAYA; SALVENDY, GAVRIEL. 1986. The Contri-
    bution of Cognitive Engineering to the Effective Design and Use of
    Information Systems. Information Services and Use. 1986; 6(5/6): 235-
    252. ISSN: 0167-5265.
GELLER, V.J.; LESK, M.E. 1983. User Interfaces to Information Systems:
    Choices vs. Commands. In: Kuehn, Jennifer J., ed. Proceedings of the
    Association for Computing Machinery Special Interest Group on Infor-
    mation Retrieval (ACM SIGIR) 6th Annual International Conference
    on Research and Development in Information Retrieval; 1983 June 6-8;
    Bethesda, MD. New York, NY: ACM; 1983. 130-135. ISBN: 0-89791-
    107-5; ACM order number: 606830.
GOMOLL, KATHLEEN. 1990. Some Techniques for Observing Users. In:
    Laurel, Brenda, ed. The Art of Human-Computer Interface Design.
    Reading, MA: Addison-Wesley; 1990. 85-90. ISBN: 0-201-51797-3; LC:
    90-34470.
GUINDON, RAYMONDE, ed. 1988. Cognitive Science and Its Applications
    for Human-Computer Interaction. Hillsdale, NJ: Lawrence Erlbaum
    Associates; 1988. 338p. ISBN: 0-89859-884-2; LC: 87-36523.
HANCOCK, P.A.; CHIGNELL, MARK H., eds. 1989. Intelligent Inter-
    faces: Theory, Research and Design. Amsterdam, The Netherlands:
    Elsevier Science Publishers; 1989. 390p. ISBN: 0-444-87313-9; LC:
    88-36512.
HARRISON, NANCY; MURPHY, BROWER. 1987. Multisensory Public
    Access Catalogs on CD-ROM. Library Hi Tech. 1987 Fall; 5(3): 77-80.
    ISSN: 0737-8831.

HARTSON, H. REX; HIX, DEBORAH. 1989. Human-Computer Interface Development: Concepts and Systems for Its Management. ACM Computing Surveys. 1989 March; 21(1): 5-92. ISSN: 0360-0300.

HELANDER, MARTIN, ed. 1988. Handbook of Human-Computer Interaction. Amsterdam, The Netherlands: North-Holland; 1988. 1167p. ISBN: 0-444-70536-8; LC: 88-25981.

HILDRETH, CHARLES R. 1982. Online Public Access Catalogs: The User Interface. Dublin, OH: OCLC, Inc.; c1982. 263p. ISBN: 0-933418-34-5; LC: 82-8224.

HILDRETH, CHARLES R. 1985. Online Public Access Catalogs. In: Williams, Martha E., ed. Annual Review of Information Science and Technology: Volume 20. White Plains, NY: Knowledge Industry Publications, Inc. for the American Society for Information Science; 1985. 233-285. ISSN: 0066-4200; ISBN: 0-86729-175-3; LC: 66-25096; CODEN: ARISBC.

HILDRETH, CHARLES R., ed. 1989. The Online Catalogue: Developments and Directions. London, England: The Library Association; 1989. 212p. ISBN: 0-85365-708-4.

HJERPPE, ROLAND. 1989. HYPERCAT at LIBLAB in Sweden: A Progress Report. In: Hildreth, Charles R., ed. The Online Catalogue: Developments and Directions. London, England: The Library Association; 1989. 177-209. ISBN: 0-85365-708-4.

HOLLANDS, J.G.; MERIKLE, PHILIP M. 1987. Menu Organization and User Expertise in Information Search Tasks. Human Factors. 1987 October; 29(5): 577-586. ISSN: 0018-7208; CODEN: HUFAA6.

JACOB, ROBERT J.K. 1989. Direct Manipulation in the Intelligent Interface. In: Hancock, P.A.; Chignell, Mark H., eds. Intelligent Interfaces: Theory, Research and Design. Amsterdam, The Netherlands: Elsevier Science Publishers; 1989. 165-212. ISBN: 0-444-87313-9.

JONES, RICHARD M. 1989. Online Catalogue Research in Europe. Journal of the American Society for Information Science. 1989 May; 40(3): 153-157. ISSN: 0002-8231; CODEN: AISJB6.

JORNA, RENÉ. 1988. A Comparison of Presentation and Representation: Linguistic and Pictorial. See reference: VAN DER VEER, GERRITT C.; MULDER, GIJSBERTUS, eds. 172-185.

JOSEPH, BIJU; STEINBERG; ESTHER R.; JONES, A. RUSSELL. 1989. User Perceptions and Expectations of an Information Retrieval System. Behaviour & Information Technology (England). 1989 March-April; 8(2): 77-88. ISSN: 0144-929X.

KAHN, PAUL. 1987. Outline for Research in Large Data Base Resources. Providence, RI: Institute for Research in Information and Scholarship, Brown University; 1987. 1 microfiche; 15p.; 24X reduction. Available from: ERIC Document Reproduction Service. ERIC: ED-296737.

KAHN, PAUL. 1988a. Information Retrieval as Hypermedia: An Outline of InterBrowse. Providence, RI: Brown University; 1988. 1 microfiche; 10p.; 24X reduction. Available from: ERIC Document Reproduction Service. ERIC: ED-298968.

KAHN, PAUL. 1988b. Making a Difference: A Review of the User Interface Features in Six CD-ROM Database Products. Optical Information Systems. 1988 July-August; 8(3): 169-183. ISSN: 0886-5809; CODEN: OISYE4; OCLC: 12930983.

KLEMPERER, KATHARINA. 1987. Common Command Language for Interactive Information Retrieval. Library Hi Tech. 1987 Winter; 5(4): 7-12. ISSN: 0737-8831.

KLOCKE, H.; TRISPEL, S.; RAU, G. 1984. Entwicklung einer Mensch-Rechner Schnittstelle für ein Anästhesie-Informationssystem unter Berücksichtigung ergonomischer Gesichtspunkte [Development of a Human-Computer Interface for an Anaesthesia Information System Considering Ergonomic Aspects]. Angewandte Informatik (Germany). 1984 May; 26(5): 197-208. ISSN: 0013-5704; CODEN: AWIFA7.

KOENIG, MICHAEL E.D. 1990. Linking Library Users: A Culture Change in Librarianship. American Libraries. 1990 October; 21(9): 844-849. ISSN: 0002-9769.

KOVED, LARRY; SHNEIDERMAN, BEN. 1986. Embedded Menus: Selecting Items in Context. Communications of the ACM. 1986 April; 29(4): 312-318. ISSN: 0001-0782; CODEN: CACMA2.

KREIGH, ROBERT J.; PESOT, JOSEPH F.; HALCOMB, CHARLES G. 1990. An Evaluation of Look-Ahead Help Fields on Various Types of Menu Hierarchies. International Journal of Man-Machine Studies. 1990 June; 32(6): 649-661. ISSN: 0020-7373; CODEN: IJMMBC.

LANCASTER, F. WILFRID, ed. 1987. What Is User Friendly?: Papers Presented at the 23rd Clinic on Library Applications of Data Processing; 1986 April 20-22; Urbana, IL. Urbana, IL: Graduate School of Library and Information Science, University of Illinois at Urbana-Champaign; 1987. 128p. ISSN: 0069-4789; ISBN: 0-87845-072-6.

LANCASTER, F. WILFRID; ELLIKER, CALVIN; CONNELL, TSCHERA HARKNESS. 1989. Subject Access. In: Williams, Martha E., ed. Annual Review of Information Science and Technology: Volume 24. Amsterdam, The Netherlands: Elsevier Science Publishers for the American Society for Information Science; 1989. 35-84. ISSN: 0066-4200; ISBN: 0-444-87418-6; LC: 66-25096; CODEN: ARISBC.

LANSDALE, M.W. 1988. On the Memorability of Icons in an Information Retrieval Task. Behaviour & Information Technology (England). 1988 April-June; 7(2): 131-151. ISSN: 0144-929X.

LANSDALE, M.W.; SIMPSON, M.; STROUD, T.R.M. 1990. A Comparison of Words and Icons as External Memory Aids in an Information Retrieval Task. Behaviour & Information Technology (England). 1990 March-April; 9(2): 111-131. ISSN: 0144-929X.

LARSON, RAY R. 1989. Rapid Prototyping and Code Generation for Direct Manipulation Interfaces. See reference: DILLON, MARTIN, ed. 1.

LAUREL, BRENDA, ed. 1990. The Art of Human-Computer Interface Design. Reading, MA: Addison-Wesley; 1990. 523p. ISBN: 0-201-51797-3; LC: 90-34470.

LAVERSON, ALAN; NORMAN, KENT; SHNEIDERMAN, BEN. 1987. An Evaluation of Jump-Ahead Techniques in Menu Selection. Behaviour & Information Technology (England). 1987 April-June; 6(2): 97-108. ISSN: 0144-929X.

LEE, ERIC; MACGREGOR, JAMES. 1985. Minimizing User Search Time in Menu Retrieval Systems. Human Factors. 1985 April; 27(2): 157-162. ISSN: 0018-7208; CODEN: HUFAA6.

LI, TIAN-ZHU. 1989. Generic Approach to CD-ROM Systems: A Formal Analysis of Search Capabilities and Ease of Use. See reference: DILLON, MARTIN, ed. 35.

LIBERATORE, MATTHEW J.; TITUS, GEORGE J.; VARANO, MICHAEL W.; DIXON, PAUL W. 1989. An Experimental Investigation of the Effects of Some Information System Design Variables on Performance, Preference, and Learning. Information Processing & Management. 1989; 25(5): 563-577. ISSN: 0306-4573; CODEN: IPMADK.

LIBRARY AND INFORMATION TECHNOLOGY ASSOCIATION (LITA). CD-ROM CONSISTENT INTERFACE COMMITTEE (CD-CINC). 1991. Report. 1991 April. 27p. Available from: Susan David, Congressional Research Service, Library of Congress, Washington, DC 20540.

LINDE, LENA; WAERN, YVONNE. 1985. On Search in an Incomplete Database. International Journal of Man-Machine Studies. 1985 May; 22(5): 563-579. ISSN: 0020-7373; CODEN: IJMMBC.

LINDEMAN, MARTHA J. 1989a. Beyond Standards and Guidelines. See reference: DILLON, MARTIN, ed. 14.

LINDEMAN, MARTHA J. 1989b. The User Interface. Bulletin of the American Society for Information Science. 1989 April-May; 15(4): 16-17. ISSN: 0095-4403; CODEN: BASICR.

LIPSCOMB, KAREN J.; LYNCH, MICHAEL F.; WILLETT, PETER. 1989. Chemical Structure Processing. In: Williams, Martha E., ed. Annual Review of Information Science and Technology: Volume 24. Amsterdam, The Netherlands: Elsevier Science Publishers for the American Society for Information Science; 1989. 189-238. ISSN: 0066-4200; ISBN: 0-444-87418-6; LC: 66-25096; CODEN: ARISBC.

LYNCH, CLIFFORD A. 1987. The Use of Heuristics in User Interfaces for Online Information Retrieval Systems. In: Chen, Ching-chih, ed. ASIS '87: Information: The Transformation of Society: Proceedings of the American Society for Information Science (ASIS) 50th Annual Meeting; 1987 October 4-8; Boston, MA. Medford, NJ: Learned Information, Inc. for ASIS; 1987. 148-151. ISSN: 0044-7870; ISBN: 0 938734-19-9; LC: 64-8303; CODEN: PAISDQ

LYNCH, CLIFFORD A. 1989. Applications and Limitations of the Z39.50 Information Retrieval Protocol Standard: Can the User Interface and Database Servers Be Separated? See reference: DILLON, MARTIN, ed. 14.

MACGREGOR, DONALD; FISCHHOFF, BARUCH; BLACKSHAW, LYN. 1987. Search Success and Expectations with a Computer Interface.

Information Processing & Management. 1987; 23(5): 419-432. ISSN: 0306-4573; CODEN: IPMADK.

MACGREGOR, JAMES N.; LEE, ERIC S. 1987a. Menu Search: Random or Systematic? International Journal of Man-Machine Studies. 1987 May; 26(5): 627-631. ISSN: 0020-7373; CODEN: IJMMBC.

MACGREGOR, JAMES N.; LEE, ERIC S. 1987b. Performance and Preference in Videotex Menu Retrieval: A Review of the Empirical Literature. Behaviour & Information Technology (England). 1987 January-March; 6(1): 43-68. ISSN: 0144-929X.

MARCHIONINI, GARY. 1989a. Information-Seeking Strategies of Novices Using a Full-Text Electronic Encyclopedia. Journal of the American Society for Information Science. 1989 January; 40(1): 54-66. ISSN: 0002-8231; CODEN: AISJB6.

MARCHIONINI, GARY. 1989b. Making the Transition from Print to Electronic Encyclopedias: Adaptation of Mental Models. International Journal of Man-Machine Studies. 1989 June; 30(6): 591-618. ISSN: 0020-7373.

MARCHIONINI, GARY; TEAGUE, JERRY. 1987. Elementary Students' Use of Electronic Information Services: An Exploratory Study. Journal of Research on Computing in Education. 1987 Winter; 20(2): 139-155. ISSN: 0888-6504; LC: 88-654875; OCLC: 13696457.

MARTIN, THOMAS H. 1988. Office Automation. In: Williams, Martha E., ed. Annual Review of Information Science and Technology: Volume 23. Amsterdam, The Netherlands: Elsevier Science Publishers for the American Society for Information Science; 1988. 217-235. ISSN: 0066-4200; ISBN: 0-444-70543-0; LC: 66-25096; CODEN: ARISBC.

MARTIN, THOMAS H. 1989. Standards for Case Studies in Human-Computer Interaction. Bulletin of the American Society for Information Science. 1989 April-May; 15(4): 19-20. ISSN: 0095-4403; CODEN: BASICR.

MATTHEWS, JOSEPH R. 1987. Suggested Guidelines for Screen Layouts and Design of Online Catalogs. Library Trends. 1987 Spring; 35(4): 555-570. ISSN: 0024-2594.

MATTHEWS, JOSEPH R.; LAWRENCE, GARY S. 1984. Further Analysis of the CLR Online Catalog Project. Information Technology and Libraries. 1984 December; 3(4): 354-376. ISSN: 0730-9295; CODEN: ITLBDC.

MATTHEWS, JOSEPH R.; LAWRENCE, GARY S.; FERGUSON, DOUGLAS, eds. 1983. Using Online Catalogs: A Nationwide Survey. New York, NY: Neal-Schuman; 1983. 255p. ISBN: 0-918212-76-6; LC: 83-8061; OCLC: 9464790.

MATTHEWS, JOSEPH R.; WILLIAMS, JOAN FRYE. 1984. The User Friendly Index: A New Tool. Online. 1984 May; 8(3): 31-34. ISSN: 0146-5422.

MCALEESE, R.; DUNCAN, E.B. 1987. The Graphical Representation of "Terrain" and "Street" Knowledge in an Interface to a Database System. In: Online Information 87: Proceedings of the 11th International

Online Information Meeting; 1987 December 8-10; London, England. Oxford, England: Learned Information; 1987. 443-456. ISBN: 0-904933-62-8.

MCDONALD, JAMES E.; SCHVANEVELDT, ROGER W. 1988. The Application of User Knowledge to Interface Design. In: Guindon, Raymonde, ed. Cognitive Science and Its Applications for Human-Computer Interaction. Hillsdale, NJ: Lawrence Erlbaum Associates; 1988. 289-338. ISBN: 0-89859-884-2; LC: 87-36523. ·

MCMATH, CHARLES F.; TAMARU, ROBERT S.; RADA, ROY. 1989. A Graphical Thesaurus-Based Information Retrieval System. International Journal of Man-Machine Studies. 1989 August; 31(2): 121-147. ISSN: 0020-7373; CODEN: IJMMBC.

MEADOW, CHARLES T.; CERNY, BARBARA A.; BORGMAN, CHRISTINE L.; CASE, DONALD O. 1989. Online Access to Knowledge: System Design. Journal of the American Society for Information Science. 1989 March; 40(2): 86-98. ISSN: 0002-8231; CODEN: AISJB6.

MISCHO, WILLIAM H.; LEE, JOUNGHYOUN. 1987. End-User Searching of Bibliographic Databases. In: Williams, Martha E., ed. Annual Review of Information Science and Technology: Volume 22. Amsterdam, The Netherlands: Elsevier Science Publishers for the American Society for Information Science; 1987. 227-263. ISSN: 0066-4200; ISBN: 0-444-70302-0; LC: 66-25096; CODEN: ARISBC.

MITEV, NATHALIE N. 1989. Ease of Interaction and Retrieval in Online Catalogues: Contributions of Human-Computer Interaction Research. In: Hildreth, Charles R., ed. The Online Catalogue: Developments and Directions. London, England: The Library Association; 1989. 142-176. ISBN: 0-85365-708-4.

NELSON, MICHAEL J.; NICHOLLS, PAUL T. 1989. Evaluation of CD-ROM Interfaces. See reference: DILLON, MARTIN, ed. 11.

NICHOLLS, PAUL TRAVIS. 1989. Information on Disk: An Update. In: Online '89: Proceedings of the Online, Inc. Conference; 1989 November 7-9; Chicago, IL. Weston, CT: Online, Inc.; 1989. 119-121. ISSN: 1051-9890; OCLC: 20720710.

NICHOLLS, PAUL TRAVIS; HAN, ISAAC; STAFFORD, KAREN; WHITRIDGE, KATHERINE. 1990. A Framework for Evaluating CD-ROM Retrieval Software. Laserdisk Professional. 1990 March; 3(2): 41-46. ISSN: 0896-4149.

NIELSEN, JAKOB; MOLICH, ROLF. 1990. Heuristic Evaluation of User Interfaces. In: Chew, Jane Carrasco; Whiteside, John, eds. Empowering People: CHI '90 Conference Proceedings of the Association for Computing Machinery's Special Interest Group on Computer and Human Interaction (ACM/SIGCHI); 1990 April 1-5; Seattle, WA. New York, NY: ACM; 1990. 249-256. ISBN: 0-89791-345-0; ACM order no. 608900.

NOORDMAN, LEO G.M. 1988. Visual Presentation of Text: The Process of Reading from a Psycholinguistic Perspective. See reference: VAN DER VEER, GERRITT C.; MULDER, GIJSBERTUS, eds. 104-124.

NORMAN, DONALD A.; DRAPER, STEPHEN W., eds. 1986. User Centered System Design. Hillsdale, NJ: Lawrence Erlbaum Associates; 1986. ISBN: 0-89859-781-1; LC: 85-25207.

OSTROFF, DANIEL; SHNEIDERMAN, BEN. 1988. Selection Devices for User [sic] of an Electronic Encyclopedia: An Empirical Comparison of Four Possibilities. Information Processing & Management. 1988; 24(6): 665-680. ISSN: 0306-4573; CODEN: IPMADK.

PAAP, KENNETH R.; ROSKE-HOFSTRAND, RENATE J. 1986. The Optimal Number of Menu Options per Panel. Human Factors. 1986 August; 28(4): 377-385. ISSN: 0018-7208; CODEN: HUFAA6.

PAAP, KENNETH R.; ROSKE-HOFSTRAND, RENATE J. 1988. Design of Menus. See reference: HELANDER, MARTIN, ed. 205-235.

PAZ, NOEMI; LEIGH, WILLIAM; YIM, ROGER. 1989. Using Graphical Study Trees to Present HELP Knowledge. Microcomputers for Information Management. 1989 March; 6(1): 47-67. ISSN: 0742-2442.

PEJTERSEN, ANNELISE MARK; GOODSTEIN, L.P. 1990. Beyond the Desktop Metaphor: Information Retrieval with an Icon-Based Interface. In: Gorny, P.; Tauber, M.J., eds. Visualization in Human-Computer Interaction: Selected Contributions from the 7th Interdisciplinary Workshop on Informatics and Psychology; 1988 May 24-27; Schärding, Austria. Berlin, Germany: Springer-Verlag; 1990. 149-182. ISBN: 0-387-52698-6; LC: 90-9971; OCLC: 21761072.

PENNIMAN, W. DAVID. 1982. Domesticating the Computer Terminal: A Plan to Increase Our Understanding of How Men Use Machines. Bulletin of the American Society for Information Science. 1982 December; 9(2): 30-33. ISSN: 0095-4403; CODEN: BASICR.

PERCIVAL, J. MARK. 1990. Graphic Interfaces and Online Information. Online Review. 1990 February; 14(1): 15-20. ISSN: 0309-314X.

PETERS, CHARLES. 1988. CD-ROM and Optical Technology: The User Interface. In: Williams, Martha E.; Hogan, Thomas H., comps. Proceedings of the 9th National Online Meeting; 1988 May 10-12; New York, NY. Medford, NJ: Learned Information, Inc.; 1988. 311-314. ISBN: 0-938734-26-1.

PHILLIPS, K.E. 1989. The Computer Human Factors Database. In: Megaw, E.D., ed. Contemporary Ergonomics 89: Proceedings of the Ergonomics Society's 1989 Annual Conference; 1989 April 3-7; Reading, England. London, England: Taylor & Francis; 1989. 125-130. ISSN: 0267-4718; ISBN 0-85066-484-5.

PIEKARA, FRANK H.; ULRICH, REGINE; MUTHIG, KLAUS-PETER. 1986. Benutzererwartungen und Informationsabruf in Btx [User Expectations and Information Retrieval in Btx]. Psychologie und Praxis (Munich, Germany). 1986; 30(1): 25-33. ISSN: 0033-2992; CODEN: PSYPBH.

POLLITT, ARTHUR STEVEN. 1987. CANSEARCH: An Expert Systems Approach to Document Retrieval. Information Processing & Management. 1987; 23(2): 119-138. ISSN: 0306-4573; CODEN: IPMADK.

POLSON, PETER G. 1988. The Consequences of Consistent and Inconsistent User Interfaces. In: Guindon, Raymonde, ed. Cognitive Science and Its Applications for Human-Computer Interaction. Hillsdale, NJ: Lawrence Erlbaum Associates; 1988. 59-108. ISBN: 0-89859-884-2; LC: 87-36523.

PUTTAPITHAKPORN, SOMPORN. 1990. Interface Design and User Problems and Errors: A Case Study of Novice Searchers. RQ. 1990 Winter; 30(2): 195-204. ISSN: 0033-7072.

RAFAELI, SHEIZAF; ENGEL, SCHMUEL. 1989. Selection Mechanism and Menu Depth: Direct Manipulation Theory vs. Empirically Derived Approaches. See reference: DILLON, MARTIN, ed. 2.

RAY, WILLIAM J.; RAVIZZA, RICHARD. 1985. Methods toward a Science of Behavior and Experience. 2nd edition. Belmont, CA: Wadsworth Publishing Co.; 1985. 414p. ISBN: 0-53404-041-1; LC: 84-17414; OCLC: 11088913.

RICE, JOHN F. 1991. Display Color Coding: 10 Rules of Thumb. IEEE Software. 1991 January; 8(1): 86-88. ISSN: 0740-7459.

ROBINSON, D. 1989. End-User Reactions toward Working with Computer-Based Information Retrieval Systems (CBIRS). Applied Ergonomics. 1989 September; 20(3): 174-180. ISSN: 0003-6870; CODEN: AERGBW.

ROSEN, LINDA. 1990. CD-ROM User Interfaces: Consistency or Confusion? Database. 1990 April; 13(2): 101-103. ISSN: 0162-4105.

ROWLEY, J.E. 1989. CD-ROM versus Online: An Evaluation of the Effect of the User Interface on Search Effectiveness: A Pilot Study. In: Online Information 89: Proceedings of the 13th International Online Information Meeting; 1989 December 12-14; London, England. Oxford, England: Learned Information; 1989. 183-193. ISBN: 0-904933-72-5.

SCHWARTZ, CANDY. 1989. Trends in Interface Design in the CD-ROM Database Environment. In: Online '89: Proceedings of the Online Inc. Conference; 1989 November 7-9; Chicago, IL. Weston, CT: Online, Inc.; 1989. 139-142. ISSN: 1051-9890; OCLC: 20720710.

SELLEN, ABIGAIL; NICOL, ANNE. 1990. Building User-Centered On-Line Help. In: Laurel, Brenda, ed. The Art of Human-Computer Interface Design. Reading, MA: Addison-Wesley; 1990. 143-153. ISBN: 0-201-51797-3; LC: 90-34470.

SHAW, DEBORA; CZAJA, RONALD. 1991. User Interaction with the PDQ Information System. Bulletin of the Medical Library Association (in press). ISSN: 0025-7338. Available from: the authors, School of Library and Information Science, Indiana University, Bloomington, IN 47405.

SHAW, WARD; CULKIN, PATRICIA B. 1987. Systems That Inform: Emerging Trends in Library Automation and Network Development. In: Williams, Martha E., ed. Annual Review of Information Science and Technology: Volume 22. Amsterdam, The Netherlands: Elsevier Science Publishers for the American Society for Information Science; 1987. 265-292. ISSN: 0066-4200; ISBN: 0-444-70302-0; LC: 66-25096; CODEN: ARISBC.

SHINAR, DAVID; STERN, HELMAN I. 1987. Alternate Option Selection Methods in Menu-Driven Computer Programs. Human Factors. 1987 August; 29(4): 453-459. ISSN: 0018-7208; CODEN: HUFAA6.

SHNEIDERMAN, BEN. 1982. Fighting for the User: How to Test and Evaluate Human Performance with Information Systems. Bulletin of the American Society for Information Science. 1982 December; 9(2): 27-29. ISSN: 0095-4403; CODEN: BASICR.

SHNEIDERMAN, BEN. 1983. Direct Manipulation: A Step Beyond Programming Languages. Computer. 1983 August; 16(8): 57-69. ISSN: 0018-9162; CODEN: CPTRB4.

SHNEIDERMAN, BEN. 1986. Designing Menu Selection Systems. Journal of the American Society for Information Science. 1986 March; 37(2): 57-70. ISSN: 0002-8231; CODEN: AISJB6.

SHNEIDERMAN, BEN. 1987. Designing the User Interface: Strategies for Effective Human-Computer Interaction. Reading, MA: Addison-Wesley; c1987. 448p. ISBN: 0-201-16505-8; LC: 85-28765.

SHNEIDERMAN, BEN. 1990. Protecting Rights in User Interface Designs. SIGCHI Bulletin. 1990 October; 22(2): 18-19. ISSN: 0736-6906; CODEN: SGBUD4; OCLC: 8814572.

SMITH, KAREN E. 1988a. Hypertext and Information Retrieval. Online. 1988 March; 12(2): 32-40. ISSN: 0146-5422.

SMITH, KAREN E. 1988b. Providing Access to Large Databases in Intermedia. In: Online '88 Conference Proceedings; 1988 October 10-12; New York, NY. Weston, CT: Online, Inc.; 1988. 137. ISSN: 1051-9890; OCLC: 20405997.

SMITH, LINDA C. 1987. Artificial Intelligence and Information Retrieval. In: Williams, Martha E., ed. Annual Review of Information Science and Technology: Volume 22. Amsterdam, The Netherlands: Elsevier Science Publishers for the American Society for Information Science; 1987. 41-77. ISSN: 0066-4200; ISBN: 0-444-70302-0; LC: 66-25096; CODEN: ARISBC.

SMITH, SIDNEY L. 1986. Standards Versus Guidelines for Designing User Interface Software. Behaviour & Information Technology (England). 1986 January-March; 5(1): 47-61. ISSN: 0144-929X.

SMITH, SIDNEY L. 1988. Standards Versus Guidelines for Designing User Interface Software. See reference: HELANDER, MARTIN, ed. 877-889.

SMITH, TIMOTHY WILLIAM. 1988. Assessing the Usability of User Interfaces: Guidance and Online Help Features. Tucson, AZ: University of Arizona; 1988. 378p. (Ph.D. dissertation). Available from: University Microfilms International, Ann Arbor, MI. (UM order no. ADG88-09947).

SPAVOLD, JANET. 1990. The Child as Naive User: A Study of Database Use with Young Children. International Journal of Man-Machine Studies. 1990 June; 32(6): 603-625. ISSN: 0020-7373.

TAGUE, JEAN. 1989. Negotiation at the OPAC Interface. In: Hildreth, Charles R., ed. The Online Catalogue: Developments and Directions.

London, England: The Library Association; 1989. 47-60. ISBN: 0-85365-708-4.

TAGUE, JEAN; SCHULTZ, RYAN. 1988. Some Measures and Procedures for Evaluation of the User Interface in an Information Retrieval System. In: 11th International Conference on Research and Development in Information Retrieval; 1988 June 13-15; Grenoble, France. New York, NY: Association for Computing Machinery; 1988. 371-385. ISBN: 2-7061-0309-4.

TAGUE, JEAN; SCHULTZ, RYAN. 1989. Evaluation of the User Interface in an Information Retrieval System: A Model. Information Processing & Management. 1989; 25(4): 377-389. ISSN: 0306-4573; CODEN: IPMADK.

TAYLOR, RODERICK A. 1986. Using Multiple Dialog Modes in a User-System Interface to Accomodate [sic] Different Levels of User Experience: An Experimental Study. Austin, TX: University of Texas at Austin; 1986. 178p. (Ph.D. dissertation). Available from: University Microfilms International, Ann Arbor, MI. (UMI order no: 87-06113).

THORELL, LISA G.; SMITH, W.J. 1990. Using Computer Color Effectively: An Illustrated Reference. Englewood Cliffs, NJ: Prentice Hall; 1990. 258p. ISBN: 0-13-939852-X; LC: 88-18613; OCLC: 18321247.

TOLIVER, DAVID E. 1987. Design Issues in Automatic Translation for Online Information Retrieval. In: Lancaster, F. Wilfrid, ed. What Is User Friendly?: Papers Presented at the 23rd Clinic on Library Applications of Data Processing; 1986 April 20-22; Urbana, IL. Urbana, IL: Graduate School of Library and Information Science, University of Illinois at Urbana-Champaign; 1987. 96-107. ISSN: 0069-4789; ISBN: 0-87845-072-6.

TRENNER, LESLEY. 1989. A Comprehensive Study of the Friendliness of Online "Help" in Interactive Information Retrieval Systems. Information Processing & Management. 1989; 25(2): 119-136. ISSN: 0306-4573; CODEN: IPMADK.

TUFTE, EDWARD R. 1983. Visual Display of Quantitative Information. Cheshire, CT: Graphics Press; 1983. 197p. OCLC: 9480885.

TUFTE, EDWARD R. 1989. Visual Design of the User Interface: Information Resolution, Interaction of Design Elements, Color for the User Interface, Typography and Icons, Design Quality. Armonk, NY: IBM; 1989. 1 volume (unpaged). OCLC: 20425355.

TUFTE, EDWARD R. 1990. Envisioning Information. Cheshire, CT: Graphics Press; 1990. 126p. LC: 90-166920; OCLC: 21270160.

VAN DER VEER, GERRITT C.; MULDER, GIJSBERTUS, eds. 1988. Human-Computer Interaction: Psychonomic Aspects. Berlin, Germany: Springer-Verlag; c1988. 458p. ISBN: 0-387-18901-7.

VAN HOE, RUDY; POUPEYE, KAREL; VANDIERENDONCK, ANDRÉ; DE SOETE, GEERT. 1990. Some Effects of Menu Characteristics and User Personality on Performance with Menu-Driven Interfaces. Behaviour & Information Technology (England). 1990 January-February; 9(1): 17-29. ISSN: 0144-929X.

VAN NES, FLORIS L. 1988. The Legibility of Visual Display Texts. See reference: VAN DER VEER, GERRITT C.; MULDER, GIJSBERTUS, eds. 14-25.

VICENTE, KIM J.; HAYES, BRIAN C.; WILLIGES, ROBERT C. 1987. Assaying and Isolating Individual Differences in Searching a Hierarchical File System. Human Factors. 1987 June; 29(3): 349-359. ISSN: 0018-7208; CODEN: HUFAA6.

VIGIL, PETER J. 1983. The Psychology of Online Searching. Journal of the American Society for Information Science. 1983 July; 34(4): 281-287. ISSN: 0002-8231; CODEN: AISJB6.

VIGIL, PETER J. 1986. The Software Interface. In: Williams, Martha E., ed. Annual Review of Information Science and Technology: Volume 21. White Plains, NY: Knowledge Industry Publications, Inc. for the American Society for Information Science; 1986. 63-86. ISSN: 0066-4200; ISBN: 0-86729-209-1; LC: 66-25096; CODEN: ARISBC.

WAERN, YVONNE. 1989. Cognitive Aspects of Computer Supported Tasks. New York, NY: John Wiley & Sons; c1989. 327p. ISBN: 0-471-91141-0; LC: 88-33929; OCLC: 18981386.

WALKER, STEPHEN. 1989. The Okapi Online Catalogue Research Projects. In: Hildreth, Charles R., ed. The Online Catalogue: Developments and Directions. London, England: The Library Association; 1989. 84-106. ISBN: 0-85365-708-4.

WARNER, AMY J. 1987. Natural Language Processing. In: Williams, Martha E., ed. Annual Review of Information Science and Technology: Volume 22. Amsterdam, The Netherlands: Elsevier Science Publishers, for the American Society for Information Science; 1987. 79-108. ISSN: 0066-4200; ISBN: 0-444-70302-0; LC: 66-25096; CODEN: ARISBC.

WEERDMEESTER, BERNARD A. 1988. Keywords Instead of Hierarchical Menus. See reference: VAN DER VEER, GERRITT C.; MULDER, GIJSBERTUS, eds. 392-403.

WILLIAMS, MARTHA E. 1985. Highlights of the Online Database Industry: Gateways, Front Ends and Intermediary Systems. In: Williams, Martha E.; Hogan, Thomas H., comps. Proceedings of the 6th National Online Meeting; 1985 April 30-May 2; New York, NY. Medford, NJ: Learned Information, Inc.; 1985. 1-4. ISBN: 0-938734-09-1.

WILLIAMS, MARTHA E. 1986. Transparent Information Systems through Gateways, Front Ends, Intermediaries, and Interfaces. Journal of the American Society for Information Science. 1986 July; 37(4): 204-214. ISSN: 0002-8231; CODEN: AISJB6.

WILLIAMS, MARTHA E.; KINNUCAN, MARK; SMITH, LINDA C.; LANNOM, LAURENCE; CHO, DONGSUNG. 1986. Comparative Analysis of Online Retrieval Interfaces. In: Hurd, Julie M., ed. ASIS '86: Proceedings of the American Society for Information Science (ASIS) 49th Annual Meeting; 1986 September 28-October 2; Chicago, IL. Medford, NJ: Learned Information, Inc. for ASIS; 1986. 365-370. ISSN: 0044-7870; OCLC: 15077010.

WILLIAMS, PHIL. 1985. Intelligent Access to Remote Computer Systems. Library and Information Research News (Loughborough, England). 1985; 8(29): 5-10. ISSN: 0141-6561.

WOODSMALL, ROSE MARIE; LYON-HARTMANN, BECKY; SIEGEL, ELLIOT R., eds. 1989. MEDLINE on CD-ROM: National Library of Medicine Evaluation Forum; 1988 September 23; Bethesda, MD. Medford, NJ: Learned Information; 1989. 498p. ISBN: 0-938734-36-9; OCLC: 19780482.

WRIGHT, P.; LICKORISH, A. 1988. Color Cues as Location Aids in Lengthy Texts on Screen and Paper. Behaviour & Information Technology (England). 1988 January-March; 7(1): 11-30. ISSN: 0144-929X.

YANKELOVICH, NICOLE; HAAN, BERNARD J.; MEYROWITZ, NORMAN K.; DRUCKER, STEVEN M. 1988. Intermedia: The Concept and the Construction of a Seamless Information Environment. Computer. 1988 January; 21(1): 81-96. ISSN: 0018-9162.

YERMISH, IRA. 1976. An Interactive Bibliographic Information Retrieval System Using Graphical Display Techniques. Paper presented at: 4th Annual Conference on Computer Graphics and Interactive Techniques; 1977 July 20-22; San Jose, CA. Available from: the author, Institute for Scientific Information, 3501 Market Street, Philadelphia PA 19104.

ZIEGLER, J.E.; FÄHNRICH, K-P. 1988. Direct Manipulation. See reference: HELANDER, MARTIN, ed. 123-133.

ZIPF, GEORGE KINGSLEY. 1965. Human Behavior and the Principle of Least Effort: An Introduction to Human Ecology. New York, NY: Hafner Publishing Co.; c1949, 1965. 573p. LC: 65-20086; OCLC: 165502.

6 Optical Disc Technology for Information Management

EUGENIA K. BRUMM
The University of Texas, Austin

INTRODUCTION

Beginning in the late 1970s and continuing through the 1980s, literature on information resources management (IRM), particularly that related to developmental stage hypotheses (GIBSON & JACKSON; KOENIG; MARCHAND; ROCKART & SCOTT), contributed to the belief that information could be regarded as a key organizational resource (MARCHAND) and that effective organizations had linked their already integrated information resources to strategic business planning. IRM supposedly had progressed beyond the point of focusing on the physical control of paperwork. In a comparative schematic of information management developmental stages, for example, Koenig excluded Marchand's first stage of physical control of information, considering it to be out of scope and precomputer. Many stage and developmental theorists have tended to assume a neatly delineated advancement involving a demise of one phase and the coincident emergence of the next, higher progressive phase. Some theoretical views have neglected to indicate that components of all phases may exist simultaneously and do, in fact, operate concurrently.

The author is grateful to Susan L. Cisco, CRM and doctoral student at the University of Texas, Austin, for her assistance with this project.

Annual Review of Information Science and Technology (ARIST), Volume 26, 1991
Martha E. Williams, Editor
Published for the American Society for Information Science (ASIS)
By Learned Information, Inc., Medford, N.J.

Earlier *ARIST* chapters (LEVITAN; LYTLE) included descriptions of information's being treated as a common resource, efficiently integrated, linked to an organization's strategy, and managed by a chief information officer (CIO). The study of Fortune 500 companies by BRUMM, however, revealed that in this large sample of organizations, information activities lack a central or coordinating focus and are not managed through an integrated IRM approach. Despite claims by authors such as MILLICAN that information management now encompasses the concept of information as a common resource, theories have far outpaced the reality of fragmentation that prevails.

In contrast, CWIKLO argues cogently that in most organizations information still exists on separate systems that share little or no data. Most information, in fact, still is stored in typed lists, books, binders, and file cabinets and on index cards. The study commissioned by the ASSOCIATION FOR INFORMATION AND IMAGE MANAGEMENT (AIIM) (1989) supports this view. Statistics indicate that in most organizations, paper remains the dominant information medium, while storage and retrieval activities continue to be disconnected from operations involved with data processing (DP). While the AIIM study of 1987 revealed that a meager 1% of the nation's information is in electronic form, Cwiklo states that as much as 10–15% of revenues in major industries are used to support DP and information management systems, but the results have been disappointing. Little has been done to increase the productivity of white collar workers during the past 30 years (DATAPRO).

There appears to be little relationship between the strategic importance of information and the investment in and level of technology applied to its management (CWIKLO). Despite many claims in the literature on the value of information in decision making and strategy formulation and as a means of gaining a competitive edge, the value of information, for the most part, has been indicated by its form, format, and residence. Although 95% of the nation's information is stored on paper (ASSOCIATION FOR INFORMATION AND IMAGE MANAGMENT, 1987), attention and resources have been focused for the past 30 years on the 1% that is stored electronically. Because of the seductive nature of information technology, the value of information stored in electronic format has been inflated, as evidenced by the resources allocated to support technology and applications.

The 95% of information that is on paper has remained undervalued, neglected, and not well managed. Most literature devoted to the management of information has disregarded this issue, suggesting an ignorance of the significance of paper-based systems in the scheme of information management.

The following facts show that the "paperless office" remains an elusive goal: over 21 trillion documents are on file in the United States (BLACK), the demand for paper grades most commonly used for business between 1976 and 1986 increased between 160% and 225%, greater than the growth of the U.S. economy (ASSOCIATION FOR INFORMATION AND IMAGE MANAGEMENT, 1987; L. M. FISHER), and companies continue to create about one million documents during every minute of business (BLACK).

Widespread advances in office automation (OA) have exponentially increased paper output, and FERRY notes that most organizations today are plagued with an overabundance of paper-based systems, while the costs of managing information in such paper-based systems have been largely undocumented (MCDOLE). When costs are calculated, they often do not include the costs of processing, retrieval time, and the search for the average 3% of misfiled or lost documents, at an estimated $120 per lost document (CARROLL).

O'DONNELL reports that the time, cost, and staggering investment required by paper-based solutions and technologies are driving organizations to examine the feasibility of optical disc (OD) document management systems. Numerous predictions indicate that OD technology will have great impact on information management in the 1990s. For example, the number of optical disc document management systems has increased dramatically, with the worldwide installed base skyrocketing from 4,230 in 1987 to 9,812 in 1988 (MAY, 1989/1990). The ASSOCIATION FOR INFORMATION AND IMAGE MANAGEMENT (1989) has estimated sales at just under $2 billion in 1989 and has projected sales to be above $5 billion in 1992, and $6.3 billion in 1993.

Scope and Terminology

This chapter summarizes the literature on document image processing from 1988 through the summer of 1990, with occasional reference to earlier literature, focusing on what has appeared since the 1987 *ARIST* chapter by LUNIN on electronic image information. Since this is the second *ARIST* chapter on document image processing, background information is not included, except where advances or changes are noteworthy. Rather than emphasizing technology, this review is devoted to either new issues or those that have been more fully discussed in the past three years—viz., cost, legality, standards, records management topics, conversion, major vendor commitment, software, networking, integration, indexing, and performance capabilities.

Over 600 sources were consulted. Some sources provide objective information, but much literature consists of application descriptions and opinion pieces in the popular press. Twenty-four percent of the 408 journal articles consulted, for example, were published in *Inform* (formerly the *Journal of Information and Image Management*), the official periodical of AIIM.

More than 30 terms were applied to OD document image processing systems (electronic imaging, optical data storage systems, document image management systems, electronic document processing), indicating a lack of standard terminology. The most common terms are used interchangeably throughout this chapter, which is confined to optical disc document image processing systems. This chapter focuses on WORM (write once, read many) technology and on rewritable (erasable) optical discs. Literature on CD-ROM is excluded since these discs are read-only devices and have limited application in document image processing systems.

Literature on image processing seems to be following a pattern similar to the data processing literature of the 1960s. The initial emphasis is on hardware, storage capacities, and processing speeds, while application software and ancillary services have received little attention.

Important Sources

Because so much literature has appeared on the subject of optical disc document management systems during the past few years, it is important to distinguish the significant from the mediocre. In general, literature produced by the Meckler Corp., especially that authored by Saffady and Roth, is worth serious examination. Other authors to consult are CINNAMON, D'ALLEYRAND, and WAEGEMANN. SKUPSKY (1990a, 1990b) has distinguished himself on legal issues, and the publication edited by WILLIAMS is also noteworthy.

Among the serials, *Optical Information Systems* (published by Meckler) contains informative, documented articles devoted solely to the topic, *Inform,* the official magazine of AIIM, regularly reports on current industry developments, and *IMC Journal,* although often vendor-based, does contain important information on recent product announcements and applications.

In addition, special attention is drawn to several reports. AIIM's annual industry studies give comprehensive pictures of the imaging industry and predict the next decade's trends. The report of a joint survey by Datapro Research and AIIM, detailing user needs for electronic document processing and how current products meet those needs, provides a wealth of valuable information and is highly recommended (DATAPRO).

VENDORS AND PRODUCTS

In 1987 LUNIN noted the lack of major vendor commitment, but that is no longer the case. IBM, Wang, Kodak, Bell & Howell, 3M, Canon, Minolta, and other vendors now have successful imaging systems in place. In addition to suppliers of full OD systems, tool-set firms, peripheral firms, and PC LAN (local-area network) firms are now providing applications and support equipment (PAPERMASTER & GUENGERICH).

Segmentation by Size and Price

DATAPRO provides a thorough and complete description of OD systems segmented by type of platform—i.e., system size and price. Intended for applications that can support over 1,000 workstations, large systems feature a medium- to large-sized CPU (central processing unit) (e.g., IBM 9370) and cost between $800,000 and $2,000,000. The principal imaging vendors in this area are Alpharel, Integrated Automation, and IBM (DATAPRO). Small- to medium-sized CPUs (e.g., Wang VS 5000) support from 10 to 300 workstations and cost between $140,000 and $800,000; the main vendors are 3M, FileNet, IBM, Kodak, and Wang.

Small systems can be networked via multiple 80286- or 80386-based microcomputers on a LAN, or they can stand alone, configured to include a workstation and relevant optical storage media, placed on a single 80286- or 80386-based processor, with software for indexing images and some workstations capable of displaying multiple images on the screen (SKINNER). Stand-alone systems, often called "electronic filing cabinets," allow direct storage and retrieval of images online with no data or text relationships within the system. Vendors such as 3M, AGA, Bell & Howell, LaserData, and Micro Dynamics produce networked systems that cost between $100,000 and $150,000, while stand-alone units are being sold for $30,000 to $60,000 (DATAPRO).

Segmentation by Levels of Integration

SKINNER provides the following summary of system functions by using the level of integration to categorize the immense scope and diversity of OD systems.

Image server to mainframe system. An image server system adds an electronic file cabinet to an existing data processing system, permitting both data and images to be accessed from and displayed on one workstation (SKINNER). The processor's software provides for indexing and communications link into external host services, while workstations display multiple images and also provide multiple data "windows."

Integrated image servers. In this environment, the imaging system can make both logical and physical connections to a host system. Logical connections allow data to be interchanged between the imaging system's application and the mainframe system's application, with information automatically downloaded into the image processor and integrated into the image database; the entire process is transparent to the user (SKINNER). Searches made within the imaging application retrieve both image and host data information, with mainframe data and image data presented to the user within one access, using only one window on the workstation. Logical connections permit data to be passed back to the host system, providing automatic mainframe updating.

Fully integrated systems. In this most sophisticated level of implementation, images form a single component of a total solution that manages text and data as well as voice (SKINNER). The user has full access to all information related to work tasks—electronic mail (E-mail), word processing documents, database applications, spreadsheets running on a host system, and images. Each task is accomplished from a single workstation, and all information is displayed concurrently through workstation windows.

Support equipment vendors. Based on products displayed at the 1990 AIIM conference, Alsup separated vendors into four categories: (1) full service, (2) PC LAN, (3) tool set, and (4) peripheral (PAPERMASTER & GUENGERICH). Full-service firms provide all components as well as software. PC LAN firms consist of software houses that provide a set of applications and tools (PAPERMASTER & GUENGERICH). Tool set firms supply tools and software that can form the nucleus of an integrator's tool kit. Peripheral firms supply optical discs, jukeboxes, scanners, and printers.

The *1990 Optical Information Systems Buyer's Guide and Consultant Directory* (ROTH, 1989a) provides a comprehensive list of names, addresses, and phone numbers of major firms involved in the read-only, write-once, and erasable (rewritable) optical information field; their products include WORM, erasable optical, CD-ROM, compact disc-video, interactive disc, compact disc-interactive, interactive compact videodisc, Digital Video Interactive, and optical memory cards. In addition Roth summarizes recent advances and presents information on new optical disc technologies, such as digital paper and floppy WORMs (ROTH, 1989a).

ADVANTAGES

Objective evaluation of actual vs. perceived advantages across product types is difficult because of the variety of configurations and the many variables on which performance depends. SAFFADY (1988b; 1990b) details capacity and performance capabilities that allow intelligent assessment. His works also reveal the complexities associated with citing cost and performance advantages of one system over another.

The following six advantages of OD document image processing systems have been cited in the literature. The first is high-density storage capacity (GRIGSBY, 1988). As their most distinctive characteristic, write-once and erasable (rewritable) optical disc systems offer much greater areal densities and storage capacities than their equivalently sized magnetic platters, and storage capacities have increased steadily and significantly since the mid-1980s (SAFFADY, 1990b). Since 1987, Hitachi, Fujitsu, Laser Magnetic Storage International, Mitsubishi, and others have introduced ISO-compatible (International Organization for Standardization) systems that can store 300–328 MB on each side of a 5.25-inch write-once cartridge (SAFFADY, 1990b). Among nonstandard 5.25-inch optical discs, the Panasonic LF-5010 can store 470 MB per recording surface, and the ISI 525GB can store 640 MB on each side of a 5.25-inch optical disc cartridge (SAFFADY, 1990b). Depending on the compression ratio and the dots-per-inch (DPI) resolution and assuming an average image size of 50 KB, each 5.25-inch optical disc cartridge capable of 470 MB per side can store 18,800 images, equivalent to over seven filing cabinet drawers (at 2,500 document images per drawer (WANG LABORATORIES).

Twelve-inch optical discs today store a minimum of 1GB per side, and even these discs can accommodate ca. 20,000 images per side (SAFFADY, 1990b; WANG). A capacity of 2 GB per surface is not unusual.

Eastman Kodak currently markets a 6.8-GB 14-inch optical disc that stores images equivalent to 100 four-drawer file cabinets (approximately 275,000 documents) or 40 reels of magnetic tape. In late 1989 Eastman Kodak announced its intention to manufacture a second-generation 14-inch, double-sided WORM cartridge capable of

4.1 GB per recording surface (*IMC JOURNAL*, 1990b; SAFFADY, 1990b). Increased storage capacity results in improved space use (BLACK) that provides such cost savings as lower-storage real estate costs and reduced storage material costs.

The second advantage of OD systems is ease of access. Because images are referenced and retrieved using computer-based index and search criteria, parameters can be used to initiate a multilevel or relational search, allowing access to specific page or document images and also to groups of related images (CINNAMON; MURPHY; SAFFADY, 1989a).

The third advantage is speed of access and delivery (GRIGSBY, 1988). Access times vary from one product to another and range from one second to several minutes (MURPHY; WAEGEMANN, 1990a).

WAEGEMANN (1988) is one of few authors who correctly notes that retrieval time depends on many variables: (1) speed of processor, (2) RAM capacity, (3) database search time, (4) access time, (5) decompression time, (6) transfer time, (7) data communications, (8) manual or automatic disc changing time, (9) time of data communications to users, and (10) screen-building time. SAFFADY (1988b; 1990b) also provides much detail on access and retrieval times in two publications.

The design of the disc itself can affect access and delivery times, depending on whether the disc tracks are arranged in a constant linear velocity (CLV) or a constant angular velocity (CAV). To achieve a compromise between high storage densities and rapid access speeds, hybrid CAV/CLV systems, such as Kodak's Quantitized Linear Velocity (QLV) disc, have been developed.

A fourth advantage is document integrity and security. Once entered, images cannot be misplaced, misfiled, altered, mutilated, or inadvertently destroyed. ATTINGER, BLACK, CINNAMON, and MURPHY believe that security is enhanced because access can be restricted by establishing computer identification and authorization procedures.

Multiuser, multilocation access (BLACK; TAUBER) is the fifth advantage of OD systems. FARMER notes that the image can be replicated electronically, transferred to multiple users at different sites, and viewed simultaneously. Such capability is impossible with paper files unless copies are made and distributed (MURPHY).

Finally, OD systems offer data-document integration and cooperative processing. As MURPHY, CINNAMON, D'ALLEYRAND, and TAUBER note, image systems can work in concert with a DP or OA application to automatically retrieve or integrate images of source or background documents that are stored on optical disc systems. Such linking also can be used to couple documents produced using application software with related background documents stored on optical disc.

Comment

In conclusion, linking promises, perhaps for the first time, a truly integrated information environment and a fulfillment of the IRM concept. Paper documents that are entered into electronic files can be acted on by using linked data-document electronic "action" forms. Users can key, hand write, or dictate (voice-annotate) information onto such forms and "electronically staple" that information to the source document image. The electronic form and document image then can be distributed electronically.

STANDARDS

As yet, little formal standardization of OD equipment and media exists, although its importance and need are widely discussed and acknowledged (CINNAMON; D'ALLEYRAND; PALINET; SAFFADY, 1990b). One problem is the many components and variety among the components of any optical disc system.

Optical discs themselves come in a range of physical sizes (4.72 inches to 14 inches) and vary in cartridge design, thickness, jukebox compatibility, and center-hole size. To promote the interchangeability of media and equipment, the TC97/SC23 committee of ISO has emphasized the standardization of the magnetic clamp method, hub diameter, and central-hole diameter for 5.25-inch optical discs (SAFFADY, 1988b). CINNAMON explains that recording techniques and media compositions also vary among devices, and these issues must be resolved before there can be an industry-wide standard disc. Although proprietary designs prohibit the physical interchange of recording media, OD document systems do store images in a digitized format that is suitable for electronic transfer to other systems and media, and it is becoming more important to transfer documents electronically than to transfer the discs (CINNAMON).

Currently no accepted industry standard exists for measuring the longevity of optical discs. B. THOMPSON reports on current work at the National Institute of Standards and Technology (a federal agency) to develop a single protocol for testing the retention span of optical discs that could be adopted by the industry. Meanwhile most states are limiting the types of documents that may be stored solely on optical disc to those that carry legally mandated retention periods of ten years or less (see section on Legal Issues).

Data standardization is more difficult since it involves comprehensive software standards. Different control computer systems rely on various operating systems and data formats. In addition to PCs, different micro, mini, and mainframe computer systems, database application software, and operating systems are used for document storage and retrieval, and there is little standardization among these. CINNAMON points to the difficulty of transferring data or substituting components among systems developed by different vendors, even when identical control computers and operating systems are used. The standards of the Consultative Committee on International Telephony and Telegraphy (CCITT) Group 3 and 4 for image compression and expansion remain ineffective since many systems are virtually incompatible in practice; they still use different compression algorithms, pattern dictionaries, compression file header information, and file formats (CINNAMON; D'ALLEYRAND). Interfaces also are not standardized. Many components require specialized interface hardware as well as dedicated driver software. Cinnamon correctly notes, however, that as long as the vendor has done a good job in delivering a complete turnkey system, the users should not become overly concerned with such integration issues.

The most important standardization issue in the long run is the most difficult: application software standards, which include standardized formats for document images, document processing activities, database structures, document indexes, and user interfaces (CINNAMON).

A new Federal Information Processing Standard (FIPS) guideline, Publication 157, entitled *Guideline for Quality Control of Image Scanners,* has been adopted to assist users in setting up their own quality control program for calibrating and testing monochrome, digital 8.5 x 11-inch image scanners (BARONAS). FIPS 157 was developed by adopting a voluntary industry standard, formerly known as the American National Standard for Information and Image Management: "Recommended Practice for Quality Control of Image Scanners, ANSI/AIIM MS44-1988."

Comment

To conclude, neither the American National Standards Institute (ANSI) nor any government agency has promulgated national standards for optical data storage media at this time. The development of technical standards is extremely important to justify confidence in the longevity and stability of OD media. It is also important that industry standards for recording and reading optical data storage formats be established. A machine purchased before industry-wide standards are established may not be supported by the vendor in a few years, resulting in documents and information that will be inaccessible. On the other hand, considerable experimentation is necessary with any set of new technologies to achieve overall optimality. Attempts to standardize can be too early as well as too late.

COMPARISON OF STORAGE MEDIA

Seventy-three sources compare micrographics and magnetic storage with optical disc systems (BANKS, 1985a, 1985b, 1988; BARR; GALLENBERGER; GOULARD; LACY, 1988, 1989; PAZNIK), but the most thorough and detailed analysis on both topics is provided by SAFFADY (1988b; 1990b). In *Optical Disks vs. Micrographics* (SAFFADY, 1988b), a survey of published opinions about the competitive relationship of micrographics and optical discs is followed by a review of read-only and read/write optical disc formats and the extent to which they compete with microforms in specific records management situations. A detailed, point-by-point comparison of computer-assisted microfilm retrieval (CAR) systems and optical disc systems analyzes input methodologies and equipment, storage media characteristics, and retrieval capabilities.

Optical Discs vs. Magnetic Storage (SAFFADY, 1990b) follows the same approach and offers a detailed comparison on storage, performance, and costs of typical optical and magnetic discs as well as magnetic tapes. The many figures and tables present cost categories, computations, and estimating methods for a broad range of applications.

Hybrid Systems

For GALLENBERGER the true distinguishing feature of electronic systems is the mobility of images. Some optical disc-based imaging systems offer integration with micrographics (BURGER; CANNING, 1987a; DATAPRO; SAFFADY, 1988b)—integrated capture, manipulation, storage, conversion, movement, and processing, generally by digitizing the microfilm images. Kodak, Imnet, and others offer such hybrid units.

Optical Disc and COM

Several authors discuss the feasibility of replacing computer output microfilm/microfiche (COM) with OD storage systems (BANKS,

1985a, 1988; MCDOLE; RAMSAY), suggesting that data be retained within the host environment and that optical disc be used for data/information storage and distribution. Conceding that individual pages of a computer-generated report have different values to users, MCDOLE suggests valuing report data by the page and merging a descending value of pages with a descending cost/performance of storage in order to demonstrate whether or not optical storage of computer data would be economically justified in the process.

Comments

One of COM's most valuable features is its ease and low cost of duplication and distribution. A mastering process, similar to CD-ROM, would be required to satisfy the wide and frequent distribution needs of COM, making the cost differential between the two technologies and support equipment a major consideration. In addition, the speed of a COM recorder in capturing data output is far beyond the current capabilities of data transfer to OD from mainframe. Further, as MCDOLE indicated, not all paper computer output is suitable for transfer to OD. His suggestion of valuing computer-generated report data page by page raises many questions. How is value to be determined? Several criteria could be used: frequency of access, the status of the person who requires access, the speed of retrieval that is necessary, the importance of retrieval to the nature of the inquiry. Who will determine the criteria to be used? What will be the cost of assigning value on a per-page basis? This is particularly difficult when assigning complex and multiple variables to computer-generated data reports that run to thousands of pages.

SOFTWARE

Software is the driving strength of electronic document management systems (SCELI, 1988) and usually overwhelms all other factors (ABRAMS) as virtually all capabilities result directly from software (GRAFF). Authors predict that innovations in software will be instrumental in putting OD technology in the forefront (ZIMMERMAN), while the lack of appropriate software can hamper wide acceptance of OD document management systems (SILVER, 1989a; WALTRIP & BLAKE, 1988). Silver explains that while compression and decompression, scanning, printing, and display components have been reduced to board-level products designed around IBM's AT platform, the software is still missing. Because much software is media dependent and often must be customized

(SCELI, 1988), the need for standard software platforms is paramount (CASTLE, 1988). While Castle calls for intensive software development to integrate and refine OD systems, Abrams and Silver fear that the skill and knowledge needed to develop and integrate necessary software components for OD image processing is beyond the reach of the MIS staff.

Software Types

Because of the high storage capacity of optical disc, PALINET explains the importance of having software that supports implementation of file structures that minimize the effects of bottlenecking and reduce the effect of relatively slow access times and data transfer rates of optical disc drives. CINNAMON and PALINET provide lucid descriptions of software types: operating system software, driver software, database software, and utility software. Several operating systems are used for optical disc system applications, including proprietary operating systems as well as those not restricted to use on specific equipment, such as MS DOS and UNIX. Device driver software, which provides the interface between peripherals and the computer's processor, directs the operating system to perform standard system functions in an unusual way. Database software consists of two components: a standardized database management system (DBMS) and database application software. The capabilities of the DBMS largely determine the overall capabilities of the OD system, while database application software incorporates movement of document images through an organization. Utility software includes that for word processing, forms design, desktop publishing, backup utilities, and emulation utilities (CINNAMON; PALINET).

Several vendors, such as FileNet and Wang, have incorporated enhanced elements of software into their packages, including workstation windowing software, facsimile server software, and computer-output-to-laser-disc software (DATAPRO; FILENET CORPORATION). FileNet also offers Document Interchange Software to allow various computers to access and store images, data, and text on any type of a FileNet system (FILENET CORPORATION).

GRAFF reports that document management software is moving toward application-specific software that is independent of the storage medium. CASTLE (1988) predicts that future developments will focus on connectivity and communications interfaces over a range of hardware platforms and enhancement of workstations.

LEGAL ISSUES

Legal questions about the admissibility of records maintained on OD, the submission of information on OD to government agencies, and the use of OD systems by government agencies have prevented some organizations from embracing OD technology. SKUPSKY (1988; 1990a; 1990b) offers a clear description of the difficult legal issues and a lucid interpretation of the laws affecting those issues.

SKUPSKY (1990a) professes that the admissibility as evidence of information on OD can be determined from existing laws: The Uniform Photographic Code of Business and Public Records as Evidence Act (UPA) (U.S. 1128-0020-00), as well as the Uniform Rules of Evidence (U.S. 128-0060-00 to 0170-00). Both laws permit admitting duplicate records into evidence if they accurately reproduce the original. Based on the UPA and the Uniform Rules of Evidence, in fact, the Internal Revenue Service is implementing image processing with the intention of destroying original documents, such as tax returns, after they have been stored on optical disc (ALTER, 1988a; SKUPSKY, 1990a).

Skupsky also emphasizes that records required by regulatory agencies can be maintained legally on OD systems for operating purposes. Paper copies from the system must be submitted to the regulatory agency, which can require that the originals also be maintained.

SKUPSKY (1990a) explains that use of OD by government agencies is the most troublesome issue affecting this technology since many government records must be kept for long periods. U.S. government agencies may use optical disc systems for managing and retrieving information and can destroy originals of short-term records but must retain the originals of long-term or permanent records in either paper or microfilm. State and federal archivists have stipulated that historical and archival records must be preserved either on paper or on archival quality microfilm, and, to date, OD has not been considered permanent or archival in nature. Several states such as Texas, Alabama, and Maine permit OD storage for records with a ten-year retention period (ASSOCIATION OF RECORDS MANAGERS AND ADMINISTRATORS; *RMD TECHNICAL BULLETIN*). To date, only Missouri, Louisiana, and Virginia have modified existing laws to include the admission of optical disc documents as evidence (SKUPSKY, 1990a).

Comment

An undeniable link exists between the development of standards and the legal acceptance of optical disc as a storage medium. Several ANSI standards pertaining to microforms, such as film composition, storage conditions, and stability of film as a medium, ensure that information recorded on microfilm will be retrievable and readable without deterioration for at least 100 years. Standards for OD manufacturing and storage are at a rudimentary stage of development, and stability claims based on the results of accelerated aging tests are disputable (SAFFADY, 1988b). Documents routinely encountered in government and business such as copyrights, patents, trademarks, annual reports, board minutes, and others must be retained for 30 years or longer. The lack of standards can affect the readability of long-term information stored on OD and thus negatively impact the legal acceptance of such information.

JUSTIFYING OPTICAL DISC SYSTEMS

Because imaging systems are still evolving, there is no formal body of knowledge that establishes a standard method for justifying or evaluating them (BENEDETTI). MATTOX takes the approach of analyzing image systems by the potential functionality they provide to the organization. She distinguishes among infrequent, active, and enterprise-wide information and examines the monetary benefits that could accrue. She describes how reduced storage costs and rapid retrieval of fugitive information can justify the replacement of stored, infrequently accessed materials. The cost of those OD systems that replace active records, on the other hand, can be justified by increased user productivity of 20–40%, reduced clerical staff, and reduced equipment and storage costs for maintaining paper-based systems. Enterprise-wide strategic OD systems focus on competitive advantage. MATTOX reports on organizations reaping monetary benefits and competitive advantages from bringing new products and services to market faster.

VALDERRAMA proposes the strategic approach by first identifying information that is critical to an organization's strategic plans. Second, a structured methodology known as information engineering is used, which involves combining business, data, and process models to assist management in designing and developing systems. He argues that this approach would put imaging systems on a more solid ground because it takes into account the organization's management style. Information engineering further ensures that information resources are focused in support of the organization's mission, direction, and critical success factors (CSFs). It also identifies information that makes possible the measurement of CSF performance, and it permits the organization to adapt systems to changing external environments. DATAPRO suggests the following success factors for OD systems: (1) greater integrity (lower misfile rates), (2) greater accuracy (ratio of documents retrieved to the total documents requested), (3) greater availability (total system uptime), (4) improved security, (5) improved access and retrieval speed, (6) improved processing (average time per transaction), (7) greater cost effectiveness, (8) ease of installation, (9) ease of use, (10) simultaneous access to both data and document bases, (11) image clarity or resolution, (12) modularity (ability to expand a system configuration without significant conversion costs), (13) compatibility in interfacing with office automation, data processing, communications, or microfilm equipment, and (14) the capability to monitor key activities, performance levels, and turnaround time.

Most authors advocate traditional methods of systems analysis to determine need and cost (ALSUP ET AL.; WALTER, 1989a), although MINKLER (1988b) points out that such studies do not address storage, retrieval, or rate of flow of information. Nevertheless, SKINNER writes that both vendors and customers are beginning to realize that an understanding of work task stages through an organization is imperative to the success of an imaging system. This has led to a renewed interest in work flow and information flow analysis (WALTER, 1989a). As an alternative to detailed systems analysis and design, both DATAPRO and MINKLER (1988b) indicate that some organizations have installed trial experimental digital imaging systems to locate errors before deciding on a major procurement. However, most of these are not true scientific pilot projects. They fail to meet the rigorous criteria of experimental design and scientific testing. MINKLER (1988b) is not alone in stating that few people are experienced in purchasing electronic image management technologies, and he points to published bid specifications that show a lack of understanding of the complexity of OD technology and its use. KALTHOFF also points out that during a prolonged acquisition process, ignorance results in wasted time and money, cost overruns, and the installation of systems that do not perform to expectations. He advocates separate funding of the buying process to include education for staff members involved in acquiring OD technology.

New Paradigm for Justification

MAY (1990) proposes a complete change in the cost justification paradigm. Based on a survey by the Nolan Norton Institute of 400 organizations that were seeking to justify imaging technology, May identified five basic justification strategies and advocated the proactive approach that he termed "Select and Populate." This involves selecting a target technology and launching a program to provide seed money and expert assistance, much like grant funding. May proposes changing traditional cost-containment approaches inasmuch as they fail to attribute value to such intangibles as customer service, brand image, or time to market. He warns that organizations that adhere to cost-containment methods will not develop the vocabulary or attitude necessary to function effectively within the complex economic environment of the 1990s.

RECORDS MANAGEMENT TOPICS

In a sense, all issues pertaining to OD systems here can be viewed as records management issues since OD image systems have been viewed as a way to solve the problem of paper-based information systems and to address record storage, organization, maintenance, and retrieval. As DYKEMAN (1990) notes, records management programs provide the infrastructure for organizational information resources and ensure that corporate and regulatory standards are met. Despite this, literature on OD systems is sparse as it pertains to specific records management topics, such as retention requirements, vital records, disposition, security, and indexing.

Retention

Lee Crawford notes that the competing claims of various storage media should be evaluated in terms of the document-handling needs of the organization particularly by asking: (1) which documents should be retained, and (2) how long should they be retained (*IMC JOURNAL*, 1987). BURGER concurs about the importance of evaluating document use in terms of the properties of each medium. In general, WORM optical disc is appropriate in low-volume, high-retrieval applications that do not require open-ended retention, while microfilm is good for high-volume, low-retrieval applications where long retention periods are common. In some open-ended and long-term situations—e.g., trusts, deeds, and mortgages—microfilm's archival capabilities are a benefit (BURGER).

ATTINGER discusses retention and disposition from a records management perspective, explaining that these issues become much more difficult in an optical disc environment. Retention and disposition policies could result in a complex system of allocation of images to optical discs, depending on retention periods, so that documents can be disposed of uniformly. Otherwise, documents with different

retention periods would be stored on the same disc, making it necessary to erase addresses to individual documents.

Security and Vital Records

ATTINGER explains that the protection of vital records can be
greatly enhanced with optical disc if the organization already uses
standard backup procedures. With an OD system, however, it may
be all the more necessary to devise a comprehensive disaster recovery plan, particularly because recovery requires the use of additional
computing facilities to handle OD technology beyond that required
to recover essential records that exist in paper or on microfilm.

Indexing

Indexing of images on OD document management systems receives short shrift in the literature. Although good indexing is the
most important part of an optical system (PAZNIK) and is essential
to the efficient management of information (GOULARD), little attention is devoted to it. An outstanding exception is the spring 1990
issue of *Library Trends* (RORVIG), which is concerned with graphical objects—i.e., pictures, line drawings, and images of pages. Also
Image Storage and Retrieval Systems (D'ALLEYRAND) discusses
OD systems within the context of records management.

As RORVIG points out (p. 640): "the beautiful systems that retrieve images of documents as pages. . .without an index and browsing tools they are as dumb as fishes and pigs." In the first section of
this journal issue, articles pertaining to the listing of graphic records
by descriptive rules and intellectual content are presented. The chief
tools are controlled vocabularies applied by automated techniques.
SELOFF details the steps used to create a subset of the *NASA Thesaurus of Technical Descriptors* for application to photographs, with
his final production tool—a "visual thesaurus"—incorporating relational database technology for the presentation of descriptors and
the machine linking of image and text to add greater uniformity to
term assignments. The second section of this journal issue describes
current technology and its application to the retrieval of graphic
records. WALKER & THOMA detail the latest product of the National Library of Medicine's (NLM) long-standing program for optical disc publication of journal articles.

BESSER explains how the management of image collections in a
large organization poses intellectual and physical access problems
and bemoans the inadequacy of text-based intellectual access sys-

tems for describing the many access points to recall the image. CHEN concurs that most existing manual image-picture indexing methods are inadequate for retrieving text since they serve only as location guides. Many images deal with the same topic but present different pictures. Using a keyword approach, Chen believes, results in imprecise and oversimplified image retrieval because images often contain information that can be useful to researchers across diverse disciplines. In a research environment, even an enormous amount of descriptive text cannot adequately substitute for viewing the image itself.

D'ALLEYRAND explains that the design of a good indexing scheme is often complex and that the development of relevant descriptors requires an understanding of both the subject matter and retrieval. Both D'Alleyrand and MCNURLIN (1989b) explain that indexing costs can become a significant portion of the operating expenses of a storage and retrieval system, and D'Alleyrand cautions against the temptation to regard indexing as low-level clerical work lest the entire system be jeopardized. CARDEN & BARR agree, noting that the extra cost is minor when compared to the costs of storage and retrieval during the entire life of the information.

In the ARMA (Association of Records Managers and Administrators) workbook, SAFFADY (1988a) also includes a discussion of indexing for OD systems, emphasizing that the determination of relevant indexing categories is an important preparatory step. He explains the nature of computer-assisted indexing and retrieval methods, whereby assigned index terms, stored and manipulated by computers, reflect conceptual relationships among the stored document images and permit the on-demand assembly of "files" in response to specific retrieval requirements.

Automatic indexing. Because indexing can represent over 50% of the total document entry time, techniques to accelerate it are being explored. Automatic indexing currently requires that either the index field be in the same place on each document or that the index be printed on a cover sheet. Two different versions of automatic indexing used in OD systems are optical character recognition and bar code indexing.

Optical character recognition. OCR software converts digitized information in a predefined area of the image into ASCII text. Three developments have made OCR technology feasible in imaging systems: (1) improvements in recognition capability, (2) software developments in automated indexing and in combined image and database structures, and (3) implementation of high-speed networks linking the central processor, OCR, and data storage media (SCHEIN). In a clear article, NATRAJ explains how OCR technology can be combined with document imaging systems. BALBAN discusses matrix matching and feature extraction and describes some advanced feature extraction systems that use artificial intelligence (AI) techniques to provide a degree of judgmental capability. Some systems have the capacity to "learn" characteristics and idiosyncrasies of a new font. Some newer systems are attempting to read handwriting. Industry vendors are addressing issues of font learning, selection of portions of documents to be read, multiple word processor/spreadsheet compatibility, automatic graphics/text differentiation, multiple column handling, and document size determination (BALBAN; CASEY & FERGUSON).

Bar code indexing. Bar code indexing is appropriate for applications in which documents are already indexed on a computer database and a correspondence must be established between each existing index entry and each document page. Because bar codes are more standardized and consistent than textual characters, bar code indexing is generally simpler and more reliable than standard OCR indexing (CINNAMON).

Two different kinds of errors can occur in any type of automated capture, the misread and substitution; the latter is potentially the more dangerous because of data corruption. D'ALLEYRAND shows that the capture of bar-coded data is more precise than OCR, with a misread rate near 0% vs. the OCR rate of 5–10%, and a substitution rate of 0.0001% vs. an OCR rate of 0.01%.

NETWORKS

At first, digital-based document management was seen as a replacement for cumbersome paper files stored at the department level. Now organizations are interested in digital document management systems that enable users to route, annotate, and transmit images in networks that are now used for data and word processing (MILLER).

PAPERMASTER & GUENGERICH overview the status of network capability of OD systems. They report that because the PC LAN market has solved incompatibility problems more quickly than expected, imaging is now viable on PC LANs, and this has changed the nature of the imaging industry. New and better technologies, such as higher network bandwidths, PC standards, and more powerful workstations, have helped make imaging an increasingly important PC LAN application (PAPERMASTER & GUENGERICH). Until recently, imaging had been done primarily on large and expensive proprietary systems. Now imaging systems are shifting to standard network technologies (WEBB), and popular LANs are handling most imaging applications, making imaging one of a suite of applications on a network instead of the reason the network was purchased (PAPERMASTER & GUENGERICH). Image servers make digitized source documents another kind of data available to PC users on existing networks, and images now can be communicated to remote sites over dedicated fiber-optic lines as well as through facsimile (WEBB).

CONVERSION

Conversion is the process of preparing documents collected under an old system for storage in a new system. Medium conversion is vitally important, although MINKLER (1988b) examined digital imaging design systems studies and learned to his dismay that a missing ingredient in nearly all of them was conversion and related aspects, such as the volume of documents, the quality of existing documents, requirements for preparing the materials to be scanned, and the quality of output documents. MCNURLIN (1989b) reports that people usually underestimate the effort required to change a document from paper to digital form.

D'ALLEYRAND is one of few authors who points out that documents to be entered into an imaging system first must be handled physically: staple removal, unwrinkling of paper, and verification of file integrity. The document then must be scanned and indexed, and the image must be checked for quality. Every time the information is touched, being converted or indexed, a cost is incurred. MCNURLIN (1989b) reports that the cost to scan and index one side of a document is $0.28, while M. J. FISHER, MATTOX, and ZIMMERMAN indicate that conversion costs can run as high as twice the cost of the total system, with costs usually averaging about 50% of the hardware and software.

Because of the growth in OD document management systems, opportunities have been created for extremely high-volume conversion services (FLUTY, 1988) since organizations with new OD systems often lack the resources for backfile conversion (GOLDBERG).

Service bureaus also convert engineering drawings from aperture cards or paper, transfer data from optical discs to CD-ROM discs, and read and transcribe documents into machine-readable code (GORDON & ETHERINGTON). Some film imaging service bureaus have incorporated optical imaging technology, but technological and financial barriers as well as lack of standardization pose major problems (WALTRIP & BLAKE, 1989).

Comment

Organizations are not always choosing complete retrospective conversion of paper-based documents. Some, like the U.S. Automobile Association (USAA) (see Section on Applications—Insurance Services), are providing access to only the most recent materials in their systems since the heaviest use of a document is at the early part of its life.

NEW PRODUCTS

Rewritable Optical Discs

Currently all commercially available rewritable (erasable) optical disc drives use magneto-optical (MO) recording (SAFFADY, 1990b). This technology uses a reversible phase transition in which a laser selectively heats areas of a magnetic disk to shift the reflective substrate between crystalline and amorphous states. Canon plans to market a high-speed rewritable MO-5001S magneto-optic disk (MOD) system as a complete, ready-to-use subsystem. Until now, this has been available only as a component used in such applications as Canon's Canofile 250 electronic desktop filing system and in Steven Jobs's NeXT computer. The complete MOD subsystem will include all necessary software and hardware, as well as an IBM PC or Macintosh interface kit, along with the disk drive, a 5.25-inch 256-MB-per-surface magneto-optic disk, and a power cable (*IMC JOURNAL*, 1990c). Kodak's high-capacity Model 560 Automated Disk Library (ADL), offering up to 75 GB of storage, can be fitted with erasable as well as WORM drives or a combination of both (*IMC JOURNAL*, 1990d).

FINLAY reports that the U. S. government has installed many rewritables. NASA is in the process of qualifying an erasable optical disc system supplied by Sundstrand, anticipating that it will be used to store programs to control robots in space (HUGHES).

WORM protects information already recorded, but because of unresolved legal issues, D'ALLEYRAND believes that it is unlikely that rewritable technology will be fully integrated in imaging systems in the near future. The possibility of altering historical records could be especially dangerous because rewritables allow erasures and changes to all of the stored information.

Optical Tape

Optical tape consists of a ribbon of film coated with an optical recording material. The technical characteristics and information storage potential of such products have been discussed for more than a decade (SAFFADY, 1990b). Despite R&D interest, optical tape systems currently exist only as prototypes. CREO Products, Inc., has demonstrated such a subsystem based on digital paper with one terabyte (one trillion bytes) of recording capacity per 12-inch reel, supplied in 880-meter lengths. The 35-mm write-once optical tape is produced by ICI Electronics and is intended for data collection, archiving, and backup in mainframe computer installations for high-volume applications (ROTH, 1989a; SAFFADY, 1990b).

Optical Cards

An optical memory card is a credit card-sized data storage medium containing a reflective laser/optical recording area that stores information using laser technology. Digital data are stored as microscopic bits on the subsurface of the card, and a beam of low-powered light records and reads the data bits (CORY). Optical memory cards have been thoroughly described (CINNAMON; CORY; D'ALLEYRAND). They can be configured as either read-only or WORM devices. CORY presents an excellent description of the optical card system, its manufacturers, configurations, and applications.

Other Advances

Imperial Chemical Industries has announced Digital Paper, a dye-polymer, infrared-sensitive write-once optical recording material coated on a flexible polyester substrate, suited for discs, tapes, cylinders, cards, strips, and tags (D'ALLEYRAND; ROTH, 1989a; SAFFADY, 1990b).

Adaptive Information Systems has added a telephone voice-response option to its document image processing, which allows users to access optical-disc-based information via touch-tone telephone 24 hours a day. The AdapTel processor links remote telephones with AdaptFile document image processing systems, providing the capability of accessing image databases and retrieving documents via mail or facsimile (*IMC JOURNAL,* 1990e).

Wang's Freestyle enhancement allows personal computers to accept handwritten notes through a pencil-like stylus and voice messages through a telephone and combine them with electronic pages displayed on the screen (MCNURLIN, 1989b). The entire multimedia package can be routed to other Freestyle users.

USER EVALUATIONS

A 1990 joint study by DATAPRO and AIIM analyzed how well vendors are meeting users' current and expected future needs. The study found that buyers are more interested in improving their organization's handling of information than in reducing information-handling costs and seek compatibility with existing equipment, access speed, and ease of use. More than half of those polled indicated that they either have implemented OD systems or are considering doing so. Respondents also noted that their organizations expect to triple in five years the percentage of documents stored in digital form and to more than double the budgets devoted to electronic document processing and retrieval equipment. DATAPRO contains a wealth of educational information on optical disc systems for those interested in this topic.

APPLICATIONS

Because of the many articles that describe applications of OD document management systems, applications can be discussed only in a general way, with certain high-profile examples highlighted. Most often targeted for document imaging systems (DATAPRO) are: paper-intensive industries, such as insurance (BUCHANAN; KAEBNICK, 1989a), health care/pharmaceutical (GARDNER; NELSON), banking/finance (COHEN; FRIIS; HAAS; KEOUGH; KLEIN), law enforcement, state (KAEBNICK, 1989b) and federal government, transportation, engineering (KAEBNICK, 1988b), law firms, and manufacturing.

Each type of application usually has special requirements. For example, engineering and manufacturing require extensive handling of large drawings. The 3M Doculink 7500 Optical Recording System was designed specifically for these documents. Scanners can accommodate paper from 8 1/2 x 11 inches to sizes A through J, aperture card images can be transferred directly to optical disc, and documents from size A to E can be printed (*IMC JOURNAL*, 1989b). The EDMS (engineering document management system) from Formtek combines both vector technology (used in computer-aided design) and raster images (dot patterns) into a document (LEINHARDT), resulting in intelligence that includes information embodied in vector elements. Finance companies use imaging systems especially for customer service, where prompt, accurate responses are important.

Government

Federal and regulatory agencies are using OD document management systems for personnel information administration, contract management, and document retention (FILENET CORPORATION). The Office of Finance of the U.S. House of Representatives, which must maintain personnel and payroll records for ca. 11,000 employees (*IMC JOURNAL*, 1989c), has converted one million documents to optical disc by downloading employee names and Social Security numbers with a FileNet Computer Output to Laser Disk software from the mainframe computer to a FileNet System (FILENET CORPORATION).

The Nuclear Regulatory Commission (NRC) has applied a microcomputer-based OD system to storage and retrieval of documents pertaining to the high-level nuclear waste repository program (BENDER, 1987a; KAEBNICK, 1988a). It has also agreed to accept OD to satisfy quality assurance requirements for storing documents associated with the design, construction, start-up, and operation of nuclear power plants (RENUART & VENKATRAMAN). The Government Relations Department of the U.S. Postal Service uses a 3M Docutron 2000 to store and retrieve letters written to the public by congressional representatives (*IMC JOURNAL*, 1988b).

At the state level, OD systems are used to administer Uniform Commercial Code (UCC) filings, pension funds, and tax information management. At the local level, city police departments use OD systems to manage criminal information, enabling detectives to access files in seconds (*IMC JOURNAL*, 1988a).

Aerospace/Aviation

Once an aircraft is built, manufacturers must be able to track part numbers for repair purposes. The tracking process involves enormous numbers of requests, purchase orders, invoices, shipping documents, and government paperwork. The Kodak KIMS system installed by Continental Airlines provides maintenance records on demand to the Federal Aviation Administration (FAA), whose auditors require original documents complete with the mechanics' signatures (YOUNG). Northwest Airlines uses a Metafile OD system for managing its technical documentation to retrieve single pages from thousand-page manuals that mechanics are required to reference while working on an aircraft (FINLAY).

The Information Systems Development Branch at the Space Telescope Science Institute is building a data archive based on WORM and jukebox technology in collaboration with the Space Telescope-

European Coordinating Facility (RUSHTON ET AL.). The archive supports the Hubble Space Telescope operationally, handling approximately 2GB of data per day and will be used for scientific analysis of the data.

Archives

The National Archives and Records Administration (NARA) in Washington, D.C., has put over 230,000 Civil War and Revolutionary War Army personnel files on WORM technology (FINLAY). The State District Archive in Banska Bystrike, Czechoslovakia, plans to introduce a document imaging system primarily to protect precious documents against wear and tear (*IMC JOURNAL*, 1990a). Plans are to permit archivists and researchers to view the full text as document images and to discourage viewing of original documents.

Insurance Services

The major need driving the insurance industry is a desire to improve employee productivity, efficiency, and customer service (L. FISHER). Major technical concerns include an emphasis on relatively quick retrieval of documents, complete case management software to link related documents, and full integration of voice, image, and data (DATAPRO).

The most highly profiled OD document management system of the past three years has been IBM ImagePlus at the U.S. Automobile Association (USAA) in San Antonio, Tex. A pioneer in large-scale optical disc-based systems, USAA served as the prototype for the IBM MVS/ESA ImagePlus product (ALTER, 1988a; CROAFF & GASAWAY; HOFFMAN, 1989; LEINFUSS; PLESUMS, 1989, 1990; PLESUMS & BARTELS; TRAMMELL). The system became operational in July 1988, with 25 terminals to automate certain customer service operations in the area of property and casualty policy service and underwriting. The system now supports 1,455 terminals for over 2,000 users, handling over two million files. Each day, USAA receives 10,000 letters (over 25,000 pages), which are scanned, indexed, stored, and delivered for processing. Computer-generated data, approaching one million pages per day, are stored for display or print on image-stored overlay forms. For delivery of information to image workstations, a dedicated 4361 mainframe, running CICS as the transaction processing monitor, acts as a front-end processor for the three 3090 IBM mainframes. USAA has improved customer service, has saved 39,000 square feet of office space, has reassigned 120 people to more meaningful tasks, and has claimed improved productivity because of automated assignment of work tasks and tracking of work flow (PLESUMS & BARTELS). At the end of the seven-year life span for documents, over one billion pages (200 million documents) will be on the system.

USAA has started a second image project to support property and casualty claims processing, that will require an additional 3,000-4,000 terminals and will include facilities to store color photographs and recorded statements. Work has also begun on a third project to store applications and correspondence for the bank credit card center.

The Montgomery Mutual Insurance Co. (BROWN & RODERICK), General American Life, and New York Based Empire Blue Cross and Blue Shield (CROAFF) are but three of the insurance companies that have adopted OD document management systems to improve productivity and gain greater control over their information.

Pharmaceuticals

Managing information in a pharmaceuticals firm is complicated because large volumes of information are collected on each new drug that must be submitted to the Food and Drug Administration (FDA) for approval. In addition, most of the information that is collected is recorded on paper, and much of it originates outside of the organization. Research reports, clinical case report forms, and technical literature appear in various physical formats and must be filed by the drug manufacturer with FDA as part of the drug approval process (ALTER, 1988a). Major drug companies, such as Glaxo (DIERS), Lederle, Upjohn, Marion, ICI Pharmaceuticals (ALTER, 1988a) and Pfizer are using OD technology to submit new drug information to FDA (ROTH, 1990a). Because documents on OD systems have been indexed, they are more readily accessible and can be randomly retrieved by multiple parameters. The ease with which documents can be accessed and retrieved on OD systems speeds drug review and approval. Approval of a drug even one month sooner than with the submission of paper records can be worth millions of dollars to the drug manufacturer.

NEEDED RESEARCH

Because there have been few, if any, in-depth research studies on OD technology other than those commissioned by AIIM, the area is ripe for research. Contemporary topics that can be pursued are the effect of imaging systems on the operations and structure of an organization, the effect of human factors on the success of implementation, and the alteration in human/social interactions as a result of implementing optical disc systems. In addition, little is known about the appropriate kinds of data to collect in order to implement an OD system successfully. Because this is an emerging discipline, virtually any relevant topic begs for empirical research and analysis. In addition there is a lack of formal education on the topic. Most education is received at workshops, seminars, and through vendors. The Graduate School of Library and Information Science at the University of Texas at Austin is one of few departments that offers academic courses in image processing and management.

TRENDS AND CONCLUSIONS

As with any emerging technology, predictions about OD systems abound. PEMBERTON believes that optical disc may become the universal information storage medium because more data, text, voice, graphics, and music can be accepted and stored on it than on any other equivalently sized format or medium. Office automation experts predict that OD document management systems will revolutionize the way information is handled (ANDERSON; CASTLE, 1988; FRIIS) and will significantly alter human factors in the work environment (L.M. FISHER; MAINELLI). ASHMORE predicts increases in industry-specific applications, while DYKEMAN (1989) indicates that OD system vendors will become more software based.

Although these predictions are important, the most profound change will be the ability of the organization to fully integrate its management of information. Once documents can be scanned, digitized, and read onto optical discs, they can be accessed together with pertinent electronic data and information from other sources in the system. A complete electronic information package, accessible from one workstation, then replaces the uncoordinated information modules that consist of a conglomeration of mixed-media files. No longer will it be necessary to piece together paper documents, which must be retrieved from physical storage, with electronic data that are logically unconnected to the documents. Until recently, a distinct demarcation has existed between paper-based and micrographic storage on the one hand, and digital mass storage on the other (ASSOCIATION FOR INFORMATION AND IMAGE MANAGEMENT, 1987). With OD systems, it is now possible to integrate text, data, and graphics, with seamless links among mechanical, electronic, and photographic capture and with seamless interactivity among different methods of storage, conversion, and movement, and with seamless integrated processing (ASSOCIATION FOR INFOR-MATION AND IMAGE MANAGEMENT, 1989).

The management of information has become far more complex than had been generally anticipated. Information resources management (IRM) encompasses the concept of information as a common resource, involving a variety of media and formats. It requires the integration of technology with strategy. It serves to integrate all information channels, utilizing expertise in varied areas. In addition to focusing on technology, IRM should provide for the comprehensive administration of information by seeking solutions to massive paper problems. As image management matures as an industry, it promises to contribute to the discipline of IRM by providing not only an added empirical basis for the development of theory but the development and deployment of new theoretical constructs. Such developments might integrate and productively direct the full spectrum of information resources of an organization and advance its scientific basis.

BIBLIOGRAPHY

ABA BANKING JOURNAL. 1989. Shrinking the "Paper Iceberg." ABA Banking Journal. 1989 May; 81(5): 82-87. ISSN: 0194-5947.

ABBOTT, GEORGE L. 1987. Optical Disk Technology. Bulletin of the American Society for Information Science. 1987 August-September; 13(6): 20-29. ISSN: 0095-4403.

ABBOTT, STEVEN J. 1990. Digital Paper: Flexible Optical Data Storage Media. SMPTE Journal. 1990 February; 99(2): 142-144. ISSN: 0036-1682.

ABRAMS, CHARLES J. 1989. Optical Disk: Image vs. Reality. Inform. 1989 January; 3(1): 32-35. ISSN: 0892-3876.

ADAM, BRUCE O. 1988. Publishing on Demand—Potential Becomes Reality. EP&P. 1988 April; 3(3): 38-46. ISSN: 0887-1876.

ALSUP, MICHAEL; BYNAN, GREG; HENNESSEY, DAN; HOLSTON, RICK; LAUFER, MARY; ROWLAND THOMAS; WILSON, JOHN L. 1986. Image Processing: Document Imaging for the Future. Journal of Information and Image Management. 1986 November; 19(11): 10-21, 46-47. ISSN: 0745-9963.

ALTER, ALLAN E. 1988a. Image Meets Reality. CIO. 1988 October; 2(1): 28-33. ISSN: 0894-9301.

ALTER, ALLAN E. 1988b. The Unpapering of America. CIO. 1988 October; 2(1): 16-26. ISSN: 0894-9301.

ANDERSON, LESTER. 1989. Optical Storage: A Growth Technology. Office. 1989 March; 109(3): 67-69. ISSN: 0030-0128.

ANDREWS, HARRY C. 1989. Technological Advances and the Future of Electronic Imaging. IMC Journal. 1989 September/October; 25(5): 6-10. ISSN: 0019-0012.

ASHMORE, G. MICHAEL. 1989. The Emerging Benefits of Image Technology. Journal of Business Strategy. 1989 May/June; 10(3): 43-46. ISSN: 0275-6668.

ASSOCIATION FOR INFORMATION AND IMAGE MANAGEMENT (AIIM). 1987. Information & Image Management: The Industry & the Technologies. 79p. (Report of study conducted for AIIM by Coopers & Lybrand). Available from: Association for Information and Image Management, 1100 Wayne Avenue, Suite 1100, Silver Spring, MD 20910, 301/587-8202.

ASSOCIATION FOR INFORMATION AND IMAGE MANAGEMENT (AIIM). 1989. Information & Image Management: The State of the Industry 1989. 88p. (Report of survey conducted for AIIM by Temple, Barker & Sloan). Available from: Association for Information and Image Management, 1100 Wayne Avenue, Suite 1100, Silver Spring, MD 20910, 301/587-8202.

ASSOCIATION OF RECORDS MANAGERS AND ADMINISTRATORS (ARMA). IAC U.S. STATE GOVERNMENT. 1990. News Bulletin No. 1-90. Report on Survey Results. 1990 March 30. 13p. Available from: ARMA International, 4200 Somerset Dr., Suite 215, Prairie Village, KS 66208.

ATTINGER, MONIQUE L. 1990. Imaging Systems and Records Management. ARMA Records Management Quarterly. 1990 January; 24(1): 9-11. ISSN: 0191-1503.

BALBAN, MORTON. 1990. OCR: What's Needed Next. Datamation. 1990 April 15; 36(8): 98-99. ISSN: 0011-6963.

BANK SYSTEMS AND EQUIPMENT. 1989. Banks Eye Image Processing as 1990 Deadline Approaches. Bank Systems and Equipment. 1989 March; 26(3): 60-63. ISSN: 0146-0900.

BANKS, RICHARD L. 1985a. COM Versus Optical Disk. Canadian Datasystems. 1985 November; 17(11): 59-67. ISSN: 0008-3364.

BANKS, RICHARD L. 1985b. Optical Disk Storage and Microfilm Systems Find Separate Applications. Computer Technology Review. 1985 December; 5(4): 95-99. ISSN: 0278-9647.

BANKS, RICHARD L. 1988. COM and Optical Recording—Change and Challenge. IMC Journal. 1988 May/June; 24(3): 18-20. ISSN: 0019-0012.

BARONAS, JEAN. 1990. A Guide to Quality Scanning. Datamation. 1990 April 15; 36(8): 96-97. ISSN: 0011-6963.

BARR, ROBERT D. 1988. Microfilm or Optical Disk: The Choice Is between Systems, Not Media. IMC Journal. 1988 March/April; 24(2): 7-8. ISSN: 0019-0012.

BENDER, AVI. 1987a. Full Text Search and Image Retrieval. IMC Journal. 1987 July/August; 23(4): 28-30. ISSN: 0019-0012.

BENDER, AVI. 1987b. Text/Image Management and Optical Disk System Design. Inform. 1987 February; 1(2): 20-23. ISSN: 0892-3876.

BENDER, AVI. 1988. An Optical Disk-Based Information Retrieval System. Library Hi Tech. 1988 July-August-September; 6(3): 81-85. ISSN: 0737-8831.

BENEDETTI, JEF. 1989. Optical Storage: Devices and Applications. Systems/3X & AS World. 1989 September; 17(9): 54-70. ISSN: 1044-1239.

BERG, BRIAN A. 1987. Critical Considerations for WORM Software Development. Optical Information Systems. 1987 September/October; 7(5): 329-333. ISSN: 0886-5809.

BERG, BRIAN A.; ROTH, JUDITH P., eds. 1989. Software for Optical Storage. Westport, CT: Meckler; 1989. 230p. ISBN: 0-88736-379-2.

BESSER, HOWARD. 1990. Visual Access to Visual Images: The UC Berkeley Image Database Project. In: Rorvig, Mark E., ed. Intellectual Access to Graphic Information. Library Trends. 1990 Spring; 38(4): 787-798. ISSN: 0024-2594.

BLACK, DAVID. 1989. The New Breed of Mixed-Media Image Management Systems. IMC Journal. 1989 January/February; 25(1): 9-13. ISSN: 0019-0012.

BOGUE, DAVID T. 1987. The Information Challenge and the Film/Computer/Optical Age. Inform. 1987 April; 1(4): 14-16. ISSN: 0892-3876.

BOOKER, ELLIS. 1990. Imaging Keeps on Trucking: North American Van Lines Wants System to Drive Down Costs, Save Time. Computerworld. 1990 February 12; 24(7): 25. ISSN: 0010-4841.

BORDAS, RICHARD R. 1987. Maximized Management and Emerging Electronic Systems. Inform. 1987 August; 1(8): 39-41. ISSN: 0892-3876.

BORDAS, RICHARD R. 1988. Engineering Document Management Systems. IMC Journal. 1988 March/April; 24(2): 43-45. ISSN: 0019-0012.

BOUGHTON, BRIAN. 1989. COM in Future Document Management Systems. IMC Journal. 1989 January/February; 25(1): 17-19. ISSN: 0019-0012.

BOZEVICH, KEN. 1988. Document Management: Business Insurance That Pays for Itself. IMC Journal. 1988 January/February; 24(1): 22-23. ISSN: 0019-0012.

BRAMBERT, DAVE. 1988. On-Demand Printing Speeds Navy's Information Flow. EP&P. 1988 January; 2(6): 52-54. ISSN: 0887-1876.

BREUER, JAMES E. 1989. The Big Squeeze: Source Document Service Companies Must Time Their Move to EIM Carefully. Inform. 1989 May; 3(5): 10-11. ISSN: 0892-3876.

BRIGHT, ROBERT E. 1988. A Global View of the Engineering Market...Today and Tomorrow. IMC Journal. 1988 May/June; 24(3): 7-8. ISSN: 0019-0012.

BRINDZA, STEPHEN. 1989. Will the Early Birds Get the Worms? Modern Office Technology. 1989 January; 34(1): 97-104. ISSN: 0746-3839.

BROWN, ADRIAN; RODERICK, STEVEN J. 1990. A Document Image Management System Tames the Insurance Industry's Paper Tiger. In: Roth, Judith P., ed. Case Studies of Optical Storage Applications. Westport, CT: Meckler; 1990. 25-36. ISBN: 0-88736-535-3.

BRUMM, EUGENIA K. 1990. Chief Information Officers in Service and Industrial Organizations. Information Management Review. 1990 Winter; 5(3): 31-46. ISSN: 8756-1557.

BUCHANAN, NEIL. 1988. Integrated Information Systems Offer Plusses to the Industry. Canadian Insurance. 1988 September; 93(10): 16-20. ISSN: 0008-3879.

BURGER, ANDREW. 1990. Integrating Optical Disk, Microfilm in Electronic Imaging Applications. IMC Journal. 1990 March/April; 26(2): 6-8. ISSN: 0019-0012.

BYLES, TORREY. 1989. Information Technology: A Year in Review. Wilson Library Bulletin. 1989 March; 63(7): 55-57. ISSN: 0043-5651.

CANNING, BONNIE. 1987a. Converting Documents into Computer Data. Administrative Management. 1987 May; 48(5): 55. ISSN: 0884-5905.

CANNING, BONNIE. 1987b. Optical Disk Systems—Pros and Cons. Administrative Management. 1987 March; 48(3): 51. ISSN: 0884-5905.

CANNING, BONNIE; CINNAMON, BARRY. 1988. Optical Disk Systems: New Hub for Integrated Office Automation. IMC Journal. 1988 July/August; 24(4): 19-22. ISSN: 0019-0012.

CARDEN, RAY; BARR, ROBERT D. 1988. Options for Effective Integration. Inform. 1988 February; 2(1): 48-52. ISSN: 0892-3876.

CARROLL, PAM. 1989/90. AAA Manages Its Travel Publication Archive with New Imaging System. Integrated Image. 1989/90 Winter; 1(1): 8-9. ISSN: 1046-932X.

CASEY, R. G.; FERGUSON, D. R. 1990. Intelligent Forms Processing. IBM Systems Journal. 1990 April/May/June; 29(3): 435-450. ISSN: 0018-8670.

CASTLE, ROBERT L. 1988. Software Technology and Image Processing. Optical Information Systems. 1988 March/April; 8(2): 78-80. ISSN: 0886-5809.

CASTLE, ROBERT L. 1989. Complex Software Architecture Required for Image Processing. Computer Technology Review. 1989 Summer; 9(10): 97-101. ISSN: 0278-9647.

CHEN, CHING-CHIH. 1987. Large-Scale Image Processing. Bulletin of the American Society for Information Science. 1987 August/September; 13(6): 15-16. ISSN: 0095-4403.

CINNAMON, BARRY. 1988. Optical Disk Document Storage and Retrieval Systems. Silver Spring, MD: Association for Information and Image Management; 1988. 98p. (AIIM Catalog No. R030). Available from: Association for Information and Image Management, 1100 Wayne Avenue, Suite 1100, Silver Spring, MD 20910, 301/587-8202. ISBN: 0-89258-116-6.

CLITES, LORRAINE; TUTTLE, WILLIAM. 1987. Industrial Document Management: An Optical System Alternative. Inform. 1987 August; 1(8): 30-33. ISSN: 0892-3876.

COHEN, HOWARD. 1989. First Washovia's Walt Leonard Dismisses "Leading Edge" Tag. Bank Systems and Equipment. 1989 January; 26(1): 40-41. ISSN: 0146-0900.

COLOMBETTI, CECILIA. 1988. Merging to Manage Engineering Documents. Inform. 1988 July/August; 2(7): 31-32, 39. ISSN: 0892-3876.

COMPUTERDATA. 1988. Gain Control of the Paper Environment. ComputerData. 1988 February; 13(2): 12-13. ISSN: 0383-7319.

CORTISSOZ, ANNE; DENNIS, RAY. 1987. Telco Transition: Online Document Management. Inform. 1987 March; 1(3): 14-18. ISSN: 0892-3876.

CORY, CHARLES E. 1990. Implementing Optical Memory Card Technologies. In: Roth, Judith P., ed. Case Studies of Optical Storage Applications. Westport, CT: Meckler; 1990. 1-24. ISBN: 0-88736-535-3.

CROAFF, MARTHA J. 1990. Insurance Takes on Image. Insurance Software Review. 1990 June/July; 15(3): 24-26, 30, 72. ISSN: 0892-8533.

CROAFF, MARVA J.; GASAWAY, MARILYN. 1988. Case Study: Image Processing at USAA. Insurance Software Review. 1988 August; 13(3): 54-55. ISSN: 0892-8533.

CROWLEY, MAY JO. 1988. Optical Digital Disk Storage: An Application for News Libraries. Special Libraries. 1988 Winter; 79(1): 34-42. ISSN: 0038-6723; CODEN: SPLBAN.

CUMMINS, JOHN. 1988. Networks—Getting Image Documents to the "Point of Need." See reference: HENDLEY, TONY, ed. 47-56.

CWIKLO, WILLIAM E. 1989. Learning How to Look Ahead: Information Management Planning. Inform. 1989 October; 3(10): 10-12, 14. ISSN: 0892-3876; CODEN: JMGPBN.

D'ALLEYRAND, MARC R. 1989. Image Storage and Retrieval Systems. New York, NY: McGraw-Hill; 1989. 246p. ISBN: 0-07-015231-4.

DAS, MUKTI; BLACK, W. WAYNE. 1988. Storing Drawings on Optical Disks. Civil Engineering. 1988 June; 58(6): 63-65. ISSN: 0360-0556.

DATAPRO. 1990. Datapro Reports on Document Imaging Systems. New York, NY: McGraw-Hill; 1990. 548p. (approx.) Available from: Datapro Research, 600 Delran Parkway, P.O. Box 1066, Delran, NJ 08075, 1-800-328-2776.

DIERS, FRED V. 1990. Technology Integration at Glaxo. Inform. 1990 February; 4(2): 18-19. ISSN: 0892-3876.

DOUGLAS, PAUL E. 1988. The Power of Integration: Issues for Engineering Data Management. Inform. 1988 February; 2(2): 25-27. ISSN: 0892-3876.

DUKE, DAVID. 1987. Electronic Records: Access Documents Instantly. Administrative Management. 1987 October; 48(10): 28-32. ISSN: 0884-5905.

DYKEMAN, JOHN. 1989. What's Ahead for Optical Disk? Modern Office Technology. 1989 June; 34(6): 83-90. ISSN: 0746-3839.

DYKEMAN, JOHN. 1990. Records Management Priorities of the 90s. Modern Office Technology. 1990 February; 35(2): 49-54. ISSN: 0746-3839.

EASTMAN KODAK. 1989. Go for the Gold. Rochester, NY: Eastman Kodak; 1989. 3p. (Brochure). Available from: Eastman Kodak Company, 343 State Street, Rochester, NY 14652-3801, 1-800-44-KODAK, ext. 993.

EDWARDS, IAN C. 1987. Optical Storage Developments—Write-Once Media. Electronic and Optical Publishing Review. 1987 March; 7(1): 16-20. ISSN: 0951-7154.

EGOL, LEN. 1990. The Focus Is on Imaging. Chemical Engineering. 1990 February; 97(2): 149-154. ISSN: 0009-2460.

EISENBERG, BART. 1989. Streamlining Legal Research. Inform. 1989 July/August; 3(7): 28-30. ISSN: 0892-3876.

ERICH, NIELS. 1989. The Vanishing File Cabinet. D&B Reports. 1989 September/October; 37(5): 42-43. ISSN: 0746-6110.

ETHERINGTON, NIGEL; GORDON, DOUG. 1989. Document Conversion: Part 2—An Evolving Industry and Optical Disk Service Bureaus. Inform. 1989 June; 3(6): 22-25. ISSN: 0892-3876.

EXPRESS-NEWS. 1990. Docucon Gets Extension on Contract with Navy. Express-News, San Antonio, TX. 1990 May 25; 3c. ISSN: 8750-3115.

FARMER, GERALD. 1990. From Concept to Commitment. Today's Office. 1990 April; 24(11): 45. ISSN: 0744-2815.

FERRY, MICHAEL J. 1988. Image Processing Systems. Journal of Information Management. 1988 Spring; 9(1): 35-52. ISSN: 0198-9839.

FILENET CORPORATION. 1989. Filenet. Costa Mesa, CA: FileNet Corporation; 1989 May 9. 25p. (FileNet Brochure). Available from: FileNet Corporation, 3565 Harbor Boulevard, Costa Mesa, CA 92626, 714/966-3400.

FINLAY, DOUGLAS. 1990. Optical Disk Technology: Is Its Future Here Now? The Office. 1990 April; 111(4): 75-77. ISSN: 0030-0128.

FISHER, LAWRENCE M. 1990. Paper, Once Written Off, Keeps a Place in the Office. New York Times. 1990 July 7; 139(48,289): 1, 30. ISSN: 0362-4331.

FISHER, LEE. 1989. Image Processing: Turning Costs into Profits. Insurance Software Review. 1989 August/September; 14(4): 64-66. ISSN: 0892-8533.

FISHER, MARSHA J. 1989. User Visions of Imaging. Datamation. 1989 May 1; 35(9): 65-70. ISSN: 0011-6963.

FLUTY, STEVE. 1987. Engineering System Integration: A Team Approach. Inform. 1987 September; 1(9): 26-31. ISSN: 0892-3876.

FLUTY, STEVE. 1988. The Service Sector at Work—Forging Market Success with Niche Strategies and Value-Added Services. Inform. 1988 June; 2(6): 22-25. ISSN: 0892-3876.

FRANK, JOHN W. 1988. Micrographics and Optical Disk—Friends or Foes? IMC Journal. 1988 July/August; 24(4): 7-9. ISSN: 0019-0012.

FRIIS, M. WILLIAM. 1989. Goodbye to Paper? ABA Banking Journal. 1989 March; 81(3): 61-73. ISSN: 0194-5947.

GALBRAITH, IAN A. 1988. Converting Paper Documents into Digital Format. See reference: HENDLEY, TONY, ed. 29-40.

GALE, JOHN C. 1987. Current Trends in the Optical Storage Industry. Bulletin of the American Society for Information Science. 1987 August/September; 13(6): 12-14. ISSN: 0095-4403.

GALLENBERGER, JOHN. 1989. EIM: Electronic Image Micrographics? Inform. 1989 April; 3(4): 14-17. ISSN: 0892-3876.

GALLENBERGER, JOHN; BATTERTON, JOHN. 1989. Kodak Optical Disk and Microfilm Technologies Carve Niches in Specific Applications. Optical Information Systems. 1989 May/June; 9(3): 127-130. ISSN: 0886-5809.

GARDNER, ELIZABETH. 1988. Automated Medical Chart Becoming a Priority. Modern Healthcare. 1988 September 2; 18(36): 29-52. ISSN: 0160-7480.

GIBSON, CYRUS F.; JACKSON, BARBARA B. 1987. The Information Imperative: Managing the Impact of Information Technology on Business and People. Lexington, MA: D.C. Heath; 1987. 160p. ISBN: 0-669-12338-2.

GOLDBERG, MICHAEL. 1988. The Conversion Challenge: Optical Disk Service Bureaus Examine Their Options. Inform. 1988 September; 2(8): 10-12. ISSN: 0892-3876.

GORDON, DOUG; ETHERINGTON, NIGEL. 1989. Document Conversion: Part 1—What Do Optical Disk Service Bureaus Have to Offer? Inform. 1989 May; 3(5): 28-29. ISSN: 0892-3876.

GOULARD, CLAUDE. 1987. What Will Tomorrow Bring in Terms of Storage and Access to Information? IMC Journal. 1987 May/June; 23(3): 6-7. ISSN: 0019-0012.

GRAFF, MICHAEL W. 1989. Document Management Software Borrows from Data Processing. Inform. 1989 January; 3(1): 24-36. ISSN: 0892-3876.

GRIGSBY, MASON. 1987. The Integration and Use of Write-Once Optical Information Systems. IMC Journal. 1987 July/August; 23(4): 9-13. ISSN: 0019-0012.

GRIGSBY, MASON. 1988. Optical Disk: Vision to Payoff. Modern Office Technology. 1988 November; 33(11): 60-66. ISSN: 0746-3839.

HAAS, PAMELA. 1988. Why Image Processing Is Banking's Next Strategic System. Banking Software Review. 1988 Spring; 13(1): 37-43. ISSN: 0872-6778.

HARTMANN, K. 1988. An Electronic Archive Based on Optical Disk Technology. See reference: HENDLEY, TONY, ed. 117-124.

HENDLEY, TONY. 1988a. The Developing Market for Document Imaging Systems in the UK. See reference: HENDLEY, TONY, ed. 1-8.

HENDLEY, TONY, ed. 1988b. Document Image Processing: The 1st European Conference on the Commercial Applications of Electronic Document Management Systems; 1988 March 22-24; London, England. London, England: Online Publications; 1988. 151p. ISBN: 0-86353-141-5.

HOFFMAN, THOMAS. 1989. The Image of Success. Information Week. 1989 August 21: 25-26, 28. ISSN: 0199-0691.

HOFFMAN, THOMAS. 1990a. An Image Problem. Information Week. 1990 March 5: 30-34. ISSN: 0199-0691.

HOFFMAN, THOMAS. 1990b. Taking AIIM. Information Week. 1990 April 16: 44. ISSN: 0199-0691.

HUGHES, DAVID. 1990. NASA Will Fly Computer Processor, Erasable Optical Disk on Space Shuttle. Aviation Week & Space Technology. 1990 January 15; 132(3): 47. ISSN: 0005-2175.

IBM SYSTEMS JOURNAL. 1990. IBM Systems Journal. 1990 April/May/June; 29(3): 175p. (Entire issue devoted to optical disk image processing systems). ISSN: 0018-8670.

IMC JOURNAL. 1987. Alternative Storage Media: An Interview with Lee Crawford. IMC Journal. 1987 November/December; 23(6): 43-45. ISSN: 0019-0012.

IMC JOURNAL. 1988a. Police Find "Investigative Aide" in Optical Disk System. IMC Journal. 1988 November/December; 24(6): 38-39. ISSN: 0019-0012.

IMC JOURNAL. 1988b. U.S. Postal Service Stores Constituent Letter Files on Optical Disk. IMC Journal. 1988 July/August; 24(4): 43-44. ISSN: 0019-0012.

IMC JOURNAL. 1989a. Canada's Investor's Group and Document-Image Processing. IMC Journal. 1989 March/April; 25(2): 24-26. ISSN: 0019-0012.

IMC JOURNAL. 1989b. New 3M Optical Disk System for High Volume Engineering Applications. IMC Journal. 1989 January/February; 25(1): 28. ISSN: 0019-0012.

IMC JOURNAL. 1989c. Paper Woes Thwarted on Capitol Hill. IMC Journal. 1989 September/October; 25(5): 15-16. ISSN: 0019-0012.

IMC JOURNAL. 1990a. Czech Archive to Install Imaging System. IMC Journal. 1990 May/June; 26(3): 34. ISSN: 0019-0012.

IMC JOURNAL. 1990b. Kodak's 8.2 Gigabyte Optical Disk. IMC Journal. 1990 July/August; 26(4): 28. ISSN: 0019-0012.

IMC JOURNAL. 1990c. Magneto-Optic Disk System. IMC Journal. 1990 May/June; 26(3): 33. ISSN: 0019-0012.

IMC JOURNAL. 1990d. New 5-1/4 Inch Optical ADL. IMC Journal. 1990 May/June; 26(3): 30. ISSN: 0019-0012.

IMC JOURNAL. 1990e. Touch-Tone Telephone Document-Access. IMC Journal. 1990 May/June; 26(3): 30. ISSN: 0019-0012.

INFORMATION WEEK. 1990. Image Systems. Information Week. 1990 February 5: 5. ISSN: 0199-0691.

KAEBNICK, GREGORY E. 1988a. DOE's Proposed Optical Disk System: More with LSS. Inform. 1988 November/December; 2(10): 12-14. ISSN: 0892-3876.

KAEBNICK, GREGORY E. 1988b. Engineering Takes Cautious Steps to Optical: Prognostications from AIIM's Engineering Division. Inform. 1988 October; 2(9): 14-17. ISSN: 0892-3876.

KAEBNICK, GREGORY E. 1989a. A New Lease on Life Insurance. Inform. 1989 July/August; 3(7,8): 20, 46-67. ISSN: 0892-3876.

KAEBNICK, GREGORY E. 1989b. Notes from Underground: Walter Corbitt Talks about Monitoring Paperwork for 35,000 Underground

Storage Tanks. Inform. 1989 July/August; 3(7,8): 21-22, 48. ISSN: 0892-3876.

KALTHOFF, ROBERT J. 1990. The Electronic Image Management [EIM] Buying Process. IMC Journal. 1990 July/August; 26(4): 14-19. ISSN: 0019-0012.

KEOUGH, LEE. 1989. Information Management: The End of the Paper Chase. Institutional Investor. 1989 July; 23(8): 203-209. ISSN: 0020-3580.

KER, NIEL. 1987. Storage: Retrieval Alternatives. Systems International. 1987 April; 15(4): 105-106. ISSN: 0305-1668.

KLEIN, JUNE R. 1989. Image Processing: New Solutions in Bank Information Management. Bank Systems and Equipment. 1989 July; 26(7): 105-106. ISSN: 0146-0900.

KLEINSCHROD, WALTER A. 1989. Optical Disk: Growth Spurts in an Emerging Technology. Today's Office. 1989 June; 24(1): 44C-44K. ISSN: 0744-2815.

KNISKERN, JAMES. 1990. Engineering a Visionary Solution. Datamation. 1990 April 15; 36(8): 90-91. ISSN: 0011-6963.

KOENIG, MICHAEL E. 1986. The Convergence of Computers and Telecommunications. Information Management Review. 1986 Winter; 1(3): 23-33. ISSN: 8756-1557.

LACY, JOHN A. 1988. Integrated Information Systems: A Look at the 1990s. IMC Journal. 1988 May/June; 24(3): 16-17. ISSN: 0019-0012.

LACY, JOHN A. 1989. The Benefits of Image-Based Document Management. The Office. 1989 January; 109(1): 132-137. ISSN: 0030-0128.

LANDRUM, CRAIG. 1987. Digital Document Automation and the Mark of Quality. Inform. 1987 November; 1(11): 22-23. ISSN: 0892-3876.

LEINFUSS, EMILY. 1990. USAA's Image of Success. Datamation. 1990 May 15; 36(10): 77-78, 80, 82. ISSN: 0011-6963.

LEINHARDT, SAMUEL. 1988. Engineering Systems: The Raster-Vector Connection. Inform. 1988 March; 2(3): 22-24. ISSN: 0892-3876.

LEVITAN, KAREN B. 1982. Information Resource(s) Management— IRM. In: Williams, Martha E., ed. Annual Review of Information Science and Technology: Volume 17. White Plains, NY: Knowledge Industry Publications, Inc. for the American Society for Information Science; 1982. 227-266. ISSN: 0066-4200; CODEN: ARISBC.

LIDDLE, LINUS L. 1988. Implementing a High Speed Patent Image Retrieval System. See reference: HENDLEY, TONY, ed. 125-136.

THE LOCAL RECORD. 1987. Optical Disk Storage Systems. The Local Record. 1987 September: 1-4. ISSN: 0887-0721. Available from: Local Records Division, Texas State Library, P.O. Box 12927, Austin, TX 78711-2927.

THE LOCAL RECORD. 1988. Attorney General Issues Optical Disk Opinion. The Local Record. 1988 Fall: 1-3. ISSN: 0887-0721. Available from: Local Records Division, Texas State Library, P.O. Box 12927, Austin, TX 78711-2927.

LUNIN, LOIS F. 1987. Electronic Image Information. In: Williams, Martha E., ed. Annual Review of Information Science and Technology: Volume 22. Amsterdam, The Netherlands: Elsevier Science Publishers for the American Society for Information Science; 1987. 179-224. ISSN: 0066-4200; CODEN: ARISBC.

LYTLE, RICHARD H. 1986. Information Resource Management: 1981-1986. In: Williams, Martha E., ed. Annual Review of Information Science and Technology: Volume 21. White Plains, NY: Knowledge Industry Publications, Inc. for the American Society for Information Science; 1986. 310-335. ISSN: 0066-4200; CODEN: ARISBC.

MACADAM, ROSS. 1988. Document Processing: Operational Control vs. Library Storage. See reference: HENDLEY, TONY, ed. 41-46.

MAINELLI, MICHAEL R. 1988. Operations, Human Factors, and Organization. See reference: HENDLEY, TONY, ed. 17-28.

MALLINSON, JOHN C. 1988. On the Preservation of Human- and Machine-Readable Records. Information Technology and Libraries. 1988 March; 7(1): 19-23. ISSN: 0730-9295.

MARCHAND, DONALD A. 1985. Information Management: Strategies and Tools in Transition. Information Management Review. 1985 Summer; 1(1): 27-34. ISSN: 8756-1557; ISBN: 0-87189-125-5.

MARKOWSKI, MICHAEL J. 1988. A Digital Hardware Design of an Electronic Filing Cabinet. Newark, DE: University of Delaware; 1988. 114p. (Master's thesis). OCLC: 19476813.

MATTOX, ADDIE. 1990. Justifying Imaging Systems. Presented at: ARMA International 35th Annual Conference; 1990 November 4-11; San Francisco, CA. (Handout from conference). 22p. Available from: The Mattox Group, 1354 North Castle Road, Sonoma, CA 95476, 707/935-0753.

MAY, THORNTON A. 1989/90. Imaging Gives "Break-Away" Advantage to Organizations. Integrated Image. 1989/90 Winter; 1(1): 4. ISSN: 1046-932X.

MAY, THORNTON. 1990. Justifying the Image. Datamation. 1990 April 15; 36(8): 82-84. ISSN: 0011-6963.

MCCREADY, SCOTT. 1989. Optical Disk-Based Systems: Japanese and American Approaches. IMC Journal. 1989 March/April; 25(2): 33-34. ISSN: 0019-0012.

MCDOLE, V. O. 1990. Optical Storage Technology. Mainframe Journal. 1990 September; 5(9): 36, 38. ISSN: 0892-8444.

MCNURLIN, BARBARA C., ed. 1989a. Electronic Document Management: Part I. I/S Analyzer. 1989 May; 27(5): 1-16. ISSN: 0896-3231.

MCNURLIN, BARBARA C., ed. 1989b. Electronic Document Management: Part II. I/S Analyzer. 1989 June; 27(6): 1-16. ISSN: 0896-3231.

MILLER, RANDY. 1989. Advances in Digital Technology Bring Images to the Desktop. IMC Journal. 1989 July/August; 25(4): 19-21. ISSN: 0019-0012.

MILLICAN, DENNIS D. 1989. Teaching Old Pros New Tricks. Inform. 1989 October; 3(10): 18-20. ISSN: 0892-3876.

MINKLER, WHITNEY S. 1988a. Image Communications: Linking Information Management. Inform. 1988 July/August; 2(7): 33-38. ISSN: 0892-3876.

MINKLER, WHITNEY S. 1988b. An Objective Overview of Digital Imaging (Optical Disk) Systems Procurements. ARMA Records Management Quarterly. 1988 October; 22(4): 3-4, 6-7. ISSN: 0191-1503.

MOORE, FRANK. 1987. Records Management at IRS: The Ultimate Paper Challenge. Inform. 1987 November; 1(11): 12-16. ISSN: 0892-3876.

MOORE, FRANK. 1988. Image Processing in the Internal Revenue Service. See reference: HENDLEY, TONY, ed. 75-86.

MORAN, ROBERT. 1988. Choosing an Image Strategy. Computer Decisions. 1988 November; 20(11): 57-60. ISSN: 0010-4558.

MURPHY, JOHN A. 1990. Document/Image Management Systems: Their Advantages Are Not Optical Illusions. Today's Office. 1990 April; 24(11): 36-38, 40. ISSN: 0744-2815.

NARA BULLETIN. 1988. Use of Optical Disk Systems to Store Permanent Federal Records. NARA Bulletin 88-8. 1988 September 19. 2p. Available from: U.S. National Archives and Records Administration, Washington, DC 20408.

NATRAJ, NAT D. 1990. OCR Integrated with Imaging Systems: Reducing Data Entry Costs. IMC Journal. 1990 January/February; 26(1): 11-15. ISSN: 0019-0012.

NELSON, NANCY. 1989. Maimonides Medical Center Uses Workflow Management System. Computers in Healthcare. 1989 March; 10(3): 45-52. ISSN: 0745-1075.

NIKOLAISON, RAY A. 1988. A University's Approach to Information-Handling. The Office. 1988 November; 108(5): 120, 125-128. ISSN: 0030-0128.

NOLAN, RICHARD L. 1979. Managing the Crises in Data Processing. Harvard Business Review. 1979 March/April; 57(2): 115-126. ISSN: 0017-8012.

NOVINGER, WALTER B. 1987. Optical Storage: A Conversion Perspective. Inform. 1987 September; 1(9): 22-23, 46. ISSN: 0892-3876.

O'DONNELL, MICHAEL J. 1988. Optical Document Processing Is Business's Paperwork Reduction Act. Computer Technology Review. 1988 April; 8(4): 20-26. ISSN: 0278-9647.

PALINET. 1989. Optical Disk Storage: Technology and Applications. Philadelphia, PA: Palinet; 1989. 357p. Available from: PALINET, 3401 Market Street, Philadelphia, PA 19104. (Looseleaf). ISBN: 0-912803-15-3.

PAPERMASTER, STEVE; GUENGERICH, STEVE. 1990. Image Management and LANs. LAN Technology. 1990 July; 6(7): 17-18. ISSN: 8750-9482.

PATCH, KIMBERLY. 1990. Document Image Processing for Picture-Perfect Payback. Digital Review. 1990 June 25; 5(25): 49-53. ISSN: 0739-4314.

PAZNIK, MEGAN JILL. 1988. Optical Disks vs. Micrographics. Administrative Management. 1988 April; 49(3): 18-23. ISSN: 0884-5905.

PEMBERTON, J. MICHAEL. 1989. Optical Disk—Super Media, Super Systems. ARMA Records Management Quarterly. 1989 April; 23(2): 64-67. ISSN: 0191-1503.

PLESUMS, CHARLES A. 1989. An Image Worth a Thousand Files. Best's Review (Property and Casualty). 1989 May; 90(1): 54-58. ISSN: 0161-7745.

PLESUMS, CHARLES A. 1990. Image Processing at USAA. Mainframe Journal. 1990 June; 5(6): 8, 10, 12, 14-15. ISSN: 0892-8444.

PLESUMS, CHARLES A.; BARTELS, R. W. 1990. Large-scale Image Systems: USAA Case Study. IBM Systems Journal. 1990 April/May/June; 29(3): 343-355. ISSN: 0018-8670.

PLUME, TERRY. 1988. Optical Disk Systems—Technology. IMC Journal. 1988 January/February; 24(1): 29-32. ISSN: 0019-0012.

RAMSAY, NANCY. 1988. Using Optical Disk in Non-Image Applications. Optical Information Systems. 1988 July/August; 8(4): 164-168. ISSN: 0886-5809.

RANADE, SANJAY. 1990. Optical Storage Jukebox Technology: A Systems Integrator's Perspective. Westport, CT: Meckler; 1990. 275p. ISBN: 0-88736-571-X.

RANADE, SANJAY; NG, JAMES. 1989. Systems Integration for Write-Once Optical Storage. Westport, CT: Meckler; 1989. 160p. ISBN: 0-88736-366-0.

RENUART, ROBERT F.; VENKATRAMAN, RAJU. 1989. Electronic Document Management Improves Design Change Process. Power Engineering. 1989 April; 93(4): 48-50. ISSN: 0032-5961.

RMD TECHNICAL BULLETIN. 1989. Optical Data Storage Systems. RMD Technical Bulletin Number 1. 1989 January: 1-4. Available from: Texas State Library, Records Management Division, Publications, P.O. Box 12917, Austin, TX 78711, 512/454-2705.

ROCKART, JOHN F.; SCOTT, MORTON M. 1984. Implications of Changes in Information Technology for Corporate Strategy. Interfaces. 1984 January/February; 14(1): 84-95. ISSN: 0092-2102.

RORVIG, MARK E., ed. 1990. Intellectual Access to Graphic Information. Library Trends. 1990 Spring; 38(4): 639-836. ISSN: 0024-2594.

ROTH, JUDITH P. 1989a. 1990 Optical Information Systems Buyer's Guide and Consultant Directory. Optical Information Systems. 1989 November-December; 9(6): 93p. (Entire issue devoted to sources for optical disc products and consultants in this area). ISSN: 0886-5809.

ROTH, JUDITH P., ed. 1989b. Optical Information Systems '89: Proceedings of the 9th Annual Conference and Exhibition; 1989 September 6-8; Hyatt Regency, Crystal City, Arlington, VA. Westport, CT: Meckler Corp.; 1989. 450p. ISBN: 0-88736-553-1.

ROTH, JUDITH P., ed. 1990a. Case Studies of Optical Storage Applications. Westport, CT: Meckler; 1990. 139p. ISBN: 0-88736-535-3.

ROTH, JUDITH P. 1990b. Converting Information for WORM Optical Storage: A Case Study Approach. Westport, CT: Meckler; 1990. 184p. ISBN: 0-88736-380-6.

ROTH, JUDITH P. 1990c. Rewritable Optical Storage Technology. Westport, CT: Meckler; 1990. 150p. ISBN: 0-88736-534-5.

RUNYAN, LINDA. 1990. PTO's Inventive Ways with Imaging. Datamation. 1990 April 15; 36(8): 92-95. ISSN: 0011-6963.

RUSHTON, A. MINICK; HUNT, L.; MCGLYNN, T.; OCHSENBEIN, F.; PERRINE, B.; RICHMOND, A.; ROMELFANGER, F.; RUSSO, G.; SHAMES, P. M. B.; WILLARD, L.; ZELLER, S. 1990. The Universe Online: Optical Disks for Astronomical Archiving. Optical Information Systems. 1990 January/February; 10(1): 35-39. ISSN: 0886-5809.

SAFFADY, WILLIAM. 1987. Optical Disks at the 1987 AIIM Conference. Optical Information Systems. 1987 September/October; 7(5): 321-328. ISSN: 0886-5809.

SAFFADY, WILLIAM. 1988a. Optical Disk Systems for Records Management. Prairie Village, KS: ARMA International; 1988. 61p. (Accompanying slides available). Available from: ARMA International, 4200 Somerset Drive, Suite 215, Prairie Village, KS 66208, 913/341-3808.

SAFFADY, WILLIAM. 1988b. Optical Disks vs. Micrographics. Westport, CT: Meckler; 1988. 101p. ISBN: 0-88736-345-8.

SAFFADY, WILLIAM. 1989a. Electronic Document Imaging Using Write-Once Optical Disks: An Overview of Concepts and Components. International Journal of Micrographics and Optical Technology. 1989; 7(3): 91-98. ISSN: 0743-9636.

SAFFADY, WILLIAM. 1989b. Optical Storage Technology: A Bibliography. Westport, CT: Meckler; 1989. 158p. ISBN: 0-88736-231-1.

SAFFADY, WILLIAM. 1990a. Micrographics and Optical Storage Equipment Review 1990 Edition. Westport, CT: Meckler; 1990. 150p. ISBN: 0-88736-661-9.

SAFFADY, WILLIAM. 1990b. Optical Disks vs. Magnetic Storage. Westport, CT: Meckler; 1990. 122p. ISBN: 0-88736-703-8.

SAFFADY, WILLIAM. 1990c. Optical Storage Technology 1990: A State of the Art Review. Westport, CT: Meckler; 1990. 200p. ISBN: 0-88736-594-9.

SCELI, W. CLAIR. 1987. The Promise That Document Management Can Keep. Bulletin of the American Society for Information Science. 1987 June/July; 13(5): 24-25. ISSN: 0095-4403.

SCELI, W. CLAIR. 1988. Micrographics? Optical Disk? Hardware? Software? Service? How to Make the Tough Decisions. Inform. 1988 September; 2(8): 9, 39. ISSN: 0892-3876.

SCHALKOFF, ROBERT J. 1989. Digital Image Processing and Computer Vision. New York, NY: Wiley; 1989. 489p. ISBN: 0-471-85718-1.

SCHEIN, ALAN. 1989. Optical Storage and OCR—Key Components of Automated Information Management Systems. Optical Information Systems. 1989 January/February; 9(1): 9-15. ISSN: 0886-5809.

SCHINDLER, PAUL E.; HOFFMAN, THOMAS. 1990. Banking on IBM's Image. Information Week. 1990 March 19; 26. ISSN: 0199-0691.

SCHNITTER, DON. 1987. Image Processing Paying Dividends. Computing Canada. 1987 October 15; 13(21): 48-49. ISSN: 0319-0161.

SCHROEDER, CHRIS. 1987. Information Standards and Optical Disk Systems. Inform. 1987 February; 1(2): 12-13. ISSN: 0892-3876.

SCIENTIFIC AMERICAN. 1990. Not Just a Pretty Face: Compressing Pictures with Fractals. Scientific American. 1990 March; 262(3): 77-78. ISSN: 0036-8733.

SEELEY, DONN E. 1989. Electronic EDMS Searches for Its Stride. Inform. 1989 January; 3(1): 27-30. ISSN: 0892-3876.

SEIGLE, DAVID C. 1988. Office Economics and Document Image Processing. Inform. 1988 January; 2(1): 34-36. ISSN: 0892-3876.

SELOFF, GARY A. 1990. Automated Access to the NASA-JSC Image Archives. In: Rorvig, Mark E., ed. Intellectual Access to Graphic Information. Library Trends. 1990 Spring; 38(4): 682-696. ISSN: 0024-2594.

SHEA, KELLY. 1987. Interview: Archiving the Archives. Computerworld. 1987 August 24; 21(34): 63. ISSN: 0010-4841.

SILVER, DAVID. 1989a. Integrated Electronic Document Management: Beyond Storage and Retrieval. IMC Journal. 1989 July/August; 25(4): 16-18. ISSN: 0019-0012.

SILVER, DAVID. 1989b. The PC Puzzle: Soon to Be Solved for Document Image Processing. Inform. 1989 June; 3(6): 14, 53. ISSN: 0892-3876.

SKINNER, CHRIS. 1989. Workflow in an Integrated Environment. IMC Journal. 1989 July/August; 25(4): 12-15. ISSN: 0019-0012.

SKUPSKY, DONALD S. 1988. Recordkeeping Requirements. Denver, CO: Information Requirements Clearinghouse; 1988. 323p. ISBN: 0-929316-18-5.

SKUPSKY, DONALD S. 1990a. Legal Requirements for Business Records: Federal Requirements. Denver, CO: Information Requirements Clearinghouse; 1990. (Looseleaf). ISBN: 0-929316-11-8.

SKUPSKY, DONALD S. 1990b. Legal Requirements for Business Records: State Requirements. Denver, CO: Information Requirements Clearinghouse; 1990. (Looseleaf). ISBN: 0-929316-12-6.

SMITH, ALAN D. 1990. The Infancy of Optical Storage. Design Management. 1990 April; 14(4): 11-14. ISSN: 1042-8534.

STURGIS, INGRID. 1988. Newest Record Filing Systems to Have Multi-Media Base. Bank Systems and Equipment. 1988 May; 25(5): 78-81. ISSN: 0146-0900.

TARGET DATA INCORPORATED. 1989. Computer & Image Processing Glossary. Northbrook, IL: Target Data Inc.; 1989 November. 15p. (Brochure). Available from: Target Data Inc., 630 Dundee Road, Suite 215, Northbrook, IL 60062-2745, 708/480-0066, FAX 708/480-0787.

TAUBER, AL. 1988. A Nontechnical Introduction to Integrated Document Processing Systems Using Optical Disks. ARMA Records Management Quarterly. 1988 April; 22(2): 16-22. ISSN: 0191-1503.

THOMPSON, BOYCE. 1990. Image Processing vs. the Ever-Growing Stack of Paper. Governing. 1990 April; 3(7): 50-55. ISSN: 0894-3842.

THOMPSON, JOHN S. 1988. Optical System Streamlines Record Keeping. Computer Technology Review. 1988 March; 8(3): 28. ISSN: 0278-9647.

TRAMMELL, BRINK. 1989. Too Little, Too Late? Not at USAA. Inform. 1989 July/August; 3(7,8): 24-26. ISSN: 0892-3876.

UPDATE. 1988. AG Says Disks Not Original Records. UPDATE. 1988 August; 1(2): 3-4. (Monthly newsletter regarding Texas statutes relating to open government). Available from: Update Publishing Company, 4406 Grey Dawn, Arlington, TX 76017, 817/572-7209.

URROWS, HENRY; URROWS, ELIZABETH. 1988. Optical Disks Compete with Videotape and Magnetic Storage Media. Optical Information Systems. 1988 May/June; 8(3): 101-109. ISSN: 0886-5809.

UTTAMCHANDANI, DEEPAK; ANDONOVIC, IVAN. 1989. Principles of Modern Optical Systems. Boston, MA: Artech House; 1989. 590p. ISBN: 0-89006-351-6.

VALDERRAMA, RAMIRO. 1989. Putting the Business Back into Imaging. Inform. 1989 October; 3(10): 16-17, 34. ISSN: 0892-3876.

VERITY, JOHN W.; BROWN, CORIE. 1988. The Graphics Revolution. Business Week. 1988 November 28; (3081): 142-153. ISSN: 0007-7135.

WAEGEMANN, C. PETER. 1988. The Handbook of Optical Memory Systems. Boston, MA: Optical Disk Institute; 1988. Paging varies. (Ring-binder format, bi-monthly updating service available). ISBN: 0-9621815-0-1.

WAEGEMANN, C. PETER. 1990a. How to Avoid Pitfalls with Optical Disk Systems. Presented at: ARMA International 35th Annual Conference; 1990 November 4-11; San Francisco, CA. 16p. (Handout from conference). Available from: C. Peter Waegemann, P.O. Box 289, Newton, MA 02160, 617/964-3923.

WAEGEMANN, C. PETER. 1990b. Strategy for Information and Image Management for the 1990s. Boston, MA: Optical Disk Institute; 1990. 250p. (approx.) ISBN: 0-9621815-2-8.

WALKER, FRANK L.; THOMA, GEORGE R. 1990. Access Techniques for Document Image Databases. In: Rorvig, Mark E., ed. Intellectual Access to Graphic Information. Library Trends. 1990 Spring; 38(4): 751-786. ISSN: 0024-2594.

WALTER, GERRY. 1988. An Overview: Technology and Application Status of Optical Disk Systems. IMC Journal. 1988 July/August; 24(4): 10-13. ISSN: 0019-0012.

WALTER, GERRY. 1989a. Making Optical Disks Pay. Inform. 1989 January; 3(1): 18-22. ISSN: 0892-3876.

WALTER, GERRY. 1989b. What Have We Learned from 12,000+ Installations? Inform. 1989 June; 3(6): 16-20. ISSN: 0892-3876.

WALTRIP, STEPHEN M.; BLAKE, ROGER P. 1988. The Software Factor. Inform. 1988 February; 2(2): 22-24. ISSN: 0892-3876.

WALTRIP, STEPHEN M.; BLAKE, ROGER P. 1989. Converting Conversion Bureaus: A Strategy for the Future. Inform. 1989 May; 3(5): 26-27. ISSN: 0892-3876.

WANG, FREDERICK A. 1987. The Promise and Peril of Information Integration. Manufacturing Systems. 1987 December; 5(12): 53-54. ISSN: 0748-948X.

WANG LABORATORIES, INC. 1990. Wang Integrated Image Systems (WIIS) 5 1/4-Inch Optical Disk Products. Lowell, MA: Wang Laboratories; 1990. 4p. (Product data sheet). Available from: Wang Laboratories, Inc., One Industrial Avenue, Lowell, MA 01851; 508/459-5000. Document No. 715-3017; 3/90.

WEBB, DAVE. 1990. Users Get Glimpse of New Generation. Computer Systems News. 1990 April 16: 37-38. ISSN: 0164-9981.

WILLIAMS, ROBERT F., ed. 1987. Legality of Optical Storage: Admissibility in Evidence of Optically Stored Records. Chicago, IL: Cohasset Associates; 1987. Paging varies. (Looseleaf-binder format; update service available). LC: 87-24280.

YOUNG, GREGORY. 1990. Effective Management of Maintenance Records at Continental Airlines. In: Roth, Judith P., ed. Case Studies of Optical Storage Applications. Westport, CT: Meckler; 1990. 37-44. ISBN: 0-88736-535-3.

ZIMMERMAN, KIM ANN. 1989. Banks Gearing Up for New Wave of Storage Technology. Bank Systems and Equipment. 1989 June; 26(6): 60-64. ISSN: 0146-0900.

III

Applications

Section III includes two chapters, a chapter entitled "Information Technology and Services in Schools" by Michael B. Eisenberg of Syracuse University and Kathleen L. Spitzer, consultant of Liverpool, New York, and one entitled "Information Systems, Services, and Technology for the Humanities" by Helen R. Tibbo of the University of North Carolina.

Michael B. Eisenberg and Kathleen L. Spitzer have done the first analysis of information technology and services in schools for *ARIST*. Their chapter provides: (1) a broad overview of the administrative and instructional uses of information technology in K-12 schools, and (2) an exposition of the current status of information technology and services of the library and information program in the United States with references to the United Kingdom and Australia.

Topics covered include: microcomputers, computers, computer-assisted instruction, integrated learning systems, distance education, interactive video, networks, information services, databases, curriculum mapping, online catalogs (OPACs), CD-ROM, CD-ROM networks, viewdata, information literacy, information skills, reading guidance and literacy, the instructional consultant role of the library media specialist, instructional television, library media program management, collection management, collection mapping, retrospective conversion, and resource sharing. The authors anticipate large increases in the number of computer-based information systems available to schools and for greater use by a younger clientele. For this reason Eisenberg and Spitzer think that information science professionals should pay more attention to the young people's interaction with the systems.

The chapter concludes with a view of short- and long-term technological trends in schools and library media programs and notes that while technology may well enhance education, students must be information literate in order to incorporate technology into their learning. "Those who are information literate will truly have the ability to be lifelong learners and fully participate in the information society."

Humanities computing has grown tremendously since the last *ARIST* chapter on this topic appeared in 1981. Helen Tibbo points out in her chapter on "Information Systems, Services, and Technology for the Humanities" that while many of the developments support traditional research activities, computer-based technologies are opening up entirely new avenues for research, teaching, and scholarly communication. Tibbo covers the English-language literature concerning information technologies in service to the humanities that appeared during the period 1981 through 1990, with an emphasis on writings published in the last five years.

Much of the material represents North American work but a significant portion originates in the United Kingdom, indicative of the attention Europeans have devoted to humanities computing. The term "humanities" has been interpreted broadly. Detailed discussions of computing applications are limited to archaeology, Biblical and classical studies, and philosophy. Information systems designed for institutions such as libraries, archives, manuscript repositories, and museums which support humanistic research are also discussed.

7 Information Technology and Services in Schools

MICHAEL B. EISENBERG
Syracuse University and
ERIC Clearinghouse on Information
Resources

KATHLEEN L. SPITZER
Library and Information Consultant

INTRODUCTION

This chapter reviews the substantial development of information technology in K–12 educational settings. To date, most discussions of the implementation, use, and impact of information technology and systems focus on corporate, academic, and government settings. However, there are widespread and varied uses of computer and information technology in elementary and secondary school situations as well. The K–12 educational environment encompasses multiple interconnected information systems for administrative and instructional functions. School library media programs, whose primary functions are to provide information service and instruction in information skills to students, teachers, counselors, administrators, and parents, are in a central position among these systems.

Technological applications in the educational arena range from routine computer applications (word processing, accounting, and scheduling) to cutting-edge applications (interactive media, simulations, and remote access to databases) (U.S. CONGRESS. OFFICE OF TECHNOLOGY ASSESSMENT, 1988). In academic, corporate, and government settings, library and information professionals are responsible for meeting information needs through service, systems design, management, and training. Similarly, school library media

Annual Review of Information Science and Technology (ARIST), Volume 26, 1991
Martha E. Williams, Editor
Published for the American Society for Information Science (ASIS)
By Learned Information, Inc., Medford, N.J.

specialists are the logical information professionals to perform these same vital functions in K–12 settings.

There is a growing realization that the educational system is the foundation of society and that many of our successes and failures can be traced back to the K–12 environment. In 1989 President Bush and state governors met to confirm the importance of education in the United States, stating that, "Education is central to our quality of life. It is at the heart of our economic strength and security, our creativity in the arts and letters, our invention in the sciences, and the perpetuation of our cultural values" (U.S. DEPARTMENT OF EDUCATION, p. 1).

Technology is recognized as a vital educational means and educational end. Technology links the classroom to the information resources of the world and can foster flexible, creative, and precise instruction that is targeted to the individual. In addition, if today's students are to function in tomorrow's world, they must be able to use the tools of tomorrow's world. One goal of education, therefore, is to develop students' abilities to use computers, telecommunications, and other information technologies for work, pleasure, and continued learning.

The information professions have much to contribute to elementary and secondary schools. Some of the major concerns of the information field—integrating technology with real needs, facilitating information transfer, establishing a user and service orientation, and instructing in essential information skills—are specific concerns in K–12 schools as well.

In defining the term "information technology," one could argue that since the goal of education is the transfer of information, all educational technology is essentially information technology. While an in-depth examination of the pedagogical implications of educational technology is beyond the scope of this chapter, we do provide a brief overview of the nature, scope, range, and extent of information technology in elementary and secondary schools. The primary focus is on the current status of information technology and services of the library and information program in the United States, with references to the United Kingdom and Australia. The literature covers the period 1986–1990.

INFORMATION TECHNOLOGY IN SCHOOLS

The vast array of information technology and systems in schools includes local- and wide-area networks, distance learning, interactive video, hypermedia, multimedia, and instructional television.

However, it is the computer that is the focal point of technology applied to education (ELY ET AL.).

No data are lacking concerning the use of computers in schools. *Power On! New Tools for Teaching and Learning,* a report from the Office of Technology Assessment (OTA) (U.S. CONGRESS. OFFICE OF TECHNOLOGY ASSESSMENT, 1988), examines the history of microcomputer use in schools and shows that the percentage of schools with microcomputers increased from 18% in 1981 to 95% in 1987. A more recent study by QUALITY EDUCATION DATA (QED) indicates that 96% of all public and private elementary and secondary U.S. schools have computers (ELY).

When computers were first introduced in schools ten years ago, the student-to-computer ratio was high, but it has dropped drastically over the past decade (see Figure 1). The improvement in this ratio is important because it indicates that students today (microdensity of 20 students per computer) are likely to have more time on a computer than did students in 1983 (microdensity of 125 students per computer). QED predicts that by 1995 there will be about 11 students per computer. A survey of school district superintendents ($n = 205$) conducted by the American Association of School Administrators validates this prediction, indicating that most superintendents are committed to improving the student-to-computer ratio (RICKETTS). In fact, 20% of them envision between one and three students per computer in the future.

At present, many schools locate computers in a self-contained computer laboratory. This means that an entire class can work in the computer lab at the same time. However, if the computer lab is always scheduled for full class use, which is often the case, individual students have limited access to computers.

SALOMON asserts that isolating computers in such a manner is the vestige of the erroneous assumption that computers should be taught as a separate subject rather than integrated with curricula. As we move toward increasing the use of computers in the general curriculum (as a source of information, for example), the need for computer labs is lessened. Instead, as Salomon states, the computer should be viewed as a tool and should be as available in the classroom as the pencil.

Applications of Technology in Schools

Technology is used in teaching, in administration, and for direct information service. The first two uses are considered here, and the

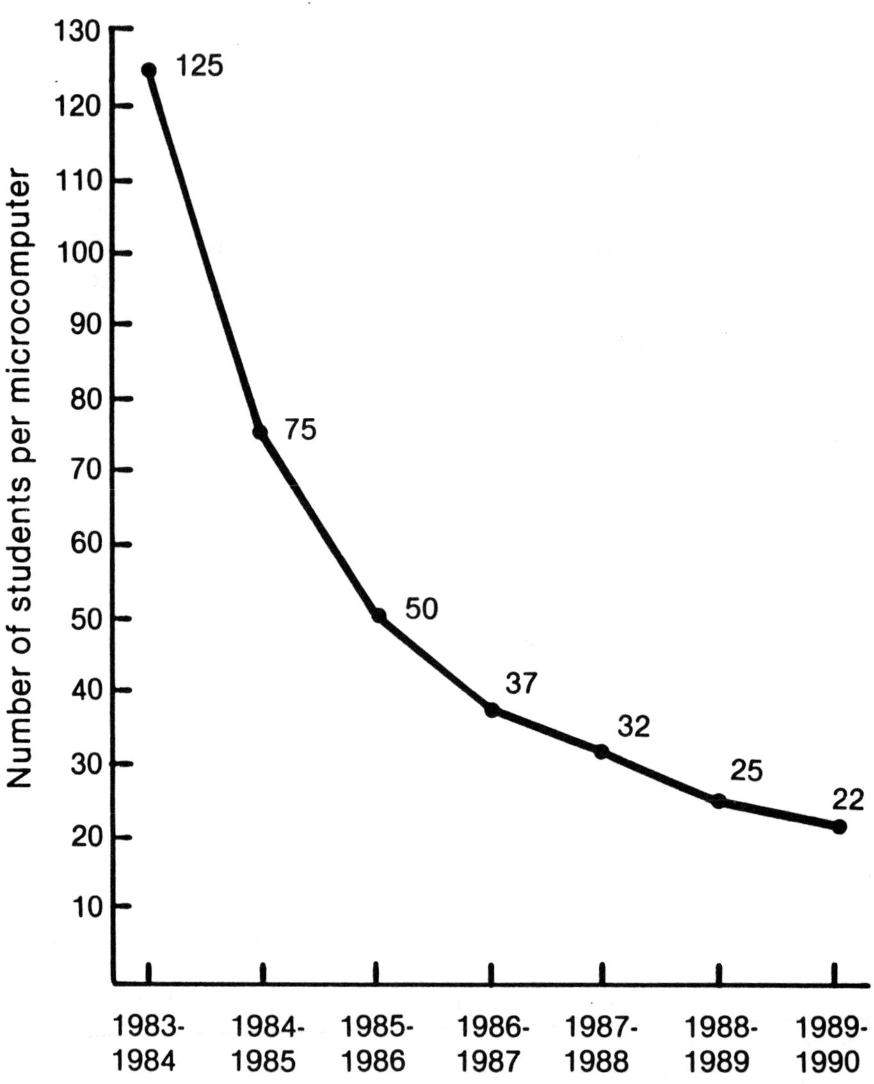

Figure 1. Microcomputer density trends. Source: QUALITY EDUCATION DATA, *Microcomputer Usage in Schools. A 1989-90 QED Update.* Denver, CO: Quality Education Data; 1990, p.1. Reprinted with permission.

use of technology for direct information service is covered in the section on the library media program.

Instructional uses. According to HAWKRIDGE (p. 1-2), there are four basic rationales for justifying computers in schools: (1) the social rationale: children should have an awareness of computers unafraid of them; (2) the vocational rationale: computers are likely to be part of the workplace of the future, so children should be taught how to operate them; (3) the pedagogic rationale: "computers can teach"; and (4) the catalytic rationale: computers can change schools for the better.

The extent of and emphasis on computer use depends on the rationale for introducing computers. HAWKRIDGE (p. 1) reports that students use computers:

- To become generally aware of the uses and limitations of computers;
- To learn computer programming (usually in BASIC but sometimes other languages such as Pascal or LOGO,
- To learn to use programs for word processing, spreadsheet analysis, graphics process control, and information retrieval from databases; and
- To learn selected topics from school subjects right across the curriculum, with the computer and educational software either complementing or temporarily replacing the teacher.

A 1989 survey of K–12 teachers ($n = 1,100$) by the WIRTHLIN GROUP of McLean, Va., indicates that teachers are quite positive about the impact of computers on American education. Most teachers believe that computers can be effective in helping students develop basic reading and writing skills, problem-solving abilities, and greater self-confidence and creativity. SHEINGOLD & HADLEY surveyed software use by teachers who have integrated the computer into the curriculum (see Figure 2). Most of the programs shown in the instructional software category in Figure 2 are commonly referred to as computer-assisted instruction (CAI).

CAI, which developed in earnest in the 1970s and 1980s, is used primarily in elementary schools. PRICE (p. 154), in a historical review of CAI, notes that "research has consistently found CAI to be effective in terms of improving student achievement, saving student time, and fostering positive attitudes on the part of both teachers and students." Others who have reviewed CAI research point out that much of the instruction is drill and practice and that the quality of such instruction varies (BOZEMAN & HOUSE). Teachers in the Wirthlin Group survey

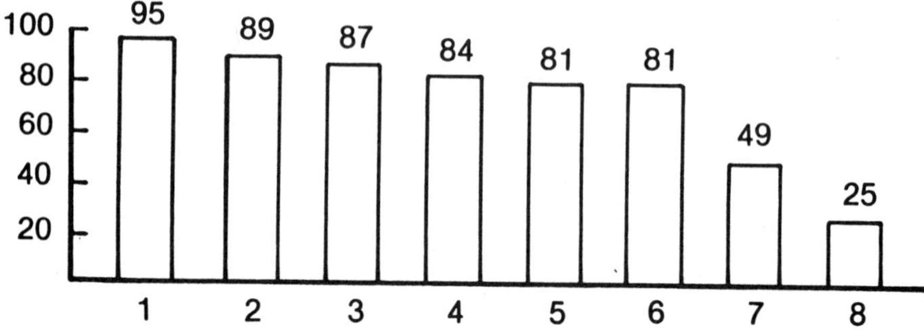

1. Text processing tools
2. Instructional software
3. Analytic and information tools
4. Programming and operating systems
5. Games and simulations
6. Graphics and operating tools
7. Communications
8. Multimedia

Figure 2. Percent of teachers using computer-based practices ($n = 608$) (Multiple mentions). Source: SHEINGOLD, KAREN; HADLEY, MARTHA. *Accomplished Teachers: Integrating Computers into Classroom Practice*, New York, NY: Center for Technology in Education; 1990, p. 8. Reprinted with permission.

believe that a weakness of CAI is that it does not generally develop critical thinking skills, a current focus of education.

The use of integrated instructional systems (IIS) (also called integrated learning systems), which include CAI as one of the components, is increasing. These systems usually consist of: (1) specific subject-oriented courseware spanning several grade levels (e.g., K–8 reading); (2) a management system that can generate reports and assign individual lessons to students according to an analysis of such reports; (3) a link to a standard curriculum; (4) provision of upgraded software as it is developed; and (5) a network of computers or terminals that may or may not be a part of the purchased package. A recent Educational Products Information Exchange (EPIE) survey of IIS use reported in SHERRY found that although students, teachers, and administrators view such systems positively, most schools were not making optimal use of them. To date, IIS are not seen as an integral part of the curriculum but rather as a supplement.

Computerized instructional management (CIM) systems contain some of the elements of the IIS and are used for management and diagnostic purposes. A CIM system is generally comprised of a curriculum database containing instructional objectives, tests, and answer keys, and a student database. Objective tests can be scored electronically and the outcomes analyzed in terms of whether or not instructional objectives have been achieved. CIM systems can generate both individual and group progress reports (HOFFMANN).

Other instructional management uses featured in the literature are:

- Record keeping via an electronic grade book or spreadsheet;
- Communications through networks with other teachers, supervisors, and professional groups; and
- Instructional material requests sent to the district office via telecommunications.

Computers have great possibilities for management and instruction. However, ELY ET AL. (p. 17) note that "the potential for computers in teaching and learning has not been advancing. The lack of progress can be attributed to the lack of teacher knowledge and skills, the lack of time to create and adapt materials, and the lack of support for introducing ideas." As teachers become more familiar with computers in their professional and personal lives, we can expect the quality of computer use in instruction to improve.

Distance education is a related instructional development that involves the use of information technology. Schools are currently implementing a variety of distance education systems to provide instruction that might not otherwise be available to students in rural and isolated areas. Examples of current distance education systems include: (1) telephone audio conferences; (2) computer-based messages via bulletin board systems; (3) audiographic conferences (incorporating a light pen or graphics tablet); (4) interactive television fixed service (ITFS) (generally used to deliver two-way interactive television over distances of fewer than 40 miles); and (5) satellite broadcast.

The Star Schools Program, established in 1988 by Public Law 100-297, dominates the literature of satellite-delivered distance education. The program, which is currently being implemented in 40 states, delivers instruction in specialized subjects to students in rural areas. QED reports that 21% of districts with fewer than 1,000 students use satellite dishes (KOBER). During the 1989–1990 school year, approximately 12,000 to 15,000 students participated in distance education through the Star Schools Program to learn such subjects as foreign languages and advanced topics for college credit.

Broadcast and recorded television and optical disc technologies are alternative instructional delivery methods that may be especially effective with visual learners. Broadcast and recorded television, in use in virtually every school in the nation, is used to enhance instruction and to provide professional development (WILSON).

Video also includes a variety of optical disc technologies such as compact disc (CD-ROM), videodisc, and interactive video. As of 1989, QUALITY EDUCATION DATA (QED) estimated that 8,776 schools had CD-ROM. CD-ROM is more extensively discussed in the section on the library media program.

ELY ET AL. note that videodiscs are only just emerging in schools. There are several levels of videodisc software currently in use: (1) level I, which allows for linear presentation without the capability for computer control; (2) level II, which contains a computer program on audio track II and allows interactivity via a microprocessor built into the videodisc player; and (3) level III, which consists of a videodisc and a computer disk (therefore requiring a computer) to allow for enhanced interactivity (SALES). QED reports that there are 1,077 videodisc players in schools and that 805 of these have interactive capability (ELY ET AL.).

Interactive video is defined as "any video program in which the sequence and selection of messages is determined by the user's response to the material" (FLOYD, p. 2). Its advantage is that teachers can customize the navigation of the videodisc for content purposes and to reflect the needs of individual learners. Examples of videodiscs in use in U.S. schools include ABC News Interactive's "The '88 Vote," which gives students and teachers access to one hour of video of the 1988 presidential campaign including speeches and press conferences, and "The National Gallery of Art," which allows students and teachers to access various periods of art, particular artists, or a sequential guided tour of the gallery. The BBC's "Domesday Project" represents a unique collaborative effort among corporations, government, education, and the public to produce a compendium of contemporary life in Great Britain. The videodiscs that resulted from the project, so named because it commemorates William the Conqueror's Domesday survey of 1086, provide a wealth of geographic, political, and sociological information that can be incorporated into instruction (BLIZZARD).

Administrative uses. The administrative use of microcomputers in schools has grown since the 1970s when mainframes were generally employed for this purpose (BLUHM). Prominent administrative uses include: (1) student registration, (2) class scheduling, (3) test scoring, (4) grade reporting, (5) attendance tracking, and (6) payroll processing. Other applications such as word processing, spreadsheet, and database programs are useful for correspondence, proposals, budgets, and record keeping (KEARSLEY).

Educational administrators, like their corporate counterparts, realize that computer applications provide optimal data manipulation capabilities to produce reports that can be analyzed for decision making. Although decision support systems (DSS) can assist administrators in making decisions, they have not been developed for the K–12 environment (TELEM, 1990a). Improved performance at the school and district levels and the renewal of educational leadership are two of the possible benefits of DSS in schools (TELEM, 1990b).

Local-area and wide-area networks can facilitate communication and increase the efficiency of administrative functions. As of 1986, more than 35,000 local-area networks (LANs) had been installed in schools in the United States (REINHOLD). LANs for schools often include management systems and security features designed to control student access to confidential records and software. For example, through IBM's IClass LAN management system, the network manager can configure students' accounts so that when they are participating in a mathematics class via computer they have access only to the instructional courseware and applications that the teacher has requested. The advantages of using a LAN within a school are: (1) multiple users can access the same program, thereby eliminating the necessity of purchasing and storing multiple copies of floppy disks; (2) student data can be accessed at networked computers throughout the school and district; and (3) expensive peripherals can be shared (REINHOLD).

Wide-area networks are used by educators to communicate with those beyond the local school district, particularly at the state level where educational policy is administered. According to QED, approximately 25% of U.S. school districts already have modems and thus are poised to access the full range of network resources. Many states are either planning a statewide network or have one. According to a Merrimack Education Center survey of every state in the United States:

> Approximately 60% [of those states] now operate a statewide computer or telecommunications network. Major functions of these networks include state reporting, student information systems, E-mail, financial management systems, electronic bulletin boards (BBSs), instructional resource databases, instructional management tools and teacher certification records. According to the survey, states reported that primary network users, ranked in order of frequency, are: principals, state departments, business managers, superintendents, teachers, curriculum specialists, librarians, personnel at institutions of higher education, researchers, and school board members. (LAVIN & PHILLIPO, p. 69)

Table 1
Computer Use by School Counselors in Ohio

Use	Percent Using:		
	Mainframe	Microcomputer	Total
College searches	42	21	63
Financial aid	38	19	57
Career planning	36	22	58
Student data	35	28	63
Word processing	5	38	43
Scheduling	45	5	50
Testing	10	6	16

Source: WRONKOVICH, MICHAEL. The Use of Computers by School Counselors: A Statistical Survey. *Journal of Educational Technology Systems.* 1989-90; 18(3): 255. Reprinted with permission © Baywood Publishing.

Guidance counselors fulfill a number of administrative duties as well as instructional functions. Their role is to advise students and parents on schedules, careers and vocations, continuing education, and financial aid opportunities. WRONKOVICH surveyed computer use by counselors in Ohio ($n = 250$) and found that more than half of them use computers for college searches, student data, financial aid, and career planning (see Table 1).

Career Information Delivery Systems (CIDS) are currently available in 46 U.S. states in the United States. These computer-based resources provide information on occupations and related education and training opportunities. They are used to explore careers and make decisions and have become a major information resource for vocational guidance and career development (LESTER & OLLIS).

During the past year, 6.1 million career seekers accessed computer-based career systems at 13,742 sites. However, CIDS systems "have impacted a mere 5.8% of the K–12 educational market in America" (JARVIS, p. 157-158).

Summary

Although there has been a steady increase in the use of computer and related technologies in schools, computers are still generally considered as an add-on rather than an integral part of the curriculum and day-to-day instruction. However, a general awareness by most teachers and administrators regarding the potential of a technological future shows that we are moving in the right direction. The widely reported National Geographic Society's Kids' Network Acid Rain Unit (WILLIAMS), which involved students from 48 states and 18 foreign countries in gathering, uploading, and analyzing data on acid rain, illustrates how technology can be incorporated into the curriculum and involve students in exploring a real problem.

Further, the Kids' Network Acid Rain Unit represents a curriculum application that is information-oriented. Educators are just beginning to recognize what has long been known in the information field—i.e., the computer has a more general information role to play, a role that underlies all administrative and instructional functions in schools. The next stage is to investigate the use of the computer as an all-purpose "information appliance." Here it is the library media programs and professionals who are assuming leadership roles.

INFORMATION TECHNOLOGY AND SERVICES IN LIBRARY MEDIA PROGRAMS

Three dimensions must be considered when speaking about the use of technology in library media programs: (1) the technology itself (e.g., computer systems, telecommunications, and networks), (2) the traditional functions of library media work (e.g., budget, acquisitions, circulation, and cataloging), and (3) the services that the library media program provides to students, teachers, and administrators (e.g., resource provision and access, consultation, and information skills instruction). Since the primary concern is the impact and use of technology in areas that "make a difference," the logical approach is to consider technology and its application to library media functions within a services context. As with any information system, the success and value of library media programs must be judged on the output side—on the services provided and how well they meet the needs of users. Therefore, the central focus must be on how technology is used to fulfill library media functions in order to provide meaningful services.

Information Power (AMERICAN LIBRARY ASSOCIATION. ASSOCIATION FOR EDUCATIONAL COMMUNICATIONS AND TECHNOLOGY, p. 1), the national guidelines for library media programs published in 1988, champions an ambitious service mission for the library media program: "to ensure that students and staff are effective users of ideas and information." Library media specialists fulfill this mission through three related roles:

- Information specialist, providing information service and expertise;

- Teacher, providing appropriate information skills instruction to students; and
- Instructional consultant, providing guidance in the integration of information resources, technologies, and skills into the curriculum.

In fulfilling these roles, library media specialists meet both the immediate and the future needs of students. Immediate needs are met by information services whereas future needs are met by integrated information skills instruction (EISENBERG & BERKOWITZ, 1988).

Information Services

The importance of a rich information base for education cannot be overemphasized. Education is fundamentally affected by the "information explosion." No textbook can possibly keep pace with all the rapid changes in the world. In science, social studies, health and other subjects, teachers must go beyond merely supplementing their textbook-based curriculum. They must revamp their approach and center instruction on the availability and use of up-to-date information sources. Further, the current emphasis on teaching critical thinking skills and transferable processes requires the use of resources to meet real needs (GOODMAN). The library media program is a key component in expanding the information base by providing access to information services and resources both within and outside of the physical confines of the school.

Access to local information. It is easy to create and use local databases to improve information access in the library media center. Such databases may range from simple bibliographies and resource lists to more formalized information retrieval sources. Databases likely to be of use include telephone directories, audiovisual files, school–community calendars, and files that provide access to human resources who may contribute their expertise to enhance instruction (e.g., community resource files).

The creation of local databases presents an opportunity for student involvement. For example, students at Dyce Academy (Dyce, Scotland) were responsible for all phases of creating a community information database, including planning, gathering the information, organizing the database, and assigning the keywords (BAIN & SADDLER). The database, created using COMMUNITEL, a teletext emulator that offers options similar to Prestel,[1] includes information

---

[1] Prestel is a viewdata system available in the United Kingdom and is explained further in the information services section of this chapter.

on local community events, statistics, transportation, and employment opportunities.

Hypermedia is another option for organizing and accessing information. An interesting example is the electronic Zuni/English Dictionary that was created by the Zuni Literacy Project and used in the Zuni Public School District (Zuni, N. M.). The electronic dictionary, accessible via Macintosh computers, is complete with pictures and audible pronunciations for 700 words (JENSEN ET AL.). At Caribou Hills High School (Burnaby, British Columbia, Canada), a 12th grader developed a hypermedia tour of the school accessible on any of 125 networked computers. By clicking on the icon for the library, students can obtain information about the online catalog, CD-ROM workstations, videodisc players, or satellite facilities (JENSEN ET AL.).

As part of its information service to professionals, the library media program provides access to state and local curriculum guides. However, information about the "real" curriculum represented by actual classroom instruction is far more valuable in the administration of the instructional program (ENGLISH). This kind of information is essential for successful planning, implementation, and evaluation of educational programs. For example, administrators need such information to set schedules, deploy staff, and identify areas of duplication or overlap; teachers need to know the sequence of content and skills in developing new units and lessons; library media specialists must use curriculum information to match services and resources to instructional objectives.

Curriculum mapping, a technique based on the procedures of content analysis, has the potential for managing curriculum information (EISENBERG & BERKOWITZ, 1988; 1990). The technique, which is a systematic process for collecting, organizing, and viewing information that represents the "real" curriculum, requires the ability to store, manipulate, and update large amounts of data. Database management systems (DBMSs) are appropriate tools for this purpose. By collecting and organizing curriculum information (e.g., name of instructional unit, subject, periods of instruction, time frame, grade, name of instructor, necessary resources, and method of evaluation), library media specialists provide a valuable information service to the school.

Access to the library media center collections. Although manual card catalogs still exist in many locations, library media programs are increasingly converting to online public access catalogs (OPACs). Surveys by MILLER & SHONTZ verify that in 1984 only 6% of those library media centers surveyed had automated their catalog, whereas in 1989 that figure had grown to 42%.

MURPHY (1988, p. 42), who has written extensively about OPACs in school library media programs, notes that the first OPACs developed for microcomputers were "essentially replicas of the card catalog, with searching options limited to first word or letters of the author, title and subject." However, as a result of demands by library media and other information professionals, Boolean and keyword searching are now available. OPACs may be purchased as standalone systems or as integrated systems that share data among cataloging, circulation, and acquisitions.

HERRING (1988, p. 35) ventures that "one of the most significant changes which will occur in the 1990s is the gradual disappearance of the card catalogue." He advises that OPACs be implemented not as a convenience for the library media program but as a way to expand access to resources for students. Because of the nature of collections in school library media centers, Herring suggests that subject access keywords be formulated by consulting with teachers who can identify the terminology most likely to be used in conjunction with the curriculum. However, expanded subject access should not replace the use of standard keywords necessary for resource sharing through union catalogs. The uniform promotion of the MARC standard in the library media literature on OPACs is a similar reaction to the need for standardization to facilitate resource sharing.

To date, there has been little research on children's interactions with OPACs. In fact, according to HOOTEN, as of 1989, there had been only one such study, that by Leslie Edmonds and co-workers, who studied children's interaction with touch-screen terminals and concluded that children have difficulty in using OPACs. Hooten recommends that studies of children's needs be undertaken and suggests some interim steps for library media specialists and public librarians: (1) enhance the readability of search screens and help messages on those online systems that allow customization of design; (2) provide clear labels in addition to MARC fields for screen display; (3) design a simplified version of menus and help screens for children to access on those online systems that allow multiple languages for menus and help screens; (4) encourage library automation software vendors to include features such as spell-checkers; (5) create a network among public libraries and school library media centers so that all are aware of the status of automation within each institution; and (6) encourage the creation of joint pubic library–school library media center automation projects so that students will use the same technology at each site. Hooten concludes (p. 272) by stating that "there is too little evidence to say exactly what effect online catalogs will have on children or what the magnitude of their needs will be regarding these new access tools."

While not a study of children's interaction with OPACs per se, BORGMAN ET AL. (1989b) conducted a pilot study to determine children's information retrieval needs. Because "information retrieval is among the applications for personal computers in the school, both as a component of other computing applications and as a primary function" (p. 81), the study was done to explore how children organize their knowledge so that an information retrieval interface for elementary school libraries could be designed. Results of the study show that "children can think in categorical terms about the domain of the database, provided they are given vocabulary terms that they understand" (p. 86).

In a related study, BORGMAN ET AL. (1989a) describe the design of a HyperCard-based prototype graphic information retrieval interface. The interface, a series of increasingly smaller bookshelves that represent a hierarchical structure of concepts, is accessed by pointing and clicking. This unique design is "intended to convey the concept of a hierarchy...in a way children can easily understand" (p. 98). The developers emphasize that studies of children's information retrieval needs are lacking but nonetheless important.

The addition of speech and graphics to a CD-ROM-based OPAC, as described by HARRISON & MURPHY, offers promise in the design of interfaces for children. These authors describe an expanded OPAC, which provides a human voice to aid in the formulation of search strategies and has enhanced graphics capabilities, such as pictures and maps of the library, state, or world. The system also features "an internal logic system that employs artificial intelligence techniques, hypertext, and thesaurus substitution [to help] prevent a patron's search from failing" (p. 79).

Access to periodical and full-text sources. Access to periodicals and full-text reference sources has been revolutionized by the introduction of compact disc–read only memory (CD-ROM) technology. CD-ROMs present a distinct advantage to library media programs in that the costs for searching via CD-ROM can be more readily estimated and budgeted for than the costs of searching online. More importantly, CD-ROMs can provide access to a variety of information for students, teachers, and administrators.

The number of CD-ROM offerings is rapidly expanding as evidenced by the increase in the number of CD-ROM titles listed in the *Optical Publishing Directory*—from 42 in 1986 to 320 in 1989 (NICHOLLS). Of particular interest to school library media programs are CD-ROMs that provide access to bibliographic databases (e.g., ERIC, WILSONDISC, and Magazine Index Plus) and full-text reference sources (e.g., Grolier's New Electronic Encyclopedia,

Compton's Multimedia Encyclopedia, Facts on File News Digest, Microsoft Bookshelf, Peterson's College Database). Public domain software (e.g., PC-SIG) and selection tools (e.g., Books in Print, Ulrich's Plus) on CD-ROMs are also popular.

The National Educational Resources Information Service (NERIS) Database on CD-ROM is currently offered by library media programs in the United Kingdom (MOORE). NERIS was established in 1986 and provides access to the National Curriculum of England and Wales, to specific resources to support the curriculum in Northern Ireland, Scotland, and Wales, to software reviews, and to original lessons developed by teachers. According to Moore, NERIS on CD-ROM is currently used by 180 subscribers who receive updated versions at the beginning of each academic term.

CD-ROM products that provide full-text periodical access are also emerging. For example, University Microfilms International's General Periodicals Ondisc features cover-to-cover reproduction of 150 periodicals. Users can search via discrete terms or can simply browse the periodical of their choice. Cover-to-cover reproduction allows users to browse for information in advertisements or in unindexed articles. Once users have identified an article of interest, they can print a copy of it right at their workstations. The ability to search and be guaranteed access to information through one system is a tremendous convenience for users. This is especially true for users in schools who may not be able to wait for interlibrary loan.

In an overview of CD-ROM technology for school library media programs, BAUMBACH (1990a) states that CD-ROMs offer advantages in that they provide: (1) an efficient way to search databases; (2) feedback that allows students to refine their searches; (3) motivation and self-confidence; (4) a way to develop problem-solving skills; (5) opportunities to explore information; and (6) an easy way to create bibliographies. Disadvantages include: (1) cost for the CD-ROM drive, computer, and peripherals; (2) lack of standardization in search protocols and screen design; (3) unavailability of materials identified in a search; (4) lack of coverage (CD-ROMs generally cannot provide information for historical searches); (5) difficulty of use by students with poor reading skills; and (6) lack of availability due to single-user access to the CD-ROM itself. Baumbach notes that because CD-ROMs make a great deal of information readily available to students, the information skills program must develop students' abilities to identify, filter, and use the information most appropriate to their needs.

Although CD-ROMs were originally designed for single users, multi-user access is a serious concern for library media programs since many class assignments require numerous students to access the same database or reference source within a limited time. Emerging technology to network CD-ROM drives provides multi-user access.

A CD-ROM network typically consists of an optical server that runs CD-ROM networking software and is connected to numerous CD-ROM drives shared across a LAN. CD-ROM drives may be contained within tower units that are designed for compact storage of multiple internal CD-ROM drives. Tower units may contain a variable number of internal drives. For example, towers offered by CBIS Inc. hold seven drives, while those sold by Meridian Data hold fourteen. Drive capability can be extended with expansion hardware that links towers together. According to BUERGER (and promotional material from networking vendors), the numbers of users and linked CDs are limited only by the hardware and software in place. That is, additional servers, drives, towers, wiring, and software can be installed to greatly increase the overall system capacity.

CD-ROMs shared via optical server software may result in faster access times than CD-ROMs accessed in a single-user environment because of caching abilities that store information from a user's previous search (HERTHER). In addition, mirroring, which comes into play when users run multiple copies of the same CD-ROM database, speeds searching by accessing the compact disc on which the read head is closest to the requested information. This latter ability is useful because library media programs may find it necessary to purchase and install several copies of popular databases.

Although LANs may exist within the library media center itself, many schools are broadening this vision. The provision of LAN access to library media resources throughout the school is a reality at Quince Orchard High School in Gaithersburg, Md.[2] The school, built in 1988, has more than 270 computers which are located in five computer labs, in each classroom, and in administrative, guidance, and department offices. Network access to resources such as Magazine Index Plus, DIALOG OnDisc, MEDLINE, Microsoft Bookshelf, and the Grolier's New Electronic Encyclopedia is provided to every computer in the school. The school is conducting a pilot project to provide telecommunications access to its resources to other schools within the county. In addition, telecommunications access to library media resources is provided after hours and on weekends. Union-

---

[2] Information about Quince Orchard High School was provided by Jean Judd in her presentation "The Networking Angle—Quince Orchard Style" given at the Conference of School Library Media Supervisors sponsored by the Division of Public Schools, Florida Department of Education, Tallahassee, Fl., September 12–14, 1990.

Endicott High School (Endicott, N.Y.) is another example of the keen interest by library media programs to provide dial-up access to library media resources after hours and on weekends.

The proliferation of electronic access to information in schools emphasizes the importance of studies of children's interaction with such systems. MARCHIONINI (1989) describes a study to explore students' use of and interaction with a full-text electronic encyclopedia. In examining the information-seeking strategies of third, fourth, and sixth graders, the author concludes that "in general, young novice users could successfully use a full-text, electronic encyclopedia with minimal introductory training. Subjects in third or fourth grade were less successful and took more time than subjects in the sixth grade" (p. 64). Marchionini notes that the "addition of a thesaurus or usage-sensitive search aid would certainly lead to more efficient searches and likely to more effective ones as well" (p. 64-65).

Another study, involving high school students, was designed by LIEBSCHER & MARCHIONINI (p. 232) to determine if "a sophisticated, analytical mental model for search queries yields better results than a simpler browse model for well-defined questions searched in an electronic, full-text encyclopedia." Students in one treatment group were given instruction in Boolean searching, while students in the other were encouraged to use browsing. The results did not support the hypothesis, and the authors conclude that "the simple browse model can be used effectively when the system presents a suitable interface" (p. 232).

Access to remote online sources. By participating in networks, school library media programs expand their collections. TUROCK notes that multitype library networks are the fastest growing cooperatives in the United States. Schools have as much to contribute to networks as they have to gain from such participation. Within multitype networks, school library media programs provide access to their unique resources such as audiovisual, professional, ethnic, career education, high interest/low reading level, and young adult collections (DOAN). VAN ORDEN & WILKES (p. 125) enumerate the advantages of network participation: "Students can access information located outside of the schools. Teachers have available an increased range of materials and information about materials, including human resources. Administrators can use data collection agencies and information services. Specialists can obtain professional materials, such as public health and guidance materials. Parents can access information about children's emotional and intellectual development." Since the fulfillment of the demands of the curriculum is a goal of library media programs, increased interlibrary loan (ILL) cooperation fostered by participation in networks can avoid problems such as the lack of sufficient materials when topics are assigned to many students.

An example of enhanced collection access through a multitype library network is provided by FITZWATER & FRADKIN. An Illinois project, called Reference by GammaFax, which is aimed at improving access to remotely held CD-ROM databases through telefacsimile, involves a multitype network of academic, public, and school libraries. Each of five source libraries is equipped with an IBM-compatible PC linked to a CD-ROM player and equipped with "Gammafax" software and circuit board. Each of four receiving libraries is equipped with a telefacsimile machine for the purpose of exchanging information with source libraries. Queries that can be searched through one of the CD-ROM databases are faxed to the source library, which then executes the search. The results are directly uploaded via "Gammafax" and received on the fax equipment at the receiving library. Participants in the project note that benefits include shared resources, shared expertise, and timely reference service.

JONES reports on the use of telefacsimile in ILL delivery for school library media centers located in the state of Washington. She notes that before the use of telefacsimile, the average fill rate for periodical requests at area high schools was 50%, but it rose to 95% after the implementation of a telefacsimile network. Student reaction to the increased access to periodicals and timeliness of the service was favorable.

Many school library media programs in the United States and abroad now offer remote, dial-up access to commercial online databases. Some of the online services available to library media users in the United States include: BRS, CompuServe, DIALOG Information Services, Inc., Dow Jones News/Retrieval Service, Einstein, The Source Telecomputing Company, and WILSONLINE. DIALOG, BRS, and WILSONLINE provide reduced classroom rates, and Einstein and Dow Jones offer flat rates to educational customers (HAND).

Radnor High School (Radnor, Pa.) pioneered the first online classroom account in 1979 with DIALOG (FIEBERT). Recent statistics show a vast increase in the use of such accounts. Anne Caputo of DIALOG reports that as of the end of January 1990, there were 5,241 educational users of DIALOG and that roughly 3,000 of these were from K–12 populations.[3] According to Caputo, of the 541,960 students currently accessing, half of these are K–12 students. A 1986 study by AVERSA & MANCALL shows that 50% of library media programs offering remote online services accessed DIALOG, 40% BRS, and 20%

---

[3] Personal communication with the authors.

WILSONLINE. Therefore, the total number of K–12 students using remote online services may well approach half a million.

In a survey by CLYDE & KIRK, Australian schools using online databases were asked to rank the three that were used most frequently. The most popular sources were: (1) Viatel, Telecom Australia's videotex service; (2) ASCIS (Australian Schools Catalogue Information Service)/ACIN (Australian Curriculum Information Network), which provides online cataloging, review, and curriculum information; and (3) sources such as PressCom and QNIS (Queensland Newspapers Information System), which represent full-text newspaper services. Keylink was also indicated as a popular electronic mail service. Two of the most significant drawbacks perceived by the schools were the high cost and limited access to equipment within the school.

Other reported studies include: (1) that by IRVING (1990) of six schools in the United Kingdom to determine the educational value and use of online service in schools; (2) the survey by LATHROP (1989b) of 73 secondary school programs in 19 states in the United States to study instructional objectives, student and staff training, curriculum uses, database selection, funding, and equipment; and (3) the survey by AVERSA & MANCALL of 45 schools across the United States to determine use, policies, and resources.

AVERSA ET AL. note the following advantages of online searching in schools: (1) an increased number of potential sources of information; (2) access to the most current information; (3) reduced search time compared with manual searching; (4) more accurate searching due to the availability of multiple access points; and (5) formation of positive attitudes toward the research process. Disadvantages include: (1) unavailability of materials retrieved in the search; (2) nonavailability of suitable databases for every subject area; (3) potential difficulties when telephone communications are disrupted; (4) potential costs; and (5) time needed to manage the online searching program.

The state of Pennsylvania has planned and provided a comprehensive online searching program for schools. Its Project LIN–TEL (Linking Information Needs—Technology, Education, Libraries) was instituted by the Pennsylvania Department of Education in 1982 to provide a statewide network to school libraries to access to online sources (EPLER, 1988). An extensive support system is provided to participants that includes training sessions, a newsletter, user meetings, and electronic mail support. A committee was formed to integrate online searching into the curriculum, and it produced *Pennsylvania Online: A Curriculum Guide for School Library Media Centers* (PENNSYLVANIA STATE LIBRARY), which provides management advice, a scope and sequence, expected outcomes, and sample lesson plans.

The Pennsylvania Department of Education realized that one of the implications of providing such access is an increased need for expanded resource provision through ILL. Arrangements were made with three universities in the state to provide copies of journal articles on request. A systematic program of resource sharing and retrospective conversion was also instituted through the formation of ACCESS PENNSYLVANIA, which provides a union catalog of resources from school, public, and academic libraries on CD-ROM. EPLER (1988, p. 54) emphasizes the positive impact of ACCESS PENNSYLVANIA on participants noting that: "The average school library in Pennsylvania has a collection of 11,500 resources. Schools participating in the CD-ROM union catalog can provide their students access to 1,000,532 items."

Many school libraries in the United Kingdom offer access to electronic information through Prestel, a viewdata system developed by the Post Office Research Laboratories and made available to the British public in 1979 as a means of information access and communication (CONDON). Prestel information is accessed via viewdata terminal or microcomputer with modem over telephone lines. According to Condon, Prestel is used in school libraries to access: (1) up-to-date information, (2) educational information, (3) remote databases, (4) other viewdata systems, (5) electronic communications, (6) software, and (7) microviewdata to allow the creation of databases. For example, students can access the Educational Counseling and Credit Transfer Information Service (ECCTIS), a career and higher education database, or use national statistical information and travel information in conjunction with curriculum.

MARCHIONINI & TEAGUE (p. 139) note that "electronic information services allow students to use an array of current information not generally available in schools and to acquire practical experience with a world-wide communication/retrieval environment." The authors designed a study to explore the effectiveness of elementary students' use of such services. Students in grades 2–3 and 4–6 were successful at using CompuServe to access an electronic bulletin board and an electronic encyclopedia. The authors caution that although the generalizability of the study is limited because of the sample size, the results encourage further study of this topic.

Student success in using front-end software in end-user searching was examined by CALLISON & DANIELS. They concluded that high school students were successful with the end-user interface but noted that students' use of online searching needs further study and should include the effect of students' independence or dependence on others in learning search strategies and the effect of online searching on ILL requests.

The computer-based information systems explored in the preceding sections may expand students' options to resources. However, HERRING (1988, p. 39) cautions that:

> There is danger in thinking that the application of new technology in information retrieval in schools will solve all the problems which pupils have in handling information about or within resources. To effectively use any retrieval system—manual or computerized, pupils will need the skills to understand why they are searching, what they are searching for and how they will use the information found. The *educational* value of using information does not lie in the pupils' mechanical ability to use a card catalogue or a database but in the learning skills involved in the exploitation of the information resources for curricular ends.

The development of such skills forms the focus of the information skills instruction program.

Information Skills Instruction

Library and information professionals are committed to developing an information literate population. Information literacy was first defined by Zurkowski (KUHLTHAU, 1987, p. 18) in 1974 as the ability to use techniques and skills "for utilizing the wide range of information tools as well as primary sources in molding information-solutions to. . .problems." A more recent definition of the term is provided by the AMERICAN LIBRARY ASSOCIATION. PRESIDENTIAL COMMITTEE ON INFORMATION LITERACY (p. 1), which states:

> To be information literate, a person must be able to recognize when information is needed and have the ability to locate, evaluate, and use effectively the needed information. Producing such a citizenry will require that schools and colleges appreciate and integrate the concept of information literacy into their learning programs and that they play a leadership role in equipping individuals and institutions to take advantage of the opportunities inherent within the information society.

The fully articulated information skills instruction program fosters information literacy by going beyond the teaching of the traditional "library skills" of location and access. Instead, these traditional skills are incorporated into a process approach that is transferable to contexts beyond school. A number of researchers and practitioners have sought to define the nature and scope of information processes. Examples include: KUHLTHAU (1985), who identified a process model for library research; CUTLIP, who viewed library media skills within the broad framework of the "Learning and Information Model;" STRIPLING & PITTS, who described library research as a thinking process with ten steps; IRVING (1985), who identified a nine-step information process; and EISENBERG & BERKOWITZ (1988; 1990), who presented the "Big Six" information problem-solving framework.

An important underlying assumption of the library media program is that information skills must be presented within the context of the curriculum. Integrated instruction is effective in that information skills are taught at the point of need. Instruction in technology is seen as a vital part of the overall information skills instructional program. Hardware and software systems provide important tools to use in meeting information needs and in solving information problems. Therefore, instruction in technology must be taught in two contexts—as part of the overall information skills effort, and in relation to a genuine need. For instance, the use of the online catalog should be taught as a tool for finding information in conjunction with a specific assignment. When presented in this way, technology and skills in using technology become inherent parts of the information process.

Those outside of the information profession also embrace this view. DE CORTE (p. 80) states that "computer learning environments should not so much provide the knowledge and intelligence to guide and structure the learning processes, but should rather create situations and offer tools that stimulate students to make maximum use of their own cognitive potential."

The key to creative and meaningful use of technology is to link it to information skills. Conversely, technology can amplify and expand students' capacities to use and process information. For example:

- Hardware and software systems offer new tools, options, and approaches for defining and completing a task;
- Computer databases and information systems expand the range and improve the possibility of retrieving relevant sources of information;

- Telecommunications and retrieval systems make it easier to locate and access information;
- Interactive multimedia systems provide multisensory interactions with information;
- Word processing, outlining, paint-and-draw programs, hypermedia, and other novel software allow for unique organization and presentation of information; and
- Computer-based capabilities change the standards for evaluating effectiveness and efficiency of information skills.

Computer skills can be developed in isolated, narrow contexts, but their value expands when they are used to solve information problems. By integrating such skills with the curriculum, technology becomes a powerful means for augmenting and expanding human capacities and fulfills the role as defined by De Corte.

Reading guidance and literacy. Traditionally, library media specialists have offered reading guidance by creating displays, giving book talks, preparing bibliographies, and recommending titles. Today, the computer can be used as a motivational tool to engender literacy through reading and writing. BEAZLEY, founder of the Computer Pals Around the World Project, relates the use of computers to promote reading and writing through electronic mail (E-mail). Children from schools throughout the world exchange personal correspondence, poetry, original stories, news items, and comments about literature through the Computer Pals project. The author states "the school library has been seen to be an extension of the global classroom as students are led through their electronic communications to seek further information from books, or simply to engage in reading for leisure, having been stimulated by a particular electronic communication" (p. 603-604).

DOWD & SINATRA report on software programs that encourage writing. For example, "Story Tree" allows students to compose an interactive story, "Newsroom" helps children produce a class newspaper complete with illustrations and layout, and "The Children's Writing and Publishing Center" combines word processing and illustration.

Databases of recommended titles may be created in-house or purchased. Fiction Finder (now commercially available) is a database program developed at Wichita State University to match literature with a child's interests (MCKENNA). The program was developed using information from students, library media specialists, and teachers to determine the most useful classification categories for recommending literature. The result is a classification scheme that includes 19 main categories (e.g., growing up, animals or things as characters, people facing problems). The program also specifies interest levels as well as book length and provides a brief commentary.

Examples of commercial annotated database systems include "BookBrain" from Oryx Press and "Bookwhiz" from Educational Testing Service (LOERTSCHER, 1988a). Available for either Apple or IBM computers, both can be customized to the school library media program's collection. While allowing students to search by title or author, these programs go beyond simple information retrieval. "BookBrain," for example, is a software package that allows students to complete a story and then uses the results to suggest titles.

Bibliographies are another way to interest students in reading. Bibliographic software, such as "Pro-Cite," can be used to produce bibliographies in various predefined formats. Some OPACs can also generate bibliographies. The inclusion of graphics through clip-art software can make the bibliographies into a visually interesting product (JENSEN ET AL.).

Information Technology in Consultation Services

The impact of technology on education is recognized by *Information Power* (AMERICAN LIBRARY ASSOCIATION. ASSOCIATION FOR EDUCATIONAL COMMUNICATIONS AND TECHNOLOGY, p. 10), which outlines an important role for the library media specialist:

> All aspects of education are significantly influenced by major technological advancements. The complexity of instructional technologies can, at times, overwhelm educators seeking ways to integrate them into the school curriculum. By assuming a leadership role in the use of technology in the school, the library media specialist promotes effective use of instructional technologies and facilitates their *full integration* (emphasis added) into the curriculum.

SCHIFFMAN (p. 43) notes that library media specialists are in a unique position to provide instructional consultation since the " [school library media program] is the only part of the school that cuts across all discipline areas. School library media specialists have contact with all teachers and administrators, unlike most others in instructional roles." Therefore, library media specialists have both the opportunity and the responsibility to make a positive impact on the quality of learning by providing expertise in the selection, use, and integration of information technology in instruction.

Several major authors address the role of the instructional consultant (e.g., CLEAVER & TAYLOR; LOERTSCHER, 1988b; TURNER) at various levels. Turner notes four levels: (1) no involvement, (2) passive participation (the library media specialist selects and maintains collections but has little interaction with faculty), (3) reaction (the library media specialist responds to teacher requests), and (4) action education (the library media specialist works as part of a team, jointly planning with teachers for the use of library media services and integrated instruction in information skills).

The 1990 edition of *School Library Media Annual* features several articles on the instructional consultant role. CRAVER, in a historical review, provides background knowledge of education trends within the past decade and current publications, research, and standards. Within the same tome, CURTIS (p. 63-64) enumerates six responsibilities of library media specialists as instructional consultants: (1) advisor to provide expertise in the adoption of new technologies; (2) change agents to act as "catalysts for change. . .through their knowledge of and competence in a wide range of learning technologies"; (3) designer to combine knowledge of curricular goals with sound instructional design principles; (4) instructor to provide instruction in the use of new technologies; (5) producer to use knowledge of media production to "provide advice and assistance to teachers and students to produce customized materials, tailor made to specific instructional or learning needs and situations"; and (6) evaluator to "provide guidance to teachers in the selection and evaluation of appropriate instructional technologies." CURTIS concludes that the shift from teacher-centered to learner-centered teaching environments provides opportunites for school library media specialists to make important contributions to improving education.

Part of that contribution involves consultation in the creation of alternatives to the overused "research paper" assignment. Library media specialists and teachers can cooperate to design projects that allow students to synthesize information through the use of various media. For example, students in a 10th grade class at Millard North High School (Omaha, Neb.) created and videotaped a news program on the greenhouse effect and the environment (EPSTEIN). Other options include speeches, short plays, slide/tape shows, physical projects, maps and other graphics.

As instructional consultants, library media specialists also advise on the use and integration of instructional television defined as "any in-school uses of television (either broadcast or recorded) for instructional purposes" (DIRR, p. 24). WILSON reports that the use of instructional video has increased from 31% in 1981–1983 to 99% in 1988–1989. A recent survey (WILSON, p. 94) shows that 77% of teachers "viewed the school library media specialist as the predominant source of information about video and related materials."

Library media specialists often coordinate distance education through the library media center. Technology such as the Voice Video Data System networks all available media (e.g., video tape, videodisc, CD-ROM, satellite cable feed) from the library media center to individual classrooms throughout the building. Using this convenience, teachers order direct delivery of media via special keypad wall units placed in classrooms (*MEDIA & METHODS*).

Information Technology in Library Media Program Management

The use of computer technology for library media management tasks (e.g., correspondence, bibliographies, overdue lists, mailings, statistics, budget) is widespread. Technology can improve the effectiveness and efficiency of library media program management. For example, catalog card production software can accomplish in two hours a task that may take up to 18 hours manually, thus allowing library media specialists to spend more time on service and less time on clerical tasks (EVERHART).

Technology also enhances the effectiveness of management tasks. Spreadsheets provide more varied and complex views of information about budgeting and accounting; DBMSs make it easier to manage personnel, collections, and patron data; and graphics and statistical packages improve the ability to analyze data and make projections. All management functions— planning, organizing, controlling, staffing, and leading—benefit from technology.

Collection management. Many of the tedious chores of the past may now be performed with the computer. Stand-alone programs are available for circulation, bibliography production, catalog card production, inventory, acquisitions, and budget (SKAPURA, 1990). Most integrated OPAC systems offer various management options, including inventory procedures and reports and overdue tracking and reporting.

MURPHY (1990b) notes that library media specialists have three options for converting records from a manual to an online system: (1) in-house conversion, requiring the entry of all necessary information for the MARC (Machine-Readable Cataloging) record; (2) partial in-house conversion, requiring the entry of information such as the

ISBN or LCCN as well as the call number on a disk which is sent to the vendor for matching and conversion to a MARC record; and (3) full vendor conversion, requiring the preparation of the shelf list before it is sent to the vendor for conversion to MARC records. The conversion option chosen depends on the size of the budget and the size of the collection.

Collection development is an essential management function of school library media programs. Library media specialists are responsible for maintaining a collection that reflects the needs of students, teachers, and administrators. In meeting these primarily curriculum-related needs, library media specialists can analyze information from both curriculum mapping (described in an earlier section of this chapter) and collection mapping to ensure systematic collection development.

In collection mapping the collection is divided into three areas for analysis: (1) the basic collection, which supports a variety of needs, (2) general emphasis area collections, which support broad, general areas of instruction, and (3) in-depth specific collections, which support single units of instruction (LOERTSCHER & HO). The results of a collection assessment are graphed via software and analyzed in terms of how well the collection is meeting users' needs. In determining the latter, it is necessary to consult curricular information (e.g., through curriculum mapping) and the users themselves. After identifying strengths and weaknesses, library media specialists can construct a collection development plan.

OPACs, which combine cataloging and circulation functions, enable library media specialists to generate reports to be used in collection management (MURPHY, 1987). For example, reports representing the number and type of materials in various Dewey ranges and the actual circulation statistics of these same materials can be graphed as Loertscher and Ho suggest. In addition, Murphy notes that a graph representing the number of unsuccessful searches in particular subject categories may reveal collection inadequacies.

Resource Sharing. Limited finances and common sense dictate that collection development be undertaken in light of network involvement (FISHER). Results of an exploratory study by VAN ORDEN & WILKES confirm that library media programs participating in networks are cooperatively developing and sharing collections. In addition to sharing material resources, network participation and telecommunications technology provide opportunities to share human resources. SWISHER ET AL. describe a joint project between the University of Oklahoma School of Library and Information Studies and the Library Resources/Technology Section of the Oklahoma State Department of Education. In 1980 the section began a program of cooperative selection by providing the state's school library media specialists with semiannual recommendations of new books for children and young adults, audiovisual materials, and special subject bibliographies. The program was initiated to fulfill a need of many isolated, rural school library media programs that had limited material and human resources. In 1986 a means of sharing the selection of information via the University of Oklahoma School of Library and Information Studies bulletin board system was developed to facilitate information transfer among users with disparate types of computers. Library media specialists also access the bulletin board system to participate in statewide teleconferences, access the University of Oklahoma online catalog, and access the Oklahoma State Department of Education database records.

Summary

Library media specialists use various technological developments to improve their programs. These developments are consistent with approaches taken by academic, public, and other library and information professionals. In addition, library media specialists emphasize the implementation of technology in context. That is, technology is considered an integral part of information skills instruction, information services, collection management, and consultation services.

FUTURE TRENDS

The literature offers predictions about both the short-term and long-term trends of technology. For the short term:

- Microdensity will continue to lower the student-to-computer ratio (QUALITY EDUCATION DATA; RICKETTS);
- Network installations of computers and CD-ROM will increase and will prompt educators to demand district-wide licensing availability from software publishers (BLASCHKE; FLANDERS);
- Distance education will expand and will eventually reach most rural areas in the United States (JEFFERSON & MOORE);

- Industry, recognizing that investments in the educational system are essential to corporate productivity, will increase its participation by providing technology and consultations to schools (National Alliance of Business as cited in BARTON & KIRSCH);
- Inquiry learning, based on using technology to access information beyond the textbook, will increase as students are encouraged to investigate various aspects of the world (D'IGNAZIO);
- Telecommunications will foster student-to-student and adult-to-student exchange of ideas and cooperative learning (D'IGNAZIO); and
- New interactive multimedia systems, which incorporate the capabilities of the VCR, CD-ROM, and the computer within one device, will emerge (Nicholas Negroponte as cited in NELSON).

For the library media program, the implications of these and other short-term trends include:

- The need for library media professionals to provide individualized service and to act as a filter between the increasing information resources and the user thereby bridging the gap between information and people (IRVING, 1988; Nicholas Negroponte as cited in NELSON);
- An expansion of library media services to offset the decreasing emphasis on textbook learning and an increasing emphasis on integrating various information sources into the curriculum (AMERICAN LIBRARY ASSOCIATION. PRESIDENTIAL COMMITTEE ON INFORMATION LITERACY);
- A resource-sharing orientation that delivers full-text information and arranges for loan of print resources electronically (SUMMERS);
- An increase in the quantity and quality of access points to resources so that potential information sources can be more readily identified by retrieval systems (MURR & WILLIAMS; SUMMERS);
- Coordinated collection development and resource sharing through participation in multitype library networks (SUMMERS);

- A major emphasis on information skills and technology use as part of information skills instruction (BREIVIK & GEE);
- The replacement of slide and filmstrip collections by interactive multimedia systems (GALBRAITH ET AL.);
- The availability of multimedia information systems through local- and wide-area networked environment (BULICK).

Long-term conjectures about technology in schools revolve around the concept of the "virtual school," wherein learning is not tied to a physical place or to a time-bound school day (BLYSTONE; PAULSEN). BLYSTONE (p. 144–148) notes that the virtual school will offer numerous advantages:

- It will be open 24 hours a day via telecommunications;
- The instructional scope and sequence of subjects will be individualized with the aid of technology;
- Text and graphics, delivered electronically, will be easier to evaluate, transmit, and store;
- Educational systems will cater not only to a K–12 environment but to learners of all ages;
- Children and adults will exchange ideas electronically and will learn from each other.

Library media futurists also talk about a "virtual library," not bound by time or place, that would allow electronic access to information and information services throughout the world (RYLAND). SLONIM & BAUER predict transparent access to worldwide information resources, foreseeing a time when the user will be able to request information electronically without contemplating source or location of use. IRVING (1988, p. 13) states that "Today's delivery systems don't recognise the distinctions between home, school, education, leisure, training or play." She also notes that the technology to bring about the "entirely electronic library" is available right now. Electronic superhighways, such as the proposed National Research and Education Network (NREN), are the first steps in fulfilling this vision (BISHOP).

Although technology may radically alter the nature of library media facilities, collections, and delivery mechanisms, the fundamental role of school library media specialists remains the same—to meet the needs of users.

CONCLUSION

This chapter provided an overview of technologies in schools and a detailed discussion of technologies and services in school library media programs. Schools provide a rich domain for study, a domain that represents our future. Since the future bodes large increases in the number of computer-based information systems, young people's interactions with such systems need to be addressed by information science professionals.

A quotation from the Colloquy on Computerised School Links (CARPENTER, p. 2) summarizes the emphasis of this exploration of information technology in schools:

> Information technology is the great enabler. It provides for those who have access to it an extension of their powers of perception, comprehension, analysis, thought, concentration and articulation through a range of activities which include: writing, visual images, mathematics, music, physical movement, sensing the environment, simulation and communication. The intellectual amplification it provides, when properly exploited in education, can deliver self-confidence and openness of mind which is indispensable for learning and development.

Information technology offers both an opportunity and a challenge and may, indeed, be the great enabler. However, information technology can only enable those individuals who possess the requisite skills for incorporating such technologies into their learning. These skills form the basis of information literacy, which is the goal of school library media programs. Those who are information literate will truly have the ability to be lifelong learners and fully participate in the information society.

BIBLIOGRAPHY

AMERICAN LIBRARY ASSOCIATION (ALA); ASSOCIATION FOR EDUCATIONAL COMMUNICATIONS AND TECHNOLOGY. 1988. Information Power: Guidelines for School Library Media Programs. Chicago, IL: ALA; 1988. 171p. ISBN: 0-8389-3352-1; LC: 88-3480.

AMERICAN LIBRARY ASSOCIATION (ALA). PRESIDENTIAL COMMITTEE ON INFORMATION LITERACY. 1989. Final Report. Chicago, IL: ALA; 1989. 21p. Available from: ALA, 50 East Huron St., Chicago, IL 60611.

AVERSA, ELIZABETH SMITH; MANCALL, JACQUELINE C. 1987. Online Users in Schools: A Status Report. Online. 1987 May; 11(3): 15-19. ISSN: 0146-5422.

AVERSA, ELIZABETH SMITH; MANCALL, JACQUELINE C.; OESAU, DIANE. 1989.   Online Information Services for Secondary School Students: A Current Assessment. 2nd edition. Chicago, IL: ALA; Syracuse, NY: ERIC Clearinghouse on Information Resources; 1989. 83p. ISBN: 0-8389-0524-2.

BAIN, LYNDA M. ; SADDLER, JOAN. 1987. Dyce Academy: Dyce Community Information Database. In: Herring, James E., ed. The Microcomputer, the School Librarian and the Teacher. London, England: Clive Bingley; 1987. 24-27. ISBN: 0-85157-399-1.

BARTON, PAUL E.; KIRSCH, IRWIN S., eds. 1990. Workplace Competencies: The Need to Improve Literacy and Employment Readiness. Washington D.C.: Office of Educational Improvement; 1990 July. 44p. (Policy perspective series; Report no. IS-90-0-987). Available from: Superintendent of Documents, U.S. Government Printing Office, Washington, DC 20402; ERIC Document Reproduction Service. ERIC: ED-317873.

BAUMBACH, DONNA J. 1990a. CD-ROM: Information at Your Fingertips! School Library Media Quarterly. 1990 Spring; 18(3): 142-149. ISSN: 0278-4823.

BAUMBACH, DONNA J. 1990b. Instructional Consultant: A Timely Role. In: Smith, Jane Bandy, ed. School Library Media Annual: Volume 8. Englewood, CO: Libraries Unlimited, Inc.; 1990. 15-23. ISSN: 0739-7712; ISBN: 0-87287-850-3.

BEAZLEY, MALCOLM R. 1989. Reading for a Real Reason: Computer Pals Around the World. The Journal of Reading. 1989 April; 32(7): 598-605. ISSN: 0022-4103.

BERTLAND, LINDA H. 1988. Usage Patterns in a Middle School Library: A Circulation Analysis. School Library Media Quarterly. 1988 Spring; 16(3): 200-203. ISSN: 0278-4823.

BISHOP, ANN P. 1990. The National Research and Education Network (NREN): Promise of a New Information Environment. ERIC Digest. Syracuse, NY: ERIC Clearinghouse on Information Resources; 1990 November. 1p. (EDO-IR-90-4). Available from: ERIC Clearinghouse on Information Resources, 030 Huntington Hall, Syracuse, NY 13244-2340.

BLASCHKE, CHARLES L. 1990. Integrated Learning Systems/Instructional Networks: Current Uses and Trends. Educational Technology. 1990 November; 30(11): 20-23. ISSN: 0013-1962.

BLIZZARD, ANDREW. 1989. 1986 and All That: The BBC Domesday Project. School Librarian. 1989 August; 37(3): 94-96. ISSN: 0036-6595.

BLUHM, HENRY P. 1987. Administrative Uses of Computers in Schools. Englewood Cliffs, NJ: Prentice-Hall, Inc.; 1987. 310p. ISBN: 0-13-008467-0; LC: 86-25335.

BLYSTONE, KENNETH E. 1989. An Introduction to Virtual Schools Using Telecommunications to Cross Old Boundaries. Computers in the Schools. 1989; 6(3-4): 141-153. ISSN: 0738-0569.

BORGMAN, CHRISTINE L.; BOWER, JAMES; AUTH, MICHAEL J.; KRIEGER, DAVID. 1989a. From Hands-On Science to Hands-On Information Retrieval. In: Katzer, Jeffrey; Newby, Gregory B., eds. ASIS '89: Managing Information and Technology: Proceedings of the American Society for Information Science (ASIS) 52nd Annual Meeting: Volume 26; 1989 October 30-November 2; Washington, DC. Medford, NJ: Learned Information, Inc. for ASIS; 1989. 96-103. ISSN: 0044-7870; ISBN: 0-938734-40-7; LC: 64-8303.

BORGMAN, CHRISTINE L.; CHIGNELL, MARK H.; VALDEZ, FELIX. 1989b. Designing an Information Retrieval Interface Based on Childrens' Categorization of Knowledge: A Pilot Study. In: Katzer, Jeffrey; Newby, Gregory B., eds. ASIS '89: Managing Information and Technology: Proceedings of the American Society for Information Science (ASIS) 52nd Annual Meeting: Volume 26; 1989 October 30-November 2; Washington, DC. Medford, NJ: Learned Information, Inc. for ASIS; 1989. 81-95. ISSN: 0044-7870; ISBN: 0-938734-40-7; LC: 64-8303.

BORGMAN, CHRISTINE L.; KRIEGER, DAVID; GALLAGHER, ANDREA L.; BOWER, JAMES. 1990. Children's Use of an Interactive Science Library: Exploratory Research. School Library Media Quarterly. 1990 Winter; 18(2): 108-112. ISSN: 0278-4823.

BOZEMAN, WILLIAM C.; HOUSE, JESS E. 1988. Microcomputers in Education: The Second Decade. Technological Horizons in Education Journal. 1988 February; 15(6): 82-86. ISSN: 0192-592X.

BREIVIK, PATRICIA SENN; GEE, E. GORDON. 1989. Information Literacy: Revolution in the Library. New York, NY: Macmillan Publishing Co.; 1989. 250p. ISBN: 0-02-911440-3.

BUERGER, DAVID. 1989. CD-ROM Servers Capitalize on LAN Connectivity Potential. Infoworld. 1989 October 23; 11(43): 41. ISSN: 0199-6649.

BULICK, STEPHEN. 1990. Future Prospects for Network-based Multimedia Information Retrieval. The Electronic Library. 1990 April; 8(2): 88-99. ISSN: 0264-0473.

CALLISON, DANIEL. 1988. Methods of Measuring Student Use of Databases and Interlibrary Loan Materials. School Library Media Quarterly. 1988 Winter; 16(2): 138-142. ISSN: 0278-4823.

CALLISON, DANIEL; DANIELS, ANN. 1988. Introducing End-User Software for Enhancing Student Online Searching. School Library Media Quarterly. 1988 Spring; 16(3): 173-181. ISSN: 0278-4823.

CARPENTER, J.P. 1989. Using the New Technologies to Create Links between Schools throughout the World: Colloquy on Computerised School Links; 1988 October 17-20; Exeter, Devon, UK. Strasbourg, France: Council for Cultural Cooperation, School Education Division; 1989 May 12. 38p. Available from: ERIC Document Reproduction Service. ERIC: ED-318658.

CHEN, LIN CHING. 1990-91. Interactive Video Technology in Education: Past, Present, and Future. Journal of Educational Technology Systems. 1990-91; 19(1): 5-19. ISSN: 0047-2395.

CLARK, CHRIS. 1989. Distance Education in United States Schools. The Computing Teacher. 1989 March; 16(6): 7-11. ISSN: 0278-9175.

CLEAVER, BETTY; TAYLOR, WILLIAM. 1989. Instructional Consultant Role of the School Library Media Specialist. Chicago, IL: American Library Association; 1989. 88p. ISBN: 0-8389-3377-7.

CLYDE, LAUREL A. 1988. Online Information Services in Schools. The Electronic Library. 1988 April; 6(2): 126-134. ISSN: 0264-0473.

CLYDE, LAUREL A.; KIRK, JOYCE. 1989. The Use of Electronic Information Systems in Australian Schools: A Preliminary Survey. School Library Media Quarterly. 1989 Summer; 17(4): 193-199. ISSN: 0278-4823.

CONDON, JAN. 1987. Prestel in the School Library. In: Herring, James E., ed. The Microcomputer, the School Librarian and the Teacher. London, England: Clive Bingley; 1987. 79-100. ISBN: 0-85157-399-1.

COSTA, BETTY; COSTA, MARIE. 1991. A Micro Handbook for Small Libraries and Media Centers. Englewood, CO: Libraries Unlimited, Inc.; 1991. 325p. ISBN: 0-87287-901-1.

CRAVER, KATHLEEN W. 1990. The Instructional Consultant Role of the School Library Media Specialist 1980-1989. In: Smith, Jane Bandy, ed. School Library Media Annual: Volume 8. Englewood, CO: Libraries Unlimited, Inc.; 1990. 4-14. ISSN: 0739-7712; ISBN: 0-87287-850-3.

CURTIS, RUTH V. 1990. The Contributions of Technology to Instruction and Learning. In: Smith, Jane Bandy, ed. School Library Media Annual: Volume 8. Englewood, CO: Libraries Unlimited, Inc.; 1990. 59-66. ISSN: 0739-7712; ISBN: 0-87287-850-3.

CUTLIP, GLEN W. 1988. Learning and Information: Skills for the Secondary Classroom and Library Media Program. Englewood, CO: Libraries Unlimited, Inc.; 1988. 134p. ISBN: 0-87287-580-6; LC: 88-27190.

DECORTE, E. 1990. Learning with New Information Technologies in Schools: Perspectives from the Psychology of Learning and Instruction. Journal of Computer Assisted Learning. 1990 June; 6(2): 69-87. ISSN: 0266-4909.

D'IGNAZIO, FRED. 1990. An Inquiry-Centered Classroom of the Future. The Computing Teacher. 1990 March; 17(6): 16-19. ISSN: 0278-9175.

DIRR, PETER. 1977. The Use of Instructional TV: A Report on a New Study. Educational and Industrial Television. 1977 November; 9(11): 23-25. ISSN: 0046-1466.

DOAN, JANICE K. 1985. School Library Media Centers in Networks. School Library Media Quarterly. 1985 Summer; 13(4): 191-199. ISSN: 0278-4823.

DOWD, CORNELIA A.; SINATRA, RICHARD. 1990. Computer Programs and the Learning of Text Structure. Journal of Reading. 1990 October; 34(2): 104-112. ISSN: 0022-4103.

EISENBERG, MICHAEL B., ed. 1990a. Technology. School Library Media Quarterly. 1990 Spring; 18(3): 71p. (Theme issue). ISSN: 0278-4823.

EISENBERG, MICHAEL B. 1990b. Technology and the Library Media Program: Focus on Potential and Purpose. School Library Media Quarterly. 1990 Spring; 18(3): 139-141. ISSN: 0278-4823.

EISENBERG, MICHAEL B.; BERKOWITZ, ROBERT E. 1988. Curriculum Initiative: An Agenda and Strategy for Library Media Programs. Norwood, NJ: Ablex Publishing Corp.; 1988. 180p. ISBN: 0-89391-486-X; LC: 88-1598.

EISENBERG, MICHAEL B.; BERKOWITZ, ROBERT E. 1990. Information Problem-Solving: The Big Six Skills Approach to Library & Information Skills Instruction. Norwood, NJ: Ablex Publishing Corp.; 1990. 156p. ISBN: 0-89391-757-5; LC: 90-22681.

ELY, DONALD P. 1990. Computers in Schools and Universities in the United States of America. Paper presented at the Association for the Development of Computer-based Instructional Systems 32nd International Meeting; 1990 October 31; San Diego, CA. 14p. Available from: ERIC Document Reproduction Service. ERIC: ED-327150.

ELY, DONALD P.; LEBLANC, GLENN; YANCEY, CRYSTAL. 1989. Trends and Issues in Educational Technology 1989. Syracuse, NY: ERIC Clearinghouse on Information Resources; 1989. 57p. ISBN: 0-937597-26-0.

ENGLISH, FENWICK W. 1979. Re-tooling the Curriculum with On-going School Systems. Educational Technology. 1979 May; 19(5): 7-13. ISSN: 0013-1962.

EPLER, DORIS. 1988. Networking in Pennsylvania: Technology and the School Library Media Center. Library Trends. 1988 Summer; 37(1): 43-55. ISSN: 0024-2594.

EPLER, DORIS. 1989. Online Searching Goes to School. Phoenix, AZ: The Oryx Press; 1989. 149p. ISBN: 0-89774-546-9.

EPLER, DORIS M.; CASSEL, RICHARD E. 1987. ACCESS PENNSYLVANIA: A CD-ROM Database Project. Library Hi Tech. 1987 Fall; 5(3): 81-92. ISSN: 0737-8831.

EPSTEIN, ANDREA. 1990. Math and Science Curricula: The Role of Media Specialists. Media & Methods. 1990 March/April; 26(4): 34-37. ISSN: 0025-6897.

EVERHART, NANCY. 1987. MMI Model Library. Small Computers in Libraries. 1987 March; 7(3): 10-15. ISSN: 0275-6722.

FIEBERT, ELYSE EVANS. 1987. Online at Radnor High: A Pattern of Change. Online. 1987 May; 11(3): 19-21. ISSN: 0146-5422.

FISHER, PHYLLIS. 1986. Extending the Carpet: School Libraries, Access and the Information Implosion. The Bookmark. 1986 Spring; 44(3): 148-151. ISSN: 0006-7407.

FITZWATER, DIANA; FRADKIN, BERNARD. 1988. CD-ROM + Fax = Shared Reference Resources. American Libraries. 1988 May; 19(5): 385. ISSN: 0002-9769.

FLANDERS, BRUCE L. 1990. Spinning the Hits: CD-ROM Networks in Libraries. American Libraries. 1990 December; 21(11): 1032-1033. ISSN: 0002-9769.

FLOYD, STEVE. 1982. Thinking Interactively. In: Floyd, Steve; Floyd, Beth, eds. Handbook of Interactive Video. White Plains, NY: Knowledge Industry Publications, Inc.; 1982. 1-14. ISBN: 0-86729-019-6.

GALBRAITH, P.L.; GRICE, R.D.; CARSS, M.C.; ENDEAN, L.; WARRY, M. 1990. Instructional Technology in Education? Whither Its Future? Educational Technology. 1990 August; 30(8): 18-25. ISSN: 0013-1962.

GLUCK, MYKE. 1990. Hypermedia: Information Done Your Way. School Library Media Quarterly. 1990 Summer; 18(4): 215-222. ISSN: 0278-4823.

GOODMAN, KENNETH S. 1989. Whole-Language Research: Foundations and Development. The Elementary School Journal. 1989 November; 90(2): 207-221. ISSN: 0013-5984.

HAND, DORCAS. 1988. Online Searching Educational Bargain. In: Smith, Jane Bandy, ed. School Library Media Annual: Volume 6. Englewood, CO: Libraries Unlimited, Inc.; 1988. 141-149. ISSN: 0739-7712; ISBN: 0-87287-635-7.

HARRISON, NANCY; MURPHY, BROWER. 1987. Multisensory Public Access Catalogs on CD-ROM. Library Hi Tech. 1987 Fall; 5(3): 77-80. ISSN: 0737-8831.

HAWKRIDGE, DAVID. 1990. Who Needs Computers in Schools, and Why? Computers & Education. 1990; 15(1-3): 1-6. (Special issue: Computer Assisted Learning, Selected Proceedings from the CAL '89 Symposium). ISSN: 0360-1315; ISBN: 0-08-040249-6.

HERRING, JAMES E. 1987a. The Electronic School Library. The Electronic Library. 1987 August; 5(4): 230-236. ISSN: 0264-0473.

HERRING, JAMES E., ed. 1987b. The Microcomputer, the School Librarian and the Teacher. London, England: Clive Bingley; 1987. 150p. ISBN: 0-85157-399-1.

HERRING, JAMES E. 1988. School Librarianship. 2nd edition. London, England: Clive Bingley; 1988. 81p. ISBN: 0-85157-423-8.

HERTHER, NANCY K. 1988. CD-ROM Standards, Networking and the Future: A Conversation with Meridian Data's Fred Meyer. Laserdisk Professional. 1988 September; 1(3): 41-49. ISSN: 0896-4149.

HOFFMANN, WILLIAM. 1990. Dade County Teachers Aided by Instructional Management Systems. Technological Horizons in Education Journal. 1990 September; 18(2): 79-81. ISSN: 0192-592X.

HOOTEN, PATRICIA A. 1989. Online Catalogs: Will They Improve Children's Access? Journal of Youth Services in Libraries. 1989 Spring; 2(3): 267-272. ISSN: 0894-2498.

IMMROTH, BARBARA FROLING. 1990. Networking: Studies of Multitype Library Networking with Implications for School Library Media Practice. In: Woolls, Blanche, ed. The Research of School Library Media Centers: Papers of Treasure Mountain Research Retreat; 1989 October

17-18; Park City, UT. Castle Rock, CO: Hi-Willow Research and Publishing Co.; 1990. 175-187. ISBN: 0-931510-30-9.

IRVING, ANN. 1985. Study and Information Skills across the Curriculum. London, England: Heinemann Educational Books; 1985. 228p. ISBN: 0-435-80520-7.

IRVING, ANN. 1988. School Libraries: Fifty Years Ahead, Are You Ready Yet? School Librarian. 1988 February; 36(1): 10-13. ISSN: 0036-6595.

IRVING, ANN. 1990. Wider Horizons: Online Information Services in Schools. London, England: British Library; 1990. 138p. (Library and Information Research Reports 80). ISBN: 0-7123-3224-3.

JARVIS, PHILLIP S. 1990. A Nation at Risk: The Economic Consequences of Neglecting Career Development. Journal of Career Development. 1990 Spring; 16(3): 157-171. ISSN: 0894-8453.

JEFFERSON, FRANCINE E.; MOORE, O.K. 1990. Distance Education: A Review of Progress and Prospects. Educational Technology. 1990 September; 30(9): 7-12. ISSN: 0013-1962.

JENSEN, ERIC; GANN, LINDA; CARSON, CHRIS; MEHARG, JEREMY. 1990. Libraries Designing Online Databases via Hypermedia. Media & Methods. 1990 November/December; 27(2): 34-35, 46. ISSN: 0025-6897.

JONES, SALLY L. 1991. Just the FAX for High School Students. School Library Journal. 1991 January; 37(1): 42. ISSN: 0362-8930.

KEARSLEY, GREG. 1988. What Should Today's School Administrators Know about Computers? Technological Horizons in Education Journal. 1988 November; 16(4): 65-69. ISSN: 0192-592X.

KOBER, NANCY. 1990. Think Rural Means Isolated? Not When Distance Learning Reaches into Schools. School Administrator. 1990 November; 47(10): 16-24. ISSN: 0036-6439.

KUHLTHAU, CAROL C. 1985. Teaching the Library Research Process. West Nyack, NY: The Center for Applied Research in Education; 1985. 190p. ISBN: 0-87628-804-2; LC: 85-3773.

KUHLTHAU, CAROL C. 1987. Information Skills for an Information Society: A Review of Research. Syracuse, NY: ERIC Clearinghouse on Information Resources; 1987. 28p. ISBN: 0-937597-14-7.

KUHLTHAU, CAROL C. 1989. Developing a Model of the Library Search Process: Cognitive and Affective Aspects. RQ. 1989 Winter; 28(2): 232-242. ISSN: 0033-7072.

LATHROP, ANN, comp. 1989a. Online and CD-ROM Databases in School Libraries: Readings. Englewood, CO: Libraries Unlimited, Inc.; 1989. 375p. ISBN: 0-87287-756-6.

LATHROP, ANN. 1989b. Online Information Retrieval as a Research Tool in Secondary Schools. In: Lathrop, Ann, comp. Online and CD-ROM Databases in School Libraries: Readings. Englewood, CO: Libraries Unlimited, Inc.; 1989. 287-303. ISBN: 0-87287-756-6.

LAVIN, RICHARD J.; PHILLIPO, JOHN. 1990. Improve School-Based Management through Intelligent Networking. Technological Horizons in Education Journal. 1990 November; 18(4): 69-71. ISSN: 0192-592X.

LESTER, JULIETTE N.; OLLIS, HARVEY T. 1988. Future Challenges to Career Information Providers: A NOICC Perspective. Journal of Career Development. 1988 Spring; 14(3): 205-215. ISSN: 0894-8453.

LIEBSCHER, PETER; MARCHIONINI, GARY. 1988. Browse and Analytical Search Strategies in a Full-Text CD-ROM Encyclopedia. School Library Media Quarterly. 1988 Summer; 16(4): 223-233. ISSN: 0278-4823.

LOERTSCHER, DAVID. 1988a. High Technology for School Libraries. Media & Methods. 1988 September/October; 25(1): 21-24. ISSN: 0025-6897.

LOERTSCHER, DAVID. 1988b. Taxonomies of the School Library Media Program. Englewood, CO: Libraries Unlimited, Inc.; 1988. 336p. ISBN: 0-87287-662-4.

LOERTSCHER, DAVID; HO, MAY LIEN. 1986. Computerized Collection Development for School Library Media Centers. Englewood, CO: Libraries Unlimited, Inc. 1986. 250p. ISBN: 0-931510-19-8.

MANCALL, JACQUELINE C.; AARON, SHIRLEY L.; WALKER, SUE A. 1986. Educating Students to Think: The Role of the School Library Media Program. School Library Media Quarterly. 1986 Fall; 15(1): 18-27. ISSN: 0278-4823.

MARCHIONINI, GARY. 1989. Information-Seeking Strategies of Novices Using a Full-Text Electronic Encyclopedia. Journal of the American Society for Information Science. 1989 January; 40(1): 54-66. ISSN: 0002-8231.

MARCHIONINI, GARY. 1990. Educational Computing Research: Status and Prospectus. In: Woolls, Blanche, ed. The Research of School Library Media Centers: Papers of Treasure Mountain Research Retreat; 1989 October 17-18; Park City, UT. Castle Rock, CO: Hi-Willow Research and Publishing Co.; 1990. 189-200. ISBN: 0-931510-30-9.

MARCHIONINI, GARY; TEAGUE, JERRY. 1987. Elementary Students' Use of Electronic Information Services: An Exploratory Study. Journal of Research on Computing in Education. 1987 Winter; 20(2): 139-155. ISSN: 0888-6504.

MARTIN, LAURA M.W. 1989. Synthesis. In: U. S. Department of Education Office of Educational Research and Improvement. To Support the Learner: A Collection of Essays on the Applications of Technology in Education. Washington, DC: U.S. Department of Education; 1989. 3 microfiche; 216p.; 24x reduction. (Report No. PIP-89-873). Available from: ERIC Document Reproduction Service. ERIC: ED 310763.

MCDONALD, FRANCES BECK, comp. 1988. The Emerging School Library Media Program. Englewood, CO: Libraries Unlimited; 1988. 328p. ISBN: 0-87287-660-8; LC: 88-6784.

MCKENNA, MICHAEL C. 1987. Using Micros to Find Fiction: Issues and Answers. School Library Media Quarterly. 1987 Winter; 15(2): 92-95. ISSN: 0278-4823.

MEDIA & METHODS. 1990. Short Takes Column. Media & Methods. 1990 May/June; 26(5): 6-7. ISSN: 0025-6897.

MILLER, MARILYN L.; SHONTZ, MARILYN L. 1989. Expenditures for Resources in School Library Media Centers, FY '88-'89. School Library Journal. 1989 June; 35(10): 31-40. ISSN: 0362-8930.

MOORE, MICHAEL. 1990. NERIS on CD-ROM. CD-ROM EndUser. 1990 September; 2(5): 36-38. ISSN: 1042-8623.

MURPHY, CATHERINE. 1987. The Online Catalog: A Tool for Collection Management. School Library Media Quarterly. 1987 Spring; 15(3): 154-157. ISSN: 0278-4823.

MURPHY, CATHERINE. 1988. The Time Is Right to Automate. School Library Journal. 1988 November; 35(3): 42-47. ISSN: 0362-8930.

MURPHY, CATHERINE. 1990a. Access to Information: The Effect of Automation. In: Woolls, Blanche, ed. The Research of School Library Media Centers: Papers of Treasure Mountain Research Retreat; 1989 October 17-18; Park City, UT. Castle Rock, CO: Hi-Willow Research and Publishing Co.; 1990. 163-174. ISBN: 0-931510-30-9.

MURPHY, CATHERINE. 1990b. Questions to Guide Retrospective Conversion. School Library Media Quarterly. 1990 Winter; 18(2): 79-81. ISSN: 0278-4823.

MURR, LAWRENCE E.; WILLIAMS, JAMES B. 1987. The Roles of the Future Library. Library Hi Tech. 1987 Fall; 5(3): 7-23. ISSN: 0737-8831.

NELSON, NANCY. 1990. Future Information Technology: Transcoders and Filters. Computers in Libraries. 1990 March; 10(3): 8-12. ISSN: 1041-7915.

NEUMAN, DELIA. 1990. Beyond the Chip: A Model for Fostering Equity. School Library Media Quarterly. 1990 Spring; 18(3): 158-164. ISSN: 0278-4823.

NICHOLLS, PAUL TRAVIS. 1990. A Buyer's Guide to CD-ROM Selection: CD-ROM Product Directories and Review Tools. CD-ROM Professional. 1990 May; 3(3): 13-21. ISSN: 1049-0833.

PAIN-LEWINS, HELEN; WATSON, LINDA. 1990a. Microcomputers and School Libraries in the United Kingdom: Part I. Computers in Libraries. 1990 January; 10(1): 22-24. ISSN: 1041-7915.

PAIN-LEWINS, HELEN; WATSON, LINDA. 1990b. Microcomputers and School Libraries in the United Kingdom: Part II. Computers in Libraries. 1990 February; 10(2): 48-50. ISSN: 1041-7915.

PAULSEN, MORTEN FLATE. 1987/88. In Search of a Virtual School. Technological Horizons in Education Journal. 1987/88 December/January; 15(5): 71-76. ISSN: 0192-592X.

PENNSYLVANIA STATE LIBRARY. 1990. Pennsylvania Online: A Curriculum Guide for School Library Media Centers. Harrisburg, PA: Pennsylvania Department of Education; 1990. 110p. Available from: ERIC Document Reproduction Service. ERIC: ED-324009.

PRICE, ROBERT. 1989. An Historical Perspective on the Design of Computer Assisted Instruction: Lessons from the Past. Computers in the Schools. 1989; 6(1/2): 145-157. ISSN: 0738-0569.

QUALITY EDUCATION DATA. 1990. Microcomputer Usage in Schools. A 1989-90 QED Update.   Denver, CO: Quality Education Data; 1990. 17p. Available from: Quality Education Data, 1600 Broadway, Twelfth Floor, Denver, CO 80202.

REINHOLD, FRAN. 1987. Educators Explore the Lay of the LAN.   Electronic Learning. 1987; (Special Supplement): 34-37. ISSN: 0278-3258.

RICKETTS, DICK. 1990. Superintendents Say: Much Done, Much to Do. School Administrator. 1990; (Special issue: Computer Technology Report): 10-13. ISSN: 0036-6439.

RYLAND, JANE N. 1990. A Step toward the Virtual Library.   Edutech Report. 1990 August; 6(5): 6-7. ISSN: 0883-1327.

SALES, GREGORY C. 1989. Videodisc Software: Levels and Use.   The Computing Teacher. 1989 March; 16(6): 35-36. ISSN: 0278-9175.

SALOMON, GAVRIEL. 1990. The Computer Lab: A Bad Idea Now Sanctified. Educational Technology. 1990 October; 30(1): 50-52. ISSN: 0013-1962.

SCARDAMALIA, MARLENE; BEREITER, CARL; MCLEAN, ROBERT S.; SWALLOW, JONATHAN; WOODRUFF, EARL. 1989. Computer-supported Intentional Learning Environments. Journal of Educational Computing Research. 1989; 5(1): 51-68. ISSN: 0735-6331.

SCHIFFMAN, SHIRL S. 1987. Influencing Public Education: A "Window of Opportunity" through School Library Media Centers.   Journal of Instructional Development. 1987; 10(4): 41-44. ISSN: 0162-2641.

SHEINGOLD, KAREN; HADLEY, MARTHA. 1990. Accomplished Teachers: Integrating Computers into Classroom Practice. New York, N Y : Center for Technology in Education; 1990. 41p. Available from: Center for Technology in Education, 610 West 112th Street, New York, NY 10025.

SHERRY, MARK. 1990. An EPIE Institute Report: Integrated Instructional Systems.   Technological Horizons in Education Journal. 1990 September; 18(2): 86-89. ISSN: 0192-592X.

SKAPURA, ROBERT. 1987. Automating the Small Library.   Media & Methods. 1987 September/October; 24(1): 10-11. ISSN: 0025-6897.

SKAPURA, ROBERT. 1990. A Primer on Automating the Card Catalog. School Library Media Quarterly. 1990 Winter; 18(2): 75-78. ISSN: 0278-4823.

SLONIM, JACOB; BAUER, MICHAEL A. 1990. The Information Utility Project: A Glimpse into the Library of the Future.   Information Processing & Management. 1990; 26(4): 467-488. ISSN: 0306-4573.

STRIPLING, BARBARA K.; PITTS, JUDY M. 1988.   Brainstorms and Blueprints: Teaching Library Research as a Thinking Process. Englewood, CO: Libraries Unlimited; 1988. 181p. ISBN: 0-87827-638-1.

SUMMERS, F. WILLIAM. 1989. A Vision of Librarianship. School Library Journal. 1989 October; 35(14): 25-30. ISSN: 0362-8930.

SWISHER, ROBERT; SPITZER, KATHLEEN L.; SPRIESTERSBACH, BARBARA; MARKUS, TIM; BURRIS, JERRY. 1991. Telecommunications for School Library Media Programs. School Library Media Quarterly. 1991 Spring; 19(3): 153-160. ISSN: 0278-4823.

TELEM, MOSHE. 1990a. DSS in Educational Organizations. Computers & Education. 1990; 14(1): 61-69. ISSN: 0360-1315.

TELEM, MOSHE. 1990b. Educational DSS: Potential Services, Benefits, Difficulties and Dangers. Computers & Education. 1990; 14(1): 71-80. ISSN: 0360-1315.

TURNER, PHILIP M. 1985. Helping Teachers Teach: A School Library Media Specialist's Role. Englewood, CO: Libraries Unlimited; 1985. 259p. ISBN: 0-87827-456-7.

TURNER, PHILIP M.; ZSIRAY, STEPHEN W., JR. 1990. The Consulting Role of the School Library Media Specialist: A Review of the Literature. In: Woolls, Blanche, ed. The Research of School Library Media Centers: Papers of Treasure Mountain Research Retreat; 1989 October 17-18; Park City, UT. Castle Rock, CO: Hi-Willow Research and Publishing Co.; 1990. 1-20. ISBN: 0-931510-30-9.

TUROCK, BETTY J. 1986. Organization Factors in Multitype Library Networking: A National Test of the Model. Library and Information Science Research. 1986 April-June; 8(2): 117-154. ISSN: 0740-8188.

U.S. CONGRESS. OFFICE OF TECHNOLOGY ASSESSMENT (OTA). 1988. Power On! New Tools for Teaching and Learning. Washington, DC: Government Printing Office; 1988 September. 263p. (OTA-SET-379). LC: 88-600551; GPO: 052-003-01125-5. Available from: Superintendent of Documents, U.S. Government Printing Office, Washington, DC 20402-9325.

U.S. CONGRESS. OFFICE OF TECHNOLOGY ASSESSMENT (OTA). 1989. Linking for Learning. Washington, DC: Government Printing Office; 1989 November. 191p. (OTA-SET-430). LC: 89-600723; GPO: 052-003-01170-1. Available from: Superintendent of Documents, U.S. Government Printing Office, Washington, DC 20402-9325.

U.S. DEPARTMENT OF EDUCATION. 1990. National Goals for Education. Washington, DC: U.S. Department of Education; 1990. 16p. Available from: ERIC Document Reproduction Service. ERIC: ED-319143.

U.S. DEPARTMENT OF EDUCATION. OFFICE OF EDUCATIONAL RESEARCH AND IMPROVEMENT. 1989. To Support the Learner: A Collection of Essays on the Applications of Technology in Education. Washington, DC: U.S. Department of Education; 1989. 3 microfiche; 216p.; 24x reduction. (Report no. PIP-89-873). Available from: ERIC Document Reproduction Service. ERIC: ED-310763.

VAN ORDEN, PHYLLIS J.; WILKES, ADELINE W. 1989. Networks and School Library Media Centers. Library Resources and Technical Services. 1989 April; 33(2): 123-133. ISSN: 0024-2527.

WILLIAMS, SHARON K. 1991. Mapping Acid Rain. Teacher Magazine. 1991 January; 2(4): 43. ISSN: 1046-6193.

WILSON, SAVAN W. 1990. Television Is for Learning. In: Smith, Jane Bandy, ed. School Library Media Annual: Volume 8. Englewood,

CO: Libraries Unlimited, Inc.; 1990. 93-113. ISSN: 0739-7712; ISBN: 0-87287-850-3.

WIRTHLIN GROUP. 1989. The Computer Report Card: How Teachers Grade Computers in the Classroom. TechTrends. 1989 October; 34(5): 30-35. ISSN: 8756-3894.

WITHROW, FRANK. 1990. Star School Distance Learning: The Promise. Technological Horizons in Education Journal. 1990 May; 17(9): 62-64. ISSN: 0192-592X.

WOOLLS, BLANCHE. 1988. A Rose by Any Other Name. School Library Media Activities Monthly. 1988 December; 5(4): 28-29. ISSN: 0889-9371.

WOOLLS, BLANCHE; LOERTSCHER, DAVID V., eds. 1986. The Microcomputer Facility and the School Library Media Specialist. Chicago, IL: American Library Association; 1986. 204p. ISBN: 0-8389-3325-4; LC: 85-26827.

WRONKOVICH, MICHAEL. 1989-90. The Use of Computers by School Counselors: A Statistical Survey. Journal of Educational Technology Systems. 1989-90; 18(3): 251-256. ISSN: 0047-2395.

YOUNG, ROBERT J. 1990. Artificial Intelligence and School Library Media Centers. School Library Media Quarterly. 1990 Spring; 18(3): 150-157. ISSN: 0278-4823.

8 Information Systems, Services, and Technology for the Humanities

HELEN R. TIBBO
University of North Carolina, Chapel Hill

INTRODUCTION

Long "a fringe activity confined to a small band of enthusiasts" (KATZEN, 1986, p. 259), humanities computing has grown tremendously since the last *ARIST* chapter on this topic appeared in 1981 (RABEN & BURTON). While many of the developments support traditional research activities, computer-based technologies are opening up new avenues for research, teaching, and scholarly communication. The availability of lengthy machine-readable texts (MRTs) and complex text-analysis software is allowing scholars to explore stylistic features of literary works at a micro level they could only imagine a few years ago. With computerized census and other demographic data, historians can now study large segments of society as once they studied only the elite ranks and can link records documenting various aspects of individuals' lives. Hypermedia, a technology capable of interactive, nonlinear display of textual, graphic, and aural materials, is a potentially revolutionary tool that may one day provide humanities instructors with a radically new type of "holistic textbook" well suited to the artifactual and multifaceted nature of many humanistic subjects. Electronic bulletin boards or lists and electronic mail (E-mail) are shrinking the communication gap of scholars working at scattered institutions while allowing for a tremendously fast and responsive interchange of ideas.

Annual Review of Information Science and Technology (ARIST), Volume 26, 1991
Martha E. Williams, Editor
Published for the American Society for Information Science (ASIS)
By Learned Information, Inc., Medford, N.J.

The goal of this chapter is to provide a framework with which to assess the impact of recent technological developments for the humanities. Projects and texts that exemplify new directions in humanistic research, teaching, and communication are presented and analyzed. It is useful to classify the computing applications discussed into three categories: (1) those that all scholars use, such as word processing or electronic mail; (2) general-purpose technologies that humanists tailor to their materials, such as CAI (computer-assisted instruction) programs; and (3) technologies that have unique significance for humanistic research, such as concordance programs for literary studies. The last category receives the most attention here.

The term "humanities" is interpreted broadly in most sections of this chapter, with detailed discussions of computing applications limited to archaeology, Biblical and classical studies, history, linguistics in support of literary studies, and philosophy. Information systems designed for institutions such as libraries, archives, manuscript repositories, and museums that support humanistic research are also discussed. Developments in the allied arts, such as dance, drama, and the fine arts, are not included. It should be noted that while the term "humanities" is used to refer to a wide range of disciplines, each of these fields has its own information processing requirements and may thus approach and use specific technologies in different ways.

This chapter covers the English-language literature concerning information technologies in service to the humanities that appeared during the period 1981 through 1990, with an emphasis on North American and British writings published in the past five years. Of necessity, much worthy and pertinent work is not mentioned because of space limitations and the size and dispersal of the humanities computing literature. Emphasis is on identifying types of work being done and categories of computing tools rather than on providing details of specific software, which tends to have a short life span. More complete listings of humanistic computing projects, including software development, can be found in *The Humanities Computing Yearbook—1988* (LANCASHIRE & MCCARTY), the second volume of which is scheduled for publication in 1991. The *COMPUTERS AND THE HUMANITIES* journal, a publication of the American-based Association for Computers and the Humanities (ACH), is an excellent source of book and software reviews.

Much of the material is included here because of its groundbreaking or influential nature, while some is simply representative of the types of work in which humanists are engaged. Key works are noted throughout the text. Many of the examples of literature that represent general trends and areas of activity are taken from *Computers and the Humanities* because of this journal's central role in reporting these developments. Because of the relative youth of humanities computing, the literature tends to be reportorial and isolated. Debates and theoretical discussions are conspicuously lacking, although there remain ongoing tensions between traditional scholars and computing humanists evident in the slow acceptance of computer-aided research as true humanistic scholarship.

As RABEN & BURTON note in their *ARIST* chapter, identification of relevant scholarship concerned with humanities computing is difficult. While *Computers and the Humanities* publishes articles that both report on humanities computing and that are the result of the application of this technology, this type of literature is found in a wide array of discipline-specific journals, serials, and monographs representing all the humanistic studies. There is no easily searched core of journals that publish most of the important articles and project descriptions in this area. Access to this literature through abstracting and indexing tools presents additional problems. The following online databases were searched via DIALOG Information Services in preparation for writing this chapter: America: History and Life, Historical Abstracts, Library and Information Science Abstracts (LISA), Modern Language Association (MLA) Bibliography, Philosopher's Index, and Religion Index. The difficulty in identifying relevant materials from these sources is twofold: (1) some areas, such as archaeology, are not adequately covered, and (2) nonstandardized indexing practices concerning the representation of the technology aspect of a work do not ensure comprehensive retrieval.

Because much of this work is so new and innovative, the best way to track some of it is through humanities computing newsletters rather than published articles. A sampling of relevant newsletters includes: the *AMERICAN SOCIETY FOR INFORMATION SCIENCE (ASIS) SIG/AH NEWSLETTER, ARCHIVES AND MUSEUM INFORMATICS*, the *ASSOCIATION FOR COMPUTERS AND THE HUMANITIES (ACH) NEWSLETTER, CANADIAN HUMANITIES COMPUTING* from the Centre for Computing in the Humanities at the University of Toronto, *CSA NEWSLETTER* from the Center for the Study of Architecture, which frequently discusses computer-aided design (CAD) issues, and *REACH: RESEARCH & EDUCATIONAL APPLICATIONS OF COMPUTERS IN THE HUMANITIES* published by the Humanities Computing Facility of the University of California at Santa Barbara.

HUMANISTS, INFORMATION, AND TECHNOLOGY

The Humanist's Relationship to Technology

Information technology can improve humanistic research in many ways. It can take the drudgery out of lengthy philological, linguistic, or text analysis while providing a measure of accuracy normally unattainable by human effort alone. Computers can facilitate research that would be impractical if done manually because of its time-consuming nature or human imprecision and provide quantitative analysis to be used along with traditional qualitative approaches, leading to more holistic perspectives across the humanities. In the early years of humanistic computing, many researchers who rushed to embrace technology and those who renounced it as unscholarly and nontraditional overlooked the symbiotic relationship of qualitative and quantitative research. As the technology, applications, and scholarship mature, an integration of the two approaches continues to increase.

In her survey, KATZEN (1983) reports that while humanists were using word processors, online searching, and quantitative data analysis in the early 1980s, much work was needed to bring the potential of humanities computing to the majority of humanistic scholars in the United Kingdom. Three years later, a survey by the American Council of Learned Societies (ACLS) found that conditions and attitudes were changing. MORTON & PRICE report that 45% of their respondents owned a personal computer or had exclusive access to one, 90% had access to a computer on campus, and over 50% used a computer regularly. Respondents reported that the following areas were improved by computer use (in order of degree of change): writing efficiency, research productivity, enjoyment of work, writing quality, research quality, research creativity, and teaching quality. ACLS scholars cited the following specific applications as being important to their work: word processing, maintaining note files, compiling a bibliography or index, statistical analysis, graphics, accessing online databases or the library's online catalog, computer-assisted instruction, budget preparation, preparing and grading tests, E-mail both within and outside of their institutions, and text analysis. While the ACLS survey did include political scientists and sociologists and did canvass a different population (U.S. vs. British), KATZEN (1986) confirms its findings, which are indicative of the growth in humanities computing during the period.

Since Katzen's 1983 study and the ACLS survey, much of the technological and academic infrastructure necessary for the adoption of computing applications by humanists has taken shape. Universities and colleges today offer their faculty vastly more powerful computing facilities than they did a decade ago. Many humanities departments have microcomputers available to faculty, and some even provide machines for each scholar, although this remains an area of disappointment on many campuses. To fill this void, many scholars have purchased their own machines and thus are able to explore various computing applications in addition to having the word processing convenience they initially sought. A growing corpus of software, including both programming languages such as SNOBOL, SPITBOL, PASCAL, and applications designed specifically for the humanities are now available (HOCKEY; IDE, 1987; UNIVERSITY OF TORONTO). Although much of the software still requires a good deal of computing knowledge on the part of users, guides, such as the one by ANDREWS & GREENHALGH, are helpful. Perhaps most importantly, computing is gaining respect in humanities departments as computers are becoming more deeply enmeshed in academic life. Legitimization of this scholarship within the disciplines can be seen in the growth of peer-reviewed articles and monographs reporting on computer-aided humanities research during the second half of the 1980s as compiled in *The Humanities Computing Yearbook—1988* (LANCASHIRE & MCCARTY). The adoption and acceptance of such research, however, has been at an evolutionary rather than revolutionary pace.

Despite improving conditions throughout the 1980s, funding remains a major obstacle to widespread humanities computing. The costs in certain areas such as creating and using bibliographic files, software development for special applications, database development, and the creation of machine-readable texts remain high because of the labor-intensive nature of this work. Unfortunately, the humanities have not traditionally benefited from the same level of funding as the sciences have, yet many humanities computing projects require such resources.

Informal Communication

Writing from the perspective of an editor of a scholarly philosophy journal, POPKIN indicates the importance of informal channels of communication for humanists by explaining that they frequently "work out their ideas in tentative ways, often first proposing them to colleagues, to correspondents, and as presentations at colloquia, seminars, and professional meetings" (p. 25). The international conferences on Computers and the Humanities (BAILEY; BURTON &

SHORT; LUSIGNAN & NORTH; OAKMAN, 1989), recently sponsored by either or both the ACH and its sister organization in Great Britain, the Association for Literary and Linguistic Computing (ALLC), is one of the most important meetings for computing humanists. Another significant conference is the biennial International Conference on Data Bases in the Humanities and Social Sciences (R.F. ALLEN, 1985; MCCRANK, 1989; MOBERG). Due to the subjective and reflective nature of humanistic scholarship, interpersonal communication can play a great role in shaping ongoing analyses. Following this line of thought, CRAWFORD argues for improved communication networks on the national and international levels. He notes that although humanists have been slow to adopt information technologies that go beyond word processing, there are thousands of private databases that are potentially of interest to a range of scholars. He concludes that the most pressing need confronting humanists is the creation of a means of communication that transcends disciplinary and political boundaries to help network such resources so that scholars may exchange data and avoid duplication of effort. Such work is in progress today at the Center for Machine-Readable Texts in the Humanities, a joint enterprise of Princeton and Rutgers universities, partially funded by the National Endowment for the Humanities (NEH) (GAUNT; HOLLANDER, 1990).

Conferences play a role in facilitating scholarly communication for humanists, but electronic bulletin boards and discussion groups are more responsive vehicles for day-to-day informal communication. The most important discussion group in North America for computing humanists is aptly titled HUMANIST. Begun at the University of Toronto by Willard McCarty in 1987 and now located at Brown University since 1990 under the editorship of Elaine Brennan and Allen Renear, HUMANIST is affiliated with the ACH and ALLC, but it is open to all interested individuals. It has more than 900 members from over two dozen countries around the world. Subscribers raise specific and general questions related to hardware, software, philosophical orientation, and appropriate research methodologies. This group also functions as an "early warning" service for calls for papers and conference announcements. Perhaps its most important roles are those of allowing individuals to exchange information quickly, to learn of projects similar to their own, and to locate electronic data banks. For example, HUMANIST lists catalogs of MRTs maintained by the Oxford University Text Archive and the ARTFL (American and French Research on the Treasury of the French Language) project based at the University of Chicago. In addition, some authors distribute bibliographies, book and software reviews, and even columns, such as "OFFLINE: Computer Research for Religious Studies," also published in the *CSSR BULLETIN*. HUMANIST is a mediated discussion group, meaning that subscribers send their messages to the editors who group messages topically. This approach decreases the total number of messages that subscribers receive and adds order to the operation.

Other growing discussion groups accessible through BITNET include: TEI-L, based at the University of Illinois at Chicago, which focuses on the Text-Encoding-Initiative; RPSDISTRB, which disseminates news about the Rutgers/Princeton text-encoding project; WORDS-L at Yale University, which focuses on literary and language studies; ENGLISH at the University of Texas, Arlington, which discusses the English language; and SHAKESPER and FINICO (Renaissance and Reformation topics) based at the University of Toronto. The Office of Humanities Communication at the University of Leicester, England, sponsors a mediated electronic, interactive newsletter, *HUMBUL*, which is very similar to HUMANIST (BOOTH; KATZEN, 1988, p. 210). Because these discussion groups often move with their sponsoring editors, it is best to check recent humanities computing newsletters for electronic addresses.

Information-Seeking and -Use Behaviors

Humanists in general.   Although they are growing in number, relatively few studies of humanistic information seeking and use, especially regarding new technologies, have been completed. A good review of some of the earlier material and general discussion of humanistic information needs is given by STONE. While primarily a guide to reference materials in the humanities, the text by BLAZEK & AVERSA reviews humanistic information-seeking research in its introduction. In a lucid and powerful essay, WEINTRAUB offers his insight into the nature of humanistic scholarship and its implications for library and information services. STOAN discusses the importance of library services that are being designed around users' information-seeking behaviors and needs and argues for closer communication and more respect between scholars and librarians. Both Stoan and Weintraub capture much of the essence of what it means to be a humanistic scholar. These articles should be the starting point for any nonhumanist who wishes to learn about the humanistic perspective and its relationship to information services.

Several researchers have used surveys and interviews to ascertain how scholars go about locating relevant scholarly materials.

WIBERLEY & JONES describe how fellows in a year-long seminar at the Institute for the Humanities (University of Illinois at Chicago) seek information. They note that although their subjects tend not to use online bibliographic databases or consult reference librarians, they do seek assistance from archivists and special-collection librarians. Wiberley and Jones also find that humanists tend to make little use of formal bibliography, an observation GUEST confirms in her questionnaire study of humanities faculty at the State University of New York at Albany. Guest conjectures that the humanist's indifference to bibliographic aids may be due to the noncumulative nature of humanistic scholarship or the fact that many of the tools present in libraries are not of high quality. More recently the Institute for the Humanities sponsored a symposium on how humanists work (UNIVERSITY OF ILLINOIS AT CHICAGO). Included in the proceedings are personal statements regarding research and information seeking from anthropologists, historians, literary scholars, philosophers, and sociologists. Moving beyond the task of locating relevant information, CASE (1986) focuses on how humanists organize the information they have found and speculates as to how librarians and publishers might facilitate this process.

Disciplinary studies. Studies that range across all the humanistic disciplines can provide the data for broad frameworks and comparisons across fields, but they typically do not generate the detailed information necessary for system design. Discipline-specific behavioral studies are needed, and the greatest number of information-needs and -use studies have been done in the area of history. STIEG assesses the needs of historians by looking at their information-gathering behaviors via a survey sent to 767 American historians. Finding that historians tend to rely on "mining" footnotes from known relevant sources rather than using printed or electronic indexes, Stieg concludes that historians are frequently unsystematic researchers who could benefit from more knowledge of how to use the library effectively. In her dissertation, TIBBO (1989) explores the nature of historical scholarship and the information-seeking behaviors of historians so as to develop a framework for abstracting historical discourse. In one segment of this three-part study, she replicates Stieg's survey, supplementing these data with extensive in-depth interviews. Her findings largely corroborate Stieg's but view historical research in a more positive light. They also add important new data concerning historians' views of the nature of historical research and its methodology and of the ideal elements needed for abstracts of historical writing to be used in a user-oriented retrieval system. In another interview study, CASE (1991a) explores the motivations for and results of historians' use of libraries and specific types of materials. In a related paper, CASE (1991b) extends his discussion of historians' conceptual organization to the retrieval of text and how it affects the design of computerized systems.

Case's research as well as Tibbo's dissertation represent the evolving nature of information-needs and -use studies in that they are concerned with "actual behavior" rather than "artifacts of behavior," such as literature or citations. Through in-depth interviews and other qualitative methodologies, such researchers are fleshing out the data from earlier surveys and quantitative studies. What is beginning to evolve, at least in the area of history, is a more holistic and realistic view of scholarship and information use. The same techniques also need to be applied to all of the humanities and other fields as well. Before information scientists can supply this audience with knowledge-based and artificial intelligence (AI) technology, they must come to a better understanding of the nature of the humanities, humanistic research approaches, and the range of information needs of humanistic scholars.

INFORMATION TECHNOLOGIES THAT SUPPORT THE USE OF SCHOLARLY MATERIALS IN THE HUMANITIES

Preservation

Technology influences humanists' use of published and unpublished research materials primarily by providing the means for physical preservation and intellectual access. Both microfilming and videodisc technologies are coming to the forefront to preserve the intellectual content of selected paper documents. The Mellon Foundation, working with the New York Public Library, has sought to improve in-house processing and control of microforms (PERSKY). The Mellon Microform Master Program has also added numerous records to the database of RLIN (Research Libraries Information Network), thus supplementing the *National Register of Microform Masters* (U.S. LIBRARY OF CONGRESS) and helping to set standards for the exchange of information about preservation. The National Endowment for the Humanities (NEH), OCLC, and the Library of Congress (LC) are presently working together with state agencies to inventory, catalog, and preserve approximately 250,000 newspaper titles published in this country since 1690 on microfilm through the U.S. Newspaper Project (USNP) (T. BUTLER). Due to the costly, labor-intensive nature of such work, NEH preservation grants require libraries to communicate information about preserved materials to avoid duplication of effort. JENNY & CLARESON report that OCLC is now including preservation data in its national database to assist in this process. The end result will be more titles preserved with less collection overlap. This type of cooperative collection management should lead to more resource sharing in the coming years, another facet of library work that OCLC and RLIN support. The Library of Congress is also working on the American Memory Project, which will preserve and disseminate important holdings on videodisc, starting with 18th century Continental Congress broadsides and 19th century daguerreotypes (*LIBRARY OF CONGRESS INFORMATION BULLETIN*). STERN & CAMPBELL describe the British Library's unique ADONIS project, a joint effort of publishers and the library to preserve the content of more than 200 biomedical journals on CD-ROM (compact disc–read-only memory).

Large collections and new types of archival media such as machine-readable records are also requiring new solutions for storage and preservation on a grand scale. The U.S. NATIONAL ACADEMY OF SCIENCES. NATIONAL RESEARCH COUNCIL reports on its study of the preservation challenges facing the National Archives and Records Administration (NARA). This report also includes a method for scoring and assessing the condition of collections and producing a strategic preservation plan for any archival agency. In two separate NARA Technical Information Papers issued in 1990, HARRIS ET AL. and RITZENTHALER describe ongoing preservation activities and priorities at the National Archives. GWINN has produced an excellent, step-by-step guide to the planning and implementation of preservation microfilming projects for both librarians and archivists. The spring 1990 issue of the *AMERICAN ARCHIVIST* (1990a) is devoted to preservation issues, including microfilming. See also the 1987 chapter by LUNIN on electronic image information.

Collection Management

As KOENIG argues, citation and referencing studies possess great potential as tools for rational collection management in the arts and humanities. Noting such characteristics as the format, age, and language of the materials humanists cite in their writing should assist librarians in purchasing and weeding decisions. Studies conducted during the 1980s reveal the types of information that citation analysis can provide for collection management. Findings indicate the importance of the monograph as a scholarly vehicle in the humanities, the enduring nature of humanistic sources and scholarship, and the humanist's extensive use of primary sources such as manuscripts (BUDD; CULLARS, 1985, 1988, 1989; HEINZKILL; M. STERN). Typical of later studies, Heinzkill found that 75% of all citations in English literary studies refer to monographs, with approximately 70% referring to material more than ten years old. Such data, although they need corroboration from many more studies, hold significant implications for library collection management and the coverage afforded by abstracting and indexing services.

Because so much more research has been done on the nature of referencing and use patterns in the sciences than in the humanities, librarians may not consider the unique characteristics of humanistic resource use when they form their collection management plans. For example, in discussing a serials review project at the University of Arizona, OLSRUD & MOORE note special difficulties for subscription cancellations in the humanities. The unique, rather than cumulative, nature of humanistic materials causes subscription cancellations to adversely influence future scholarship for years to come. STIELOW & TIBBO (1989) propose the framework for a multidimensional collection development model based on the Research Libraries Group's (RLG) online Conspectus that would be sensitive to such considerations. The Conspectus breaks library collections into over 2,000 categories to assess the holdings for cooperative collection development. Stielow and Tibbo point out the usefulness of such a rational and flexible model for developing precise plans for each element and medium represented in a collection with respect to an institutional assessment. In 1989 OCLC introduced a Collection Analysis CD, a compact disc tool that allows OCLC-member academic libraries to compare their collections with the holdings of peer institutions. Bibliographic and holdings data are taken from the OCLC Online Union Catalog (DILLON ET AL.; GETZ).

Such collection assessment and planning are particularly important in times of shrinking budgets and increased resource sharing when the idea of a "complete" collection of even newly published materials is unrealistic for most if not all libraries. PERRAULT synthesizes the findings from user and bibliometric studies with discussions of the need for preservation, the challenges of retrospective purchasing, the role of special collections, and the need for foreign-language materials in an excellent article on humanities collection management. She concludes that while it was once an "art," collection development is becoming more of a "science" with tools such as the Conspectus.

Intellectual Access and Dissemination

Monographic literature.   A continuously growing and increasingly diversified corpus of humanistic scholarship and a movement toward cooperative collection development and resource sharing point to the need for more elaborate and better-organized retrieval systems in the humanities, both for monographic and serial publications. Today, most research libraries provide access to their monographic collections through online catalogs that can speed the retrieval of items and allow for lists of retrieved materials to be printed on the spot, thus saving the researcher extensive note taking. In an OCLC-sponsored study of subject searching in library catalogs, MARKEY speculates that humanists may be one group to express a less-than-favorable opinion concerning the emergence of online library catalogs (p. 2). Markey's point is not an unreasonable one considering that many humanists use a library's catalog as a bibliographic tool rather than as an aid for locating known items. Specifically, TIBBO (1989) found historians to be critical of the online catalog because it lacked the cross references traditionally present in card catalogs that facilitate subject searching. Exploring the notion that humanists may be critical of online catalogs, BROADBENT surveys humanities faculties regarding their use of online catalogs and relates her results to system design. One interesting finding, in light of growing cooperative collection development, is that Broadbent's respondents call for more in-depth coverage of the local library collection rather than better access to other library collections or online databases. FROST examines scholars' use of subject searching in card and online catalogs and finds that scientists tend to do more subject searching than humanists do, but this area needs more research. LEHMANN & RENFRO describe the results of an experiment conducted by the University of Pennsylvania Library between October 1989 and the spring of 1990 to bring RLIN access directly to faculty in their offices. While only 40 humanists had used RLIN accounts for four months or more at the time Lehmann and Renfro reported their findings, comments from this small group lead the authors to believe that humanists would come to rely on bibliographic utilities such as RLIN in the near future.

Journal literature.   Although not as vital as monographs, the journal literature appears to be gaining importance for the humanities. BROADUS reports on an information use study of humanities scholars in residence at the National Humanities Center (NHC) in Research Triangle Park, N. C. He analyzes requests made over a two-year period for published materials by format, date of publication, subject, and language and concludes that the scholars tend to request more journal articles and newer materials than those kinds most often cited by humanists. Despite such findings, relatively few online databases cover aspects of the scholarly serial literature in the humanities. P. STERN cites inadequate services as the primary problem for online searching in the humanities. According to M. E. WILLIAMS, 84 databases in 1988 (2% of all databases) related to the humanities, 184 (3%) did so in 1989, and 216 (4%) were relevant to the humanities in 1990. While these figures appear substantial, they represent very small percentages of the total number of publicly available databases for each of these years. Many of the databases included in these totals may be of use to humanists but are not focused on humanistic topics. Many others are either very small or are produced outside the United States and are thus not readily available to scholars through academic-library computerized reference services because database vendors such as DIALOG Information Services and BRS Information Technologies do not host them. Of major U.S. vendors, DIALOG Information Services offers the largest number of humanities bibliographic databases. Many aspects of the humanities are not represented, while others are covered only thinly. Lack of interest in and use of these tools by humanists may be responsible for the paucity of databases (STEBELMAN); conversely, a lack of coverage may impede humanists' adoption of this information technology. Several researchers looking at humanists' information-seeking behaviors (e.g., STIEG; TIBBO, 1989) as well as the ACLS survey (MORTON & PRICE) and HORNER & THIRLWALL have found humanists to be interested in the potential of online databases, but little evidence of actual use of mediated or end-user search facilities exists. LOUGHRIDGE calls for university librarians to increase their emphasis on technologies to support humanistic research, such as online searching in preparation for the "electronic campus."

Contrary to what many users may think, database coverage is not the only matter of concern. Several factors make database searching in the humanities particularly difficult. Chief among these is the semantic ambiguity attached to many humanistic terms. Using the Brown Corpus of American English for a study of automatic indexing, ROWBOTTOM & WILLETT find that a humanistic article yields far fewer index terms than does a scientific document. The high occurrence of "natural language" in humanistic writing that impedes the selection of index terms also presents great difficulties for bibliographic retrieval. At this time, Boolean search techniques cannot compensate to any great extent for these vocabulary problems; the result is frequently large retrieval sets with many false drops or irrelevant citations. Conversely, if several other terms are *"AND ed"* with an ambiguous term, retrieval may easily drop to zero.

In a study of terms taken from encyclopedias and dictionaries in the humanities, WIBERLEY (1983) confirms the imprecise nature of humanists' language but observes the importance of singular proper terms, especially the names of persons or single creative works. He concludes that subject access is far more straightforward than has been recognized if subjects are expressed through such proper names. This method of retrieval is quite similar to provenance access systems used in archives. In a later study, WIBERLEY (1988) compares the vocabulary for several humanistic disciplines and discovers great differences in the density of use of proper and common terms across specific fields. Some humanistic literatures, such as those in art and literary studies, contain a relatively precise vocabulary while philosophy and religious studies have much more ambiguous vocabularies, at least for indexing and online searching. The importance of such discipline-oriented text characteristics holds serious implications for cataloging, indexing, and online retrieval and reveals the dangers of "lumping" all humanists and their literatures into one category. TIBBO (1989; 1992) reaches similar conclusions regarding the importance of discipline-oriented retrieval systems in her study of historical abstracting. She demonstrates the inappropriateness of the *American National Standard for Writing Abstracts* (AMERICAN NATIONAL STANDARDS INSTITUTE) for abstracting historical discourse and questions its application to any humanistic abstracting. She further suggests a new framework and associated guidelines for abstracting in history and calls for more author-generated abstracts in the humanities.

In those databases that lack abstracts, such as the MLA Bibliography, searchers must depend entirely on titles and index terms. Since humanists frequently use metaphorical language in their titles and since indexing is notoriously difficult in the humanities, searchers must work particularly hard. KIBBEE reports on a folklore search on the topic of the symbolism of quilts in the MLA Bibliography, which yielded no hits despite the fact that the file contained at least three relevant records. GARFIELD describes how the Institute for Scientific Information "enriches" nondescriptive titles in the *Arts and Humanities Citation Index* with added entry terms to improve retrieval. As Garfield notes, citation searching holds great promise for information retrieval in the humanities in that it overcomes vocabulary and indexing problems. Surprisingly, little has been written concerning humanists' use of this tool.

The desire for an exhaustive bibliography makes online searching in the humanities even more problematic. STIELOW & TIBBO (1988) discuss the difficulties associated with one type of exhaustive bibliography—the "negative" search—and note the absence of any discussion of this topic in the library literature. Due to the noncumulative nature of humanistic inquiry, scholars frequently request searches to see if anything has been published on a topic, hoping that the results will be negative so that they can pursue this area. When a topic is truly virgin territory, these negative searches share the difficulties of patent searching wherein the searcher never knows what has been missed and gets little or no feedback from the database to alter the search tactics. The interdisciplinarity of the humanities presents further difficulties in that only certain aspects of a research question may be available in a particular database. Lack of records for retrospective and primary materials in most bibliographic databases is an additional problem that searching skill cannot overcome.

CD-ROM databases present new challenges, especially in terms of end-user searching. DESMARAIS provides a user's perspective on the WILSONDISC CD-ROM version of the MLA Bibliography. Although this format should speed document retrieval from the serial literature in the area of language study, Desmarais correctly notes several factors that may confuse users; these include conflicting numbers between postings for a search and actual citations retrieved. Extensive research is called for in end-user CD-ROM searching, especially with the difficulties posed by humanistic databases. While clients can quickly learn to manipulate user-friendly search commands if help screens are well designed and documentation is available, can they grasp the intricacies of index terms, thesauri (or the lack thereof), and heuristics that are designed to improve recall or precision? These questions are central to humanities databases that even the experts have trouble searching. WALKER & ATKINSON raise these and other questions concerning the efficacy of end-user searching in this domain.

Archival and manuscript sources. During the past decade, information technologies have had a dramatic impact on the materials that archivists collect and on the ways in which archivists process these materials whether they be personal papers or institutional archival holdings (COOK, 1986, 1989; MCCRANK, 1981). Despite visions of a "paperless society," the use of computers and word processors has generated massive amounts of unpublished information. To make modern records useful for researchers, archivists and manuscript curators have had to devise methods to control such bulk. The abundance of recorded information has forced archivists and manuscript curators to make disciplined collecting and appraisal decisions (HAM) and to focus on large groups of records rather than individual documents or folders of documents (MILLER). Increasingly, archivists must preserve and provide access to machine-readable records themselves as well as the paper documentation produced from them. The archival community's growing concern with these records is seen in the Society of American Archivists' (SAA) recent bibliography on automated records and techniques in archives (MATTERS).

Archivists and curators also face the challenge of automating their own operations. COX & BEARMAN have compiled a very thorough and useful directory of software for archives and museums. They describe and compare various software and systems for applications, including cataloging and description, collections management, membership and development, and records management. BEARMAN (1987/88) has also written a report that outlines the basic acquisition and implementation issues involved with automated systems for archives and museums. This report should be required reading for archivists and curators before they draw up any automation plans for their institutions.

National bibliographic information systems have had the most problematic impact of any technological development on archival and curatorial work in recent years. By sending collection descriptions to utilities such as RLIN or OCLC, archivists and curators can widely disseminate collection information to researchers (BOWER; MICHELSON, 1987). However, it has been much more difficult for archivists to embrace these systems than it was for librarians because of the unique nature of archival materials, the varying degrees of description needed to represent different collections adequately, and archivists' frequent insistence that they must have freedom to describe their institution's materials in their own ways. The archival community has had to struggle with developing and implementing the standardization necessary for participation in these national networks, including the development of the machine-readable cataloging format for archives and manuscript control, called MARC/ AMC (BEARMAN, 1987a).

SAA has published three key works related to the MARC/AMC format. A description and explanation of the format, *MARC for Archives and Manuscripts: The AMC Format* (SAHLI), has been instrumental in introducing the AMC format to archivists and has been widely used in workshops on this topic. *MARC for Archives and Manuscripts: A Compendium of Practice* (EVANS & WEBER) is a companion to the Sahli text that provides examples of actual use of the format. The manual, *Archives, Personal Papers, and Manuscripts* (HENSEN), which thoroughly explains issues such as the choice of access points for a record and the specific form of entry for persons, geographic names, and corporate bodies, has become the de facto standard for cataloging archival and manuscript materials.

Such work continues. The fall 1989 and winter 1990 issues of the *AMERICAN ARCHIVIST* (1989; 1990b) contain several reports, recommendations, and papers of the SAA's Working Group on Standards for Archival Description. Work on name and subject authority files (MICHELSON, 1988) has also gone forward as have investigations of data dictionaries and models of the logical architecture of archives and museum information systems (BEARMAN, 1990). Even full-text retrieval systems have been discussed (NOLTE). What makes information retrieval so difficult in archives is the necessity for enormous data compression in the access tools. Collections extending to hundreds of linear feet must be described in a MARC record to be entered into OCLC with only 4,096 characters; large collections of letters may be described by a single line—Letters by Soandso, 1800–1865. Electronic image processing holds out great promise to make such materials available, both over networks for viewing and by disseminating detailed archival finding aids that may extend to several hundred pages for very large collections. The realization of this promise, however, lies well in the future for most small and underfunded archival repositories although the publishing company of CHADWYCK-HEALEY has microfilmed finding aids from large archival and manuscript collections throughout the United States for their National Inventory of Documentary Sources in the United States (NIDS US).

Physical objects. Along with archaeologists, museum curators who preserve their "finds" have perhaps the widest variety of information processing needs of any scholars because of the large array of data types collected, from text to physical objects. Curators with live exhibits may have collections of animal sounds or preserved specimens. The functional link among museums is the activity of providing public access to the collections and collateral information about them. Museums do not exist simply to collect but to disseminate information. In large institutions this function requires a sophisticated information resources management (IRM) system to control and integrate collection, institutional, and external data (STAM, 1989a).

The primary computer applications for most museums are extensive database management systems (DBMSs) used to store and retrieve information about specific objects and the collection as a whole. Acceptance of the ideas that information, regardless of its content, has certain definable properties and that an information system, regardless of its context, needs to provide a framework or container for the information, makes control of all of this material less arduous than it might at first appear. Specific challenges lie in identifying core data elements necessary to describe certain types of holdings and in developing retrieval mechanisms, including indexing languages, thesauri, and authority files, that create records flexible enough to meet local needs yet universal enough to be exchanged through international databases (STAM, 1989b). This was the primary goal of the Getty Museum Prototype Project begun in 1982 (N. S. ALLEN).

Other interesting areas include the use of videodiscs, hypermedia, and expert systems to store and disseminate images of physical collections as well as analytical information. These tools will not only improve collection management and preservation but will also democratize museum collections by making them readily available outside of the institutions. BEARMAN (1987b) has produced a useful guide that describes closely related technologies such as videodiscs, compact discs, and optical digital discs and outlines appropriate applications and development costs. One of the earliest hypermedia applications to use museum and archaeological material was the experimental PROJECT EMPEROR-I produced at Simmons College for educational and information retrieval purposes (CHEN, 1986; CHEN ET AL.). The two videodiscs in this project contain text and images concerning the reign of Qin Shi Huang Di, the first emperor of China, who ruled about 2,200 years ago. The project is significant for its pioneering role in the investigation of picture management by documentary systems. Chen and her colleagues (CHEN, 1990) continue work on this project, integrating emerging information technologies, such as high-resolution image digitization, into the existing configuration. BESSER reports on the Berkeley University Art Museum's project to make digitized images of objects in its collection available throughout the campus on high-resolution computer displays with zooms, pans, windowing, and dynamic color change enhancements. The quality of images in such a project is a key issue, especially if these images are to be viewed in place of the object in a classroom or exhibit setting. In a more recent project to link art objects and related information, MOLINE presents a model combining hypertext and an expert system. LIGHT ET AL. include a discussion of museum documentation systems used around the world.

The *Art and Architecture Thesaurus* (*AAT*) (OXFORD UNIVERSITY PRESS), developed by the Getty Art History Information Program, is a key tool in the control of information about art, architecture, and museum collections. Over ten years in the making, *AAT* provides a standard, controlled vocabulary to be used by museums, archives, libraries, and indexing scrvices to describe artistic and architectural materials. Available as a three-volume printed set or in an electronic edition, *AAT* is a list of terms showing synonyms, variants, and term relationships, including hierarchies. It should improve information retrieval from bibliographic databases, such as the Avery Index and RILA, which are available from DIALOG Information Services. The first edition with 23 hierarchies was published in 1990. The entire *AAT*, including 17 new hierarchies and all new terms entered in the interim, is scheduled for publication in 1993.

INFORMATION TECHNOLOGIES THAT SUPPORT SELECTED RESEARCH IN THE HUMANITIES

Archaeology

After finding remains of past civilizations, archaeologists face three primary research problems: (1) how to understand the physical evidence they uncover, (2) how to document and store descriptions of the evidence, and (3) how to construct models of earlier cultures based on partial physical remains. To solve their first problem, archaeologists use scientific techniques, such as carbon dating and pollen analysis. More recently, however, they have turned to sophisticated information systems to assist with the other challenges of culture study. LOCK & WILCOCK and RICHARDS & RYAN describe the various computer capabilities that archaeologists can productively use at different stages of their work. Three types of applications appear most useful: (1) database management systems, (2) statistical packages, and (3) graphics software. There is also a need for electronic databases to control the discipline's current and retrospective literature (FARRUGGIA & MARTLEW; MARTLEW; C. OPPENHEIM).

Archaeological excavations can produce massive amounts of descriptive data, which researchers must mine for meaning. The ability to store, retrieve, and relate this information easily and reliably is essential to any form of data analysis or, more importantly, synthesis. To structure their data, archaeologists frequently use computers to do cluster analysis (especially for classification and scaling) and seriation studies (dating of sites based on data from objects found there). GAINES (1984) provides a good overview of the impact of computerized information systems on American archaeology. As with all such work, definition of data elements and terminological standardization are key issues (CARVER; CHENHALL; COOPER) especially if large data banks are to be constructed for interproject use, which is the case with regional analyses. RICHARDS argues that standardization in categorizing excavation data will stifle creativity and hypothesis building and prefers the concept of data compatibility but does not adequately define or illustrate the term to make it useful for database design. SCHOLTZ & MILLION look beyond standard DBMSs to control collection data and argue that management information systems (MISs) are needed to integrate multiple files, including site inventories, land use records, project lists, and graphic displays. Several instructive examples of DBMSs, MISs and data banks for archaeological research are presented by GAINES (1981).

Moving away from time-space studies, the "new archaeology" of the past 25 years has sought to understand the economic and social nature of past cultures. To deal with highly complex but frequently incomplete data, archaeologists have used statistics and modeling (SABLOFF). DAY argues that such techniques are increasingly important to a discipline in which explanation and interpretation are more valuable than description alone.

The most exciting aspect of archaeological computing today is graphics. Plotters can create two-dimensional landscapes that incorporate statistical data (EFFLAND), but complex three-dimensional maps of pre- and post-excavation sites are also possible. Topographic plots or wire-frame diagrams built from thousands of site grid readings can be viewed from any perspective to help identify potential dig sites and to interpret excavations (ARNOLD; LOCK & WILCOCK). Architectural archaeologists have become strong users of computer-assisted drafting and design (CADD) software. Scholars no longer have to worry about making field drawings to scale; they simply enter all known measurements taken from monuments or excavations into the CADD database, thus avoiding the need to translate three-dimensional information into two-dimensional drawings (W. WILLIAMS). Photogrammetry, the science of determining dimensions through the analysis of photographs, is another computerized information tool of architectural archaeologists that allows rapid and accurate data collection via photographs.

ALLEN ET AL. bring together 29 essays discussing how archaeologists can use geographic information systems (GISs) to interpret human behavior and material culture over space. GISs can help the archaeologist model the spatial dimensions in which a past culture existed. These essays cover a range of material, including general introductions to GIS, discussions of theory and methodology, hardware and software considerations, and specific applications. The text will undoubtedly become an important resource for archaeologists.

Biblical and Classical Studies

Biblical and classical scholars use computers primarily as text analyzers. Numerous tagged and untagged electronic versions of Masoretic, Semitic, Septuagint, and Greek texts, both in ancient and modern languages, are available on tape, disk, and CD-ROMs from projects worldwide. These MRTs allow researchers to study orthographical, lexical, morphological, syntactic, grammatical, and semantic features as well as textual variations. Examples of such research include Kenny's work on an MRT version of the New Testament to explore the relationship between the books of Luke and the Acts of the Apostles and the authorship of Revelations and the Pauline Epistles (KENNY, 1986). Similarly, LEDGER uses various statistical procedures to analyze Platonic dialogs by letter frequency. Such work could not be accomplished without the aid of the computer owing to the enormity of the texts and the data collection tasks.

Several electronic text archives exist in support of Biblical studies. These include the Thesaurus Linguae Graecae (TLG), a data bank of the entire corpus of ancient Greek literature extant from the period between Homer (approximately 750 B.C.) and 600 A.D. (held at the University of California, Irvine) as well as the complementary Duke Data Bank of Documentary Papyri, which includes all Greek and Latin words found in the documentary papyri from the fourth century B.C. to the seventh century A.D. (located at Duke University, Durham, N.C.). The Center for Computer Analysis of Texts at the University of Pennsylvania maintains a data bank supporting Septuagint studies. The Oxford University Computing Service Text Archive has several classical MRTs, including the Hebrew Bible, Septuagintal texts, and the Greek New Testament. HUGHES provides detailed information on these and several other projects in his *Bits, Bytes and Biblical Studies,* the outstanding text in the area of computers and religion. This "review-oriented reference book" examines products, projects, and resources, including word processing, Bible concordance programs, computer-assisted language learning for ancient and Biblical languages, online services, archaeological programs, and machine-readable ancient texts and text archives. Hughes updates the material in this text through his newsletter, *BITS & BYTES REVIEW.*

History

In their introduction to the proceedings of the second Association for History and Computing (AHC) conference, DENLEY ET AL. state that "the idea that the discipline of history has much to gain from the widespread use of computers in teaching and research is nowadays uncontroversial, accepted by almost all but the most determined of technological reactionaries" (p. ix). With the goal of demonstrating "that computers have much more to offer the historian than mere secretarial or numerical assistance" (p. ix), this volume discusses the methodological innovation that has accompanied the use of technology that can keep track of large quantities of data. While several historical applications for computing technologies do exist, one is struck by such journal articles as: "Statistical Fantasies and Historical Facts: History in Crisis and Its Methodological Implications" (FITCH) and "Cliometrics: The State of the Science (or Is It Art or, Perhaps, Witchcraft?)" (DAVIS & ENGERMAN), which reflect the continuing anti-quantification sentiment within the discipline.

Since the first computer-aided demographic studies in the 1960s, historians have struggled to develop valid and reliable methods of data analysis and, as THALLER discusses, they have sought a theory of historical computing. To date, much of the historical computing, especially in the United States, has involved the use of data banks, containing such material as census returns, customs records, voting returns, and tax data, such as the Domesday Book (available from the University of California at Santa Barbara) and the Massachusetts Tax Valuation List at the University of Delaware. Thaller argues that this kind of work is limited because the data cannot completely reflect the complexities of life. He calls for software that can take into account the temporal context within which the data originated and that can deal with the inherently fuzzy nature of information in historical source materials. Much of the work reported at the two AHC conferences on History and Computing (DENLEY & HOPKIN; DENLEY ET AL.) reflects Thaller's concerns and the European trend toward studies built on complex data links to reveal the richness of human life rather than the social scientific quantifying that is popular in the United States.

Many historians are presently constructing their own specialized databases. GUTMANN ET AL. discuss the use of relational database software for such projects because it facilitates record links. Some of this work is quite different from earlier demographic studies. DUNK & RAHTZ present strategies for gravestone recording using a conceptual scheme and a table of iconographical motifs. Data modeling and simulations are assuming a growing importance in historical computing (E. A. ALLEN; HANNEMAN & HOLLINGSWORTH; MCGREGOR). Historians are also exploring the potential role of AI and expert systems in their work. ENNALS addresses how AI applications can help with logical and historical reasoning and how such programs can be used in the classroom. He devotes a chapter to the use of PROLOG, a popular computing language in Europe for such applications. Most of this work is only in the conceptual or elementary stages of development, and, as SCHULTE points out, such technologies are probably best suited to the minute examination of very limited problems rather than the "wide generalizations" and "deep underlying causes" of which historians are so fond. With the development of more capable expert systems, historians should find computers more useful for analyzing the social and cultural data necessary to understand the complexities of the past.

Literary Text Analysis

A preponderance of humanities computing work falls in the area of literary and linguistic analysis. OAKMAN (1984), in the second edition of a key humanities computing text, gives a thorough overview of the fundamentals of literary computing and the variety of possible research. RUDALL & CORNS present a practical guide to literary computing appropriate for the novice in this area. BRAINERD provides a brief but detailed discussion of computerized concordance production and automated text analysis. C. BUTLER also provides a good overview of activities in this area, including discussions of various types of linguistic analyses (graphological, lexical, syntactic, phonological, and semantic) and their uses in computational stylistics, lexicography, text editing, language instruction, the simulation of human-language processing, and corpus-based descriptive linguistics. Graphological analysis produces word lists, indexes, concordances, and word-frequency and -length statistics. Because these are simple tasks for computers and because scholars have readily found critical applications for these products, much of the literary computing done to date has been conducted at this level.

Twenty-five years ago when even large computers had very limited processing capacity, such counting activities were considered to be "computational linguistics" (CL). Over the past three decades much has changed. Today's computational linguists generally consider these analyses with regard to issues such as authorship attribution for a particular literary work as being "literary and linguistic computing" (GAZDAR & MELLISH, p. 3) or "computational stylistics" (POTTER, 1989). Most of this section focuses on literary and linguistic computing because although other areas of linguistic analysis, including natural-language processing (NLP), are keenly interesting and promising, they are beyond the computing power and expense accounts of many literary scholars. Development in these areas falls primarily to computational linguists and computer and information scientists who may have access to powerful parsers and comprehensive electronic dictionaries. This chapter allows only a brief discussion of CL and NLP, areas that deserve fuller treatment such as the 1987 *ARIST* chapter on NLP by WARNER.

Computational linguistics is a broad, interdisciplinary field that involves the perspectives and research of computer and information scientists, philosophers, psychologists, and linguists in building computer models of natural language production and comprehension. J. ALLEN (p. 1) cites two primary motivations for this type of research: (1) a technological motivation to build AI systems to function as natural-language interfaces to databases, automatic machine translators, and text analysis systems; and (2) a linguistic motivation to understand how humans use and understand natural language. Allen summarizes the ultimate goal of CL as being the ability to "specify a theory of language comprehension and production to such a level of detail that a person could write a computer program that can understand and produce natural language" (p. 1).

Beyond the early programs that counted tokens, such as the number of times a particular word appeared in a text, some of the first work in CL and NLP was machine translation (MT). Because of the limitations of early computers and the complexity of the task, little was accomplished in this domain in the 1950s and 1960s. TUCKER & NIRENBURG survey this and more recent advances in MT in a 1984 *ARIST* chapter. The greatest problems for computational linguists have been natural language's inherent ambiguity and the task of devising effective and efficient ways of representing knowledge. During the 1970s, much of the activity in CL and NLP involved procedural logic and approaches such as augmented transition networks. This work was followed by research with declarative formalisms, which tell a computer "what" but leave the "how" to the machine, and data structures identified by parsers. Parsers are algorithms designed to "recognize" various, predetermined linguistic structures. Computational linguists have been concerned with parsers for over 20 years. Most of the earlier work involving parsers focused on isolated sentences; today, more sophisticated parsers are able to make "sense" of larger text segments and factor context into the interpretation of text blocks.

Ambiguity and the need for contextual knowledge resident in large lexicons and program instructions remain major problems for the foreseeable future, but computational linguistics and NLP have progressed in many ways. GAZDAR & MELLISH note both the partial success of natural-language translation programs (partial because they require pre-editing of the input or post-editing of the output to correct passages their formal rules cannot handle) and natural-language front ends for databases that translate a restricted subset of natural language into database query language. Some limited commercial applications of NLP are becoming practical. Gazdar and Mellish speculate that the next generation of NLP software will function more like humans but that it will be a long time before programs "understand" the text they analyze and generate complicated explanations for expert systems.

J. ALLEN has written a fairly thorough NLP text, introducing many ideas about syntax and semantics, grammars, and natural-language representation. *Automatic Text Processing* by SALTON is not as technical as Allen's text but covers some basic ideas in text processing, including discussion of information retrieval and automatic indexing. GROSZ ET AL. have edited a collection of papers to provide an introduction for NLP students and a reference collection for researchers. It provides convenient access to a number of technical reports and articles that appeared in scattered journals while giving a sense of the history of NLP and the key issues and developments.

GAZDAR ET AL. compiled an unannotated but fairly comprehensive bibliography of NLP work covering 1980 to early 1987. The 1,764 entries appear alphabetically by author with a KWIC index of titles. The core of this bibliography consists of papers from the journal *COMPUTATIONAL LINGUISTICS*, a key journal published quarterly by the MIT Press for the Association for Computational Linguistics (ACL). The proceedings of the ACL's annual meeting is also a source of current research in the field (ASSOCIATION FOR COMPUTATIONAL LINGUISTICS, 1962-). ACL's conferences on applied NLP are useful for reports on NLP applications (ASSOCIATION FOR COMPUTATIONAL LINGUISTICS, 1988). Presently, literary computing and computational linguistics are drawing closer together. Literary scholars have found that to probe deeply into the nature of literature, they need the sophisticated parsing programs of the computational linguists, while the linguists must use the MRTs and corpora that computing humanists have compiled.

Any discussion of computer-aided text analysis presupposes the availability of MRTs. Three corpora of English, the Brown Corpus of American English (FRANCIS), the Lancaster-Oslo-Bergen (LOB) Corpus of British English (JOHANSSON; MARSHALL), and the London-Lund Corpus of spoken, educated British English (SVARTVIK & EEG-OLOFSSON; SVARTVIK ET AL.; SVARTVIK & QUIRK) and associated concordances are available on magnetic and CD-ROM media for descriptive studies. AARTS & MEIJS cover many aspects of such work as it relates to any corpus. GARSIDE ET AL. report on the work of the Unit for Computer Research on the English Language (UCREL) at the University of Lancaster (England) from 1979 to 1986 concerning natural-language processing of the LOB Corpus. Topics include challenges of using a tagged corpus, the UCREL probabilistic parsing system, and problems associated with orthography.

In addition to samplings of entire languages, specific texts and the collected works of significant authors are available in MRT, including several versions of the Bible and Shakespeare's works (BOLTON). When completed, Dartmouth University's Dante Project will make the full text of the *Divine Comedy*, along with the texts of over 60 commentaries written during the past 600 years, available online (HOLLANDER, 1989). Villanova University now maintains the Wurzburg collection of the critical Latin editions of St. Augustine's works. The Center for Text and Technology at Georgetown University is an example of a nonprofit institution involved in the creation and dissemination of electronic versions of important texts in the humanities and social sciences. It is currently involved in preparing a number of MRTs for the works of Hegel. Analytical bibliographers and rare book scholars will find three databases of particular interest: (1) the Incunable Short Title Catalogue (ISTC), developed by the British Library (HELLINGA & GOLDFINCH); (2) the Wing Short-Title Catalogue, 1641–1700, an MLA project; and (3) the Eighteenth-Century Short-Title Catalogue (ESTC), produced by the University of California at Riverside and available on RLIN.

Machine-readable dictionaries (MRDs) are a particularly rich source of information for NLP and literary research. If NLP projects are to have wide applicability, they require extensive lexical information that accounts for the range of meaning and use for each word entered. The compilation of sizable lexicons that extend beyond particular domains has been a significant task for NLP researchers. The difficulty, cost, and labor-intensive nature of such work has generally limited it to laboratory prototypes and naturally makes machine-readable dictionaries attractive. NLP researchers may use entire MRDs or extract specific segments and tailor them to their research domain, thus eliminating an enormous amount of work.

Extensive work on MRDs was done during the 1980s. The proceedings of a symposium on lexicography in the electronic age held in Luxembourg in 1981 report on then state-of-the-art projects worldwide (GOETSCHALCKX & ROLLING). AMSLER provides a useful overview of the nature, compilation, and potential uses of MRDs in a 1984 *ARIST* chapter on this topic. More recently, BOGURAEV & BRISCOE provide a thorough introduction to computational lexicography for NLP. They discuss the nature of dictionary entries, dictionary organization and representation, and various NLP applications of MRD data, including word lists, taxonomies, semantic processing, and browsing possibilities. They also provide an excellent bibliography on this topic. In a special 1990 issue of *Computers and the Humanities* devoted to humanities computing in Italy, NENCIONI describes various electronic lexicographical projects of the Accademia della Crusca, located in Florence, Italy. He notes that while dictionary production has benefited from computerized input for over two decades, it is only the recently developed data bank that allows for highly flexible lexical tools.

While several dictionaries are now available in electronic versions (e.g., *The Merriam-Webster Seventh New Collegiate Dictionary*, *The Merriam-Webster New Pocket Dictionary*, and the *Longman Dictionary of Contemporary English*), the most important one for English-language literary studies is the *New Oxford English Dictionary*, produced at the Centre for the New OED at the University of Waterloo, Canada, for the Oxford University Press. Potential uses of the *New OED* for literary scholars include: online word look-up for definitions, synonyms, and related terms; the use of a particular word at a particular time in history; the earliest use of a word; and study of various patterns in the language as a whole facilitated by the *OED's* extensive etymological information. LOGAN describes the OED project and the problems associated with the production of an MRD. He also discusses tests the Centre ran to ensure quality control in the corpus.

With the growing availability of optical scanning technology, researchers can create their own MRTs from printed material. If the resulting file is to be useful for text analysis, the scanner must be able to derive an ASCII text from the bit-mapped images of the scanned material. All scanners can convert documents, both images and text, to bit-mapped graphics images that can be stored and retrieved. This technology has extensive applications for archival storage in which users are satisfied with viewing entire pages of material at a time. No manipulation of the text on any page stored in this fashion can take place as display software can recognize only the bit-mapped image as an intact entity. Optical character recognition (OCR) technology can "recognize" type fonts and convert that information into ASCII code that can be manipulated through word processors or spreadsheets. Limitations to OCR include scanning resolution, the ability to recognize a wide variety of type fonts and to "learn" new fonts, and scanning and translating accuracy. Scanners and OCR technology have yet to replace the proofreader. GROTOPHORST provides a clear explanation of how OCR works and discusses the integration of OCR and full-text retrieval systems. CAHAN and PEREZ both survey the OCR marketplace and provide prospective consumers of OCR systems with useful insights into the capabilities and limitations of various low-priced systems.

Until recently, more sophisticated scanners that could deal with many different fonts, especially proportional print, were prohibitively expensive for all but well-funded institutions. The price of OCR technology has fallen precipitously, and it can be expected that more and more businesses, agencies, and educational institutions will be able to purchase optical scanners that create flexible files suitable for text analysis rather than just archival images. SCHEIN reports on the recent development and expansion of text-recognition capabilities at affordable prices. He cites the introduction of TrueScan, a PC recognition card selling for less than $2,500 from Calera Recognition Systems (Santa Clara, Ca.). He notes that by attaching a scanner to a PC equipped with TrueScan, users can convert text in a wide variety of type fonts to electronic files at "one-tenth the cost of an earlier generation of recognition equipment" (p. 68).

While scanning technology may facilitate textual and natural-language research on a local level, data entry must be standardized if texts are to be shared. Supported by an NEH grant, the ACH, ACL, and ALLC are presently involved in creating guidelines for encoding and interchanging MRTs. Draft version 1.1 of the Text Encoding Initiative's (TEI) Guidelines (SPERBERG-MCQUEEN & BURNARD) was published in November 1990, with the editors asking for comments regarding usability. The TEI guidelines are based on the INTERNATIONAL ORGANIZATION FOR STANDARDIZATION (ISO) Standard 8879: *Standard Generalized Markup Language* (SGML) that BRYAN fully discusses for prospective users. BARNARD ET AL., while noting the need for a markup standard, argue that SGML is not designed to maintain multiple views of a document's structure and that an SGML-based standard entails more markup than researchers are likely to accept. The work of TEI appears to deal with the first problem but does require a good deal of tagging and keyboarding.

Several researchers use computer analysis to investigate the particular style of texts. This work has come to be known as stylometric analysis or stylometry. The collection of essays on literary computing and criticism edited by POTTER (1989) provides a sound overview of the issues related to this research. Potter's bibliography should be useful for anyone exploring literary computing and stylistics. KENNY (1982) surveys various types of stylometric analysis in the introduction to his literary statistics text. GILMOUR-BRYSON provides a more specific introduction to the use of computers in medieval studies. R.F. ALLEN (1984; 1988) presents the stylo-statistical method of literary analysis, in which a computer identifies a text's keywords, thus identifying vocabulary that the author stresses and that characterizes the text. One of the chief goals of such research is to explore the elements of an author's style that create the atmosphere of a particular work or body of literature by identifying and analyzing its "keywords." Allen (1988, p. 1) explains that in stylo-statistics the term "keyword" has a restricted meaning of "one of the most frequently used words of the text that deviates significantly in a positive sense from the norm." In studying French literature, Allen uses the vocabulary norm frequencies that have been established by the Institut National de la Langue Française at Nancy, France, based on a corpus of more than 70 million words taken from examples of 19th and 20th century literature and are broken down by time period. He then compares the word profiles of selected pieces of literature with the frequencies appearing in the natural language of the period, looking specifically for how an author's "style" varies from the linguistic norms of a particular culture and time. Analysis involves identifying those words that appear at a higher frequency than would be their random distribution in the language as a whole. Allen discusses many of the technical problems associated with word forms and homographs.

Stylo-statistical research is not without its detractors (see VAN PEER for an opposing view that stresses the importance of literary and cultural contextuality for stylistic analysis). DELCOURT provides a summary of the theoretical issues surrounding stylo-statistics, including primarily French controversies concerning this type of analysis. He supports his points with a small mathematical example from Laclos's novel, *Les Liaisons Dangereuses*. He concludes that statistical linguistic analysis is appropriate for stylistic studies but that researchers must be careful when selecting linguistic models and should not be "satisfied with the easy identification of monsters, i.e. literary phenomena unexplained by wrong models" (p. 285). He further observes that the identification of appropriate models is difficult and time consuming but that it can lead to precise insights. It must be again noted that computers are simply a tool for humanists and not an end in themselves. Computer-aided analysis of texts can lead to either intensive and insightful critiques or shallow statistical reports that offer little meaning. Appropriately the quality of the research continues to lie with the scholar and not the technical apparatus. In a very lucid article POTTER (1988) explains how literary computing can support meaningful literary criticism. She points out that literary computing does not replace any traditional scholarship such as historical study or criticism but may augment it by providing specific evidence as to the nature of literary works. She concludes by explaining why the synthesis of literary computing and literary criticism will be difficult.

Computers and the Humanities includes numerous examples of computer-assisted literary analysis and tools created to support this work. CANNON & OAKMAN describe one such tool, the URICA program—User Response Interactive Collation Assistant—designed to collate two works to determine textual variants. This program allows a researcher to match a machine-readable "master text" to another existing machine-readable text or one that is being keyed in by a user. At each point of difference, the user may determine the point at which the two texts again match. URICA output is a file indicating variants, their locations, and the type of variant, such as an insertion, deletion, or typographical error. This type of program allows researchers to compare two texts and identify variations between them efficiently.

Computer-assisted literary research includes the study by BURROWS (1989) of the frequency profiles of all common words in Jane Austen's works to show differences among the word profiles of Austen's characters. This work is different from much of the other stylo-statistical analysis, such as Allen's research discussed above, in that Burrows correlates the frequency profiles of all the very common words from many of Austen's novels rather than viewing word-frequency patterns as discrete phenomena. Burrows uses multiple regression analysis and presents his findings graphically. In a related monograph, BURROWS (1987) thoroughly discusses the statistical procedures underlying this type of analysis. FRAUTSCHI uses word frequencies and measures of narrative voice to highlight the distinctiveness of the characters in Rousseau's *Emile*. Based on several different analyses of text from the *Profession de foi du vicaire savoyard* embedded in Book IV of Rousseau's novel, *Emile,* and other parts of the narrative, Frautschi finds quantitative evidence that there are narratological differences between the novel and this component. This finding supports the observation of other Rousseau scholars that the verbal textures of these two texts are different.

Moving beyond word frequencies, R. OPPENHEIM studies variations in sentence length and attempts to correlate the length of successive sentences in portions of Joyce's *Ulysses* and *The Dubliners* and of Hemingway's *In Our Time*. She concludes that this type of analysis is not useful for author identification since similar patterns occur in the writing of both Joyce and Hemingway but that it is a useful tool to analyze various aspects of literary works. SIMONTON analyzes various aspects of 154 Shakespearean sonnets, finding that the popular poems contain language and images that are significantly different from the obscure pieces. IDE (1989) describes a computer-assisted analysis of semantic patterning in Blake's *The Four Zoas* to study theme and structure. This work is significant in that it is an attempt to move beyond word and sentence counting to a type of quantitative analysis that involves contextual considerations. Ide is interested not only in locating general thematic groupings of images across the text but also in exploring how these images relate to the remainder of the text.

Scholars also use literary statistics to solve problems of ascription or authorship attribution. Key works in this area include those by MORTON and by MOSTELLER & WALLACE. Morton examines various features of language that are of particular interest in stylometry and provides examples of how these linguistic characteristics can be explored with regard to authorship and literary fraud. Mosteller and Wallace discuss specifically how Bayesian inference works in a large-scale data analysis and apply it to assess the authorship of the *Federalist Papers*. MERRIAM also uses the *Federalist Papers* in his examination of Morton's claim (discussed by Mosteller and Wallace in their second edition) that certain word habits show random variation in the works of a single author. Merriam's work demonstrates that Hamilton's and Madison's use of "on" and "upon" were consistently different from one another. M.W.A. SMITH (1988; 1989), again using Morton's approach, explores the authorship of Acts I and II of *Pericles* by analyzing the first words of speeches and finds evidence for George Wilkins's participation in writing this play by examining pairs of consecutive words.

Philosophy

Philosophers appear to have embraced information technologies more slowly than many other humanistic scholars. Based on a study of philosophers at Big Eight and Big Ten universities, SIEVERT &

SIEVERT report that many of their respondents use computers for word processing but that few employ other information technologies in their work. They note that although 75% of the philosophers knew that *Philosopher's Index* and *Arts and Humanities Citation Index* were available in an online format, only 50% had ever used a remote database and most were content to use printed tools for gathering information. Conversely, SLOMAN argues that computers—especially the development of AI—have produced a revolution in philosophy. This revolution lies not so much in the use of computers but in the way computers have changed philosophers' concepts of such "human" processes as perceiving, inferring, remembering, recognizing, understanding, and learning.

The minority of philosophers who do use computers directly in their research most frequently use applications for text analysis, theorem proving and the study of logic, which in recent years has merged with mathematics (COVEY; WALL). WOS (also WOS ET AL.) has produced important work that merges logic, mathematics, and computer science and probes numerous problems associated with automated reasoning. Classroom instruction, especially in logic and simulations, is also a growing application (CROY, 1986; HARGROVE) along with work in database building for philosophical dictionaries.

Some philosophers are concerned with the impact of information technologies on human communication, thought processes, and learning. Working from a phenomenological perspective, HEIM (1986) examines how humanistic discussion is facilitated or hampered in an online conference or bulletin board environment. He explains that while the immediacy, speed, and informality of such communication media encourage interactive conversations, they may also curtail the background warmth of such interchanges and shorten the gestation periods for thought. HEIM (1987) extends this analysis to word processing, speculating on how technology will influence thought and creativity. The concern here is that people may become more productive, but they may also lose the imaginative connections and associations that characterize genuine humanistic knowledge. SIMONS is equally concerned about the ethical and creative ramifications of the computer in musical composition. He argues that when composers use computers to write their music (rather than to record the music), the normal relationships among the composer, the work, future performances, and sound complexes are disturbed and creative identity is obscured. CROY (1985) discusses the ethical concerns in computer-assisted instruction, focusing on the responsibility of educators to use available technology "in a way that explores its potential for attaining educational aims" (p. 348).

INFORMATION TECHNOLOGIES THAT SUPPORT TEACHING AND LEARNING IN THE HUMANITIES

Humanities scholars and teachers at all educational levels are using an ever-increasing variety of software in their classrooms. College professors might find any of the research tools and approaches discussed above useful for explicating the structure and content of objects of humanistic inquiry. Yet, such sophisticated research tools are only a small segment of what is available to teachers of humanistic studies. Computer-assisted instruction (CAI) or computer-assisted-learning (CAL) software is designed specifically for use in the classroom. Much of it holds great promise for improving basic education in English and foreign language acquisition, composition skills, and a fundamental understanding of the human condition, past and present.

Designed for students rather than experts, CAI and CAL tools comprise a large percent of humanistic computing software. Depending on their application and the amount of control they wish to exercise over course development, teachers can find both off-the-shelf CAI software packages and authoring systems with which they can compose their own course materials using the format provided by the program. Two compilations of conference papers from the 1980s focusing specifically on CAL applications in the humanities provide overviews of recent work on an international basis. The compilation edited by OLSEN contains papers given at an NEH/MLA (Modern Language Association)-sponsored conference on CAI in high school and undergraduate humanities curricula. Topics range from CAI in history and logic to courseware development for language instruction. In their book KENT & LEWIS include papers presented at an international research seminar on CAL held at the University of London Institute of Education in 1986. The content is arranged around six central themes: (1) handling data, (2) curriculum developments, (3) teaching strategies, (4) child learning, (5) software development, and (6) strategies for CAI.

During the past decade, extensive work has been done in English and foreign language acquisition (see, for example, CAMERON ET AL. and ZOCK ET AL.). Classroom instruction using programs developed by computer-assisted language learning (CALL) authoring systems is becoming increasingly common on college campuses and in elementary and secondary schools. HUGHES describes and evaluates several CALL programs for the study of Biblical languages, including Sumerian, Egyptian, Hebrew, classical Greek, and Latin; he calls attention to Duke University's MicroCALIS Program, an authoring system produced as part of Duke's COLOE (Computerization of Language Oriented Enterprises) project. Other language-based programs support the development of composition skills (JOHNSON; SELFE & WAHLSTROM), poetics (NEWBOLD & STAHLKE), correction of spelling and phonographic errors (VERONIS), and linguistics and morphology (HOLMAN). STEVENS ET AL. provide an extensive bibliography on CALL programs and projects through 1985.

During the 1980s, the journal *Computers and the Humanities* devoted two issues to CAI. A comparison of their content illustrates the growth and potential trends in this area. The first issue, July-December 1984, included an introduction entitled, "The Adolescence of Computer-Assisted Instruction" and an article on the coming of age of computers in writing instruction (C. R. SMITH ET AL.). Most of the other articles addressed such issues as the introduction of CAI into a curriculum (AGER), the challenges of CAI (BURNS), and the promise of CAI (WATSON). Indicative of what was to come, two articles discussed videodisc technology (DEBLOOIS; WYATT). One 1989 *Computers and the Humanities* issue was devoted to intelligent computer-assisted language instruction (ICALI), a small but growing area that seeks to devise and implement computer-assisted learning environments that are modeled on human cognitive behavior (BAILIN & LEVIN; CHAPELLE). The topics covered reflect the evolving nature of the field: syntactic parsing (SANDERS & SANDERS), semantic processing for communicative exercises in foreign language learning (MULFORD), and intelligent tutoring systems (NEUWIRTH). UNDERWOOD argues that CALL systems that are based on the best of modern technology rather than those that are simply the easiest and most obvious will radically improve classroom instruction. In another 1989 issue of this journal, FARGHALY presents a model for ICALI based on a natural-language processing system that offers an interactive environment for students. Because of the complexity of natural language, such systems are presently limited to domain-specific knowledge representations, but future work may significantly enlarge these domains.

Programs that facilitate language acquisition are only one segment of the CAI market available to humanists. CROY (1988) describes the use of CAI to enhance human interaction in learning deductive proof construction in logic courses. Much historical computing has focused on the classroom with simulations to provide students with "you are there" experiences (BLOW & DICKINSON). DENLEY ET AL. include essays on the teaching of history in both secondary schools and colleges, and WILKES provides an overview of the history of CAI being used in Great Britain. Possibly the most significant developments in computer-assisted learning tools have taken place in the area of hypertext and hypermedia design.

MARCHIONINI (1988) identifies a chief value of hypertext by describing it as "the electronic representation of text that takes advantage of the random access capabilities of computers to overcome the strictly sequential medium of print on paper" (p. 8). Users of hypertext systems are no longer bound to follow the text or lesson (if it is a CAI application) from beginning to end. Students are empowered by highly individualized, interactive, and self-directed learning experiences. This capacity to access the content of a hyperdocument in a nonlinear manner allows the use of a glossary and movement to other relevant text, such as notes, details, refutations, or supporting arguments, to explicate something the reader has encountered earlier, which may include text, pictures, animation, and sound.

Hypermedia applications are still in the developmental stage so it is difficult to assess their full impact, but clearly they are an interesting and innovative way to present a large amount of material on a subject; as YANKELOVICH ET AL. argue, they may one day become standard textbooks. KINNELL points out that their potential seems greatest in the humanistic disciplines in which text is so often enhanced by the presence of images or sounds. One significant advantage over printed books on art, architecture, or archaeology is that by viewing a series of images, students can examine all sides of a three-dimensional object. Proponents of hypermedia, such as CONKLIN, argue that because hypermedia models human associative memory, it can influence how individuals perceive and think about subject matter.

The Perseus Project, developed at Harvard University, is an example of a hypermedia project that combines texts, art, and archaeological materials on Greek civilization (CRANE & MYLONAS; MYLONAS ET AL.). It includes translations of major Greek texts with notes, texts in Greek for advanced students, color images, archaeological drawings with texts, maps and plans, Landsat images, essays, an historical overview, and a classical encyclopedia. The major objective of this project is to provide an interactive curriculum, supported by both text and images, in which the student can experience an integrated view of Greek culture.

In support of university education and scholarship, the Institute for Research in Information and Scholarship (IRIS), housed at Brown University, is engaged in developing Intermedia, a flexible authoring system for creating and reading hypermedia databases (KAHN ET AL.; LANDOW; K. E. SMITH; WALTER). As humanists become more familiar and comfortable with hypermedia, numerous smaller, home-grown projects will undoubtedly develop. What also must be developed along with the technology are educationally sound design principles and rigorous methodologies to test the effects of hypermedia against pedagogical objectives.

While hypertext and hypermedia provide educators great opportunities, consumers should be warned that, as with any other educational technology, the finished products and the learning experiences will only be as good as the content. Key challenges exist in the establishment of appropriate nodes and links as well as in screen design for these media. The development of excellent hypermedia packages for the humanities will require both technology and insightful and pedagogically sound input from humanistic scholars. In addition, instructors using hyperdocument courseware must also help students gain a new type of literacy for this environment. Because hypermedia is an enabling rather than directive technology, MARCHIONINI (1990) observes that "undisciplined traversal of a hyperdocument is entertaining at best and may be disorienting and confusing" (p. 356-357). Another challenge is in the area of student assessment. Since hypermedia supports individualized and independent learning, student self-assessment may become an important part of the learning environment.

CONCLUSIONS AND OUTLOOK FOR THE FUTURE

So much has changed since RABEN & BURTON wrote the last *ARIST* chapter on this topic in 1981 that only a portion of the relevant material could be included here. Yet the adoption of information technologies by humanists has been and remains an evolutionary process. Progress has been piecemeal rather than systematic, with individuals working on isolated projects for the most part. In a few areas, such as archaeology, computers are becoming an integral tool, but in most humanistic fields few scholars use computers for anything more than word processing. With an increase in interdisciplinarity, some humanists have looked to the social sciences for methodological and computing support. Although there is a growing acceptance and respect for such investigations, most humanists continue their work with traditional methods. The great promise of humanistic computing for research lies in the integration of traditional and innovative approaches to materials. Such a holistic approach could truly enhance our understanding of mankind's creations and its past.

Humanists tend to use or benefit from information technologies primarily in four ways. First, perhaps the least glamorous but potentially most important technological impact lies with the preservation of humanistic research materials on storage media such as CD-ROMs. No matter what sort of computer program humanists may have, if primary sources are lost, scholars cannot study them. Second, word processing and text management software are having an enormous impact on how scholars, including humanists, manage their research notes and produce documents. The fundamentally verbal nature of humanistic scholarship makes these computer applications particularly important to humanists. Third, humanists use information technology to implement their research. The most exciting applications here include text analysis and stylometrics, graphic visualizations, and modeling. Fourth, humanists are taking advantage of a growing corpus of hypermedia and CAI software to facilitate their teaching. While it is unlikely that the book—the most enduring, random-access, portable information technology man has ever created—will soon be replaced by hypermedia and yet-to-be-developed technologies, the book will be complemented by these new tools. Hypermedia projects are of particular interest in the humanities, which often seek to relate words and images.

Two reasons for the recent growth of humanities computing—funding and the growth of technology—seem paramount. A decade ago, Raben and Burton noted the low status of humanistic studies at all educational levels in the United States and linked this to a paucity of funding for humanistic computing projects. With the return-to-basics movement in American education and an increased appreciation of our cultural heritage has come a renewed role for humanistic scholarship. There is also growing financial support from institutions and organizations such as the Annenberg Foundation, the Mellon Foundation, and NEH as well as from computer companies such as Apple and IBM. With the development of prototype and experimental projects, humanists have become increasingly aware of, interested in, and involved with computing projects. New text-intensive yet easy-to-use software along with the increased availability of powerful computers have brought many humanists into the computing fold.

The computing infrastructure that now exists in many colleges and universities supports the humanist's computing needs not only with hardware and software but also with computing personnel, thus freeing the humanist from having to become a computer expert. Many inequities still exist, however, in terms of the availability of technological approaches for scholars across this country and throughout the world. Unfortunately, many humanities computing activities remain very costly, especially database development. The sources of funding discussed above will provide for only a small percent of the potential research involving humanities computing. Humanists who wish to explore computing applications in the 1990s will need to locate new funding sources.

Not long ago humanists needed only a good library and relevant primary sources for their scholarship. Today they face some of the same challenges to obtain technological support that scientists have long known. One hopes that as the technology becomes less expensive and easier to use, it will also become more accessible to those who find it useful. Humanities computing centers will undoubtedly play an important role here. The next decade should be extremely exciting for humanists who wish to use technology to facilitate their communication, research, and teaching.

BIBLIOGRAPHY

AARTS, JAN; MEIJS, WILLEM, eds. 1984. Corpus Linguistics: Recent Developments in the Use of Computer Corpora in English Language Research. Amsterdam, The Netherlands: Rodopi B.V.; 1984. 229p. (Costerus. New Series vol. 45). ISBN: 90-6203-696-1; LC: 84-165668.

AGER, TRYG A. 1984. Computation in the Philosophy Curriculum. Computers and the Humanities (The Netherlands). 1984 July-December; 18(3/4): 145-156. ISSN: 0010-4817; CODEN: COHUAD.

ALLEN, EDWARD A. 1988. A Model and Typology of Local Political Struggle in Eighteenth-Century France. Historical Methods. 1988 Winter; 21(1): 20-28. ISSN: 0161-5440.

ALLEN, JAMES. 1987. Natural Language Understanding. Menlo Park, CA: The Benjamin/Cummings Publishing Co., Inc.; 1987. 574p (p. 1). ISBN: 0-8053-0330-8; LC: 87-24224.

ALLEN, KATHLEEN M.S.; GREEN, STANTON W.; ZUBROW, EZRA B.W., eds. 1990. Interpreting Space: GIS and Archaeology. London, England: Taylor & Francis; 1990. 398p. ISBN: 0-85066-824-7.

ALLEN, NANCY S. 1988. The Museum Prototype Project of the J. Paul Getty Art History and Information Program: A View from the Library. Library Trends. 1988 Fall; 37(2): 175-193. ISSN: 0024-2594.

ALLEN, ROBERT F. 1984. A Stylo-Statistical Study of "Adolphe" Preceded by Indexes and a Description of Computer Programming for Language Analysis. Genève-Paris: Slatkine-Champion; 1984. 391p. (Travaux de Linguistique Quantitative no. 22). ISBN: 2-05-100561-3; LC: 84-212430.

ALLEN, ROBERT F., ed. 1985. Data Bases in the Humanities and Social Sciences: [Proceedings of the] International Conference on Data Bases in the Humanities and Social Sciences: Volume 2; 1983; Rutgers, The State University, New Brunswick, NJ. Osprey, FL: Paradigm Press, Inc.; 1985. 434p. (ICDBHSS '83). Available from: Learned Information, Inc., Medford, NJ. ISBN: 0-931351-00-6.

ALLEN, ROBERT F. 1988. The Stylo-Statistical Method of Literary Analysis. Computers and the Humanities (The Netherlands). 1988; 22(1): 1-10. ISSN: 0010-4817; CODEN: COHUAD.

AMERICAN ARCHIVIST. 1989. Standards for Archival Description. American Archivist. 1989 Fall; 52(4): 163p. ISSN: 0360-9081.

AMERICAN ARCHIVIST. 1990a. Special Preservation Issue. 1990 Spring; 53(2): 190p. ISSN: 0360-9081.

AMERICAN ARCHIVIST. 1990b. Standards for Archival Description: Background Papers. American Archivist. 1990 Winter; 53(1): 178p. ISSN: 0360-9081.

AMERICAN NATIONAL STANDARDS INSTITUTE. 1979. American National Standard for Writing Abstracts. New York, NY: ANSI; 1979. 15p. (ANSI Z39.14-1979). Available from: American National Standards Institute, 1430 Broadway, New York, NY 10018.

AMERICAN SOCIETY FOR INFORMATION SCIENCE (ASIS) SIG/AH NEWSLETTER. 1987-. Gilmore, Matthew B., ed. Silver Spring, MD: American Society for Information Science (ASIS). Available from: American Society for Information Science, 8720 Georgia Avenue, Suite 501, Silver Spring, MD 20910-3602.

AMSLER, ROBERT A. 1984. Machine-Readable Dictionaries. In: Williams, Martha E., ed. Annual Review of Information Science and Technology: Volume 19. White Plains, NY: Knowledge Industry Publications, Inc. for the American Society for Information Science; 1984. 161-209. ISSN: 0066-4200; ISBN: 0-86729-093-5; CODEN: ARISBC; LC: 66-25096.

ANDREWS, DEREK; GREENHALGH, MICHAEL. 1987. Computing for Non-Scientific Applications. [Leicester, England]: University of Leicester Press; 1987. 346p. ISBN: 0-7185-1252-9.

ARCHIVES AND MUSEUM INFORMATICS. 1987-. Bearman, David, ed. Pittsburgh, PA: Archives & Museum Informatics. ISSN: 1042-1467.

ARNOLD, J. BARTO, III. 1979. Archaeological Applications of Computer-Drawn Contour and Three Dimensional Perspective Plots. In: Upham, Steadman, ed. Computer Graphics in Archaeology: Statistical Cartographic Applications to Spatial Analysis in Archaeological Contexts. [Tempe, AZ]: Arizona State University; 1979. 1-15. (Arizona State University Anthropological Research Papers no. 15). ISSN: 0271-0641; LC: 79-620035.

ASSOCIATION FOR COMPUTATIONAL LINGUISTICS. 1962-. Proceedings of the Association for Computational Linguistics Annual Meeting. Available from: Donald E. Walker (ACL), Bellcore, MRE 2A379, 445 South Street, Box 1910, Morristown, NJ 07960-1910.

ASSOCIATION FOR COMPUTATIONAL LINGUISTICS. 1988. Proceedings of the 2nd Conference on Applied Natural Language Processing; 1988 February 9-12; Austin, TX. n.p.: Association for Computational Linguistics; 1988. 259p. Available from: Donald E. Walker (ACL), Bellcore, MRE 2A379, 445 South Street, Box 1910, Morristown, NJ 07960-1961.

ASSOCIATION FOR COMPUTERS AND THE HUMANITIES (ACH) NEWSLETTER. 1978-. Walsh, Vicky A., ed. Washington, DC: Association for Computers and the Humanities. ISSN: 0190-6631.

BAILEY, RICHARD W., ed. 1982. Computing in the Humanities: Papers from the 5th International Conference on Computing in the Humanities; 1981 May 17-20; Ann Arbor, MI. Amsterdam, The Netherlands: North-Holland Publishing Co.; 1982. 191p. (ICCH/5). ISBN: 0-444-86423-7; LC: 82-7856.

BAILIN, ALAN; LEVIN, LORI. 1989. Introduction: Intelligent Computer-Assisted Language Instruction. Computers and the Humanities (The Netherlands). 1989 January-March; 23(1): 3-11. ISSN: 0010-4817; CODEN: COHUAD.

BARNARD, DAVID; HAYTER, RON; KARABABA, MARIA; LOGAN, GEORGE; MCFADDEN, JOHN. 1988. SGML-Based Markup for Literary Texts: Two Problems and Some Solutions. Computers and the Humanities (The Netherlands). 1988; 22(4): 265-276. ISSN: 0010-4817; CODEN: COHUAD.

BEARMAN, DAVID. 1987a. The National Information Systems Task Force (NISTF) Papers, 1981-1984. Chicago, IL: Society of American Archivists; 1987. 119p. ISBN: 0-931828-39-2.

BEARMAN, DAVID. 1987b. Optical Media: Their Implications for Archives and Museums. Pittsburgh, PA: Archives & Museum Informatics; 1987, c1989. 74p. (Archives and Museum Informatics Technical Report no. 1. Originally published as Archival Informatics Technical Report Vol. 1 No. 1, Spring 1987). ISSN: 1042-1459.

BEARMAN, DAVID. 1987/88. Automated Systems for Archives and Museums: Acquisition and Implementation Issues. Pittsburgh, PA: Archives & Museum Informatics; 1987/88, c1989. 88p. (Archives and Museum Informatics Technical Report no. 4. Originally published as Archival Informatics Technical Report Vol. 1 No. 4, Winter 1987-88). ISSN: 1042-1459.

BEARMAN, DAVID. 1990. Archives & Museum Data Models and Dictionaries. Pittsburgh, PA: Archives & Museum Informatics; 1990. 100p. (Archives and Museum Informatics Technical Report no. 10). ISSN: 1042-1459.

BESSER, HOWARD. 1987. The Changing Museum. In: Chen, Ching-chih, ed. ASIS '87: Information: The Transformation of Society: Proceedings of the American Society for Information Science (ASIS) 50th Annual Meeting: Volume 24; 1987 October 4-8; Boston, MA. Medford, NJ: Learned Information, Inc. for ASIS; 1987. 14-19. ISSN: 0044-7870; ISBN: 0-938734-19-9; CODEN: PAISDQ.

BITS & BYTES REVIEW. 1987-. Hughes, John J., ed. Whitefish, MT: Bits & Bytes Computer Resources. (Short title: B & B Review; Looseleaf format; Back issues available). ISSN: 0891-2955.

BLAZEK, RON; AVERSA, ELIZABETH. 1988. The Humanities: A Selective Guide to Information Sources. 3rd edition. Englewood, CO: Libraries Unlimited, Inc.; 1988. 382p. (Library Science Text Series). ISBN: 0-87287-558-X; ISBN: 0-87287-594-6 (pbk); LC: 87-33907.

BLOW, FRANCES; DICKINSON, ALARIC, eds. 1986. New History and New Technology: Present into Future. London, England: The Historical Association; 1986. 76p. ISBN: 0-85278-282-9.

BOGURAEV, BRAN; BRISCOE, TED, eds. 1989. Computational Lexicography for Natural Language Processing. London, England and New York, NY: Longman and John Wiley & Sons, Inc.; 1989. 310p. ISBN: 0-582-02248-7; LC: 88-18077.

BOLTON, WHITNEY. 1990. The Bard in Bits: Electronic Editions of Shakespeare and Programs to Analyze Them. Computers and the Humanities (The Netherlands). 1990 August; 24(4): 275-287. ISSN: 0010-4817; CODEN: COHUAD.

BOOTH, ANTHONY. 1988. Bulletin Boards and Libraries: The HUMBUL Experience. Library Association Record (England). 1988 November; 90(11): 666, 668, 670. ISSN: 0024-2195.

BOWER, JAMES M. 1988. One-Stop Shopping: RLIN as a Union Catalog for Research Collections at the Getty Center. Library Trends. 1988 Fall; 37(2): 252-262. ISSN: 0024-2594.

BRAINERD, BARRON. 1987. Textual Analysis and Synthesis by Computer. Abacus. 1987 Winter; 4(2): 8-18. ISSN: 0724-6722.

BROADBENT, ELAINE. 1986. A Study of Humanities Faculty Library Information Seeking Behavior. Cataloging and Classification Quarterly. 1986 Spring; 6(3): 23-37. ISSN: 0163-9374; CODEN: CCQUDE.

BROADUS, ROBERT N. 1987. Information Needs of Humanities Scholars: A Study of Requests Made at the National Humanities Center. Library and Information Science Research. 1987 April-June; 9(2): 113-129. ISSN: 0740-8188.

BRYAN, MARTIN. 1988. SGML: An Author's Guide to the Standard Generalized Markup Language. Workingham, England: Addison-Wesley Publishing Co.; 1988. 364p. ISBN: 0-201-17535-5 (pbk); LC: 88-24193.

BUDD, JOHN. 1986. Characteristics of Written Scholarship in American Literature: A Citation Study. Library and Information Science Research. 1986; 8(2): 189-211. ISSN: 0740-8188.

BURNS, HUGH. 1984. The Challenge for Computer-Assisted Rhetoric. Computers and the Humanities (The Netherlands). 1984 July-December; 18(3/4): 173-181. ISSN: 0010-4817; CODEN: COHUAD.

BURROWS, J. F. 1987. Computation into Criticism: A Study of Jane Austen's Novels and an Experiment in Method. Oxford, England: Clarendon Press; 1987. 255p. ISBN: 0-19-812856-8; LC: 86-12482.

BURROWS, J. F. 1989. "An Ocean Where Each Kind...": Statistical Analysis and Some Major Determinants of Literary Style. Computers and the Humanities (The Netherlands). 1989 August-October; 23(4-5): 309-321. ISSN: 0010-4817; CODEN: COHUAD.

BURTON, SARAH K.; SHORT, DOUGLAS D., eds. 1983. [Transactions of the] 6th International Conference on Computers and the Humanities; 1983 June 6-8; North Carolina State University, Raleigh, NC. Rockville, MD: Computer Science Press; 1983. 782p. (ICCH/6: Computers: Coming of Age in the Humanities). ISBN: 0-914894-96-X; LC: 83-7479.

BUTLER, CHRISTOPHER. 1985. Computers in Linguistics. Oxford, England: Basil Blackwell, Ltd.; 1985. 266p. ISBN: 0-631-14266-5; ISBN: 0-631-14267-3 (pbk); LC: 85-7540.

BUTLER, TODD. 1985. U.S. Newspaper Program Gains Momentum. OCLC Newsletter. 1985 April; 157: 6-7. ISSN: 0163-898X.

CAHAN, MITCHELL A. 1989. Optical Character Readers/Text Scanners: A Market Analysis. Information Technology and Libraries. 1989 June; 8(2): 186-196. ISSN: 0730-9295.

CAMERON, K. C.; DODD, W. S.; RAHTZ, S. P. Q., eds. 1986. Computers and Modern Language Studies. Chichester, England: Ellis Horwood Ltd.; New York, NY: Halsted Press; 1986. 160p. (Ellis Horwood Series in New Technologies in Training). ISBN: 0-7458-0057-2 (Ellis Horwood Ltd.); ISBN: 0-470-20343-9 (Halsted Press); LC: 86-009408.

CANADIAN HUMANITIES COMPUTING. 1987-. McCarty, Willard; Doutrelepont, Charles, eds. Toronto, Ontario, Canada: Centre for Computing in the Humanities. (Produced for the Consortium for Computers in the Humanities / le Consortium pour ordinateurs en sciences humaines (COCH/COCH) by the Centre for Computing in the Humanities at the University of Toronto). ISSN: 0843-2562.

CANNON, ROBERT L.; OAKMAN, ROBERT L. 1989. Interactive Collation on a Microcomputer: The URICA! Approach. Computers and the Humanities (The Netherlands). 1989 December; 23(6): 469-472. ISSN: 0010-4817; CODEN: COHUAD.

CARVER, MARTIN O. H. 1985. The Friendly User. In: Cooper, Malcolm; Richards, Julian, eds. Current Issues in Archaeological Computing: [Proceedings of] the 3rd Annual Conference on Techniques of Archaeological Excavation; 1984 December 8; Birmingham, England. Oxford, England: B.A.R. (British Archaeological Reports, Ltd.); 1985. 47-61. (BAR International Series no. 271). ISBN: 0-86054-344-7; LC: 86-134209.

CASE, DONALD O. 1986. Collection and Organization of Written Information by Social Scientists and Humanists: A Review and Exploratory Study. Journal of Information Science (England). 1986; 12(3): 97-104. ISSN: 0165-5515.

CASE, DONALD O. 1991a. The Collection and Use of Information by Some American Historians: A Study of Motives and Methods. Library Quarterly. 1991 January; 61(1): 61-82. ISSN: 0024-2519.

CASE, DONALD O. 1991b. Conceptual Organization and Retrieval of Text by Historians: The Role of Memory and Metaphor. Journal of the American Society for Information Science. 1991; 42. (In press). ISSN: 0002-8231; CODEN: AISJB6.

CHADWYCK-HEALEY. 1984-. National Inventory of Documentary Sources in the United States (NIDS US). Alexandria, VA: Chadwyck-Healey. (Microfiche copies of finding aids; published in 10 units per year with index). Available from: Chadwyck-Healey, 1101 King Street, Suite 380, Alexandria, VA 22314.

CHAPELLE, CAROL. 1989. Using Intelligent Computer-Assisted Language Learning. Computers and the Humanities (The Netherlands). 1989 January-March; 23(1): 59-70. ISSN: 0010-4817; CODEN: COHUAD.

CHEN, CHING-CHIH. 1986. Potential of Videodisc Technology for International Information Transfer. Journal of Library and Information Science (Rep. of China). 1986 October; 12(2): 105-120. ISSN: 0363-3640.

CHEN, CHING-CHIH. 1990. Hypermedia/Multimedia Technology and New Opportunities for Libraries in the 1990s. In: Helal, Ahmed H.; Weiss, Joachim W., eds. Developments in Microcomputing—Discovering New Opportunities for Libraries in the 1990s. Essen, Germany: Essen University Library; 1990. 1-23. (Festschrift in honor of Richard De Gennaro; 12th International Essen Symposium; 1989 October 23-26). ISSN: 0931-7503; ISBN: 3-922602-13-4.

CHEN, CHING-CHIH; MIRANDA, S.; SEIDEL, S. 1988. The New Concept of Hyperbase and Its Experimentation on the "First Emperor of China" Videodisc. Microcomputers for Information Management. 1988 December; 5(4): 217-246. ISSN: 0742-2342.

CHENHALL, ROBERT G. 1981. Computerized Data Bank Management. In: Gaines, Sylvia W., ed. Data Bank Applications in Archaeology. Tucson, AZ: University of Arizona Press; 1981. 1-8. ISBN: 0-8165-0686-8; LC: 81-901.

COMPUTATIONAL LINGUISTICS. 1976-. Allen, James F., ed. Cambridge, MA: MIT Press for the Association for Computational Linguistics. (Formerly the American Journal of Computational Linguistics). ISSN: 0891-2017; CODEN: AICLD9.

COMPUTERS AND THE HUMANITIES. 1966-. Holmes, Glyn, ed. Dordrecht, The Netherlands: Kluwer Academic Publishers. (Official Journal of the Association for Computers and the Humanities). ISSN: 0010-4817; CODEN: COHUAD.

CONKLIN, J. 1987. Hypertext: An Introduction and Survey. IEEE Computer. 1987 September; 20(9): 17-41. ISSN: 0018-9162.

COOK, MICHAEL. 1986. Archives and the Computer. 2nd edition. London, England: Butterworths-Heinemann, Ltd.; 1986. 176p. ISBN: 0-408-10882-7; LC: 85-019533.

COOK, MICHAEL. 1989. The Role of Computers in Archives. Information Development (England). 1989 October; 5(4): 217-220. ISSN: 0266-6669; CODEN: INDEE8.

COOPER, MALCOLM A. 1985. Computers in British Archaeology: The Need for a National Record. In: Cooper, Malcolm; Richards, Julian, eds. Current Issues in Archaeological Computing: [Proceedings of] the

3rd Annual Conference on Techniques of Archaeological Excavation; 1984 December 8; Birmingham, England. Oxford, England: B.A.R. (British Archaeological Reports, Ltd.); 1985. 79-91. (BAR International Series no. 271). ISBN: 0-86054-344-7; LC: 86-134209.

COVEY, PRESTON K. 1981. Formal Logic and Philosophic Analysis. Teaching Philosophy. 1981 July-October; 4(3-4): 277-301. ISSN: 0145-5788.

COX, LYNN; BEARMAN, DAVID, comps. and eds. 1990. 1990 Directory of Software for Archives and Museums. Pittsburgh, PA: Archives & Museum Informatics; 1990. 196p. (Archives and Museum Informatics Technical Report no. 12. Originally published as Archival Informatics Technical Report Vol. 3 No. 4). ISSN: 1042-1459.

CRANE, GREGORY; MYLONAS, ELLI. 1988. The Perseus Project: An Interactive Curriculum on Classical Greek Civilization. Educational Technology. 1988 November; 28(11): 25-32. ISSN: 0013-1962.

CRAWFORD, DAVID. 1986. Meeting Scholarly Information Needs in an Automated Environment: A Humanist's Perspective. College and Research Libraries. 1986 November; 47(6): 569-574. ISSN: 0010-0870.

CROY, MARVIN J. 1985. Ethical Concerns in Computer-Assisted Instruction. Metaphilosophy. 1985 October; 16(4): 338-349 (p. 348). ISSN: 0026-1068.

CROY, MARVIN J. 1986. The Current State of Computer-Assisted Instruction for Logic. Teaching Philosophy. 1986 December; 9(4): 333-350. ISSN: 0145-5788.

CROY, MARVIN J. 1988. The Use of CAI to Enhance Human Interaction in the Learning of Deductive Proof Construction. Computers and the Humanities (The Netherlands). 1988 October-December; 22(4): 277-284. ISSN: 0010-4817; CODEN: COHUAD.

CSA: NEWSLETTER OF THE CENTER FOR THE STUDY OF ARCHITECTURE. 1988-. Eiteljorg, Harrison, II, ed. Bryn Mawr, PA: Center for the Study of Architecture. Available from: Center for the Study of Architecture, P.O. Box 60, Bryn Mawr, PA 19010.

CSSR BULLETIN. 1985-. Busse, Rick; Mills, Watson, eds. Macon, GA: Council of Societies for the Study of Religion. Available from: The editors, Mercer University, Macon, GA 31207.

CULLARS, JOHN. 1985. Characteristics of the Monographic Literature of British and American Literary Studies. College and Research Libraries. 1985 November; 46(6): 511-522. ISSN: 0010-0870.

CULLARS, JOHN. 1988. Characteristics of the Monographic Scholarship of Foreign Literary Studies by Native Speakers of English. College and Research Libraries. 1988 March; 49(2): 157-170. ISSN: 0010-0870.

CULLARS, JOHN. 1989. Citation Characteristics of French and German Literary Monographs. Library Quarterly. 1989 October; 59(4): 305-325. ISSN: 0024-2519.

DAVIS, LANCE E.; ENGERMAN, STANLEY. 1987. Cliometrics: The State of the Science (or Is It Art or, Perhaps, Witchcraft?). Historical Methods. 1987 Summer; 20(3): 97-106. ISSN: 0161-5440.

DAY, RICHARD H. 1981. Dynamic Systems and Epochal Change. In: Sabloff, Jeremy A., ed. Simulations in Archaeology. Albuquerque, NM: University of New Mexico Press; 1981. 189-227. (School of American Research Advanced Seminar Series). ISBN: 0-8263-0576-8; LC: 80-54568.

DEBLOOIS, MICHAEL. 1984. Designing Instructional Materials for the Humanities: Is There a Role for Interactive Videodisc Technology? Computers and the Humanities (The Netherlands). 1984 July-December; 18(3/4): 189-194. ISSN: 0010-4817; CODEN: COHUAD.

DELCOURT, CHRISTIAN. 1989. Where Have All the Key Words Gone? Computers and the Humanities (The Netherlands). 1989 August-October; 23(4-5): 285-291 (p. 285). ISSN: 0010-4817; CODEN: COHUAD.

DENLEY, PETER; FOGELVIK, STEFAN; HARVEY, CHARLES, eds. 1989. History and Computing II. Manchester, England: Manchester University Press; 1989. 290p (p. ix). ISBN: 0-7190-2877-9; ISBN: 0-7190-2971-6 (pbk); LC: 88-013542.

DENLEY, PETER; HOPKIN, DEIAN, eds. 1988. History and Computing. Manchester, England: Manchester University Press; 1988. 224p. ISBN: 0-7190-2484-6.

DESMARAIS, NORMAN. 1989. MLA Bibliography on CD-ROM: A User's Perspective. Optical Information Systems. 1989 May-June; 9(3): 138-143. ISSN: 0886-5809.

DILLON, MARTIN; STEPHENS, DAVE; FLASH, KEVIN; CROOK, MARK. 1988. Design Issues for a Microcomputer-Based Collection Analysis System. Microcomputers for Information Management. 1988 December; 5(4): 263-273. ISSN: 0742-2342.

DUNK, JULIE; RAHTZ, SEBASTIAN. 1989. Strategies for Gravestone Recording. In: Denley, Peter; Fogelvik, Stefan; Harvey, Charles, eds. History and Computing II. Manchester, England: Manchester University Press; 1989. 72-80. ISBN: 0-7190-2877-9; ISBN 0-7190-2971-6 (pbk); LC: 88-013542.

EFFLAND, RICHARD W. 1979. Statistical Distribution Cartography and Computer Graphics. In: Upham, Steadman, ed. Computer Graphics in Archaeology: Statistical Cartographic Applications to Spatial Analysis in Archaeological Contexts. [Tempe, AZ]: Arizona State University; 1979. 17-29. (Arizona State University Anthropological Research Papers no. 15). ISSN: 0271-0641; LC: 79-620035.

ENNALS, RICHARD. 1985. Artificial Intelligence: Applications to Logical Reasoning and Historical Research. Chichester, England: Ellis Horwood, Ltd.; New York, NY: Halsted Press; 1985. 172p. (Ellis Horwood Series in Computers and Their Applications). ISBN: 0-85312-856-1 (Ellis Horwood Ltd.); ISBN: 0-470-20181-9 (Halsted Press); LC: 85-804.

EVANS, MAX J.; WEBER, LISA B. 1985. MARC for Archives and Manuscripts: A Compendium of Practice. Madison, WI: The State Historical Society of Wisconsin; 1985. 262p. (Distributed by the Society of American Archivists, 600 South Federal Street, Suite 504, Chicago, IL 60605). ISBN: 0-87020-232-4; LC: 85-11457.

FARGHALY, ALI. 1989. A Model for Intelligent Computer Assisted Language Instruction (MICALI). Computers and the Humanities (The Netherlands). 1989 October-December; 23(4): 235-250. ISSN: 0010-4817; CODEN: COHUAD.

FARRUGGIA, J. P.; MARTLEW, ROGER. 1984. Retrieving Information from Computerised Data-Bases: Keywords and FRANCIS. In: Martlew, Roger, [ed.]. Information Systems in Archaeology. Gloucester, England: Alan Sutton Publishing Ltd.; 1984. 106-110. (New Standard Archaeology). ISBN: 0-86299-116-1; LC: 84-131183.

FITCH, NANCY. 1984. Statistical Fantasies and Historical Facts: History in Crisis and Its Methodological Implications. Historical Methods. 1984 Fall; 17(4): 239-254. ISSN: 0161-5440.

FRANCIS, W. NELSON. 1980. A Tagged Corpus—Problems and Prospects. In: Greenbaum, Sidney; Leech, Geoffrey; Svartvik, Jan, eds. Studies in English Linguistics for Randolph Quirk. London, England: Longman; 1980, 1979c. 192-209. ISBN: 0-582-55079-3; LC: 79-41023.

FRAUTSCHI, RICHARD L. 1989. Lexical and Focal Preferences in Rousseau's Profession de foi du Vicaire Savoyard (Book IV of Emile). Computers and the Humanities (The Netherlands). 1989 August-October; 23(4-5): 347-355. ISSN: 0010-4817; CODEN: COHUAD.

FROST, CAROLYN O. 1987. Faculty Use of Subject Searching in Card and Online Catalogs. Journal of Academic Librarianship. 1987 May; 13(2): 86-92. ISSN: 0099-1333.

GAINES, SYLVIA W., ed. 1981. Data Bank Applications in Archaeology. Tucson, AZ: University of Arizona Press; 1981. 142p. ISBN: 0-8165-0686-8; LC: 81-901.

GAINES, SYLVIA W. 1984. The Impact of Computerized Systems on American Archaeology: An Overview of the Past Decade. In: Martlew, Roger, [ed.]. Information Systems in Archaeology. Gloucester, England: Alan Sutton Publishing Ltd.; 1984. 63-76. (New Standard Archaeology). ISBN: 0-86299-116-1; LC: 84-131183.

GARFIELD, EUGENE. 1980. Is Information Retrieval in the Arts and Humanities Inherently Different from That in Science? The Effect That ISI's Citation Index for the Arts and Humanities Is Expected to Have on Future Scholarship. Library Quarterly. 1980 January; 50(1): 40-57. ISSN: 0024-2519.

GARSIDE, ROGER; LEECH, GEOFFREY; SAMPSON, GEOFFREY, eds. 1987. The Computational Analysis of English: A Corpus-Based Approach. London, England: Longman Goup UK Ltd.; 1987. 196p. ISBN: 0-582-29149-6; LC: 86-33738.

GAUNT, MARIANNE I. 1990. Machine-Readable Literary Texts: Collection Development Issues. Collection Management. 1990; 13(1/2): 87-96. ISSN: 0146-2679; CODEN: COMADF.

GAZDAR, GERALD; FRANZ, ALEX; OSBORNE, KAREN; EVANS, ROGER. 1987. Natural Language Processing in the 1980s: A Bibliography.

Stanford, CA: Center for the Study of Langauge and Information; 1987. 240p. (CSLI Lecture Notes no. 12). ISBN: 0-937073-26-1; ISBN: 0-937073-28-8 (pbk); LC: 87-71618.

GAZDAR, GERALD; MELLISH, CHRIS. 1989. Natural Language Processing in PROLOG: An Introduction to Computational Linguistics. Workingham, England: Addison-Wesley Publishing Co.; 1989. 504p. ISBN: 0-201-18053-7; LC: 88-16667.

GETZ, MALCOLM. 1989. Managing the Collecting Effort. The Bottom Line. 1989; 3(1): 41-43. ISSN: 0888-045X.

GILMOUR-BRYSON, ANNE, ed. 1984. Computer Applications to Medieval Studies. Kalamazoo, MI: Western Michigan University, Medieval Institute Publications; 1984. 194p. (Studies in Medieval Culture no. 17). ISBN: 0-918720-25-7; ISBN: 0-918720-18-4 (pbk); LC: 84-4519.

GOETSCHALCKX, J.; ROLLING, L., eds. 1982. Lexicography in the Electronic Age: Proceedings of a Symposium; 1981 July 7-9; Luxembourg. Amsterdam, The Netherlands: North-Holland Publishing Co; 1982. 276p. ISBN: 0-444-86404-0; LC: 82-6341.

GROSZ, BARBARA J.; SPARCK JONES, KAREN; WEBBER, BONNIE LYNN, eds. 1986. Readings in Natural Language Processing. Los Altos, CA: Morgan Kaufmann Publishers, Inc.; 1986. ISBN: 0-934613-11-7; LC: 86-18488.

GROTOPHORST, CLYDE W. 1989. Keyless Entry: Building a Text Database Using OCR Technology. Library Hi Tech. 1989; 7(1): 7-15. ISSN: 0737-8831.

GUEST, SUSAN S. 1987. The Use of Bibliographic Tools by Humanities Faculty at the State University of New York at Albany. Reference Librarian. 1987 Summer; 18: 157-172. ISSN: 0276-3877; CODEN: RELBD6.

GUTMANN, MYRON P.; FLIESS, KENNETH H.; HOLMES, AMY E.; FAIRCHILD, AMY L.; TEAS, WENDY A. 1989. Keeping Track of Our Treasures: Managing Historical Data with Relational Database Software. Historical Methods. 1989 Fall; 22(4): 128-143. ISSN: 0161-5440.

GWINN, NANCY E., ed. 1987. Preservation Microfilming: A Guide for Librarians and Archivists. Chicago, IL: American Library Association; 1987. 212p. ISBN: 0-8389-0481-5; LC: 87-10020.

HAM, F. GERALD. 1984. Archival Choices: Managing the Historical Record in an Age of Abundance. In: Peace, Nancy E., ed. Archival Choices: Managing the Historical Record in an Age of Abundance. Lexington, MA: D.C. Heath and Co.; 1984. 133-147. (The Lexington Books Special Series in Libraries and Librarianship). ISBN: 0-669-05354-6; LC: 81-48395.

HANNEMAN, ROBERT; HOLLINGSWORTH, J. ROGERS. 1984. Modeling and Simulation in Historical Inquiry. Historical Methods. 1984 Summer; 17(3): 150-163. ISSN: 0161-5440.

HARGROVE, EUGENE C. 1986. Moria: A Computer Simulation for Introductory Philosophy. Teaching Philosophy. 1986 September; 9(3): 219-236. ISSN: 0145-5788.

HARRIS, KENNETH E.; LEE-BECHTOLD, SUSAN; WILSON, WILLIAM K.; MAYN, CHARLES W.; HOLMES, WILLIAM M.; CLAMES, ALAN R. 1990. National Archives Preservation Research Priorities: Past and Present. Washington, DC: National Archives and Records Administration; 1990. 21p. (NARA Technical Information Paper no. 7). NTIS: PB90-206210.

HEIM, MICHAEL. 1986. Humanistic Discussion and the Online Conference. Philosophy Today. 1986 Winter; 30: 278-288. ISSN: 0031-8256.

HEIM, MICHAEL. 1987. Electric Language: A Philosophical Study of Word Processing. New Haven, CT: Yale University Press; 1987. 305p. ISBN: 0-300-03835-6; LC: 86-28247.

HEINZKILL, RICHARD. 1980. Characteristics of References in Selected Scholarly English Literary Journals. Library Quarterly. 1980 July; 50(3): 352-365. ISSN: 0024-2519.

HELLINGA, LOTTE; GOLDFINCH, JOHN, eds. 1987. Bibliography and the Study of 15th-Century Civilisation: Papers Presented at a Colloquium at the British Library 1984 September 26-28: Organised in Conjunction with the Warburg Institute of the University of London. London, England: The British Library; 1987. 260p. (British Library Occasional Papers no. 5). ISBN: 0-7123-0049-X.

HENSEN, STEVEN L., comp. 1989. Archives, Personal Papers, and Manuscripts: A Cataloging Manual for Archival Repositories, Historical Societies, and Manuscript Libraries. 2nd edition. Chicago, IL: Society of American Archivists; 1989. 196p. ISBN: 0-931828-73-2; LC: 89-063416.

HOCKEY, SUSAN M. 1985. Snobol Programming for the Humanities. Oxford, England: Clarendon Press; 1985. 178p. ISBN: 0-19-824675-7; ISBN: 0-19-824676-5 (pbk); LC: 85-15422.

HOLLANDER, ROBERT. 1989. The Dartmouth Dante Project. Quaderni d'italianistica (Canada). 1989 Spring and Fall; 10(1-2): 287-298. (Special issue, Dante Today, ed. A. A. Iannucci). ISSN: 0226-8043.

HOLLANDER, ROBERT. 1990. Conference on a National Center for Machine-Readable Texts in the Humanities. Association for Computers and the Humanities (ACH) Newsletter. 1990 Summer; 12(2): 4-6. ISSN: 0190-6631.

HOLMAN, EUGENE. 1988. FINNMORF: A Computerized Reference Tool for Students of Finnish Morphology. Computers and the Humanities (The Netherlands). 1988 July-September; 22(3): 165-172. ISSN: 0100-4817; CODEN: COHUAD.

HORNER, JAN; THIRLWALL, DAVID. 1988. Online Searching and the University Researcher. Journal of Academic Librarianship. 1988 September; 14(4): 225-230. ISSN: 0099-1333.

HUGHES, JOHN J. 1987. Bits, Bytes and Biblical Studies: A Resource Guide for the Use of Computers in Biblical and Classical Studies. Grand Rapids, MI: Zondervan Publishing House; 1987. 643p. (Regency Reference Library). ISBN: 0-310-28581-X; LC: 87-6163.

IDE, NANCY M. 1987. Pascal for the Humanities. Philadelphia, PA: University of Pennsylvania Press; 1987. 320p. ISBN: 0-8122-1242-8.

IDE, NANCY M. 1989. A Statistical Measure of Theme and Structure.
Computers and the Humanities (The Netherlands). 1989 August-
October; 23(4-5): 277-283. ISSN: 0010-4817; CODEN: COHUAD.

INTERNATIONAL ORGANIZATION FOR STANDARDIZATION (ISO).
1986. Information Processing—Text and Office Systems—Standard
Generalized Markup Language (SGML). 1st edition. Geneva, Switzerland: ISO; 1986 October 15. 155p. (ISO 8879). Available from: ISO, 1
Rue De Varembe, Case Postale 56, CH-1121, Geneva 20, Switzerland.

JENNY, KRISS; CLARESON, TOM. 1990. OCLC Announces Bibliographic
Capabilities for Preservation. OCLC Newsletter. 1990 July/August;
186: 16-22. ISSN: 0163-898X.

JOHANSSON, STIG. 1985. Word Frequency and Text Type: Some Observations Based on the LOB Corpus of British English Texts. Computers
and the Humanities (The Netherlands). 1985 January-March; 19(1):
23-36. ISSN: 0010-4817; CODEN: COHUAD.

JOHNSON, ERIC. 1990. Project Report: Strong Writer. Computers and
the Humanities (The Netherlands). 1990 August; 24(4): 289-294. ISSN:
0010-4817; CODEN: COHUAD.

KAHN, PAUL; LAUNHARDT, JULIE; LENK, KRZYSZTOF; PETERS,
RONNIE. 1990. Design of Hypermedia Publications: Issues and Solutions. In: Furuta, R., ed. EP90: Electronic Publishing, 1990: Proceedings of the International Conference on Electronic Publishing, Document Manipulation, and Typography; 1990 September 18-20;
Gaithersburg, MD. Cambridge, England: Cambridge University Press;
1990. 107-124. (Series on Electronic Publishing no. 4). ISBN: 0-521-
40246-8.

KATZEN, MAY. 1983. An Office for Humanities Communication. Scholarly Publishing (Canada). 1983 February; 14(2): 179-186. ISSN: 0036-
634X.

KATZEN, MAY. 1986. The Application of Computers in the Humanities: A
View from Britain. Information Processing and Management. 1986;
22(2): 259-267 (p. 259). ISSN: 0306-4573; CODEN: IPMADK.

KATZEN, MAY. 1988. A National Information Network. Scholarly Publishing (Canada). 1988 July; 19(4): 210-216 (p. 210). ISSN: 0036-634X.

KENNY, ANTHONY. 1982. The Computation of Style: An Introduction to
Statistics for Students of Literature and Humanities. Oxford, England:
Pergamon Press; 1982. 176p. (Pergamon International Library of
Science, Technology, Engineering, and Social Studies). ISBN: 0-08-
024282-0; ISBN: 0-08-024281-2 (pbk); LC: 81 19221.

KENNY, ANTHONY. 1986. A Stylometric Study of the New Testament.
Oxford, England: Clarendon Press; 1986. 127p. ISBN: 0-19-826178-0;
LC: 86-8436.

KENT, W. A.; LEWIS, R., eds. 1987. Computer Assisted Learning in the
Humanities and Social Sciences. Oxford, England: Blackwell Scientific
Publications; 1987. 213p. ISBN: 0-632-01555-1; LC: 87-9419.

KIBBEE, JO. 1987. Tradition Meets Technology: Searching Folklore Online.
Database. 1987 February; 10(1): 24-26. ISSN: 0162-4105.

KINNELL, SUSAN K. 1988. Information Retrieval in the Humanities Using Hypertext. Online. 1988 March; 12(2): 34-35. ISSN: 0146-5422.

KOENIG, MICHAEL E.D. 1978. Citation Analysis for the Arts and Humanities as a Collection Management Tool. Collection Management. 1978 Fall; 2(3): 247-261. ISSN: 0146-2679.

LANCASHIRE, IAN; MCCARTY, WILLARD, eds. 1988. The Humanities Computing Yearbook—1988. Oxford, England: Clarendon Press; 1988. 396p. ISBN: 0-19-824442-8.

LANDOW, GEORGE P. 1989. Hypertext in Literary Education, Criticism, and Scholarship. Computers and the Humanities (The Netherlands). 1989 July-September; 23(3): 173-198. ISSN: 0010-4817; CODEN: COHUAD.

LEDGER, GERALD R. 1989. Re-counting Plato: Computer Analysis of Plato's Style. Oxford, England: Oxford University Press; 1989. 254p. ISBN: 0-19-814684-7; LC: 89-015979.

LEHMANN, STEPHEN; RENFRO, PATRICIA. 1991. Humanists at the Keyboard: Faculty Use of the RLIN Database. Computers and the Humanities (The Netherlands). 1991 Summer; 25. 11p. (In press). ISSN: 0010-4817; CODEN: COHUAD.

LIBRARY OF CONGRESS INFORMATION BULLETIN. 1989. American Memory. Library of Congress Information Bulletin. 1989 May 29; 48(22): 193-194. ISSN: 0041-7904.

LIGHT, RICHARD B.; ROBERTS, D. ANDREW; STEWART, JENNIFER D. 1986. Museum Documentation Systems: Developments and Applications. London, England: Butterworths & Co. Ltd.; 1986. 332p. ISBN: 0-408-10815-0; LC: 85-11003.

LOCK, GARY; WILCOCK, JOHN. 1987. Computer Archaeology. Aylesbury, Bucks, England: Shire Publications Ltd.; 1987. 64p. (Shire Archaeology). ISBN: 0-85263-877-9.

LOGAN, HARRY M. 1989. Report on a New OED Project: A Study of the New Words in the New OED. Computers and the Humanities (The Netherlands). 1989 August-October; 23(4-5): 385-395. ISSN: 0010-4817; CODEN: COHUAD.

LOUGHRIDGE, BRENDAN. 1989. Information Technology, the Humanities, and the Library. Journal of Information Science (The Netherlands). 1989; 15(4-5): 277-286. ISSN: 0165-5515.

LUNIN, LOIS F. 1987. Electronic Image Information. In: Williams, Martha E., ed. Annual Review of Information Science and Technology: Volume 22. Amsterdam, The Netherlands: Elsevier Science Publishers B.V. for the American Society for Information Science; 1987. 179-224. ISSN: 0066-4200; ISBN: 0-444-70302-0; CODEN: ARISBC; LC:66-25096.

LUSIGNAN, SERGE; NORTH, JOHN S., eds. 1977. Computing in the Humanities: Proceedings of the 3rd International Conference on Computing in the Humanities; 1977 August 2-6; Waterloo, Ontario, Canada. Waterloo, Ontario, Canada: University of Waterloo Press; 1977. 365p. (ICCH/3). ISBN: 0-88898-014-0.

MACKESY, EILEEN M. 1982. A Perspective on Secondary Access Services in the Humanities. Journal of the American Society for Information Science. 1982 May; 33(3): 146-151. ISSN: 0002-8231; CODEN: A1SJB6.

MARCHIONINI, GARY. 1988. Hypermedia and Learning: Freedom and Chaos. Educational Technology. 1988 November; 28(11): 8-12 (p. 8). ISSN: 0013-1962.

MARCHIONINI, GARY. 1990. Evaluating Hypermedia-Based Learning. In: Jonassen, D.; Mandl, H., eds. Designing Hypermedia for Learning. New York, NY: Springer-Verlag; 1990. 355-373 (p. 356-357). ISBN: 0-38752-958-6.

MARKEY, KAREN. 1984. Subject Searching in Library Catalogs before and after the Introduction of Online Catalogs. Dublin, OH: OCLC Online Computer Library Center, Inc.; 1984. 176p (p. 2). (OCLC Library, Information and Computer Science Series no. 4). ISBN: 0-933418-54-X; LC: 84-7226.

MARSHALL, IAN. 1983. Choice of Grammatical Word-Class without Global Syntactic Analysis: Tagging Words in the LOB Corpus. Computers and the Humanities (The Netherlands). 1983 September; 17(3): 139-150. ISSN: 0010-4817; CODEN: COHUAD.

MARTLEW, ROGER. 1984. Bibliographical Data-Bases in Archaeology. In: Martlew, Roger, [ed.]. Information Systems in Archaeology. Gloucester, England: Alan Sutton Publishing Ltd.; 1984. 99-105. (New Standard Archaeology). ISBN: 0-86299-116-1.

MATTERS, MARION, ed. 1990. Automated Records and Techniques in Archives: A Resource Directory. Chicago, IL: Society of American Archivists; 1990. 75p. Available from: The Society of American Archivists, 600 South Federal Street, Suite 504, Chicago, IL 60605.

MAWDSLEY, EVAN, ed. 1990. History and Computing III: Historians, Computers and Data: Applications in Research and Teaching. Manchester, England: Manchester University Press; 1990. 213p. ISBN: 0-7190-3051-X; ISBN: 0-7190-3211-3 (pbk); LC: 09-036568.

MCCRANK, LAWRENCE J., ed. 1981. Automating the Archives: Issues and Problems in Computer Applications. White Plains, NY: Knowledge Industry Publications, Inc. for the American Society for Information Science; 1981. 363p. ISBN: 0-914236-95-4; ISBN: 0-914236-86-5 (pbk); LC: 81-11732.

MCCRANK, LAWRENCE J., ed. 1989. Databases in the Humanities and Social Sciences: Proceedings of the International Conference on Databases in the Humanities and Social Sciences: Volume 4; 1987 July 11-13; Auburn University, Montgomery, AL. Medford, NJ: Learned Information, Inc.; 1989. 718p. (ICDBHSS '87). ISBN: 0-938734-37-7.

MCGREGOR, ROBERT KUHN. 1989. An Algorithmic Model of Forest Consumption in the Nineteenth-Century Northeast. Historical Methods. 1989 Winter; 22(1): 9-12. ISSN: 0161-5440.

MERRIAM, THOMAS. 1989. An Experiment with the Federalist Papers. Computers and the Humanities (The Netherlands). 1989 June; 23(3): 251-254. ISSN: 0010-4817; CODEN: COHUAD.

MIALL, DAVID S., ed. 1990. Humanities and the Computer: New Directions. Oxford, England: Clarendon Press; 1990. 222p. ISBN: 0-19-824244-1.

MICHELSON, AVRA. 1987. Description and Reference in the Age of Automation. American Archivist. 1987 Spring; 50(2): 192-208. ISSN: 0360-9081.

MICHELSON, AVRA, ed. 1988. Archives and Authority Control. Pittsburgh, PA: Archives & Museum Informatics; 1988, c1989. 63p. (Archives and Museum Informatics Technical Report no. 6). ISSN: 1042-1459.

MILLER, FREDRIC M. 1990. Arranging and Describing Archives and Manuscripts. Chicago, IL: Society of American Archivists; 1990. 131p. ISBN: 0-931828-75-9.

MOBERG, THOMAS F., ed. 1987. Data Bases in the Humanities and Social Sciences: Proceedings of the International Conference on Data Bases in the Humanities and Social Sciences: Volume 3; 1985 June 22-24; Grinnell College, Grinnell, IA. Osprey, FL: Paradigm Press; 1987. 533p. (ICDBHSS '85). Available from: Learned Information, Inc. ISBN: 0-931351-07-3; ISBN: 0-931351-02-2 (pbk).

MOLINE, JUDI. 1991. The User Interface: A Hypertext Model Linking Art Objects and Related Information. In: Interfaces for Information Retrieval. Westport, CT: Greenwood Publishing Group; 1991. (Paper presented at the American Society for Information Science Mid-Year Meeting; 1989 May 21-24; San Diego, CA). (In press). Available from: the author, Office Systems Engineering Group, National Computer Systems Laboratory, National Institute of Standards and Technology, Bldg. 225 Room B266, Gaithersburg, MD 20899.

MORTON, ANDREW Q. 1978. Literary Detection: How to Prove Authorship and Fraud in Literature and Documents. New York, NY: Charles Scribner's Sons; 1978. 223p. ISBN: 0-684-15516-8; LC: 78-67672.

MORTON, HERBERT C.; PRICE, ANNE J. 1989. The ACLS Survey of Scholars: Final Report of Views on Publications, Computers, and Libraries. Washington, DC: American Council of Learned Societies and University Press of America, Office of Scholarly Communication and Technology; 1989. 137p. ISBN: 0-8191-7260-X; ISBN: 0-8191-7261-8 (pbk); LC: 88-39482.

MOSTELLER, FREDERICK; WALLACE, DAVID L. 1984. Applied Bayesian and Classical Inference. 2nd edition. New York, NY: Springer-Verlag; 1984. 303p. (Springer Series in Statistics; 2nd edition of Inference and Disputed Authorship: The Federalist). ISBN: 0-387-90991-5; LC: 84-5489.

MULFORD, GEORGE W. 1989. Semantic Processing for Communicative Exercises in Foreign-Language Learning. Computers and the Humanities (The Netherlands). 1989 January-March; 23(1): 31-44. ISSN: 0010-4817; CODEN: COHUAD.

MYLONAS, ELLI; CRANE, GREGORY; MORRELL, KENNY; SMITH, D. NEEL. 1991. The Perseus Project: Data in the Electronic Age. 19p.

Available from: Dr. Elli Mylonas, Perseus Project, Dept. of the Classics, 319 Boylston Hall, Harvard University, Cambridge, MA 02138.

NENCIONI, GIOVANNI. 1990. The Accademia della Crusca: New Perspectives in Lexicography. Computers and the Humanities (The Netherlands). 1990 December; 24(5-6): 345-352. ISSN: 0010-4817; CODEN: COHUAD.

NEUWIRTH, CHRISTINE M. 1989. Intelligent Tutoring Systems: Exploring Issues in Learning and Teaching Writing. Computers and the Humanities (The Netherlands). 1989 January-March; 23(1): 45-57. ISSN: 0010-4817; CODEN: COHUAD.

NEWBOLD, W. WEBSTER; STAHLKE, HERBERT F. W. 1990. POETRY I: Teaching Verse with CAI. Computers and the Humanities (The Netherlands). 1990 June; 24(3): 177-185. ISSN: 0010-4817; CODEN: COHUAD.

NOLTE, WILLIAM. 1987. High-Speed Text Search Systems and Their Archival Implications. American Archivist. 1987 Fall; 50(4): 580-584. ISSN: 0360-9081.

OAKMAN, ROBERT L. 1984. Computer Methods for Literary Research. Revised, paperback edition. Athens, GA: University of Georgia Press; 1984. 235p. ISBN: 0-8203-0686-X (pbk); LC: 83-9273.

OAKMAN, ROBERT L., ed. 1989. 8th International Conference on Computers and the Humanities. Computers and the Humanities. 1989 August-October; 23(4-5): 178p. (Special issue devoted to the proceedings of the 8th International Conference on Computers and the Humanities (ICCH/8); 1987 April 9-11; Columbia, SC). ISSN: 0010-4817; CODEN: COHUAD.

OLSEN, SOLVEIG, ed. 1985. Computer-Aided Instruction in the Humanities: Papers from the Conference on Computer-Aided Instruction in the High School and Undergraduate Humanities Curriculum Organized by the Modern Language Association of America (MLA); 1983 February 3-4. New York, NY: MLA; 1985. 266p. (Technology and the Humanities no. 2). ISBN: 0-87352-522-3; ISBN: 0-87352-553-1 (pbk); LC: 85-13740.

OLSRUD, LOIS; MOORE, ANNE. 1989. Serials Review in the Humanities: A Three-Year Project. Collection Building. 1989; 10(3-4): 2-10. ISSN: 0160-4953.

OPPENHEIM, CHARLES. 1984. Online Information Retrieval, Data-Bases and Networks. In: Martlew, Roger, [ed.]. Information Systems in Archaeology. Gloucester, England: Alan Sutton Publishing Ltd.; 1984. 90-98. (New Standard Archaeology). ISBN: 0-86299-116-1.

OPPENHEIM, ROSA. 1988. The Mathematical Analysis of Style: A Correlation-Based Approach. Computers and the Humanities (The Netherlands). 1988; 22(4): 241-252. ISSN: 0010-4817; CODEN: COHUAD.

OXFORD UNIVERSITY PRESS. 1990. Art and Architecture Thesaurus. Oxford, England: Oxford University Press; 1990. 3 volumes: 1782p. ISBN: 0-19-506403-8.

PEREZ, ERNEST. 1990. Low-Budget, Cost-Effective OCR: Optical Character Recognition for MS-DOS Micros. Library Software Review. 1990 July/August; 9(4): 209-217. ISSN: 0742-5759.

PERRAULT, ANNA H. 1983. Humanities Collection Management—An Impressionistic/Realistic/Optimistic Appraisal of the State of the Art. Collection Management. 1983 Fall/Winter; 5(3/4): 1-23. ISSN: 0146-2679.

PERSKY, GAIL. 1984. The Mellon Microform Master Project at the New York Public Library. Microform Review. 1984 Winter; 13(1): 11-16. ISSN: 0002-6530.

POPKIN, RICHARD H. 1990. The Scholarly Communication Process in the Humanities: The Role of the Editor. Serials Librarian. 1990; 17(3/4): 25-32 (p. 25). ISSN: 0361-526X; CODEN: SELID4.

POTTER, ROSANNE G. 1988. Literary Criticism and Literary Computing: The Difficulties of a Synthesis. Computers and the Humanities (The Netherlands). 1988; 22(1): 91-97. ISSN: 0010-4817; CODEN: COHUAD.

POTTER, ROSANNE G., ed. 1989. Literary Computing and Literary Criticism: Theoretical and Practical Essays on Theme and Rhetoric. Philadelphia, PA: University of Pennsylvania; 1989. 276p. ISBN: 0-8122-8156-X; LC: 88-38159.

RABEN, JOSEPH; BURTON, SARAH K. 1981. Information Systems and Services in the Arts and Humanities. In: Williams, Martha E., ed. Annual Review of Information Science and Technology: Volume 16. White Plains, NY: Knowledge Industry Publications, Inc. for the American Society for Information Science; 1981. 247-266. ISSN: 0066-4200; ISBN: 0-914236-90-3; CODEN: ARISBC; LC: 66-25096.

RAHTZ, SEBASTIAN, ed. 1987. Information Technology in the Humanities: Tools, Techniques and Applications. Chichester, England: Ellis Horwood, Ltd.; New York, NY: Halsted Press; 1987. 188p. (Ellis Horwood Series in Computers and Their Applications). ISBN: 0-7458-0148-X (Ellis Horwood Ltd.); ISBN: 0-470-20852-X (Halsted Press); LC: 87-4258.

REACH: RESEARCH & EDUCATIONAL APPLICATIONS OF COMPUTERS IN THE HUMANITIES. 1989-. Dahlin, Eric, ed. Santa Barbara, CA: University of California at Santa Barbara, Humanities Computing Facility. Available from: The Humanities Computing Facility of the University of California at Santa Barbara, Santa Barbara, CA 93106.

RICHARDS, JULIAN D. 1985. Standardising the Record. In: Cooper, Malcolm; Richards, Julian, eds. Current Issues in Archaeological Computing: [Proceedings of] the 3rd Annual Conference on Techniques of Archaeological Excavation; 1984 December 8; Birmingham, England. Oxford, England: B.A.R. (British Archaeological Reports, Ltd.); 1985. 93-102. (BAR International Series no. 271). ISBN: 0-86054-344-7; LC: 86-134209.

RICHARDS, JULIAN D.; RYAN, N. S. 1985. Data Processing in Archaeology. Cambridge, England: Cambridge University Press; 1985. 232p. (Cambridge Manuals in Archaeology). ISBN: 0-521-25769-7; LC: 84-9523.

RITZENTHALER, MARY LYNN. 1990. Preservation of Archival Records: Holdings Maintenance at the National Archives. Washington, DC:

National Archives and Records Administration; 1990. 29p. (NARA Technical Information Paper no. 6). NTIS: PB90-168733.

ROBERTS, D. ANDREW. 1985. Planning the Documentation of Museum Collections. Duxford, Cambridge, England: Museum Documentation Association; 1985. 568p. ISBN: 0-905963-53-9.

ROWBOTTOM, MARY E.; WILLETT, PETER. 1982. The Effect of Subject Matter on the Automatic Indexing of Full Text. Journal of the American Society for Information Science. 1982 May; 33(3): 139-141. ISSN: 0002-8231; CODEN: AISJB6.

RUDALL, B. H.; CORNS, T. N. 1987. Computers and Literature: A Practical Guide. Cambridge, MA: Abacus Press; 1987. 129p. ISBN: 0-85626-340-0; LC: 85-13370.

SABLOFF, JEREMY A. 1981. Background. In: Sabloff, Jeremy A., ed. Simulations in Archaeology. Albuquerque, NM: University of New Mexico Press; 1981. 3-9. (School of American Research Advanced Seminar Series). ISBN: 0-8263-0576-8; LC: 80-54568.

SAHLI, NANCY. 1985. MARC for Archives and Manuscripts: The AMC Format. Chicago, IL: Society of American Archivists; 1985. 261p. ISBN: 0-931828-65-1; LC: 85-25039.

SALTON, GERARD. 1989. Automatic Text Processing: The Transformation, Analysis, and Retrieval of Information by Computer. Reading, MA: Addison-Wesley Publishing Co.; 1989. 530p. (Addison-Wesley Series in Computer Science). ISBN: 0-201-12227-8; LC: 88-467.

SANDERS, ALTON F.; SANDERS, RUTH H. 1989. Syntactic Parsing: A Survey. Computers and the Humanities (The Netherlands). 1989 January-March; 23(1): 13-30. ISSN: 0010-4817; CODEN: COHUAD.

SCHEIN, ALAN. 1990. The Recognition-Linked Information Management System (IIMS): The Next Major Advance in Computing. Optical Information Systems. 1990 March/April; 10(2): 66-69 (p. 68). ISSN: 0886-5809.

SCHOLTZ, SANDRA C.; MILLION, MICHAEL G. 1981. A Management Information System for Archaeological Resources. In: Gaines, Sylvia W., ed. Data Bank Applications in Archaeology. Tucson, AZ: University of Arizona Press; 1981. 15-26. ISBN: 0-8165-0686-8; LC: 81-901.

SCHULTE, THEO J. 1989. Artificial Intelligence Techniques for Historians: Expert Systems, Knowledge Representation and High-Level Programming. In: Denley, Peter; Fogelvik, Stefan; Harvey, Charles, eds. History and Computing II. Manchester, England: Manchester University Press; 1989. 90-96. ISBN: 0-7190-2877-9; ISBN: 0-7190-2971-6 (pbk); LC: 88-013542.

SELFE, CYNTHIA L.; WAHLSTROM, BILLIE J. 1988. Computers and Writing: Casting a Broader Net with Theory and Research. Computers and the Humanities (The Netherlands). 1988 January-March; 22(1): 57-66. ISSN: 0010-4817; CODEN: COHUAD.

SIEVERT, DONALD; SIEVERT, MARYELLEN. 1988. Humanists and Technology: The Case of Philosophers. In: Borgman, Christine L.; Pai, Edward Y. H., eds. ASIS '88: Information and Technology: Planning for the Second 50 Years: Proceedings of the American Society for Information Science (ASIS) 51st Annual Meeting: Volume 25; 1988 October 23-27; Atlanta, GA. Medford, NJ: Learned Information, Inc. for ASIS; 1988. 94-99. ISSN: 0044-7870; ISBN: 0-938734-29-6; CODEN: PAISDQ.

SIMONS, PETER M. 1988. Computer Composition and Works of Music: Variation on a Theme of Ingarden. Journal of the British Society for Phenomenology (England). 1988 May; 19(2): 141-154. ISSN: 0007-1773.

SIMONTON, DEAN KEITH. 1990. Lexical Choices and Aesthetic Success: A Computer Content Analysis of 154 Shakespeare Sonnets. Computers and the Humanities (The Netherlands). 1990 August; 24(4): 251-264. ISSN: 0010-4817; CODEN: COHUAD.

SLOMAN, AARON. 1978. The Computer Revolution in Philosophy: Philosophy, Science and Models of Mind. Hassocks, Sussex, England: Harvester Press, Ltd.; 1978. 304p. (Harvester Studies in Cognitive Science). ISBN: 0-85527-389-5; ISBN: 0-85527-542-1 (pbk); LC: 79-308001.

SMITH, CHARLES R.; KIEFER, KATHLEEN E.; GINGRICH, PATRICIA. 1984. Computers Come of Age in Writing Instruction. Computers and the Humanities. 1984 July-December; 18(3/4): 215-224. ISSN: 0010-4817; CODEN: COHUAD.

SMITH, KAREN E. 1988. Hypertext—Linking to the Future. Online. 1988 March; 12(2): 32-40. ISSN: 0146-5422.

SMITH, M. W. A. 1988. The Authorship of Acts I and II of Pericles: A New Approach Using First Words of Speeches. Computers and the Humanities (The Netherlands). 1988 February; 22(1): 23-41. ISSN: 0010-4817; CODEN: COHUAD.

SMITH, M. W. A. 1989. A Procedure to Determine Authorship Using Pairs of Consecutive Words: More Evidence for Wilkins's Participation in Pericles. Computers and the Humanities (The Netherlands). 1989 April; 23(2): 113-129. ISSN: 0010-4817; CODEN: COHUAD.

SPERBERG-MCQUEEN, C. MICHAEL; BURNARD, LOU, eds. 1990. Guidelines for the Encoding and Interchange of Machine-Readable Texts. Chicago, IL and Oxford, England: ACH, ACL, ALLC; 1990 October. 290p. (Draft: Version 1.1). Available from: Dr. Sperberg-McQueen, Computer Center (M/C 135), University of Illinois at Chicago, Box 6998, Chicago, IL 60680. Document no.: TEI P1.

STAM, DEIRDRE C. 1989a. Public Access to Museum Information: Pressures and Policies. Curator. 1989 September; 32(3): 190-198. ISSN: 0011-3069; CODEN: CRTRAH.

STAM, DEIRDRE C. 1989b. The Quest for a Code, or a Brief History of the Computerized Cataloging of Art Objects. Art Documentation. 1989 Spring; 8(1): 7-15. ISSN: 0730-7187.

STEBELMAN, SCOTT D. 1981. On-Line Searching and the Humanities: Relevance, Resistance, and Marketing Strategies. In: Williams, Martha E.; Hogan, Thomas H., comps. Proceedings of the 2nd National Online

Meeting; 1981 March 24-26; New York, NY. Medford, NJ: Learned Information, Inc.; 1981. 443-453. ISBN: 0-938734-02-4.

STERN, BARRIE T.; CAMPBELL, ROBERT. 1989. International Document Delivery: The ADONIS Project. Wilson Library Bulletin. 1989 February; 63(6): 36-41. ISSN: 0043-5651.

STERN, MADELEINE. 1983. The Characteristics of the Literature of Literary Scholarship. College and Research Libraries. 1983 July; 44(4): 199-209. ISSN: 0010-0870.

STERN, PETER. 1988. Online in the Humanities: Problems and Possibilities. Journal of Academic Librarianship. 1988 July; 14(3): 161-164. ISSN: 0099-1333.

STEVENS, VANCE; SUSSEX, ROLAND; TUMAN, WALTER V. 1986. A Bibliography of Computer-Aided Language Learning. New York, NY: AMS Press, Inc.; 1986. 140p. (AMS Studies in Education no. 6). ISSN: 0882-438X; ISBN: 0-404-12666-9; LC: 86-17450.

STIEG, MARGARET F. 1981. The Information Needs of Historians. College and Research Libraries. 1981 November; 42(6): 549-560. ISSN: 0010-0870.

STIELOW, FREDERICK J.; TIBBO, HELEN R. 1988. The Negative Search and the Humanities: A Critical Essay in Library Literature. RQ. 1988 Spring; 27(3): 358-365. ISSN: 0033-7072.

STIELOW, FREDERICK J.; TIBBO, HELEN R. 1989. Collection Analysis in Modern Librarianship: A Stratified, Multidimensional Model. Collection Management. 1989; 11(3/4): 73-91. ISSN: 0146-2679; CODEN: COMADF.

STOAN, STEPHEN K. 1984. Research and Library Skills: An Analysis and Interpretation. College and Research Libraries. 1984 March; 45(2): 99-109. ISSN: 0010-0870.

STONE, SUE. 1982. Humanities Scholars: Information Needs and Uses. Journal of Documentation (England). 1982 December; 38(4): 292-313. ISSN: 0022-0418.

SVARTVIK, JAN; EEG-OLOFSSON, MATS. 1982. Tagging the London-Lund Corpus of Spoken English. In: Johansson, Stig, ed. Computer Corpora in English Language Research. Bergen, Norway: Norwegian Computer Centre for the Humanities; 1982. 85-109. ISBN: 82-7283-027-2.

SVARTVIK, JAN; EEG-OLOFSSON, MATS; FORSHEDEN, OSCAR; ORESTROM, BENGT; THAVENIUS, CECILIA. 1982. Survey of Spoken English: Report on Research 1975-1981. Lund, Sweden: LiberLaromedel Lund; 1982. 108p. (Lund Studies in English no. 63). ISBN: 91-40-04822-5.

SVARTVIK, JAN; QUIRK, RANDOLPH, eds. 1980. A Corpus of English Conversation. Lund, Sweden: LiberLaromedel Lund; 1980. 893p. (Lund Studies in English no. 56). ISBN: 91-40-04740-7.

THALLER, MANFRED. 1989. The Need for a Theory of Historical Computing. In: Denley, Peter; Fogelvik, Stefan; Harvey, Charles, eds. History and Computing II. Manchester, England: Manchester University Press; 1989. 1-11. ISBN: 0-7190-2877-9; ISBN: 0-7190-2971-6 (pbk).

TIBBO, HELEN R. 1989. Abstracts, Online Searching, and the Humanities: A Study of the Structure and Content of Abstracts of Historical Discourse. College Park, MD: University of Maryland; 1989. 879p. (Ph.D. dissertation). Available from: University Microfilms, Ann Arbor, MI. (UMI order no. AAD89-24240).

TIBBO, HELEN R. 1992. Abstracting across the Disciplines: A Content Analysis of Abstracts from the Natural Sciences, the Social Sciences, and the Humanities with Implications for Standardization and Online Information Retrieval. Library and Information Science Research. 1992; 14. (In press). Available from: the author, School of Information and Library Science, 100 Manning Hall, CB# 3360, University of North Carolina at Chapel Hill, Chapel Hill, NC 27599-3360.

TUCKER, ALLEN B., JR.; NIRENBURG, SERGEI. 1984. Machine Translation: A Contemporary View. In: Williams, Martha E., ed. Annual Review of Information Science and Technology: Volume 19. White Plains, NY: Knowledge Industry Publications, Inc. for the American Society for Information Science; 1984. 129-160. ISSN: 0066-4200; ISBN: 0-86729-093-5; CODEN: ARISBC; LC: 66-25096.

U.S. LIBRARY OF CONGRESS. 1965-. National Register of Microform Masters. Washington, DC: Library of Congress, Catalog Publication Division. (Superseded by New Serial Titles ISSN: 0028-6680). ISSN: 0090-3299; LC: 65-029419.

U.S. NATIONAL ACADEMY OF SCIENCES. NATIONAL RESEARCH COUNCIL. COMMITTEE ON PRESERVATION OF HISTORICAL RECORDS. 1986. Preservation of Historical Records. Washington, DC: National Academy Press; 1986. 108p. ISBN: 0-309-03681-X; LC: 86-12718.

UNDERWOOD, JOHN. 1989. On the Edge: Intelligent CALL in the 1990s. Computers and the Humanities (The Netherlands). 1989 January-March; 23(1): 71-84. ISSN: 0010-4817; CODEN: COHUAD.

UNIVERSITY OF ILLINOIS AT CHICAGO. THE UNIVERSITY LIBRARY. 1989. Humanists at Work: Papers Presented at a Symposium [on] Disciplinary Perspectives and Personal Reflections; 1989 April 27-28; University of Illinois at Chicago. Chicago, IL: University of Illinois at Chicago, The University Library; 1989. 131p. Available from: The University Library, University of Illinois at Chicago (M/C 234), Box 8198, Chicago, IL 60680.

UNIVERSITY OF TORONTO. CENTRE FOR COMPUTING IN THE HUMANITIES. 1989. Tools for Humanists, 1989. Toronto, Canada: University of Toronto, Centre for Computing in the Humanities; 1989. 140p. (A guidebook to the software and hardware fair held in conjunction with The Dynamic Text Conference, 1989 June 6-9). Available from: The Centre for Computing in the Humanities, University of Toronto, Toronto, Ontario M5S 1A1 Canada.

VAN PEER, W. 1989. Quantitative Studies of Literature: A Critique and an Outlook. Computers and the Humanities (The Netherlands). 1989 August-October; 23(4-5): 301-307 (p. 301). ISSN: 0010-4817; CODEN: COHUAD.

VERONIS, JEAN. 1988. Computerized Correction of Phonographic Errors. Computers and the Humanities (The Netherlands). 1988 January-March; 22(1): 43-56. ISSN: 0010-4817; CODEN: COHUAD.

WALKER, G.; ATKINSON, S. D. 1988. Online Searching in the Humanities: Implications for End-Users and Intermediaries. In: [Online Information 88]: Proceedings of the 12th International Online Information Meeting: Volume 1; 1988 December 6-8; London, England. Oxford, England: Learned Information (Europe) Ltd.; 1988. 401-412. ISBN: 0-904933-68-7.

WALL, ROBERT. 1985. The "New" Logics and Natural Language Processing. Computers and the Humanities (The Netherlands). 1985 April-June; 19(2): 123-129. ISSN: 0010-4817; CODEN: COHUAD.

WALTER, MARK. 1989. IRIS Intermedia: Pushing the Boundaries of Hypertext. The Seybold Report on Publishing Systems. 1989 August 7; 18(21): 21-32. ISSN: 0736-7260.

WARNER, AMY J. 1987. Natural Language Processing. In: Williams, Martha E., ed. Annual Review of Information Science and Technology: Volume 22. Amsterdam, The Netherlands: Elsevier Science Publishers B.V. for the American Society for Information Science; 1987. 79-108. ISSN: 0066-4200; ISBN: 0-444-70302-0; CODEN: ARISBC; LC: 66-25096.

WATSON, DERYN M. 1984. Computer-Assisted Learning for School Pupils of History, French and English in the UK. Computers and the Humanities. 1984 July-December; 18(3/4): 233-242. ISSN: 0010-4817; CODEN: COHUAD.

WEINTRAUB, KARL J. 1980. The Humanistic Scholar and the Library. Library Quarterly. 1980 January; 50(1): 22-39. ISSN: 0024-2519.

WIBERLEY, STEPHEN E., JR. 1983. Subject Access in the Humanities and the Precision of the Humanist's Vocabulary. Library Quarterly. 1983 October; 53(4): 420-433. ISSN: 0024-2519.

WIBERLEY, STEPHEN E., JR. 1988. Names in Space and Time: The Indexing Vocabulary of the Humanities. Library Quarterly. 1988 January; 58(1): 1-28. ISSN: 0024-2519.

WIBERLEY, STEPHEN E., JR.; JONES, WILLIAM G. 1989. Patterns of Information Seeking in the Humanities. College and Research Libraries. 1989 November; 50(6): 638-645. ISSN: 0010-0870.

WILKES, JOHN, ed. 1985. Exploring History with Microcomputers. London, England: Council for Educational Technology; 1985. 178p. (Microelectronics Education Programme Readers no. 6). ISSN: 0264-4142; ISBN: 0-86184-137-9.

WILLIAMS, MARTHA E. 1991. The State of Databases Today: 1991. In: Marcaccio, Kathleen Young, ed. Computer-Readable Databases: A Directory and Data Sourcebook. 7th edition. Detroit, MI: Gale Research, Inc.; 1991. ix-xviii (p. xv). ISSN: 0271-4477; ISBN: 0-8103-2945-X.

WILLIAMS, WARREN. 1989. Exploring Ancient Civilization. Cadence. 1989 September; 4(9): 67-70. ISSN: 0887-9141.

WOS, LARRY. 1988. Automated Reasoning: 33 Basic Research Problems. Englewood Cliffs, NJ: Prentice-Hall; 1988. 319p. ISBN: 0-13-054552-X (pbk); LC 87-13148.

WOS, LARRY; OVERBEEK, ROSS; LUSK, EWING; BOYLE, JIM. 1984. Automated Reasoning: Introduction and Applications. Englewood Cliffs, NJ: Prentice-Hall, Inc.; 1984. 482p. ISBN: 0-13-054453-1; ISBN: 0-13-054446-9 (pbk); LC: 83-22968.

WYATT, DAVID. 1984. ESL Applications of the Computer-Controlled Videodisc Player. Computers and the Humanities (The Netherlands). 1984 July-December; 18(3/4): 243-250. ISSN: 0010-4817; CODEN: COHUAD.

YANKELOVICH, NICOLE; MEYROWITZ, N.; VAN DAM, A. 1985. Reading and Writing the Electronic Book. IEEE Computer. 1985 October; 18(10): 15-30. ISSN: 0018-9162.

ZOCK, M.; LAROUI, A.; FRANCOPOULO, G. 1989. SWIM: A "Natural" Interface for the Scientifically Minded Language Learner. Computers and the Humanities (The Netherlands). 1989 October-December; 23(4): 411-422. ISSN: 0010-4817; CODEN: COHUAD.

IV

The Profession

Section IV includes a chapter on "Human Networks in Organizational Information Processing" by Kerry Grosser of the Royal Melbourne Institute of Technology in Melbourne Australia. Kerry Grosser's chapter is the first *ARIST* chapter to deal with the question of human networks in organizational information processing. Human networks are central to information dissemination in organizations as for most of us it is people rather than printed or computer-based information resources that are our primary information sources.

In the information management and information science literatures, the main focus has been on the technology and physical resource dimensions of information in organizations. In this chapter Grosser argues that what is lacking is the human dimension. As long as the human factor remains unacknowledged, organizations will never achieve optimal effectiveness from their information resources. Information transfer in organizations occurs within a definite human and social context, with process dimensions of information as significant as content factors.

The chapter reviews a wide and multidisciplinary literature relating to human networks and information processing in organizations for insights into how information professionals can better adapt their services and systems to accommodate the realities of human information handling in organizations. The review commences with a consideration of formal and informal structures and associated information flows in organizations and their interactions, then focuses on a range of literature pertaining to informal networks and information processing, the informational role of corporate cultures, and an examination of the how the human element has been treated in theories of organizational information processing. Grosser concludes by analyzing implications of human networks for the effective management of information in organizations.

9 Human Networks in Organizational Information Processing

KERRY GROSSER
Royal Melbourne Institute of Technology

INTRODUCTION

Despite significant advances in information technology and the development of highly sophisticated information systems, there is mounting concern in many organizations that substantial investments in information technology have not yielded the expected returns. In the literatures of information management and information science, the main focus has been on information technology and physical information resources in organizations. In this chapter, it is argued that human networks play a crucial informational role in organizations and that unless information professionals acknowledge their existence and learn to work through them in the planning and provision of information services, organizations will never achieve optimal effectiveness from their information resources. A product or resource approach to information is too limited. Information transfer in organizations occurs within a definite human and social context, with process dimensions of information as significant as content factors.

Human networks are central to information dissemination in organizations. With most of us, it is people rather than printed or computer-based information resources that constitute our primary

The author would like to express her appreciation to Carey Butler for her assistance in locating and procuring materials for this review and to the reviewers who provided invaluable feedback on the first draft of this chapter.

Annual Review of Information Science and Technology (ARIST), Volume 26, 1991
Martha E. Williams, Editor
Published for the American Society for Information Science (ASIS)
By Learned Information, Inc., Medford, N.J.

information source. Studies of managers' information sources show that most of their information (75–95%) comes from direct human contact (e.g., MINTZBERG, 1973). In organizations, much of the information consumed comes indirectly, via human mediators, from those respected as experts or trusted as reliable information sources. Part of this is related to human needs for social interaction and to the high premium placed on developing meaningful relationships with others, to working in a conducive and mutually supportive environment. But it can also be the quickest and most efficient means of procuring information—e.g., overcoming problems of information overload and adding value by interpreting the meaning or significance of a piece of information.

For the information manager, a recognition of the informational role of human networks simultaneously provides a threat and a challenge. If an information professional is not attuned to informal networks, it is likely that the information service will be increasingly viewed as peripheral and irrelevant, a prime candidate for "pruning" in times of economic downturn. On the other hand, for the alert it can provide the key to enhancing the effectiveness of information systems and services within the organization.

This chapter reviews a wide and multidisciplinary literature relating to human networks and information processing in organizations in order to gain insights into how information professionals can better adapt their services and systems to accommodate the realities of human information handling in organizations. The focus of the review is on people as information sources, within an organizational context. As this is the first time this theme has been reviewed in *ARIST*, the author considers it necessary to include a historical perspective in the analysis. Because of space constraints, it is not possible to provide a comprehensive review of all component themes. The aim is to provide an introduction to the area, to identify major themes and trends in the literature in this field, and to give illustrative examples of relevant writings and research. Any one of the component areas here could constitute a major review in its own right. Inevitably certain important, related literatures are excluded or treated cursorily, the most notable being the human information processing literature derived from a cognitive psychology framework, decision-theory approaches to management decision making, and the end-user computing literature. A subsequent volume of *ARIST* will address some of the other "human factors" omitted from this chapter.

Throughout the 1970s and 1980s, rapid developments in information technology and the associated difficulties of information professionals' keeping pace with innovations seem to have had the impact of a strong focus on information systems, technologies, and a product orientation to information. Human sources of information were largely ignored in library and information science writings of this period. Most of the insights into the role of people as information sources come from literature outside this field. Reviews of information resources management (IRM) (e.g., LEVITAN, 1982; LYTLE, 1986) tended to focus on changes in technology, computing and communications hardware and software, and issues in integrating and managing an organization's total physical information resource, but there was little recognition that people may constitute the most important information resource in any organization. HIRSCHHEIM notes a similar tendency in the office systems implementation literature, which, he claims, has focused almost exclusively on the analytic/technical perspective to the detriment of the social; he concludes that approaches based on the interpretive paradigm are more likely to lead to successful office austomation implementation. Here it is argued that there is a need for a "renaissance" in the information science and management literatures to incorporate an understanding of human networks and people as information sources, elements that have been recognized for decades—and that we all intuitively acknowledge in our own information use practices—but that have not been accorded the attention they deserve in the recent literature or in current information management practices in organizations.

For regular *ARIST* readers, a review of the treatment of human factors in previous *ARIST* volumes may be useful. No chapter has focused specifically on human networks and people as information sources in organizations, although several authors occasionally refer to this area. Several chapters on "Information Needs and Uses" have appeared in *ARIST* volumes since 1966. The review under this title by T. J. ALLEN in 1969 came closest to the scope of the current paper, with some attention devoted to the role of informal structures and people as information sources in science and engineering. The 1978 review by CRAWFORD mentioned cognitive and social aspects of information use. In 1986, DERVIN & NILAN reviewed literature calling for a greater user orientation vs. technological orientation in information systems, and they concluded that there are utilities to be gained from both approaches. The authors stressed the need for a significant paradigm shift in information needs and use research toward methods that take into account situational/contextual and cognitive factors. HILLS in 1983 mentioned invisible colleges and gatekeeper roles in scholarly communication. The other major related themes presented in *ARIST* reviews have been human factors in computer use in 1983 (RAMSEY & GRIMES) and impacts of computer-mediated communication systems on interpersonal communication and organizational structures in 1980 (RICE) and 1986 (STEINFIELD). Passing reference is made in the current chapter to some of the findings on human impacts of computer systems, but no systematic review is attempted due to space constraints and scope considerations.

The review commences with a consideration of informal networks and associated information flows in organizations from a number of distinct perspectives; it then focuses on the related theme of the informational role of corporate cultures and on management writings that yield insights into the role of human networks in information dissemination in organizations. It concludes by analyzing implications of human networks for the effective management of information in organizations.

INFORMAL NETWORKS AND INFORMATION FLOWS IN ORGANIZATIONS

Overview

The distinction between formal and informal structures in organizations has long been recognized. Most sources on informal structures at some point contrast communication and information dissemination in the informal network with formal communication channels and information sources.

The formal structure as embodied in the organization chart represents an ordered system that regulates authority and communication flows, links decision makers at different levels with defined data-transmission channels, and generates an orderly flow of information and decision processes. In the formal structure, information flows are primarily vertical—communication down the line relays information about organizational ideologies, policies, procedures and practices, work directives, and feedback on performance—and upwards communication provides management with feedback on performance and problems at lower levels. Lateral communication comprises interactions between those within one department or work group, formal cross-department liaison positions, or staff units (e.g., personnel department) feeding information into the formal structure. Other formal positions are established to transmit relevant external data needed for strategic decision making to top management (e.g., a market analysis role).

Although formal information flows can be seen as an orderly grid, the regulated channels in practice are often rigid, slow, unreliable, and of finite carrying capacity. Major communication dysfunctions include significant losses in data transmission as information is transmitted from the top to the bottom of a complex organizational structure, or vice versa, and a high probability of miscommunication. To survive, organizations operating in complex and turbulent environments must seek out supplementary or alternative communication channels. MINTZBERG (1983) provides a set of diagrams illustrating the interconnections between formal and informal information flows, demonstrating how informal communication patterns and flows can be overlaid on the formal structure.

The informal structure represents the social interactions that occur naturally within organizations irrespective of the defined structures. While the two concepts are not necessarily mutually exclusive, a distinction is sometimes made between friendship networks and advice networks in organizations (e.g., KRACKHARDT, 1990a). The former concerns the networks that emerge to satisfy human social needs for friendship and recognition, a sense of belonging, for a sharing of interests, experiences, values, and feelings. Advice networks involve interactions with significant individuals in the informal structure who are perceived to possess important information that will facilitate the achievement of work goals. Advice networks, and to a lesser extent friendship networks, are sources of considerable power and political influence within an organization. Another categorization of communication networks in organizations is by function: (1) social network (for the sharing of non-work-related information), (2) authority network (for communicating information dealing with authority and responsibility relationships among organization members), and (3) expertise network (pertaining to communication of a technical nature, associated with the performance of work tasks) (MCCLURE).

In contrast to formal flows, informal communication patterns tend to be spontaneous, unregulated, and unstructured. While most informal communication is lateral, certain individuals within one work group play a key role in organizational communication, linking different hierarchical levels, or divisions, or acting as "gatekeepers" of strategically important data emanating from outside organizational boundaries. The informal network exerts a powerful and constant influence in organizations; however, it will make its presence more obvious at times of organizational tension and uncertainty—i.e., in situations eliciting fear and anxiety and stimulating social interaction and especially when formal communications systems are not functioning effectively in keeping employees informed of problems and issues affecting them.

Interrelationships of Formal and Informal Networks and Information Sources

Formal and informal communication networks should not be viewed as a simple dichotomy but as interdependent, inextricably intertwined. A substantial body of management literature over the past decade has focused on the nature of and interconnections between formal and informal structures, usually concluding that management success correlates with an ability to utilize effectively the informal as well as the formal networks (e.g., BUTLER; FARRIS; C. HALL; HAN; MINTZBERG, 1983; WOOTEN).

A review of the literature on informal networks back to the early 1970s shows that some themes apppear perennially while others wax and wane. Component literatures include sociology, organizational theory, organizational behavior, social psychology, management, marketing, information science, and communication studies. Reviews of major themes follow.

The Nature of Informal Networks and Associated Informational Roles: The Sociological Perspective

In the analysis of informal networks, the organization is regarded as a mutually interdependent social system made up of "components" (communication groups, cliques) and "connections" among those groups. Within a group, communication activity is intense. Certain individuals act as links between discrete groups. A "bridge agent" is an individual with a strong primary group affiliation who interacts regularly with a person from another group. A "liaison agent" acts as a link among groups but does not share in intensive group activity. "Isolates" are those who do not share in communication (T. H. ALLEN; RICHARDS). Derived from a sociological framework, this approach has been extended in writings emanating from other disciplines (e.g., management and communications).

Since the late 1960s, T. J. Allen and others from the Sloan School at MIT have been involved in research into communication networks within scientific and technological research laboratories. They have identified particular informal communicative and informational roles within these settings: the "technological gatekeeper," the "internal communication (or technical discussion) star," and the "external communication star" (T. J. ALLEN, 1971; HALL & RITCHIE; TAYLOR). Internal communication or technical discussion stars are approached by others within their work group for advice on technical matters due to their perceived knowledge and expertise. Because of their professional and personal links with significant "others" outside the organization, external communication stars are regarded as important information sources. Technological gatekeepers are *both* internal and external communication stars: they are relatively few in number and form an elite within a laboratory. Compared with their colleagues, technological gatekeepers have a much higher incidence of exposure to the professional literature: they make more oral contacts outside the organization, have published more, hold more patents, have more professional affiliations, attend more conferences, present more conference papers, and are more likely to hold influential positions. They perform a vital informational role within the work group and are approached in preference to documentary or computer-based information sources, due both to inherent inadequacies of other information media and to a need for interpersonal interaction in the discussion of complex technical problems (TAYLOR). Also there is a high positive correlation between intense communication activity characteristic of the technological gatekeeper and high levels of job performance (HALL & RITCHIE).

Allen's concept of technological gatekeepers in R&D establishments has been applied more generally to other organizations in writings on the role of "boundary-spanning individuals" in information transfer. TUSHMAN & SCANLAN provide a comprehensive review of the role of boundary-spanning individuals in importing strategic information into organizations. The authors postulate that communication barriers develop between different organizations (or between major divisions of one organization) due to different cultures, conceptual frameworks, and terms of reference. Information transfer across organizational boundaries requires effective boundary spanning, which Tushman and Scanlan see as a two-step process, searching out relevant information from one side and disseminating it on the other side of the boundary. Hence, the boundary-spanning role requires a thorough understanding of the local coding schemes and conceptual frameworks from both sides of the boundary, an ability to translate from one "language" to the other, and highly developed information and communication skills. Boundary-spanning individuals play a key role in overcoming the problems associated with communication "at the boundaries." Like Allen's technological gatekeepers, they are well connected internally and externally, are technically competent, and are effective communicators, occupying a central role in the informal network. In Tushman and Scanlan's research, boundary spanners were those most frequently nominated by their colleagues as being the most technically competent and the most valuable sources for external information and new ideas. They had significant informal power, prestige, and status within the organization. The authors' model of informational boundary spanning requires that the individual:

- Develop competence specific to the internal unit, then gain access to the internal dissemination network and become an internal communication star; and
- Develop competence specific to the external area, then gain access to relevant external sources of information and become an external communication star to a specific area.

In another study, TUSHMAN & ROMANELLI demonstrated that the influence of boundary-spanning individuals within an organization is greatest under conditions of high environmental or task uncertainty and that internal communication stars exert more influence when task requirements are clear and more routine.

MCCLURE provides an excellent overview on a related theme, the role of the "information rich" in organizations, "the phenomenon by which certain individuals are better able to acquire, process and utilize information than are other individuals in the organization" (p. 381). These persons, due to their cognitive and communicative abilities, play a significant role in organizational communications; they have access to more sources of information, and "better" information, and are able to identify information of greater value to their work group. McClure reviews previous literature on the role of the information rich in organizations and notes that they have been variously termed "liaison person," "information specialist," "internal consultant," "technological gatekeeper," "group expert," "special communicator," "early adopter," and so forth. They function as information carriers, selectively filtering and transmitting relevant outside information to the group; they act in a current-awareness role; they are able to answer technical questions from their colleagues; they are seen by their colleagues as the most valuable sources of information and are most likely to be consulted as a first source; they know where to obtain relevant information, from both informal networks and other data sources; and they are innovators and informal opinion leaders, with a significant impact on organizational decision making. Due to their distinctive skills and qualities and outstanding performance, they possess high status, formal or informal, within their work group.

While the most intensive study on informal communication networks has been conducted within R&D establishments, there have been other significant applications. REINGEN & KERNAN report on the use of network analysis in marketing as a means of investigating referral behavior (i.e., word-of-mouth referrals) and customer networks—i.e., how information about a product flows within and among social groups in large-scale transfer.

Informal Networks and the Diffusion of Technological Innovations in Organizations

Links have subsequently been made between technological gatekeepers/boundary-spanning individuals and innovators. In a study of three applied R&D organizations, KELLER & HOLLAND found a high correlation between the roles of "communicator" and "innovator"; communicators tended to be innovators and vice versa. Both communicators and innovators were characterized by an innovative orientation, a low need for clarity, high self-esteem, a higher educational level, a higher level of journal reading, a higher job level, and centrality in the communication network. PETERS & WATERMAN (1982) in their classic work, *In Search of Excellence,* stress the links among intense informal communication activity, openness of communication, and successful innovations in "excellent" companies.

Considerable research has been conducted by Leonard-Barton and others at Harvard Business School on the role of informal networks in the process of technological diffusion in organizations (LEONARD-BARTON, 1985, 1986, 1987, 1988a, 1988b, 1990; LEONARD-BARTON & DESCHAMPS; LEONARD-BARTON & KRAUS). Findings have shown that a technological innovation tends to spread in two distinct stages with the rate of adoption determined by the nature of the communication process. In the initial decision to adopt a technological innovation, a few significant individuals ("experts," "technological gatekeepers," "boundary spanners," "champions," or "assassins") act as positive or negative opinion leaders, exerting a disproportionate influence on opinion among their peers. Active supporters or active rejecters of the innovation tend to be more tied into social communication networks than the "hedgers" or opinion avoiders. Overt management support can encourage fence sitters to adopt the innovation.

Implementation of a technological innovation in an organization is often a prolonged process. After management makes the initial adoption decision, it takes time for the decision to filter down to all levels of the organization. Depending on the nature of the technology, each individual may need to make his/her own adoption decision. These "secondary adoption decisions" do not necessarily follow automatically from the organizational decision; there can be sabotage or delay tactics resisting the innovation at any point. Positive or negative opinion leaders exert an ongoing influence over their colleagues throughout this phase. Also, early adopters influence later adopters, and later adopters in turn influence earlier adopters to continue or discontinue using the technology (MARKUS, 1990b). To ensure the successful adoption of an innovation, LEONARD-BARTON (1986; 1987) stresses the need for managers to recognize the importance of informal networks in individuals' secondary adoption decisions and to work through informal communication channels, which are the most credible sources of influence on opinion and trial of the technology. There is a greater chance of successful implementation of a technological innovation when relevant social links are established—i.e., if system designers and managers treat potential users as codevelopers rather than passive receivers of the new technology and set up support mechanisms such as user groups. After the successful implementation of a technological innovation throughout an organization, in the maintenance phase, the role of the internal communication or technical discussion stars becomes more important than that of the boundary spanner.

Rarely will an organization use a technology exactly as it was conceived by the system designers. New uses emerge unexpectedly when individuals apply the technology in unintended ways or modify the system to better suit their needs or preferred modes of working. Through informal communication processes, such uses permeate the organization. This has been evidenced in the research of LEONARD-BARTON (1986; 1987; 1988a; 1988b) into the adoption of an expert system by sales staff in the field and by recent research into uses of computer-mediated communication technologies, such as electronic mail, electronic bulletin boards, computer conferencing, and group decision-support systems (CULNAN & MARKUS; HAUSER & BYRD; MARKUS, 1990a, 1990b; RICE; SPROULL & KIESLER; STEINFELD). The uses to which such technologies are put is largely a function of the experience and characteristics of the user(s). Although intended for the exchange of work-related information, there is considerable evidence that computer-mediated communication systems in organizations are widely used for socio-emotional purposes, for communication of a personal nature, providing an alternative medium for face-to-face communication. Research has also demonstrated that with the absence of the nonverbal dimension of face-to-face communication, there is a tendency for users to be less inhibited in their interpersonal communication, saying much more than they would be prepared to say face to face. Computer-mediated communication systems tend to equalize participation (c.f. natural social processes in face-to-face groups); for example, in group decision support systems, there is less of a tendency for leader emergence.

Inevitably, the introduction of new communication technologies triggers changes in organizational communication processes, information flows, and structures. The number of messages transmitted rises dramatically after the introduction of a new technology, at least in the short term. There is increased cross-unit and cross-locational communication and external communication. As the technology facilitates direct communication between employees and senior management, hierarchical authority relationships may be eroded, with the potential of information overload at higher levels in the absence of natural organizational information-filtering mechanisms. In some cases, technology will substitute for structure—e.g., a functional organization using the technology to achieve some of the advantages of a project structure or vice versa (ALLEN & HAUPTMAN, 1990; HAUSER & BYRD; OGILVIE ET AL.).

However, the new communication technologies certainly do not eliminate the need for interpersonal interaction. They are suited for certain types of communication (e.g., transmitting technical information, asking questions, exchanging opinions, keeping in touch) but not for others (e.g., bargaining, resolving disagreements, tasks requiring constant, focused discussion, "equivocal" situations—in which social context cues are important) (HAUSER & BYRD; RICE). T. J. ALLEN (1990) has observed that the use of different media tends to be directly correlated. Those who interact regularly face to face are also likely to communicate regularly by telephone or by E-mail, and the existence of these new media does not appear to reduce the need for face-to-face communication. Informal networks in organizations remain just as important as they have always been; the difference today is that network members have greater choices in the modes of communication they use: face-to-face or electronic. Further research is needed into the circumstances and factors that influence the choice of medium for communication.

Managers and Informal Communication Networks

To what extent are the significant information and communication roles in informal networks occupied by managers with formal authority? The literature suggests that many managers occupy central roles in informal communication networks. Certainly promotion to senior management positions would appear to require the type of skills that are characteristic of the "boundary spanner" or "nerve center." However, this does not always pertain, and significant roles are often assumed by individuals outside the formal hierarchy.

In Mintzberg's research (MINTZBERG, 1973; 1975) senior managers' informational and decisional roles were demonstrated to depend largely on their liaison role—i.e., their making contacts outside the formal chain of command. "The manager cultivates such contacts largely to find information. In effect, the liaison role is devoted to building up the manager's own external information system—informal, private, verbal, but, nevertheless, effective" (MINTZBERG, 1975, p. 55). By developing an extensive network of contacts inside and outside the organization, managers emerged as "nerve centers" of their organizational units, not knowing everything, but typically knowing more than the rest of the staff.

Based on research findings related to boundary-spanning roles, some technical organizations over recent years have formalized such roles, filling the positions with high-performing technical professionals. In an interesting recent Working Paper, NOCHUR & ALLEN pose the question: "Do nominated boundary spanners become effective technological gatekeepers?" Their research findings into the effectiveness of nominated boundary spanners in the transfer of technologies from the R&D center of a large energy resources company to its operating units showed that more than half of the designated liaison agents did not function as gatekeepers, lacking either the internal or external communication networks essential for effectiveness in that role. The authors conclude that "effective gatekeeping cannot be mandated by assigning people to fill that role. Effective communication networks are formed over a period of time as formal and informal contacts are developed and cultivated" (p. 14). Implications for management include appointing to formal positions those who have already proven themselves as effective gatekeepers or, if that is not an option, selecting internal or external communication stars and providing them training and other opportunities to develop the "missing" component.

The "Invisible College" Phenomenon as a Special Type of Informal Network

In the late 1960s and early 1970s there was a considerable level of interest in the invisible college phenomenon as one aspect of the role of scientific and technical information in national economic development. In two much-quoted review articles, PRICE (1971a; 1971b) observed that there was an elite of high-performing scientists who produced about half of the published work in the field, whose number was equal to the square root of the population. CRAWFORD (1971) performed a sociometric analysis of an informal communication network of 218 scientists working in the field of sleep research. Using the criterion of contacts with six other scientists as her cutoff point for central figures in the network, she identified 33 key scientists who were the focus of considerable communication activity. Over 60% of the population of sleep researchers worked in clusters involving these central scientists. These individuals formed a cohesive group, communicating intensively among themselves and to a lesser extent with others in the research community. Reexamining these data on sleep researchers three years later, KORFHAGE observed that if Crawford had used ten contacts as her cutoff point, there would have been 14 or 15 central figures in the network, the number predicted by Price's formula.

Although geographically dispersed, the key specialists within an international invisible college network appear to perform the same type of role as do technological gatekeepers or boundary spanners within one organization. Using sociometric techniques and ratings of professional status as a researcher by their peers, ZALTMAN identified a highly elite invisible college in high-energy physics that crossed international boundaries. From 977 responses, 27 key scientists who were doing the most significant work in this field were identified. They were in frequent contact with each other and performed an important gatekeeping and linking function within the broader scholarly community. Highly visible in their communication activity, members of this elite group were both the most active communicators (e.g., presenting papers at conferences, publishing articles, and disseminating preprints) and the highest recipients of information from a diversity of channels (e.g., journals, reprints, manuscripts, reports from their own and other institutions, telephone, face-to-face discussions, oral and written conference reports, and private correspondence). Zaltman emphasizes the importance of such an elite in scientific communication. They become familiar with new ideas as they are formulating them long before publication and have a direct influence on the dissemination and utilization of scientific information and an indirect influence on the discovery of new knowledge.

A number of other studies on the invisible college phenomenon have been reported since—e.g., the 1983 study by LACY & BUSCH on informal scientific communication in the agricultural sciences. These authors comment that the relative importance of the informal network of scientific communication and the published literature varies with the field of research, with informal communication being more important in rapidly developing fields and more important in applied science/engineering than in the basic sciences. More intense periods of communication were associated with the establishment of research agenda or publication of research products.

An excellent review of the current state of invisible college research appears in the book edited by BORGMAN on scholarly communication and bibliometrics (see especially the chapters by Lievrouw and Griffith). The reports on the impacts of computer-mediated communication technologies, such as E-mail, fax, and computer conferencing, on scholarly communication are of particular interest.

Techniques for Recording and Analyzing Network Structures

Network analysis involves the identification and recording of communication activities of individuals within an organization and analysis of the dynamic processes relating its components. If network analysis data are subsequently compared with/superimposed over the formal organization chart, the extent to which the informal and formal structures are consistent can be determined. Deviations highlight communication problems. Managerial analysis of these data might involve, for example, considerations of how to integrate isolates more into communication processes or whether those acting as bridges are the most suitable in terms of their knowledge and experience or whether there is a too-high connectivity within a group and sufficient links among groups. Network analysis provides a powerful tool for managers who wish to enhance organizational effectiveness (T. H. ALLEN).

"Sociograms," or sociometric diagrams, developed from J. Moreno's research into sociometry from the 1930s, and "adjacency matrices," based on matrix algebra, are the two major techniques used in recording network structures (GEORGE & ALLEN; RICE & RICHARDS). The two methods are technically equivalent. With either technique, a questionnaire, interview, or direct observation is first used to establish communication and interaction patterns— viz., who communicates with whom within the organization. Sociograms record dyadic relationships among individuals in the form of a simple diagram, wherein individuals are represented as nodes (numbers within a circle) and communication links are shown with lines. A development of this involves the use of "directed graphs," adding arrows to the lines, indicating communication direction—i.e., one-way to or from a node or two-way interaction. Sociograms are ideal for analyzing relatively small networks (e.g., up to 100 people) but become complex and unwieldy, difficult to interpret, and extremely time consuming to construct for larger structures.

An adjacency matrix is a square divided into rows, columns, and cells. Each individual in the network is represented as a number at the top of a column and row. Cells record whether or not there is interaction between two individuals: using binary data, either filled vs. blank cells or "1" vs. "0." It is possible to record more detailed information in cells of the matrix—e.g., a different symbol is used to indicate varying frequencies of interaction, such as every day, once or twice a week, once a month, once a year, and less frequently than yearly. Matrices have become the most prevalent technique used for network analysis in organizations because they are more suited to an analysis of large, complex structures and are amenable to computer manipulation. From the 1950s to the 1970s there were a number of attempts to utilize different mathematical approaches to rearrange matrix data in order to derive meaningful configurations (RICHARDS). Such procedures are complex and involved manually but lend themselves to computerization.

Various matrix-based software is being used for network analysis. One promising technique is the "Netgraph" software currently under development at Sloan School (MIT) by George and others (T. J. ALLEN, 1990; GEORGE & ALLEN). The program enables rows and columns of the matrix to be permuted according to key variables and has sophisticated graphics capabilities, including color coding. Drawing on an organizational communication matrix of about 500 people, George and Allen provide a set of "Netgraph" printouts, demonstrating different manipulations of data—e.g., sorting communication patterns by age group, by number of communication partners, by physical location (sites, buildings, floors, wings), and by organizational location (sections, departments). Color coding is used in different ways—e.g., to indicate whether one member of the communication pair is a manager or an engineer. Such technology has added a significant dimension to network analysis—viz., the ability to link demographic, structural, or other characteristics with network data and to provide insights into the nature of group interaction that would be impossible with manual techniques.

Effects of Physical and Organizational Proximity on Informal Communication

Perhaps the two most important determinants of organizational communication are physical and organizational location, a fact that is readily demonstrable in any diagrammatic representation of informal networks and communication activity in an organization. Intensive communication activity is more likely to occur when individuals are located within the same department, unit, project team, and so forth.

Since the 1950s there have been numerous studies on the effect of spatial factors on human interaction. Some of the most significant research into the effects of physical proximity on informal communication within an organizational context has been conducted by Allen and others. In a classic early study done in 1975, ALLEN & FUSFELD demonstrated that physical proximity had a substantial impact on the nature and frequency of communication among scientists or engineers in research laboratories. The physical and architectural arrangement of the laboratory greatly influenced communication patterns: the greater the physical distance either horizontally or vertically, the less the interaction. The researchers measured distance in meters from desk to desk. Probability of communication fell off sharply after 30 meters. In a multistory building, placement on different floors was a strong deterrent to communication. Similarly, interaction was limited when individuals were located in separate wings, buildings, or sites. Implications for architectural design of laboratories were drawn by the authors. Square or circular structures promote interaction more than elongated rectangular buildings. Locating shared facilities centrally, such as laboratories, lunch rooms, or coffee machines, encourages a higher degree of interaction among staff. Managers located on the top floor in the room with the best view may unintentionally isolate themselves and inhibit communication with their subordinates. Since this early study, there has been some ongoing research at MIT into the effects of physical proximity and architectural design on communication behavior, with further research yet to be published.[1]

Informal Networks from the Corporate Culture Perspective

In the foregoing discussion, the analysis of the informal communications network has assumed that there is an elite in each organization, those who possess a high level of technical and professional expertise, who have access to a greater number and range of information sources inside and outside the organization than do most others and who are widely recognized and valued for their skills. The

---

[1]T. J. Allen, personal communication, 1990.

other major approach to informal networks is the corporate culture perspective, which has been popularized throughout the 1980s. It comes with a very different underlying philosophy and set of assumptions, much of which is difficult to reconcile with the former view. Much less "scientific" in approach (e.g., less concerned with a formal mapping of information networks), it stresses more the qualitative, intangible, human, value-laden aspects of communication.

In a paper presented at an Office Systems Conference, HIRSCHHEIM makes a similar distinction, defining two conflicting views of "the office." On the one hand, there is the formal view, the rational or analytic perspective, in which the office is an environment where people engage in clearly defined, structured activities to support the effective running of the organization—an approach amenable to formal observations, quantitative measurement, and empirical testing. The other perspective, the "agent" or "culture" view, "conceives of the office in terms of mostly unstructured and informal human action" (p. 31), small social groupings in which people create for themselves shared meanings and rituals to maintain meaningful interpersonal interactions. With this "interpretive" approach, research is qualitative and phenomenological, concerned with understanding social actions and meanings within a particular organizational setting. To Hirschheim, the analytic and interpretive perspectives form extreme types at either end of a continuum. Along the continuum he identifies seven views of the office that emerge from the literature: (1) office activities, (2) office functions, (3) office semantics, (4) decision taking, (5) work roles, (6) transactional, and (7) language action.

The most comprehensive and systematic analysis of the corporate culture perspective is that provided by DEAL & KENNEDY in their 1982 best seller, *Corporate Cultures*. A substantial proportion of subsequent writings on this theme are heavily indebted to this source. In this approach, the "cultural network" of an organization tends to be treated as synonymous with the "informal network." Deal and Kennedy perceive the informal network as the primary means of communication within an organization, a carrier of corporate values, a hidden hierarchy of power. The cultural network bypasses the organization's formal structure, tying together all levels of the organization without respect to position. Not only is this network largely independent of formal information systems, but it also overcomes many of the problems of such systems. Unlike the formal systems, the informal network transmits information with lightning speed. It is highly selective, differentiating the significant from the less significant, overcoming problems of information overload. Most of all, however, the cultural network "adds value" to the raw data of formal communications, assigning meaning, interpreting significance for employees, and embellishing events to make them exciting and more palatable for human digestion. Key "characters" in the informal network include storytellers, priests, whisperers, gossips, secretarial sources, spies, and cabals. Managerial success depends on a conscious cultivation of influential contacts within the cultural network and working through this channel as well as through formal systems.

The "Organizational Grapevine"

There has been a considerable body of "organizational grapevine" literature in management journals throughout the 1980s. Most of these articles are extensions of the corporate culture perspective on informal networks. The grapevine can be defined as the communications network of the informal group.

The so-called organizational "grapevine" or "rumor mill" tends to have negative connotations: a reputation of unreliability, inaccuracy, unconscious or deliberate distortion of information, even maliciousness. However, most recent articles follow the lead of Deal and Kennedy in viewing the grapevine as a vital communication network that supplements (rather than replaces) formal channels, which can and must be managed effectively for optimal organizational performance. Article titles such as "Harvesting Your Employee Grapevine" (ARNOLD), "Tapping into the Employee Grapevine" (VICKERY), "Fighting the Fertile Grapevine" (HUNTER), and "More than Rumors: Understanding the Organizational Grapevine" (ZAREMBA) exemplify this trend. In these writings, the grapevine is described as: pervasive; an extremely fast and efficient means of conveying a message throughout the organization; resilient, difficult to stop; generally accurate and reliable, contrary to popular myth (with inaccuracies usually attributable to incomplete or filtered information more than wrong information); exerting a greater influence on employees (who regard the information as accurate) than do formal communications; and a source of invaluable management information relating to employee perceptions, anxieties, hopes, and expectations.

ECCO analysis (Episodic Communication Channels in Organizations) is one research technique that has been used in grapevine research (ARNOLD). This involves the release of an important piece of information into the informal network and subsequently tracing its communication path throughout the organization.

Message Distortion and Information Filtration
through the Informal Network

Much of the research on information filtration and message distortion dates from the early 1970s to early 1980s. In 1973, ATHANASSIADES investigated links between motivational factors and information distortion in an upward direction (i.e., from subordinates to their supervisors) in two hierarchical organizations, a police department and a university department. Distortion of upward communication was found to be negatively correlated with level of security and positively related to achievement (ascendancy motivation) needs of the subordinate. A year later, O'REILLY & ROBERTS conducted three experiments on selective filtration of information in upward, downward, and lateral information transmission in organizational hierarchies. Directionality of information flow and the nature of the sender–receiver relationship were key variables. Results indicated that senders filtered out different types of information, depending on the direction of the flow of information and on the sender's degree of trust in the receiver. A tendency to pass more favorable and important information upward and to filter out the negative and unimportant was noted—i.e., management would be denied access to important but unfavorable information. More total information was shared laterally than either upward or downward, as was more unfavorable information. When senders had a high degree of trust in the receiver, they tended to pass more information, including unfavorable information, but when trust was low, they passed only favorable information. This was strongest with upward communication (vs. downward or lateral communication). The authors express their concern over the implications of their findings for the quality of management decision making: managers who rely totally on formal channels of information transmission are making decisions with incomplete and at times deliberately distorted information.

O'REILLY (1978) followed up the set of laboratory studies with field research in an organizational context and obtained similar results. One dimension added by the field studies was the understanding that the degree of information distortion is significantly and inversely associated with job satisfaction and individual and group performance factors—i.e., the lower the level of satisfaction with the job, supervision, or co-workers or the lower the level of individual or group performance, the greater the intentional distortion of information passed upward. Those with high job mobility aspirations tended to engage in less information distortion. GAINES conducted similar research in an industrial organization but with less conclusive results.

In a 1989 experiment with college students, KURKE ET AL. demonstrated that information loss could be reversed over a limited period (three hours). As information was relayed through a chain, details were dropped, interpretations added, and implications altered. However, when the simplified information was relayed back through the chain, subjects were able to restore edited material, with reconstructions approximating the original input (in terms of themes/content of messages rather than exact words).

DELANEY suggests that ideally the process of information filtration in organizations should operate in the same way as filters that are used to eliminate static or extraneous signals; that is, the "noise" should be removed, but important and meaningful information should be transmitted. He provides some guidelines for managers on how to minimize the frequent problems experienced with information transmission in organizations with inadequate filtering of information (i.e., including the trivial and unimportant along with the important) or deliberate withholding of information.

Informal Networks: The Social Psychological Perspective

Krackhardt and others (KRACKHARDT, 1987, 1990a, 1990b; KRACKHARDT & PORTER, 1985, 1986; KRACKHARDT & STERN) provide one of the clearest expositions of the social psychological perspective on informal networks. Rather than proceeding from the macro level of the organization as a functioning system (the organizational sociology view), this school of thought approaches networks from the viewpoint of the individual within the organization. It is based on the assumption that individual behavior is affected by a person's perceptions of significant others in the social network and involves a microanalysis of the individual's values, beliefs, perceptions, motives, and behavior within this context.

Network links among partners can be measured along three dimensions: (1) extent of dependence on another in terms of work assignment for effective performance on the job; (2) intensity of interaction (i.e., the frequency and total amount of time spent together); and (3) affect, the strength of feelings between partners, positive or negative. These three factors are linked in sequence: a high task dependence creates a demand for frequent interaction, and a prolonged intensity of interaction in turn triggers strong feelings. If affect reactions are strongly negative, there will be a tendency where possible to seek out alternative connections. People have a finite capacity for networking and close emotional bonds. Weak ties are not necessarily undesirable since they involve less personal cost to maintain. Also, in information terms, strong ties tend to be associated with a high degree of redundancy of information (i.c., they draw on similar information sources), while weak links will tend to introduce new perspectives and innovative or different ideas and can be associated with more creative solutions. Within an organization, newcomers will find it difficult to infiltrate an established network of stable bonds but will tend to mix with others who are available and not already overloaded with stable links. This situation promotes the development of cliques (e.g., the "old guard" vs. the "young turks"), which can be dysfunctional in organizational terms.

Managing the Informal Network for Optimal Organizational Performance

General management writings. A popular and recurring theme in management books and journals over the past decade has been the need for managers to recognize the existence of informal networks and their informational role, to acknowledge their importance in getting things done within an organization, and to learn to work effectively through them.

DEAL & KENNEDY provide a useful analysis of ways in which managers can capitalize on the informal cultural network, which has been drawn on extensively in subsequent writings in the popular management press. They stress that managers need consciously to cultivate a network of appropriate and influential contacts in the cultural network and to work through this hidden hierarchy. This requires that they be able to recognize and to identify the influential characters, the vital links in the network who act in a key role in gathering and disseminating information. Tapping into such networks calls for subtlety from the manager. A warm, caring personality, an approachable manner, and an openness of communication help establish credibility and trust. Managers need to spend a lot of their time talking with and developing friendships with the key characters in the network, showing a genuine interest and asking for details and for personal evaluations of meaning and significance of situations or events. Socializing outside work can help develop close ties. Deal and Kennedy claim that effective managers learn to rely on the cultural network for the bulk of their communications within the organization. When they wish to relay an important message, they should release it into informal as well as formal channels, realizing that employees will tend to pay more attention to a message conveyed from a trusted human source close at hand. If the message is not too involved but is short, concise, and repeatable, there is less chance of its content being distorted as it passes through the informal network.

Other articles that convey a similar message are those by BAKER, BISTLINE, BUTLER, C. HALL, HAN, and WOOTEN. Butler draws on E. E. Jennings's dichotomy of the "maze-bright" vs. the "maze-dull" manager, based on a behavioral psychology analogy of rats learning to find their way through a maze in response to positive and negative reinforcement, such as cheese and electric shocks. According to Butler, the "maze-dull" manager is attuned only to the formal organization, to mechanistic, impersonal factors, formal written communications, rules and regulations, authority structures, and the like. In contrast, the "maze-bright" manager understands that the informal organization is far more important, and is sensitive and perceptive to the less tangible dimensions of interpersonal relationships within the organization, recognizing the centrality of culture, values, social power, and informal communications. Butler's message is that managers who wish to advance their careers must tune into the "real" picture of the organization and learn where the power really lies.

The organizational grapevine literature (ARNOLD; HUNTER; VICKERY; ZAREMBA) poses various suggestions for "managing the rumor mill." Potentially rumors can be negative, involve information distortion, trigger employee resentment, and embarrass managers. On the positive side, rumors can provide managers with an early warning about employee discontent, sources of uncertainty and anxiety, fears, and so forth, which may be alleviated if acted on promptly. Hence there is a need to pay heed to rumors and to openly refute those that are without foundation. Some of the suggested ways of obviating problems of persistent or damaging rumors in organizations are: mixing informally with employees; practicing MBWA (management by walking around) (PETERS & WATERMAN, 1982; 1984); keeping an ear to the ground; maintaining open and honest communication with employees; having a policy of keeping employees informed on issues that concern them; and admitting mistakes.

Research literature on informal networks and various aspects of organizational effectiveness. A considerable body of literature has examined relationships between informal networks and different aspects of organizational effectiveness. However, this material tends to be uncoordinated and lacking conceptual integration. Some of the aspects represented in the literature are outlined below with illustrative examples. No attempt is made to be exhaustive.

In terms of informal networks and leadership effectiveness, research by HOLLINGSWORTH involving foremen from a utility company established that the most effective leaders among the group were those who perceived the *actual* strength of the informal organization within their work group.

In terms of informal networks and task performance, relationships have been documented. KATZ & TUSHMAN detected distinctly different communication patterns among high-performing (vs. low-performing) project teams in the R & D laboratory of a large U.S. corporation. Better-performing project teams appeared to develop particular types of communication networks that would enable them to deal effectively with their information needs. Complex tasks were found to require widespread face-to-face contacts with other areas/individuals inside and outside the organization, while more routine tasks required greater reliance on the formal hierarchy. The researchers conclude that organizational communication should be considered as an organizational design variable, which is amenable to managerial influence, and they stress the importance of managers organizing and managing communication networks for optimal performance.

For informal networks and strategic decision making, FARRIS claims that the informal organization has a crucial role in strategic decision making in organizations, both as a center of political activity and of intellectual activity in terms of its information processing capacity. He offers three detailed cases of such influence in different types of organizations to substantiate his assertion.

As far as informal networks and turnover are concerned, in a longitudinal study in three restaurants in a fast-food chain, KRACKHARDT & PORTER (1985; 1986) established that friendship had a substantial influence on the relationship between turnover and stayers' attitudes; generally close friends tended to leave together or to stay together. If one left and the other stayed, the latter tended to resolve the cognitive dissonance thus created by increasing his/her own satisfaction with the job to justify the decision to stay. Rather than following a regular, consistent pattern, turnover was seen to occur in clusters related to the degree to which employees occupied similar informal roles in a communication network. Implications for management in trying to reduce turnover are not to spread resources evenly across the organization but rather to analyze perceived social networks to identify groups of similar co-workers who are most likely either to leave together or to stay together.

Informal networks also affect organizational crises. In a 1988 article, KRACKHARDT & STERN developed a theory linking informal networks with organizational response to a crisis. This theory was tested in a series of experimental simulations and was basically supported. Given the tendency for dense friendship networks (cliques/coalitions) to develop within organizational subunits rather than between subunits, and for such subunits to compete with each other, the authors speculate that in a major crisis such informal networks would be seriously dysfunctional to the organization. When facing a serious situation or high degree of uncertainty, an organization needs to centralize control, to coordinate its resources, and to ensure that all units pull together to counter the threat to survival. However, the nature of most informal networks in organizations would engender a lack of overall cohesion, with increased conflict among subunits, each fighting for its own needs. In a crisis, it would appear that the more effective organizations would be those that have developed strong friendship networks, cooperation, and trust *between* units. It is important to point out, however, that in stable times, with normal routine operations, effective group functioning requires strong friendship networks *within* subunits. This article exemplifies a relatively new emphasis in the literature: the idea that although informal structures in organizations occur naturally, they can be deliberately adapted or modified by an alert management for optimal organizational performance. In contrast, the cultural networks perspective tends to regard informal networks as a given, which managers can tap into and work through but not manipulate or change in any fundamental way. However, there are exceptions to this in some of the cultural networks literature. In several articles, Krackhardt stresses the importance of managers' understanding the nature of the current informal networks in their organizations, identifying cliques and power groups, and then evaluating whether or not the existing configuration is best serving organizational needs. Without conscious design, he believes that informal networks tend to develop in ways that are suboptimal or even dysfunctional for an organization. Management can be proactive in terms of determining an appropriate informal network structure to facilitate the achievement of organizational goals and can provide a climate and facilities to encourage the development of such a network.

Informal networks are also influential in organizational power and promotion. In a recent article, KRACKHARDT (1990a) argued that an accurate cognition of informal networks is in itself a base of power, over and above power attributable to informal and formal structural positions. In a small entrepreneurial firm, perceptions of friendship networks and advice networks were compared with actual networks. Those with a more accurate understanding of the advice network were rated as more powerful by others in the organization, although accuracy of the friendship network was not related to reputational power. Note here the links between perceived power and information flows within the organization. On a similar theme,

BASA ET AL., in a longitudinal study of promotion among engineers in an R & D laboratory over a ten-year period, found that professionals most likely to be promoted to management positions were those who were active participants in the informal network within the organization, those who fit in well with the prevalent social system and culture and had a positive affective response to the organization.

THE INFORMATIONAL ROLE OF
ORGANIZATIONAL CULTURE

The informational role of organizational or corporate cultures has been a major theme in the management, sociological, social psychological, and information systems/technology literatures for the past decade. The terms "organizational culture" and "corporate culture" tend to be used interchangeably in the literature (and are used in this way in this chapter). Organizations develop their own distinctive cultures in the same way as discrete groups do within the wider community. Newcomers are socialized into the prevailing culture through a combination of formal and informal means. While company orientation and training programs, special meetings, and functions represent a formal indoctrination attempt, informal social networks existing within the organization constitute the most potent purveyor of organizational values and beliefs.

Organizational culture is defined as the set of values and beliefs shared by those working in an organization, which has a dramatic impact on employee behavior and on organizational performance, acting as a unifying force to bind employees together (DEAL & KENNEDY). There is a distinct informational role implied here: in organizations with strong cultures, employees know what is expected of them and do not need to waste time figuring out what to do or how to do it; such a culture provides security and guidance for action (DRAKE).

Within the organizational culture literature, two distinct approaches can be identified, although neither is developed to the extent of possessing a fully unified and coherent set of theoretical constructs. The most pervasive is the dominant culture approach, which is based on a sociological perspective and has been developed particularly in the popular management literature. A more recent emphasis has been that of cultural diversity within an organization, propounded by social psychologists and industrial anthropologists. Both approaches assume the centrality of informal structures, but, as explained in the first part of the chapter, they have entirely different views on the nature and function of human networks in organizations.

The Dominant Culture Perspective

Introduction.   DEAL & KENNEDY provide a comprehensive review of the dominant culture perspective. They define elements of culture as including the organization's: (1) distinct business environment; (2) values, or set of beliefs, about itself, which define success and establish standards and goals to achieve; (3) heroes, current or past, who make success attainable and human and provide viable role models; (4) rites and rituals; and (5) cultural network.

PETERS & WATERMAN (1982) demonstrated that a strong and coherent culture was a key ingredient in the success of "excellent" companies. It engenders a sense of confidence and encourages entrepreneurial experimentation; employees are convinced that they belong to an outstanding organization and have a positive self-image of their performance and of their contribution to corporate performance. By contrast, weak cultures do not tend to provide an environment conducive to change. Typologies of organizational cultures are provided by HANDY, DEAL & KENNEDY, and SCHOLZ.

Some "informational" elements of organizational culture. Several recent articles focus on particular informational elements of culture in an organizational setting. Corporate folklore and its role in organizational culture is the theme of a review article by M.O. JONES. Folklore genres include jargon, traditional sayings, nicknames, anecdotes, jokes, rumors, myths and legends, and songs as well as customs, ceremonies, rituals, and the like. MYRSIADES reviewed the literature on corporate stories/myths as a source of studying organizational communications. Organizational stories constitute more than information transmission: they are cultural communications, symbolic realities of extended real-life metaphors, which help create and sustain organizational groups. Studying stories emanating from different parts of an organization will show whether there is a unifying dominant culture (or competing subcultures) and reveal much about informal structures within the organization. Myrsiades argues that an analysis of an organization's oral tradition as contained in corporate stories is an important tool in the repertoire of methodologies available for organizational studies and urges its adoption by organizational ethnographers, organization development specialists, and communciations researchers.

Exploring links between imagery and organizational strategy, SAPIENZA used ethnographic techniques to trace the development of strategic decisions in two hospitals facing extreme environmental uncertainty. Over a six-month period, Sapienza attended relevant meetings as a nonparticipant observer and tracked executives, focusing on the language managers used and the extent to which they used imagery in the strategic decision-making process. She found that many strategy statements were rich in imagery and that managers made strategic decisions in partial response to their figures of speech. A three-stage process by which imagery emerges and influences decision making is postulated: after collective discussion of individual perceptions of the stimuli, a common vocabulary and syntax tends to develop, which gives way to the emergence of a reigning image describing the stimuli to which top managers respond strategically.

Corporate culture as a means of enhancing organizational effectiveness.   Reference was made earlier to the informational role of strong corporate cultures that provide shared understandings and a guide for action. Over the past decade, numerous management writings have focused on this theme, stressing that the development of a strong corporate culture is a means of enhancing organizational performance and effectiveness. The findings of PETERS & WATERMAN (1982) relating to the importance of a dominant culture have been extensively cited in this context (e.g., LISTON).

There has been a widespread fascination with identifying the cultural characteristics of high-performing companies and emulating those principles in other organizations. Some of this literature underestimates the impact of a "culture clash" between divergent value systems and fundamentally different sets of shared understandings that underlie any culture. While this is most evident with national differences, strong variations in culture can exist between different organizations in the same city. The literature reviewed in this section provides examples of each scenario: importing a foreign culture to the West and attempting to merge cultures in company takeovers or amalgamations. Importing a technological innovation from overseas can be problematic because the technology may come with its own set of cultural attributes, which may clash with those of the prevailing company culture and trigger industrial unrest.

A popular theme has been what western managers can learn from Japanese companies, an interest triggered by declining levels of productivity in the West compared with Japan. Most articles conclude that a dominant company culture constitutes the "magic" ingredient in corporate growth and success in Japan, and that, although national cultures differ, there is much that western companies can learn from their Japanese counterparts. MARSLAND & BEER highlight the centrality of the human resource and the efficiency of information flows in Japanese companies. A vast amount of information is gathered and circulated about competitors and comparative performance statistics; informal networks, partly due to "lifetime" employment policies and a teamwork emphasis, are highly developed and effective, enabling the location of desired information within minutes. More recent articles (e.g., KENNEDY) stress the success of the Japanese with total quality management (TQM) as a function of company culture and the adoption of Japanese solutions such as "Just In Time" and "Quality Control Circles" in the West. KING & WOOD identify culture as "the missing ingredient in the recipe for maximum productivity in a manufacturing environment"; they attribute problems in the implementation of advanced manufacturing technologies to a culture clash between existing company values and the principles underlying the new technology (e.g., continual improvement, faster throughput, elimination of waste, teamwork, participative problem solving, and conformity to customer specifications). Successful implementation of new technology is contingent on addressing social and cultural factors along with technological considerations.

Another related theme has been the impact on organizational culture of privatization or takeovers. It is argued that while cultures are difficult to change, this can be done through careful planning and management development programs—when managers are given the means and the opportunity to make the change themselves (SMITH ET AL.)—and by controlling corporate information resources/systems (VINCENT). Shorter-term mergers of two cultures through joint venture projects in information technology are the focus of an exploratory study by CARTWRIGHT & COOPER. The researchers hypothesized that cultural compatibility between merger partners and the extent to which a single coherent culture emerged would be predictors of organizational success; however, results were inconclusive.

Successful organizations tend to be those that can change their structures and cultures appropriately to cope with radical environmental changes. A U.K. survey demonstrated that culture change was being treated strategically in progressive British companies, with the key agents of culture change being improved communications, structural changes, and management development programs (COWLING). A more theoretical approach to the link between organizational culture and strategy is provided by SCHOLZ, who argues that corporate culture is an important part of corporate strategy (a crucial element in solving the problem of strategic fit) and analyzes why strong cultures are associated with corporate success.

SERPA focuses on the ethical dimensions of culture; he claims that a key to corporate success is the development of "a candid corporate culture," enshrining honesty as a central cultural value, encouraging open communication, and facilitating the free flow of information throughout the organization.

"Politicking" in organizations, according to MILGROM & ROBERTS, is counterproductive to economic efficiency; employees put time and effort into individually focused "influence activities" rather than into maximizing organizational outcomes. Suggestions for minimizing the negative impact of such activities include selective closure of communication channels (i.e., limiting access to certain decision makers), altering decision making criteria to favor those performing well with productive activities, and rewarding the productive with financial and other incentives.

Information technology and corporate culture. In the management, computing, and information systems literatures, information technology and corporate culture has been a recurrent theme. With the dominant culture perspective, it is assumed that the successful implementation of an information system in an organization depends on compatibility with the organization's "umbrella" culture. Early sources focused on the likely impacts of new information technology on organizational cultures and the nature of work. For example, in 1982 OLSON speculated that the technology could have a substantial social impact, with more employees choosing to work from home for lifestyle reasons. This trend would have significant implications for the organization of work, authority structures, the nature of the physical environment, communication systems, performance evaluation, promotion policies, and so forth. However, the past decade has not seen these potential impacts of information technology realized on the scale envisaged, perhaps due to the social function of work and the human need for meaningful social interaction and regular face-to-face communication.

A more recent emphasis in the literature has been the need to ensure that information systems are culturally consistent with the dominant organizational culture. For instance, a centralized information system may be inappropriate in an organization in which decision making is highly decentralized. LINDNER equates success of the information system's function in organizations with the recognition by the information systems professionals of the importance of a strong corporate culture, understanding of that culture, and use of policies and approaches that are compatible with that culture.

OGILVIE ET AL. identify three major information processors at an organizational level: (1) the computer-based information system (CBIS), (2) organizational structure, and (3) organizational culture, which, they argue, must be congruent and held in balance for optimal organizational effectiveness. To some extent, a CBIS can replace structure within an organization. However, for successful implementation of a CBIS, the system must support key cultural values. "The CBIS should always be viewed as a means to accomplish larger organizational objectives in a way that is consistent with organizational values. The CBIS is never simply a technical mechanism for reducing labor costs" (p. 237).

MORIEUX & SUTHERLAND combine two theoretical approaches: use of corporate culture to help achieve organizational goals, and use of information technology (IT) as a crucial element in strategic planning processes. The authors stress the interaction of these factors: cultural changes affect attitudes toward the use of IT, and in turn the use of IT changes the culture. Information systems professionals need to be aware of cultural factors in the introduction of IT. For example, does the prevailing organizational climate engender IT phobia, a tendency to reject new technology out of hand, or IT mania, an unquestioning acceptance of information technology proposals, or something in between? Are staff accustomed to participative decision making, and should they be involved in the design phase? What type and level of training and support are required and for what period? Senior executives may resent being taught by their inferiors and find it difficult to admit ignorance. Is there a role for user support groups? There will be differences among departments in the speed and extent of integrating new IT into their operations. Sharing facilities is a significant deterrent to use. In time, the technology tends to adopt a life of its own within an organization, being used in new and innovative ways.

Many sources stress the inappropriateness of the traditional, technically oriented culture of the centralized information systems department in current environments. In a stirring article, R. JONES challenges information systems professionals to abandon the culture of the data processing era and to adopt a more pivotal role in their organizations, developing an information systems culture that is business oriented. The major current information systems problem, the author claims, is that information systems professionals are technically competent but are not tuned into the business; they are preoccupied with maintaining old systems rather than spending time developing new software tailored to organizational needs. Proposed solutions include developing an understanding of the nature of the business, improving communication among users and information systems staff, and exploiting new generation software, such as computer-assisted software engineering (CASE) tools in the pursuit of corporate goals.

The Cultural Diversity Perspective

Although less pervasive than the dominant culture approach, the cultural diversity perspective, which is a relatively recent phenomenon, adds a valuable dimension to an understanding of corporate culture. The product of social psychologists and industrial anthropologists, this perspective views organizational cultures as fragmented and diverse, composed of distinct subcultures that are based on friendship patterns among different social groups within an organization. ROSE and KRACKHARDT & KILDUFF provide clear overviews of this approach.

KRACKHARDT & KILDUFF (p. 142) describe corporate culture as "an emergent property of informal relationships within work groups," a cognitive system negotiated between interacting individuals who create locally shared systems of meaning. Research in this tradition focuses on "how norms, beliefs, attributions, behaviors, and other aspects of organizational culture are controlled through the informal networks of coworkers." In Krackhardt and Kilduff's research in a medium-sized entrepreneurial firm employees rated each other along seven cultural dimensions. As anticipated, friends tended to have similar cultural attributions compared with those who were not friends, and there was a trend for those who disagreed with their friends to experience lower levels of job satisfaction. The researchers concluded: "People's attributions are to some extent controlled by the need to be in harmony with others in their friendship networks. These networks are likely to resist management attempts to initiate discrepant cultural values or interpretations" (p. 151). Managers who ignore the cultural diversity that exists within an organization can trigger unexpected internal conflict.

Drawing on the CMM (Coordinated Management of Meaning) theoretical framework, ROSE explicates the concept of corporate culture in terms of rules internalized as cognitions by individuals, with consequent action being the product of a complex interplay between values that are inherent in the dominant culture espoused by management and values embedded in different subcultures. Three distinct types of subculture identified include: (1) the enhancing subculture, in which members adhere more fervently than the rest of the organization to the values of the dominant culture; (2) the orthogonal subculture, in which members adhere to the core values of the dominant culture but as well have an additional, nonconflicting set of values of their own; (3) and the counterculture, characterized by a set of values that are in direct conflict with those of the core culture.

THOMPSON & WILDAVSKY use a cultural diversity perspective to explain the phenomenon of information bias in organizations.

They argue that different types of cultures tend to produce a distinctive information bias since each is disposed to learn different things and to accept or to reject different types of information. Hierarchies, which emphasize status, correct procedures, and maintaining the existing order, tend to retain old truths as long as possible and to search for new information which will support the status quo. Markets are characterized by competitive individualism and a relatively weak group identity, concerned with maximizing results, achieving the greatest gain for the least effort, and they will seek out just enough information to justify a decision, with a minimum of search. Sects are more concerned with equalizing outcomes from the vantage point of the worst off and will seek evidence of inequality and new information on how to reduce inequality.

THE HUMAN ELEMENT IN ORGANIZATIONAL INFORMATION PROCESSING AND DECISION MAKING

Numerous theories and models of organizational information processing are expounded in the literature. This chapter does not attempt to review these theories but selectively highlights research relevant to the central theme of this paper—viz., that human networks play a central role in information dissemination in organizations. In this section, three major strands of the management and organizational theory literatures are examined for insights into the role of human networks in organizations. These include research into: (1) the nature of managerial work, (2) strategic decision processes in organizations, and (3) human information sources in models of organizational information processing.

The Nature of Managerial Work

Early research by MINTZBERG (1973; 1975) shattered the popular myth of managers' being rational and deliberate problem solvers who make intensive use of formal information systems for input. His study involved tracking five CEOs from medium to large organizations in different industries and collecting 25 days of detailed observations relating to all the executives' activities (e.g., every piece of mail perused, each meeting, each face-to-face contact or phone call).

Mintzberg found senior level managers overburdened with work, their individual tasks characterized by "brevity, variety and fragmentation," yet unable to delegate many tasks because of the nature of their information. They manifested an action orientation, focusing on the immediate and the tangible, making snap decisions in response to stimuli or making major decisions in small increments, even though the complex problems facing them might call for reflection and long-range planning. There seemed to be no deliberate or systematic planning apart from flexible plans in their own heads. Overwhelmingly, their major sources of information were other people: interpersonal contacts in scheduled meetings, face-to-face contact, phone calls, or observational tours. Mintzberg's subjects spent 78% of their time in verbal communication. Other studies in Mintzberg's extensive literature review on the nature of managerial work produced similar figures. Rather than drawing on the aggregated information in management information systems set up to serve their needs or on documentary sources or files, most of the subjects used data for decision making that were stored in their own brains or the brains of others with whom they interacted. Compared with interpersonal sources, formal information systems tended to be regarded as too limited in scope, too general, not sufficiently up to date, and unreliable.

A significant amount of subsequent research has substantiated Mintzberg's findings. For example, ACHLEITNER & GROVER recently studied information-transfer patterns among managers in the finance department of a large corporation and found that oral communication was the predominant format for information transfer, consuming 92% of managers' work time. People were the major information source, and a large proportion of information received was unrecorded. In a study of marketing managers, PERKINS & RAO found experience to be an important deteminant of managerial behavior for relatively unprogrammed decisions, impacting on managers' evaluation and use of "soft" information, the amount of information used, and the nature of the resulting decision.

Analyzing his own data, and synthesizing the findings of others on the nature of managerial work, Mintzberg identified ten major management roles which cluster around three areas: (1) interpersonal roles (figurehead, leader, and liaison), (2) informational roles (monitor, disseminator, and spokesperson), and (3) decisional roles (entrepreneur, disturbance handler, resource allocator, and negotiator). Mintzberg stresses that these roles are not discrete or easily separable but very much intertwined and overlapping. From their interpersonal contacts (liaison role), managers develop a powerful database of information, the processing of which is a key part of the job. In Mintzberg's study, CEOs spent 40% of their time on tasks devoted exclusively to the transmission of information and 70% of incoming mail they processed was purely informational. The "monitoring"

informational role was largely derived from the well-developed network of liaison contacts both in the external environment and internal
sources, with managers receiving a wealth of solicited and unsolicited
information. The other two informational roles involve sharing the
information gleaned from this extensive personal network—the disseminator role being that of passing on important information to
subordinates, who generally would not have access to that information
otherwise, and the spokesperson role being that of sharing information
with those external to the organization. Decisional roles flow on from
informational roles, with managers possessing information on which to
base decisions.

Although Mintzberg's original research is now dated, in his most
recent work (MINTZBERG, 1989), he argues that little has changed;
despite major technological advances, information technology has
had relatively little impact on the nature of managerial work, which
is very much the same today as it was decades ago and probably
centuries ago.

Strategic Decision Processes in Organizations

A considerable amount of research into the process of strategic
decision making in organizations tends to support the composite
picture of managerial work defined by Mintzberg and to refute any
notion of logical, step-by step decision processes assumed by rational
models of organizational decision making. Much of the research
involves ethnographic approaches: using observation and interviews
to trace the development of particular strategic decisions in organizations. Recurrent examples are technological innovations, major
investments, developing new services or products, and structural
changes, such as internal reorganizations, mergers, or takeovers.

By their nature, strategic decision processes are unstructured
and nonprogrammable, less amenable to precise description or the
application of operations research and quantitative modeling techniques than are routine operational decisions. HICKSON, in an
excellent review article on strategic decision making in organizations,
contrasts two opposing schools of thought: the "management sys-
tematizers," who advocate the use of rational, analytical techniques
in strategic planning and decision making, and the "behavioral
debunkers," who highlight the mental and political limits of such
methods. SCHILIT criticizes the limited world view of the various
normative approaches to strategic planning, such as comprehensive
planning models, mathematical models, game theory, growth share,
and business planning matrices; these share the basic underlying

assumptions of rational decision making, optimization or maximization, and the single goal of long-term profitability. Such analytical models, he claims, fail to acknowledge the importance of multiple goals, bargaining and negotiation, and coalition behavior. The reality of organizational decision making is much more complex—i.e., decisions are often based on illogical, emotional, or irrational factors, and there is a tendency to adopt solutions that "satisfice" rather than "optimize."

According to Hickson, earlier writers on organizational decision making tended to focus on the concepts of problems and solutions and their associated information requirements, while the more recent emphasis has been on political and process aspects: power and the influence ability of key players and interest groups and the crucial nature of timing. Hickson distinguishes two overlapping but complementary theories of the *process* of organizational decision making that are opposed to traditional rational models: incrementalism and the "garbage can" model; he adds a third model of his own, the dual rationality model.

Incrementalism assumes that in the process of gathering information, alternatives are identified and evaluated immediately and that these successive evaluations are logical increments that lead to a final decision over time. "Garbage can" models are discussed in some detail below. "Dual rationality" is an attempt to draw together the dual strands of the problem and the politics of strategic decisions. This model involves "an implicit interest-accommodating rationality that weighs up what is at stake for each interested party, and what the range of acceptable alternatives may be" (p. 186). Each matter for decision simultaneously raises problems and implicates interests in a unique combination. Different decision processes are evidenced in varying combinations of these two factors. Vortex decisions are those involving highly complex and highly political matters; tractable decisions are unusual but noncontroversial, less complicated, and less political; and familiar decisions are routine and recurrent and least complex but may be highly political in nature. ENK & HART outline an interactive process for working toward integrative decisions, which is designed to accommodate situations of high complexity and uncertainty and to reconcile multiple political interests and concerns.

Based on their observations of strategic decision processes in universities that bore no relation to rational models, COHEN ET AL., in a seminal article, postulated the "garbage can model" of organizational decision making. They argued that major policy decisions of organizations tend to be the result of chance interactions among four relatively independent elements: (1) choice opportuni-

ties, (2) problems, (3) potential solutions, and (4) participants; like
the garbage in a trash can, the decision depends on the mix currently
available. There are "collections of choices looking for problems,
issues and feelings looking for decision situations in which they
might be aired, solutions looking for issues to which they might be
the answer, and decision makers looking for work" (p. 1). The authors
developed these ideas into a computer-simulation model, which they
subsequently tested. Rational means of problem resolution were
rarely found; as load on the system increased (i.e., problem activity,
decision-maker activity, decision difficulty), decisions made by flight
and oversight increased.

The literature since has evidenced a good deal of fascination with,
and some support for, the garbage can model. Recently, MANDELL
devised a computer simulation model to test the consequences of
improving dissemination in garbage can decision processes. SCHMID
ET AL. report on a research project that involved three months of
observing decision-making processes in board meetings of two human
service agencies; observations tended to reinforce the garbage can
model. Difficulties in the decision-making process included: insuffi-
cient information to make informed decisions; crucial information
not available at the time the decision was being made; "group think"
processes that encouraged the grasping and unanimous acceptance
of one solution; an unequal utilization of human energy, with a clear
dominance of the few key participants regarded as the most expert
or knowledgeable; failure to prioritize, with inconsequential decisions
frequently consuming more time than significant strategic decisions;
and many important decisions made by oversight (i.e., with a minimum commitment of time and energy or by flight (e.g., postponing
the decision to a future unspecified time and/or delegating it to a
subcommittee)) and not by resolution. The researchers conclude that
their observations are typical of most organizations, with post hoc,
reactive decision making more prevalent than deliberate, longer-
range, proactive strategic planning. Enhancement of management
information systems and more adequate training of committee
members in meeting processes and their personal roles and responsibilities are among the suggested solutions for improving organizational decision processes.

A range of other studies based on case histories of strategic
decisions reinforces the various nonrational models of organizational decision making identified above. Perhaps the best known of
these is the 1976 analysis of 25 cases of strategic decision processes
in Canadian organizations by MINTZBERG ET AL. The composite
picture to emerge was one of muddling through, characterized by

disjointed decision processes, interrupts, cycling and recycling, and logical incrementalism rather than any rational deductive ideal of systematically working through defined phases. There was a widespread belief that it was not possible to derive all relevant information and a tendency to be content with limited information. Seven kinds of decision processes were identified: (1) the simple impasse, (2) political design, (3) basic search, (4) modified search, (5) basic design, (6) blocked design, and (7) dynamic design.

A large-scale study of 150 cases in 30 organizations in the United Kingdom by HICKSON and others highlighted great variance in strategic decision processes: sporadic processes, characterized by irregular bursts of activity; fluid processes, which were rapid and steadily paced; and constricted processes, narrowly channelled, for example, around the CEO.

Human Information Sources in Models of Organizational Information Processing

Early theories of organizational information processing were based on the premise that organizations process information to reduce uncertainty—i.e., obtain data in response to explicit questions. Increasing amounts of information are processed in situations in which there are high levels of environmental or task uncertainty. Organizational structures develop in response to such information processing requirements. GALBRAITH, integrating the perspectives of organizational theorists such as T. Burns and G. Stalker, J. Woodward, and P.R. Lawrence and J.W. Lorsch, provided the foundation for this approach, which subsequently became the focus of much research over the next decade.

However, the uncertainty reduction theory of organizational information processing failed to explain adequately the human and social aspects of information processing in organizations. A valuable dimension was added by WEICK, who postulated another theory: organizations process information to reduce equivocality. In its dictionary sense, equivocality involves different meanings that are equally possible, ambiguous interpretations, or something of uncertain significance. Stimuli may be so complex and confusing that managers do not even know the right questions to ask, and there may be conflicting and multiple interpretations of the same set of data. PUTNAM & SORENSON provide a useful overview of the concept of equivocality in an organizational context.

Some of the most promising recent developments in theories of organizational information processing have built on the conceptual foundation laid by Weick. Most notable in this context has been the work of Daft, Lengel, Huber, and others, who have proposed models of organizational information processing that integrate the perspectives of uncertainty reduction and equivocality reduction (DAFT; DAFT & HUBER; DAFT & LENGEL, 1984, 1986; DAFT & MACINTOSH; DAFT & WEICK; HUBER; HUBER & DAFT; HUBER & MCDANIEL; LENGEL; TREVINO ET AL.).

These theories better accommodate the role of informal information/communication networks in organizations and observations on the nature of managerial work. Organizational information processing is seen to be closely linked with structural design, with managers able to manipulate structural factors and communication media for optimal information processing. Some structural mechanisms and communication media are more suited to reducing uncertainty, others to equivocality reduction. Mechanisms that facilitate the supply of large volumes of data (e.g., documentary sources and computer-based information systems) exemplify the former, and mechanisms that permit debate, clarification, and immediate feedback (e.g., face-to-face media) illustrate the latter.

In connection with equivocality reduction, DAFT & LENGEL (1984; 1986) defined the concepts of information richness and media richness. Information richness is the ability of information to change understanding within a time interval. The authors rank different communication media on their ability to facilitate the processing of rich information. The highest-ranking media are those that clarify ambiguities and different frames of reference quickly. They are characterized by immediate (vs. delayed/slow) feedback, involvement of multiple senses (vs. just the visual), and use of personal (vs. impersonal) sources. On this scale, face-to-face contact ranks highest, followed by telephone interaction, personal documents, such as letters and memos, impersonal written documents, and, lowest, numeric sources such as MIS or CBIS. Media that are high in richness become more important at higher levels of an organization and in complex, dynamic environments in which equivocality is high (c.f. at operational levels where tasks are more routine and more clearly defined). A seven-phase continuum of the relative ability of different structural mechanisms to reduce uncertainty and to reduce equivocality is postulated, which assumes an inverse relationship between the two factors. Mechanisms high in uncertainty reduction appear at one end of the continuum, and those high in equivocality reduction appear at the other. The order is: rules and regulations, formal information systems, special reports, planning, direct contact, integrator positions, and group meetings/collaborative teams. Increasingly, organizations are facing high degrees of environmental uncertainty and complexity, ill-defined situations and conflicting perspectives, for which structural mechanisms and communication media suited to equivocality reduction are essential. However, with more recent technological developments in computer-mediated communication systems and group decision support systems/computer supported cooperative work (an active area of research worldwide), these distinctions are blurring. A separate review article is necessary to do justice to the human impacts of these technologies.

Recent research (e.g., GOLDSTEIN & ZACK; TREVINO ET AL.; ZACK & MCKENNEY, 1989a) has linked managerial effectiveness with appropriate choice of communication media—e.g., using "rich" media for equivocal messages and "lean" media for unequivocal messages. While no model offers any final answers and logical flaws can be identified, these models provide a significant advance on earlier theories and explain some of the human factors in information processing that form the substance of this chapter.

CONCLUSIONS AND IMPLICATIONS

Traditionally the major focus in the information management, information science, and information systems literatures has been on the physical nature of the information resource and its enabling technology rather than on the "soft," more qualitative, human dimensions of information processing. Understanding the human factors behind information transfer and the nature and role of informal communication networks in organizations, including the primacy of interpersonal sources of information, is crucial to the effective management of the organizational information resource.

The literature cited here has identified an overwhelming preference for human as opposed to document- or computer-based information sources. Despite the sophisticated technology available, people still prefer to interact with other people for many different reasons:

- People have a natural, human need for social interaction, for developing meaningful relationships with others;
- People desire to establish or promote a conducive and mutually supportive working climate, to nurture personal links through frequent interaction;

- It is often the quickest and most efficient means of procuring the desired information, avoiding problems of information overload required in the process of identifying, sifting, and evaluating information sources;
- It seems easier to ask someone nearby rather than spend time and effort locating the answer personally;
- Expert advice is available from someone who is more familiar with the area;
- More up-to-date information may be gleaned than is available in physical sources; and
- People add value to information, interpreting its meaning and significance in a particular context; this cannot be derived from documents or computer-based information sources.

Because of the natural human inclination to seek out human information sources first, it appears that there is an important ongoing role for information professionals with highly developed interpersonal and communication skills, who can function effectively as information intermediaries, human links between organizational members and recorded sources of data. Despite the rapid advances in end-user computing, people still feel more comfortable interacting with other people. Recognizing the human phenomenon in organizational information processing in no way diminishes the value of organizational information systems and services, but it does lead the information professional to reassess his or her role, aspects of service, and expectations of usage.

The literature surveyed here highlights the fallacy of the ideal of providing direct access to information for all members of an organization. However, an information service may permeate indirectly to most employees through the mediation of certain high-information consumers who act as "communication stars" within the organization, transmitting the content of information they assimilate to their work colleagues. One of the major challenges for the information professional is to be able to identify these individuals and to work through them within the organization. According to the "80/20 law," maximum gains can be made by selectively targeting those who are likely to yield the highest returns rather than dissipating energy unnecessarily. Having identified the "information rich" or "communication stars" within the organization, information professionals need to ensure that there are mechanisms in place to keep these individuals informed. As voracious information consumers, they will tend rapidly to assimilate information that is directed their way and to play a key role in the dissemination of that information within the organization.

A specific targeting of information services to a select minority within an organization meshes well with marketing theory, but it does raise ethical problems and some cognitive dissonance for a profession based on a service mentality. Statements on "Freedom to Read" and other creeds of the library profession that espouse the democratic ideal of equal access to information and equal service to all, irrespective of race, color, political, or religious affiliation do not sit easily with this approach. Perhaps this has been a part of the problem with the profession. Success in attracting funds for information services within an organization has much to do with the political skills of the information center manager. Targeting communication stars involves making links with the sources of power in an organization. Many of these individuals will be managers, and those who are not will have a strong influence on the organizational decision-making processes through their status in the informal structure. There is no better way to ensure ongoing financial support of the information service function within the organization. Few courses in library and information science have developed adequately the skills required for this process: skills in network analysis, personal networking and liaison, lobbying, and negotiation and conflict resolution.

Ideally, the information professional should occupy a central position in the informal network and be one of the "communication stars" of the organization. Unfortunately, in many organizations the information service remains peripheral, irrelevant to most organizational members. A preoccupation with systems and physical resources rather than people may be a contributing factor here. Facing a hostile economic climate, organizations are increasingly placing their information systems and services under the microscope, evaluating their performance, and where they have not demonstrated their value, downsizing or dispensing with them, drastically reducing budgets and staff. In this environment, it is imperative that information professionals reassess their own service role within their organizations.

For too long the human factor has been the forgotten resource in information service provision in organizations. Information professionals need to focus more on coordination of the organization's total information resource, including its people. Analyzing information flows through interpersonal communications networks inside and outside the organization and diagnosing information needs and patterns of information/media use are as central to this function as designing, evaluating, and managing automated information systems. More than that, however, effective management of the organizational information resource requires that the information professional become an integral part of the organization's informal network.

BIBLIOGRAPHY

ACHLEITNER, HERBERT K.; GROVER, ROBERT. 1988. Managing in an Information-Rich Environment: Applying Information Transfer Theory to Information Systems Management. Special Libraries. 1988 Spring; 79(2): 92-100. ISSN: 0038-6723.

ALLEN, T. HARRELL. 1976. Communication Networks: The Hidden Organizational Chart. Personnel Administrator. 1976 September; 21(6): 31-35. ISSN: 0031-5729.

ALLEN, THOMAS J. 1969. Information Needs and Uses. In: Cuadra, Carlos A., ed. Annual Review of Information Science and Technology: Volume 4. Chicago, IL: Encyclopaedia Britannica, Inc.; 1969. 3-29. ISSN: 0066-4200.

ALLEN, THOMAS J. 1971. Communication Networks in R&D Laboratories. R&D Management. 1971; 1(1): 14-21. ISSN: 0033-6807.

ALLEN, THOMAS J. 1977. Managing the Flow of Technology. Cambridge, MA: MIT Press; 1977. 320p. ISBN: 0-262-01048-8.

ALLEN, THOMAS J. 1986. Organizational Structure, Information Technology, and R&D Productivity. IEEE Transactions on Engineering Management. 1986 November; EM-33(4): 212-217. ISSN: 0018-9391.

ALLEN, THOMAS J. 1990. People and Technology Transfer. Cambridge, MA: MIT, Sloan School of Management, International Center for Research on the Management of Technology (ICRMOT); 1990. 23p. (Working Paper; WP # 10-90). Available from the Center: ICRMOT Working Papers, MIT, Room E56-304, Cambridge, MA 02139.

ALLEN, THOMAS J.; FUSFELD, A.R. 1975. Research Laboratory Architecture and the Structuring of Communications. R & D Management. 1975 February; 5(2): 153-164. ISSN: 0033-6807.

ALLEN, THOMAS J.; HAUPTMAN, OSCAR. 1987. The Influence of Communication Technologies on Organizational Structure: A Conceptual Model for Future Research. Communication Research. 1987 October; 14(5): 575-587. ISSN: 0093-6502.

ALLEN, THOMAS J.; HAUPTMAN, OSCAR. 1990. The Substitution of Communication Technologies for Organizational Structure in Research and Development. In: Fulk, Janet; Steinfield, Charles, eds. Organizations and Communication Technology. Newbury Park, CA: Sage; 1990. 275-294. ISBN: 0-8039-3530-7; 0-8039-3531-5 (pbk.).

ARNOLD, VANESSA DEAN. 1983. Harvesting Your Employee Grapevine. Management World. 1983 July; 12(6): 26-28, 37. ISSN: 0090-3825.

ATHANASSIADES, JOHN C. 1973. The Distortion of Upward Communication in Hierarchical Organizations. Academy of Management Journal. 1973 June; 16(2): 207-226. ISSN: 0001-4273.

BACHARACH, SAMUEL B.; AIKEN, MICHAEL. 1977. Communication in Administrative Bureaucracies. Academy of Management Journal. 1977 September; 20(3): 365-377. ISSN: 0001-4273.

BAKER, H. KENT. 1981. Tapping into the Power of Informal Groups. Supervisory Management. 1981 February; 26(2): 18-25. ISSN: 0039-5919.

BASA, FRANK; ALLEN, THOMAS J.; KATZ, RALPH. 1990. Work Environment, Organizational Relationships and Advancement of Technical Professionals: A Ten Year Longitudinal Study in One Organization. Cambridge, MA: MIT, Sloan School of Management, International Center for Research on the Management of Technology (ICRMOT); 1990. 32p. (Working Paper; WP #9-90). Available from the Center: ICRMOT Working Papers, MIT, Room E56-304, Cambridge, MA 02139.

BATT, ROBERT. 1982. Putting on a New Face: The Need for Behavioral Skills in MIS. Computerworld. 1982 December 28/January 4; 16(1): 77-81. ISSN: 0010-4841.

BELL, PETER. 1978. How to Cope with Uncertainty. Management Today. 1978 April: 67-69, 126. ISSN: 0025-1925.

BISTLINE, SUSAN MITCHELL. 1985. After-Hours Socializing. Association Management. 1985 February; 37(2): 89-93. ISSN: 0004-5578.

BLANDIN, J.S.; BROWN, W.B. 1977. Uncertainty and Management's Search for Information. IEEE Transactions on Engineering Management. 1977; 4: 114-119. ISSN: 0018-9391.

BOLAND, RICHARD J. 1987. The In-Formation of Information Systems. In: Boland, R.J.; Hirschheim, R.A., eds. Critical Issues in Information Systems Research. New York, NY: Wiley; 1987. 363-379. ISBN: 0-471-91281-6.

BORGMAN, CHRISTINE L., ed. 1990. Scholarly Communication and Bibliometrics. Newbury Park, CA: Sage Publications; 1990. 363p. ISBN: 0-8039-3879-9.

BOWMAN, JOEL P.; TARGOWSKI, ANDREW S. 1987. Modelling the Communication Process: The Map Is Not the Territory. Journal of Business Communication. 1987 Fall; 24(4): 21-34. ISSN: 0021-9436.

BURTON, PAUL F. 1988. Information Technology and Organisational Structure. Aslib Proceedings. 1988 March; 40(3): 57-68. ISSN: 0001-253X.

BUTLER, JOHN K. 1986. A Global View of Informal Organization. Advanced Management Journal. 1986 Summer; 51(3): 39-43. ISSN: 0036-0805.

CARTWRIGHT, SUSAN; COOPER, CARY L. 1989. Predicting Success in Joint Venture Organizations in Information Technology. Journal of General Management. 1989 Autumn; 15(1): 39-52. ISSN: 0306-3070.

COHEN, MICHAEL D.; MARCH, JAMES G.; OLSEN, JOHAN P. 1972. A Garbage Can Model of Organizational Choice. Administrative Science Quarterly. 1972; 17(1): 1-25. ISSN: 0001-8392.

COWLING, ALAN. 1989. Personnel's Strategic Role in Culture Change. Personnel Management. 1989 December; 21(12): 10-11. ISSN: 0031-6761.

COX, ALLAN J. 1986. The Corporate Management Trap: Beware of the Hidden Agenda. Advertising Age. 1986 December 6; 47(49): 33, 36. ISSN: 0001-8899.

CRAWFORD, SUSAN Y. 1971. Informal Communication among Scientists in Sleep Research. Journal of the American Society for Information Science. 1971; 22(5): 301-310. ISSN: 0002-8231.

CRAWFORD, SUSAN Y. 1978. Information Needs and Uses. In: Williams, Martha E., ed. Annual Review of Information Science and Technology: Volume 13. White Plains, NY: Knowledge Industry Publications, Inc. for the American Society for Information Science (ASIS); 1978. 61-81. ISSN: 0066-4200.

CULNAN, MARY J. 1983. Chauffered Versus End User Access to Commercial Databases: The Effects of Task and Individual Differences. MIS Quarterly. 1983 March; 7(1): 55-67. ISSN: 0276-7783.

CULNAN, MARY J.; MARKUS, M. LYNNE. 1987. Information Technologies. In: Jablin, Frederick M.; Putnam, Linda L.; Roberts, Karlene H.; Porter, Lyman W., eds. Handbook of Organizational Communication: An Interdisciplinary Perspective. Newbury Park, CA: Sage; 1987. 420-443. ISBN: 0-8039-2387-2.

CZEPIEL, JOHN A. 1975. Patterns of Interorganizational Communications and the Diffusion of a Major Technological Innovation in a Competitive Industrial Community. Academy of Management Journal. 1975 March; 18(1): 6-24. ISSN: 0001-4273.

DAFT, RICHARD L. 1989. Organization Theory and Design. 3rd edition. St Paul, MN: West; 1989. 602p. ISBN: 0-314-46341-0.

DAFT, RICHARD L.; HUBER, GEORGE P. 1987. How Organizations Learn: A Communication Framework. In: DiTomaso, N.; Bacharach, S.B., eds. Research in the Sociology of Organizations: Volume 5. Greenwich, CT: JAI Press; 1987. 1-36. ISBN: 0-89232-637-9.

DAFT, RICHARD L.; LENGEL, ROBERT H. 1984. Information Richness: A New Approach to Managerial Information Processing and Organization Design. In: Staw, B.; Cummings, L.L., eds. Research in Organizational Behavior: Volume 6. Greenwich, CT: JAI Press; 1984. 191-233. ISBN: 0-89232-351-5.

DAFT, RICHARD L.; LENGEL ROBERT H. 1986. Organizational Information Requirements: Media Richness and Structural Design. Management Science. 1986 May; 32(5): 554-571. ISSN: 0025-1909.

DAFT, RICHARD L.; MACINTOSH, NORMAN B. 1981. A Tentative Exploration into the Amount and Equivocality of Information Processing in Organizational Work Units. Administrative Science Quarterly. 1981; 26: 207-224. ISSN: 0001-8392.

DAFT, RICHARD L.; WEICK, K.E. 1984. Toward a Model of Organizations as Interpretation Systems. Academy of Management Review. 1984; 9: 284-295. ISSN: 0363-7425.

DASTMALCHIAN, ALI. 1986. Environmental Characteristics and Organizational Climate: An Exploratory Study. Journal of Management Studies. 1986 November; 23(6): 609-633. ISSN: 0022-2380.

DAVIS, KEITH. 1978. Methods for Studying Informal Communication. Journal of Communication. 1978 Winter; 28(1): 112-116. ISSN: 0021-9916.

DEAL, TERRENCE E.; KENNEDY, ALLAN A. 1982. Corporate Cultures: The Rites and Rituals of Corporate Life. Reading, MA: Addison-Wesley; 1982. 232p. ISBN: 0-201-10277-3; 0-201-10287-0 (pbk.).

DELANEY, W.A. 1979. The Art of Filtering. Supervisory Management. 1979 July; 24(7): 9-12. ISSN: 0039-5919.

DERVIN, BRENDA; NILAN, MICHAEL. 1986. Information Needs and Uses. In: Williams, Martha E., ed. Annual Review of Information Science and Technology: Volume 21. White Plains, NY: Knowledge Industry Publications, Inc. for the American Society for Information Science (ASIS); 1986. 3-33. ISSN: 0066-4200.

DRAKE, MIRIAM A. 1984. Information and Corporate Cultures. Special Libraries. 1984 October; 75(4): 263-269. ISSN: 0038-6723.

DRISKILL, L.P.; GOLDSTEIN, JONE RYMER. 1986. Uncertainty: Theory and Practice in Organizational Communication. Journal of Business Communication. 1986 Summer; 23(3): 41-56. ISSN: 0021-9436.

ENK, GORDON A.; HART, STUART L. 1985. An Eight-Step Approach to Strategic Problem Solving. Human Systems Management. 1985; 5(3): 245-258. ISSN: 0167-2533.

ESTRIN, TEVIAH L. 1990. The Roles of Information Providers in Decision Making. Journal of General Management. 1990 Spring; 15(3): 80-95. ISSN: 0306-3070.

FARRIS, GEORGE F. 1979. The Informal Organization in Strategic Decision-Making. International Studies of Management & Organization. 1979 Winter; 9(4): 37-62. ISSN: 0020-8825.

FELDMAN, MARTHA S.; MARCH, JAMES G. 1981. Information in Organizations as Signal and Symbol. Administrative Science Quarterly. 1981; 26: 171-186. ISSN: 0001-8392.

FORGIONNE, GUISSEPPI A. 1988. A Strategy for Technology Management. Journal of Information Systems Management. 1988 Winter; 5(1): 42-51. ISSN: 0739-9014.

FOSTER, LAWRENCE W.; FLYNN, D.M. 1984. Management Information Technology: Its Effects on Organizational Form and Function. MIS Quarterly. 1984 December; 8(4): 229-236. ISSN: 0276-7783.

FRANK, ALLAN D. 1984. Can Water Flow Uphill? Training & Development Journal. 1984 May; 38(5): 118-128. ISSN: 0041-0861.

FREEDMAN, DAVID H. 1987. IS and the Corporate Culture. Infosystems. 1987 December; 34(12): 30-32. ISSN: 0364-5533.

GAINES, JANET H. 1980. Upward Communication in Industry: An Experiment. Human Relations. 1980 December; 33(12): 929-942. ISSN: 0018-7267.

GALBRAITH, J. 1973. Designing Complex Organizations. Reading, MA: Addison-Wesley; 1973. 150p. ISBN: 0-201-02559-0.

GEORGE, VARGHESE P.; ALLEN, THOMAS J. 1989. Netgraphs: A Graphic Representation of Adjacency Matrices as a Tool for Network Analysis. Cambridge, MA: MIT, Sloan School of Management, International Center for Research on the Management of Technology (ICRMOT);

1989. 31p. (Working Paper; WP # 1-89). Available from the Center: ICRMOT Working Papers, MIT, Room E56-304, Cambridge, MA 02139.

GILCHRIST, ALAN. 1985. The Flow and Management of Information in Organisations. In: Cronin, Blaise, ed. Information Management: From Strategies to Action. London, England: Aslib; 1985. 55-71. ISBN: 0-85142-193-8.

GOLDSTEIN, DAVID K.; ZACK, MICHAEL H. 1989. The Impact of Marketing Information Supply on Product Managers: An Organizational Processing Perspective. Office: Technology & People. 1989 July; 4(4): 313-336. ISSN: 0167-5710.

GRANOVETTER, M.S. 1972. The Strength of Weak Ties. American Journal of Sociology. 1972; 78: 1360-1380. ISSN: 0002-9602.

HALL, CHARLES. 1986. The Informal Organization Chart. Supervisory Management. 1986 January; 31(1): 40-42. ISSN: 0039-5919.

HALL, KEVIN R.; RITCHIE, ERIC. 1975. A Study of Communication Behaviour in an R&D Laboratory. R&D Management. 1975; 5(3): 243-245. ISSN: 0033-6807.

HALL, M.F. 1965. Communication within Organizations. Journal of Management Studies. 1965; 2: 54-69. ISSN: 0022-2380.

HAN, PYUNG E. 1983. The Informal Organization You've Got to Live With. Supervisory Management. 1983 October; 28(10): 25-28. ISSN: 0039-5919.

HANDY, CHARLES. 1985. On the Cultures of Organizations. In: Understanding Organizations. 3rd edition. Harmondsworth, England: Penguin; 1985. 185-221. ISBN: 0-140-09110-6.

HAUSER, RICHARD D.; BYRD, TERRY A. 1990. The Effects of Computer-Mediated Communication on Inter-departmental Relationships: Propositions for Research. Information Resources Management Journal. 1990 Fall; 3(4): 30-40. ISSN: 1040-1628.

HELLWEG, SUSAN A. 1983. Organizational Grapevines: A State-of-the-Art Review. Paper presented at the International Communication Association Annual Meeting; 1983 May 26-30; Dallas, TX.

HENDERSON, LINDA S. 1987. The Contextual Nature of Interpersonal Communication in Management Theory and Research. Communication Quarterly. 1987 August; 1(1): 7-31. ISSN: 0146-3373.

HICKSON, DAVID J. 1987. Decision-Making at the Top of Organizations. Annual Review of Sociology. 1987; 13: 165-192. ISSN: 0360-0572.

HILLS, P.J. 1983. The Scholarly Communication Process. In: Williams, Martha E., ed. Annual Review of Information Science and Technology: Volume 18. White Plains, NY: Knowledge Industry Publications, Inc. for the American Society for Information Science (ASIS); 1983. 99-125. ISSN: 0066-4200.

HIRSCHHEIM, R.A. 1986. Perspectives and Views of the Office: Alternative Approaches to Understanding the Office. In: Verrijn-Stuart, A.A.; Hirschheim, R.A., eds. Office Systems: Proceedings of the IFIP TC 8 Working Conference on Office Systems; 1985 September 29-October 2; Helsinki, Finland. New York, NY: Elsevier; 1986. 29-56. ISBN: 0-444-70105-2.

HOFFMAN, ERIC; ROMAN, PAUL M. 1984. Information Diffusion in the Implementation of Innovation Process. Communication Research. 1984 January; 11(1): 117-140. ISSN: 0093-6502.

HOLLINGSWORTH, A. THOMAS. 1974. Perceptual Accuracy of the Informal Organization as a Determinant of the Effectiveness of Formal Leaders. Journal of Economics and Business. 1974 Fall; 27(1): 75-78. ISSN: 0148-6195.

HUBER, GEORGE P. 1990. A Theory of the Effects of Advanced Information Technologies on Organizational Design, Intelligence, and Decision Making. In: Fulk, J.; Steinfield, C., eds. Organizations and Communication Technology. Newbury Park, CA: Sage; 1990. 237-274. ISBN: 0-8039-3530-7; 0-8039-3531-5 (pbk.).

HUBER, GEORGE P.; DAFT, RICHARD L. 1987. The Information Environments of Organizations. In: Jablin, Frederick M.; Putnam, Linda L.; Roberts, Karlene H.; Porter, Lyman W., eds. Handbook of Organizational Communication: An Interdisciplinary Perspective. Newbury Park, CA: Sage; 1987. 130-164. ISBN: 0-8039-2387-2.

HUBER, GEORGE P.; MCDANIEL, REUBEN R. 1986. Exploiting Information Technologies to Design More Effective Organizations. In: Jarke, M., ed. Managers, Micros and Mainframes. New York, NY: Wiley; 1986. 221-236. ISBN: 0-471-90988-2.

HUNTER, BILL. 1984. Fighting the Fertile Grapevine. Communication World. 1984 September; 1(11): 13-16. ISSN: 0744-7612.

IATUL QUARTERLY. 1988. Information Culture and Business Performance. IATUL Quarterly. 1988 June; 2(2): 93-106. ISSN: 0950-4117.

JONES, MICHAEL OWEN. 1990. A Folklore Approach to Emotions in Work. American Behavioral Scientist. 1990 January; 33(3): 278-286. ISSN: 0002-7642.

JONES, R. 1989. Time to Change the Culture of Information Systems Departments. Information & Software Technology. 1989 March; 31(2): 99-102. ISSN: 0950-5849.

KATZ, RALPH; ALLEN, THOMAS J. 1985. Project Performance and the Locus of Influence in the R&D Matrix. Academy of Management Journal. 1985 March; 28(1): 67-87. ISSN: 0001-4273.

KATZ, RALPH; TUSHMAN, MICHAEL. 1979. Communication Patterns, Project Performance, and Task Characteristics: An Empirical Evaluation and Integration in an R&D Setting. Organizational Behavior & Human Performance. 1979 April; 23(2): 139-162. ISSN: 0030-5073.

KELLER, ROBERT T.; HOLLAND, WINFORD E. 1983. Communicators and Innovators in Research and Development Organizations. Academy of Management Journal. 1983 December; 26(4): 742-749. ISSN: 0001-4273.

KENNEDY, CAROL. 1987. Can We Catch Up in the Quality Race? Director. 1987 November; 41(4): 44-46. ISSN: 0012-3242.

KENNY, GRAHAM K.; BUTLER, RICHARD J.; HICKSON, DAVID J.; CRAY, DAVID; MALLORY, GEOFFREY R.; WILSON, DAVID C. 1987. Strategic Decision Making: Influence Patterns in Public and Private

Sector Organizations. Human Relations. 1987 September; 40(9): 613-631. ISSN: 0018-7267.

KING, ROBERT A.; WOOD, G. CHRISTOPHER. 1989. Overcome Cultural Barriers to Manufacturing Improvement. Journal of Business Strategy. 1989 May/June; 10(3): 59-60. ISSN: 0275-6668.

KNIGHT, KENNETH E.; MCDANIEL, REUBEN R. 1979. Organizations: An Information Systems Perspective. Belmont, CA: Wadsworth; 1979. 191p. ISBN: 0-534-00583-7.

KORFHAGE, ROBERT R. 1974. Informal Communication of Scientific Information. Journal of the American Society for Information Science. 1974 January/February; 25(1): 25-32. ISSN: 0002-8231.

KRACKHARDT, DAVID. 1987. A Preliminary Note on Networks of Informal Relations in Organizations. Ithaca, NY: Cornell University, Johnson Graduate School of Management; 1987 October. 8p. (Draft Paper). Available from: the author, Graduate School of Business Administration, Harvard Business School, Soldiers Field, Boston, MA 02163.

KRACKHARDT, DAVID. 1989. Graph Theoretical Dimensions of Informal Organizations. Paper presented at the National Meeting of the Academy of Management; 1989 August; Washington, DC. 43p. Available from: the author, Graduate School of Business Administration, Harvard Business School, Soldiers Field, Boston, MA 02163.

KRACKHARDT, DAVID. 1990a. Assessing the Political Landscape: Structure, Cognition, and Power in Organizations. Administrative Science Quarterly. 1990 June; 35: 342-369. ISSN: 0001-8392.

KRACKHARDT, DAVID. 1990b. The Strength of Strong Ties: The Importance of Philos in Organizations. Boston, MA: Harvard Business School; 1990 August. (Draft Paper).

KRACKHARDT, DAVID; KILDUFF, MARTIN. 1990. Friendship Patterns and Culture: The Control of Organizational Diversity. American Anthropologist. 1990 March; 92(1): 142-154. ISSN: 0002-7294.

KRACKHARDT, DAVID; PORTER, LYMAN W. 1985. When Friends Leave: A Structural Analysis of the Relationship between Turnover and Stayers' Attitudes. Administrative Science Quarterly. 1985 June; 30: 242-261. ISSN: 0001-8392.

KRACKHARDT, DAVID; PORTER, LYMAN W. 1986. The Snowball Effect: Turnover Embedded in Communication Networks. Journal of Applied Psychology. 1986 February; 71(1): 50-55. ISSN: 0021-9010.

KRACKHARDT, DAVID; STERN, ROBERT N. 1988. Informal Networks and Organizational Crises: An Experimental Simulation. Social Psychology Quarterly. 1988; 51(2): 123-140. ISSN: 0190-2725.

KURKE, LANCE B.; WEICK, KARL E.; RAVLIN, ELIZABETH C. 1989. Can Information Loss Be Reversed? Evidence for Serial Reconstruction. Communication Research. 1989 February; 16(1): 3-24. ISSN: 0093-6502.

LACY, WILLIAM B.; BUSCH, LAWRENCE. 1983. Informal Scientific Communication in the Agricultural Sciences. Information Processing & Management. 1983; 19(4): 193-202. ISSN: 0306-4573.

LENGEL, ROBERT H. 1983. Managerial Information Processing and Media Selection Behavior. College Station, TX: Texas A&M University; 1983. 188p. (Ph.D. dissertation). Available from: University Microfilms International, Ann Arbor, MI. (UM order no. 83-23685).

LEONARD-BARTON, DOROTHY. 1985. Experts as Negative Opinion Leaders in the Diffusion of a Technological Innovation. Journal of Consumer Research. 1985 March; 11: 914-926. ISSN: 0093-5301.

LEONARD-BARTON, DOROTHY. 1986. The Secondary Adoption Decision: Implementing a New Technology within an Organization. Boston, MA: Harvard Business School, Division of Research; 1986. 27p. (Working Paper; 9-787-006). Available from: the author, Harvard Business School, Soldiers Field, Boston, MA 02163.

LEONARD-BARTON, DOROTHY. 1987. The Case for Integrative Innovation: An Expert System at Digital. Sloan Management Review. 1987 Fall; 29(1): 7-19. ISSN: 0019-848X.

LEONARD-BARTON, DOROTHY. 1988a. Implementation as Mutual Adaption of Technology and Organization. Research Policy. 1988; 17: 251-267. ISSN: 0048-7333.

LEONARD-BARTON, DOROTHY. 1988b. Implementation Characteristics of Organizational Innovations. Communication Research. 1988 October; 15(5): 603-631. ISSN: 0093-6502.

LEONARD-BARTON, DOROTHY. 1990. Modes of Technology Transfer with Organizations: Point-to-Point Versus Diffusion. Boston, MA: Harvard Business School, Division of Research; 1990. 30p. (Working Paper; 90-060). Available from: the author, Harvard Business School, Soldiers Field, Boston, MA 02163.

LEONARD-BARTON, DOROTHY; DESCHAMPS, ISABELLE. 1988. Managerial Influence in the Implementation of New Technology. Management Science. 1988 October; 34(10): 1252-1265. ISSN: 0025-1909.

LEONARD-BARTON, DOROTHY; KRAUS, WILLIAM A. 1985. Implementing New Technology. Harvard Business Review. 1985 November-December; 63(6): 102-110. ISSN: 0017-8012.

LEVITAN, KAREN B. 1982. Information Resource(s) Management—IRM. In: Williams, Martha E., ed. Annual Review of Information Science and Technology: Volume 17. White Plains, NY: Knowledge Industry Publications, Inc. for the American Society for Information Science (ASIS); 1982. 227-266. ISSN: 0066-4200.

LINDNER, JANE. 1985. Harnessing Corporate Culture. Computerworld. 1985 September 23; 19(38): 'InDepth' 1-10. ISSN: 0010-4841.

LIPPERT, FRED G. 1982. Cliques: Good or Bad? Supervision. 1982 August; 44(8): 16-17. ISSN: 0039-5854.

LISTON, WILLIAM T. 1984. Exploring In Search of Excellence: America's Best-Run Companies: How Do They Do It? Management World. 1984 January; 13(1): 28-30. ISSN: 0090-3825.

LYTLE, RICHARD H. 1986. Information Resource Management: 1981-1986. In: Williams, Martha E., ed. Annual Review of Information

Science and Technology: Volume 21. White Plains, NY: Knowledge Industry Publications, Inc. for the American Society for Information Science (ASIS); 1986. 309-336. ISSN: 0066-4200.

MAGJUKA, RICHARD. 1988. Garbage Can Theory of Organizational Decision Making: A Review. In: DiTomaso, Nancy; Bacharach, Samuel B., eds. Research in the Sociology of Organizations: Volume 6. Greenwich, CT: JAI Press; 1988. 225-259. ISBN: 0-89232-881-9.

MANDELL, MARVIN B. 1988. The Consequences of Improving Dissemination in Garbage-Can Decision Processes: Insights from a Simulation Model. Knowledge: Creation, Diffusion, Utilization. 1988 March; 9(3): 343-361. ISSN: 0164-0259.

MARKUS, M. LYNNE. 1990a. Asynchronous Technologies in Small Face-to-Face Groups. Los Angeles, CA: University of California, Los Angeles, John E. Anderson Graduate School of Management; 1990 May. (Draft Paper). Available from: the author, UCLA John E. Anderson Graduate School of Management, Los Angeles, CA 90024-1481.

MARKUS, M. LYNNE. 1990b. Toward a "Critical Mass" Theory of Interactive Media. In: Fulk, J.; Steinfield, C., eds. Organizations and Communication Technology. Newbury Park, CA: Sage; 1990. 194-218. ISBN: 0-8039-3530-7; 0-8039-3531-5 (pbk.).

MARSLAND, STEPHEN; BEER, MICHAEL. 1983. The Evolution of Japanese Management: Lessons for U.S. Managers. Organizational Dynamics. 1983 Winter; 11(3): 49-67. ISSN: 0090-2616.

MARTIN, LINDA J. 1985. Uncertain? How Do You Spell Relief? Journal of Portfolio Management. 1985 Spring; 11(3): 5-8. ISSN: 0095-4918.

MCCLURE, CHARLES R. 1978. The Information Rich Employee and Information for Decision Making: Review and Comments. Information Processing & Management. 1978; 14: 381-394. ISSN: 0306-4573.

MCKENNA, R.F. 1975. A Description of the Organizational Interfaces of the Formal and Informal Systems. Industrial Management. 1975 November; 17(11): 1-7. ISSN: 0019-8471.

MILGROM, PAUL; ROBERTS, JOHN. 1988. An Economic Approach to Influence Activities in Organizations. American Journal of Sociology. 1988; 94(Supplement): S154-S179. ISSN: 0002-9602.

MINTZBERG, HENRY. 1973. The Nature of Managerial Work. Englewood Cliffs, NJ: Prentice-Hall; 1973. 298p. ISBN: 0-13-610402-9.

MINTZBERG, HENRY. 1975. The Manager's Job: Folklore and Fact. Harvard Business Review. 1975 July/August; 53(4): 49-61. ISSN: 0017-8012.

MINTZBERG, HENRY. 1983. Structures in Fives: Designing Effective Organizations. Englewood Cliffs, NJ: Prentice-Hall; 1983. 312p. ISBN: 0-13-854191-4.

MINTZBERG, HENRY. 1989. Mintzberg on Management: Inside Our Strange World of Organizations. New York, NY: Free Press; 1989. 418p. ISBN: 0-02-921371-1.

MINTZBERG, HENRY; RAISINGHANI, DURU; THEORET, ANDRE. 1976. The Structure of "Unstructured" Decision Processes. Administrative Science Quarterly. 1976 June; 21: 246-275. ISSN: 0001-8392.

MORIEUX, YVES V.; SUTHERLAND, EWAN. 1988. The Interaction between the Use of Information Technology and Organizational Culture. Behaviour & Information Technology. 1988 April-June; 7(2): 205-213. ISSN: 0144-929X.

MYRSIADES, LINDA SUNY. 1987. Corporate Stories as Cultural Communications in the Organizational Setting. Management Communication Quarterly. 1987 August; 1(1): 84-120. ISSN: 0893-3189.

NEWSTROM, JOHN W.; MONCZKA, ROBERT E.; REIF, WILLIAM E. 1974. Perceptions of the Grapevine: Its Value and Influence. Journal of Business Communication. 1974 Spring; 11(3): 12-20. ISSN: 0021-9436.

NOCHUR, KUMAR S.; ALLEN, THOMAS J. 1990. Do Nominated Boundary Spanners Become Effective Technological Gatekeepers? Cambridge, MA: MIT, Sloan School of Management, International Center for Research on the Management of Technology (ICRMOT); 1990 June. 15p. (Working Paper; WP # 6-90). Available from the Center: ICRMOT Working Papers, MIT, Room E56-304, Cambridge, MA 02139.

OGILVIE, JOHN R.; POHLEN, MICHAEL F.; JONES, LOUISE H. 1988. Organizational Information Processing and Productivity Improvement. National Productivity Review. 1988 Summer; 7(3): 229-237. ISSN: 0277-8556.

OLSON, MARGRETHE H. 1982. New Information Technology and Organizational Culture. MIS Quarterly. 1982 December; Special Issue: 71-92. ISSN: 0276-7783.

O'REILLY, CHARLES A. 1978. The International Distortion of Information in Organizational Communication: A Laboratory and Field Investigation. Human Relations. 1978 February; 31(2): 173-193. ISSN: 0018-7267.

O'REILLY, CHARLES A. 1980. Individuals and Information Overload in Organizations: Is More Necessarily Better? Academy of Management Journal. 1980 December; 23(4): 684-696. ISSN: 0001-4273.

O'REILLY, CHARLES A.; ROBERTS, KARLENE H. 1974. Information Filtration in Organizations: Three Experiments. Organizational Behavior & Human Performance. 1974 April; 11(2): 253-265. ISSN: 0030-5073.

PAYNE, STEPHEN L.; PETTINGILL, BERNARD F. 1986. Coping with Organizational Politics. Supervisory Management. 1986 April; 31(4): 28-31. ISSN: 0039-5919.

PENLEY, LARRY E. 1982. An Investigation of the Information Processing Framework of Organizational Communication. Human Communication Research. 1982 Summer; 8(4): 348-365. ISSN: 0360-3989.

PERKINS, W. STEVEN; RAO, RAM C. 1990. The Role of Experience in Information Use and Decision Making by Marketing Managers. Journal of Marketing Research. 1990 February; 27(1): 1-10. ISSN: 0022-2437.

PETERS, THOMAS J.; AUSTIN, NANCY A. 1985. A Passion for Excellence: The Leadership of Difference. New York, NY: Random House; 1985. 437p. ISBN: 0-394-54484-6.

PETERS, THOMAS J.; WATERMAN, ROBERT H. 1982. In Search of Excellence: Lessons from America's Best Run Companies. New York, NY: Harper & Row; 1982. 360p. ISBN: 0-06-015042-4.

PETERS, THOMAS J.; WATERMAN, ROBERT H. 1984. Nurturing Growth and Innovation. Modern Office Technology. 1984 March; 29(3): 16-22. ISSN: 0746-3839.

PRICE, DEREK J. DE SOLLA. 1971a. Invisible College Research: State of the Art, Informal Communication among Scientists. Proceedings of a Conference on Current Research; 1971 February 22. Chicago, IL: American Medical Association; 1971.

PRICE, DEREK J. DE SOLLA. 1971b. Some Remarks on Elitism in Information and the Invisible College Phenomenon in Science. Journal of the American Society for Information Science. 1971 March/April; 22(2): 74-75. ISSN: 0002-8231.

PUTNAM, LINDA L.; SORENSON, RITCH L. 1982. Equivocal Messages in Organizations. Human Communication Research. 1982 Winter; 8(2): 114-132. ISSN: 0360-3989.

RAMSEY, H. RUDY; GRIMES, JACK D. 1983. Human Factors in Interactive Computer Dialog. In: Williams, Martha E., ed. Annual Review of Information Science and Technology: Volume 18. White Plains, NY: Knowledge Industry Publications, Inc. for the American Society for Information Science (ASIS); 1983. 29-59. ISSN: 0066-4200.

REINGEN, PETER H.; KERNAN, JEROME B. 1986. Analysis of Referral Networks in Marketing: Methods and Illustration. Journal of Marketing Research. 1986 November; 23(4): 370-378. ISSN: 0022-2437.

RICE, RONALD E. 1980. The Impacts of Computer-Mediated Organizational and Interpersonal Communication. In: Williams, Martha E., ed. Annual Review of Information Science and Technology: Volume 15. White Plains, NY: Knowledge Industry Publications, Inc. for the American Society for Information Science (ASIS); 1980. 221-249. ISSN: 0066-4200.

RICE, RONALD E.; RICHARDS, WILLIAM D. 1985. An Overview of Network Analysis Methods and Programs. In: Dervin, B.; Voigt, M. J., eds. Progress in Communication Sciences: Volume 6. Norwood, NJ: Ablex; 1985. 105-165. ISBN: 0-89391-306-5.

RICHARDS, WILLIAM D. 1971. An Improved Conceptually-Based Method for Analysis of Communication Network Structure of Large Complex Organizations. East Lansing, MI: Michigan State University, Department of Communication; 1971. 27p. ERIC: ED 064876.

ROSE, RANDALL A. 1988. Organizations as Multiple Cultures: A Rules Theory Analysis. Human Relations. 1988 February; 41(2): 139-170. ISSN: 0018-7267.

SAPIENZA, ALICE M. 1987. Imagery and Strategy. Journal of Management. 1987 Fall; 13(3): 543-555. ISSN: 0149-2063.

SCHILIT, WARREN KEITH. 1987. An Examination of the Influence of Middle-Level Managers in Formulating and Implementing Strategic Decisions. Journal of Management Studies. 1987 May; 24(3): 271-293. ISSN: 0022-2380.

SCHMID, HILLEL; DODD, PAMELA; TROPMAN, JOHN E. 1987. Board Decision Making in Human Service Organizations. Human Systems Management. 1987; 7(2): 155-161. ISSN: 0167-2533.

SCHOLZ, CHRISTIAN. 1987. Corporate Culture and Strategy: The Problem of Strategic Fit. Long Range Planning. 1987 August; 20(4): 78-87. ISSN: 0024-6301.

SERPA, ROY. 1985. Creating a Candid Corporate Culture. Journal of Business Ethics. 1985 October; 4(5): 425-430. ISSN: 0167-4544.

SHARMA, JITENDRA M. 1979. Organizational Communications: A Linking Process. Personnel Administrator. 1979 July; 24(7): 35-39, 43. ISSN: 0031-5729.

SMITH, PETER E.; BARNARD, JOHN M.; SMITH, GEOFFREY. 1988. When Public Becomes Private. Management Decision. 1988; 26(1): 11-15. ISSN: 0025-1757.

SPROULL, LEE; KIESLER, SARA. 1986. Reducing Social Context Cues: Electronic Mail in Organizational Communication. Management Science. 1986 November; 32(11): 1492-1512. ISSN: 0025-1909.

STEINFIELD, CHARLES W. 1986. Computer-Mediated Communication Systems. In: Williams, Martha E., ed. Annual Review of Information Science and Technology: Volume 21. White Plains, NY: Knowledge Industry Publications, Inc. for the American Society for Information Science (ASIS); 1986. 167-202. ISSN: 0066-4200.

TAYLOR, ROBERT L. 1975. The Technological Gatekeeper. R&D Management. 1975; 5(3): 239-242. ISSN: 0033-6807.

THOMAS, VICKI. 1985. We've Gotta Stop Meeting Like This! Communication World. 1985 March; 2(5): 18-20. ISSN: 0744-7612.

THOMPSON, MICHAEL. 1979. Rubbish Theory. London, England: Oxford University Press; 1979. 228p. ISBN: 0-19-217658-7.

THOMPSON, MICHAEL; WILDAVSKY, AARON. 1986. A Cultural Theory of Information Bias in Organizations. Journal of Management Studies. 1986 May; 23(3): 273-286. ISSN: 0022-2380.

TREVINO, LINDA KLEBE; DAFT, RICHARD L.; LENGEL, ROBERT H. 1990. Understanding Managers' Media Choices: A Symbolic Interactionist Perspective. In: Fulk, J.; Steinfield, C., eds. Organizations and Communication Technology. Newbury Park, CA: Sage; 1990. 71-94. ISBN: 0-8039-3530-7; 0-8039-3531-5 (pbk.).

TUSHMAN, MICHAEL L.; NADLER, DAVID A. 1978. Information Processing as an Integrating Concept in Organization Design. Academy of Management Review. 1978; 3: 613-624. ISSN: 0363-7425.

TUSHMAN, MICHAEL L.; ROMANELLI, ELAINE. 1983. Uncertainty, Social Location and Influence in Decision Making: A Sociometric Analysis. Management Science. 1983 January; 29(1): 12-23. ISSN: 0025-1909.

TUSHMAN, MICHAEL L.; SCANLAN, THOMAS. 1981. Boundary Spanning Individuals: Their Role in Information Transfer and Their Antecedents. Academy of Management Journal. 1981 June; 24(2): 289-305. ISSN: 0001-4273.

VICKERY, HUGH B. 1984. Tapping into the Employee Grapevine. Association Management. 1984 January; 36(1): 59-63. ISSN: 0004-5578.

VINCENT, DAVID. 1984. Corporate Culture. Computerworld. 1984 November 5; 18(45): 'In-depth' 21-30. ISSN: 0010-4841.

WARD, JOHN M. 1987. Integrating Information Systems into Business Strategies. Long Range Planning. 1987; 20(3): 19-29. ISSN: 0024-6301.

WEICK, KARL E. 1979. The Psychology of Organizing. 2nd edition. Reading, MA: Addison-Wesley; 1979. 121p. ISBN: 0-201-08593-3.

WOOTEN, BOB E. 1981. Organizational Communication: The Channel vs. the Grapevine. Management World. 1981 March; 10(3): 39-40. ISSN: 0090-3825.

ZACK, MICHAEL H.; MCKENNEY, JAMES L. 1989a. Characteristics of the Organizational Information Domain: An Organizational Information Processing Perspective. Boston, MA: Harvard Business School, Division of Research; 1989. 50p. (Working Paper; No. 89-027). Available from: the authors, Graduate School of Business Administration, Harvard Business School, Soldiers Field, Boston, MA 02163.

ZACK, MICHAEL H.; MCKENNEY, JAMES L. 1989b. Organizational Information Processing and Work Group Effectiveness. Boston, MA: Harvard Business School, Division of Research; 1989 February. 88p. plus Appendices. (Working Paper; No. 89-054). Available from: the authors, Graduate School of Business Administration, Harvard Business School, Soldiers Field, Boston, MA 02163.

ZALTMAN, GERALD. 1974. A Note on an International Invisible College for Information Exchange. Journal of the American Society for Information Science. 1974 March/April; 25(2): 113-117. ISSN: 0002-8231.

ZAREMBA, ALAN. 1988. More Than Rumors: Understanding the Organizational Grapevine. Boston, MA: Northeastern University; 1988. 12p. ERIC: ED 296434.

Introduction to the Index

Index entries have been made for names of individuals, corporate bodies, subjects, geographic locations, and author names included in the text pages and for author and conference names from the bibliography pages. The page numbers referring to the bibliography pages are set in italics and are listed after the page numbers relating to the text pages. This format allows one to distinguish references to bibliographic materials from references to text.

Acronyms are listed either under the acronym or under the fully spelled-out form, depending on which form is more commonly used and known. In either case a cross reference from the alternate form is provided. Postings associated with PRECIS, for example, would be listed under PRECIS as readers are generally less familiar with the full name, "Preserved Context Index System." In a few cases, such as names of programs, systems, and programming languages, there is no spelled-out form either because there is none or because the meaning has been changed or is no longer used.

The index is arranged on a word-by-word basis. The sort sequence employed follows the University of Chicago Press and British Standards BS3700 and BS1749. In general, special characters are listed first, followed by numbers, then alpha characters. Thus, 3M Company would file before the "A"s, and O'Neill would precede Oakman. Government organizations are generally listed under country name, with *see* references provided from names of departments, agencies, and other subdivisions. While index entries do correspond precisely in spelling and format, they do not follow the typographical conventions used in the text. Author names, which are all upper case in the text, and programming languages, which are in small caps in the text, are in upper and lower case or normal upper case in the index.

Subject indexing is by concepts rather than by words. When authors have used different words or different forms of the same word to express the same or overlapping concepts, the terminology has been standardized. An effort was made to use the form of index entries for concepts that had previously appeared in *ARIST* indexes. Cross references have been used freely to provide access to subject concepts. *See also* references are used for overlapping or related (but not synonymous) concepts; *see* references are used to send the reader to the accepted form of a term used in the index.

The index was prepared by Debora Shaw, using the MACREX Plus Indexing Program, version 4.01 developed by Hilary and Drusilla

Calvert and distributed in the United States by Bayside Indexing. The overall direction and coordination of the index were provided by Martha E. Williams. Comments and suggestions should be addressed to the Editor.

Index*

Introduction to the Keyword and Author Index

473

The following section is an author and keyword index to *ARIST* chapters for Volumes 1 through 26 . It has been produced to assist users in locating specific topics, chapters, and author names for all *ARIST* volumes to date. The index terms are sorted alphabetically and include all author names and content words from titles (a stop-word list of articles, conjunctions, and other non-content words was used). The sort word is followed by the author(s) name(s) and the *ARIST* citation.

Keyword and Author Index
of *ARIST* Titles
for Volumes 1-26

Lytle, Richard H.
      Lytle, Richard H. Information Resource Management: 19811986. **21**, p309

Machine
      Amsler, Robert A. **19**, p161; Davis, Ruth M. **1**, p221; Gechman, Marvin
      C. **7**, p323; Hjerppe, Roland, **21**, p123; Meadow, Charles T. and Meadow,
      Harriet R. **5**, p169; Mills, R.G. **2**, p223; Schipma, Peter B. **10**, p237;
      Shoffner, Ralph M. **3**, p137; Tucker, Allen B., Jr. and Nirenburg, Sergei,
      19, p129; Wilde, Daniel U. **11**, p267; Williams, Martha E. **9**, p221
Magnino, Joseph J., Jr.
      Magnino, Joseph J., Jr. Document Retrieval and Dissemination. **6**, p219
Mailloux, Elizabeth
      Mailloux, Elizabeth. Engineering Information Systems. **24**, p239
Maintenance
      Meadow, Charles T. and Meadow, Harriet R. **5**, p169; Shoffner, Ralph M.
      3, p137
Man
      Davis, Ruth M. **1**, p221; Licklider, J.C.R. **3**, p201; Mills, R.G. **2**, p223
Management
      Broadbent, Marianne and Koenig, Michael E.D. **23**,1 p237; Brumm,
      Eugenia. **26**, p197; Buckland, Michael K. **9**, p335; Eastman, Caroline M.
      20, p91; Holm, Bart E. **5**, p353; Huffenberger, Michael A. and Wigington,
      Ronald L. **14**, p153; Leimkuhler, Ferdinand F. and Billingsley, Alice. **7**,
      p499; Levitan, Karen B. **17**, p227; Lytle, Richard H. **21**, p309; Minker,
      Jack and Sable, Jerome. **2**, p123; Murdock, John and Sherrod, John. **11**,
      p381; Senko, Michael E. **4**, p111; Wasserman, Paul and Daniel, Evelyn.
      4, p405; Weiss, Stanley D. **5**, p299
Marketing
      Freeman, James E. and Katz, Ruth M. **13**,1 p37; Tucci, Valerie K. **23**, p59
Markey, Karen
      Markey, Karen. Visual Arts Resources and Computers. **19**, p271
Markuson, Barbara Evans
      Markuson, Barbara Evans. Automation in Libraries and Information
            Centers. **2**, p255
Marron, Beatrice
      Marron, Beatrice and Fife, Dennis. Online Systems—Techniques and
            Services. **11**, p163
Martin, Susan K.
      Martin, Susan K. Library Automation. **7**, p243
Martin, Thomas H.
      Martin, Thomas H. The User Interface in Interactive Systems. **8**, p203;
      Martin, Thomas H. Office Automation. **23**, p217
Martyn, John
      Martyn, John. Information Needs and Uses. **9**, p3
Maskewitz, Betty F.
      Carroll, Bonnie (Talmi) and Maskewitz, Betty F. Information Analysis
            Centers. **15**, p147

6, p41; Coyne, Joseph G., Carroll, Bonnie C., and Redford, Julia S. **18**, p231; Debons, Anthony and Montgomery, K. Leon. **9**, p25; Drenth, Hilary, Morris, Anne, and Tseng, Gwyneth. **26**, p113; Eastman, Caroline M. **20**, p91; Frank, Robyn C. **22**, p293; Gannett, Elwood K. **8**, p243; Grattidge, Walter and Creps, John E., Jr. **13**, p297; Griffiths, José-Marie. **17**, p269; Hawkins, Donald T. **16**, p171; Hearle, Edward F.R. **5**, p325; Hersey, David F. **13**, p263; Huffenberger, Michael A. and Wigington, Ronald L. **14**, p153; Kantor, Paul B. **17**, p99; Katter, Robert V. **4**, p31; King, Donald W. **3**, p61; Lancaster, F. Wilfrid and Gillespie, Constantine J. **5**, p33; Lerner, Rita G., Metaxas, Ted, Scott, John T., Adams, Peter D., and Judd, Peggy. **18**, p127; Levy, Richard P. and Cammarn, Maxine R. **3**, p397; Luedke, James A., Jr., Kovacs, Gabor J., and Fried, John B. **12**, p119; Mailloux, Elizabeth. **24**, p239; Marron, Beatrice and Fife, Dennis **11**, p163; Martin, Thomas H. **8**, p203; McCarn, Davis B. **13**, p85; Mick, Colin K. **14**, p37; Neufeld, M. Lynne and Cornog, Martha. **18**, p151; Raben, Joseph and Burton, Sarah K. **16**, p247; Raben, Joseph and Widmann, R.L. **7**, p439; Raitt, David I. **20**, p55; Rees, Alan M. **2**, p63; Saracevic, Tefko, Braga, Gilda, and Quijano Solis, Alvaro. **14**, p249; Senko, Michael E. **4**, p111; Shaw, Ward and Culkin, Patricia B. **22**, p265; Sieck, Steven K. **19**, p311; Silberman, Harry F. and Filep, Robert T. **3**, p357; Smith, Linda C. **15**, p67; Sowizral, Henry A. **20**, p179; Steinfield, Charles W. **21**, p167; Summit, Roger K. and Firschein, Oscar. **9**, p285; Swanson, Rowena Weiss. **10**, p43; Tate, F.A. **2**, p285; Tibbo, Helen R. **26**, p287; Vaupel, Nancy and Elias, Arthur. **16**, p267; Vinsonhaler, John F. and Moon, Robert D. **8**, p277; Voges, Mickie A. **23**, p193; Wanger, Judith. **14**, p219; Weiss, Stanley D. **5**, p299

Tannehill, Robert S., Jr.
> Tannehill, Robert S., Jr. Bibliographic and Information-Processing Standards. **18**, p61

Tate, F.A.
> Tate, F.A. Handling Chemical Compounds in Information Systems. **2**, p285

Taulbee, Orrin E.
> Taulbee, Orrin E. Content Analysis, Specification, and Control. **3**, p105

Taylor, Robert S.
> Taylor, Robert S. Professional Aspects of Information Science and Technology. **1**, p15

Technical
> Griffin, Hillis L. **3**, p241

Techniques
> American Institute of Physics Staff. **2**, p339; Bates, Marcia J. **16**, p139; Belkin, Nicholas J. and Croft, W. Bruce. **22**, p109; Climenson, W. Douglas. **1**, p107; Marron, Beatrice and Fife, Dennis. **11**, p163; McCarn, Davis B. **13**, p85; McGill, Michael J. and Huitfeldt, Jennifer. **14**, p93; Summit, Roger K. and Firschein, Oscar. **9**, p285; Wyllys, Ronald E. **14**, p3

Technologies
> Goldstein, Charles M. **19**, p65

About the Editor . . .

Professor Martha E. Williams assumed the Editorship of the *ANNUAL REVIEW OF INFORMATION SCIENCE AND TECHNOLOGY* with Volume 11 and has produced a series of books that provide unparalleled insights into, and overviews of, the multifaceted discipline of information science.

Professor Williams holds the positions of Director of the Information Retrieval Research Laboratory and Professor of Information Science in the Coordinated Science Laboratory (CSL) as well as affiliate of the Computer Science Department at the University of Illinois, Urbana-Champaign, Illinois. As a chemist and information scientist Professor Williams has brought to the Editorship a breadth of knowledge and experience in information science and technology.

She serves as a Director and was formerly the Chairman of the Board of Engineering Information, Inc.; she is founding editor of *COMPUTER-READABLE DATABASES: A DIRECTORY AND DATA SOURCEBOOK;* Editor of *ONLINE REVIEW* (Learned Information, Ltd., Oxford, England); and Program Chairman for the National Online Meetings which are sponsored by *ONLINE REVIEW.* She was appointed by the Secretary of Health, Education and Welfare, Joseph Califano, to be a member of the Board of Regents of the National Library of Medicine (NLM) in 1978 and has served as Chairman of the Board. She has been a member of the Numerical Data Advisory Board of the National Research Council (NRC), National Academy of Sciences (NAS). She was a member of the Science Information Activities task force of the National Science Foundation (NSF), was chairman of the Large Database subcommittee of the NAS/NRC Committee on Chemical Information, and was Chairman of the Gordon Research Conference on Scientific Information Problems in Research in 1980.

Professor William is a Fellow of the American Association for the Advancement of Science, Honorary Fellow of the Institute of Information Scientists in England, and recipient of the 1984 Award of Merit of the American Society for Information Science. She is a member of, has held offices in, and/or is actively involved in various committees of the American Association for the Advancement of Science (AAAS), the American Chemical Society (ACS), the Association for Computing Machinery (ACM), the American Society for Information Science (ASIS), and the Association of Information and Dissemination Centers (ASIDIC). She has published numerous books and papers and serves on the editorial boards of several journals. She is the founder and President of Information Market Indicators, Inc., and consults for many governmental and commercial organizations.

ASIS and Its Members

For over 50 years the leading professional society for information professionals, the American Society for Information Science is an association whose diverse membership continues to reflect the frontiers and horizons of the dynamic field of information science and technology. ASIS owes its stature to the cumulative contributions of its members, past and present.

ASIS counts among its membership some 4000 information specialists from such fields as computer science, management, engineering, librarianship, chemistry, linguistics, and education. As was true when the Society was founded, ASIS membership continues to lead the information profession in the search for new and better theories, techniques, and technologies to improve access to information through storage and retrieval advances. And now, as then, ASIS and its members are called upon to help determine new directions and standards for the development of information policies and practices.

Individual Membership Application

New Member
Renewal

asis AMERICAN SOCIETY FOR INFORMATION SCIENCE

Please print or type in black ink.

Name (Last, First, Middle) _______________________ Day Phone(___) ___________ Ext: _______

Title ____

Organization ____

Mailing Address ____

City ___________________________ State _______ Zipcode _________ Plus 4: _______

Province (Outside U.S.) _____________ Country ____________ Mail Code __________

Check One—The Above Address Is My ☐ Work ☐ Home

Please select category of membership:

☐ Regular $85 $ _______

☐ Student $20 $ _______

I am a full-time student at ___________________

Faculty advisor's signature ___________________

Special Interest Group (SIG) Dues

☐ Check here if one free SIG selected.

Additional SIGs _______ x $6 each $ _______

Total Membership and SIG Dues $ _______

Contribution to ASIS Scholarship Fund $ _______

Contribution to ASIS Development Fund $ _______

Total Payment Enclosed $ _______ (US)

Chapter Membership: You will automatically become a member of the chapter serving your geographic area (if one exists). Information about your chapter and additional chapters you may want to join will be sent to you upon receipt of your membership application.

Check or money order enclosed (Payable to ASIS)
or charge my   ☐ VISA   ☐ Mastercard

Account # _______________________________

Expiration Date _________________________

Signature _______________________________

Because your ASIS membership is individual rather than organizational, your membership goes with you if you make a career move. All membership fees and contributions are tax-deductible to the full extent of the law in the United States. You will receive notification of your active membership when your application form is processed. Please allow 4-6 weeks for delivery. For new members, membership is for one year from the month in which dues are received. Membership fees are non-refundable.

Of the annual membership dues, $11 is payment for the *Bulletin*; $15 is payment for the *Journal*.

All ASIS members may select one SIG at no charge. You may join additional SIGs at $6 each. Please note *all* selections here. Enclose payment of $6 for the second and succeeding selections.

☐ **Arts and Humanities** (AH)
☐ **Automated Language Processing** (ALP)
☐ **Biological and Chemical Information Systems** (BC)
☐ **Behavioral and Social Sciences** (BSS)
☐ **Classification Research** (CR)
☐ **Computerized Retrieval Services** (CRS)
☐ **Education for Information Science** (ED)
☐ **Foundations of Information Science** (FIS)
☐ **Human-Computer Interaction (HCI)**
☐ **Information Analysis and Evaluation** (IAE)
☐ **International Information Issues** (III)
☐ **Library Automation and Networks** (LAN)
☐ **Law and Information Technology** (LAW)
☐ **Medical Information Systems** (MED)
☐ **Management** (MGT)
☐ **Numeric Data Bases** (NDB)
☐ **Office Information Systems** (OIS)
☐ **Personal Computers** (PC)
☐ **Information Generation and Publishing** (PUB)
☐ **Storage and Retrieval Technology** (SRT)
☐ **Technology, Information and Society** (TIS)

Please mail this form with your payment to
American Society for Information Science
Ben Franklin Station
P.O. Box 554
Washington, DC 20044-0554

All other correspondence to ASIS Headquarters,

8720 Georgia Avenue, Suite 501, Silver Spring, MD 20910
Tel. 301-495-0900 FAX 301-495-0810